Tupolev Tu-16

TUPOLEV
Tu-16

Versatile
Cold War Bomber

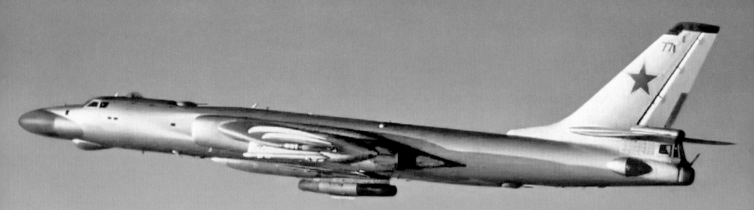

Schiffer Publishing Ltd

4880 Lower Valley Road • Atglen, PA 19310

Yefim Gordon | Dmitriy Komissarov | Vladimir Rigmant

Type set in Times New Roman
Book Design by Polygon Press Ltd., Moscow.

ISBN: 978-0-7643-5418-2
Printed in China

Published by Schiffer Publishing, Ltd.
4880 Lower Valley Road
Atglen, PA 19310
Phone: (610) 593-1777; Fax: (610) 593-2002
E-mail: Info@schifferbooks.com
Web: www.schifferbooks.com

For our complete selection of fine books on this and related subjects, please visit our website at www.schifferbooks.com. You may also write for a free catalog.

Schiffer Publishing's titles are available at special discounts for bulk purchases for sales promotions or premiums. Special editions, including personalized covers, corporate imprints, and excerpts, can be created in large quantities for special needs. For more information, contact the publisher.

We are always looking for people to write books on new and related subjects. If you have an idea for a book, please contact us at proposals@schifferbooks.com.

Contents

Acknowledgments

This book is illustrated with photos by Yefim Gordon, Oleg Buga-kov, Vadim Kondratenkov, Vladimir Nazarov, Sergey Popsuyev-ich, Sergey Sergeyev, the late Sergey Skrynnikov, Guido Bühlmann, Peter Davison, as well as from the archives of the Tupolev PLC, the Kazan' Aircraft Factory (KAPO), the M. M. Gromov Flight Research Institute (LII), the ITAR-TASS News Agency, the US Air Force, the US Navy, the Royal Swedish Air Force, the Russian Aviation Research Trust (RART), the Russian State Archive of the Economy (RGAE) and the personal archives of Yefim Gordon and Viktor Kudryavtsev.

The authors wish to express special thanks to Viktor Kudryavtsev who supplied valuable materials.

The authors have also used the following web sources: www. testpilot.ru, www.forum.vahtubinske.ru, www.topwar.ru, www. retrovtap.ru, www.bagerovo.ru, www.urban3p.ru, www.airwar. ru, www.rbase.new-factoria.ru, www.militaryrussia.ru, www. engine.aviaport.ru, www.indiandefence.com, www.sinodefence-forum.com, www.mreadz.com, www.military-today.com, www. bbs.huanqiu.com, www.popsci.com, www.janes.com, www. ausairpower.net, www.russianplanes.net, www.carpenterdata. net, www.strategycenter.net, www.forum.faleristika.info.

Line drawings by Viktor Mil'yachenko, Andrey Yurgenson and the Tupolev PLC.

Colour artwork by Andrey Yurgenson.

Tu-16K-10-26 '23 Red' flies over the *Forrestal* class aircraft carrier USS *Ranger* (CV-61) during her 1989 WESTPAC cruise. The white radomes are noteworthy; usually the *Badger-C* had dark radomes.

Introduction

The second half of the 1940s found the aircraft industries of the major world powers, including the Soviet Union, faced with the task of producing long-range bombers powered by turbojet and turboprop engines. The aircraft were required to fly at cruising speeds close to Mach 1 while retaining the payload and range capabilities of such bombers as the wartime American Boeing B-29 Stratofortress or its Soviet clone, the Tupolev Tu-4 (NATO reporting name *Bull*). This necessity was dictated not only by the overall thrust of progress in aviation technology (the availability of gas-turbine engines and advancements in aerodynamics) – in particular, the increased potential of fighter aviation, with wide-scale introduction of jet fighters capable of speeds around 1,000 km/h (621 mph) that rendered slow piston-engined aircraft vulnerable – and air defence systems with long-range detection radars. An equally important reason was the advent of a new weapon – the nuclear bomb, which enabled a comparatively small number of bombers to inflict catastrophic damage on an enemy.

The United States was the first to produce a long-range bomber powered by gas-turbine engines. As early as 1945, the Boeing Company initiated work on the Model 450 six-turbojet bomber, which made its first flight in December 1947, and achieved initial operational capability (IOC) with the US Air Force's Strategic Air Command as the B-47 Stratojet in 1951, being officially termed a 'medium-range strategic bomber'. It was closely followed by Great Britain with its trio of four-turbojet 'V-Bombers' – the Vickers Type 660 Valiant (which first flew in May 1951, and entered service with the Royal Air Force in January 1955), Avro 698 Vulcan (first flown in August 195, and inducted in July 1956) and Handley Page HP.80 Victor (first flown in December 1952, and inducted in April 1958). These were also medium-range strategic bombers, which served for many years as the basis for the British nuclear deterrent.

For the Soviet Union the production of a long-range bomber with an operational radius up to 3,000 km (1,863 miles) was vital. Such an aircraft would form an effective counter to the Western threat, being able to strike at American military bases in Europe and Asia, the political, economic and military centres of the USA's allies, and American and British naval concentrations – particularly aircraft carrier task forces (CTFs), which presented a major threat to the USSR. It would also be capable of attacking the transatlantic supply routes, without which the ability of America's European allies to fight a protracted defensive war against the USSR would be highly questionable.

These naval considerations were, it should be said, crucial for the Soviet Union in developing its long-range bombers and then, from the late 1950s onwards, equipping them to carry air-to-surface missiles. The need to counter the West's enormous naval superiority, both in size and expertise, demanded the development of aircraft in a new class able to operate effectively against the surface ships of a potential enemy over the expanse of the world's oceans. This is the reason why the USSR, and later the Russian Federation, has constantly produced and developed this particular type of aircraft – a long-range bomber equipped with air-to-surface missiles – while its potential adversaries in the West have not. From the 1950s through the 1980s the strategic bomber arm of the Soviet Air Force (VVS – *Voyenno-vozdooshnyye seely*) and the Soviet Naval Aviation (AVMF – *Aviahtsiya Voyenno-morskovo flota*) were equipped with a steady succession of such aircraft, one of whose basic applications was against naval targets, particularly aircraft carriers with their formidable anti-aircraft defences.

In the West the category of medium-range strategic bombers and air-to-surface missile carriers gradually died out (unlike the long-range strategic bombers). The B-47 was retired as a bomber in 1965, leaving only the reconnaissance variants to soldier on until 1969; the handful of Convair B-58 Hustler supersonic bombers fielded from 1960 onwards were withdrawn in 1970 due to design failings and changing operational conditions that severely limited the Hustler's value as a bomber. It was replaced by a limited number of General Dynamics FB-111As developed from the F-111 Aardvark tactical fighter-bomber – but even these inadequately filled the role of the extinct medium-range bomber, and eventually all of them were reconverted to their original role. The British V-bombers were soon progressively withdrawn from service, the Valiant being forced into early retirement in 1965 by fatigue life issues and the Victor B.2 in 1968 for the same reason, the Victor B.1s having been converted into in-flight refuelling (IFR) tankers earlier; the Vulcan survived in the bomber role until 1984. The French Dassault Mirage IV twin-engined nuclear-capable bomber introduced in 1964 can be placed in the medium-range strategic bomber category, but only at a stretch due to its comparatively small bomb load and relatively small combat radius; it was withdrawn from the nuclear role in 1996.

Thus the USSR remained alone among the world's major powers, designing and building aircraft in the long-range bomber category with a persistence born of its unique geopolitical and techno-military situation, endowing them with ever new roles.

These aircraft were a permanent, potent and continually updated response in the ruthless military-political game with the West known as the Cold War – or, as some people now tend to put it, the First Cold War. For many years one of the most prominent pieces in this game of world chess was a Soviet aircraft that is the subject of this book – the Tupolev Tu-16 *Badger* twin-turbojet long-range bomber.

Its importance can hardly be overestimated. As far as performance is concerned, the Tu-16 was superior to any other aircraft in its class existing at the time. It had up-to-date avionics and equipment (by the day's standards) and featured potent and rationally laid out defensive armament. It incorporated all the then-latest achievements of both the Soviet aircraft design school and world aircraft design; specifically regarding structural design, this included extruded metal profiles of large cross-section, large stamped parts (including, for the first time in Soviet practice, large stamped subassemblies made of AK-8 aluminium alloy for the wing spar root portions), magnesium alloy castings and new structural materials. In particular, the Tu-16's airframe made large-scale use of the new V95 high-strength aluminium alloy. Subsequently the Tu-16's long service career gave proof positive of this alloy's good properties. In contrast, it was the *Valiant*'s primary structural material, the DTD683 aluminium alloy with poorly studied properties, that proved to be the bomber's undoing because of its inadequate fatigue resistance. The corrosion protection techniques used in the Tu-16's airframe turned out to be highly effective; the new plastic materials used for insulating its electric system components also proved to be highly durable.

For the Soviet aeronautical science the Tu-16 was a groundbreaking project – the first in the heavy transonic aircraft class. Its testing and subsequent operation opened a whole can of worms… that is, revealed a number of previously unknown theoretical problems concerning aeroelasticity and dynamic stressing of the airframe, particularly on take-off and landing. In the instances of dynamic stressing the fuselage was subjected to greater bending loads than the designers had anticipated, using the traditional structural strength calculation techniques and the then-current structural strength standards to which the Tu-16 had been designed. This was demonstrated by several cases when the forward fuselage failed catastrophically in a hard, messed-up landing during the bomber's service introduction period. Once the dynamic stressing had been analysed, the weak spots in the airframe were identified and reinforced, and the Tu-16's flight manual was appropriately amended. Learning from this experience, the designers considered possible dynamic stressing in various flight modes for all subsequent Tupolev aircraft.

The Tu-16's rapid production entry at several aircraft factories, its constant refinement in the course of production and service, the extension of its designated service life to an acceptable figure and its steady operation were largely made possible by the persistent work of the engineering team of OKB-156 (*opytno-konstrooktorskoye byuro* – experimental design bureau; the number is a code allocated for security reasons) headed by General Designer Andrey Nikolayevich Tupolev. A measure of their work is that, typically of a Soviet aircraft, the Tu-16 spawned a multitude of versions – more than 50 versions were developed during its 40-year service career to meet the changing demands of the customer. Another important fact is that the bomber was extremely prolific, ranking second in its class only to the B-47 (which had a production run of 2,032). 1,510 copies of the type were manufactured in the USSR alone, not to mention licence production in China, which has developed its own versions (Chinese production of the *Badger* is past 200 and counting).

The success of the Tu-16 paved the way for large-scale introduction of heavy swept-wing aircraft of various classes in the Soviet Union, providing invaluable information for the development of later Tupolev aircraft designed in the 1950s and 1960s. Most importantly perhaps, the *Badger* itself became the basis for another ground-breaking project – the Tu-104 *Camel* twin-turbojet medium-haul airliner with which it shared the powerplant and much of the airframe structure, only the fuselage being designed anew. The Tu-104 not only took Soviet civil aviation into the jet age but also gained the distinction of being the world's first jet airliner in sustained commercial service – albeit not the *first-ever* jet airliner, as Soviet propaganda was apt to put it.

For the Soviet military the Tu-16 was the first heavy aircraft capable of speeds close to 1,000 km/h (621 mph). In the 1950s and 1960s the airmen flying the type in the VVS and the AVMF could justly take pride in the fact that they were flying what was then one of the world's most modern combat aircraft. The Tu-16 was the Soviet Air Force's first long-range delivery vehicle for free-fall nuclear weapons, and later its first stand-off air-to-surface missile platform, to be fielded in really large numbers; after all, the Tu-4A nuclear-capable bomber and the Tu-4KS missile strike aircraft made up only a small proportion of the *Bull* 'herd'. It was the same story with in-flight refuelling: the Tu-16 was the first Soviet bomber to introduce IFR capability on a large scale, unlike the Tu-4 where only a few examples had refuelling receptacles.

Equally importantly, operational experience with the *Badger* made it possible to train highly professional aircrews and ground crews who later transitioned to progressively more advanced supersonic bombers – the Tu-22 *Blinder*, Tu-22M *Backfire* and Tu-160 *Blackjack*. Moreover, the Tu-16 was instrumental in expediting the Tu-104's service entry with Aeroflot Soviet Airlines – and not only as a crew trainer; when the Soviet Armed Forces were subjected to large-scale cuts in the early 1960s, many former Tu-16 pilots found new jobs as airline captains and first officers – also on the Tu-104.

The Tu-16 remained in first-line service until the late 1980s; the last survivors were retired in Russia in 1993. Thus it outlasted both the country in which it was developed and all the other aircraft in its class, being comparable in longevity to such heavy strategic bombers as the Boeing B-52 Stratofortress and the Tu-95/Tu-142 *Bear* bomber/anti-submarine warfare aircraft family, both of which are still in service as of this writing. Unlike the B-52 and the Tu-95, the *Badger* did not require major design changes in its lifetime. Like a faithful soldier, the good old Tu-16 has served its country well, and a few have been preserved for posterity in Russia (not to mention the fact that the aircraft got a new lease of life in China). This book charts the development and service history of this remarkable aircraft.

Chapter 1

Antecedents and Precursors: In Search of the Optimum Solution

The Soviet Air Force began to formulate its requirements for a future long-range jet bomber immediately after the Tu-4 entered service with the heavy bomber arm of the VVS – the Long-Range Aviation (DA – *Dahl'nyaya aviahtsiya*). The turbojet- or turbo-prop-powered long-range bomber category appeared in its planning as early as 1947-48.

The aircraft was to have the following preliminary specifications:

• maximum speed at 1,000 m (3,280 ft), 900 km/h (559 mph);
• service ceiling, 15,000 m (49,210 ft);
• range at optimum speed with a 3,000-kg (6,610-lb) bomb load, 6,000 km (3,720 miles);
• climb time to 10,000 m (32,810 ft), 10 minutes;
• take-off run, 1,200 m (3,940 ft);
• landing run, 800 m (2,625 ft);
• bomb load: normal, 3,000 kg (6,610 lb); maximum, 20,000 kg (44,010 lb).

The eight-man crew was to be accommodated in pressurised compartments. The defensive armament was to consist of nine 20-mm (.78 calibre) or 23-mm (.90 calibre) cannons – two with 200 rounds per gun (rpg) in a forward-firing remote-controlled chin turret, two with 400 rpg in a remote-controlled dorsal turret, two with 400 rpg in a remote-controlled ventral turret and three with 400 rpg in a tail turret.

The bomb armament was to include all types of conventional bombs carried by the Tu-4; additionally, provision was to be made

OKB-156 General Designer Andrey N. Tupolev (right) and his First Deputy Aleksandr A. Arkhangel'skiy. Both are wearing the Gold Star Medal indicative of their Hero of Socialist Labour title.

The Tupolev OKB design staff, most of whom participated in the development of the Tu-16. Front row, left to right: Kurt V. Minckner, Aleksandr A. Arkhangel'skiy, Andrey N. Tupolev, Nikolay I. Bazenkov and Dmitriy S. Markov; rear row: Aleksandr R. Bonin, Aleksandr E. Sterlin, Sergey M. Yeger, Ivan S. Lebedev, Konstantin P. Sveshnikov, Dmitriy A. Gorskiy, Aleksey M. Cheryomukhin and Nikolay V. Kirsanov.

for carrying the forthcoming Soviet nuclear bomb, the work on which was going ahead rapidly. Special importance was attached to the ability to carry stand-off air-to-surface missiles (referred to in Soviet terminology of the time as *samolyot-snaryad* – lit. 'missile aircraft' or aircraft-type missile) with a launch weight of up to 7,000 kg (15,430 lb).

The following essential navigation and targeting equipment was to be installed: an AP-5 autopilot; a celestial compass; an aircraft sextant; an automatic direction finder (ADF); an RV-2 *Kristall* (Crystal) low-altitude radio altimeter and an RV-10 high-altitude radio altimeter (RV = *rahdiovysotomer*); a Meridian short-range radio navigation (SHORAN) system; a long-range radio navigation (LORAN) system; an 'autonavigator' (that is, navigation computer); *Kadmiy* (Cadmium) gun laying radars ('radar sights', in Soviet terminology) for the gunners' stations; an overall fire control radar; a vector-synchronised optical bomb sight linked to the autopilot and to the bomb-aimer's panoramic radar. Other avionics were to include enemy radar detection and countermeasures equipment, identification friend-or-foe (IFF) equipment, a radar warning receiver (RWR) alerting the crew of enemy fighter attacks, RSB-D communications radio (*rahdiostahntsiya bombardirovshchika* – bomber-type radio) and RSIU-3 command radio sets, and a Bendix Aviation Ltd. SCR-578 emergency radio with a BC-778 'Gibson Girl' transmitter as used on

American bombers of the day. Reconnaissance equipment intended mainly for bomb damage assessment (BDA) was to comprise two AFA-33-50 or AFA-33-75 cameras (*aerofotoapparaht* – aerial camera) with mountings for vertical and oblique photography. An auxiliary power unit (APU) similar to the M-10 used on the Tu-4 (a generator driven by a two-stroke petrol engine) was to be fitted.

It is evident from these specifications for a future long-range bomber that the Soviet Air Force Command was calling for a high-speed aircraft fitted with the very latest systems and able to carry out missions in the teeth of strong enemy air defences at any time of day or night, in any weather and in a variety of theatres of operations. The early interest in the aircraft's ability to carry a large cruise missile is also noteworthy.

The new bomber was to replace the Tu-4 in the early 1950s, as the VVS Command was aware that the Tu-4 was becoming obsolescent even as it was being fielded (after all, the B-29, from which the *Bull* had been copied, had first flown in 1942). It was already obvious that by the early 1950s a piston-engined bomber's chances of breaking through the ever-developing American air defence system would be comparable to a snowball's chance in hell. This supposition was soon confirmed when the Korean War broke out in 1951 and US Air Force B-29s encountered Soviet Mikoyan/ Gurevich MiG-15 *Fagot* jet fighters which took a heavy toll on the slow bombers. The further career of piston-engined long-range and intercontinental bombers had come to an end; the future lay with turbojet and turboprop aircraft. On both sides of the 'Iron Curtain', work on piston-engined bombers was being wound up (in the USSR, development of the Tu-85 *Barge* four-engine bomber was terminated in 1951, and in the USA production of the Convair B-36 Peacemaker was curtailed in 1954), while development of jet bombers was accelerated. The advent of the B-47 evoked the crash programme to create a counterpart to the Stratojet.

However, before a long-range bomber able to fly at transonic speeds could be created by Soviet designers, a whole series of theoretical and practical questions in the fields of aerodynamics, structural design and propulsion had to be resolved. Without the answers, such an aircraft could not come into being.

For a while the Soviet endeavours to create a viable long-range jet bomber were hampered by the lack of sufficiently powerful and fuel-efficient engines. Fortunately this situation did not last long; in the late 1940s several Soviet engine design bureaux set about developing turbojet and turboprop engines. Thus, from the Tu-80 heavy bomber prototype of 1947-49 the Tupolev OKB's work in this field took two directions. One was a 'bigger/heavier/farther is better' approach that led to the short-lived Tu-85 of 1951 – the last-ever straight-wing, piston-engined intercontinental bomber (though it was soon revived on a new technological level as the swept-wing, four-turboprop Tu-95 *Bear*). The other was smaller but fast medium bombers – a direction that led to the Tu-16.

It deserves mention that OKB-156 was one of the first in the Soviet Union to build a jet-powered bomber. Several 'clean sheet of paper' tactical bomber projects with a powerplant consisting of two 2,040-kgp (4,500-lbst) Rolls-Royce Nene I centrifugal-flow turbojets were running at the Tupolev OKB in 1946-47, but when the Soviet Air Force issued a revised operational requirement the projected 'aircraft 73' (provisional service designation Tu-20) had

to be radically reworked. This meant the aircraft surely could not be flown in time for the Aviation Day flypast at Moscow-Tushino airfield on the third Sunday of August 1947 – an all-important event at which the latest achievements of the national aircraft industry would be demonstrated to the Soviet political and military leaders. In order to 'show the flag' at Tushino the OKB took the decision to build a 'quick fix' jet bomber – 'aircraft 77' (originally called Tu-10 but later redesignated Tu-12), a heavily-modified Second World War-vintage Tu-2S *Bat* tactical bomber refitted with the same Nene I turbojets instead of Shvetsov ASh-82 radial engines, a new nose and a new tricycle landing gear. Even though the Tu-12 made its 18-minute maiden flight on 27th July 1947 in time for the flypast, it was only second – the Il-22 four-turbojet bomber created concurrently by OKB-240 under General Designer Sergey V. Ilyushin beat it by just three days, taking to the air on 24th July as the first Soviet jet bomber! Also, the Tu-12 was basically a technology demonstrator, whereas the Il-22 – the first aircraft thus designated – was developed as a fully capable bomber, with all due attention to detail.

In the second half of the 1940s, drawing on their experience with the first swept-wing jet fighters, the results of aerodynamic research in the wind tunnels at the Central Aerodynamics & Hydrodynamics Institute named after Nikolay Ye. Zhukovskiy (TsAGI – *Tsentrahl'nyy aero- i ghidrodinamicheskiy institoot*) and the study of captured German material, Soviet designers were able to embark on the design of swept-back wings for bombers. In the process they had to solve a new set of problems in aerodynamics, in calculating the strength of high aspect ratio swept wings, and in studying stability/control characteristics and the behaviour of swept wings at speeds close to the speed of sound.

Again, the Tupolev OKB was one of the first in the Soviet Union to start work on fast bombers with swept wings and tail surfaces. Assisted by colleagues from TsAGI and leading special-

The one-off Tu-12 ('aircraft 77') was the Tupolev OKB's first jet. Its Tu-2 lineage is obvious – the wings, tail unit and most of the fuselage are taken straight from the wartime piston-engined bomber.

ists in the field of aircraft structural strength, the OKB designed, built and bench-tested models of swept wings with varying sweepback and rigidity. Research was undertaken into wings with constant 35° sweep at quarter-chord (in passing, this would become a sort of standard for Tupolev aircraft for many years to come) and an aspect ratio of 6 to 11. The calculations for the root section of the swept wings posed particular problems for the structural strength specialists since, in the preferred two-spar structure, the forward spar was longer than the rear spar and carried the greater load. The distribution of stress flows in the wing centre section torsion box and outer wing panels were studied in detail by the OKB's structural strength department under Aleksey M. Cheryomukhin, using scale models made initially of paper, then of metal.

Above and above left: A desktop model of the 'aircraft 82' jet tactical bomber with pre-1955 placement of the star insignia.

Below: A three-view drawing of the '82' from the ADP documents.

Above right: Front view of the sole 'aircraft 82' prototype during manufacturer's flight tests. Note the landing lights built into the air intake centrebodies.

Right: A three-quarters front view of the 'aircraft 82'.

Below right: This photo accentuates the bomber's small size. Note the provisional service designation Tu-22 on the nose and tail. The shape of the nose and the tailcone differs from the drawing.

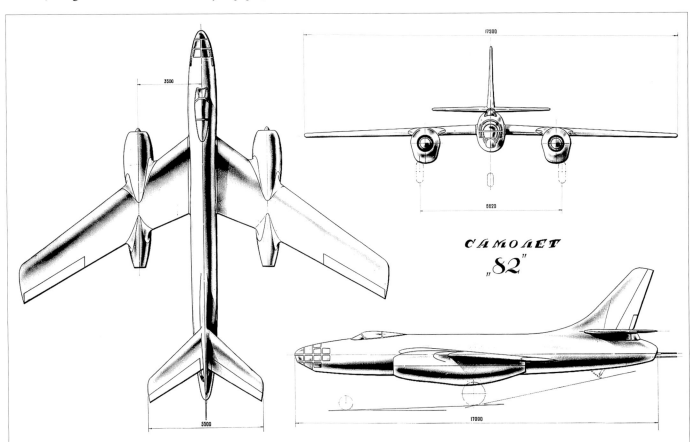

The test results were used to formulate an engineering methodology for swept-back wings and tail surfaces. Three eminent TsAGI experts on the structural strength of swept wings, Saveliy N. Kan, Iosif A. Sverdlov and Vladimir F. Kiselyov, also had a hand in this research work, contributing to the theory and practice of swept wing design in the Soviet Union. As a result, when the Tupolev OKB started work on designing its first swept-wing bombers it already possessed an understanding of how the wing structure would behave and a formulated methodology for its design.

As for TsAGI itself, the institute had begun research into swept wings immediately after the Second World War, largely falling back on captured German materials (the aviation specialists of the Third Reich had made considerable progress in this field). At TsAGI this direction of work was headed by Professor Vladimir V. Stroominskiy, who was an avid proponent of swept wings; OKB-156 General Designer Andrey N. Tupolev favoured swept wings, sharing Stroominskiy's views on the subject. TsAGI paid particular attention to swept wings in the context of long-range bombers, which were a high-priority programme, and to selecting

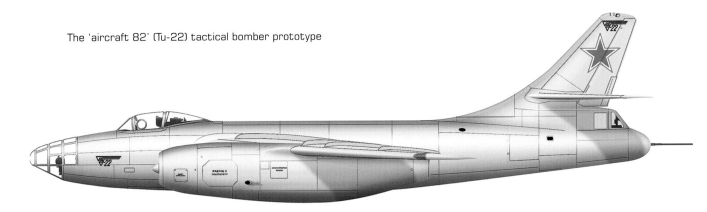

The 'aircraft 82' (Tu-22) tactical bomber prototype

the optimum general arrangement for such aircraft. The latter bit was tricky because, firstly, a high lift/drag ratio at high subsonic Mach numbers was required to ensure adequate range; secondly, there was the need to choose the best location for the multiple engines that were needed to provide the required thrust. Thirdly, it was necessary to ensure acceptable field performance in spite of the higher wing loading (as compared to piston-engined aircraft), the lower lift generated by the new high-speeds airfoils and the relative reduction of the high-lift devices' efficiency on swept wings as compared to straight wings.

Proceeding from the results of the large scope of work carried out by OKB-156 and TsAGI, in April 1948 the OKB's preliminary design (PD) project section headed by Gheorgiy A. Cheryomukhin (the son of Aleksey M. Cheryomukhin; he became the OKB's chief aerodynamicist in 1974) prepared a comprehensive summary titled *Research into the Flight Characteristics of Heavy Swept-wing Jet Aircraft*. It concerned the choice of the parametrical limits of a jet bomber designed to meet the Air Force's general operational requirement for 1947-48. Aircraft with 35° wing sweep at quarter-chord and an all-up weight ranging from 80,000 to 160,000 kg (from 176,370 to 352,730 lb) were contemplated. The powerplant consisted of six or eight turbojets giving an overall thrust of 12,000-24,000 kgp (26,455-52,910 lbst). Two models came into consideration – the Klimov RD-45 (a Soviet version of the RR Nene I reverse-engineered under Vladimir Ya. Klimov;

RD = *re'aktivnyy dvigatel'* – jet engine) or the indigenous 3,300-kgp (7,275-lbst) Mikulin AM-TKRD-01 axial-flow turbojet developed by OKB-300 under Chief Designer Aleksandr A. Mikulin. (AM stands for Aleksandr Mikulin, while TKRD means *toor-bokompressornyy re'aktivnyy dvigatel'* – 'turbo-compressor jet engine', that is, turbojet.) The wing loading varied from 300 to 500 kg/m² (from 61.5 to 102.5 lb/sq ft). Thus the summary covered a hypothetical range of aircraft from a medium-range bomber to an intercontinental strategic bomber. This summary had a considerable influence on the choice of the aircraft's basic parameters at the practical stage of the Tupolev OKB's work on heavy jets.

Analysis showed that with the available low-powered engines the required range could only be obtained if the maximum possible dimensions and weight were selected for the bomber. The German designers had taken this approach during the Second World War; so had the Boeing Company when developing the six-engined B-47. The Soviet designers, however, chose a different approach: in order to achieve acceptable aerodynamic parameters, operational qualities and operating economics it was decided to use two or four really powerful engines. The practical effort proceeded in two directions, the first of which was to verify swept wings in actual flight. Therefore in February 1948, the Tupolev OKB started work on an experimental swept-wing tactical bomber. Known in house as **'aircraft 82'** (and sometimes referred to as the Tu-82), it was to fly at speeds close to the speed of sound (Mach 0.9-0.95). As mentioned earlier, the Ilyushin OKB was 'the first past the post' with the Il-22; now, adding offence to injury, the Soviet Air Force selected Ilyushin's Il-28 *Beagle* twin-turbojet tactical bomber over the Tu-14 *Bosun*. On the other hand, 'aircraft 82', which was developed as an unsolicited venture (without an official order), was the first Soviet bomber with swept wings.

The 'aircraft 82' was a radical redesign of the 'aircraft 73' three-turbojet tactical bomber (the initial prototype version of the twinjet Tu-14). Actually it was, to all intents and purposes, a new aircraft; quite apart from the swept wings, it had all-swept tail surfaces (on the '73' only the horizontal tail was swept). It was to be powered by two 2,270-kgp (5,000-lbst) RD-45F engines (*for-seerovannyy* – uprated) – the Soviet copy of the RR Nene II – or 2,700-kgp (5,950-lbst) Klimov VK-1 turbojets, a further uprated version of the RD-45, in wing-mounted nacelles, whereas the '73' had two RD-45 cruise engines and a 1,530-kgp (3,350-lbst) RD-500 centrifugal-flow turbojet (a reverse-engineered Rolls-

Performance of the 'aircraft 82' during manufacturer's flight tests	
Empty weight	11,226 kg (24,749 lb)
All-up weight:	
normal	14,919 kg (32,890 lb)
maximum	18,339 kg (40,430 lb)
Maximum speed:	
at sea-level	870 km/h (540 mph)
at 4,000 m (13,120 ft)	931 km/h (578 mph)
Cruising speed	798 km/h (495 mph)
Climb time to 5,000 m (16,400 ft)	5.8 minutes
Range	2,395 km (1,490 miles)
Service ceiling	11,400 m (37,400 ft)
Take-off run	1,100 m (3,610 ft)
Landing run	550 m (1,805 ft)

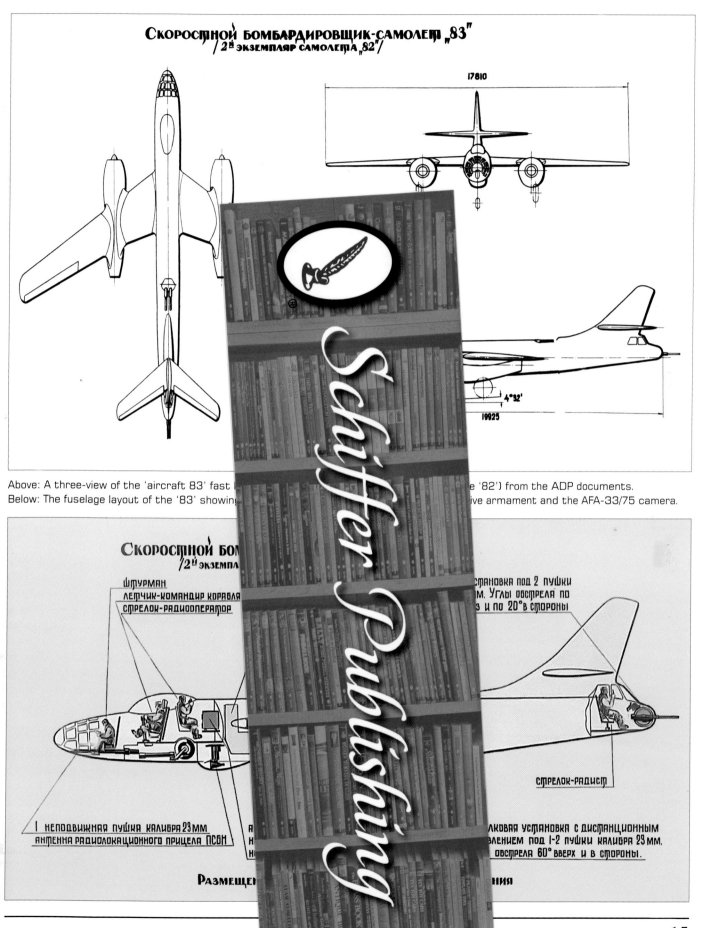

Скоростной бомбардировщик-самолет „83"
/2^й экземпляр самолета „82"/

17810

4°32'

19925

Above: A three-view of the 'aircraft 83' fast [...] e '82') from the ADP documents.
Below: The fuselage layout of the '83' showing [...] ive armament and the AFA-33/75 camera.

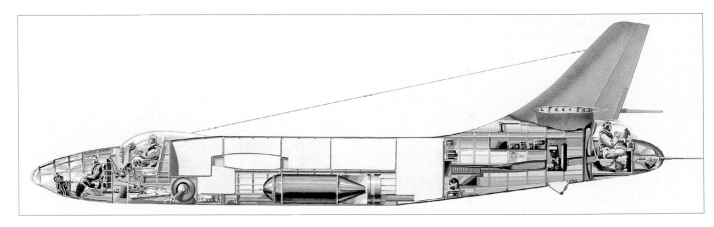

Above: A different projected fuselage layout of the '83' with a crew of three, no dorsal cannon barbette and no radar.
Below: A projected fuselage layout of the '83' (again with a three-man crew) showing a reshaped nose and a different tail barbette with twin cannons. The shape of the fuselage and the tail turret design are the same as on the 'aircraft 82' drawing on page 12.

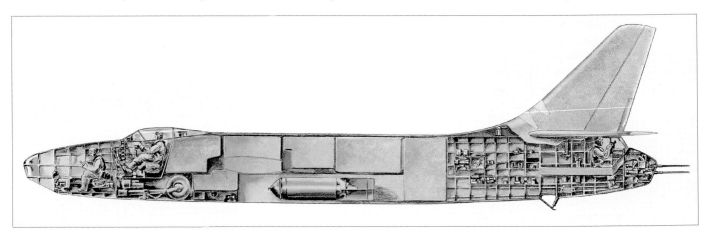

Royce Derwent V) as a booster for take-off or for a burst of speed over the target. The crew was reduced from four to three – the pilot, the navigator/bomb-aimer and the gunner/radio operator (GRO); the dorsal and ventral gun barbettes were deleted and replaced by a glazed gunner's station at the aft extremity of the fuselage with a ventral access hatch and a single twin-cannon powered turret. (A similar crew reduction and optimisation of the powerplant and armament was done when 'aircraft 73' evolved into the twinjet 'aircraft 81' and then into 'aircraft 81T' – the production Tu-14T torpedo-bomber for the AVMF.) Moreover, 'aircraft 82' was significantly smaller and lighter than its precursor, with an overall length of 17.57 m (57 ft 7⁴⁷⁄₆₄ in), a wing span of 17.81 m (58 ft 5³⁄₁₆ in, a wing area of 46.24 m² (497.72 sq ft) and a normal take-off weight of about 13,000 kg (28,660 lb).

The PD project was completed in March 1948. On 12th June, that year the Soviet Council of Ministers (that is, government) issued directive No.2052-804, giving 'aircraft 82' official status and allocating the provisional service designation Tu-22 (which would later be reused for another bomber). Work on the advanced development project (ADP), which differed only slightly from the original version, was concluded ten days later on 22nd June.

Construction of the 'aircraft 82' at the OKB's prototype manufacturing facility in Moscow (MMZ No.156 'Opyt') began in July 1948. (MMZ = *Moskovskiy mashinostroitel'nyy zavod* – Moscow Machinery Plant; *opyt* translates as either 'experiment' or 'experi-

ence'.) The sessions of the so-called mock-up review commission (*maketnaya komissiya*) – an expert panel composed of industry and Air Force representatives whose task was to detect and eliminate any obvious errors at an early stage – took place on 16th-18th August, though normally such sessions take place before the first metal is cut. Powered by RD-45F engines, the sole prototype was rolled out on 15th February 1949, and submitted for manufacturer's flight tests. It differed from the ADP version in having four pairs of boundary layer fences on the wings and lacking the originally envisaged reversible hydraulic actuators (the decision to remove them was prompted by the results of the '73' and '78' bombers' tests). The offensive and defensive armament was not fitted either because the '82' was considered a development aircraft.

The '82' made its first flight on 24th March 1949, from the airfield of the Flight Research Institute named after Mikhail M. Gromov (LII – *Lyotno-issledovatel'skiy institoot*) in Zhukovskiy near Moscow with Tupolev OKB chief test pilot Aleksey D. Perelyot at the controls. The manufacturer's flight tests report noted that the bomber was stable and could be flown by a pilot with average skills. There were no nasty surprises – the bomber's handling was much more docile than that of the first swept-wing fighters.

Concurrently with the tests, 'aircraft 82' was being prepared to take part in the annual Aviation Day flypast at Tushino. During the dress rehearsal of the event in the summer of 1949, while the bomber was flying low over the Moskva River on the approaches to Tushino, it was caught in a series of thermals of varying intensity causing a phenomenon that was later called 'recurrent turbulence' – an effect arising when an aircraft flies at low altitude over complex terrain (for instance, plain/river/woodland). The G loads were so severe that the port engine partly broke free from the bearer, which was overstressed; test pilot Aleksey D. Perelyot was injured when he was tossed around in the cockpit, hitting his face on the instrument panel, but managed to shut down the affected engine and make a safe single-engine landing at Zhukovskiy. This incident necessitated the introduction of the new 'recurrent turbulence' concept into the structural strength calculation norms. After a series of tests, a calculation method allowing for 'recurrent turbulence' was introduced into aircraft design practice; Aleksey M. Cheryomukhin played a key role in this, identifying the cause of the phenomenon.

The 'aircraft 82' was essentially an experimental machine – a proof-of-concept vehicle for the swept-wing design, and it served its purpose, confirming the viability of swept wings on large aircraft and allowing the first practical step towards the creation of the Tu-16 to be taken. In parallel, OKB-156 was working on its fully combat-capable version designated **'aircraft 83'**, which featured a full complement of offensive and defensive armament. This bomber differed from the '82' prototype in having a longer fuselage measuring 19.925 m (65 ft 4^{29}/$_{64}$ in) and a crew of four, which included an aft-facing GRO seated behind the pilot and controlling a dorsal cannon barbette (the tail gunner was now a pure gunner); the shape and size of the cockpit canopy and the navigator's station glazing were altered. VK-1 engines were to be fitted to cater for the higher weight, and the configuration of the fuselage fuel tanks was also revised. The bomber was to be equipped with a PSBN navigation/bomb-aiming radar (*pribor slepovo bombometaniya i navigahtsii* – 'blind bombing and navigation device') aft of the nosewheel well, with the option of replacing this with an alternative targeting system called Rym-S (the Russian word *rym* – originally a nautical term of Dutch origin – means 'ring bolt'). This was a rangefinding system that allowed the bomber to attack a stationary target with known co-ordinates, using triangulation from a pair of ground-based or heliborne transmitters. An AFA-BA/40 camera replaced the AFA-33/75.

Construction of the 'aircraft 83' prototype began at MMZ No.156 but was never completed because all further work on swept-wing tactical bombers was wound up in 1949. This was because the Il-28 straight-wing tactical bomber was due to enter

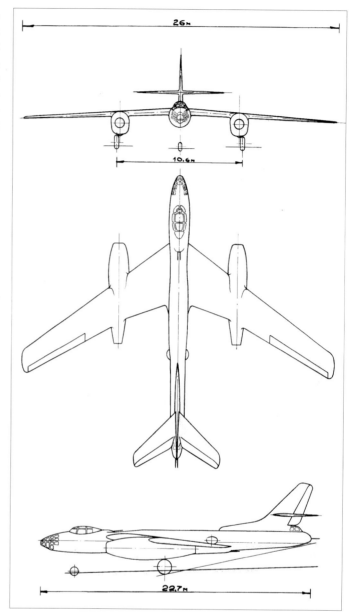

Above: A three-view drawing of the 'aircraft 486' from the ADP documents, showing its larger size and the waist gunner's station with lateral sighting blisters for the ventral cannon barbette.

Below: The fuselage layout of 'aircraft 486'.

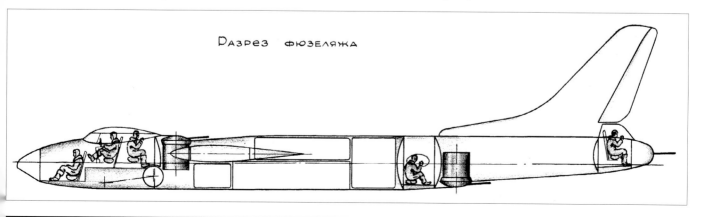

Left and below left: A desktop model of 'aircraft 486'. Note the recess for the dorsal cannon barbette aft of the fighter-type canopy, the reduced wing trailing edge sweep inboard of the engine nacelles and the 'dimples' aft of the waist gunner's sighting blisters meant to improve his rearward field of view. Unlike the 'aircraft 83', there appears to be no radar.

Opposite page: The fuselage layout of the 'aircraft 86' bomber – the next phase in the project's evolution. The redesigned flight deck remarkably similar to that of the future Tu-16, with side-by-side seating for the two pilots, and the chin radome are clearly visible.

Preliminary project specifications of the 'aircraft 486'	
Length	22.75 m (74 ft 7⁴⁵⁄₆₄ in)
Wing span	26.0 m (85 ft 3⅝ in)
Height on ground	7.2 m (23 ft 7¹⁵⁄₃₂ in)
Wing area	83.0 m² (893.4 sq ft)
Wing sweep	34°30'
Wing aspect ratio	8.15
Wing taper	2.0
Vertical tail area	11.205 m² (120.61 sq ft)
Horizontal tail area	13.695 m² (147.41 sq ft)
Empty weight	18,500 kg (40,790 lb)
All-up weight:	
normal	26,000 kg (57,320 lb)
maximum (in overload configuration)	31,500 kg (69,450 lb)
Wing loading	380 kg/m² (77.91 lb/sq ft)
Maximum speed:	
at sea level	990 km/h (615 mph)
at 6,000 m (19,685 ft)	1,030 km/h (639 mph)
Range with a 1,000-kg (2,205-lb) bomb load	3,500-4,000 km (2,173-2,484 miles)
Take-off run:	
with a 32,000-kg (70,550-lb) TOW	1,700 m (5,580 ft)
with a 26,000-kg TOW	1,100 m (3,610 ft)
Crew	5

mass production and Soviet Air Force service imminently. It was almost equal to the future Tu-22 in most performance aspects (and actually superior in field performance) while being much easier to build and operate thanks to certain clever design features; the Air Force was quite happy with the Il-28 as it was. Moreover, at the aircraft technology level of the day swept wings did not confer any tangible advantage on a subsonic tactical bomber anyway. The Il-30 of 1949, a swept-wing derivative of the *Beagle* similar to the '82', also remained a purely experimental aircraft for this very reason; as a matter of fact, it was built but never flown.

Attempting to save the project, the Tupolev OKB proposed a long-range interceptor version of the bomber designated '83P' (*perekhvatchik* – interceptor) to the Soviet Air Defence Force (PVO – *Protivovozdooshnaya oborona*). However, the latter showed a complete lack of interest, being unable at the time to recognise the potential of such an aircraft. It was not until ten years later that a heavy interceptor with a take-off weight of 15,000-18,000 kg (33,070-39,680 lb) suddenly became a priority programme for the PVO.

The other direction of development work was originally to develop a scaled-up version of the Tu-14 powered by bigger turbojet engines. Thus, 'aircraft 82'/'aircraft 83' was followed by a succession of progressively larger and heavier bombers – the '486', '86', '87', and '491' designs which did not progress beyond the project stage. However, the cumulative experience gained with these projects allowed the Tupolev OKB to develop the 'aircraft 494' and 'aircraft 495' projects – the Tu-16's immediate precursors – and eventually turn the Tu-16 into the outstanding long-range bomber that it was. These projects warrant a closer look.

'Aircraft 486' medium bomber (project)

Back in mid-1948 OKB-156 began developing a version of the straight-wing 'aircraft 73' bomber powered by new indigenous turbojets in the 3,000 to 5,000-kgp (6,610 to 11,020-lbst) thrust class. The original project studies envisaged substituting the existing two RD-45 cruise engines yielding a total of 4,080 kgp (8,990 lbst) with two Mikulin AM-TKRD-01s yielding 6,600 kgp (14,550 lbst); together with the RD-500 booster engine they increased the total take-off thrust from 5,600 to 8,120 kgp (from 12,345 to 17,900 lbst). A Council of Ministers directive stipulating these engines was issued in September 1949, requiring the re-engined aircraft to enter flight test in the fourth quarter of the year. Yet, it turned out that flight performance would be almost unchanged – there was no improvement over the 'aircraft 73', so it wasn't worth the sweat. Therefore the designers soon switched to even more powerful AM-TKRD-02 (alias AM-02) axial-flow turbojets rated at 4,780 kgp (10,540 lbst) for take-off. At the same time the booster engine was deleted and the defensive armament was reworked to feature a tail gunner's station as used on the 'aircraft 81' (Tu-14). Even so, the total thrust of 9,560 kgp (21,075 lbst) was greater than in the previous three-engined version.

Work on the AM-TKRD-02 powered version commenced in January 1949. However, preliminary calculations undertaken by the OKB's aerodynamics department showed that the increased thrust of the new engines would increase the aircraft's speed so much that it would reach critical Mach numbers, leading to the onset of Mach tuck (a tendency to enter a dive spontaneously at high speed that afflicted straight-wing aircraft). On the 'aircraft 73' this phenomenon manifested itself at speeds above Mach 0.8. Under these conditions, retaining the unswept wings was no longer viable; a transition to swept wings became imperative. Added to this, the considerably higher fuel consumption of the new engines necessitated an increase in the fuel load to 10,000-12,000 kg (22,045-26,455 lb). This, in turn, led to a significant increase of the take-off weight – from the 20,140-24,200 kg (44,400-53,350 lb) of the 'aircraft 73' to 30,000 kg (66,140 lb) – and to a major revision of the fuselage's internal layout.

An extensive redesign ensued, changing the aircraft's appearance completely. In the resulting new high-speed medium-range bomber project, which bore the provisional in-house designation 'aircraft 486' (denoting the sixth project undertaken in 1948), the fuselage still featured a fighter-style bubble canopy for the single pilot and the GRO plus an extensively glazed parabolic nose for the navigator/bomb-aimer, as on the 'aircraft 73' and the Tu-14 (the cockpit and the navigator's station formed a single pressurised cabin). As on the '73' (but not the Tu-14), a pressurised gunner's compartment with a ventral entry hatch was located aft of the bomb bay, featuring lateral elliptical blisters for observation and gun aiming. The blisters protruded only a little beyond the fuselage contour to minimise drag, and to provide the waist gunner with an acceptable field of view rearwards and downwards the fuselage sides had characteristic depressions or 'dimples' downstream of the blisters, giving an hourglass cross-section. The tail gunner's station was not connected to this compartment (there was an avionics/equipment bay between them). The project drawings and an available desktop model of the 'aircraft 486' do not show any radar.

The high aspect ratio wings with 3° anhedral were still mid-set; however, because of the wing sweep the wing/fuselage joint was moved forward from a position amidships to a position immediately aft of the cockpit, changing the bomber's proportions appreciably. The conventional tail surfaces had roughly the same sweepback as the wings, and the horizontal tail was mounted a short way above the root of the fin, which had a large root fillet. In similar manner to the 'aircraft 73' the engines were housed in large conformal nacelles of variable cross-section that adhered directly to the wing underside, dividing the flaps into two sections; the wing trailing-edge sweep inboard of the nacelles was slightly less than outboard. The landing gear design was also similar to the '73', the twin-wheel nose unit retracting aft (the ADP drawing shows a single nosewheel, though!) while the single-wheel main units retracted forward into the underside of the nacelles, giving a wide wheel track of 10.6 m (34 ft 9²¹⁄₆₄ in). During retraction the large mainwheels located on the outboard side of the struts turned through 90° by means of simple mechanical linkages to lie flat beneath the engines. This was a bit more difficult because the axial-flow engines had a fairly constant cross-section, leaving less room for the wheel wells. In contrast, on the '73' the difference between the diameters of the centrifugal-flow engine's combustion chamber section and the jet-pipe allowed the mainwheels to be comfortably accommodated beneath the jetpipes with no increase in the nacelle cross-section.

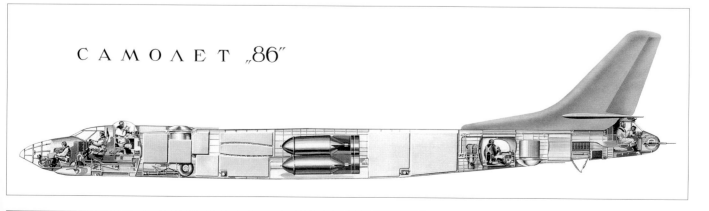

С А М О Л Е Т „86"

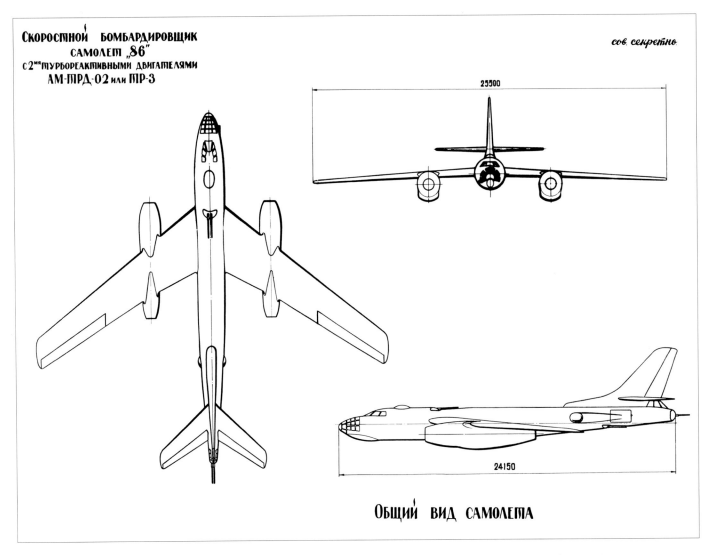

Скоростной бомбардировщик
самолет „86"
с 2-мя турбореактивными двигателями
АМ-ТРД-02 или ТР-3

сов. секретно

25500

24150

Общий вид самолета

The bomb bay of 'aircraft 486' located between two groups of fuel tanks was able to accommodate large bombs, including the 3,000-kg (6,610-lb) FAB-3000 M-46 bomb (*foogahsnaya aviabomba* – high-explosive bomb, 1946 model). The defensive armament comprised seven cannons – a fixed forward-firing 23-mm Nudelman/Rikhter NR-23 cannon with 180 rounds on one side of the nose and three pairs of 20-mm Berezin B-20E cannons with 200 rpg in a remote-controlled dorsal barbette aft of the cockpit, a remote-controlled ventral barbette aft of the waist gunner's station and the tail turret.

Developed in 1944 by Mikhail Ye. Berezin, the B-20 was a 'king size' version of the 12.7-mm (.50 calibre) UB machine-gun, differing from the latter mainly in having a new barrel of larger calibre; the B-20E version of 1946 had an electric charging mechanism, hence the suffix. The NR-23 (*izdeliye* 150P) cannon was developed in 1947 by Aleksandr E. Nudel'man and Aron A. Rikhter at OKB-16 of the Ministry of Armament based in Tula. (*Izdeliye* (product) such-and-such is a code for Soviet/Russian military hardware items commonly used in paperwork to confuse outsiders.) It was a derivative of the 1944-vintage Nudelman/ Suranov NS-23 with a breechblock accelerator increasing the rate of fire from 550 to 850 rounds per minute for virtually no increase

in weight. As compared to the B-20E, the NR-23 had more than twice the weight of fire – 2.66 kg/sec (5.86 lb/sec) versus 1.32 kg/ sec (2.91 lb/sec) – and a higher rate of fire (800-950 rpm versus 600-800 rpm) but was slightly heavier, weighing 39 kg (86 lb) versus 25 kg (55 lb).

Work on the '486' was halted at the initial design stage but served as the basis for the 'aircraft 86' long-range bomber project.

'Aircraft 86' and 'aircraft 87' medium bombers (projects)
At the end of 1948 the Tupolev OKB set to work on the 'aircraft 86' long-range bomber – a larger and heavier aircraft powered by two Mikulin AM-02 turbojets or two slightly smaller 4,500-kgp (9,920-lbst) Lyul'ka TR-3 axial-flow turbojets (*toorbore'aktivnyy [dvigatel']* – turbojet engine) developed by OKB-165 under Arkhip M. Lyul'ka. The work was performed in the OKB's technical projects department under the guidance of Sergey M. Yeger.

The designers took the general arrangement of 'aircraft 486' as a starting point, but the '86' had a fuselage of greater diameter and a larger bomb bay which accommodated a normal bomb load of 2,000 kg (4,410 lb) and a maximum load of 6,000 kg (13,230 lb). As originally conceived, the Mikulin-powered version was to have a range of 4,000 km (2,485 miles) with a normal bomb load, a

Above: Four aspects of a rather crude-looking wooden model of 'aircraft 86'.

Left: A three-view drawing of the '86' marked *Sov[ershenno] sek**ret**no* (Top secret). Note the airbrakes on the rear fuselage sides. The upper view appears to suggest a single-pilot cockpit, but the drawing on this page shows otherwise!

Below: A different fuselage layout of the '86' showing the weapons and equipment placement.

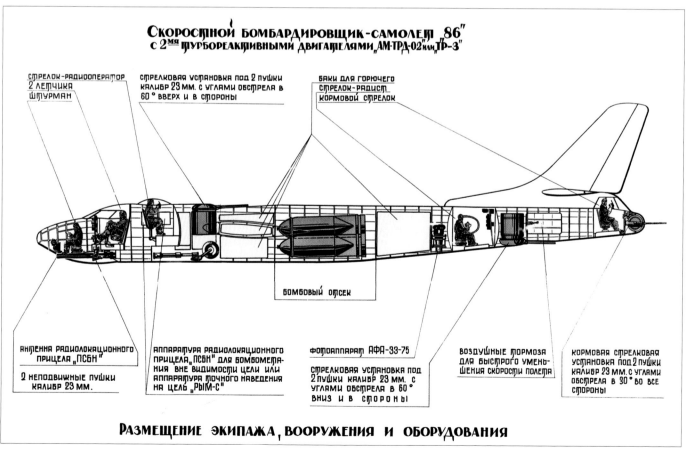

Left: An artist's impression of the 'aircraft 86'.

Right: A three-view of the 'aircraft 491' bomber that evolved from the '86', showing the stronger sweep-back of the wings and the tail surfaces.

Below right: The fuselage layout of the '491' from the ADP documents. Note the two 'plugs' inserted into the fuselage of the original '86' fore and aft of the wings.

maximum speed of 980 km/h (609 mph) at 6,000 m (19,685 ft) and a service ceiling of 13,400 m (43,960 ft). The all-up weight was increased to 40,000 kg (88,180 lb) and the fuel load was to be 5,200-17,200 kg (11,460-37,920 lb).

To ease the pilot workload during the longer missions, a co-pilot was included in the crew, increasing the latter to six; the pilots were seated side by side in what was now a flight deck. Hence the forward pressurised cabin was completely reconfigured to feature a stepped windscreen and a roof level with the fuselage top instead of the predecessor's bubble canopy under which the pilot and the gunner/radio-operator (GRO) sat back to back. The GRO was repositioned to a separate aft-facing workstation at the back of this cabin, sitting above and behind the pilots under an observation/sighting blister. At the same time the PSBN radar was moved forward to a chin position (ahead of the nosewheel well), its teardrop radome blending with the navigator's station glazing. A pair of fighter-type airbrake flaps were installed on the rear fuselage – an unusual feature for a bomber. The nose gear strut was lengthened, and the main gear units were given twin wheels. The defensive armament was augmented by a second fixed forward-firing NR-23 cannon.

The PD project of 'aircraft 86' was completed in March 1949; the OKB immediately set about building a full-size wooden mock-up of the bomber and issuing detail drawings to MMZ No.156 for

prototype construction. As early as 19th March, the mock-up, which was then only 50% complete, was inspected by the mock-up review commission. Meanwhile, a large model of 'aircraft 86' was undergoing wind tunnel tests at TsAGI.

In the course of the design work on 'aircraft 86' the Tupolev OKB jointly with TsAGI was exploring the influence of varying wing areas and aspect ratios on the flight performance of a swept-wing aircraft. As a result, the project was revised. The definitive version had wings of greater span with an aspect ratio of 10, the wing area was increased to 100-110 m² (1,075-1,182 sq ft). The fuselage was lengthened, its nose became sharper to reduce drag, and the navigator's field of view was improved at the same time. The fuel tankage was increased, part of the additional fuel tanks being in the reconfigured fuselage. The nose gear unit was fitted with twin wheels instead of a single wheel, a retractable tail bumper was added ahead of the tail gunner's station to protect the tail turret, which mounted a single NR-23 cannon, and the PSBN radar was replaced by the improved PSBN-M (*modifitseerovannyy* – modified).

In the definitive version the design range was increased to 4,750 km (2,951 miles). In addition to the basic bomber, the OKB drafted the 'aircraft 86R' reconnaissance version (*[samolyot-] razvedchik* – reconnaissance aircraft) and the 'aircraft 86T' torpedo-bomber and minelayer (*torpedonosets*) for the AVMF.

The Lyul'ka-powered version, whose flight performance was similar to the Mikulin-powered version, was being developed in parallel as a 'belt and braces' policy in case the AM-02 was not available on time. The PD project of the version with TR-3 engines, which had some structural differences from the AM-02 powered version, was issued on 18th July 1949. One of the late project versions with TR-3 engines bore a separate designation, 'aircraft 87'. The work on these projects showed that building a transonic bomber with a range of 5,000 km (3,105 miles) was feasible.

Yet, man supposes, God disposes. In this case God took the shape of the Ministry of Medium Machinery (MSM – *Ministerstvo srednevo mashinostroyeniya*) responsible for the Soviet nuclear programme. Development of the first Soviet nuke – the RDS-1 implosion-type nuclear device (alias *izdeliye* 501 or 'nuclear device 1-200') with a yield of 22 kilotons – began in 1947. (The RDS acronym was used for early Soviet nuclear devices, gen-

Preliminary project specifications of the 'aircraft 86' (definitive form)	
Length	27.48 m (90 ft 1⁵⁄₆₄ in)
Wing span	27.49 m (90 ft 2½ in)
Height on ground	8.25 m (27 ft 0⁵⁄₆₄ in)
Wing area	100 m² (1,075.26 sq ft)
All-up weight:	
normal	30,000 kg (66,140 lb)
in overload configuration	42,000 kg (92,590 lb)
Maximum speed at 4,000 m (13,120 ft)	950-1,000 km/h (590-621 mph)
Service ceiling	13,000 m (42,650 ft)
Range with a 2,000-kg (4,40-lb) bomb load	4,000 km (2,485 miles)
Take-off run	1,000-1,200 m (3,280-3,940 ft)
Landing run	500-600 m (1,640-1,970 ft)

Preliminary project specifications of the 'aircraft 491'	
Length	26.39 m (86 ft 6½ in)
Wing span	22.5 m (73 ft 9⁵⁄₆₄ in)
Height on ground	7.5 m (24 ft 7¹⁄₆₄ in)
Wing area	81.7 m² (879.4 sq ft)
Wing sweep	45°
Wing aspect ratio	6.2
Empty weight	21,920 kg (48,330 lb)
All-up weight:	
normal	30,000 kg (66,140 lb)
in overload configuration	42,700 kg (94,140 lb)
Maximum speed at 6,500 m (21,325 ft)	1,085 km/h (674 mph)
Service ceiling	13,500 m (44,290 ft)
Range with a 2,000-kg (4,410-lb) bomb load	5,000 km (3,105 miles)
Crew	6

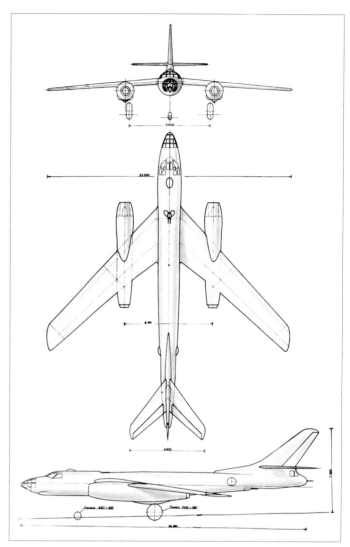

erating such explanations as *re'aktivnyy* **dvigatel'** *spetsiahl'nyy* ('special jet engine'), *re'aktivnyy* **dvigatel'** *Stalina* ('Stalin's jet engine'), *Rosseeya* **delayet** *sama* ('Russia makes [the atomic bomb] on her own') and the like.)

The first RDS-1 was detonated on 29th August 1949, at the proving ground built for this purpose 170 km (105 miles) west of Semipalatinsk, Kazakhstan, and known as the War Ministry's Practice Range No.2 (UP-2 – *oochebnyy poligon*). Pretty soon an air-droppable production version was developed – the RDS-3 (*izdeliye* 501-M) bomb with a yield of 38-42 kilotons, codenamed 'Maria'. Henceforth new Soviet long-range bombers had to be designed with the ability to carry this weapon. However, the RDS-3 weighed more than 5,000 kg (11,020 lb); with this bomb on board the 'aircraft 86' would be unable to meet the stipulated range target of 5,000 km. Moreover, special features had to be incorporated into the aircraft to make sure the bomb was thermally stable en route to the target (if the nuke got too cold it could fail to detonate) and that the crew was shielded from the effects of the nuclear explosion. In a nutshell, the VVS needed not merely a bomber with twice the speed of the Tu-4 but an aircraft capable of delivering a nuclear bomb over the same range as the Tu-4.

Research undertaken by OKB-156 in the course of work on the '86' showed that a viable long-range fast bomber could be created

by increasing the weight and dimensions of the aircraft and by increasing the engine thrust by 50-100%. As a result, work on the '86' bomber was discontinued at the PD project stage, but many of its features, including the fuselage layout, the crew complement and the armament, were subsequently used on the 'aircraft 88' – the future Tu-16.

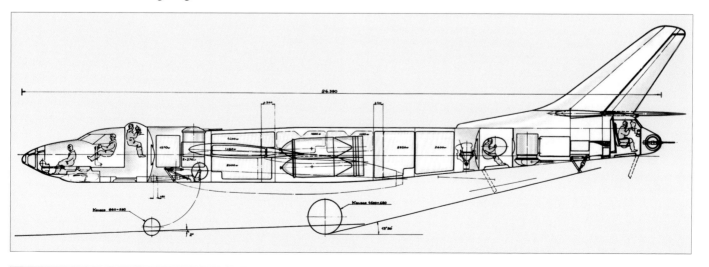

Two views of a wooden model showing the first version of the 'aircraft 494' bomber (494/1) with single-wheel main gear units retracting forward into the conformal engine nacelles.

This model shows the '494/2' version with the same engines in much smaller pylon-mounted engine nacelles and main gear bogies retracting aft into separate wing-mounted fairings outboard of them.

The '494/3' version was to have four conformal engine nacelles – two under the nose and two on the wings, B-47 style.

'Aircraft 491' medium bomber (project)

In April 1949 the Tupolev OKB produced the 'aircraft 491' bomber project (that is, the first project developed in 1949) – a faster version of 'aircraft 86'. On the latter, with a wing sweep of 35° the thrust reserve provided by the two AM-02 engines could not be used to the full; it was therefore decided to increase the wing sweep at quarter-chord to 45°. According to the designers' estimates, this would allow the bomber to reach a maximum speed of 1,085 km/h (674 mph) while meeting the stipulated range target of 5,000 km (3,105 miles).

The '494/4' was even more cartoony, with two conformal nacelles under the nose and two more atop the rear fuselage.

The '494/5' again had the nose-mounted inboard engines, while the outer engines were mounted at the wingtips.

The designers took the first version of the '86' as the starting point and made the following changes. The wing sweepback was increased to 45° and the wing anhedral to 4°; the wing centre section was completely revised and new wingtip fairings were fitted. The sweepback of the vertical and horizontal tail was also increased – from 40° to 50° at quarter-chord. The aircraft had a longer centre fuselage section with increased fuel tankage. The nose gear strut was lengthened again and the main gear units were redesigned, featuring inward-facing single wheels of a new type.

To improve the aerodynamic shape of the engine nacelles, the cross-section of the AM-02's jetpipe was altered to a figure-eight. This allowed the nacelles' cross-section area to be reduced and their aerodynamic qualities to be enhanced.

The 'aircraft 491' project did not progress beyond the proposal stage. At that time the properties of the novel wings with 45° sweep were not yet fully explored, and the Tupolev OKB (or rather General Designer Andrey N. Tupolev, who was famously conservative) decided that the speed gain of a few dozen kilometres per hour did not justify the technical risk, choosing to stick to the proven 35° wings for the time being. Later the OKB contemplated 45° wings again for a number of transonic and supersonic aircraft, but the 'aircraft 97' and 'aircraft 103' remained paper projects,

while the 'aircraft 98' (Tu-98 *Finback*) medium bomber prototype and 'aircraft 105' (the immediate precursor of the Tu-22 *Blinder*) shifted to 55-57° wing sweep before reaching the hardware stage.

'Aircraft 494' medium bomber (project)

In the autumn of 1949 the Ilyushin OKB, which had won favour from the Air Force and the Powers That Be by creating the successful Il-28 bomber, was commissioned by the VVS to design a high-speed long-range jet bomber; the appropriate Council of Ministers directive was issued shortly afterwards. Designated Il-46, the aircraft was to be powered by two Lyul'ka TR-3A turbojets (subsequently redesignated AL-5) – a version of the TR-3 uprated to 5,000 kgp (11,020 lbst). With a normal take-off weight the bomber was to have a normal bomb load of 3,000 kg (6,610 lb) and a maximum range of 3,000 km (1,863 miles); in high gross weight configuration this would increase to 5,000 kg (11,020 lb) and 5,000 km (3,105 miles) respectively.

(Jumping ahead of the story, it should be noted that, faced with a tight development schedule and a lack of prior experience with heavy swept-wing aircraft – the Il-30 was never flown, after all, – OKB-240 General Designer Sergey V. Ilyushin took the decision to break down the Il-46 programme into two stages. The aircraft

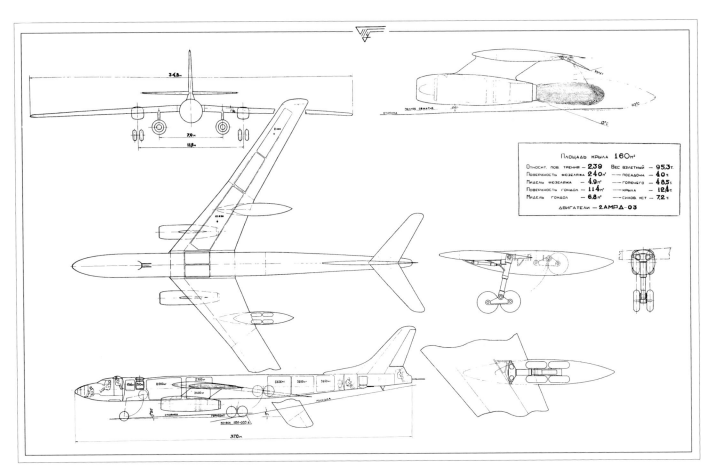

Above: A drawing of the '494-2' with two AM-RD-03 engines, showing details of the landing gear design and the engine installation.

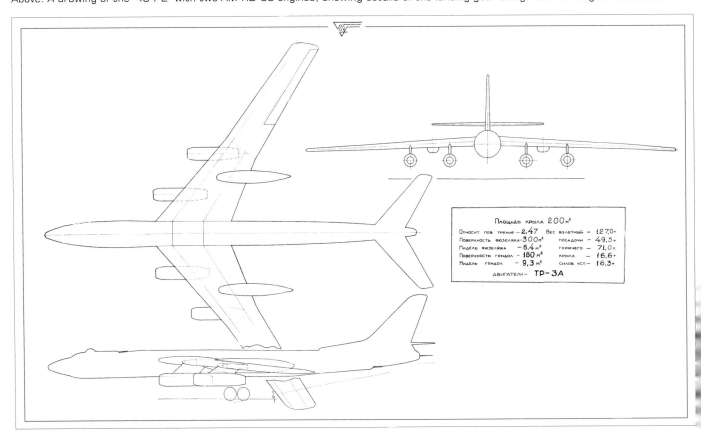

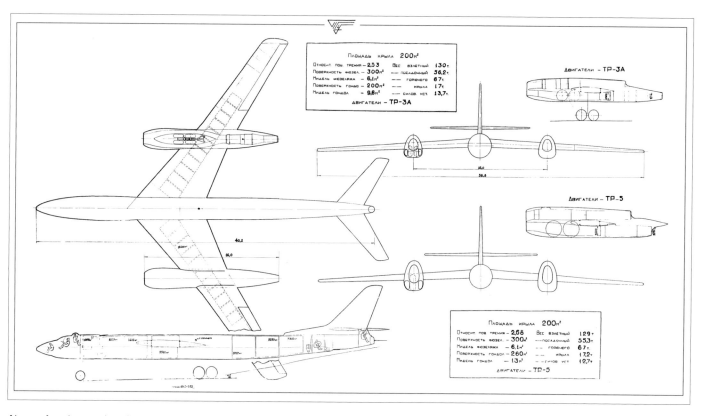

Above: Another project layout of the '494' with four TR-3A or TR-5 engines in staggered vertical pairs and an IL-18 style main gear.

Below left: This version of the '494' project had four TR-3As in individual underwing pods.

Below: A further version of the '494' with side-by-side pairs of TR-3As exhausting on both sides of the main gear fairings.

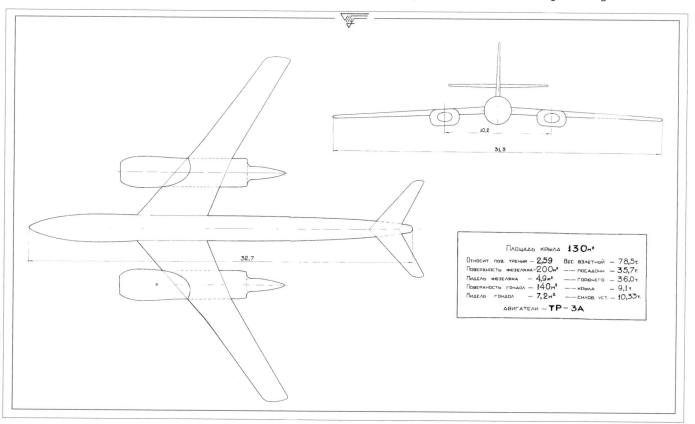

The fact that the Ilyushin OKB was commissioned to design a high-speed bomber did not put off the Tupolev OKB from developing a competing design unbidden, with the aim of producing an aircraft with higher performance than the Il-46. This project was known in house as 'aircraft 494' (the fourth project undertaken in 1949). The initial research was carried out by Boris M. Kondorskiy's projects team in which young graduates of the Moscow Aviation Institute, such as Aleksey A. Tupolev (the General Designer's son, who subsequently became head of the OKB when Andrey N. Tupolev passed away in 1972), Gheorgiy A. Cheryomukhin, Yu. Yu. Yoodin, Igor' B. Babin and Vladimir A. Sterlin, began their careers and went on to become the OKB's leading specialists. The first drafting of the layout and the first calculations were done under the close scrutiny of Andrey N. Tupolev who gave this project his particular attention. Subsequently, when the bomber's general arrangement, weights and dimensions had been decided, the technical projects department headed by Sergey M. Yeger joined in, followed by the remaining sections of the OKB.

The simultaneous quest by TsAGI and OKB-156 ended in a rational solution to the many problems involved in choosing the aerodynamic form of a heavy swept-wing aircraft. The most rapid progress was made in the research based on preliminary studies carried out by TsAGI on the chosen layout with wings having an aspect ratio of 7-9 and a sweepback of 35° at quarter-chord. The prototype of this layout was designated E-4 at TsAGI, and wind tunnel tests with a model were made between 1947 and 1950. The chosen design of the swept wings was in many ways identical to that used by German designers on the Junkers EF 132 six-turbojet long-range bomber project of 1944-45 whose development was cut short by the end of the Second World War.

While the layout of the aircraft and the proportions of its assemblies were being determined, each day Andrey N. Tupolev visited Yeger's department first thing in the morning to check up on progress; then, after a visit to his study he went to the mock-up shop of MMZ No.156 where a full-size wooden mock-up of the aircraft was being built. Kondorskiy's team had the task of setting the aircraft's basic parameters (wing area, weights and engine thrust) with which the bomber would meet the following requirements:

• normal bomb load, 6,000 kg (13,230 lb);
• maximum bomb load, 12,000 kg (26,455 lb);
• maximum speed at sea level, 950 km/h (590 mph);
• maximum speed at 10,000 m (32,810 ft), 950-1,000 km/h (590-621 mph);
• climb time to 10,000 m, 23 minutes;
• service ceiling, 12,000-13,000 m (39,370-42,650 ft);
• range with normal bomb load, 7,500 km (4,660 miles);
• take-off run without jet-assisted take-off (JATO) boosters, 1,000 m (3,280 ft);
• landing run, 900 m (2,950 ft).

The bomber was to have a crew of six. The defensive armament was identical to that of the 'aircraft 86'.

These figures (apart from range and bomb load) were essentially in line with those for the earlier 'aircraft 86' project, and the dimensions of 'aircraft 494' were based on data for the '86' project and on the aforementioned report titled *Research into the Flight Characteristics of Heavy Swept-wing Jet Aircraft*.

General Designer Andrey N. Tupolev in the late 1950s.

developed during stage A would retain the proven unswept wing design; stage B would concentrate on the definitive version with 35° wing sweep designated Il-46S (*strelovidnoye krylo* – swept wings).

Looking like a scaled-up Il-28 with twin-wheel main landing gear units having two independent shock struts side by side, the straight-wing Il-46 prototype was rolled out on 29th December 1951, and made its first flight on 3rd March 1952, with Vladimir K. Kokkinaki at the controls. Manufacturer's flight tests gave promising results – the aircraft attained a cruising speed of 700 km/h (435 mph), a maximum speed of 928 km/h (576 mph) at 5,000 m (16,400 ft) and a range of 4,845 km (3,009 miles). The state acceptance (= certification) trials were completed on 15th October, showing that the bomber fully met the operational requirement it was designed to; theoretically, the question was whether to put it into production or go ahead with the Il-46S. In the meantime, however, the Tupolev OKB had built and flown the more modern 'aircraft 88' prototype – the future Tu-16 which outperformed the Il-46 by a considerable margin; it was this aircraft that was ordered into production. Hence the Il-46S was never built, and the Tupolev OKB was vindicated for being upstaged with the Tu-14.)

Boris M. Kondorskiy, head of the Tupolev OKB's projects team.

Aleksey M. Cheryomukhin, head of the OKB's structural strength department.

Igor' B. Babin, one of the designers involved in the development of the 'aircraft 494'.

Vladimir A. Sterlin, another designer involved in the 'aircraft 494' project.

Ivan L. Golovin, the Tupolev OKB's chief metallurgist responsible for structural materials.

Sergey M. Yeger, head of the OKB's technical projects department.

Aleksandr V. Nadashkevich, head of the OKB's armament section.

Leonid L. Kerber, the OKB's equipment section chief.

Aleksandr E. Sterlin, a prominent aerodynamicist working for the Tupolev OKB.

Tupolev OKB aerodynamicist Gheorgiy A. Cheryomukhin who developed the calculation methods used in designing the Tu-16.

Abram S. Faynshtein, head of the Tupolev OKB's non-metallic materials laboratory.

Semyon A. Vigdorchik, the Tupolev OKB's chief technologist.

Preliminary project specifications of the 'aircraft 494/1'

Fuselage length	37.1 m (121 ft 8⅝ in)
Wing span	34.8 m (114 ft 2$^{5}/_{64}$ in)
Wing area	160 m² (1,722.23 sq ft)
Take-off weight	96,000 kg (211,640 lb)
Landing weight	41,000 kg (90,390 lb)
Fuel load	48,000 kg (105,820 lb)
Weight of engines	8,300 kg (18,300 lb)

Preliminary project specifications of the 'aircraft 494/2'

Fuselage length	37.0 m (121 ft 4$^{45}/_{64}$ in)
Wing span	34.8 m (114 ft 2$^{5}/_{64}$ in)
Wing area	160 m² (1,722.23 sq ft)
Take-off weight	95,300 kg (210,100 lb)
Landing weight	40,000 kg (88,180 lb)
Fuel load	48,500 kg (106,920 lb)
Weight of engines	7,200 kg (15,870 lb)

Like its competitor from the Ilyushin stable, 'aircraft 494' was to be powered by Lyul'ka TR-3A (AL-5) turbojets. As an alternative, a projected turbofan engine being developed by the Lyul'ka OKB under the provisional designation TR-5 was also considered; it had the same take-off thrust of 5,000 kgp (11,020 lbst) but a lower specific fuel consumption (SFC), which promised longer range, all other things being equal. Additionally, the Tupolev OKB contemplated the AMRD-03 axial-flow turbojet (later redesignated AM-3) then under development at the Mikulin OKB as a possible powerplant for 'aircraft 494'. With an estimated take-off thrust of 8,200 kgp (18,080 lbst), it was then the world's mot powerful jet engine; more will be said about it in Chapter 2.

The aerodynamic characteristics of the new bomber were similar to those of 'aircraft 86'; so were the geometrical parameters, including the wing planform. The maximum fuselage fineness ratio was to be similar to that of the Tu-85 strategic bomber. The stability coefficients were derived from the '86' project, providing that the rear fuselage length/wing span ratio was close to that accepted for the '86'. The parameters of the bomb bay corresponded to those of the rear bomb bay on the Tu-85, which held 6,000-12,000 kg (13,230-26,455 lb) of bombs; this required the fuselage diameter to be at least 2.5 m (8 ft 2$^{27}/_{64}$ in). The weights of the structural elements for various versions of the project were provisionally based on their equivalents for 'aircraft 86'; the crew complement, armament and equipment were to be the same as for the '86'. Even the maximum permissible tyre pressure was calculated, being 9-10 kg/cm² (128.5-142.8 psi).

Preliminary project specifications of the 'aircraft 494' with four engines in separate underwing nacelles

Wing area	200 m² (2,152.78 sq ft)
Take-off weight	127,000 kg (279,990 lb)
Landing weight	49,500 kg (109,130 lb)
Fuel load	71,000 kg (156,530 lb)
Weight of engines	16,300 kg (35,940 lb)

Preliminary project specifications of the 'aircraft 494' with four engines in vertical pairs

Engine type	TR-3A	TR-5
Length	40.2 m (131 ft 10$^{43}/_{64}$ in)	40.2 m (131 ft 10$^{43}/_{64}$ in)
Wing span	38.8 m (127 ft 3$^{9}/_{16}$ in)	38.8 m (127 ft 3$^{9}/_{16}$ in)
Wing area, m² (sq ft)	200 (2,152.78)	200 (2,152.78)
Take-off weight, kg (lb)	130,000 (286,600)	129,000 (284,400)
Landing weight, kg (lb)	56,200 (123,900)	55,300 (121,920)
Fuel load, kg (lb)	67,000 (147,710)	67,000 (147,710)
Weight of engines, kg (lb)	13,700 (30,200)	12,700 (28,000)

Preliminary project specifications of the 'aircraft 494' with four engines in side-by-side pairs

Length	32.7 m (107 ft 3$^{13}/_{32}$ in)
Wing span	31.3 m (102 ft 8$^{9}/_{32}$ in)
Wing area	130 m² (1,399.31 sq ft)
Take-off weight	78,500 kg (173,060 lb)
Landing weight	35,700 kg (78,710 lb)
Fuel load	36,000 kg (79,370 lb)
Weight of engines	10,330 kg (22,770 lb)

The work on the '494' bomber within Kondorskiy's projects team was the responsibility of Igor' B. Babin, Gheorgiy A. Cheryomukhin and Vladimir A. Sterlin. The team completed the PD project materials in June 1950, when the analysis and research resulted in a wing sweep of 36° being selected. The following alternative powerplants were considered: two AMRD-03 turbojets, four TR-3A (AL-5) turbojets or four TR-5 turbofans; additionally, the team calculated the bomber's performance with hypothetical afterburning versions of these three engines.

Various provisional layouts for 'aircraft 494' were considered, depending on the choice of engines. For the version powered by AMRD-03 engines and having a wing area of 160-200 m² (1,722-2,152 sq ft), two layouts were proposed. The first version, which was logically known in house as 'aircraft 494/1', retained the general arrangement of the 'aircraft 86' and 'aircraft 491' projects – the engines were housed in conformal nacelles located at about one-third of the wing span which also housed the main gear units.

The basic data derived from the preliminary layouts for the 'aircraft 494

'Wing area, m² (sq ft)	100 (1,076.39)	130 (1,399.31)	160 (1,722.23)	200 (2,152.78)	240 (2,588.34)
Take-off weight, kg (lb)	57,000-60,000 (125,660-132,275)	75,000-80,000 (165,340-176,370)	93,000-96,000 (205,030-211,640)	126,000-132,000 (277,780-291,000)	152,000-158,000 (335,100-348,320)
Fuel load, kg (lb)	24,000 (52,910)	36,000-39,000 (79,370-85,980)	48,500 (106,920)	71,000 (156,530)	85,600-87,500 (188,710-192,900)

The aircraft's proportions were somewhat different, though – the fuselage had a higher fineness ratio; also, the wing leading edge now had a kink just outboard of the engine nacelles, the leading-edge sweep decreasing slightly on the outer wings.

The second version ('aircraft 494/2') had the engines mounted under the wings in slender cylindrical nacelles on short forward-swept pylons located at approximately a quarter of the wing span. It was based on captured German materials delivered from Göttingen in 1947 which incorporated the results of wind tunnel research on various ways of locating the engine nacelles relative to the wings: in front, beneath, above and behind them. Placing the engine nacelles behind the wings gave the minimum drag for the wing/nacelle combination.

The main gear units were totally reworked, with four-wheel bogies somersaulting aft through 180° to stow in separate fairings at one-third of the span that projected well beyond the wing trailing edge, likewise dividing the flaps into two sections. These fairings were carefully shaped to minimise wave drag at transonic speeds; in the West, where the concept was developed almost in parallel, such fairings came to be known as anti-shock bodies, Whitcomb bodies or Küchemann carrots. Thus, for the first time, OKB-156 came up with this method of housing the main gear bogies which became a 'trademark' feature of Tupolev designs in the 1950s and 1960s up to and including the Tu-154 *Careless* medium-haul airliner. This feature was also present on most versions of the 'aircraft 494'.

For the TR-3A and TR-5 engines, several layouts were proposed, each one looking more cartoony than the previous one. On the 'aircraft 494/3', which had a wing area of 130-160 m² (1,399-1,722 sq ft), two engines were located low on the forward fuselage sides, flanking the nosewheel well and exhausting under the wing roots. They were set at a small 'toe-in' angle, the circular air intakes encroaching on the circular fuselage cross-section while the nozzles were clear of it; this was meant to direct the efflux away from the fuselage. The other two were carried in conformal nacelles on the wings between the flaps and the ailerons, like the outer engines of the B-47; as a result, the outer flap sections had a shorter span.

With a wing area greater than 130-160m², other four-engine arrangements were contemplated. On the 'aircraft 494/4', possibly the most bizarre configuration, all four engines were located on the fuselage – the front pair was in the same position as in the previous version while the rear pair sat atop the rear fuselage immediately ahead of the fin fillet, with a gap between the engine nacelles (they did not encroach on the fuselage cross-section). This necessitated a redesign of the tail unit, which differed from all the other project versions – 'aircraft 494/4' had cruciform tail surfaces, the horizontal tail being raised clear of the upper engines' efflux.

'Aircraft 494/5' had two engines in the same position under the forward fuselage and two in cylindrical nacelles at the wingtips. This version was very probably rejected because of the strong thrust asymmetry in the event one of the outer engines failed.

A version for which no designation has been quoted had four engines under the wings in individual pylon-mounted nacelles (see page 26). The data in table 3 on page 30 refers to this version.

Yet another unnamed version had the four engines housed in wing-mounted nacelles, in BAC Lightning-style vertical pairs (!); the four-wheel main gear bogies retracted forward into the engine nacelles, somersaulting forward through 180° as on the Il-18 *Coot* four-turboprop medium-haul airliner. The design performance varied, depending on the type of engines.

Yet another version powered by TR-3A turbojets also had paired engines in wing-mounted nacelles, but the latter were carried on pylons, accommodating the engines in side-by-side pairs with a considerable 'toe-in' angle. The short main gear units were attached to the same pylons, the bogies retracting aft into special boattail fairings between the engine nozzles so that the jet efflux passed on both sides of them. (As an aside, several years later, in 1960, the same nacelle/main gear fairing design was used on the would-be production form of the East German '152/II' four-turbojet short-haul airliner designed by Brunolf Baade.)

Eventually the projects team selected the version with podded engines and wing-mounted main gear fairings ('aircraft 494/2'), which was the most rational one.

The essential differences between the project versions of the '494' devolved mainly on the type of engines and their placement, while the internal layout of the fuselage was basically similar to that of the '86' in all versions.

An analysis of the layouts provided a number of practical conclusions. As the dimensions of the aircraft increased, the layout in which the main gear units were stowed in the engine nacelles became less workable due to the nacelles' greater cross-section area and wetted area and to the thrust losses caused by the long jetpipes. Conversely, the layout in which the undercarriage and engines were housed in separate fairings offered a reduction in overall drag, first and foremost wave drag. This was because the interference of the main gear fairings and the pylon-mounted engine nacelles with the wings was minimal and would not substantially increase the wave drag as the angle of attack increased. As a bonus, pylon-mounted nacelles facilitated maintenance because the engines were easily accessible from the ground.

Burying the engines in the wing roots (as on the Junkers EF 132) with a wing area of up to 300 m² (3,229 sq ft) without any corresponding increase in the wing root chord and thickness/chord ratio in comparison with the '86' was inefficient. Housing the engines in the fuselage was difficult due to the inevitable heating of the fuselage structure and interference of the jet efflux with the bomb bay doors (if the engines were mounted ahead of the wings) or with the tailplane and glazing of the tail gunner's station (if the engines were mounted aft of the wings).

As was evident from this analysis, the most efficient layout for a medium bomber was the one in which the engines were mounted on pylons and the main gear units retracted into wing fairings (as already mentioned, this was exactly the layout chosen by Boris M. Kondorskiy's team). However, TsAGI was still very cautious about the idea of pylon-mounted engines, which were therefore not widely used on Soviet aircraft at this time. Engines mounted on pylons (or, to use the Soviet term of the time, *nozhee* – 'knives'; not to be confused with the bendable trim tabs of some early jet aircraft which were referred to by the same term!) were used only on the twin-turbojet '150' bomber designed in the Soviet Union in

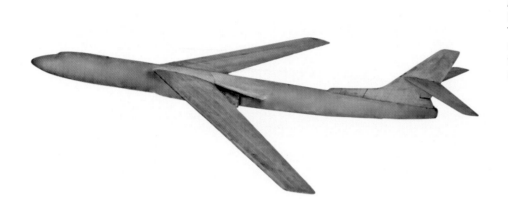

A wooden model of the 'aircraft 495'. It was much closer to the eventual Tu-16 as regards the engine placement (the two engines flanked the fuselage) but had a high-wing layout and hence cruciform tail surfaces.

1950 under the direction of the aforementioned Brunolf Baade, who was then head of a team of interned German aircraft designers at OKB-1, and later on the Il-54 *Blowlamp* experimental bomber of 1953, although pylon-mounted engines were also considered during design work on such aircraft as the Myasishchev M-4 *Bison-A* four-turbojet strategic bomber and the Tu-95.

The bomber's design performance with a 6,000-kg (13,230-lb) bomb load was examined within the confines of the 'wing area/take-off weight' ratio for seven differently powered variants:

- two AMRD-03 engines with and without afterburners;
- four TR-3A engines with and without afterburners;
- four TR-5 engines with and without afterburners;
- four afterburning AMRD-03 engines (!). (It should be noted, however, that an afterburning version of the AM-3 was never actually developed.)

The results of this analysis showed that if the maximum possible range was to be achieved, given the same SFC, the twin-engined layout using two AMRD-03 engines was preferable to the four-engined layouts due to the lower drag and weight of the powerplant. In order to achieve the stipulated range and field performance (specifically, the take-off run), the bomber had to have the following minimum parameters: a take-off weight of 60,000-70,000 kg (132,275-154,320 lb), a wing area of 150-170 m² (1,614-1,830 sq ft) and an overall take-off thrust of 14,000-16,000 kgp (30,860-35,270 lbst). If the overall thrust was reduced to a minimum possible figure of 12,000-14,000 kgp (26,455-30,860 lbst), it was necessary to increase the dimensions of the aircraft to meet the range and field performance target; the take-off weight rose to 70,000-80,000 kg (154,320-176,370 lb) and the wing area to 190-210 m² (2,045-2,260 sq ft).

The research precisely defined the parameters for the optimum number and type of engines for the subsequent development of a long-range jet bomber meeting the specified performance target. The following conclusions were drawn:

- the limits within which the stipulated performance could be achieved were significantly extended if the overall engine thrust was increased;
- the limits for a twin-engine layout (with AMRD-03 engines) were wider than for a four-engine layout (with TR-3A engines) and wider for turbofan engines (the TR-5) than for pure turbojets (the TR-3A);

- given the specified performance, the long-range bomber's TOW should be 60,000-100,000 kg (132,275-220,460 lb), the wing area 150-250 m² (1,614-2,690 sq ft), and the total available thrust greater than 12,000-14,000 kgp.

This work defined the design, and subsequent development, of a long-range subsonic jet bomber. The validity of these precepts was essentially confirmed by the creation of the Tu-16 and other aircraft of its class.

'Aircraft 495' ('aircraft 495-88') medium bomber (project)

In addition to the layouts described above, there was a PD project version proposed by Aleksey A. Tupolev. Bearing the provisional designation 'aircraft 495' to signify the fifth project evolved in 1949 (it was also known as the '495-88', hinting at the 'proper' manufacturer's designation), the aircraft differed from the '494' in having only two AL-5 engines installed in conformal nacelles flanking the fuselage, a high-wing layout and cruciform tail surfaces. Both TsAGI and the Tupolev OKB came up with this method of positioning the engines. Wind-tunnel tests of a model with this configuration yielded very good results. Moreover, the '495' had an unconventional mono-wheel undercarriage (almost like that of a sailplane) – it was not really a bicycle undercarriage, featuring a highly stressed main unit supplemented by wing-mounted outrigger struts and auxiliary fuselage struts. The wing area was to be 140 m² (1,506 sq ft).

In the summer of 1950 the different project versions of the future long-range bomber were discussed at a conference held at OKB-156. The alternative variants of the '494' project were presented by Igor' B. Babin and Gheorgiy A. Cheryomukhin, while Aleksey A. Tupolev presented his own '495' project. After lengthy discussions with his design staff Chief Designer Andrey N. Tupolev decided to go ahead with the bomber which received the in-house designation 'aircraft 88'. The bomber was to combine the best features of the two competing projects – the fuselage design and the tricycle undercarriage with wing-mounted main gear fairings were taken from the most promising versions of the '494', while the twin-engined layout and the location of the engines were to follow the '495' project. Thus, in this first approximation, the Tu-16 took shape – an aircraft which, in a few years, would evoke the admiration of the world's aviation community. The right choice of layout contributed in no small measure to the bomber's future success.

Chapter 2

Development and Testing: The Bomber Materialises

The '88' ('aircraft 88') medium bomber

The Tupolev OKB's quest for the optimum version of the new long-range bomber offering higher performance than that promised by the Il-46 was welcomed not only by the Soviet Air Force but by the Soviet government as well, and it was decided to commission such an aircraft from the Tupolev OKB. This decision followed the pattern of scientific and technological policy set by the nation's leaders in the post-war years when new types of weaponry, including aircraft, were to be created. For Andrey N. Tupolev it was an opportunity to redress his failure in the undeclared contest with OKB-240 for the USSR's first jet tactical bomber.

On 10th June 1950, the Council of Ministers issued directive No.2474-974, tasking the Tupolev OKB with designing and building a long-range jet bomber powered by two 5,000-kgp (11,020-lbst) Lyul'ka TR-3F turbojets. This was a short-lived

interim designation of the former TR-3A (the F suffix denoted *forseerovannyy* – uprated) before the engine received its definitive designation AL-5. On 14th June, the Ministry of Aircraft Industry (MAP – *Ministerstvo aviatsionnoy promyshlennosti*) followed up with order No.444 to the same effect. Pursuant to these documents the new bomber – the 'aircraft 88' – was to have performance closely matching the figures extrapolated by the OKB in the course of the PD project studies. Two prototypes were to be built, the first of these being submitted for state acceptance trials in December 1951. However, as the resources of OKB-156 were heavily taxed by the work on the Tu-85, which was still on the agenda then, on 28th November 1950, the deadlines for 'aircraft 88' were postponed by three months.

It should be noted that the commissioning documents specified that the bomber be designed around two Mikulin AMRD-03 tur-

A colourised photo of the first prototype Tu-16 ('aircraft 88/1') at Zhukovskiy during manufacturer's tests in company with production Tu-4 bombers and the sole Tu-70 airliner.

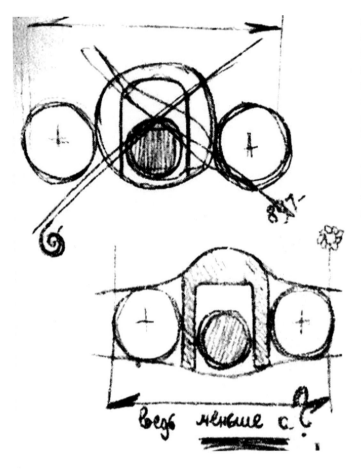

and with full-size specimens. In the course of this work it became evident that the thrust of the two AL-5 engines envisaged originally (a legacy of the 'aircraft 495' project) would be clearly inadequate to achieve the specified performance. It was therefore decided to use two AMRD-03 engines (subsequently redesignated AM-3 in production form); as a 'belt and braces' policy, the OKB considered a version with four AL-5 engines but in this form the take-off weight would be greater.

Aleksandr A. Mikulin's Moscow-based OKB-300 had begun design work on the AMRD-03 in 1949; this was the first Soviet high-powered turbojet. It had an eight-stage axial compressor, a cannular combustion chamber, a two-stage turbine and a fixed-area nozzle. The compressor featured subsonic high-pressure stages which provided a pressure ratio of 6.2; for the first time in Soviet design practice the engine incorporated such features as compressor adjustment by means of air bleed valves aft of the first compressor stages and pin-hole disc connection in the drum-type rotor facilitating blade alignment. Swirl vanes were fitted at the entry to the combustion chamber, which had ribbed walls improving flame tube cooling in similar manner to the ribbed cylinders of air-cooled piston engines. The AMRD-03 was also fitted with a so-called turbostarter (a small gas turbine engine spinning up the main engine's spool) for automatic self-contained starting, an adjustable de-icing system and an oil/fuel heat exchanger in which fuel was used for cooling the engine oil. At OKB-300 the work on this engine was headed by Prokofiy F. Zoobets, who subsequently became head of another engine design bureau – MAP's OKB-16 based in Kazan' – in 1954 (not to be confused with the OKB-16 weapons design bureau mentioned earlier).

Being fully aware of the technical risks involved in using this all-new engine, Andrey N. Tupolev visited OKB-300 to check up on progress and had consultations with Chief Designer Aleksandr A. Mikulin and his deputy Prof. Boris S. Stechkin. The results were convincing enough, and in February 1951 Tupolev decided that work would concentrate on the version with two AM-3

bojets – initially rated at 8,000 kgp (17,640 lbst) for take-off. Once the layout of the new bomber had been finalised as related in Chapter 1, the work continued at the detail design stage. The complex task of determining the dimensions and final aerodynamic and structural layout of 'aircraft 88' required large-scale parametric research and numerous experiments both with scale models

Above left: A sketch by Andrey N. Tupolev showing a conventional engine placement versus a 'squeezed' (area-ruled) fuselage. Tupolev's comment is '[The width] is smaller, isn't it?'

Left: A prototype AM-03 turbojet undergoing bench tests. The tank on the left holds petrol for the engine's S300-75 turbine starter.

Above right: Dmitriy S. Markov (left), Sergey M. Yeger (second from left) and Boris M. Kondorskiy (right) in the mid-1950s when the Tu-16 was being tested.

Right: Aleksandr A. Mikulin hands a model of an aircraft to a lustily grinning Andrey N. Tupolev as a present for his 60th birthday on 10th November 1948.

Right: OKB-300 General Designer Aleksandr A. Mikulin.

Centre right: Dmitriy S. Markov, the Tu-16's chief project engineer at OKB-156.

Far right: Aleksey A. Tupolev, who contributed significantly to the choice of the Tu-16's general arrangement.

engines. Still, the matter was not finally resolved until several months later when the Mikulin OKB built and bench-tested a prototype of the AM-3. On 24th August 1951, the Council of Ministers issued a new directive, followed on 30th August, by MAP order No.832, which posed more stringent requirements; now 'aircraft 88' was to be powered by AM-3 turbojets with a take-off thrust increased to 8,700 kgp (19,180 lbst) and an SFC of 1.0 kg/kgp·hr (lb/lbst·hr) at take-off power. The documents stipulated a thrust of 7,000 kgp (15,430 lbst) at nominal power and 6,400 kgp (14,110 lbst) at cruise power, with a corresponding SFC of 0.95 kg/kgp·hr and 0.93 kg/kgp·hr respectively. The dry weight of the AM-3 was anticipated to be 3,100 kg (6,830 lb).

Speaking of which, this high weight was the trade-off for the engine's high performance – the AM-3 was nearly twice as heavy as contemporary Soviet turbojets in the same class; for example, the AL-5 had a dry weight of 1,770 kg (3,900 lb). The AM-3 also surpassed all other engines in terms of dimensions, with a length of 5.38 m (17 ft 7¹³⁄₁₆ in) and a maximum diameter of 1.4 m (4 ft 7⁷⁄₆₄ in). Leonid L. Kerber, head of the Tupolev OKB's equipment department, described his first impression of the AM-3 thus: *'By the standards of the day this was something of a monster. The huge engine with a thrust of more than 8,000 kg, a diameter of nearly 1.5 m [4 ft 11 in] and a weight of several tons instilled doubts as to whether any aircraft designer would dare to install such a monster in his aircraft.'*

The engine was to commence its own state acceptance trials in December 1951. Hence, to speed up development work, on 22nd September 1951, MAP issued order No.948 requiring a Tu-4 to be converted as a testbed for the AM-3; the engine testbed was to be ready by November, bearing the designation Tu-4LL (*letayushchaya laboratoriya* – lit. 'flying laboratory'). (Note: In Russian the term *letayushchaya laboratoriya* is used indiscriminately to denote any kind of flying testbed or research/survey aircraft.) The first two AM-3s were scheduled for delivery to OKB-156 as early as August 1951: one for ground tests (the Tupolev OKB had its own engine test bench) and one for flight testing on the Tu-4LL. They were to be followed in November 1951, by two more engines intended for the first prototype '88', which would be completed by then, with a third example to be delivered in January 1952, as a spare engine. At this point the bomber's future depended to a con-

siderable degree on the successful completion of the engine's tests.

The Tu-4LL in question was one of eight such aircraft operated by LII and, more specifically, one of the three Tu-4LLs used to test new turbojet and turbofan engines. Actually this aircraft, which was converted from a Moscow-built Tu-4 (no Soviet Air Force serial, construction number 230113), had been modified by Vladimir M. Myasishchev's OKB-23 jointly with LII for testing the powerplant of the future M-4 bomber. At the first phase of the

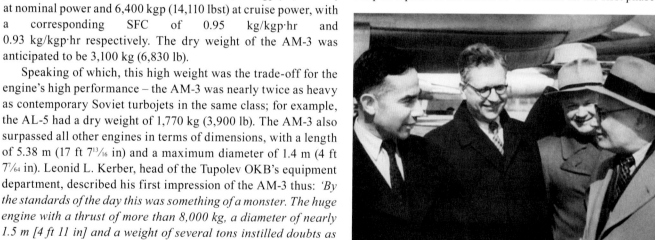

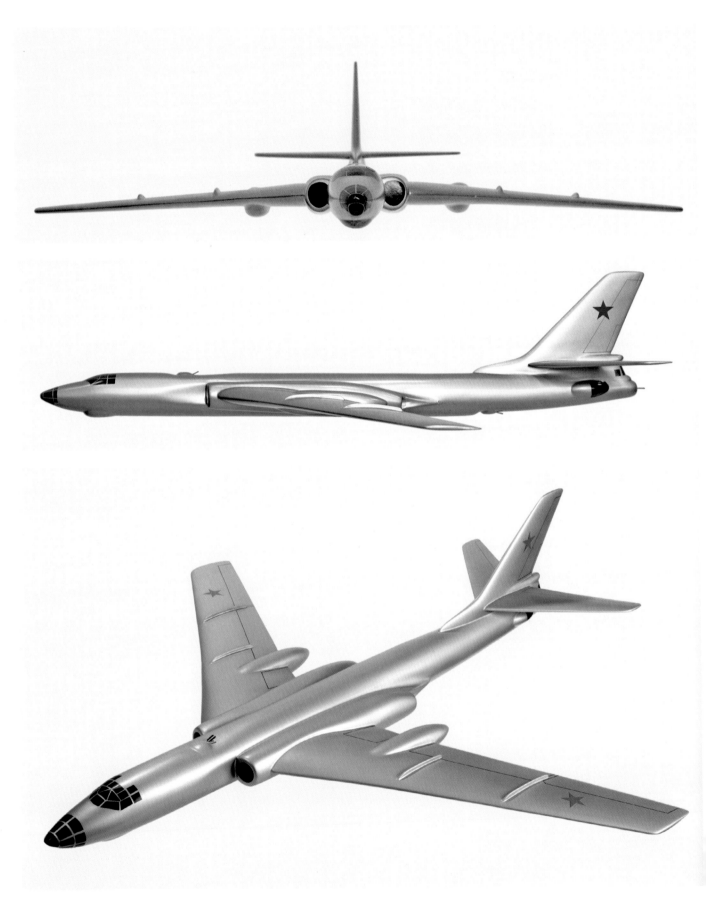

Three views of a desktop model showing 'aircraft 88'. The circular shape of the air intakes is not entirely accurate.

Three more views of the same model. The diameter of the engine nozzles is a bit too small.

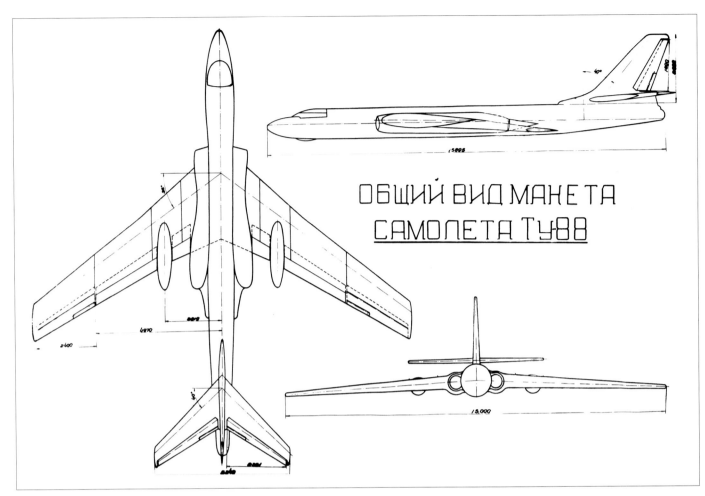

ОБЩИЙ ВИД МАКЕТА
САМОЛЕТА ТУ88

A rather basic three-view from the ADP documents inscribed 'General arrangement of the Tu-88 aircraft' (sic). The area-ruling of the fuselage and the engine nacelles is clearly visible.

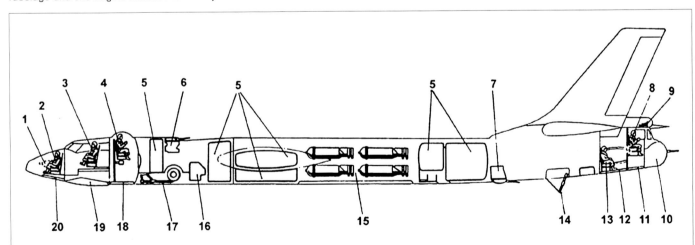

The internal layout of the fuselage of 'aircraft 88'. 1. Fixed forward-firing AM-23 cannon; 2. Navigator/bomb-aimer's station; 3. Captain's and co-pilot's stations; 4. Navigator/operator's station; 5. Fuel tanks; 6. DT-7V dorsal barbette with twin AM-23s; 7. DT-N7S ventral barbette with twin AM-23s; 8. Tail gunner's (defensive fire commander's) station; 9. PRS-1 Argon gun ranging radar antenna; 10. DK-7 tail turret with twin AM-23s; 11. Rear pressure cabin entry hatch; 12. Gunner/radio operator's ejection hatch; 13. GRO's station; 14. Retractable tail bumper; 15. Weapons bay; 16. AFA-33M camera; 17. Nose gear unit; 18. Front pressure cabin entry hatch; 19. RBP-4 navigation/bomb-aiming radar antenna; 20. Navigator/bomb-aimer's ejection hatch.

programme it had been fitted with an AL-5 development engine and known at the Myasishchev OKB as the DR-1; D stood for *dvigatel'* (engine, a reference to the engine testbed role) while *izdeliye* R was the Tu-4's product code. Later, when the AM-3 development engine was installed on Tu-4LL c/n 230113 in January 1952, the in-house designation was changed to DR-2. The AM-3 was installed in the Tu-4's front bomb bay in a special nacelle which could be raised or lowered hydraulically by a pantographic mechanism. The nacelle was semi-recessed for take-off and landing to give adequate ground clearance, extending clear of the fuselage into the slipstream before start-up; when the nacelle was stowed the air intake was blanked off by a movable shutter to prevent windmilling and foreign object damage. It was also possible to extend the engine on the ground when the aircraft was parked over a special trench for ground runs.

In 1952 the AM-3 successfully passed bench tests as part of its state acceptance trials and was put into large-scale production. It was to power several types of Soviet heavy military and commercial aircraft for many years to come.

However, we are jumping way ahead of the story and should go back in time a little. Intensive design work on 'aircraft 88' got under way immediately after a Council of Ministers directive giving the project official status was issued in June 1950. On 10th July that year the Soviet Air Force issued a specific operational requirement (SOR) for the new bomber. The general design work was finished on 20th April 1951, when the ADP was completed and submitted for review to the Soviet Air Force's Aviation Technology Committee, which signed its approval on 29th May. The ADP with AM-3 engines was finally confirmed on 5th July. The SOR was slightly amended on 11th September 1951; the aircraft's specifications in accordance with this are given in the table on page 41.

'Aircraft 88' was designed from the outset to carry not only ordinary bombs of up to 9,000 kg (19,840 lb) calibre but also naval mines and torpedoes optimised for high-altitude parachute-retarded launch, making it suitable for both Air Force and Navy use. In extreme cases a bomb load of up to 12,000 kg (26,455 lb) could be carried.

The types of ordnance envisaged by the ADP are listed in the table on page 41. AMD = *aviatsionnaya meena donnaya* – air-dropped bottom mine; *Desna* is the name of a river in European Russia; Lira (pronounced *leera*) means 'Lyre'. As for the nonsensical word *Serpey*, it is nothing more than an accidental anagram of the intended codename *Persey* (Perseus); quite simply, a typist had made an error when typing out the document clearing the weapon for service, and no-one had taken the responsibility to set her straight, believing that 'the Powers That Be know better'! Type 45-36AVA means 450-mm (17^{45}/$_{64}$ in) calibre, 1936 model, *[torpeda] aviatsionnaya, vysotnaya* – air-droppable torpedo for high-altitude attacks; TAV = *torpeda aviatsionnaya, vysotnaya*; RAT = *re'aktivnaya aviatsionnaya torpeda* – jet-powered air-droppable torpedo.

At that stage the defensive armament was to comprise seven 23-mm Nudelman/Rikhter NR-23 cannons: one fixed forward-firing cannon with 100 rounds on the starboard side of the nose, two in a dorsal barbette aft of the flight deck (with 250 rpg) to

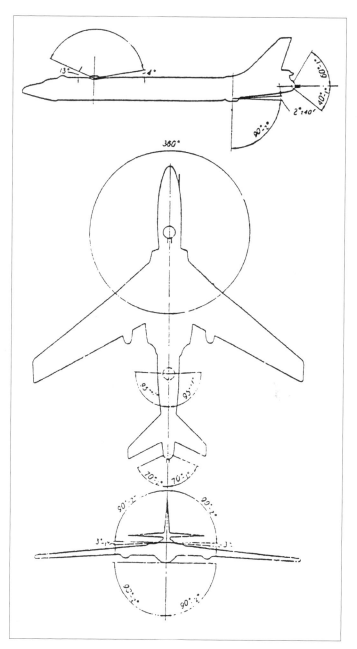

A diagram showing the field of fire of the 88's defensive armament.

cover the upper rear quadrant, two in a ventral barbette under the rear fuselage (again with 250 rpg) to cover the lower rear quadrant, and two in a tail barbette (with 300 rpg).

The crew positions were armour-protected from behind, from below and from the sides. The overall weight of the armour on the aircraft was to be 545 kg (1,201 lb).

Another peculiarity of the '88' at the ADP stage was the unconventional undercarriage design. Basically it was a tricycle landing gear; the twin-wheel nose unit and the main units with four-wheel bogies all retracted aft. For the first time in Soviet practice the nose unit was designed in such a way that the twin 900 x 275 mm (35.43 x 10.82 in) wheels mounted on a common axle acted as a vibration damper, reducing the risk of self-induced shimmy oscillations. The main units also incorporated a novel

A large model of the 'aircraft 88' (Tu-16) in the T-101 wind tunnel at TsAGI. Note the three pairs of wing fences; the innermost pair was eventually deleted.

feature – during retraction the bogies, which were fitted with 1,000 x 300 mm (39.37 x 11.81 in) wheels having a tyre pressure of 8.5-9 kg/cm² (121-128 psi), somersaulted through 180° to lie in the aforementioned fairings on the wings, back to front. The large clamshell doors in these fairings opened only when the gear was in transit, reducing drag. The Tupolev OKB even took out a patent for this main gear design. The most unusual bit was that retractable outrigger struts of the sort usually found on a bicycle-gear aircraft were fitted to the wingtips, each with a single wheel measuring 265 x 80 mm (10.43 x 3.14 in). Thus the '88' was to

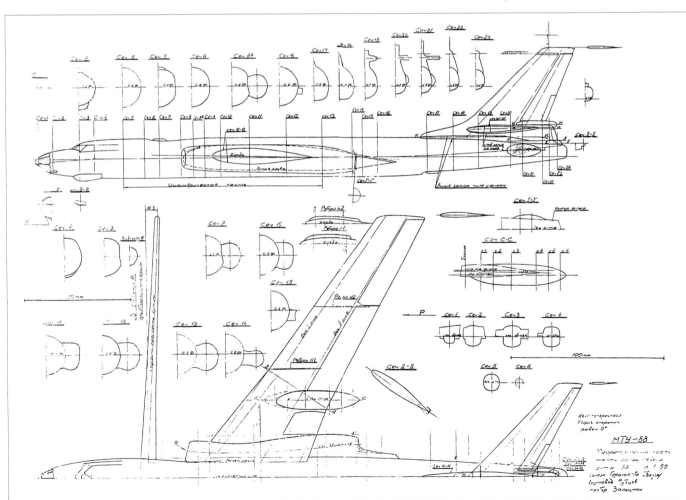

A drawing showing the cross-sections of the Tu-16's fuselage, engine nacelles, main gear fairings and wings.

have five landing gear struts (but not for long – this was soon changed).

(As an aside, somewhat later, and completely independently of the Tupolev OKB, British aircraft engineers used an almost identical main gear design and associated fairings on the one-off Vickers Valiant B.2 prototype which took to the air on 4th September 1953. The reason for the switch from the outward-retracting twin-wheel main gear units of the production Valiant B.1 high-altitude bomber was that, unlike the latter, the Valiant B.2 was intended for low-altitude operations where turbulence was likely. Hence it needed a stiffer wing structure which was not weakened by the mainwheel wells.)

The heavy-duty undercarriage enabled the aircraft to operate from both paved (concrete) runways at regular bases and unpaved (earth or snow) airstrips at forward operating locations. Normally the '88' was to rely on wheel brakes only during the landing run, but a brake parachute was provided for emergencies.

According to the ADP documents, the aircraft was to feature the following basic avionics and equipment. Electric power was provided by four 1.8-kW GSR-1800 engine-driven generators, with two 12SA-65 DC batteries as a back-up. The oxygen equipment included KP-24 breathing apparatus (*kislorodnyy pribor* – oxygen apparatus) for each of the six crew members and an SKZhU-50 liquid oxygen converter. The aircraft was to be fitted with an AP-5M electric autopilot; navigation was assisted by two (main and back-up) ARK-5 Amur (a river in the Soviet Far East; pronounced like the French word *amour*) automatic direction finders (ARK = *avtomaticheskiy rahdiokompas* – ADF), an SP-50 *Materik* (Continent) instrument landing system (ILS; SP = *[sistema] slepoy posahdki* – blind landing system), Meridian SHORAN, RV-2 and RV-10 radio altimeters. The communications equipment included two sets of 1RSB-70 command link radios, an RSIU-3 communications radio, an AVRA-45 emergency locator transmitter (*avareeynaya rahdiostahntsiya* – emergency radio, 1945 model) and an SPU-10 intercom (*samolyotnoye peregovornoye oostroystvo*). The '88' was to feature a *Rubidiy-MM II* (Rubidium) bomb-aiming radar in a chin radome, with a FARM camera photographically recording the image on the radar display, and a PRS-1 Argon gun-laying radar (*pritsel rahdiolokatsionnyy strelkovyy* – radio gunsight; NATO codename *Bee Hind*) above the tail gunner's station. The Rubidiy-MM II was based on the Tu-4's *Kobal't-1* (Cobalt) radar, with an additional module inte-

ADP data for the 'aircraft 88' bomber with two AM-3 engines (8,700-kgp version)	
Fuselage length	33.6 m (110 ft 2⅝ in)
Wing span	33.0 m (108 ft 3½ in)
Height on ground	8.9 m (29 ft 2⅝ in)
Wing sweep at quarter-chord	35°
Wing area:	
including centre section	164.59 m² (1,771.63 sq ft)
less centre section	159 m² (1,711.46 sq ft)
Empty weight	32,760 kg (72,220 lb)
Normal take-off weight	64,500 kg (142,200 lb)
Payload:	
normal	14,190 kg (31,280 lb)
in overload configuration	31,740 kg (69,970 lb)
Maximum speed:	
at sea level	840 km/h (521 mph) *
at 5,000 m (16,400 ft)	988 km/h (613 mph)
at 10,000 m (32,810 ft)	918 km/h (570 mph)
Time to height (normal all-up weight/maximum all-up weight):	
to 5,000 m	3.6/5.5 minutes
to 10,000 m	9.0/14.5 minutes
Service ceiling:	
with normal AUW	13,800 m (45,280 ft)
with maximum AUW	12,900 m (42,320 ft)
Range: †	
with a 28,500-kg (62,830-lb) fuel load	6,000 km (3,726 miles)
with a 27,500-kg (60,630-lb) fuel load	5,750 km (3,571 miles)
with a 25,500-kg (56,220-lb) fuel load	5,300 km (3,291 miles)
with a 21,500-kg (47,400-lb) fuel load	4,380 km (2,906 miles)
Endurance: †	
with a 28,500-kg fuel load	7.5 hours
with a 27,500-kg fuel load	7.3 hours
with a 25,500-kg fuel load	6.7 hours
with a 21,500-kg fuel load	5.5 hours
Take-off run with maximum AUW	1,500 m (4,920 ft)
Take-off distance to h=25 m (82 ft) with maximum AUW	3,650 m (11,980 ft)
Landing run with a 37,000-kg (81,570-lb) landing weight	670-750 m (2,200-2,460 ft)
Crew	6

Notes:
* Restricted by a dynamic pressure limit of 3,400 kg/m² (697.0 lb/sq ft) at altitudes up to 3,600 m (11,810 ft); at higher altitude the maximum permissible speed is Mach 0.86
† With a take-off weight of 64,500 kg (142,200 lb), flying at 11,200-14,400 m (36,750-47,240 ft) and a cruising speed of 780-840 km/h (484-521 mph)

The ordnance combinations carried by 'aircraft 88' as per ADP		
Type of ordnance	Maximum quantity	Total weight
1. Bombs		
FAB-250 M-46	24	6,000 kg (13,230 lb)
FAB-500 M-46	18	9,000 kg (19,840 lb)
FAB-1500 M-46	6	9,000 kg (19,840 lb)
FAB-3000 M-46	2	6,000 kg (13,230 lb)
FAB-5000 M-46	1	5,000 kg (11,020 lb)
OGAB-6000	1	6,000 kg (13,230 lb)
FAB-9000 M-46	1	9,000 kg (19,840 lb)
2. Naval mines		
AMD-500	12	6,000 kg (13,230 lb)
AMD-1000	4	4,000 kg (8,820 lb)
AMD-M	4	4,800 kg (10,580 lb)
Desna	4	3,000 kg (6,620 lb)
Serpey	4	5,000 kg (11,020 lb)
Lira	4	4,000 kg (8,820 lb)
3. Torpedoes		
45-36AVA	3	3,000 kg (6,620 lb)
TAV	3	3,800 kg (8,380 lb)
A-2 (RAT)	3	1,830 kg (4,030 lb)

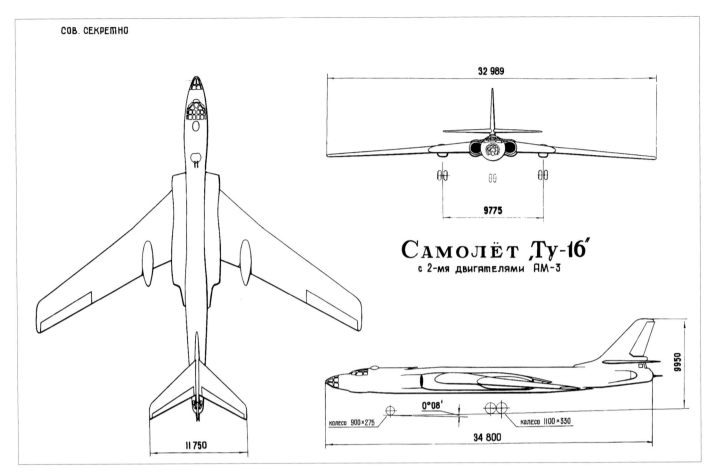

Above: A three-view drawing of the bomber (now marked 'Tu-16') with two AM-3 engines from the ADP documents. Note the shape of the gunner/radio operator's sighting blisters and their fairings.

Below: The fuselage layout of the Tu-16 from the same documents. The gunner/radio operator's sighting blisters are shown as circular, which is not entirely correct.

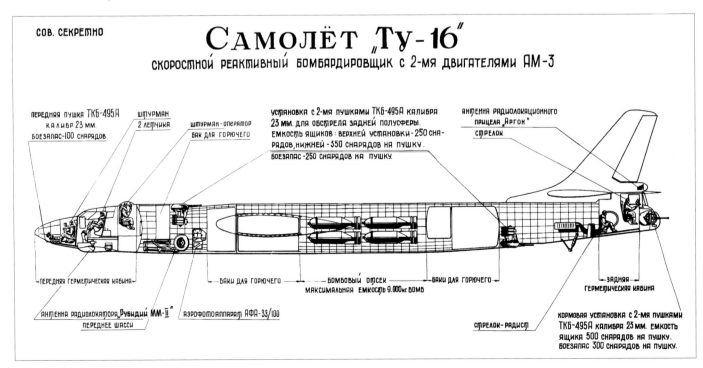

grating it with the optical bombsight. Identification friend-or-foe (IFF) equipment consisted of a *Bariy-M* (Barium) transponder and a *Magniy-M2* (Magnesium) interrogator. Photo equipment for planned reconnaissance/BDA and reconnoitring targets of opportunity comprised AFA-33/50, AFA-33/75 and AFA/33/100 day cameras or NAFA-3S/50 cameras (*nochnoy aerofotoapparaht* – aircraft camera for night operations) for vertical photography, plus AFA-33/75 and AFA-33/55 cameras for oblique photography.

Construction of a full-size mock-up at MMZ No.156 began in June 1950, and the mock-up was completed on 20th April, the following year. Its first inspection by Soviet Air Force representatives on 16th February 1951, resulted in a list of no fewer than 101 items to be corrected, and a further 25 shortcomings were pointed out during the second inspection on 8th March. All of these were taken into account during subsequent work on the aircraft. Officially the mock-up, together with the ADP, was shown to the Air Force on 20th March 1951. The mock-up review commission chaired by Col.-Gen. Sergey I. Rudenko, the then Commander-in-Chief of the Soviet Air Force, worked between 2nd June and 7th July, the C-in-C approving the mock-up on the latter date. Heated discussions broke out occasionally between the OKB specialists and the military, who sometimes made unreasonable demands. Leonid L. Kerber recalled that Andrey N. Tupolev, who was never shy to use naughty words, had an argument with one particular Air Force representative who demanded that the navigator/operator working the dorsal cannon barbette should have a view of the aircraft's lower hemisphere as well. *'[Aleksandr V.] Nadashkevich, who headed the armament department, tried in vain to explain [to this Lieutenant-Colonel] that it was impossible and, even more to point, it was unnecessary because the two tail gunners had an excellent view of the entire lower hemisphere. The Lieutenant-Colonel was adamant. Then Tupolev said with a smile: "When you grow an eye on your ass, I will provide you with a view of..." Before he could finish the phrase, a roar of laughter swept the room and the embarrassed Lieutenant-Colonel withdrew his requirement. Gradually the military stopped posing ridiculous requirements because no one wanted to be derided by Tupolev.'*

Later, the mock-up review commission had to convene again in March 1952, because additional equipment had been installed in the aircraft and major structural changes had been introduced on the second prototype 'aircraft 88' (which see). At this point the issues relating to equipment and armament were finally sorted out and the earlier criticisms taken into account.

This lengthy process of obtaining the required approvals from the military was due not only, and not so much, to bureaucratic red tape; rather, it resulted from the large number of unusual design features incorporated in 'aircraft 88', which made it rather different from its predecessors.

The fuselage's internal layout was considerably revised. The separate waist gunner's station found in the 'aircraft 486'/'aircraft 86'/'aircraft 491' series of projects was deemed to be excessive; on the 'aircraft 88' the crew of six were seated in two pressurised cabins. The front one accommodated the pilots, with the navigator/bomb-aimer ahead of them and the aft-facing dorsal gunner behind/above them. The latter was known as a 'navigator/operator' (*shtoorman-operahtor*) or Nav/Op – presumably because

he worked the aircraft systems like a flight engineer but could perform some navigation functions as well, sitting beneath an astrodome. In contrast, the 'proper' navigator in the extreme nose was tautologically referred to as *shtoorman-navigahtor* (both words mean 'navigator' in Russian). The rear pressure cabin was located at the aft extremity of the fuselage, accommodating two gunners (unlike earlier heavy bombers); this improved combat co-ordination and boosted morale – the tail gunner was no longer 'alone out there'. Hence the large elliptical observation/sighting blisters used by the GRO, who worked the ventral barbette, were now located immediately ahead of the tail gunner's station glazing. Only the rear 60% of these lateral blisters were transparencies, the front portions being metal fairings protecting the glazing from the hot jet exhaust.

Importantly, all crewmembers were provided with ejection seats – for the first time on a Soviet bomber. This improved the chances of survival in an emergency and bolstered crew confidence. In contrast, on the British V-bombers only the pilots enjoyed the luxury of ejection seats, while the other crewmembers had to bail out in the old-fashioned way. Similarly, on the Il-28 and the Tu-14 the pilot and the navigator/bomb-aimer had ejection seats while the GRO had none.

A notable attribute of the 'aircraft 88' was that the capacious bomb bay was located behind the wing centre section's rear spar. Thanks to this the bomb load was carried close to the centre of gravity (CG) and did not cause a marked change in CG position when the bombs were released, while the bay itself did not encroach on the wings' load-bearing structure. The strength and rigidity of the fuselage in the area were ensured by very strong longitudinal beams flanking the bomb bay.

The bomber was further distinguished by other special features. The high aspect ratio wings (an aspect ratio about 7 was chosen) had a two-spar design, the spar webs and the upper/lower skin panels forming a strong torsion box. The rigid wing structure of 'aircraft 88' was in stark contrast to the Boeing B-47 and B-52 long-range bombers; the American machines had aeroelastic wings which flexed in flight, damping vertical gusts due to their considerable deformation. The stiffer wings of the '88' were less prone to deformation in flight, being subjected to lower stress. Later, the wealth of operational experience amassed with the Tu-16 and the Tu-104 airliner in the USSR, as well as with the American Boeing 707, Douglas DC-8 and Convair 880 Coronado airliners, proved that the more rigid wing construction was more robust, especially from the point of view of structural fatigue. The Americans had to overcome many operational problems involving the wings of the B-47 and B-52 (namely fatigue cracks, with repeated revision and reinforcement of the wing structure as a result).

As the bomber was designed to fly at transonic speeds, its tail surfaces had stronger sweepback than the wings. Thanks to this, the 'shock stall' phenomenon affected the tail later than the wings; in practical terms, this allowed the machine to remain stable and controllable at high speeds.

The engines were located in conformal nacelles at the wing roots, flanking the centre fuselage aft of the rear spar, with lateral air intakes a short way ahead of the wing leading edge. The air intakes had a curious shape vaguely resembling a Reuleaux trian-

Top and above: A model showing how the future production Tu-16 was to look.

gle with one apex pointing downward; this became one of the most recognisable features of the bomber's appearance. This placement of the engines solved the problem of interference at the wing/fuse-lage joint – the most difficult junction in aerodynamic terms. This particular problem was solved by introducing an 'active fillet' aft of the engine nozzles: the jet exhaust sucked away the air flowing around the wing roots and fuselage, at the same time directing the airflow in that zone.

OKB-156 designers who took part in the design of the '88' recalled that the unusual layout resulted from an overpowering desire to minimise the cross-section area of the fuselage/nacelle/wing combination by all means. For this reason the engines were located as deeply as possible, and the fuselage sides ahead of the air intakes were concave (with 'dimples') so that the intakes par-tially overlapped the circular fuselage cross-section. Andrey N. Tupolev himself insistently advocated and monitored this solu-tion. He constantly inspected the proposed layout of the bomber and demanded that the designers *'squeeze, squeeze and squeeze as*

much as possible'. When a large model of the 'aircraft 88' incor-porating all these 'squeezes' was tested in the TsAGI T-101 wind tunnel, TsAGI specialists could not understand how the drag had been so drastically reduced, and it took them a long time to report the conclusion of their findings to the OKB.

(Speaking of which, the wings of the wind tunnel model had three pairs of boundary layer fences – just outboard of the engine nacelles, just outboard of the main gear fairings and in line with the ailerons' inboard ends; the innermost pair would be deleted on the actual aircraft. The engine nozzles were initially closed by conical fairings but these were soon removed.)

The chosen engine placement aft of the wing torsion box and the mid-wing layout meant that the engines' inlet ducts of necessity passed through the wing torsion box (as distinct from the high-wing 'aircraft 495' project). Hence an unusual design was developed for the wing spars and inlet ducts; the latter were divided into two channels, the main one going straight through the spars while the smaller auxiliary duct passed below them, merging with the main duct at the engine's compressor face. This arrangement ensured an adequate cross-section to cater for the AM-3's mass flow, despite the relatively small wing thickness at the roots, allowing the engines to run normally. Hence the root portions of the wing spars were designed as hollow frames, which initially were built up from sev-eral pieces; later, on the production model, these were replaced by massive one-piece extruded parts for added strength.

The central portion of the airframe (comprising the centre fuselage, wings, engine nacelles and undercarriage) was designed in accordance with the area rule, which gave the aircraft its high aerodynamic properties. This was done by 'squeezing' the fuse-lage and engine nacelles in the area of the wing/fuselage joint (the nacelles were perceptibly curved in plan view) and by installing the main gear fairings which acted as 'anti-shock bodies'. In fact, this was the first use of the area ruling concept, which was only introduced on a large scale into the world aircraft design practice in 1954. These and other aerodynamic features incorporated in the 'aircraft 88' subsequently allowed the production Tu-16 bomber to reach a speed of 1,040 km/h (645 mph) or Mach 0.92 when uprated RD-3M engines were fitted.

The bomber's defensive armament consisted of three remote-controlled twin-cannon turrets, a fixed forward-firing cannon, four optical sighting stations and a gun-ranging radar covering the rear hemisphere. This took the bomber's defensive capability to a level that was far superior to the defensive systems of contempo-rary bombers in the same class. The defensive weapons system was developed by the OKB-134 weaponry design bureau based at Tushino (an area in the north-west of Moscow) under the overall guidance of Chief Designer Ivan I. Toropov. The designers intended to use either the Topaz long-range gun ranging radar (which existed only on paper) or the aforementioned PRS-1 Argon; the latter had shorter detection range but had passed its trials and was about to enter series production. Given the tight development schedule, the Tupolev OKB preferred 'an Argon in the hand to a Topaz in the bush' and opted for the PRS-1 radar.

In the course of design work on the 'aircraft 88' the leading specialists of OKB-156 and TsAGI had a number of arguments about the use of irreversible hydraulic actuators in the bomber's control system. The specialists at TsAGI expressly recommended the use of power-assisted controls on large high-speed aircraft. However, in the opinion of the OKB's specialists, the poor reliability of the first Soviet hydraulic actuators for aircraft made them unsuitable for the new machine (as already mentioned, Andrey N. Tupolev was rather conservative, and one of his famous dictums is that *the best hydraulic actuator is the one that stays on the ground*). The designers had therefore to find a way of reducing the control forces to an acceptable level. This was not easy, considering that on such a large aircraft flying at high speed the control surfaces had to have very small hinge moments. The problem was solved after numerous scale models and full-size components had been tested in TsAGI's wind tunnels.

As 'aircraft 88' was to become the first Soviet nuclear weapons delivery vehicle to become operational in large numbers (the small fleet of Tu-4As could not provide a reliable nuclear deterrent), the Tupolev OKB, as well as other organisations working to provide the Soviet 'nuclear shield', were faced with the task of ensuring the delivery aircraft's safety from the effects of the nuclear explosion. Such new phenomena as the spread of the powerful blast wave in a heterogeneous atmosphere (taking into account the effect of wind and its altitude variance) and the flash of the nuclear explosion (which was diffused or reflected as it passed through an atmosphere charged with various particles) had to be explored. The parameters of how the nuclear explosion would affect the aircraft had to be determined. Essentially this boiled down to issues of aerodynamics and structural strength. Would the blast wave destroy the bomber? Would the aircraft be crushed by the pressure differential following the shock wave? Would the blast wave throw the bomber (flying in autopilot mode) off balance and would the crew have to take over control? One particularly important issue was how the heat generated by the flash would affect the relatively weak duralumin alloy which was the bomber's primary structural material. (Later, some participants in nuclear tests involving the Tu-16 as the delivery vehicle asserted that the duralumin skin of the aircraft's undersides was weakened by the explosion to such an extent that you could push your finger through it.) To find the answers to these questions the Tupolev OKB enlisted the help of specialists from TsAGI and other research establishments and enterprises in various industries. Experimental facilities were built to simulate the complex effects produced on the aircraft by a nuclear explosion, and by the second half of the 1950s a range of effective measures to protect the new nuclear weapons carriers in the air (from the effects of their own weapons) and on the ground (from enemy attack) had been devised and introduced.

The bomber's airframe design, the structural materials used, its equipment and systems, as well as the manufacturing technology involved, were chosen and developed with due regard to the then-current capabilities of the Soviet aircraft industry. This enabled an airborne strike system, which was to become one of the key components of the Soviet deterrent in the 'Cold War' years, to be created within the shortest possible time.

First prototype ('aircraft 88/1', 'order 881')

The blueprints for the first prototype were issued to the OKB's experimental production facility (MMZ No.156) between Febru-

ary 1951, and January 1952. The aircraft bore the in-house designation '88/1' (occasionally rendered as '*izdeliye* 88/1'). Over the years the Tu-16 was subjected to many kinds of refits and modifications which were referred to in MAP correspondence as 'order such-and-such'. Well, whether by coincidence or not, the first prototype was referred to as *zakaz* 881 ('order 881').

(A linguistic comment must be made here. There are two related Russian words which are both translated into English as 'order'. In this case 'order' means not 'a verbal or written command from a superior', such as the aforementioned MAP orders (which corresponds to the word *prikaz*), but 'an order placed by a customer' (which corresponds to the word *zakaz*). The degree of work involved in such orders varied – from replacing a certain item of equipment to a complete refit into an entirely new version. To avoid confusion, orders of the latter kind are hereinafter mentioned without a 'No.' – for example, 'order 881', the way they were listed in actual paperwork.)

The manufacturing drawings were actually issued in parallel with the machine's construction; the work went on in 'live update' mode, with reciprocal on-the-spot correction of both the actual airframe and the blueprints. Work on setting up the manufacturing jigs and tooling began in April 1951, and the forward fuselage was assembled as early as May. By the end of 1951, the first prototype had been completed. On 26th December, Andrey N. Tupolev signed order No.27 for the machine's transfer to the LII airfield in the town of Zhukovskiy south of Moscow where the Tupolev OKB, like most of the Soviet aircraft design bureaus, had its flight test facility. The latter was known as ZhLIiDB (*Zhookovskaya lyotno-ispytahtel'naya i dovodochnaya bahza* – the Zhukovskiy Flight Test & Refinement Base).

On 25th January 1952, the dismantled aircraft '88/1' was transported to Zhukovskiy for further development work and flight tests; five days later the reassembled bomber was rolled out and parked on the apron reserved for Tupolev's machines. The aircraft had a natural metal finish and wore Soviet Air Force markings but no serial; unusually for the time, the red star insignia were not applied to the rear fuselage (as they should have been up to 1955), being present on the wings and tail only.

The actual prototype differed slightly from the ADP version. Most notably, the landing gear design was revised, the wingtip-mounted outrigger struts being deleted as unnecessary thanks to the stiff wings. The nose gear unit was fitted with K2-70/2 non-braking wheels having the same 900 x 275 mm (35.43 x 10.82 in) size, whereas the main gear bogies had larger 1,100 x 330 mm KT-16 wheels (*koleso tormoznoye* – brake-equipped wheel).

From then on, the obligatory ground testing of the systems and equipment began and the engines were ground-run. Part of the equipment was still missing at the time of the rollout, and new items were installed as they were delivered by various suppliers. Even as this work was in progress, on 25th February 1952, the first prototype was submitted for manufacturer's flight tests. Installation of the principal systems was completed on 24th April – three days before the first flight.

Meanwhile, the static test airframe (*izdeliye* '88/0' or 'order 880') was built in parallel; it was also completed by the end of 1951 and delivered to TsAGI on 26th December. Static tests at TsAGI

(also in Zhukovskiy, a stone's throw from the LII airfield) took place between 15th January, and 28th November 1952. At the end of March that year OKB-156 completed the structural strength calculations. The static tests and strength calculations were based on the initial planning data given in table 1 on page 50.

The aircrew assigned to the first prototype was captained by test pilot Nikolay S. Rybko and included co-pilot M. L. Mel'nikov, engineer in charge of the flight tests Boris N. Grozdov and engineer in charge of the aircraft Igor' A. Starkov. Chief Designer Dmitriy S. Markov, one of Andrey N. Tupolev's closest aides, was the project chief of 'aircraft 88', being permanently in charge of all work on the bomber from the first prototypes to the last production version.

The defensive armament was different from the original project.

Above left: The 'aircraft 88/0', the static test airframe of the Tu-16 in its original configuration matching the first prototype. Note the large aperture for the engine inlet duct in the wing's front spar visible on the right.

Left: A view of the static test airframe's centre fuselage and starboard wing; the latter is almost hidden from view by a thicket of fixtures for applying and measuring the loads.

Above: Another view of the '88/0' with the tail surfaces not fitted. Various odds and ends are also visible, including a fighter's wing on the left and the starboard inner wing of an M-4 bomber (note the twin inlet ducts) on the right.

Right: The '88/0' with the tail surfaces installed and rigged for testing.

The 'aircraft 88/1' was to feature seven 23-mm Afanas'yev/ Makarov TKB-495A cannons. This weapon was developed by the firearms design bureau in the city of Tula (hence TKB for ***Tool'skoye konstrooktorskoye byuro*** – Tula Design Bureau), and the version with a lengthened barrel (indicated by the A suffix) later entered production as the AM-23. The following cannon installations were envisaged:

• one cannon – sometimes designated TKB-495N – with 100 rounds on an NU-88 fixed forward-firing gun mount (*nosovaya oostanovka* – nose installation for 'aircraft 88') on the starboard side of the nose;

• two cannons with 250 rpg in a DT-V7 dorsal barbette (*distantsionno [oopravlyayemaya] toorel', verkhnyaya* – remote-controlled turret, upper);

Three views of the '88/1' at Zhukovskiy during manufacturer's flight tests. Note the tapered forward main gear door segments with built-in taxi lights and the IFF rod aerials ahead of the flight deck windshield and under the wing leading edge.

Three more aspects of the first prototype. The rear cannons are at maximum elevation. The front ends of the GRO's teardrop-shaped sighting blisters are metal fairings protecting the glazing from the jet exhaust.

Design data used as the basis for the static tests of 'aircraft 88'

Fuselage length	34.6 m (113 ft 6¹³⁄₆₄ in)
Wing span	33.0 m (108 ft 3½ in)
Wing area	166.0 m² (1,786.81 sq ft)
Maximum take-off weight	64,000 kg (141,100 lb)
Normal all-up weight	48,000 kg (105,820 lb)
Landing weight (four AL-5 engines)	51,200 kg (112,880 lb)
Landing weight (two AM-3 engines)	42,500 kg (93,700 lb)
Estimated Mach number	0.86
Maximum dynamic pressure for a 64,000-kg AUW:	
with a G load of 6	3,450 kg/m² (707.34 lb/sq ft)
with a G load of 4.3	2,700 kg/m² (553.57 lb/sq ft)

Performance of the '88/1' bomber with two AM-3 engines as recorded at the start of the manufacturer's flight tests

Fuselage length	34.6 m (113 ft 6¹³⁄₆₄ in)
Height on ground	9.85 m (32 ft 3⁵⁄₆₄ in)
Wing span	32.977 m (108 ft 2⁵⁄₁₆ in)
Wing area	164.59 m² (1,771.63 sq ft)
Wing sweep at quarter-chord	35°
Operating empty weight	41,050 kg (90,500 lb)
Take-off weight:	
normal	57,720 kg (127,250 lb)
maximum	77,350 kg (170,530 lb)
Payload:	
normal	16,670 kg (36,750 lb)
maximum	37,300 kg (82,230 lb)
Fuel load:	
normal	12,470 kg (27,490 lb)
maximum	32,100 kg (70,770 lb)
Crew	6

The first prototype's ordnance load options

Type of ordnance	Maximum quantity	Total weight
1. Bombs		
SAB-100-55 *	24	2,400 kg (5,290 lb)
FAB-500 M-46	18	9,000 kg (19,840 lb)
BrAB-500 *	18	9,000 kg (19,840 lb)
FAB-1500 M-46	6	9,000 kg (19,840 lb)
FAB-3000 M-46	2	6,000 kg (13,230 lb)
BrAB-3000	2	6,000 kg (13,230 lb)
FAB-5000 M-46	1	5,000 kg (11,020 lb)
BrAB-6000	1	6,000 kg (13,230 lb)
FAB-9000 M-46	1	9,000 kg (19,840 lb)
FAB-250 M-43	16	4,000 kg (8,820 lb)
FAB-500 M-43	12	6,000 kg (13,230 lb)
FAB-1000 M-43	4	4,000 kg (8,820 lb)
FAB-2000 M-43	4	8,000 kg (17,640 lb)
2. Naval mines		
AMD-500	12	6,600 kg (14,550 lb)
AMD-1000	4	4,500 kg (9,920 lb)
AMD-2M + AMD-500	4+6	7,560 kg (16,670 lb)
AMD-2M	8	8,560 kg (18,870 lb)
IGDM *	8	8,560 kg (18,870 lb)
Serpey	6	8,700 kg (19,180 lb)
Desna	8	6,000 kg (13,230 lb)
Lira	8	7,600 kg (16,760 lb)
A-2	4	2,440 kg (5,380 lb)
3. Torpedoes		
45-36AMV	6	6,984 kg (15,400 lb)
RAT-52	4	n.a.

* SAB = svetyashchaya aviabomba – flare bomb; BrAB = *broneboynaya aviabomba* – armour-piercing bomb; IGDM = *indooktsionno-ghidrodinamicheskaya donnaya meena* – bottom mine with a combined induction/hydrodynamic detector

• two cannons with 350 rpg in a DT-N7 ventral barbette (*distantsionno [oopravlyayemaya] toorel', nizhnyaya* – remote-controlled turret, lower);

• two cannons with 500 rpg in a DK-7 tail turret (*distantsionno [oopravlyayemaya toorel'], kormovaya* – remote-controlled turret, rear).

In fact, the project materials show that the above figures were the *capacity* of the ammunition boxes and that the actual ammo supply for the ventral and tail cannons was only 250 and 300 rpg respectively. However, this armament was still experimental; it was not available when manufacturer's tests began, and the first prototype was tested in unarmed configuration. A photo of the '88/1' prior to the first flight does show at least the dorsal and ventral barbettes, but these may have been dummy versions then.

The basic equipment fit essentially corresponded to that for the draft project. Yet, again the Rubidiy-MM II (also rendered as Rubidiy MM-2) and Argon radars and the Meridian SHORAN were not yet ready for flight testing and consequently were not fitted, the radomes under the nose and above the tail gunner's station being empty. It was decided to install them later when they became available in the course of test and development work.

As soon as all available equipment had been fitted, on 24th April 1952 the '88/1' moved under its own power for the first time, undergoing taxying tests for a full hour. A second taxying test took place the next day, and on 27th April, the aircraft made its 12-minute maiden flight. Manufacturer's tests continued until 29th October 1952, the aircraft logging a total of 72 hours 12 minutes in 46 flights. During the tests a top speed of 1,020 km/h (633 mph) was attained, which was better than the stipulated figure. On the other hand, the bomber turned out to be overweight. Even with an incomplete avionics and equipment fit, the first prototype had an empty weight of 41,050 kg (90,500 lb) versus the target figure of 35,750 kg (78,820 lb) and a take-off weight of 77,350 kg (170,530 lb) instead of the estimated 64,000 kg (141,100 lb). This inevitably had a detrimental effect on performance, particularly range and field performance. A weight reduction of at least 5-6 tons (11,020-13,230 lb) was required.

Building on the results of the manufacturer's tests it was decided to submit the machine for state acceptance trials, despite the fact that it was overweight. The primary task was to evaluate the bomber as a strike system; in the meantime the designers would do their utmost to reduce its weight and achieve the specified performance. On 13th November 1952, the aircraft was handed over to the Red Banner State Research Institute of the Air Force named after Valeriy P. Chkalov (GK NII VVS – *Gosudarstvennyy Krasnoznamyonnyy naoochno-issledovatel'skiy institoot Voyenno-vozdooshnykh sil*; the 'Red Banner' bit means the institute was awarded the Order of the Red Banner of Combat). The trials commenced on 15th November, at the LII airfield in Zhukovskiy but were interrupted on 30th March 1953, when the aircraft was damaged in a heavy landing after a routine test flight. Over a comparatively short space of time GK NII VVS test pilots made 79 flights in the '88/1' totalling 167 hours 28 minutes.

In spite of the reasonably good performance, the first prototype failed its state acceptance trials for three fundamental reasons: the mission equipment did not function satisfactorily, the defensive armament was still incomplete and the radar equipment was missing. Quite apart from this, the aircraft had to be repaired. The State commission decided to continue the trials with the lightened second prototype, which was built at an accelerated tempo at MMZ No.156. The repaired '88/1' was subsequently used for testing and refining the special equipment and the engines.

Even as the state acceptance trials of the '88/1' were in progress, the bomber was ordered into production. On 10th July 1952, the Council of Ministers issued directive No.3193-1214 followed a day later by MAP order No.804. Pursuant to these documents, 'aircraft 88' was allocated the service designation Tu-16. Preparations for series production at MAP's aircraft factory No.22 in Kazan', the capital of the Tatar Autonomous SSR, were to begin

forthwith (without waiting for the completion of the state acceptance trials). Production was to commence in July 1953, according to the following schedule: one aircraft in July, one in August, two in September, three in October, three in November and five in December. Tu-4 production at plant No.22 was to be terminated.

Performance of the '88/1' during manufacturer's flight tests

Maximum speed at a weight of 57500 kg (126,765 lb):	
at sea level	690 km/h (428 mph)
at 5,000 m (126,400 ft)	1,020 km/h (633 mph)
at 7,000 m (22,965 ft)	1,002 km/h (622 mph)
at 10,000 m (32,810 ft)	962 km/h (597 mph)
at 12,000 m (39,370 ft)	930 km/h (577 mph)
Range:	
with a 77,128-kg (170,035-lb) TOW, a 3,000-kg (6,610-lb)	
bomb load and a 32,100-kg (70,770-lb) fuel load	6,050 km (3,757 miles)
with a 75,848-kg (167,213-lb) TOW, a 9000-kg (19,840-lb)	
bomb load and a 25,740-kg (56,750-lb) fuel load	6,050 km (3,757 miles)
Service ceiling over the target	12,300 m (40,350 ft)
Time to height:	
to 6,000 m (19,685 ft)	6.4 minutes
to 10,000 m	13.0 minutes
Take-off run with a TOW of 76,000-77,000 kg (167,550-169,750 lb)	1,980 m (6,500 ft)
Take-off distance to h=25 m (82 ft) with a TOW of 76,000-77,000 kg	3,750 m (12,300 ft)
Landing run with a landing weight of 50,200 kg (110,670 lb)	1,510 m (4,950 ft)
Landing distance from h=25 m with a landing weight of 50,200 kg	2,354 m (7,723 ft)

* Restricted by a dynamic pressure limit of 2,300 kg/m² (471.56 lb/sq ft) an altitudes up to 7,000 m

Performance of the '88/1' during state acceptance trials

Operating empty weight	40,940 kg (90,255 lb)
Take-off weight:	
normal	61,500 kg (135,580 lb)
maximum	77,430 kg (170,700 lb)
Payload:	
normal	20,560 kg (45,330 lb)
maximum	36,490 kg (80,445 lb)
Fuel load:	
normal	16,070 kg (35,430 lb)
maximum	32,000 kg (70,550 lb)
Maximum speed at sea level with a 57,500-kg 126,760-lb) AUW *	690 km/h (428 mph)
Maximum speed at full power:	
at 7,500 m (24,610 ft)	1,005 km/h (624 mph)
at 10,000 m (32,810 ft)	962 km/h (597 mph)
at 12,000 m (39,370 ft)	916 km/h (569 mph)
Maximum speed at nominal power:	
at 7,500 m	980 km/h (608 mph)
at 10,000 m	941 km/h (584 mph)
at 12,000 m	881 km/h (547 mph
Range with a 77,430-kg TOW, a 3,000-kg (6,610-lb) bomb load and a 32,000-kg fuel load at 10,000-13,100 m (32,810-42,980 ft) **(option A)**	5,610 km (3,484 miles)
Range with a 77,430-kg TOW, a 3,000-kg bomb load and a 32,000-kg fuel load at a constant altitude of 10,000 m **(option B)**	5,260 km (3,267 miles)
Range with a 77,430-kg TOW, a 9,000-kg (19,840-lb) bomb load and a 26,000-kg (57,320-lb) fuel load at 10,000-12,900 m (32,810-42,320 ft) **(option C)**	4,390 km (2,726 miles)
Operational range with a 77,430-kg TOW, a 3,000-kg bomb load and a 32,000-kg fuel load at 10000-13100m (with 5% fuel reserves)	5,200 km (3,230 miles)
Endurance with a 77,430-kg TOW:	
option A (see above)	7 hours 10 minutes
option B	6 hours 48 minutes
option C	5 hours 44 minutes
Maximum endurance with a 77,430-kg TOW, a 3,000-kg bomb load and a 32,000-kg fuel load at 10,000 m	8 hours 15 minutes
Service ceiling (40,030-42,980 ft)	12,200-13,100 m
Time to height:	
to 5,000 m (16,400 ft)	5.7 minutes
to 10,000 m	16.2 minutes
Take-off run with a 77,430-kg TOW	2,320 m (7,610 ft)
Take-off distance to h=25 m (82 ft) with a 77,430-kg TOW	4,000 m (13,120 ft)
Landing run with a 50,200-kg (110,670-lb) landing weight	1,540 m (5,050 ft)
Landing distance from h=25 m with a 50,200-kg landing weight	2,480 m (8,140 ft)

* Restricted by a dynamic pressure limit of 2,300 kg/m² (471.56 lb/sq ft) an altitudes up to 7,000 m

Far left: Tupolev OKB test pilot Nikolay S. Rybko, the Tu-16's project test pilot during manufacturer's tests.

Centre left: Tupolev OKB test pilot Aleksey D. Perelyot who also participated in the tests.

Left: GK NII VVS test pilot Lt.-Col. Anatoliy K. Starikov who was the institute's project test pilot during the Tu-16's state acceptance trials.

The CofM directive and the MAP order also contained the following stipulations. Series production of the AM-3 turbojet was to be organised at aero engine factory No.16 (likewise located in Kazan'), which was to deliver the first 70 engines in 1953. Not later than 1st August 1952, the repaired first prototype was to perform an additional maximum-range test flight; a new gun ranging radar capable of detecting fighter-type targets at no less than 15-17 km (9.3-10.5 miles) range – the aforementioned Topaz radar – was to be developed for the Tu-16. In accordance with the amendments to the bomber's specifications set forth in Council of Ministers directive No.3125-1469 of 24th August 1951, in September 1952 MAP and the Tupolev OKB were to submit for renewed state acceptance trials a Tu-16 with a take-off weight of 48,000-55,000 kg (195,820-121,250 lb). This was to have a bomb load of 3,000-9,000 kg (6,610-19,840 lb), a technical range of 6,000-7,000 km (3,726-4,347 miles), a service ceiling of 13,000 m (42,650 ft), a take-off run of 1,500-1,800 m (4,920-5,910 ft) and a defensive armament of seven 23-mm cannons. The state acceptance trials of the Tu-16 were to be concluded in December 1953, whereupon the Air Force was to conduct service evaluation with the first 15 production examples built in Kazan'.

The '88' had become overweight in the course of the first prototype's design and construction. The primary reason for this had been the constant over-cautiousness of the structural strength department and the designers' concern both for the aircraft and their own fates. (It should be borne in mind that the Tu-16 came into being during the ultimate years of the Stalin regime when any kind of mistake could result in imprisonment – or worse.) Everyone wanted to be on the safe side. Designers at the 'grass roots' level added an extra 10% to the strength of a specific airframe part – just in case; their bosses added a bit more for the same reason, and so on. As a result, the take-off weight exceeded the target figure by more than 10 tons (22,045 lb)! Added to this, at the outset the engine type was not yet finalised – the bomber had to be designed around either four AL-5s or two AM-3s, – which also added excess weight. As a consequence, there was more than enough weight to be trimmed off, and this was done on the second prototype of the '88'.

Second prototype ('aircraft 88/2', 'order 882')

Designated '88/2' and referred to in MAP correspondence as 'order 882', the second prototype – called *dooblyor* (lit. 'understudy', or 'back-up') in the Soviet terminology of the time – was built in accordance with the same Council of Ministers directive and MAP order as the '88/1' but without any set deadlines. Originally it was regarded merely as a 'duplicate' of the first prototype; however, by

Left: Rybko bent the first prototype a little in a landing mishap at Zhukovskiy on 30th March 1953, when the aircraft overran, collapsing the starboard main gear unit. Note the open entry hatch of the rear pressure cabin (which is also the tail gunner's ejection hatch) and the 'towel rail' aerial above the GRO's starboard blister.

Above right and right: The second prototype ('aircraft 88/2') at Zhukovskiy during manufacturer's tests. Note the additional air scoops under the engine nacelles. The nose cannon is not fitted here.

the late summer of 1951, when the '88/1' was almost completed, it became obvious that the machine was overweight. Andrey N. Tupolev tasked his design staff with reducing the aircraft's empty weight as much as possible. This involved redesigning much of the airframe structure in order to 'slim down' the machine.

This work focused on three major areas. Firstly, the non-stressed structural elements had to be lightened. Secondly, it was necessary to reduce the weight of the load-bearing elements insofar as possible without compromising their structural strength. This was achieved by reducing the number of manufacturing joints and fasteners; for example, as already mentioned, the built-up frames at the wing roots through which the inlet ducts passed were replaced by one-piece parts made of AK8 alloy (*alyuminiy kovochnyy* – aluminium optimised for forging). In certain parts of the airframe the D-16 duralumin used hitherto was replaced by the new V95 high-strength aluminium alloy (V stood for *vysokoprochnyy* – high-strength, while 95 was the number of the foundry in the Urals producing the alloy). One-piece extruded profiles of variable cross-section were incorporated, as were large extruded parts with integral stiffeners, large skin panels made of a single sheet of metal and so on.

Thirdly, with the Air Force's consent the OKB imposed a speed limit (recorded in the flight manual) at altitudes up to 6,250 m (20,510 ft), since at these altitudes the aircraft would not normally be involved in combat operations anyway. The dynamic pressure limit below this altitude was reduced from 2,700 to 2,200 kg/m² (from 553.57 to 451.0 lb/sq ft).

These measures reduced the aircraft's empty weight from 41,050 to 36,490 kg (from 553.57 to 451.0 lb) – not quite as much as the designers had hoped, but a net saving of 4,560 kg (10,050 lb) is not bad either. Design work on the lightened version was completed in November 1952. By then, however, the blueprints for the 'heavy' (overweight) version had already been supplied to plant No.22 and preparations for production were going full steam ahead. Replacing these blueprints with the ones for the 'light' version and resetting the jigs was fraught with a delay in launching production, with predictable consequences for those responsible. At this difficult moment Andrey N. Tupolev, supported by the MAP top executives, took the courageous decision to put the lightened version of the Tu-16 into production – a vital decision. At the same time every measure was taken to minimise the resulting delay until the first bombers had been produced. All the corrected blueprints had been supplied to plant No.22 by the end of 1952, and the realistic delivery deadline for the first production Tu-16 was postponed from July to October 1953.

Design work on the second prototype began in August 1951, with construction of the aircraft at MMZ No.156 taking place simultaneously. The blueprints featuring all the weight-saving measures were prepared by the OKB between May and December

Above: Head-on view of the second prototype accentuating the area-ruled nacelles and the shape of the air intakes. Note the reshaped main gear doors having less taper.

Left: Here the nose cannon and IFF aerials have been installed.

Below: A side view of the '88/2'.

Opposite page: These views of the '88/2' at Zhukovskiy show how the front fairings of the GRO's sighting blisters became progressively wider towards the front and blended smoothly into the fuselage instead of having a parabolic shape (see page 49 for comparison). This was a unique feature of the second prototype.

1952. The '88/2' was completed in early 1953 and trucked to the ZhLIiDB on 13th February.

Apart from the revisions mentioned above, a number of criticisms made during the early flights of the '88/1' were taken into account, and some changes were made when equipment not available earlier was eventually fitted. Thus, the fuselage nose was lengthened by 0.2 m (7⅞ in) to increase crew comfort and accommodate equipment more easily. Fuel tanks were installed in the outer wing panels, increasing total fuel capacity from 38,200 to 43,900 litres (from 8,404 to 9,658 Imp gal), albeit the fuel supply was initially limited to 36,200 litres (7,964 Imp gal) due to structural strength concerns. The tailplane was reinforced and given a torsion box structure similar to that of the wings; the engine nacelles were slightly widened to facilitate engine installation and maintenance; the air/air heat exchanger in the air conditioning system (ACS) was replaced by a cooling turbine and the air intake for the ACS was altered.

The criticisms voiced by the State commission on the first prototype's test results were acted upon (in particular, this concerned the fitting and operation of the mission equipment). DT-V7, DT-N7S and DK-7 barbettes with TKB-495A cannons were fitted; the latter were later replaced by TKB-495AM (*modernizeerovan-*

Left: Here the '88/2' is depicted at Chkalovskaya AB during check-up state acceptance trials at GK NII VVS to verify the performance of the lightened second prototype.

Another view of the second prototype at Chkalovskaya.

naya – updated, aka AM-23) cannons; PS-48M optical sighting stations for the cannons (borrowed from the Tu-4), a PRS-1 Argon gun ranging radar, a prototype of the Rubidiy MM-2 ground mapping radar and an OPB-11R vector-synchronised bombsight replacing the OPB-10S optical bombsight were fitted. (PS = *pritsel'naya* **stahnt**siya – sighting station; OPB = *opticheskiy pritsel bombardirovochnyy* – optical bombsight; R = *[svyazanyy s] radahrom* – linked to the radar; S = *sinkhronnyy* – synchronised.) PO-4500 dynamotors (*preobrazovahtel' odnofahznyy* – single-phase AC converter) were installed to power the radars. A modernised AP-5-2M autopilot was fitted; the oxygen system featured KP-24 breathing apparatus instead of the KP-16 model.

Once again, the '88/2' had a natural metal finish and Soviet Air Force insignia but no serial. There were subtle external differences from the '88/1'; in particular, the forward-hinged one-piece front segments of the mainwheel well doors, which were attached to the actuation rams/drag struts, were reshaped – they had an almost trapezoidal shape, with less curvature and less taper at the front. The fairings of the GRO's observation blisters were reworked, widening towards the front and blending into the fuselage. Small 'elephant's ear' air intake scoops were added below the engine nacelles half-way along their length and on top of the nacelles' rear portions. A whip aerial offset to port was located just aft of the flight deck glazing, serving the ARK-5 ADF and the Meridian

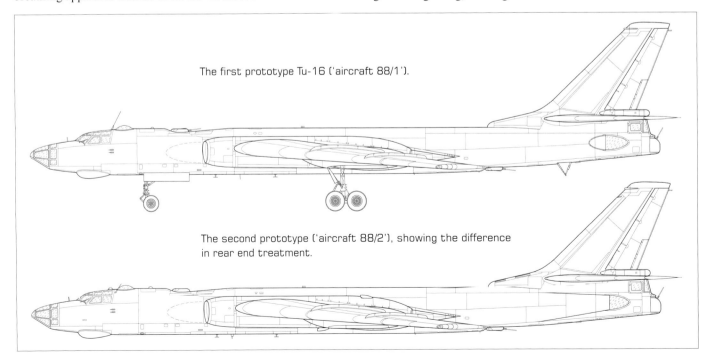

The first prototype Tu-16 ('aircraft 88/1').

The second prototype ('aircraft 88/2'), showing the difference in rear end treatment.

radio; a straight rod aerial for the Magniy-M IFF transponder was added ahead of the flight deck windshield.

On 2nd March 1953, MAP issued order No.272 'legalising' the lightened second prototype. This document restricted the take-off weight to 70,000 kg (154.320 lb) and the dynamic pressure at medium/low altitudes to 2,200 kg/m² (451 lb/sq ft) below 6,250 m (20,500 ft). The aircraft was to be ready for stage 2 of the state acceptance trials in June 1953. Furthermore, plant No.22 was required to supply TsAGI with a production Tu-16 airframe for renewed static tests in order to make sure that the lightened version conformed to structural strength standards.

The epic story of the bomber's lightening programme culminated in the following episode. Since the heads of OKB-156 had deviated from the generally accepted rules, a scapegoat had to be found. Light(e)ning causes 'thunder'! The formal pretext was the second prototype's failure to meet the stipulated speed target of 1,000-1,020 km/h (621-633 mph) – during the trials it showed a top speed of 992 km/h (616 mph). This led the then Minister of Aircraft Industry Mikhail V. Khroonichev to issue a formal rebuke to project chief Dmitriy S. Markov (which remained on his record for a long time until finally cancelled – and which he rightly and perversely could take pride in). He was 'rewarded' for the improved and, as it turned out, highly successful aircraft by a formal note in his employment certificate and personal record, but thankfully there were no more grave consequences.

By March 1953, the debugging work on the second prototype had been completed, and on 14th March, it was cleared for flight tests. Once again, test pilot Nikolay S. Rybko was the aircraft's captain and M. L. Mel'nikov was the co-pilot; the crew also included Mikhail M. Yegorov who was the engineer in charge of the test programme. Yegorov had done excellent investigative and development work on the powerplants of the Tu-4 and its Tu-70 transport derivative, as well as during the testing of the first Tupolev jets.

The '88/2' commenced taxi tests on 28th March 1953, and the thirty-minute first flight followed on 6th April. The manufacturer's tests were completed on 12th September.

On 16th September 1953, the aircraft was cleared for renewed state acceptance trials and was handed over to GK NII VVS two days later. The trials were held between 26th September 1953, and 10th April 1954, almost exactly a year after the machine's first flight; the '88/2' logged a total time of 154 hours 33 minutes in 65 flights. The trials were performed by a crew captained by Lt.-Col. Anatoliy K. Starikov, who later performed the greater part of the Tu-104 airliner's test programme. Apart from the trials of the aircraft itself, its systems were tested concurrently – in particular, the AM-3 engines, the experimental Rubidiy MM-2 bomb-aiming radar, the PS-48M optical sighting stations and the experimental Argon gun ranging radar. The data derived from these trials of the '88/2' served as a yardstick for the first production Tu-16 bombers and were used as standards in their manuals.

The '88/2' prototype passed its trials with GK NII VVS solely as a bomber. Tests of the mine and torpedo armament were deferred and were to be carried out on a specially modified production machine which would serve as the pattern aircraft for the Tu-16's torpedo bomber/minelayer version. During the trials the Tu-16 carried the following types of bombs: a 3,000-kg (6,610-lb) normal

Performance of the '88/2' during manufacturer's flight tests	
Length overall	35.2 m (115 ft 5⁵⁄₆₄ in)
Fuselage length	34.8 m (114 ft 2⁵⁄₆₄ in)
Wing span	32.989 m (108 ft 2²⁵⁄₃₂ in)
Height:	
theoretical (landing gear in no-load condition)	10.355 m (33 ft 11⁴⁵⁄₆₄ in)
practical (height on ground)	9.85 m (32 ft 3⁵⁄₆₄ in)
Wing area	164.65 m² (1,772.28 sq ft)
Wing aspect ratio	6.627
Wing taper	2.6416
Wing sweep at quarter-chord	35°
Landing gear track	9.775 m (32 ft 0²⁷⁄₃₂ in)
Landing gear wheelbase	10.913 m (35 ft 9¹⁄₆₄ in)
Empty weight	36,810 kg (81,150 lb)
All-up weight:	
normal (in maximum-range flight)	52,500 kg (115,740 lb)
maximum	71,040 kg (156,610 lb)
Payload:	
normal	15,690 kg (34,590 lb)
in overload configuration	35,230 kg (77,670 lb)
Fuel load:	
normal	11,490 kg (25,330 lb)
in overload configuration	30,030 kg (66,200 lb)
Maximum speed at take-off power with a 52,500-kg AUW:	
at 5,500 m (18,040 ft)	1,002 km/h (622 mph)
at 10,000 m (32,810 ft)	944 km/h (586 mph)
at 12,000 m (39,370 ft)	905 km/h (562 mph)
Rate of climb with a 56,000-kg (123,460-lb) AUW:	
at 2,000 m (6,560 ft)	16.3 m/sec (3,207 ft/min)
at 6,000 m (19,685 ft)	11.6 m/sec (2,282 ft/min)
at 10,000 m	7.2 m/sec (1,417 ft/min)
Time to altitude with a 56,000-kg AUW:	
to 6,000 m	6.7 minutes
to 10,000 m	13.8 minutes
Service ceiling over the target:	
before bomb release	12,900 m (42,320 ft)
after bomb release	13,200 m (43,310 ft)
Maximum technical range with 3,000 kg (6,610 lb) of bombs: *	
with a 71,040-kg AUW and a 30,030-kg fuel load	6,015 km (3,736 miles)
with a 72,000-kg (158,730-lb) TOW	5,760 km (3,577 miles)
Take-off run with 20° flap:	
with a 56,200-kg (123,900-lb) TOW	1,220 m (4,000 ft)
with a 71,000-kg (156,530-lb) TOW	1,700 m (5,580 ft)
Take-off distance to h=25 m (82 ft) with 20° flap:	
with a 56,200-kg TOW	2,215 m (7,270 ft)
with a 71,000-kg TOW	n.a.
Landing run with brake parachute and 35° flap:	
with a 43,600-kg (96,120-lb) landing weight	1,200 m (3,940 ft)
with a 47,000-kg (103,620-lb) landing weight	1,360 m (4,460 ft)
Landing distance from h=25 m with brake parachute and 35° flap:	
with a 43,600-kg landing weight	1,840 m (6,040 ft)
with a 47,000-kg landing weight	n.a.
Landing run without brake parachute †	1,760 m (5,770 ft)
Landing distance from h=25 m without brake parachute †	2,553 m (8,376 ft)

* flying a 'hi-hi-hi' mission profile
† with 35° flap and a 48,470-kg (106,860-lb) landing weight

bomb load option comprising 24 FAB-100 HE bombs; or a maximum bomb load of 9,000 kg (19,840 lb) comprising 24 FAB-250s, or 18 FAB-500s, or six FAB-1500s, or two FAB-3000s, or a single FAB-9000. Additionally, in the course of the trials twelve TsOSAB-10 marker bombs (*tsvetnaya oriyenteerno-signahl'naya aviabomba* – coloured marker/signal flare bomb) were carried in a special bay.

When creating the Tu-16 the Soviet aeronautical science and aircraft industry coped with scientific and technological challenges associated with the aerodynamics of a swept-wing aircraft at high subsonic speeds, including the basic principles of designing high-lift devices for swept wings. The Tu-16 helped study the stability and handling of such aircraft at critical angles of attack, in stall and spin mode (spin and dive recovery). It became the final stage in the development and use of manual flight controls on a heavy aircraft, showing clearly that a heavy aircraft had to have power-assisted controls by all means. It helped to improve the methods of designing swept wings and pressurised cabins and contributed to the refine-

ment of structural strength standards. The research and development work in the fields of aerodynamics, aeroelasticity and structural strength at the OKB proceeded under the direction of Aleksandr E. Sterlin, Nikolay A. Sokolov and Aleksey M. Cheryomukhin respectively, in close co-operation with TsAGI.

In designing the Tu-16 the OKB successfully resolved some technological problems having to do with large forged airframe parts, large-scale use of magnesium alloys, sealants, corrosion protection measures and so on. This work was tackled by the teams under Semyon A. Vigdorchik, Ivan L. Golovin, Abram S. Faïnshteyn and the specialists of several research institutions – first and foremost the Central Aero Engine Institute (TsIAM – *Tsentrahl'nyy institoot aviatsionnovo motorostroyeniya*). The choice of the general arrangement was the responsibility of Sergey M. Yeger's team, the work being supervised by Andrey N. Tupolev himself.

After receiving approval from the State commission 'aircraft 88/2' was recommended for series production and operational service with the Soviet Air Force.

Performance of the '88/2' during state acceptance trials

Length overall	35.2 m (115 ft 5⁵³⁄₆₄ in)
Fuselage length	34.8 m (114 ft 2²⁄₆₄ in)
Wing span	32.989 m (108 ft 2²⁵⁄₃₂ in)
Height:	
theoretical	10.355 m (33 ft 11⁴³⁄₆₄ in)
practical	9.85 m (32 ft 3⁵¹⁄₆₄ in)
Wing area	164.65 m² (1,772.28 sq ft)
Wing aspect ratio	6.627
Wing taper	2.6416
Wing sweepback at quarter-chord	35°
Landing gear track	9.775 m (32 ft 0²⁷⁄₃₂ in)
Landing gear wheelbase	10.913 m (35 ft 9⁴¹⁄₆₄ in)
Dry weight	36,600 kg (80,690 lb)
Empty weight (with trapped fuel, starter fuel and oil)	37,040 kg (81,660 lb)
All-up weight:	
normal for technical range	55,000 kg (121,250 lb)
maximum	71,560 kg (157.760 lb)
for exceptional occasions	72,000 kg (158,730 lb)
Maximum permitted landing weight	48,000 kg (105,820 lb)
Payload:	
normal	17,960 kg (39,590 lb)
in overload configuration	34,520 kg (76,100 lb)
Fuel load:	
normal	13,660 kg (30,115 lb)
in overload configuration	30,220 kg (66,620 lb)
maximum for exceptional occasions	30,660 kg (67,590 lb)
Crew weight	600 kg (1,320 lb)
Normal bomb load	3,000 kg (6,610 lb)
Weight of cannon ammunition	700 kg (1,540 lb)
Unstick speed:	
with a 57,000-kg (125,660-lb) take-off weight	250 km/h (155 mph)
with a 71,560-kg take-off weight	280 km/h (173 mph)
Maximum speed at take-off power with a 55,000 kg normal all-up weight	
at sea level	675 km/h (419 mph)
at 6,250 m (20,500 ft)	992 km/h (616 mph)
at 10,000 m (32,810 ft)	938 km/h (582 mph)

Maximum speed at nominal power with a 55,000 kg AUW:	
at sea level	675 km/h (419 mph)
at 6,250 m	958 km/h (595 mph)
at 10,000 m	915 km/h (568 mph)
Maximum Mach number	0.876
Landing speed with a 44,000-kg (97,000-lb) landing weight	223 km/h (138 mph)
Service ceiling:	
at nominal power with a 57,000-kg take-off weight	12,800 m (41,990 ft)
at nominal power with a 71,560-kg take-off weight	11,300 m (37,070 ft)
Time to reach service ceiling:	
with a 57,000-kg TOW	31 minutes
with a 71,560-kg TOW	38 minutes
Maximum technical range ('hi-hi-hi' flight profile):	
with a 57,000-kg TOW and a 3,000-kg bomb load	5,640 km (3,503 miles)
with a 71,560-kg TOW and a 3,000-kg bomb load	5,760 km (3,577 miles)
Combat radius	2,415 km (1,500 miles)
Take-off run at take-off power with 20° flap:	
with a 57,000-kg take-off weight	1,140 m (3,740 ft)
with a 71,560-kg take-off weight	1,900 m (6,230 ft)
Take-off distance to h=25 m (82 ft) at take-off power with 20° flap:	
with a 57,000-kg take-off weight	1,885 m (6,180 ft)
with a 71,560-kg take-off weight	3,165 m (10,380 ft)
Time from brake release to unstick:	
with a 57,000-kg TOW	28.7 sec
with a 71,560-kg TOW	45.0 sec
Landing run with a 44,000-kg landing weight and 35° flap:	
without brake parachute	1,655 m (5,430 ft)
with brake parachute	1,050 m (3,440 ft)
Landing distance from h=25 m with a 44,000-kg landing weight and 35° flap:	
without brake parachute	2,785 m (9,140 ft)
with brake parachute	2,180 m (7,150 ft)
Time from touchdown to standstill with a 44,000-kg landing weight:	
without brake parachute	34.5 sec
with brake parachute	28.5 sec

Chapter 3

The *Badger* in Production

As already mentioned, the 'aircraft 88' (Tu-16) bomber was ordered into production by Council of Ministers directive No.3193-1214 dated 10th July 1952 and MAP order No.804 dated 11th July 1952. The production version was to be patterned on the second prototype ('88/2').

As the type entered production, some of the Tu-16's design features necessitated the use of new manufacturing technologies and structural materials – and not only at the aircraft factories proper but at various subcontractor plants as well. For example, the aforementioned one-piece frames at the wing roots (the portions of the wing spars through which the inlet ducts passed) were introduced primarily to reduce the machine's structural weight, but there was

one more perfectly valid reason for their use. These components were manufactured in the town of Kamensk-Ural'skiy (Sverdlovsk Region, in the south of the Urals mountain range) by the Kamensk-Ural'skiy Metallurgical Works (KUMZ – *Kamensk-Oorahl'skiy metallurgicheskiy zavod*, an enterprise established specifically as a supplier of semi-finished products in aluminium and magnesium alloys to the aerospace industry), using large hydraulic extrusion presses. The latter had been brought from the Soviet Occupation Zone (one of the four Allied occupation zones of Germany) in 1948 as war reparations; a team of interned German specialists helped to commission the equipment at the new location. The three Schliemann presses – two vertical presses delivering pressures of 30,000

The final assembly shop of plant No.22 in Kazan', showing regular 'glass-nosed' Tu-16s interspersed with one of the pre-production Tu-16K-10s (right) and pre-production Tu-110 airliners (in the background).

Above: Tu-16 airframes taking shape; the inner wings and main gear fairings have been mated to the fuselage but the forward pressure cabins are still missing. The aircraft farthest from the camera has the engines and tail surfaces already installed.

Below: The fifth production Tu-16 ('1 Black', c/n 3200105) which was used for testing the bomber's ejection system. Note the underwing camera fairings and the photo calibration markings.

Opposite page: Scenes from the ejection system tests on '1 Black'. Note the escape hatch covers falling away in the third photo.

and 15,000 tons (66,137,570 and 33,068,780 lb) and a horizontal press delivering a pressure of 12,000 tons (26,455,030 lb) – were fully operational again by 1952. Yet, they were almost idle due to lack of orders from the aircraft factories because aircraft designers were still thinking in outdated technological terms; KUMZ needed to find orders that would keep its extrusion shop busy. Thus, the Tu-16 was the first Soviet aircraft built in series to make use of large extruded parts. Soon afterwards, KUMZ began manufacturing similar wing spar frames for the M-4 built at plant No.23 in Moscow; later orders included wings for the S-25 *Sosna* (Pine tree) surface-to-air missile (SAM) system (later renamed **Berkut** – Golden Eagle; NATO codename SA-1 *Guild*). By the end of the 1950s a Soviet-built hydraulic press of comparable power was commissioned at aircraft factory No.1 in Kuibyshev; later, when the plant was transferred to the missile industry, this press was used to manufacture parts for the R-7 intercontinental ballistic missile (ICBM). These advances put the USSR among the world's leading aero and space technologies.

The same CofM directive No.3193-1214 and MAP order No.804 designated the Kazan' aircraft factory No.22 named after Sergey P. Gorbunov as the pilot production plant for the Tu-16, cancelling further production of the Tu-4 which it had been building since 1947. This factory, known since 1978 as KAPO (*Kazahnskoye aviatsionnoye proizvodstvennoye obyedineniye* – Kazan' Aircraft Production Association named after Sergey P. Gorbunov), had a long history of building bombers, including heavy ones, and these were largely Tupolev types. The factory was well equipped for large-scale production of the Tu-4, which enabled it to master production of a totally new type of aircraft without undue problems – in theory at least. While the Tu-4 and the Tu-16 aircraft differed markedly in outlines and aerodynamics, there were considerable similarities as regards structural design features.

The schedule set forth in the MAP order was extremely tight. It is worth quoting a short extract from that document:

'Plant No.22 shall commence tooling up for production of the jet bomber powered by two AM-3 engines in accordance with the [OKB-156] General Designer's blueprints without waiting for the completion of the state acceptance trials; the aircraft shall be designated Tupolev-16 (Tu-16).

Iosif F. Nezval', who was head of the Tupolev OKB's Kazan' branch office when the Tu-16 entered production.

Kazan' factory test pilot Nikolay N. Arzhanov who who tested Tu-16s in 1953-63, including the first production machine.

Kazan' factory test pilot Aleksandr G. Vasil'chenko who tested Tu-16s in 1953-60, including the first production machine.

Kazan' factory test pilot Nikolay Ye. Kul'chitskiy who tested Tu-16s in 1962-63.

The delivery schedule for production Tu-16s in 1953 shall be: one aircraft in July, one aircraft in August, two aircraft in September, three aircraft in October, three aircraft in November and five aircraft in December. The first Tu-16 shall be submitted for state acceptance trials in September.'

Déjà vu. It had been the same story in 1945 when the Tu-4 (then provisionally designated B-4) was ordered into production in Kazan' – the plant had been allocated exactly one year for launching production of a completely new aircraft, while in fact the process had taken two years. It is hard to understand the reasoning of the government officials who assigned such obviously unrealistic schedules. Assuming they were not complete morons, there can be two explanations; either the MAP top brass wanted to see how the plant in general (and its director in particular) would cope with the Mission Impossible – that is, how close they would get to the deadline, or MAP was intentionally pursuing an arm-twisting policy, blackmailing the factory (which was 'not maintaining schedules')

and its director, who would be the first to take the rap. And in those days failure to cope with such an important task could easily cost the director his job, at the very least.

Meanwhile, production of the AM-3 turbojet was being organised at MAP's plant No.16, also located in Kazan'. In 1953 the plant was required to deliver 70 engines.

The launch of Tu-16 production proceeded quickly and was based on the principles tried and tested with the Tu-4. It was closely monitored by OKB-156 General Designer Andrey N. Tupolev and the bomber's project chief Dmitriy S. Markov. Speaking at a briefing in the OKB, Markov said: *'There will be no need to rework all the blueprints* (as compared to the overweight '88/1'– *Auth.*). *Speaking from experience, I can confidently say that only few parts will require major changes. We will manufacture and test them as a matter of top priority. Moreover, having done that, we will immediately manufacture enough of these parts for ten aircraft and send them to the production factory. For the purpose of holding static tests in full we will then take one of the first production machines and transfer it to TsAGI, which will test it on a top priority basis; I will arrange that with the TsAGI top brass.'* Much of the responsibility rested with Iosif F. Nezval', head of the Tupolev OKB's branch office at the Kazan' aircraft factory (formerly the factory's own design office, OKB-22).

Notwithstanding all this, the Kazan' factory was faced with many new design features and a lot of problems to be overcome.

Left: Tu-16s in flights of three come in over the History Museum, entering Red Square on 1st May 1954, when the type made its first public appearance.

Top right: An early-production Kazan'-built Tu-16 (c/n 4200204) used as an instructional airframe at the Riga Civil Aviation Engineers Institute.

Above right: The first Voronezh-built Tu-16 ('08 Red', c/n 5400001) serves for an NBC drill at the Achinsk Aviation Technical School.

Right: Tu-16 c/n 4200401 with the forward cabin entry hatch open.

Some of its older shops had to be rebuilt and re-equipped. In 1952 the capacity of the preparatory workshops (whose job was to manufacture the jigs and tooling and the half-finished articles) was increased 39% at the expense of the main assembly shops. New design teams responsible for the hydraulics, avionics, ejection seats and ground support equipment were set up. While the assembly technology was still based on the 'loft floor' technique, the curves of some airframe components (including the engine nacelles and the main gear fairings) were calculated by mathematical analysis. To ensure proper quality the lofts were made of duralumin instead of the usual plywood. A total of 1,360 lofts, no fewer than 31,010 templates, 12,110 pieces of tooling for the preparatory and machining shops, and 285 assembly jigs for the build-up and final assembly shops were manufactured.

The Tu-16's high speed, which was twice as high as the Tu-4's, required high-quality manufacturing of the airframe components whose contours had to conform strictly to the blueprints. Hence a new assembly method was introduced at plant No.22; the major airframe subassemblies were manufactured 'from the skin up' – that is, the skin panels were placed in the assembly jig first

(instead of the internal structural members, as had been the case previously), making sure that the outlines were correct when the component had been assembled.

The swept-wing configuration and the jet engines flanking the fuselage and fed by ducts passing through the wing spars demanded a special degree of care and accuracy from the assembly workers. Quite apart from the fact that the Tu-16's fuselage was crammed with equipment, its maximum diameter was 2.5 m (8 ft 2²⁷⁄₆₄ in) versus 2.9 m (9 ft 6³⁄₁₆ in) on the Tu-4, and the workers cursed between their teeth as they toiled in the cramped conditions, recall-

Left: A brand-new Kazan'-built Tu-16 bomber undergoing pre-flight checks. The c/n is taped over.

Below left: A Tu-16KS undergoing pre-flight checks. The extended radome of the Kobal't-P radar is visible, as are the missile pylons.

Bottom left: The Tu-16 pre-delivery flight line at Kazan'-Borisoglebskoye. The nearest aircraft is again a Tu-16KS.

Right: Minister of Defence Dmitriy F. Ustinov (second from right) inspects Naval Aviation Tu-16 versions at Kazan' in the early 1970s. A Tu-16K-11-16 is nearest, with a Tu-16K-10 visible beyond.

ing the Tu-4's roomy fuselage. The use of numerous large sub-assemblies and parts with integrally milled stiffeners required meticulous attention in their manufacture and assembly. A particular problem arose when KUMZ delivered imperfect wing spar frames which did not match the drawings. Close inspection and measurement was needed before these could be passed for assembly, and in some instances defective frames with deep incisions had to be scrapped.

Heightened requirements applied to the fuel system which worked at higher pressures; also, the grades of rubber used in the fuel system of the Tu-4 were resistant to aviation gasoline (Avgas) but were attacked by kerosene (Avtur), meaning that new materials had to be found for the gaskets. During the learning curve there were also many problems with debugging the avionics and equipment, particularly the defensive armament and the PRS-1 Argon gun laying radar.

To make matters worse, the OKB kept sending new drawings and the design of the Tu-16 changed even as the first production machines were being manufactured. All efforts notwithstanding, the completion schedule of the first Kazan'-built bombers was slipping – due both to discrepancies in the manufacturing documents, which were being constantly amended, and to delays in manufacturing the top-priority jigs and tooling.

Unlike the Tu-4, in the case of the Tu-16 there was no pre-production Batch Zero. The first production bomber (c/n 3200101) was finally completed and accepted by the factory's quality control department in late September 1953. It weighed in at 37,200 kg (82,010 lb), or 37,520 kg (82,720 lb) with the centreline rack for heavy-calibre bombs installed, which was within the specified limits. Contrary to everyone's expectations, there was no roll-out ceremony; at the orders of the plant's director Leonid P. Sokolov the bomber was furtively rolled out in the night of 1st/2nd October.

Speaking of construction numbers, Kazan'-built Tu-16s had two distinct c/n systems. Most of the versions (all except the Tu-16K-10) had seven-digit c/ns under the straightforward System 1 derived from the one used earlier for the Tu-4. For exam-

ple, a Tu-16KS manufactured in May 1956, was c/n 6203125, which means year of manufacture 1956, plant No.22 (the first digit is omitted to confuse hypothetical spies – a common practice in those days), production batch 031, 25th aircraft in the batch. Thus, the three-digit batch number presentation made allowance for manufacturing 100 or more batches, which was not uncommon with Soviet aircraft. (Some sources claim that the third digit was chosen randomly to complicate deciphering of the c/n for the outsider; however, this is highly unlikely because the third digit under System 1 has never been seen to be anything but zero.)

Predictably, the Tu-16 production schedule had gone to the dogs. The original plan for 15 aircraft was reduced to six, but even this target was not met – only one aircraft had been built by September and one more was nearing completion. On this pretext, on 19th October 1953, Leonid P. Sokolov was fired from his post as director of plant No.22, sharing the fate of his predecessor Vasiliy A. Okulov. He was 'kicked upstairs', becoming chief of MAP's 10th Main Directorate, and replaced by Pyotr P. Smirnov – a first-rate production man who had previously been director of aircraft factory No.1 in Kuibyshev. (The latter city has now reverted to its historic name of Samara.)

After three weeks of ground tests and checks the first flight date was set for 26th October. The Kazan' factory test crew assigned to the first production machine comprised project test pilot Aleksandr G. Vasil'chenko as captain, co-pilot Nikolay N. Arzhanov (both of them Test Pilots 1st Class), navigator Nasyr Sh. Shamilov, GRO operator Aleksey M. Kostin, Nav/Op Aleksey I. Vorob'yov, gunner Yusouf A. Gubaidoolin and flight technician Mikhail D. Shoovalov. Iosif A. Boorov was appointed engineer in charge of the flight tests, with Ghennadiy Ya. Fomin as his assistant.

As was his wont, General Designer Andrey N. Tupolev arrived at Kazan'-Borisoglebskoye, the factory airfield of plant No.22, in a MAP-owned aircraft to witness the first flight of the first production Tu-16, which was being readied on the taxiway. With typical single-mindedness, when asked by Smirnov if he'd like a cup of tea with lemon first, Tupolev replied rather brusquely: *'I did not come*

Top and above: These artist's impressions of the Tu-16 based on intelligence data appeared in the western press in the early 1950s. The upper one is fairly accurate while the lower one is obviously not.

Below: A scratchbuilt scale model of the Tu-16 manufactured in the West around the same time. Note the exaggerated wing fences and the absence of the Tu-16's trademark rear sighting blisters.

here to drink tea. Come on, show me what the heck you have assembled.' Then he briskly walked over to the aircraft, examined it and had a talk with the crew, many of whom he knew well since the days when the Tu-4 was being tested. The Old Man, as he was called (not to his face, of course), could be rather rude with designers and engineers, even with factory directors – but never with pilots and tech staff, whom he treated with respect because the prototype aircraft was in their hands.

Having done that, Andrey N. Tupolev walked along the runway and took up a position at the spot where, according to his calculations, the bomber was to lift off – a legendary habit of his. His intuition did not fail him – the Tu-16 lifted off exactly where he had predicted, to the loud cheers of the factory workers who were watching the first flight, many of them perched on the roofs like sparrows. Curiously, the exact date of the first production bomber's first flight remains unknown to this day, as different documents give different dates – 26th, 29th and even 25th October.

After the brief first flight Tupolev immediately signed an order awarding a money prize to the people who had contributed the most to this success – first of all the test crew. The aircraft was carefully draped in tarpaulins and placed under guard; Tupolev forbade anyone to approach it for the next three days until the first flight results from the flight data recorder had been analysed.

As regards stability and handling, the Tu-16 was more demanding than the Tu-4 on take-off and landing and was very sensitive to the controls. The engines turned out to be rather troublesome at first, being prone to surging at low ambient temperatures, and the skin of the inlet ducts would buckle and crack due to pressure fluctuations caused by the surge. Engine acceleration was poor by comparison with the Tu-4's piston engines, and restarting after an in-flight shutdown or flameout was difficult.

The second production Tu-16 (c/n 3200102) followed in November 1953; it was test flown by pilots Nikolay N. Arzhanov and Aleksandr S. Pal'chikov, with Ghennadiy Ya. Fomin as engineer in charge. This aircraft shared the bugs of the first one and introduced new ones – the radar was rather troublesome. Repairs and adjustments were made after every single flight, and it was not until 30th December 1953 that both aircraft were accepted by military quality control, which is regarded as their manufacture date. (Incidentally, it was not until the fourth or fifth batch that the bomber's initial bugs were eliminated on the Kazan' production line.)

Almost immediately the plant began preparing to build specialised versions of the Tu-16. As early as 17th September 1953, MAP issued an order instructing the OKB to develop a longer-range version with IFR capability, a nuclear-capable version and a version armed with stand-off air-to-surface missiles, all of which were to enter flight test in 1954.

In 1954 most of the initial difficulties were overcome and the bomber's manufacturing labour intensity was halved. As a result, the Kazan' factory delivered 70 Tu-16s that year, fulfilling the year's production plan, and the production rate kept increasing.

With the start of Tu-16 production, considerable animosity arose between the factory test pilots (who were civilian) and the military test pilots tasked with quality control, who did not trust each other. When Nikolay N. Arzhanov flatly refused to give a check ride to military test pilot Mikhail F. Otkidach, Tupolev OKB project test pilot Nikolay S. Rybko was summoned from Moscow to do it. This gave rise to a curious incident. In late 1949 a new runway (11/29) measuring 2,400 x 100 m (7,870 x 330 ft) had been commissioned at Kazan'-Borisoglebskoye, running at an angle to the old one (now no longer in existence). Yet Rybko, who had flown the first production Tu-4 from the old runway, had the visual references for the latter printed indelibly in his mind, and as he came in to land he began the approach to the old runway out of habit. Seeing that the aircraft was on the wrong course, navigator Grigoriy G. Balakin pointed this out to Rybko, who rudely told him not to interfere with the captain's actions. Sure enough, Rybko missed the runway and had to go around. After messing up the second approach, though, he had no choice but to ask Balakin for directions. After landing and listening to the factory test pilots' mocking comments about him *'running like a dog from one lamp standard to another'* Rybko immediately packed his bag and returned to Moscow with ignominy.

The original production plan for 1955 drawn up by MAP was for the Kazan' plant to build 220 Tu-16s; this was later reduced to 195, while actually the plant delivered 200 machines. Most of them were Tu-16A nuclear-capable bombers, and the first four production Tu-16KS missile strike aircraft were also built. That year no fewer than 775 design changes (including 300 major changes) concerning the ejection seats, landing gear, avionics and defensive armament were introduced on the Tu-16 production line; they mostly resulted from the check-up tests of Tu-16 c/n 4201002 at GK NII VVS. A further 62 of the above changes resulted from the state acceptance trials of the Tu-16A and Tu-16KS, plus a further 153 (associated with the defensive armament) from the tests of Tu-16 c/n 4200401.

The original production plan for 1956 required the factory to build no fewer than 330 Tu-16s (appetite comes when eating!).

Eventually this was revised to a more realistic figure of 120, and 132 aircraft were actually delivered. Again, most of them were Tu-16As. The cutback in the production plans was partly due to a fatal accident on 18th January 1956, when a brand-new Tu-16A (c/n 6202917) crashed during a pre-delivery test flight from Kazan'-Borisoglebskoye and a lengthy investigation ensued; this and other accidents involving the type are described in Appendix 2.

In 1957 the Kazan' factory began producing Tu-16s equipped with an IFR receptacle. The pre-delivery tests of such aircraft included the in-flight refuelling procedure but no Tu-16Z tanker was available (this version was outfitted exclusively by the Kuibyshev factory). Hence a production bomber was hastily converted to Tu-16Z standard; the fuel transfer hose for it was supplied by the Tupolev OKB's Tomilino branch. An immediate problem arose: the factory test pilots had no experience with the tanker version and lacked the appropriate type ratings. This problem was resolved when two experienced tanker crews were seconded to the factory from the Air Force.

In 1958 one more version – the Tu-16Ye active/passive electronic countermeasures (ECM) aircraft – entered production at plant No.22.

Between 1953 and 1958 plant No.22 built its first 42 batches of the Tu-16. Batches 1 through 10 consisted of five aircraft each; the number of aircraft per batch was increased to ten from Batch 11 onwards, then to 20 from Batch 26 onwards and finally to 30 per batch from Batch 31 onwards. The following versions were produced within this time frame: the baseline Tu-16 conventional bomber, the Tu-16A, the Tu-16KS and the Tu-16Ye. Additionally, in 1957-59 the factory converted seven production bombers as prototypes and pre-production examples of the Tu-16K-10 missile strike version; these aircraft retained their original c/ns under System 1.

In 1958 the Kazan' factory initiated production of the stretched 100-seat Tu-104B airliner; a year later it launched production of the Tu-22 supersonic bomber. Hence Tu-16 production was halted to free up capacity for the new types, by which time a total of 543 *Badgers* had been built. The final c/n under System 1 was 8204222, the last pre-production Tu-16K-10 (ZA) missile strike aircraft manufactured in December 1958; thus, Batch 42 was incomplete, with 22 aircraft instead of 30.

In the Kazan' factory's internal paperwork an abbreviated version of the c/n (the batch number and the number of the aircraft in the batch) was usually used; thus, Tu-16 c/n 3200101 was referred to as 'Tu-16 No.101'; really it should be 0101, but only three digits were used for batches 1 through 9. Tupolev OKB, GK NII VVS and (especially) LII documents sometimes quote abbreviated c/ns for Tu-16s not only from Kazan' but from other factories as well, unfortunately making it impossible to reconstruct the full c/n (unless you know when and where the aircraft was built).

The Tu-16K-10 was mostly produced by the Kuibyshev plant No.1 from 1959 onwards (see below). However, when plant No.1 was transferred from MAP to the Ministry of General Machinery (MOM – *Ministerstvo obshchevo mashinostroyeniya*) – the agency responsible for the Soviet missile and space programmes – in 1961 and switched to ballistic missiles and space launch vehicles, production of the Tu-16K-10 was urgently reinstated at plant No.22.

Tu-16 production at plant No.22 named after Sergey P. Gorbunov, Kazan'											
Version	**Year of production**										**Total**
	1953	1954	1955	1956	1957	1958	1959	1961	1962	1963	
Tu-16	2	19	1	–	19*	3*	–	–	–	–	44 (22*)
Tu-16A	–	45	189	103	57+46*	13*	–	–	–	–	453 (59*)
Tu-16KS	–	6	10	29	23+23*	16*	–	–	–	–	107 (39*)
Tu-16K-10	–	–	–	–	2 †	3* †	2* †	30	70	50	157 (5*)
Tu-16Ye	–	–	–	–	–	38*	–	–	–	–	38*
Grand total	**2**	**70**	**200**	**132**	**170 (88*)**	**73***	**2***	**30**	**70**	**50**	**799 (163*)**

Note: Here and elsewhere in the tables, only new-build aircraft are listed (conversion jobs are not included). The stated year is the year when the aircraft was accepted by military quality control, not the actual year of completion

* Aircraft built with an in-flight refuelling receptacle (designation suffixed 'ZA', see Chapter 4).

† Prototypes (1957) and pre-production aircraft (1958-59)

The first production machine was manufactured in June 1961, the last example leaving the factory in December 1963.

Unlike all other versions, Kazan'-built production Tu-16K-10s used a different construction number system – the then-current system introduced with the Tu-22; again, it had a seven-digit format but was structured quite differently. 30 batches of this version were built in Kazan', with five aircraft per batch (as was the case with the Tu-22 and subsequent Kazan'-built aircraft); oddly, the batch numbering under System 2 did not continue the sequence of the previous versions, the Tu-16K-10s being allocated the batches 51-80 (batches 43-50 did not exist). For instance, an example manufactured in May 1963 was c/n 2743054. The first and the last digits do not signify anything at all and were chosen randomly within a range of 1 to 5 to complicate c/n deciphering for the outsider; the remainder means Batch 74, year of manufacture 1963, 05th aircraft in the batch. Again, in paperwork the c/n was often abbreviated to the batch number/number in the batch; this can be regarded as the fuselage number (f/n) or line number – in this case, 7405.

The first production examples from plant No.22 became the prototypes for various versions or were used as testbeds. Details of these are given in Chapter 4.

Since the Kazan' aircraft factory alone obviously could not supply the Air Force with a sufficient number of Tu-16 bombers quickly enough, a decision was taken to widen the scope of the type's production. On 19th September 1953 the Council of Ministers issued directive No.2460-1017 a stepping up of Tu-16 production, followed on 25th September by MAP order No.77 to the same effect. Among other things, these documents ordered the aforementioned plant No.1 named after Iosif V. Stalin – one of the two aircraft factories in Kuibyshev – to commence production of the Tu-16. Unlike the co-located plant No.18 (now called Aviacor Joint-Stock Co.), which was then producing the Tu-4, plant No.1 was a 'fighter maker' manufacturing Mikoyan jet fighters; thus it had some experience with jets but none with heavy bombers. Actually, in August 1953, it had started building the Il-28 tactical bomber but managed to complete only 50 *Beagles* before MAP order No.33 required it to switch to heavier stuff – the Tu-16.

Production entry was greatly assisted both by the Tupolev OKB and the by principal manufacturer of the type, the Kazan'

factory. The latter supplied three completely knocked-down (CKD) kits to Kuibyshev in 1954 as 'starter sets' – just like it had done in 1948 when plant No.18 located next door was mastering the Tu-4. This time there was a Batch Zero (or rather 00). The first Kuibyshev-built pre-production Tu-16 (c/n 1880001) was assembled entirely from the parts of an aircraft that would have been c/n 4200505 in the Kazan' production sequence; it took to the air from Kuibyshev-Bezymyanka, the factory airfield shared by plants No.1 and No.18, in the summer of 1954. Similarly, Tu-16 c/n 1880002 was assembled from a CKD kit which would have been c/n 4200402. Ten *Badgers* were assembled in Kuibyshev in 1954, including two more built from CKD kits (c/ns 1880402 and 1880403). The first seven examples built in early 1955 (c/ns 1880404, 1880405 and 1880501 through 1880505) were likewise assembled from CKD kits supplied by plant No.22 before own production finally began.

Kuibyshev-built Tu-16s had a single construction number system – a seven-digit system similar to the one used previously for the Il-28 and, before that, the MiG-17 *sans suffixe* (*Fresco-A*). Unlike the c/n systems used by the other plants, it did not show the year of production; for instance, a Tu-16R built in December 1955 was c/n 1881809 – that is, Plant No.1, 'aircraft 88', Batch 18, 09th aircraft in the batch. In all, 41 batches of the Tu-16 were produced in Kuibyshev. Batch 0 consisted of two aircraft, Batch 1 had just a single machine, Batches 2 and 3 again had two aircraft each. From Batch 4 (December 1954) the output standardised on five aircraft per batch; the number was increased to ten from Batch 11 onwards in June 1955 and to 20 from Batch 21 onwards in February 1956, although the final Batch 40 had only 12 aircraft.

Apart from the baseline Tu-16 bomber, the following main versions were produced in Kuibyshev: the Tu-16K-10 (ZA) missile strike aircraft, the Tu-16R reconnaissance aircraft with internal SRS-1 and podded SRS-3 signals intelligence (SIGINT) sets, the Tu-16 Romb (Rhombus) reconnaissance aircraft with internal SRS-3 SIGINT set, the Tu-16SPS active ECM aircraft, and the Tu-16 *Yolka* (Spruce – or, if you like, Christmas tree) and Tu-16Ye active/passive ECM versions. There was also a one-off example with the experimental *Silikat* (Silicate) ECM system; while not officially listed as a production machine, this aircraft was built as

Tu-16 production at plant No.1, Kuibyshev								
Version	**Year of production**							**Total**
	1954	1955	1956	1957	1958	1959	1960	
Tu-16	10	80	35	46*	–	–	–	171 (46*)
Tu-16SPS (with SPS-1)	–	22	20	–	–	–	–	42
Tu-16SPS (with SPS-2)	–	–	28	70	4*	–	–	102 (4*)
Tu-16 Romb	–	–	5	–	–	–	–	5
Tu-16 Silikat (Tu-16 Fonar')	–	–	1	–	–	–	–	1
Tu-16R (with SRS-1 and SRS-3)	–	–	–	44*	26*	–	–	70*
Tu-16 Yolka (with ASO-16/7)	–	–	–	42*	–	–	–	42*
Tu-16Ye	–	–	–	4*	34*	13*	–	51*
Tu-16K-10 (ZA)	–	–	–	–	–	17*	42*	59*
Grand total	**10**	**102**	**89**	**206 (136*)**	**64***	**30***	**42***	**543 (272*)**

Note: Some sources state very different production figures for plant No.1: ten aircraft accepted in 1954, 130 in 1955, 131 in 1956, 150 in 1957, 50 in 1958, 30 in 1959 and 42 in 1960, which adds up to 545 instead of 543

* Aircraft built with an in-flight refuelling receptacle (designation suffixed 'ZA').

such, not a refit. Subsequently this Tu-16 was re-equipped with the experimental *Fonar'* (Lantern, or Streetlight) ECM set. Like the machines produced in Kazan', some of the first Tu-16s produced at plant No.1 were used as prototypes for later versions.

Even that was not enough to meet the demand. Hence on 2nd February 1955, the Council of Ministers issued directive No.163-97 followed on 1st March by MAP order No.127. Aircraft factory No.64 in Voronezh was thereby ordered to begin production of the Tu-16 – primarily the Tu-16T torpedo-bomber for the Naval Aviation, and the preparations for production there likewise proceeded with the active assistance and support of OKB-156 and the Kazan' factory. Again, there was a Batch Zero (or rather 000); the first pre-production Tu-16 (c/n 5400001) was rolled out at Voronezh-Pridacha airfield in May 1955. The first Voronezh-built Tu-16T was

assembled from a CKD kit received in February 1955, that would have been c/n 5201603 in the Kazan' production sequence.

Voronezh-built Tu-16s utilised a single construction number system which was identical to the Kazan' factory's System 1. For example, a Tu-16 (ZA) manufactured in July 1957, is c/n 7402010 – that is, year of manufacture 1957, Plant No.64 (again the first digit is omitted for security reasons), Batch 020, 10th aircraft in the batch. 23 batches of the *Badger* were built in Voronezh, with three aircraft in Batch 0, one in Batch 1, five aircraft each in Batches 2 through 11 and generally ten aircraft each in Batches 12 through 22; Batch 20 was an exception, comprising 12 aircraft.

The Voronezh plant was 'last in, first out', ceasing production of the type in December 1957. Apart from the Tu-16 and Tu-16T, it also built a small batch of Tu-16 Yolka ECM aircraft.

A mid-production Kuibyshev-built Tu-16A on a snow-covered hardstand. The huge tactical code painted directly on the forward fuselage shows the picture was taken in the late 1950s.

Tu-16 production at plant No.64, Voronezh				
Version	Year of production			Total
	1955	1956	1957	
Tu-16	8	49	22*	79 (22*)
Tu-16T	17	29	30*	76 (30*)
Tu-16 Yolka (with ASO-16/7)	–	–	10*	10*
Grand total	**25**	**78**	**62***	**165 (62*)**

* Aircraft built with an in-flight refuelling receptacle (designation suffixed 'ZA').

Like the Tu-4, Tu-16s built by all three factories originally had the c/n prominently stencilled in black on both sides of the nose (below the flight deck windows) and on both sides of the fin. Kazan'-built Tu-16K-10s sometimes had it painted on the tail only (unlike their Kuibyshev-built sister ships). In the early 1980s, however, the construction numbers were toned down to grey on white or removed altogether for security reasons, remaining only on a manufacturer's data plate inside the aircraft which was not visible to the casual observer.

Additionally, some Kazan'-built 'glass-nosed' Tu-16s had a four-digit number stencilled on the fin below the construction number in the same font and character size. Its first digit matched the first digit of the c/n (and thus the year of production), the other three ran in sequence, accruing continuously. Such aircraft were invariably missile strike versions; thus, for instance, Tu-16KS c/n 5202716 was marked 5014, Tu-16KS c/n 7203608 was marked 7124, while Tu-16K-11-16 c/n 8204022 was marked 8191. While these extra 'tail numbers' run in sequence, they were allocated singly or in groups of two or three all over the c/n range under System 1. The meaning is not 100% certain but these were very probably sequence numbers of the missile carriers – both built and converted by the Kazan' plant (the last three digits exceed by far the number of Tu-16KSs built, which is 107). The highest known example is Tu-16K-11-16 c/n 8204112 with the tail number 8212. However, far from all missile carriers sported such numbers.

Thus, the Tu-16 was produced for more than a decade – from 1953 to late 1963. The production rates varied over the years, peaking in 1955-57; more than a thousand Tu-16s were produced in the course of these three years. Between them the three production factories built 1,507 Tu-16s – 799 in Kazan', 543 in Kuibyshev and 165 in Voronezh. Together with the Moscow-built '88/1' and '88/2' prototypes and the '88/0' static test airframe, this brings the total Soviet production of the *Badger* to 1,510 – quite an impressive figure.

Only eleven versions of the Tu-16 were built as such – namely the Tu-16 and Tu-16A bombers, the Tu-16T torpedo-bomber, the Tu-16KS and Tu-16K-10 missile strike aircraft, the Tu-16R and Tu-16 Romb reconnaissance versions, and the Tu-16Ye, Tu-16 Yolka, Tu-16SPS and Tu-16P ECM aircraft. All other versions were refits of earlier production models. For example, the Tu-16R and Tu-16P were built exclusively by plant No.1 in Kuibyshev, but nevertheless Kazan'-built examples of these versions (identifiable by their construction numbers) could be seen, and these were obviously converted from bombers.

In addition to new production, all three factories were involved in various refit and upgrades programmes and in producing spares

Overall Soviet Tu-16 production by year				
Year	Plant No.22, Kazan'	Plant No.1, Kuibyshev	Plant No.64, Voronezh	Total
1953	2	–	–	2
1954	70	10	–	80
1955	200	102	25	327
1956	132	89	78	299
1957	170	206	62	438
1958	73	64	–	137
1959	2	30	–	32
1960	–	42	–	42
1961	30	–	–	30
1962	70	–	–	70
1963	50	–	–	50
Total	**799**	**543**	**165**	**1,507**

Overall Soviet Tu-16 production by version				
Version	Plant No.22, Kazan'	Plant No.1, Kuibyshev	Plant No.64, Voronezh	Total
Tu-16	44	171	79	294
Tu-16A	453	–	–	453
Tu-16KS	107	–	–	107
Tu-16K-10	157	59	–	216
Tu-16T	–	–	76	76
Tu-16R (with SRS-1 and SRS-3)	–	70	–	70
Tu-16 Romb	–	5	–	5
Tu-16Ye	38	51	–	89
Tu-16 Yolka (with ASO-16/7)	–	42	10	52
Tu-16SPS (with SPS-1)	–	42	–	42
Tu-16SPS (with SPS-2)	–	102	–	102
Tu-16 Silikat/Fonar'	–	1	–	1
Total	**799**	**543**	**165**	**1,507**

for the Air Force's operational and maintenance units. Furthermore, some specialised versions were converted by operational Soviet Air Force and Soviet Navy units. For example, a number of production Tu-16K-10 missile carriers were converted into Tu-16RM-1 reconnaissance aircraft by AVMF maintenance shops. An immense amount of work was done through the combined efforts of the Soviet military and OKB-156, since there were several dozen types of modifications carried out on Tu-16 machines while in service. Testbed examples were often converted by the organisations wishing to use them, either with the participation of OKB-156 or under its supervision.

It would be impossible to give a precise list of all the Tu-16's versions and modifications because some aircraft were modified more than once and, unfortunately, in many cases the documents that could shed light on the matter have been destroyed. Drawing on existing documents and archive material, the following two chapters contain more detailed information on the many versions of the Tu-16, as well as on a series of projected versions which never materialised.

Chapter 4

The Tu-16 Family: The Soviet Strike Versions

In the course of its production and long service career the Tu-16 spawned a multitude of versions, not all of which were destined to reach the hardware stage. Most of them fall into five distinct categories as described below, and this chapter deals with the strike variants, which were quite numerous.

I. The bombers and related aircraft

Tu-16 long-range bomber ('order 882'; *izdeliye* 88, *izdeliye* N)

The production Tu-16 bomber was patterned on the second prototype (the '88/2') and was therefore likewise referred to in MAP paperwork as 'order 882'. For security reasons a couple of product codes came into use in unclassified documents – *izdeliye* 88 and *izdeliye* N; they also served as an unclassified designation for everyday use because the actual service designation was classi-fied. (It was the same story with almost every item of Soviet military hardware in the post-war years.) Later, as new versions appeared with suffix letters to the Tu-16 designation, the same version designator letters were added to the product code, giving rise to some monstrous ciphers. Thus the Tu-16A was '*izdeliye* NA' and the Tu-16R was '*izdeliye* NR', which was tolerable; but the Tu-16REZA became '*izdeliye* NREZA' and the Tu-16KRMEZA turned into '*izdeliye* NKRMEZA', which was too much! After declassification, the *izdeliye* designations for the Tu-16 fell into disuse.

As already mentioned, plant No.22 led the way in mastering production of the Tu-16. The first Kazan'-built bomber (c/n 3200101) was rolled out in the autumn of 1953 and accepted by military quality control on 29th October, with one more production Tu-16 following by the year's end. Production was extended to Kuibyshev in 1954 and to Voronezh in 1955.

An early-production Kazan'-built Tu-16A bomber equipped with Magniy-M and Bariy-M IFF transponders. The huge tactical code on the forward fuselage indicates the picture was taken in the 1960s.

Opposite page: This uncoded early-production Tu-16 *sans suffixe* (c/n 4200403) was used by LII in several test programmes. Here it is seen with the original main gear door design patterned on that of the '88/1' (with forward-hinged one-piece forward doors which are strongly tapered).

Above and below: The same aircraft with the flaps fully deployed.

Right: The upper side of the starboard wing of Tu-16 c/n 4200403 was covered with wool tufts to record the airflow patterns; the cine camera was mounted on the fin.

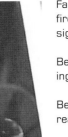

Far left and left: The tail gunner (defensive fire commander) of a Tu-16 uses the PS-53K sighting station to take aim.

Below, far left: A pursuing fighter in the aiming reticle of the PS-53K sight.

Below left: The Tu-16 fires its twin AM-23 rear cannons...

Below: ...and the fighter is hit, bursting into flames.

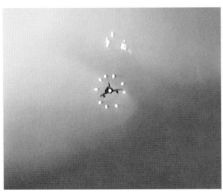

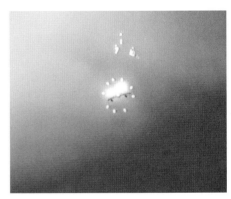

Outwardly the initial production machines differed little from the prototypes. Kazan'-built Tu-16s at least up to and including Batch 4 retained the one-piece forward-hinged main gear doors immediately ahead of the struts with circular windows for the taxi lights which were attached to the struts. Interestingly, the shape of these doors matched the first prototype, not the second one – the doors were strongly tapered at the front; so did the fairings of the GRO's sighting blisters. Rod aerials for the Magniy-M IFF interrogator, aka SRZ (*samolyotnyy rahdiolokatsionnyy zaproschik* – aircraft-mounted radar interrogator), were located atop the extreme nose (above the navigator's station) and in the front ends of the main gear fairings, with a further rod aerial for the Bariy-M IFF transponder, aka SRO (*samolyotnyy rahdiolokatsionnyy otvetchik* – aircraft-mounted radar transponder), under the fuselage in line with the wing leading edge. As on the prototypes, two 'towel rail' aerials were installed on the starboard side, serving two R-807 radios which performed different functions; the aerial on the upper forward fuselage (running from the flight deck to the wing leading edge) was for the command radio, while the one on the lower rear fuselage was for the communications radio. The empty weight of the production bomber varied from 37,200 to 37,520 kg (from 82,010 to 82,720 lb), depending on which type of bomb racks were fitted to suit different bomb loads.

The Tu-16 made its first public appearance on 1st May 1954 when a nine-ship formation flew over Moscow's Red Square during the traditional May Day parade. The West was quick to take note of the new Soviet jet bomber. NATO's Air Standards Co-ordinating Committee (ASCC) allocated the reporting name *Badger* to the Tu-16; later, when new versions were detected by western observers, the basic bomber's reporting name was amended to *Badger-A*.

On 28th May 1954 the Tu-16 was officially included into the Soviet Air Force inventory by Council of Ministers directive No.1034-43. This was confirmed by MAP order No.355 of 4th June 1954, which stipulated that an updated production machine be submitted for check-up tests at GK NII VVS in September-October that year.

The above directive stipulated the following performance for the production Tu-16:

• bomb load: normal, 3,000 kg (6,610 lb); maximum 9,000 kg (19,840 lb);

• top speed at nominal power with a 55,000-kg (121,250-lb) normal all-up weight in level flight at an altitude of 6,250 m (20,510 ft), 992 km/h (616 mph);

• ditto at 10,000 m (32,810 ft), 938 km/h (582 mph);

• service ceiling at nominal power and normal AUW, 12,900 m (42,320 ft);

• climb time to service ceiling at nominal power and normal AUW, 31 minutes;

• maximum range ('hi-hi-hi' mission profile) at optimum cruising speed with a 72,000-kg (158,730-lb) TOW and a 3,000-kg bomb load, 5,760 km (3,577 miles);

• take-off run with a 71,560-kg (157,760-lb) take-off weight, 1,900 m (6,230 ft);

• landing run with a 44,000-kg (97,000-lb) landing weight, 1,655 m (5,430 ft).

The cannon armament was stipulated as one fixed forward-firing 23-mm cannon with 100 rounds, two 23-mm cannons with 250 rpg in a dorsal turret, two 23-mm cannons with 250 rpg in a ventral turret (maximum ammunition capacity 350 rpg) and two 23-mm cannons with 350 rpg in a tail turret (maximum ammo capacity 500 rpg). The bomber was to have a crew of six.

Right: '12 Red', another Tu-16 bomber. The vehicle beyond is a 16,000-litre (3,520 Imp gal) TZ-16 refuelling bowser based on the YaAZ-210D conventional tractor unit.

Below: Soviet Air Force technicians use a ladder to check the rudder trim tab and clean the rear glazing of a Tu-16 bomber. Note the large codes on the tails. The aircraft further down the line has all the glazing under wraps.

Check-up tests of the defensive armament system components – the new PS-53 sighting station featuring a VB-53 ballistic computer (*vychislitel'nyy blok* – computation module) and the PRS-1 Argon gun ranging radar – took place in July 1954, using Tu-16 c/n 4200401. The PS-53 replaced the PS-48 after lengthy attempts to refine the latter failed to give satisfactory results.

In keeping with a MAP order yet another Kazan'-built production aircraft (c/n 4201002) was modified to extend its range by increasing the fuel tankage; this increased Its take-off weight in overload configuration to 75,800 kg (167,110 lb). Of course this was detrimental to the aircraft's field performance; check-up tests at GK NII VVS showed that with the above high gross weight, with the engines at take-off power and the flaps set at 20°, the bomber's unstick speed increased to 288 km/h (178 mph), the take-off run to 2,180 m (7,150 ft) and the take-off distance to 3,375 m (11,070 ft). On the plus side, with a 3,000-kg (6,610-lb) normal bomb load,

700 kg (1,540 lb) of cannon ammunition and 34,263 kg (75,534 lb) of fuel a range of 6,430 km (3,995 miles) was attained. The effective range with 5% fuel reserves was 5,970 km (3,709 miles). Upon completion of the check-up tests at GK NII VVS the high gross weight/extended-range Tu-16 c/n 4201002 was accepted as the *etalon* ('standard-setter', or pattern aircraft) for production examples in 1955.

On 28th September 1954, the Tu-16 suffered an accident which showed clearly that a large and heavy aircraft like the Tu-16 did require power-assisted controls after all. It also showed that the bomber was robust enough, despite the weight-saving measures. That day the first pre-production Kuibyshev-built example (c/n 1880001) was making a test flight from Kuibyshev-Bezymy-anka, captained by factory test pilot Lt.-Col. Gheorgiy S. Molchanov; the mission objective was to determine the machine's G limits. Maj. Aleksandr I. Kazakov, a young test pilot from the

same factory, was the co-pilot; in spite of this, he was flying the aircraft from the left-hand seat because Molchanov had decided to check his piloting skills. The crew also included navigator/bomb-aimer V. S. Tikhomirov, Nav/Op Yu. G. Shestakov, GRO V. D. Kalachov and tail gunner Ye. N. Serezhnikov.

At an altitude of 9,000 m (29,530 ft) and an indicated airspeed of 550-560 km/h (341-347 mph) Kazakov put the machine into a dive, pulling 3.2 Gs when recovering from the dive; however, this fell short of the target figure of 3.47 Gs. When Molchanov intervened, hauling back on his control yoke to increase the G load, the bomber reached a critical angle of attack and stalled, flicking into a spin with up to 60° bank. Descending in a tight spiral, the Tu-16 accelerated rapidly and the pilots were unable to recover from the spin because, with no hydraulic actuators to assist them, the control forces were too high. Seeing that the aircraft was out of control, at an altitude of 5,000 m (16,400 ft) Molchanov ordered the crew to eject and was the first to do so; Kalachov and Serezhnikov hastily followed suit. However, the ejection took place at excessively high speed, the captain and the GRO losing their lives (the captain was not properly strapped in and his parachute was torn to shreds, while the two occupants of the rear pressure cabin collided during ejection). The tail gunner survived, albeit with injuries.

Meanwhile, the navigator messed up the ejection procedure and his hatch cover jammed, leaving him unable to eject; the Nav/Op, too, was being tardy. Conversely, co-pilot Aleksandr I. Kazakov stayed with the aircraft, fighting doggedly to regain control. He could hear the airframe creaking under the strain and realised it was on the point of breaking up in mid-air. However, luck was on his side: the G force consecutively wrenched the starboard and port main gear units loose from the uplocks, the extended struts acting as speedbrakes. Hauling the control yoke back with a force of some 100 kgf (220 lbf), Kazakov managed a recovery to straight and level flight at an altitude of some 100 m (330 ft) and brought the aircraft back to base, landing safely.

The bomber stood up to the abuse, even though it had significantly exceeded its limits; afterwards the pilot assessed the G load at the moment of recovery as 4.2 and the airspeed as 1,000 km/h (621 mph) – way beyond the maximum permitted figure of 700 km/h (435 mph). This evoked much interest on the part of the structural strength experts, who were surprised that the aircraft had stayed in one piece; some accounts of the accident say the bomber was virtually undamaged. Contrary to what one might expect, Tu-16 c/n 1880001 was not written off (just to be on the safe side, because its structural integrity had been compromised); upon completion of the investigation it served on as a development aircraft, becoming a prototype of the Tu-16Z tanker (see Chapter 5).

The investigation panel, which included Prof. Grigoriy S. Kalachov, engineer Daniil S. Zosim and test pilot Ivan I. Shooneyko, pointed out that the Tu-16 had stability and control problems compounded by the lack of powered controls. This led to a dangerous propensity to entering a steep spiral in the event of a stall.

A month later, on 27th October 1954, Aleksandr I. Kazakov was awarded the prestigious Hero of the Soviet Union (HSU) title '*for bravery and heroism when mastering new aviation hardware*'. Tikhomirov and Shestakov were awarded the Order of the Red Banner of Combat. As for Gheorgiy S. Molchanov, his actions were

the subject of controversy for many years. Many people denounced him for 'jumping ship' (both literally and figuratively), saying he was guilty of leaving the other crewmembers to their fate. Others pointed out that 'the captain abandons the ship last' when it is controllable – which it wasn't, to all intents and purposes. They said that at worst Molchanov had made an error in judgement as to whether control could be restored, which had cost him his life, and that bad judgement is one thing and guilt is another.

The initial production version capable of carrying only conventional (non-nuclear) munitions entered service in early 1954. Much later the Mikoyan MiG-23 tactical fighter had an interim version between the initial MiG-23S *Flogger-A* and the MiG-23M *Flogger-B* that had no suffix letter to the designation, despite being the *second* version; this was popularly known as ***dvadtsat' tretiy 'bez bookvy'*** (MiG-23 with no [suffix] letter, or *sans suffixe*), and by analogy the initial 'non-nuclear' version of the bomber is hereinafter called Tu-16 *sans suffixe*. In the course of six years the three factories built a total of 294 Tu-16 *sans suffixe* bombers, which were distributed about equally between the Air Force (to be precise, the DA) and the Naval Aviation.

The Tu-16 *sans suffixe* served as the basis for all subsequent versions. Yet the basic bomber did not remain immutable; almost immediately the OKB started making various refinements to the Tu-16. As already mentioned, the first production batches built in Kazan' and Kuibyshev had a main gear door design identical to that of the '88/1'. However, it turned out that airflow departure from the forward-hinged door segments, which were at about 45° to the slipstream when the gear was down, caused vibration of the main gear fairings. To eliminate this, the one-piece doors were replaced by a second, smaller pair of clamshell doors which did not interfere with the airflow when open. The new version was tested in 1954 on an unserialled Kazan'-built Tu-16 (c/n 4200403) which had been built with the old door design. The fifth production machine (c/n 3200105) retaining the original design served as a reference. The results were good – the test pilots, including LII's project test pilot Ivan I. Shooneyko, noted a marked reduction of the vibration levels. Soon the new design was introduced on the Kazan' and Kuibyshev production lines (the first Kuibyshev-built machine to have it was a Batch 3 aircraft, c/n 1880302); Voronezh-built Tu-16s had the new door design from the outset.

Incidentally, Tu-16 c/n 4200403 was used by LII for exploring its stability and handling at high angles of attack, bank angles and G loads. The aircraft was equipped with wool tufts on the port wing's outer section and a cine camera on the port side of the fin fillet to capture the airflow patterns. Valentin F. Kovalyov was project test pilot, with M. G. Kotik as engineer in charge. Test flights were made at altitudes of 4,000-10,000 m (13,120-32,810 ft) and speeds up to Mach 0.9, with a take-off weight of 52,800 kg (116,400 lb) and a CG position of 27.2% mean aerodynamic chord (MAC). The same aircraft was used for testing a new position of the TP-156 pitot heads (*troobka Pito* – Pitot tube. OKB-156 design) for the captain's and navigator's instruments. The new placement (two in tandem on each side instead of two vertically paired pitots to port and one to starboard) was recommended by LII specialists.

Over its many years of service the bomber was repeatedly upgraded, with an increase in its take-off weight to 77,150 kg

(170,090 lb), the empty weight being 37,200 kg (82,010 lb). The original AM-3 engines gave way to an improved version designated RD-3M (*modernizeerovannyy* – updated) and its derivatives. The reason for the designation change was that in 1955 Aleksandr A. Mikulin, who had fallen out of favour with the government, was removed from his post as Chief Designer of OKB-300 and replaced by Sergey K. Tumanskiy; hence the 'AM-for-Aleksandr Mikulin' designation prefix was replaced by a depersonalised 'RD'.

The mission equipment was updated and many other systems were also changed. In particular, electronic countermeasures (ECM) equipment was fitted for individual and group protection against enemy radars – initially in the form of an ASO-16/3 chaff dispenser (*apparaht sbrosa [dipol'nykh] otrazhateley* – 'dipole reflector dispenser' with three chaff cassettes). Some of the Tu-16s remaining in service at the end of the 1970s received the latest active ECM systems, such as the SPS-151/-152/-153 Siren' jammer series (Lilac, pronounced *seeren'*), the SPS-4M *Modulyatsiya* (Modulation) jammer and the like; these updates were known as 'order 2615' and 'order 691'. (SPS = *stahntsiya pomekhovykh signahlov* – lit. 'interference signal emitter'.) For operations in large formations the bombers were retrofitted with the A-326 *Rogovitsa* (Cornea) formation-keeping system; its receiver antenna was housed in a distinctive dielectric fairing on the flight deck roof, while the transmitter aerials were located on the port side of the navigator's station (a short L-shaped aerial) and above the gun ranging radar's radome.

Export sales of the Tu-16 began in 1958. The first foreign customer for the bomber version was China, which obtained a manufacturing licence for the type and developed its own versions. (Chinese production is described in Chapter 8.)

By the early 1980s only a small number of Tu-16s in dedicated bomber versions remained in service. Very few Tu-16s originally built as bombers were destined to remain that way until retirement as time-expired. A few such relics remained at the Long-Range Aviation's 43rd TsBP i PLS (*Tsentr boyevoy podgotovki i pereoochivaniya lyotnovo sostahva* – Combat Training & Aircrew Conversion Centre) at Dyagilevo airbase near Ryazan' in central Russia; a few more served on with a training air regiment of the Chelyabinsk Military Navigator College (ChVVAUSh – *Chelyabinskoye vyssheye voyennoye aviatsionnoye oochilischche shtoormanov*).

Tu-16 (ZA) IFR-capable bomber ('order 229')

Starting in 1957, the final (?) 90 Tu-16 conventional bombers were built with provisions for in-flight refuelling (IFR) from Tu-16Z refuelling tankers using the wing-to-wing system (described in Chapter 5). Such bombers were designated Tu-16 (ZA), the suffix standing for for *zapravlyayemyy [samolyot]* (receiver aircraft). In production the IFR-capable bomber was referred to as 'order 229'. Theoretically the product code should be *izdeliye* NZA.

Digressing a little, we may mention that initially the ZA suffix was given in parentheses (this will be seen in the designations of other IFR-capable versions). The reason is that the Cyrillic letter Z, especially in upper case, is very similar to the numeral 3, and without parentheses the designation could be misread as 'Tu-163A' (or 'Tu-163', in the case of the tanker). Later the parentheses were omitted and the designation rendered as Tu-16ZA (Tu-16AZA, Tu-16KSZA, Tu-16K-10ZA, Tu-16RZA and so on) – probably on the assumption that the designations were sufficiently well known to Those Who Needed To Know and there would be no confusion.

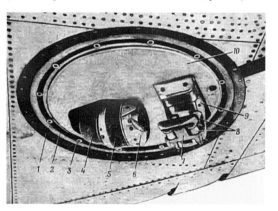

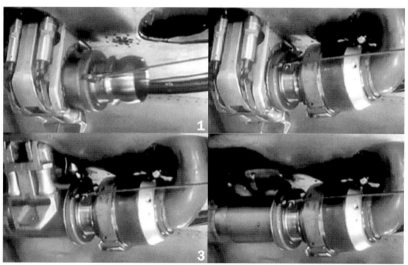

Above left: The in-flight refuelling receptacle under the port wingtip of a Tu-16 (ZA) bomber. The retractable grapple and the fuel line connector head are visible.

Left: The receptacle with the hose of a Tu-16Z tanker connected to it (note the line of the stabilising drogue parachute).

Above: Stills from a cine film showing the receptacle in action. 1. The grapple secures the end of the hose; 2. The fuel line connector locks into position; 3. The grapple retracts; 4. Contact is established and fuel transfer is in progress.

Some documents, though, had the suffix printed in lower case for the same reason (in order to avoid a misread) – Tu-16za, Tu-16Rza, Tu-16Eza and so on. Once the IFR system had become an almost standard feature of the *Badger*, the ZA suffix was dropped from everyday use and the designations reverted to their original form. To determine whether a particular aircraft was IFR-capable or not you needed to see its record card where the ZA suffix was retained.

The Tu-16 (ZA) was equipped with a pneumatically actuated IFR receptacle under the port wingtip which engaged the tanker's hose and connected it to the fuel system; appropriate modifications were made to the wing structure. A fuel line ran along the port wing's front spar from the receptacle to the Nos. 2-5 fuel tanks (the tanks of Groups 1 and 2). The receptacle also served for emergency fuel jettison from these tanks; further fuel jettison valves were located in the Nos. 16L/16R wing tanks.

In-flight refuelling and fuel quantity/usage was monitored by the SETS-60M system (*soommeeruyushchiy elektricheskiy toplivomer s signalizahtsiyey* – summing electric fuel meter with a [low fuel] warning feature) replacing the SETS-60D version used on non-IFR-capable *Badgers*. The receptacle was controlled from the GRO's station, while the refuelling control panel was located on the co-pilot's instrument panel. To facilitate refuelling the procedure was largely automated.

There were a few other associated changes. The pneumatic system was modified for operating the receptacle and scavenging the fuel transfer line after breaking contact with the tanker. To enable refuelling at night the Tu-16 (ZA) was fitted with extra lighting equipment. A light in the tailcone of the port main gear fairing illuminated the wing underside and the receptacle; a light buried in the fuselage side at fuselage frame 18 shone aft, illuminating the port wing leading edge and the tanker's fuel transfer hose. The navigator and the GRO were provided with manually trained searchlights at their workstations (in the former case, at the glazing panel between frames 2-3). Finally, a signal light the port wingtip came on when the hose was locked into place, telling the tanker's crew that fuel transfer could begin. The performance and handling of the aircraft was not affected by the addition of the IFR receptacle.

Outwardly the Tu-16 (ZA) could be identified by a small Perspex window ahead of the port air intake for the wing leading edge illumination light and by a horizontal trapezoidal winglet at the port wingtip which reduced the intensity of the wingtip vortex and moved it outward, reducing its effect on the tanker's hose. A special rod at the wing leading edge prevented the hose from being thrown on top of the winglet in a messed-up approach to the tanker. An identical winglet was fitted to the starboard wingtip of early aircraft for aerodynamic symmetry reasons but was later omitted as superfluous. The entire IFR system is described in detail in the Tu-16Z section.

Other IFR-capable versions of the *Badger* had the same equipment. The Tu-16K-10 (ZA) was an exception, having a somewhat different fuel system (see page 154).

Tu-16A nuclear-capable bomber (aircraft '88A'; 'order 191', 'order 699', *izdeliye* NA)

Being optimised for carrying a free-fall nuclear bomb, the Tu-16A was the first Soviet nuclear weapons delivery system to see serv-ice in large numbers. Its development was initiated by Council of Ministers directive No.3193 issued on 10th July 1952. The aircraft was referred to in production as 'order 191' and in operational service as 'aircraft 88A' or *izdeliye* NA (*ahtomnyy* – atomic or nuclear; in this case, nuclear-capable). Some documents erroneously call this version Tu-16N (apparently meaning *nositel' [spetsboyepripahsov]* – carrier of 'special', that is, nuclear munitions), although this designation in fact applies to an in-flight refuelling tanker (see Chapter 5).

The Tu-16A differed from the baseline Tu-16 primarily in having a heat-insulated bomb bay equipped with an environmental control system maintaining the correct temperature up to the aircraft's service ceiling. This was necessary because nuclear munitions are sensitive to sub-zero temperatures and may malfunction after having a cold soak at high altitude – the chain reaction might not go ahead, leading to non-detonation. Also, a special system performing the pre-release procedure (disengaging the multistage safety system, arming the detonator and activating the barometric sensors to explode the nuke at the preset altitude) and releasing the bomb was fitted. Last but not least, the aircraft was provided with special protection from the effects of the nuclear explosion.

Work on a version of the *Badger* capable of delivering nuclear weapons began in mid-1953. Upon completion of the design work in November 1953, two conventional Tu-16s *sans suffixe* were to be modified and delivered for testing to the Air Force's 71st Test Range at Bagerovo AB in the eastern part of the Crimea Peninsula, 14 km (8.7 miles) west of the city of Kerch. This outfit had overall responsibility for testing Soviet nuclear weapons; its head, Maj.-Gen. Viktor A. Chernorez, was a first-rate specialist who contributed immensely to equipping the Soviet Armed Forces with nuclear and thermonuclear weaponry.

Actually the designation '71st Test Range' was something of a misnomer because, in addition to an instrumented test range with a target for the bomb drops, the establishment included three Air Force units. The latter were the 35th OSBAP (*otdel'nyy smeshannyy bombardirovochnyy aviapolk* – Independent Composite Bomber Regiment) performing the test drops, the 513th IAP (*istrebitel'nyy aviapolk* – fighter regiment) providing protection, and the 647th SAPSO (*smeshannyy aviapolk spetsiahl'novo obespecheniya* – Composite Special Support Air Regiment). This latter operated a mixed bag of utility, transport and reconnaissance aircraft, which varied over the years, and was tasked with air sampling in the wake of nuclear tests, aerial photography and transport/liaison duties. Only instrumented dummy bombs were dropped at Bagerovo; nobody in their right mind would test a live nuke in the Crimea which was, to use a common Soviet cliché, *the all-Union resort*!

The two Tu-16A prototypes modified to 'order 191' standard were converted from the second and third Kazan'-built production bombers (c/ns 3200102 and 4200103). The testing was completed in April 1954, and the new version entered production at plant No.22 that same year, starting with c/n 4200502 (although some documents indicate that the first production Tu-16A was c/n 4201301). The Tu-16A became the most prolific new-build version of the *Badger* family; a total of 453 had been built when pro-

A fine shot of a Tu-16A sporting the 'anti-flash' white finish and an 'Excellent aircraft' maintenance award badge on the nose gear door.

duction ceased in 1958, accounting for almost one-third of the type's overall production run. Like the Tu-16 *sans suffixe*, the Tu-16A was delivered in approximately equal numbers to the DA and the AVMF; in squadron service it was operated both as a nuclear weapons carrier and as a conventional bomber. On 28th May 1954, the Tu-16A was included into the Soviet Air Force inventory by Council of Ministers directive No.1034-443.

For bomb-aiming the Tu-16A was equipped with an RBP-4 navigation/attack radar (***rahdiolokatsionnyy bombardirovochnyy pritsel*** – radar bomb sight; NATO codename *Short Horn*) and an OPB-11R or OPB-11RM optical bombsight, which was linked to the radar and to the AP-5-2M or AP-6E autopilot. The RBP-4 was an advanced derivative of the Rubidiy MM-2 radar (and thus fitted nicely into the existing chin radome); it was developed in 1949-52 under the guidance of V. S. Dekhtyaryov, passing its tests on a Tu-16. The radar could work in 360° search mode or scan a 45° sector whose axis could be directed incrementally within ±55° to the direction of flight. The RBP-4 could detect large targets, such as major industrial centres, at 150-180 km (93-111 miles) range and had a maximum targeting range of some 70 km (43.5 miles); it permitted bomb delivery from altitudes of 2,000-15,000 m (6,560-49,210 ft) at flight speeds of 300-1,250 km/h (186-776 mph). For better ECM resistance the radar worked in two selectable frequencies.

The cannons were aimed by means of a PKI-1 reflector sight for the fixed forward-firing cannon (*pritsel kollimahtornyy istrebitelya* – fighter-type collimator gunsight), PS-53VK, PS-53BL, PS-53BP and PS-53K optical sighting stations and the PRS-1 gun ranging radar. (The suffix letters to the designations of the PS-53 stations denoted their location: VK = ***verkhnyaya***

koopol'naya – for the dorsal dome, BL = *bortovaya **levaya*** – port lateral, BP = *bortovaya **pravaya*** – starboard lateral, K = *kormovaya* – rear. This variance was due to the fact that the four stations had different fields of view and permitted different fields of fire.)

The Tu-16A's flight and navigation equipment included an autopilot, an A-711 LORAN (with an A-713 receiver), an RSBN-2S Svod (Dome) SHORAN, an A-326 formation flying system, a ZSO celestial navigation system (comprising IAS-1M, AK-53M and DAK-2 star trackers), a compass system (comprising KI-12, GPK-52 and DIK-46M compasses), an SP-50 ILS, an NI-50B navigation display, a DISS-1 *Veter-2* (Wind) Doppler radar, an ARK-5 ADF, an RV-17M high-altitude altimeter and an RV-2 low-altitude altimeter. (RSBN = ***rahdiotekhnicheskaya sistema blizhney navigahtsiï*** – SHORAN; ZSO = ***zvyozdno-solnechnyy orientahtor*** – star & sun orientation device; DAK = *distantsionnyy **astrokompas*** – remote astrocompass; KI = ***kompas indooktsionnyy*** – induction-type compass; GPK = ***gheero-polukompas*** – gyro compass; DIK = *distantsionnyy indooktsionnyy **kompas*** – remote induction-type compass; NI = *navigatsionnyy **indikahtor*** – navigational display; DISS = ***doplerovskiy izmeritel' skorosti i snosa*** – Doppler [ground] speed and drift angle indicator.) The communications suite included an RSIU-5B (later redesignated R-802) or R-832M *Evkalipt-M* (Eucalyptus) command radio, a 1-RSB-70M communications radio with a US-9 receiver and an R-851 emergency locator transmitter (ELT). A *Sirena-2* (Siren) radar warning receiver and an SPS-5M active ECM system were provided. The flight deck featured three additional circuit breaker panels at the navigator's, captain's and navigator/operator's stations.

The Tu-16A was fitted with a special MBD6-16 or MBD6-16M centreline bomb cradle (*mostovoy bahlochnyy derzhatel'* – braced beam-type rack, Group 6, that is, for ordnance up to 9,000 kg/ 19,840 lb calibre), which was compatible with all five types of nuclear bombs at the disposal of the DA. It could also carry the same conventional bomb, anti-shipping mine or torpedo load as the Tu-16 *sans suffixe*. The variety of the Tu-16A capable of carrying naval mines was modified under the terms of 'order 699'.

To keep the delicate control system of the nuclear bomb operational the bomb bay temperature was maintained at +20°C (68°F). The environmental control system featured four *izdeliye* 107 electric heaters, four air temperature regulators, four powered fans and a temperature control system.

The aircraft, its crew and equipment were protected from the heat and flash of the nuclear explosion in the following ways. Firstly, the gaps on the aircraft's exterior were sealed or minimised; to this end, strips of metal were riveted to the perimeter of hatch covers, the edges of the bomb bay doors and wheel well doors. Secondly, glazed areas were blanked off from the inside before the bomb was dropped. Specifically, the navigator's station featured a sliding metal shutter on the optically flat lower pane and quick-fit metal blinds on the lateral panes. The flight deck side windows were closed by blinds made of a double layer of heavy fabric; the GRO's sighting blisters were closed by fixed flat blanks and multi-segment metal shutters whose shape matched the inside of the transparencies when closed, while the tail gunner's station glazing was also closed by multi-segment metal shutters.

Thirdly, some equipment items and wiring bundles were encased in wound or glued insulating materials. Finally, the aircraft received a so-called 'anti-flash' colour scheme, albeit an incomplete one – the undersurfaces and fuselage sides were given a coat of special high-gloss white paint to reflect the flash as much as possible; the upper surfaces and the vertical tail retained their

Performance of the Tu-16A with RD-3M-500 engines	
Empty weight	39,720 kg (87,570 lb)
All-up weight:	
normal	75,800 kg (167,110 lb)
maximum	79,000 kg (174,170 lb)
Maximum bomb load	9,000 kg (19,840 lb)
Maximum speed at max continuous power and	
an AUW of 55,000-70,000 kg (121,250-154,320 lb):	
at up to 500 m (1,640 ft)	670 km/h (416 mph)
at 6,250 m (20,500 ft)	890 km/h (552 mph)
at 10,000 m (32,810 ft)	960 km/h (596 mph)
Maximum permissible Mach number	0.9
Service ceiling with a take-off weight of 62,000 kg (136,690 lb)	12,800 m (41,990 ft)
Service range at optimum altitude, with bomb release at midway point	5,800 km (3,602 miles)

natural metal finish. (By comparison, the British V-bombers were initially white overall – for the same reason.) In the late 1950s all operational Tu-16A bombers were modified to ensure greater resistance to the nuclear flash, with those areas of the metal skin most exposed to the flash being made as resistant as possible.

In addition to the 'anti-flash' colour scheme which was its main identification feature, the Tu-16A had detail differences from the Tu-16 *sans suffixe* occasioned by the more modern avionics and equipment. Thus, instead of the 'towel rail' aerial low on the starboard side of the rear fuselage the R-807 communications radio had a wire aerial running from a short aerial mast on the centreline near the wing leading edge to the top of the fin. The RSIU-5B command radio was served by two distinctive L-shaped aerials located low on the starboard side of the nose (near the nose-wheel well) and under the rear fuselage (offset to starboard); later, with the R-832M radio, the rear aerial was relocated to the flight

Tu-16A '34 Red' with an SPS-100 Rezeda-AK active jammer in a fairing supplanting the DK-7 tail turret and the gunner's rear glazing.

deck roof. Some time after production entry the Bariy-M IFF transponder and Magniy-M IFF interrogator were replaced by the SRZO-2M *Khrom-Nikel'* (Chrome-Nickel) combined interrogator/transponder (*samolyotnyy rahdiolokatsionnyy zaproschik-otvetchik*, or *izdeliye* 023) with triple rod aerials ahead of the flight deck windshield and under the rear fuselage; their distinctive shape gave rise to the NATO codename *Odd Rods*.

When the RSBN-2S SHORAN was added, its presence was revealed by the flush antennas built into the fin (two on each side) immediately below the dielectric fin cap that housed the antenna of the RSIU-3M radio. Two prominent strake aerials for the ARK-5 ADF were installed high on the forward fuselage sides aft of the flight deck, the starboard one replacing the earlier 'towel rail' aerial of the command radio; the ADF loop aerials were buried in the fuselage underside. Some Tu-16As had an ARK-UD ADF with a loop aerial in a small teardrop fairing amidships. From 1962 onwards some aircraft were retrofitted with an ASO-16/3 chaff dispenser whose outlet was located on the port bomb bay door. Others had an ASO-2B *Avtomat-2* (Automatic device) chaff dispenser with a less obtrusive outlet on the rear fuselage underside. The ASO-2B, alias KDS-16GM (*kassetnyy derzhatel' spetsiahl'nyy* – special cassette), could work in six modes (incremental or continuous), jamming radars with five different wavebands; a single aircraft could leave a trail of chaff 800-1,500 m (2,620-4,920 ft) long and 400 m (1,310 ft) deep.

When the Tu-16A entered service its empty weight was 37,700 kg (83,110 lb) – just 185 kg (407 lb) greater than the basic bomber's. However, various upgrades in the course of production and service caused the empty weight to rise steadily until it reached 39,720 kg (87,570 lb); this necessitated installation of RD-3M-500 engines uprated to 9,500 kgp (20,940 lbst). Also, the higher weight caused some structural strength problems; to overcome these, narrow reinforcement plates were riveted to the lower forward/centre fuselage sides.

Since the Tu-16A had virtually no obvious external differences from the baseline bomber (apart from the white undersides), it was likewise referred to by NATO as the *Badger-A*.

During the 1960s, 155 Tu-16A bombers were converted to carry KSR-2 and KSR-11 air-to-surface missiles. Several dozen Tu-16As were still in squadron service in the early 1980s.

Tu-16A (ZA) nuclear-capable bomber with IFR capability (aircraft '88A')

The final 59 production Tu-16As built in 1957-58 were completed with an IFR receptacle under the port wingtip and all the other associated changes. These aircraft were designated Tu-16A (ZA); theoretically the product code should be *izdeliye* NAZA.

Tu-16A nuclear-capable bomber (aircraft '88A', 'order 684/1')

Analysis of the lessons learned in local conflicts at the end of the 1960s led the Soviet Air Force to enhance the Tu-16A bomber's tactical capabilities. A special variant able to carry a large number of small bombs weighing between 50 and 500 kg (110-1,102 lb) was produced as 'order 684/1'. The maximum bomb load remained unchanged at 9,000 kg (19,840 lb), but the maximum number of FAB-100 and FAB-250 bombs was increased from 16 to 24 and the maximum number of FAB-500s from 12 to 18.

All bombs were carried internally; to this end two additional KD3-488 bomb cassettes were installed on the bomb bay sidewalls between the existing pairs of such cassettes. This required the electric heaters in the bomb bay, the MBD6-16 centreline bomb cradle and the ASO-16 chaff dispenser to be removed. Modifications were made to the bomb bay doors to keep them from striking the bombs when the maximum number of FAB-500 M-62 bombs was carried.

The first example thus upgraded was Tu-16A c/n 7203829. Later, Tu-16A c/n 5201607 modified in the same fashion by plant No.22 underwent check-up tests at GNIKI VVS (as the former GK NII VVS was known since 1965) in 1969; Lt.-Col. Viktor V. Oosenko was project test pilot, with S. S. Shirokov as engineer in charge. Between 1st April and 14th May 1969, this aircraft made seven flights from Vladimirovka AB and Migalovo AB near Kalinin (now renamed back to Tver') hosting the 173rd TBAP (*tyazholyy bombardirovochnyy aviapolk* – Heavy Bomber Regiment), logging 14 hours 15 minutes. Two bombing sessions were made with the expenditure of twenty-four 75-kg (165-lb) P-50-75 practice bomblets and four FAB-500 M-62 bombs. The results were encouraging and the upgrade was recommended for service.

Tu-16A nuclear-capable bomber with active ECM equipment (aircraft '88A', 'order 2624')

In the late 1960s and early 1970s, the Kazan' aircraft factory retrofitted a small number of Tu-16A bombers with an SPS-100 *Rezeda-AK* (Mignonette) active jammer in a distinctive large parabolic fairing with flattened sides which was grafted onto the tail gunner's station, replacing its rear bulletproof glazing, the DK-7 tail turret and the PRS-1 gun-laying radar. This ECM fairing, which was unique to the Tu-16 equipped with the SPS-100, was vertically split, the halves opening like clamshell doors for maintenance access to the avionics mounted on a special truss-type bearer. The SPS-100 had both air cooling and liquid cooling; the clamshell doors featured cooling air scoops, the air escaping through the fairing's cropped rear end closed by a grille. The antennas of the SPS-100 were installed in four pairs of small dielectric blisters – three on the clamshell doors and one just ahead of the GRO's observation blisters. Additionally, an SPS-5 *Fasol'* (String bean) active jammer was installed in the forward avionics bay between fuselage frames 18-21; its swept blade aerials were located low on the forward fuselage sides, flanking the nosewheel well. The SPS-100 was mainly intended for use against anti-aircraft artillery (AAA) gun-laying radars and surface-to-air missile (SAM) guidance radars, while the SPS-5 was optimised for jamming the fire control radars of hostile fighters. An ASO-16/3 chaff dispenser was also fitted.

Tu-16As retrofitted with SPS-100 and SPS-5 jammers were referred to as 'order 2624'. The first such aircraft was a machine with the tactical code '34 Red' (c/n 7203514) which was test flown from Kazan'-Borisoglebskoye on 10th January – 4th April 1968, and underwent check-up tests at GNIKI VVS on 18th May – 29th August 1968, together with three similarly equipped Tu-16s of other versions (see Chapter 5/Tu-16 Yolka section for more details).

Left row, top to bottom:

Nuclear bombs are delivered to the aircraft on covered dollies.

The covers are removed, revealing the RDS-37 hydrogen bomb.

The RDS-37 is prepared for loading into the Tu-16V.

The area around the bomb bay was curtained off with a special quilted tent to prevent unauthorised personnel from seeing the bomb. Note the thick fabric hoses supplying warm air to the area.

Right row, top to bottom:

The Tu-16V carrying the H-bomb taxies out at Sary-Shagan AB. Note the special pressure probe on the nose for measuring the intensity of the blast wave.

The bomber takes off, heading for the Semipalatinsk Proving Ground.

The crew donned special dark goggles immediately before the explosion.

Tu-16A nuclear-capable bomber
(aircraft '88A', 'order 657')

The Tu-16A was upgraded again in the 1970s, with revisions to the electrical wiring for the nuclear bomb release system and enhanced radiation protection for the crew. This upgrade was referred to as 'order 657'.

Tu-16A nuclear-capable bomber
(aircraft '88A', 'order 260')

Among the versions with slightly revised equipment and armament were a number of Tu-16A bombers fitted with a Rubin-1 (Ruby, pronounced *roobin*) navigation/attack radar linked to an OPB-112 optical bombsight. Such refits were known as 'order 260'.

Modified Tu-16A thermonuclear weapons testbeds
(Tu-16V – first use of designation; 'order 212, 'order 468')

On 12th August 1953, the Soviet Union tested its first thermonuclear device – the RDS-6S having a maximum design yield of 400 kilotons. Dubbed 'Joe 4' by the Americans (in a rather disrespectful reference to Soviet leader Iosif V. Stalin), this was the world's first hydrogen bomb. Like all previous Soviet nuclear munitions, it was developed by the KB-11 design bureau of the Soviet Academy of Sciences' Laboratory No.2 in the town of Sarov (in what was then the Gor'kiy Region) under the guidance of Academician Yuliy B. Khariton. (Being associated with top-secret research, Sarov had various cover names, including Arzamas-75 and Arzamas-16. The *real* town of Arzamas is located further north in the same region, between Gor'kiy – now renamed back to Nizhniy Novgorod – and Sarov.) The S suffix in the designation stood for *sloyka* (layered puff pastry) because the device featured consecutive layers of fission and fusion fuel (lithium-6 deuteride); this combination of fusion energy and neutron-initiated ('boosted') fission was expected to give a tenfold increase in explosive power.

As the nuclear arms race between the Soviet Union and the USA gained momentum, KB-11 and the Moscow-based Nuclear Physics Institute headed by Academician Igor' V. Kurchatov were working on progressively more powerful thermonuclear bombs with a yield of up to 100 megatons. Known as *izdeliye* 'V' and codenamed 'Ivan', or 'Vanya' (contrary to established Soviet tradition of using female given names as codenames for nuclear bombs), the monstrous 100-megaton hydrogen bomb was to be carried by a specially modified Tu-95 *Bear-A* bomber, which was designated Tu-95V and known as 'order 242'.

In parallel with the development of the Tu-95V, the Tupolev OKB similarly adapted an early-production Kazan'-built Tu-16 (no tactical code, c/n 4200503) as a carrier for hydrogen bombs. This was done pursuant to Council of Ministers directive No.357-228 of 17th March 1956 and MAP order No.184 of 29th March. The conversion job was known as 'order 212'.

Yet, even before that a Tu-16 – possibly the same one – was used for testing the Soviet Union's first practical hydrogen bomb, the RDS-27. Created by the same KB-11, the single-stage bomb had an identical 'layered' design and the same 400-kiloton maximum yield; it was comparable in size to the largest conventional bomb carried by the Tu-16 (the FAB-9000 M-54) but had a more streamlined teardrop-shaped body.

The aircraft in question had a couple of non-standard exterior features. A long slender probe was mounted on the starboard side of the nose in lieu of the forward-firing cannon, carrying a pressure sensor for measuring the intensity of the blast wave as the latter caught up with the aircraft; more sensors were mounted in the DT-N7S ventral barbette instead of the cannons. There was no wire aerial for the R-807 radio, indicating this was a very early production bomber.

The test took place on 6th November 1955, at the Semipalatinsk Proving Ground; originally it had been scheduled for 5th November but had to be postponed because of poor weather. This was the most powerful nuke to be tested in the Soviet Union so far, therefore at Igor' V. Kurchatov's insistence a special research programme was undertaken prior to the test, confirming that the aircraft would not be endangered by the blast. Captained by Lt.-Col. Vladimir F. Martynenko, the Tu-16 took off from Zhana-Semey airfield in Kazakhstan, the nearest one to the proving ground. Mikoyan/Gurevich MiG-17 *Fresco* fighters from the 513th IAP provided escort – just in case; their pilots reputedly had orders to shoot the bomber down if it strayed from the designated course. The bomb was released at 12,000 m (39,370 ft), detonating at the preset altitude of 1,000 m (3,280 ft) at 1040 hrs local time; the actual yield was some 250 kilotons. 20 minutes later Il-28R reconnaissance aircraft from the 647th SAPSO equipped with air sampling canisters took a series of air samples in the wake of the mushroom cloud as it travelled on the wind; no radioactive contamination of the terrain was recorded within a 170-km (105-mile) radius from the hypocentre of the explosion.

A few days later the same aircraft was used to test an even more powerful weapon – the 3-megaton RDS-37 two-stage hydrogen bomb – at the Semipalatinsk Proving Ground. The bomb was outwardly almost identical to the RDS-27, having the same dimensions. It was equipped with a PG-4083 parachute retarding system developed by the Paradropping Systems Research & Experimental Institute (NIEI PDS – *Naoochno-issledovatel'skiy eksperimentahl'nyy institoot parashootno-desahntnykh sistem*), giving the bomber more time to get clear of the blast; the system was ordered on 17th October 1955, and delivered eleven days later.

Before the test the bomber received an 'anti-flash' colour scheme. The first attempt was undertaken on 20th November 1955; captained by Maj. Fyodor P. Golovashko, the Tu-16 took off from Zhana-Semey AB at 0930 hrs local time but then things started to go wrong. First, the weather turned foul, the target being obscured by clouds. The crew requested a practice run with the use of the bomber's radar and was authorised to do so, but eventually the drop had to be cancelled when the radar failed. The crew found themselves in a predicament; it was a choice of making an emergency landing with the nuke on board – for the first time in Soviet practice – or disposing of the bomb. Reporting the situation to the Central Command Post (CCP) – a special structure hardened against the nuclear blast located 25-30 km (15.5-18.6 miles) from the centre of the proving ground, the crew got a 'stand by' while the people in charge of the nuclear test racked their brains to find a solution. An emergency drop in non-detonation mode in some unpopulated area was ruled out for various reasons. Meanwhile, time was getting short because the bomber was getting low on fuel. An emergency landing was finally authorised after Academicians Yakov B. Zel'dovich (representing KB-11) and Andrey D. Sakharov (the author of the 'layered design' concept, representing the Moscow Energy Institute), who were present at the CCP, had given a written guarantee that it was safe and Air Force specialists had analysed all possible scenarios in the event of a crash. At 1200 hrs the Tu-16 landed safely at Zhana-Semey; Golovashko did his utmost to make the smoothest possible touchdown.

After the radar had been fixed and the bomb checked and re-loaded, a second attempt was made on 22nd November. This time everything worked; the bomber took off at 0834 hrs and, after the prescribed practice run, dropped the bomb at 0947 hrs from an altitude of 12,000 m (39,370 ft) at a speed of 870 km/h (540 mph). The RDS-37 detonated at 1,550 m (5,085 ft) when the aircraft was 15 km (9.3 miles) away. The blast wave caught up with the bomber (which was flown manually) 2 minutes 44 seconds after bomb release. Some seven minutes after the blast the mushroom cloud had climbed to 13-14 km (42,650-45,930 ft) and measured 25-30 km (15.5-18.6 miles) in diameter. For safety's sake the actual yield was reduced to 1.6 megatons during the test; nevertheless, it gave proof positive that yields in excess of 1 megaton could be achieved. Tragically, there were some casualties and collateral damage when structures located nearly two dozen miles away were knocked down by the blast wave; windows were shattered within a 200-km (124-mile) radius. Radiation levels measured at 25 km from the hypocentre one hour after the explosion did not exceed 0.02 R/h.

Later, two further production examples of the Tu-16A were modified for testing thermonuclear weapons (they were known as 'order 468'). The three machines are sometimes called Tu-16V by analogy with the Tu-95V; in all these cases the V was probably derived from the codename *Vanya* – or from *vodorodnaya bomba* (hydrogen bomb). They were used for testing Soviet nuclear and thermonuclear weapons.

Tu-16B experimental long-range bomber

On 28th March 1956 the Council of Ministers issued directive No.424-261 followed by MAP order No.194 to the same effect on 6th April. These documents ordered OKB-156 to develop a version of the Tu-16 powered by Zoobets M16-15 turbojets created in 1955 by OKB-16 in Kazan'. Two re-engined bombers were to be submitted for state acceptance trials in the first quarter of 1957.

Originally known as the RD-3P, the new engine was a considerably uprated version of the RD-3, having a ninth compressor stage which increased the take-off thrust to 11,000 kgp (24,250 lbst); some sources quote a slightly higher figure of 11,300 kgp (24,910 lbst). Moreover, the new powerplant had a 15% lower SFC; thus it was expected to give the aircraft a range of 7,200 km (4,472 miles) and a maximum speed of 1,030-1,050 km/h (639-652 mph). The original M16-15 had a time between overhauls of only 100 hours; a later version with a 300-hour TBO was designated RD16-15.

On 28th May 1956 MAP let loose with order No.295 instructing OKB-156 to supply the necessary conversion documentation to plant No.22 in Kazan' not later than 1st July in preparation for series production of the RD16-15 powered version. Plant No.22

itself was ordered to produce two prototypes with the new engines, one to be ready for manufacturer's tests in October and the second in November 1956, while OKB-16 was to supply four RD16-15 engines with a life of 200 hours in September.

The Tupolev OKB was quick to prepare the project documents for the new version, which was designated Tu-16B. Two versions were proposed, one of which was to carry additional external fuel tanks under the wings – probably for the first time on a Soviet bomber; both versions featured IFR capability.

The first prototype Tu-16B was converted at the end of 1956 from a brand-new Kazan'-built production machine (coded '27', c/n 6203330); some sources mistakenly quote the c/n as 6203340, which cannot be true because there were no more than 30 aircraft per batch. Testing at LII commenced in March 1957, initially with M-16-15 engines; these were later replaced with the RD16-15 version which had a longer service life. Vasiliy A. Komarov was the project test pilot. The second prototype Tu-16B (c/n 6203401) was likewise manufactured at the end of 1956 and underwent state acceptance trials at GK NII VVS until 1961. Unlike the AM-3, which was started by a turbostarter, the M-16-15 (RD16-15) had electric starting; hence additional DC batteries had to be carried and the engine nacelles lacked the usual prominent ventral air intakes (closed by rotating doors when not in use) and dorsal exhaust ports for the turbostarters. Their absence was the Tu-16B's only external difference from the standard *Badger*, yet the internal changes to the engine nacelles and the air intakes were more extensive. Thanks to the more powerful and fuel-efficient engines and greater fuel load the Tu-16B was to offer vastly improved performance – especially range, which was expected to transform it into an intercontinental bomber. Yet, even though the basic objectives were achieved and the engines proved reliable and trouble-free, the cutbacks in the Soviet bomber force initiated by the new Soviet leader Nikita S. Khrushchov (who famously preferred missile systems to manned combat aircraft) meant that neither the Tu-16B nor the RD16-15 engine entered production.

Apart from the Tu-16B, OKB-156 worked on a number of other projects relating to the bomber's powerplant. These included an attempt to equip the RD-3M engines with thrust reversers (on both the Tu-16 and the Tu-104) and the use of solid-fuel jet-assisted take-off (JATO) boosters to shorten the take-off run when the bomber was fully loaded. None of these were adopted for production machines. Later projects in 1965 included replacing the RD-3M-500 engines with the new fuel-efficient Kuznetsov NK-8-2 or NK-8-4 turbofans which were rated at 9,500 kgp (20,940 lbst) or 10,500 kgp (23,150 lbst) respectively, with an SFC of 0.83 or 0.81 kg/kgp·hr respectively – an idea that really made sense but was frustrated by problems with modifying the engine nacelles. In the mid-1970s the Tupolev OKB proposed re-engining the Tu-16 with Solov'yov D-30KP turbofans having a take-off thrust of 12,000 kgp (26,455 lbst), a cruise thrust of 2,750 kgp (6,060 lbst) and an SFC of 0.5-0.7 kg/kgp·hr, as fitted to the Ilyushin Il-76 *Candid* transport; however, on 23rd April 1975 the Soviet Air Force Command issued an explicit instruction not to go ahead with the work. Perhaps the reasoning of the VVS top brass was that the Tu-16 was getting long in the tooth and investing time and money in re-engining it was pointless. (Later, the Chinese military thought differently, and the latest Chinese derivative of the *Badger* has exactly D-30KP turbofans – see Chapter 8.)

The 'inflexible' character of the Tu-16's engine installations had been a matter of concern for the aircraft's designers for some time. As early as the beginning of the 1950s an alternative configuration for the bomber included new wings featuring leading-edge root extensions (LERXes) with 45° leading-edge sweep at the roots; the leading edges incorporated slot air intakes similar to those of the British V-bombers. The engine fairings were to be under the wing trailing edge close to the fuselage. Such a layout would have provided far more options on the type of engines fitted as the bomber was upgraded.

Project data for the Tu-16B		
	Version without drop tanks	**Version with drop tanks**
Wing area, m² (sq ft)	165 (1,776)	184 (1,980)
Empty weight, kg (lb)	38,100 (84,000)	39,440 (86,950)
Take-off weight, kg (lb)	76,800 (169,320)	90,200 (198,860)
Maximum range, km (miles)	n.a.	9,780 (6,074)
Operational range, km (miles):		
on internal fuel	7,200-7,500 (4,472-4,658)	8,950 (5,559)
with one in-flight refuelling	10,000-10,500 (6,211-6,521)	11,900 (7,391)
with two in-flight refuellings	13,200 (8,198)	15,200 (9,441)

'Aircraft 90/88' long-range bomber with TR-3F engines (project)

As the design work on the 'aircraft 88' went ahead, the Tupolev OKB continued working on an alternative configuration as an insurance policy in case of problems with the AM-3 engine. This project, the 'aircraft 90/88', had four 5,000-kgp (11,020-lbst) Lyul'ka TR-3F turbojets, but with a different configuration. Two of the engines were located at the wing roots (in the same positions as on the '88'), while the other two were carried under the wings between the flaps and ailerons.

Two versions were proposed; one had main gear fairings like the basic '88' while on the second version the main gear units retracted into fairings blended smoothly with the wing-mounted engine nacelles. In both cases the main gear units had twin wheels

instead of four-wheel bogies, and single-wheel outrigger struts were fitted to the wingtips in a similar way to that originally proposed for the '88'. The fuselage was virtually identical to the Tu-16. Further development was terminated once the success of the Tu-16 was assured.

'Aircraft 90' long-range bomber with TV-12 engines (project)

In 1954 OKB-156 designer Sergey M. Yeger proposed a version of the Tu-16 powered by two 12,000-ehp Kuznetsov TV-12 turbo-props (known as the NK-12 in production form) – the same model as fitted to the four-engined Tu-95 bomber. The engines were to drive AV-60 eight-blade contra-rotating reversible-pitch propellers of 5.6 m (18 ft 4¹⁵⁄₃₂ in) diameter developed by the Stoopino Machinery Design Bureau (SKBM – *Stoopinskoye konstrooktorskoye byuro mashinostroyeniya*), now called NPO Aerosila ('Aeropower' Research & Production Association). The turboprop derivative of the Tu-16 was designated 'aircraft 90'.

Yeger's project required the wings of the '88' to be modified; the wing root air intakes and the inlet ducts passing through the wing spars were eliminated, allowing conventional spars to be used, and the engines were mounted ahead of the wing leading edge in cylindrical nacelles between the flaps and the ailerons. In similar fashion to the Tu-95's inboard engine installations, the nacelles blended with the main gear fairings; however, the bifurcated engine exhaust pipes exited above the wings, not below them.

The more fuel-efficient turboprop engines were seen as a means of extending the bomber's range, but the associated redesign of the wings, undercarriage and fuselage looked set to be a

Basic dimensions of the 'aircraft 90'	
Length overall	35.7 m (117 ft 1³⁄₄ in)
Fuselage length	34.8 m (114 ft 2¾ in)
Wing span	32.989 m (108 ft 2²⁵⁄₃₂ in)
Stabiliser span	11.75 m (38 ft 6⁹⁄₃₂ in)
Distance between propeller axes	9.775 m (32 ft 0²⁷⁄₃₂ in)
Landing gear track	9.775 m (32 ft 0²⁷⁄₃₂ in)
Landing gear wheelbase	10.913 m (35 ft 9⁴¹⁄₆₄ in)

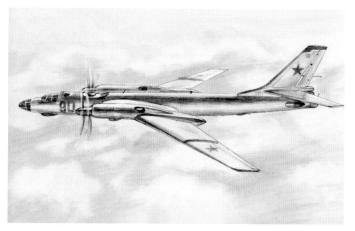
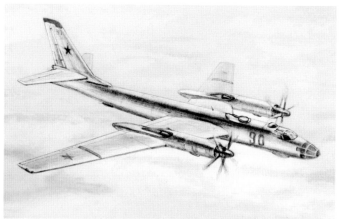

Artist's impressions of the twin-turboprop 'aircraft 90' based on the Tu-16.

Left: An artist's impression of the 'aircraft 103' bomber from the project documents, showing the stronger wing sweep, the vertically paired engines and the enlarged elliptical air intakes.

Below: The one-off Tu-16 '36 Black' (c/n 4200303) equipped for carrying SNAB-3000 Krab homing bombs.

protracted affair. Also, the Soviet Air Force was content with the performance of the Tu-16 powered by the standard AM-3 engines. The project was therefore shelved, although a project version of the Tu-104 airliner powered by two turboprops in similar nacelle/ main gear fairing combinations – either Kuznetsov NK-8s rated at 6,000-8,000 ehp (this engine never reached the hardware stage, unlike the later turbofan of the same name) or 6,250-ehp Kuznetsov TV-2Fs – was later considered as 'aircraft 118'.

'Aircraft 97' long-range supersonic bomber (project)

In the mid-1950s OKB-156 explored the idea of converting the Tu-16 into a supersonic bomber designated 'aircraft 97'. Two 13,000-kgp (28,660-lbst) Dobrynin VD-5 afterburning turbojets designed by OKB-36 in Rybinsk (Yaroslavl' Region), alias RKBM (*Rybinskoye konstrooktorskoye byuro motorostroyeniya* – Rybinsk Engine Design Bureau), were to be fitted, together with new wings swept back 45° at quarter-chord. These measures were meant to increase the bomber's top speed by at least 150-200 km/h (93-124 mph). Eventually, however, such a redesign was considered pointless because the Tupolev OKB was already working on 'clean sheet of paper' supersonic long-range bombers – notably 'aircraft 105', the immediate precursor of the Tu-22 *Blinder*.

'Aircraft 103' long-range supersonic bomber (project)

One of the last endeavours to exploit the proven design features of the successful Tu-16 was the 'aircraft 103' long-range supersonic

bomber project of 1954. The wing sweep was increased to 45° and the powerplant consisted of four Dobrynin VD-7 or Mikulin AM-13 non-afterburning turbojets, both types having a take-off rating of 11,000 kgp (24,250 lbst). Unusually, the engines were arranged in vertical pairs (*à la* English Electric Lightning) on the centre fuselage sides, the inlet ducts passing above and below the wing torsion box. The engine nacelles were enlarged accordingly, having an elliptical cross-section with the larger axis vertical, and the air intakes had the same elliptical shape.

However, it soon became clear that the machine would not be able to reach supersonic speed in this configuration even with twice the Tu-16's engine power (this became possible only with a totally different aerodynamic configuration) and the project was shelved. Still, the '103' did serve as the precursor to the work on the truly supersonic '105' bomber with two afterburning VD-7M engines.

Tu-16 with SNAB-3000 'Krab' homing bombs ('order 6625')

Back in the late 1940s the Soviet Union started experimenting with precision-guided munitions (PGMs) for tactical and long-range bombers. This work was largely inspired by German wartime research on, and operational use of, guided bombs in the Second World War. On 14th April 1947, the Council of Ministers passed directive No.1175-440 giving guidelines for guided weapons development until the mid-1950s. Among other things, the KB-2 design bureau headed by Aleksandr D. Nadiradze within the framework of the Ministry of Agricultural Machinery (which developed munitions, among other things!), was tasked with developing a 3,000-kg (6,610-lb) calibre homing bomb designated SNAB-3000 (*samonavodyashchayasya aviabomba* – homing bomb) which was also known under the codename Krab (Crab).

Development of the SNAB-3000 proceeded under the guidance of David V. Svecharnik. The design was strongly influenced by the German SD-1400X Fritz X gliding bomb of Second World War vintage, featuring the same general arrangement with four large fins in a squashed-X arrangement, with an angle of 55°15' between the planes, and cruciform tailfins within a squashed-octagon rudder arrangement; both the wings and the rudders had control surfaces. Apart from the need to provide adequate ground clearance if the bomb was carried by an aircraft with a short landing gear, this wing design was dictated by vertical and horizontal control authority requirements. Unlike the German prototype, however, the SNAB-3000's wings with an area of 3.29 m² (35.37 sq ft) had 30° leading-edge sweep and the body had a constant diameter; in contrast, the German bomb had unswept trapezoidal wings and a bulged warhead section. The wing sweep was due to the need to move the wings' centre of pressure aft, thereby compensating the Soviet bomb's aft CG position caused by the lightweight seeker head in the nose and the heavy explosive charge aft of it.

The bomb had an actual weight of 3,300-3,325 kg (7,275-7,330 lb) and a 1,285-kg (2,830-lb) high-explosive charge. The twin AV-515 impact fuses (*aviatsionnyy vzryvahtel'* – aviation-specific fuse) with an arming time of 5-60 seconds were specially developed for the bomb by GSKB-604 (*Glahvnoye spetsiahl'noye konstrooktorskoye byuro* – Chief Special Design Bureau) in the MOM framework; standard AV-139 fuses could also be fitted.

The guidance system featured an AP-55M electric autopilot developed by MAP's OKB-122 plus an infra-red seeker head for terminal guidance, with twin lenses side by side in the cropped nosecone having a ±8° field of view up/down and to the sides. Two models of the seeker developed by TsKB-393 (*tsentrahl'noye konstrooktorskoye byuro* – Central Design Bureau) were used. The Type 01-53 could detect IR radiation of at least 0.04 µW/cm², while the Type 01-54 had a minimum level of 0.018 µW/cm² and twice the detection range, locking on to large targets with a high heat signature, such as a factory or a power station, at 9 km (5.59 miles) range versus 4.5 km (2.8 miles) for the Type 01-53. However, the latter model could be used against really hot targets (such as a metal foundry) which would 'blind' the more sensitive version.

The delivery technique was as follows. The aircraft performed the bombing run in the usual way and the bomb was released automatically when the target was in the crosshairs of the bombsight. The autopilot then put the bomb into a 55° dive and the IR seeker was activated by a timer, guiding the bomb all the way in.

Trials began in 1951 when the first 20 bombs had been manufactured, initially using suitably modified Tu-4s. A 'dumb' version of the bomb without the homing system was tested first; the fully equipped 'smart' version entered test at the GK NII VVS facility in Akhtoobinsk (Astrakhan' Region, southern Russia) in late 1952. The bomb showed promising results at first, accurately homing in on pans with burning kerosene used as heat sources to simulate targets; out of the 12 inert and live bombs dropped in 1953-54, eight fell within 47 m (154 ft) of the target.

However, the piston-engined Tu-4 was slow and hopelessly outdated, so in early 1955 a decision was taken to use the state-of-the-art Tu-16 as the delivery vehicle. With a wing span of 2.52 m (8 ft 3⁷/₃₂ in) the SNAB-3000 could not be carried internally. Hence a Kazan'-built Tu-16 serialled '36 Black' (c/n 4200303), which had been transferred to the OKB's Kazan' branch on 30th August 1954, was fitted with special pylons under the wings just outboard of the inboard boundary layer fences for carrying two bombs. The conversion job was known as 'order 6625'.

It was then that problems began; the jet-powered Tu-16 turned out to be too fast for the bomb, which became unstable when

dropped at speeds around Mach 0.9, the control surfaces becoming inefficient. As a result, accuracy deteriorated dramatically. The first four drops were a total disaster; the 10,000-m (32,810-ft) altitude limit and the 840-km/h (521-mph) speed limit introduced in the course of the next 32 drops did not help. During the state acceptance trials in September 1955, the Tu-16 dropped a further 18 bombs, 12 of them on targets with a heat signature equal to or less than that of the Krasnodar Oil Refinery. Six of the bombs missed the target by as much as 80 m (260 ft) and the others failed to lock on altogether. Only two bombs dropped on a 'hot' target emulating the Azov Steel Foundry scored hits with an error of no more than 12 m (40 ft).

Moreover, the strong drag generated by the bombs reduced the bomber's range to 3,620 km (2,248 miles) with two SNAB-3000s and 4,500 km (2,795 miles) with one bomb versus 5,430 km (3,372 miles) with a 9,000-kg free-fall bomb carried internally. Finally, the guidance system was all too unreliable; 50% of the test missions flown by Tu-16 '36 Black' ended in failure due to various malfunctions of the bombs. Hence on 26th August 1956, the Council of Ministers' Scientific & Technical Board convened to assess the results of the trials, cancelling all further work on the SNAB-3000.

Tu-16 'Chaika' (Tu-16-UB) experimental guided bomb carrier

The interest of the Soviet military towards guided bombs was further spurred when the US Air Force used guided bombs (known in US Army slang as 'hobo', an acronym for 'HOming BOmb') with considerable success against North Korean targets in the Korean War of 1950-53. Therefore on 15th October 1951 the Council of Ministers issued a directive tasking the same KB-2 with developing the UB-2000F *Chaika* (Seagull) and UB-5000F Kondor radio-controlled gliding bombs (UB = *oopravlyayemaya bomba* – guided bomb). They were intended for destroying small but important targets (such as railway bridges, storage depots and administrative buildings) in a high-altitude attack. In December 1951, KB-2 merged with plant No.67 to form GSNII-642 (*Gosudarstvennyy soyooznyy naoochno-issledovatel'skiy institoot* – All-Union State Research Institute; the 'all-Union' bit indicated that the establishment had national importance). This institute carried on with the development of the bombs.

Again, outwardly the UB-2000F bore a certain resemblance to the German Fritz X bomb; the squashed-X wings arrangement had 28° dihedral for the upper pair and 28° anhedral for the lower pair. However, the wings were of cropped-delta planform with 45° leading-edge sweep (due to the high speed of the Il-28 and Tu-16 jet bombers that were to carry it), and again the casing had a constant diameter. Unlike the SNAB-3000, the UB-2F had a twin-fin tail unit with broad-chord stabilisers that was totally different from the German bomb's boxkite-like structure. Like its German forebear, it was controlled by means of oscillating spoilers and rudders. The 2,240-kg (4,940-lb) bomb had a 1,795-kg (3,960-lb) HE warhead, hence the F (*foogahsnaya* – high-explosive).

Two guidance systems were proposed. The first one made use of the 4A-N1 command line-of-sight guidance system, also known as KRU-UB (*komanhdnoye rahdio'upravleniye oopravlyayemoy* *bomb*oy – radio command guidance for guided bomb). The on-board part of the system transmitted continuous guidance signals in time/pulse modulation mode; these were picked up by the bomb's BU-2 control module (*blok oopravleniya*), which included an AP-59 autopilot. The KRU-UB system had three transmitters operating in different wavebands simultaneously to frustrate jamming; however, only one of the 600 possible frequencies was actually used at a time for bomb guidance, the other two wavebands being intended for deceiving the enemy. A special OPB-2UP periscopic synchronised bombsight was used, indicating proximity of the proper moment for bomb release and automatically dropping the bomb at the right time. It could also be used for dropping free-fall bombs in level flight.

The UB-2000F used triangulation as the principal guidance method, the bomb-aimer keeping the bomb on a straight line between the aircraft and the target (which he observed through the bombsight) by means of a joystick. To enable this, red tracer flares were mounted at the tips of the bomb's horizontal tail. Guidance was performed by superimposing the bomb's image with a moving marker in the bombsight registering the angles of divergence; the latter were derived from calculating the bomb's trajectory and generated by a special processor. If no commands were forthcoming the UB-2000F glided in a shallow dive, staying below the line connecting the aircraft and the target; therefore it needed to be guided onto this line by programmed commands before triangulation guidance could begin. As the bomb's speed was lower than that of the aircraft, triangulation could only be performed after the aircraft had passed over the target, the bomb performing a programmed turn to dive onto the target. For example, when dropped at 7,000 m (22,965 ft), it was released at a distance of 2.6 km (1.6 miles) from the target, travelling more than 4 km (2.5 miles) in the same direction and making a U-turn for the final dive when the bomber was already 5 km (3.1 miles) beyond the target. Before the attack, the bomb's gyro had to be unlocked and spun up, and the guidance system switched on at least three minutes before bomb release.

Alternatively, a television guidance system was to be used. In this case the bomb was fitted with a TV camera in the nose and a data link system transmitting a 'bomb's eye view' to a display, the weapons system operator (WSO) using the images to make course corrections through the linked radio control system. This guidance method was more accurate and less dependent on weather conditions which could impair observation of the target and the bomb's tracer flares.

The Tu-16 was seen as a suitable delivery vehicle for both types of bombs. The weapons system for the Tu-16 based on the smaller UB-2000F bomb was designated 4A-22 (although some sources attribute this designation to the bomb itself); it included two bombs, the KRU-UB guidance system, the OPB-2UP optical sight, bomb racks and auxiliary equipment. The UB-2000F had an overall length of 4.73 m (15 ft 6$^7/_{32}$ in), a body diameter of 600 mm (1 ft 11$^5/_8$ in), a wing span of 2.1 m (6 ft 10$^{43}/_{64}$ in) and a horizontal tail span of 1.56 m (5 ft 1$^{27}/_{64}$ in). This precluded internal carriage, and carrying the bombs under the fuselage (as was the case with the Il-28-131 armed with the same bomb) was considered inexpedient; hence the Tu-16 carried the bombs under the wings on short pylons identical to those of the version carrying the SNAB-3000 bomb.

The UB-2000F could be released at 5,000-15,000 m (16,400-49,210 ft) and 400-900 km/h (248-559 mph), though some sources quote a maximum speed of 1,200 km/h (745 mph). The speed required for releasing the bomb depended on the bomber's flight level, being 550 km/h (341 mph) at 5,000 m (16,400 ft), 750 km/h (466 mph) at 5,500 m (18,040 ft), 900 km/h at 6,000 m (19,685 ft) and over 900 km/h above 6,500 m (21,330 ft). As the bomb's speed was lower than that of the aircraft, the pilot was obliged to pull his machine up, reducing the ground speed, so that both the bomb and the target remained visible.

An experimental batch of UB-2000Fs was manufactured as early as 1953. Initial tests to confirm the bomb's advertised accuracy were held between November 1954, and February 1955, involving 15 drops from specially modified Il-28s. They showed that accuracy was improved by a factor of 77.8 (!) as regards range and a factor of 15.2 as regards circular error probable (CEP) by comparison with conventional free-fall bombs; for example, in a drop from 11,000 m (36,090 ft) at 720 km/h (447 mph) the UB-2000F showed a range error margin of 21.1 m (69 ft 3 in) and a CEP of 10.8 m (35 ft 5 in). In a drop from 7,000 m (22,965 ft), an experienced bomb-aimer needed just two or three such 'smart bombs' to destroy a target measuring 30x70 m (100x230 ft) which would have required the expenditure of 168 FAB-1500 'dumb bombs'. When dropped from 5,500 m at 700 km/h (435 mph), the bomb could be guided within an area measuring 3.6 km (2.24 miles) forward, 1.6 km (0.99 miles) rearward and 875 m (2,870 ft) to either side of the drop point; in a drop from 11,000 m at 720 km/h it was 26 km (16.16 miles), 19 km (11.81 miles) and ±10 km (6.2 miles) respectively.

A further 20 drops were made by Il-28s and Tu-4s during the state acceptance trials, which began on 20th July 1955, with good results. Hence on 1st December 1955 the Council of Ministers issued directive No.2000-1070, including the UB-2000F into the VVS inventory as the UB-2F Chaika (*izdeliye* 4A22); a production batch of 120 such bombs was manufactured in 1956.

A small number of Tu-16 bombers, including a Kuibyshev-built example (c/n 1881303), were equipped with the 4A-22 Chaika system; some sources call these aircraft Tu-16-UB. However, the bomb's operational use technique had several inherent flaws. For one thing, the guidance system could only be used in good visibility conditions when the bomb and the target could be observed through the sight; for another, the bomber needed to pass in a straight line directly above the target, which made it vulnerable to enemy air defences. Moreover, the system could only be used in good visibility conditions when both the bomb and the target could be observed. Hence the UB-2F was withdrawn from the inventory as early as 1957.

It may be mentioned that three other versions of the bomb were under development in addition to the standard UB-2000F. The UB-2000B (*broneboynaya* – armour-piercing) was a naval version with a shaped-charge armour-piercing (SCAP) warhead designed to burn through the armoured decks of warships, but development was discontinued in 1953. The UB-2000F Chaika-2 was to be an IR-homing version fitted with the same Type 01-54 seeker head as the SNAB-3000, while the UB-2000F Chaika-3 was to be a passive radar homing bomb with a PRG-10V seeker (*passivnaya* **rah-**

diolokatsionnaya golovka [samonavedeniya] – passive radar seeker head) for destroying enemy air defence radars; development of these versions was not completed either.

Tu-16 Condor experimental guided bomb carrier ('order 251')

The other bomb mentioned above, the UB-5000F Condor (later redesignated UB-5), was a scaled-up version of the UB-2000F. Designed for use against large surface ships, it had a weight of 5,100 kg (11,240 lb) and a 4,200-kg (9,260-lb) high-explosive warhead. The overall length increased to 6.846 m (22 ft 5^{33}/$_{64}$ in), the wing span to 2.67 m (8 ft 9^7/$_{64}$ in), the tailplane span to 1.81 m (5 ft 11¼ in) and the body diameter to 850 mm (2 ft 9^{15}/$_{32}$ in). The wings featured stronger leading-edge sweep and a kinked leading edge; the number of spoilers was doubled as compared to the Chaika and the tail section of the body had a different shape.

Development of the UB-5000F lagged behind that of the UB-2000F, as GSNII-642 wanted to make sure that any development problems encountered with the smaller bomb would be designed out of the larger one. Again, two versions were developed, one using radio command guidance and the other having TV guidance. The 4A-N1 command line-of-sight guidance system, the suspension system and other associated equipment were taken wholesale from the UB-2000F.

The radio command guided version was tested first, being dropped from a modified Tu-4 as early as September 1954. Early tests gave disappointing results, the accuracy proving significantly poorer than the UB-2F's because the heavier Condor accelerated to supersonic speed (around Mach 1.1) in the dive and became unstable in roll and yaw, deviating the from the intended course. To remedy this, the wing dihedral/anhedral was increased to 31° and special endplates were fitted to all four wings; the endplates were vertical, not at right angles to the wings.

The problems were eventually overcome and satisfactory results obtained through the speed range. In August 1955, the TV-guided version of the Condor bomb passed initial tests, again with the Tu-4 as the delivery vehicle. Tests on the Tu-16 'Condor' development aircraft (converted as 'order 251') began in March 1956. In spite of its reasonably good accuracy, the system was not accepted for operational service, as the large bombs carried externally entailed an increase in drag, reducing the Tu-16's speed and range unacceptably. Work on the TV-guided Condor was hastily terminated in the autumn of 1956 at the orders of the higher command because the Soviet government had decided to abandon guided bombs in favour of stand-off air-to-surface missiles (ASMs).

Tu-16 with the UBV-5 guided bomb

Work on a more sophisticated guided bomb, the 5,150-kg (11,350-lb) UBV-5, began in the summer of 1956. Unlike the bombs described above, the UBV-5 was designed to be carried in the bomb bay (the V stood for *vnootrennyaya [podveska]* – internal carriage). Hence it was somewhat more compact, having a length of 6.2 m (20 ft 4^3/$_{32}$ in) and a body diameter of 850 mm but much shorter cruciform wings located halfway along the body length, with a span of 1.045 m (3 ft 5^9/$_{64}$ in). These had a trapezoidal plan-

form and were at 45° to the horizontal plane, featuring inset ailerons for roll control and stabilisation. Pitch and directional control was exercised by small all-movable swept cruciform rudders at the rear end which were located in the vertical and horizontal planes.

The bomb was to have a 4,200-kg HE warhead or an SCAP warhead. Again, there was a choice of two guidance systems – a TV-guided version and an IR-homing version.

The short-span wings allowed the bomb to be carried internally, which was a prime requirement, since supersonic bombers were strongly on the agenda. An alternative version designed for semi-recessed carriage was also offered but was rejected by the Air Force. The UBV-5 underwent tests with the Tu-16 as the delivery vehicle.

A common drawback of all Soviet guided bombs was that the aircraft was obliged to release the bomb only a few kilometres from the target, increasing the risk of enemy interdiction. This negated the main advantage of guided bombs – their simplicity and low production costs as compared to ASMs. The problem could be overcome by fitting solid-fuel rocket motors on the bombs, so that they resembled ASMs, but the emphasis had already shifted to true air-launched cruise missiles able to strike at the target without taking the aircraft within range of the enemy air defences. Hence further development of the UBV-5 was abandoned. The same fate befell the 7,500-kg (16,530-lb) URB rocket-powered guided bomb (*oopravlyayemaya raketnaya bomba*) which was to be released at a range of 300-350 km (186-217 miles) from its target.

Tu-16V high-altitude bomber (project – second use of designation)

In the late 1950s OKB-156 made yet another attempt to re-engine the bomber. Designated Tu-16V (*vysotnyy* – high-altitude), the projected version was powered by two Dobrynin VD-7 non-afterburning turbojets – the same version as proposed for the 'aircraft 103'. With an 11,000-kgp (24,250-lbst) take-off thrust and an 8,600-kgp (18,960-lbst) nominal thrust, the VD-7 engine was not only more powerful than the RD-3M but also more fuel-efficient, with an SFC of 0.80-0.85 kg/kgp·hr versus 0.93 kg/kgp·hr; it was lighter and smaller into the bargain. Hence the designers estimated that the bomber's range could be increased by about 15% with the same fuel load. The ADP drawings show that the engine nacelles were revised to accommodate the new engines and extra DC batteries were installed, as the VD-7 had electrical starting.

Project work on the Tu-16V took place at the same time as Vladimir M. Myasishchev's OKB-23 was working on the 3M *Bison-B* four-engined bomber powered by the same VD-7B engines (this Dobrynin-powered version was later designated 3MN, the suffix denoting *novyye dvigateli* – new engines). Eventually, however, the project was terminated due to the general trend towards cutbacks in the manned combat aircraft programmes in the late 1950s/early 1960s – that is, during the Khrushchov era. Another reason was that the service introduction of the 3M revealed serious problems with the VD-7 engine, which even led OKB-23 to develop the 3MS version of the *Bison-B* powered by the same RD-3M engines as the M-4 *Bison-A* (hence the S for *staryye dvigateli* – old engines) as a stop-gap measure. These problems were not resolved

Left: '77 Red' (c/n 4200501), the prototype of the Tu-16T torpedo-bomber. Outwardly this version was no different from the standard bomber.

Below left: Another view of the Tu-16T prototype during state acceptance trials at NII AVMF in Feodosiya. Note how the serial is repeated in the same size on the tail.

Below: An operational Voronezh-built Tu-16T in flight. The tactical code is carried on the nose gear doors only and is not visible at this angle; for some reason it is not repeated on the tail.

by OKB-36 until series production of the Tu-16 was drawing to a close, making the Tu-16V project pointless.

Tu-16 with unguided rocket defensive armament ('order 227')

The possibility of using spin-stabilised unguided rockets as a defensive weapon for Soviet bombers was explored in the mid-1950s. The rockets were known in Soviet terminology as TRS (*toorbore'aktivnyy snaryad* – lit. 'turbojet-powered missile'); actually they had a solid-fuel rocket motor. On 3rd November

1954, the Council of Ministers issued directive No.2253-1069 requiring MAP to develop a launcher for TRS rockets that could be elevated through ±30° as a protection for the Tu-16's rear hemisphere; a bomber thus equipped was to be submitted for trials in the second quarter of 1956.

The system was developed by MAP jointly with the Ministry of Defence and the Ministry of Defence Industry (MOP – *Ministerstvo oboronnoy promyshlennosti*). The work was kicked off by MAP order No.693 issued on 13th November 1954. A production Tu-16 was made available to one of the enterprises in the MOP

framework for testing the installation, but the project was soon terminated. The reason was that, just like the Soviet Union, the 'potential adversary' (the western powers) was developing interceptors armed with medium- and long-range air-to-air missiles (AAMs); the proposed rocket installation would be useless against these threats.

Tu-16T torpedo-bomber ('order 210', *izdeliye* NT)
The use of the Tu-16 as a torpedo-bomber by the Naval Aviation (AVMF) was envisaged from the outset; pursuant to Council of Ministers instruction No.7501 issued on 12th July 1954 and MAP order No.432 on 15th July, all production Tu-16 bombers were to be capable of carrying torpedoes or naval mines as standard. The 21st production Kazan'-built Tu-16 manufactured in June 1954 and serialled '77 Red' (c/n 4200501) was earmarked for the relevant manufacturer's tests and state acceptance trials; thus it became the prototype of the version produced to 'order 210' and designated Tu-16T (*torpedonosets* – torpedo-bomber) or *izdeliye* NT in naval service. It already had the new clamshell design of the small main gear doors.

In accordance with the above CofM instruction and MAP order the aircraft was to undergo trials (which would be jointly performed by the OKB and the military) in August-September 1954. The ordnance load options included four RAT-52 rocket-propelled torpedoes, or six 45-52VT wet-heater torpedoes, or eight AMD-500M or APM mines, or an unspecified number of IGDM, AGDM-2M or Lira mines. (APM = *aviatsionnaya plavoochaya meena* – air-dropped floating mine; AGDM = *akoosticheskoghidrodinamicheskaya donnaya meena* – bottom mine with a combined acoustic/hydrodynamic detector. Some sources, though, identify the AGDM-2M and the Lira as the same weapon.)

The RAT-52 (*re'aktivnaya aviatsionnaya torpeda* – jet-powered air-droppable torpedo, 1952 model), as it was designated upon inclusion in the AVMF inventory, merits a few words. It was under development since 1945 – initially at the Ministry of Agricultural Machinery's NII-1 and then, from 1946 onwards, at NII-2 within the MAP framework. NII-2 was subsequently reorganised as the State Research Institute of Aircraft Systems (GosNII AS – *Gosudarstvennyy naoochno-issledovatel'skiy institoot aviatsionnykh sistem*), becoming the leading Soviet integrator of avionics and weapons.

The RAT-52 had been conceived as a homing torpedo, but the guidance system proved to be beyond the capabilities of the design team, requiring fundamental research, and was omitted in the final version – all the more so because it was superfluous, given the torpedo's short range. The torpedo was designed for high-altitude delivery (from 1,500-4,000 m/4,920-13,120 ft) and equipped with a parachute system and ailerons, making sure it stayed on the aircraft's course during the aerial segment of the trajectory. Together with the parachute system the torpedo weighed 627 kg (1,382 lb) and had a 243-kg (535-lb) warhead of TGA explosive (*trotil, gheksoghen, alyuminiy* – a trotyl/RDX/aluminium powder compound) detonated by two impact fuses. The RAT-52 was 3,897 mm (12 ft 9^{27}/$_{64}$ in) long, with a calibre of 450 mm (17^3/$_4$ in).

Before the attack the navigator set the torpedo's travel depth (2-8 m/6.5-26 ft, depending on the draught of the target ship),

switched its capacitors to charge mode and began the attack run. At the proper moment the bomb sight automatically released the torpedo; one second later a small propeller-shaped stabilising parachute deployed and the RAT-52 descended vertically, dropping fast like a bomb. The main parachute deployed at 500 m (1,640 ft), reducing descent speed. It separated after splashdown, whereupon a pair of foreplanes on the torpedo's extreme nose were brought into play to bring the RAT-52 from its maximum dive depth of 20 m (65 ft) to the preset depth and level it off. Next, the foreplanes were jettisoned, the solid-fuel rocket motor was ignited, delivering a thrust of 800-1,200 kgp (1,760-2,645 lbst), and the torpedo continued straight ahead on the course it had at the moment of release.

The rocket motor accelerated the torpedo to 58-68 kts (107-130 km/h); time from release at 2,000 m (6,560 ft) to impact was only 35 seconds, including 26 seconds for the aerial segment of the trajectory, which left the target no time for evasive action. By comparison, conventional wet-heater torpedoes could not travel faster than 40-45 kts (74-83 km/h). The chief shortcoming of the torpedo was the rocket motor's short burn time (16-19 seconds) giving a range of only 550-600 m (1,800-1,970 ft), which took the bomber within range of the ship's air defences. On the other hand, the torpedo could be dropped at any altitude from 1,500 m (4,920 ft) upwards at a speed up to 800 km/h (496 mph). A 'kill' was possible if the torpedo splashed down in a rectangle with two sides equalling the torpedo's range and the other two equalling target length plus a small target lead. For a ship with a hull length of 100-120 m (330-390 ft), 'kill' probability in a single-torpedo attack was 17-23%, increasing in the event of a multiple-torpedo attack.

The Tu-16T was ordered into production by Council of Ministers directive No.163-97 of 2nd February 1955 and MAP order No.127 of 1st March. Production of the torpedo-bomber (patterned on the prototype) began at plant No.64 in 1955, with orders for 25 new-build examples that year and for the conversion of 20 bombers operated by the AVMF. Production continued until 1957, by which time 76 torpedo-bombers had been built in Voronezh. The conversion of naval Tu-16 *sans suffixe* bombers to Tu-16T standard at the same factory proceeded in parallel; such aircraft were refitted to carry mines and torpedoes, featuring a revised electric weapons release system and additional control panels in the navigator's station, as well as a special safety system. On the Il-28T torpedo-bomber there were cases when the navigator forgot to set the torpedo's travel depth, whereupon the torpedo popped out of the water like a cork after splashdown, jumping as high as 5 m (16 ft), then falling flat and breaking up (remember the maxim: 'water is soft unless you hit it hard'!). The Tu-16T's safety system precluded this, preventing the torpedoes from being inadvertently released with zero travel depth.

Production examples of the Tu-16T differed from the prototype in having a revised weapons bay for carrying two RAT-52 torpedoes, six 45-54VT torpedoes with a VT-2 parachute system (that is, 450-mm calibre, 1954 model, *vysotnoye torpedometahniye* – high-altitude torpedo attack) or six 45-56NT torpedoes (that is, 450-mm calibre, 1956 model, *nizkoye torpedometahniye* – low-altitude torpedo attack). The RAT-52 required special Der-53T shackles (*derzhahtel' torpednyy* – [weapons] rack for torpedoes, 1953 model). The 45-56NT featured a travel depth stabiliser and a

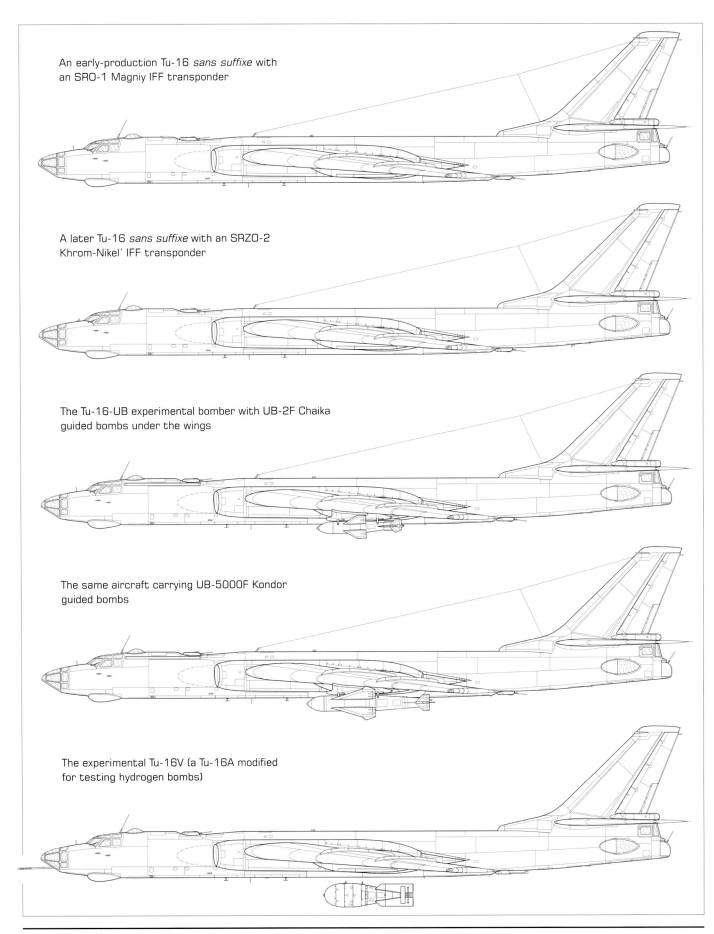

An early-production Tu-16 *sans suffixe* with
an SRO-1 Magniy IFF transponder

A later Tu-16 *sans suffixe* with an SRZO-2
Khrom-Nikel' IFF transponder

The Tu-16-UB experimental bomber with UB-2F Chaika
guided bombs under the wings

The same aircraft carrying UB-5000F Kondor
guided bombs

The experimental Tu-16V (a Tu-16A modified
for testing hydrogen bombs)

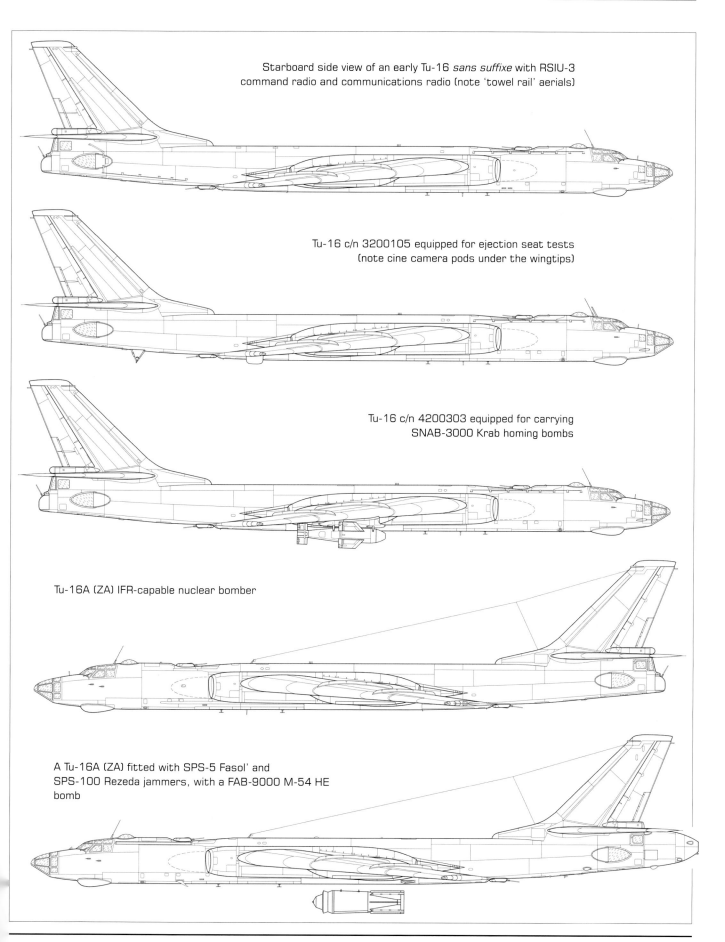

Starboard side view of an early Tu-16 *sans suffixe* with RSIU-3 command radio and communications radio (note 'towel rail' aerials)

Tu-16 c/n 3200105 equipped for ejection seat tests (note cine camera pods under the wingtips)

Tu-16 c/n 4200303 equipped for carrying SNAB-3000 Krab homing bombs

Tu-16A (ZA) IFR-capable nuclear bomber

A Tu-16A (ZA) fitted with SPS-5 Fasol' and SPS-100 Rezeda jammers, with a FAB-9000 M-54 HE bomb

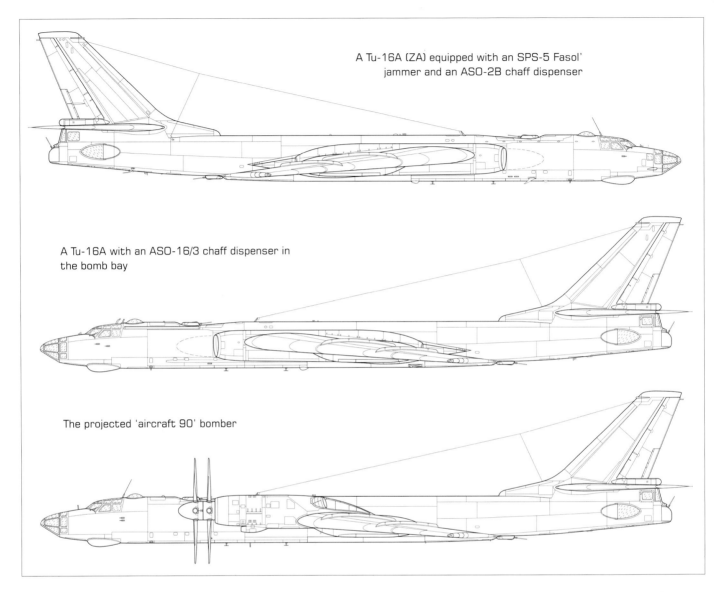

A Tu-16A (ZA) equipped with an SPS-5 Fasol' jammer and an ASO-2B chaff dispenser

A Tu-16A with an ASO-16/3 chaff dispenser in the bomb bay

The projected 'aircraft 90' bomber

stabilising parachute system borrowed from the RAT-52; the torpedo was 5,000 mm (16 ft 4^{55}/$_{64}$ in) long, with a launch weight of 1,036 kg (2,284 lb) and a 200-kg (440-lb) warhead. It could be dropped at altitudes of 120-230 m (390-750 ft) and speeds up to 700 km/h (434 mph); it had a maximum range of 4 km (2.48 miles) and travelled at 36 kts (66.6 km/h). This was the last Soviet air-droppable wet-heater torpedo; documents from first-line AVMF units show that the 45-56NT did not find practical use. Older 45-36MAV torpedoes (that is, 450-mm calibre, 1936 model, *[torpeda] modernizeerovannaya, aviatsionnaya, vysotnaya* – updated air-droppable torpedo for high-altitude attacks) could be carried as well.

Other weapons options were two VB-2F depth charges, twelve AMD-4-500 bottom mines or four AMD-4-1000 mines, RM-1 and RM-2 mines (*re'aktivno-vsplyvayushchaya meena* – rocket-propelled ascending mine), UDM versatile bottom mines (*ooniversahl'naya donnaya meena*), MDM-3, MDM-4 and MDM-5 bottom mines, the Serpey and Lira anchored mines, AMD-2M, IGDM and Desna influence mines. The RM-1 and RM-2 were equipped with a sonar-type detector and fired a rocket-

propelled charge when a ship or submarine passed above them. For weapons practice the Tu-16T could carry UPAMB-100/80 dummy mines (*oochebnaya parashootnaya aviatsionnaya meena-bomba* – parachute-retarded air-dropped practice mine/bomb) whose ballistic parameters closely replicated those of real air-dropped naval mines. On splashdown the UPAMB-100/80 released an orange-coloured buoy, making it possible to assess the bombing accuracy on post-attack reconnaissance photos.

The Tu-16T's high speed meant the aircraft would be on the attack course very briefly and the target had to be detected at a range of at least 100-120 km (62-74.5 miles). The weapons were aimed by means of the standard RBP-4 radar and OPB-11R optical bombsight; unlike the Il-28T, the Tu-16T did not have a specialised torpedo delivery sight.

The overall weapons load was 8,700 kg (19,180 lb); the Tu-16T could also carry a full 9,000-kg (19,840-lb) bomb load. Outwardly it differed from the bomber version only in having slightly modified bomb bay doors. Some aircraft were equipped with ECM gear, including the SPS-22N *Buket* (Bouquet) active jammer. The first aircraft to feature the latter was a machine coded '21' (c/n 7401706), which underwent check-up tests in 1969 together with a similarly equipped Tu-16P ECM aircraft (see Chapter 5).

Being intended for low- and high-altitude torpedo attack and mine-laying, the Tu-16T had flight performance comparable to that of the standard bomber. With an all-up weight of 55,000 kg (121,250 lb), the top speed was 992 km/h (616 mph) at 6,250 m (20,510 ft) and 938 km/h (582 mph) at 10,000 m (32,810 ft). Range at optimum altitude with a take-off weight of 72,000 kg (158,730 lb) and a 3,000-kg (6,610-lb) load of torpedoes or mines was 5,760 km (3,577 miles). The Tu-16T had a service ceiling of 12,800 m (41,990 ft), reaching this altitude in 31 minutes with the engines at nominal power. The take-off run with a 71,560-kg (157,760-lb) AUW was 1,900 m (6,230 ft), and the landing run with a 44,000-kg (97,000-lb) landing weight was 1,655 m (5,430 ft).

Like the basic bomber version of the Tu-16, the Tu-16T was known to NATO as the *Badger-A*.

By the early 1960s the more formidable anti-aircraft defences employed by naval vessels made the use of torpedo-bombers impractical; anti-shipping strike missions were taken over by missile strike aircraft, and minefields could be set up by ordinary bombers with equal ease. Therefore the Tu-16T fleet was converted into Tu-16PLO ASW aircraft or Tu-16S SAR aircraft. Six examples of the Tu-16T were supplied to Egypt.

Tu-16 minelayer upgrade ('order 699')

Some versions of the Tu-16 in AVMF service, particularly the Tu-16SPS and Tu-16 Yolka ECM versions and the Tu-16R reconnaissance aircraft (see Chapter 5), were refitted for mine-laying in accordance with 'order 699', with the option of reverting to the original version (to this end the separate pressurised capsule for the mission equipment operator in the weapons bay between fuselage frames 45-48 was retained). A few Tu-16s in service with the Red Banner Black Sea Fleet Air Arm were thus modified in the early 1970s. This involved removing superfluous equipment (ELINT gear, active and passive jammers and cameras) to save weight; KD3-416 cassettes (*kassetnyy derzhahtel'* – cassette-type rack, Group 3, that is, for ordnance up to 500 kg/1,102 lb calibre) and KD4-316 cassettes (Group 4, that is, for ordnance up to 3,000 kg/6,610 lb calibre) were installed in the weapons bay (except between frames 45-48). Possible ordnance loads were six AMD-500Ms, 12 IGDM-500s or UDM-500s, four IGDM or AMD-2M or APM or RM-1 or UDM-2 or Lira or Serpey mines.

Tu-16PLO (Tu-16PL) anti-submarine warfare aircraft ('order 649')

The military reform initiated by Nikita S. Khrushchov in 1960 boiled down to massive cutbacks of the Soviet Armed Forces – ostensibly in accordance with reduced peacetime needs but also to project a more peaceful image of the Soviet Union to the outside world. The AVMF was also hit by the cutbacks; many units were disbanded, while the minelayer and torpedo-bomber regiments (MTAP – *minno-torpednyy aviapolk*) were reorganised as maritime missile strike air regiments (MRAP – *morskoy raketonosnyy aviapolk*), re-equipping with missile carriers.

However, the MTAPs had a small number of Tu-16T torpedo-bombers, which were outdated in their original role but were still

fairly young aircraft. Hence, starting in 1962, some Tu-16Ts were converted for anti-submarine warfare duties as the Tu-16PLO (*protivolodochnaya oborona* – ASW) or Tu-16PL. These were intended for operations within a range of 1,000 km (without in-flight refuelling) from their bases. The Baku mission equipment suite fitted to the Tu-16PLO comprised the SPARU-55 Pamir receiver (*samolyotnoye priyomnoye avtomaticheskoye reghist-reeruyushcheye oostroystvo* – airborne automatic radio detector device, 1955 model), a number of sonobuoys (each one transmitting on its own frequency), an ANP-18 automatic navigation instrument (*avtomaticheskiy navigatsionnyy pribor*), an RBP-4 radar and a PP-1 panoramic receiver/display (*panorahmnyy priyomoindikahtor*).

The suite worked as follows. The sonobuoys were dropped in a pattern around the submarine's presumed location, picking up its sound and relaying information on the sub's position and parameters to the aircraft. Once a signal corresponding to the acoustic signature of a sub had been registered, the SPARU-55 got a bearing on the relevant buoy, using its own aerial and the aircraft's ADF loop aerial. At the same time the signal was displayed on the PP-1, which allowed the crew to keep an eye on all the buoys while 'listening' to the one that had detected the sub. The crew could then make a decision whether to attack, or the information received could be relayed to other aircraft.

The Tu-16PLO could be configured for the mission in three different ways. Option 1 – the search or 'hunter' configuration – carried either 24 RGB-N Iva passive sonobuoys (Willow, pronounced *eeva*; RGB = *rahdioghidroakoosticheskiy booy* – lit. 'radio-hydroacoustic buoy') or 36 RGB-NM *Chinara* (Platanus) sonobuoys. These had a detection range of 1-4 km (0.62-2.49 miles) and a data link range of 80-100 km (49-62 miles) with the aircraft patrolling at 1,000 m (3,280 ft).

Option 2 – the search/attack or 'hunter/killer' configuration – offered a choice of either 18 buoys plus two AT-1 homing torpedoes (*aviatsionnaya torpeda*) or 12 buoys plus one nuclear depth charge. Finally, Option 3 – the attack or 'killer' configuration – was armed with a choice of two AT-1 torpedoes, or 25 PLAB-50 depth charges (*protivolodochnaya aviabomba* – anti-submarine bomb) or six RM-1 rocket-propelled mines. Some sources say the Tu-16PLO carried 7.54-kg (16.62-lb) PLAB-MK depth charges (*protivolodochnaya aviabomba malovo kalibra* – small-calibre anti-submarine bomb).

The AT-1 had been under development since 1956 as the PLAT-1 (*protivolodochnaya aviatsionnaya torpeda* – air-dropped ASW torpedo), officially joining the inventory in 1962. It was powered by an electric motor fed by silver-zinc batteries; the active/passive homing system worked in two planes (azimuth and elevation). The torpedo was dropped by parachute from an altitude of 2,000 m (6,560 ft); after splashdown it travelled in circles with a 60 to 70-m (200 to 230-ft) radius until it detected the submarine, then went for the target in a straight line. The torpedo was not noted for high performance, having a range of 5 km (3.1 miles), a speed of 28 kts (51.8 km/h or 32.17 mph) and a travel depth of 20-200 m (65-660 ft). During an exercise in 1964 the instrumented inert AT-1 torpedoes dropped from a Tu-16PLO behaved erratically – seven of the eight torpedoes failed to find the sub altogether, three of them surfacing without even reaching the preset depth of 40 m (130 ft) because an electric circuit had been improperly wired by mistake. The eighth torpedo locked on to the target submarine travelling at a depth of 110 m (360 ft) but lost lock-on and returned to the preset depth. The cause was traced to the thermocline at a depth of 60-80 m (200-260 ft) affecting the propagation of sound waves and hence the operation of the AT-1's acoustic homing system.

The Tu-16PLO had a take-off weight of 79,000 kg (174,170 lb), carrying a 3,000-kg (6,610-lb) warload. Its range was 5,400 km (3,355 miles), the on-station loiter speed was 420-430 km/h (260-267 mph) and the service ceiling was 13,000 m (42,650 ft).

Conversion of the Tu-16T into the Tu-16PLO as per 'order 649' was carried out in the North Fleet Air Arm from 1962 onwards and in the Pacific Fleet Air Arm from 1963 onwards. The aircraft served for only five or six years – the Tu-16PLO was withdrawn in 1968, yielding its place to the purpose-built Ilyushin Il-38 *May* shore-based ASW aircraft and Beriyev Be-12 **Chaika** (Seagull; NATO *Mail*) ASW amphibian.

Tu-16SP anti-submarine warfare aircraft

In the 1970s a few examples of the Tu-16S search and rescue aircraft (see Chapter 5) were converted into 'hunter-killer' ASW aircraft designated Tu-16SP to meet an AVMF order. The S letter was a leftover from the previous SAR role, while the P denoted *protivolodochnyy* (ASW, used attributively). Instead of a lifeboat the aircraft carried a powerful 360° search radar enclosed by a large teardrop radome in its weapons bay, enabling it to detect surfaced submarines or submarines travelling at periscope depth, as well as surface ships. ASW torpedoes or sonobuoys could also be carried. As compared to the Tu-142 *Bear-F* dedicated long-range ASW aircraft, the Tu-16SP had far shorter range and endurance; thus, as soon as the Tu-142 was fielded in sufficient numbers the inadequate Tu-16SP was phased out.

II. The missile carriers

Tu-16KS missile strike aircraft ('order 187', *izdeliye* NKS)

After the war the Soviet work on stand-off air-to-surface weapons to be used against well-defended targets, which had started in the late 1930s, was speeded up. On 13th May 1946, the Council of Ministers issued the first directive ordering research and development work on anti-shipping cruise missiles.

Development of the weapons system codenamed *Kometa* (Comet) began pursuant to a further Council of Ministers directive (No.3140-1028) issued on 8th September 1947. Apart from the aircraft used as the missile platform, the system included the Kometa-3 (K III) missile, its Kometa-1 (K I) guidance system and the Kometa-2 (K II) targeting system installed on the aircraft. At an altitude of 1,500-4,000 m (4,920-13,120 ft) the on-board radar was to detect a surface ship with a 10,000-ton displacement at a range of 100 km (62.1 miles); the missile would be launched at 60 km (37.2 miles) range and was to have a cruising speed of at least 950 km/h (590 mph). The ADPs of the missile itself, the guidance/targeting systems and the weapons system as a whole were to be completed in the second, third and fourth quarters of 1948 respectively.

The missile platform was developed by the Tupolev OKB, where Aleksandr V. Nadashkevich, head of the OKB's Section V (*vo'oruzheniye* – armament), was in charge of the work. On 2nd June 1948, the Council of Ministers issued a directive on the creation of the Kometa weapons system, which involved adapting the Tu-4 bomber to launch the missiles over an operational range of up to 2,000 km (1,242 miles) from their bases; this was primarily an anti-shipping strike system for use against large surface ships.

The Kometa-1 guidance system was a product of the Ministry of Armament's SB-1 (*spetsiahl'noye byuro* – Special Bureau), which was created in 1949 and renamed KB-1 in 1950; it also had overall responsibility for the Kometa weapons system. It was headed by Col. Pavel N. Kooksenko, with Engineer-Maj. Sergo L. Beria – the son of the infamous Ministry of the Interior chief Lavrentiy P. Beria – as Chief Engineer. (After Stalin's death in March 1953 the new Soviet government exposed the crimes of the Stalin regime. Lavrentiy Beria was found guilty of high treason and executed, sharing the fate of many he had sent to death. Hence Beria Jr. was removed from office and replaced by Konstantin Patrookhin.)

The Kometa-2 targeting system started life in 1948 at NII-17, an avionics house headed by Chief Designer Viktor V. Tikhomirov (it is now known as the Vega-M Research & Production Association). However, pursuant to Council of Ministers directive No.1228-436 issued on 25th March 1949, SB-1 took over development of this system as well.

Development of the Kometa-3 missile was originally assigned to OKB-51, which was then headed by Vladimir N. Chelomey and specialised in missiles. However, this first version derived from the German V-1 'buzz bomb' and powered by a 900-kgp (1,980-lbst) Chelomey D-7 pulse-jet engine (as per the abovesaid directive) had the required range but not the required speed. Hence on 2nd August 1948 the Council of Ministers issued directive No.2922-1200 transferring responsibility for the missile to the OKB-155 'fighter maker' design bureau under Artyom I. Mikoyan.

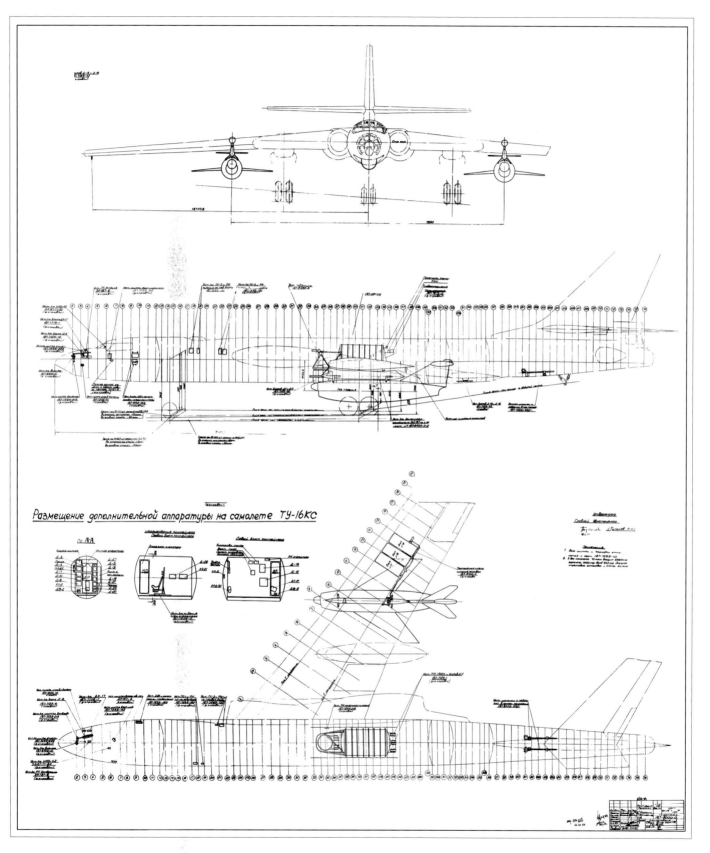

Above: A drawing from the ADP documents showing the location of the mission equipment on the Tu-16KS missile strike aircraft.

Opposite page: A production-standard KS-1 missile on a ground handling dolly. These views show the cover of the explosive charge compartment replacing the cockpit of the *izdeliye* K aircraft, the pure cigar shape of the fin tip fairing and the shape of the wingtips.

His closest aide Mikhail I. Gurevich, who headed a section of the design bureau specialising in missiles (OKB-2-155), was project chief, while Aleksandr Ya. Bereznyak led the actual design effort. (Later, in 1967, OKB-2-155 became an organisationally separate enterprise named MKB *Raduga* (*mashinostroitel'noye konstrooktorskoye byuro* – 'Rainbow' Machinery Design Bureau) headed by Bereznyak, and in this capacity it created virtually all of the air-launched cruise missiles that saw service with the Soviet Air Force and Naval Aviation, as well as many ground-launched and sea-launched anti-shipping cruise missiles.)

Mikoyan's first version of the missile designated KS – variously deciphered as *Kometa-snaryad* ('Comet missile') or *kry-lahtyy snaryad* (winged missile) – resembled a scaled-down MiG-9 *Fargo* fighter with straight wings, no cockpit canopy, a nose air intake feeding one 800-kgp (1,760-lbst) RD-20 axial-flow turbojet (a Soviet-built version of the captured BMW 003A) instead of two and guidance antenna radomes on the nose and the unswept fin. Version 2 had wings with 35° sweep at quarter-chord

Top and above: The uncoded Tu-16KS prototype (c/n 4200305) with dummy external stores resembling torpedoes on the missile pylons

Opposite page: Three views of the same aircraft with two pre-production KS-1 missiles on the pylons. Note the semi-retracted hemispherical radome borrowed straight from the Tu-4KS (its bottom portion is just visible under the centre fuselage) and the forward-hinged main gear door sections found on early-production Tu-16s.

positioned well forward; the swept tail unit (a T-tail or a cruciform tail) carried a cigar-shaped fairing housing components of the mid-course guidance system. The engine air intake was now located under the centre fuselage, and the resulting long 'snout' housing the radar seeker gave the missile a cartoony appearance. The stipulated range at a launch altitude of 4,000 m was 195 km (120 miles). The ADP was submitted for review in December 1948; however, the mock-up review commission discovered numerous faults in the project and axed it.

OKB-2-155 had to start from scratch; work on the second version of the missile – the KS-1 (in-house designation *izdeliye* E) – began on 25th March 1949. The second version looked like a scaled-down MiG-15 *Fagot* jet fighter – or rather the one-off MiG-15P*bis* (*izdeliye* SP-1) radar-equipped all-weather interceptor – minus cockpit canopy. It had a cigar-shaped fuselage, mid-set swept wings, a swept cruciform tail unit and a nose air intake with a bullet-shaped guidance antenna radome on top of the vertical splitter. The wings fitted with two pairs of boundary layer fences had unusually strong sweepback (57°30' leading-edge sweep and 55° sweepback at quarter-chord versus 37° and 35° respectively for the MiG-15) and 5° anhedral. The fin was tipped by the same fairing housing guidance system components. The KS-1 was powered by a 1,590-kgp (3,500-lbst) Klimov RD-500K centrifugal-flow turbojet – an expendable version of the RD-500 (K = *korotkoresoorsnyy* – short-life) – breathing through a nose air intake. The missile was 8.29 m (27 ft 2⅜ in) long, with a wing span of 4.722 m (15 ft 5²⁹⁄₃₂ in) and a fuselage diameter of 1.145 m (3 ft 9 in). It had a launch weight of 2,735 kg (6,030 lb) and carried a

Above left: The port BD-187 pylon of the Tu-16KS with the retractable sway braces deployed.

Left: A KS-1 is lifted off the dolly and hooked up to the port pylon of the Tu-16KS prototype by means of two hand-driven hoists; the shape of the missile's air intake makes it appear to be grinning saucily. Note the detachable panel at the front of the pylon making this possible.

Below left: Here the KS-1 missiles are in place under the wings of the Tu-16KS (the other missile is just visible).

Below: The weapons system operator's pressurised capsule and various equipment in the bomb bay of the Tu-16KS. Note the dorsal emergency exit for the WSO.

800-kg (1,760-lb) or 1,000-kg (2,205-lb) high-explosive/fragmentation warhead over a range of 70-90 km (43-55 miles), flying at a maximum speed of 1,050-1,100 km/h (652-683 mph). The ADP of this version was submitted for review on 3rd November 1949.

The guidance system devised for the KS-1 missile consisted of a K-2 radio control (command link) subsystem with a receiver antenna at the top of the fin, plus a K-1 passive radar homing set installed in the nose for terminal guidance, with an antenna in a parabolic radome on top of the air intake. The K-1 and K-2 sets were both linked to the missile's APK-5 autopilot. The K-3 component installed on the aircraft comprised the on-board part of the

Above: An operational Tu-16KS coded '25 Red'.

Top right: The final moments before launch. The radome of the Kobal't-N radar is deployed; note the angular shape of the radome on production aircraft. A window and the entry hatch for the WSO's station can be seen aft of the radome.

Above right and right: Stills from a cine film showing how the starboard missile's engine fires up and the KS-1 falls away before accelerating and heading towards the target.

Below and below right: More stills from footage filmed during the tests, showing the starboard missile being launched. Note the escorting UTI MiG-15 trainer used as a chase plane.

Operational Tu-16KSs at a Soviet Navy airbase, with missiles attached and APA-2 ground power units based on the ZiS-150 general-purpose lorry in attendance. The regiment CO accepts the squadron commander's report that the unit is ready for action.

command link subsystem and the Kobal't-1 (Cobalt) 360° search/target illumination radar. Once a target had been detected and a lock-on achieved, the target was tracked by the Kobal't radar; the KS-1 was then launched and radio-controlled by the WSO until the missile's own homing radar (picking up radar echoes from the target which was continuously illuminated by the Kobal't radar) could take over.

In 1950 the missile was ready for testing as the diminutive *izdeliye* K demonstrator aircraft (a manned version of the KS-1 with a retractable bicycle landing gear and a cockpit instead of the explosive charge), which uncannily resembled the Japanese Ohka suicide bombs. It was carried aloft by the Tu-4K (alias Tu-4KS) missile strike aircraft equipped with wing pylons and released, emulating a target run-in before being flown to a conventional landing by the pilot. The first actual missiles were tested in 1952; on 21st November that year the Tu-4K made the first successful live launch of a KS-1, destroying a decommissioned ship used as a target. At the end of 1952 the missile entered low-rate initial production at plant No.256 in Ivan'kovo township, Kalinin Region (the present-day Tver' Region). (In 1958 Ivan'kovo was transferred

A Tu-16KS coded '63' takes off, carrying a KS-1 under the port wing. The bright red colour indicates this is an inert practice round.

to the Moscow Region during an administrative reform; it was later absorbed by the neighbouring town of Doobna, and plant No.256 was henceforth regarded as located in Doobna.) The missile had the NATO reporting name AS-1 *Kennel*.

The Kometa system became operational in September 1953. Some 50 Tu-4 bombers were converted to Tu-4K standard at plant No.23 in Fili (then a western suburb of Moscow, now a part of the city), which was one of three factories building the type. They were the sole Soviet missile strike aircraft for several years, serving with AVMF units.

The availability of the Tu-16 immediately offered a better missile platform able to reach high subsonic speeds, an altitude of 12,000-13,000 m (39,370-42,650 ft) and offering a large combat radius and higher chances of survival in a combat environment. Hence the Council of Ministers directive clearing the Kometa system for Soviet Navy service contained a clause requiring a Tu-16 bomber to be modified as a prototype platform for the proven Kometa system. The resulting aircraft received the designation Tu-16KS (it was also known in service as *izdeliye* NKS and in production as 'order 187').

In 1954 a brand-new early-production Kazan'-built Tu-16 with no serial (c/n 4200305) was converted as the first prototype of the missile carrier version. The on-board components of the system were transferred to the *Badger* in almost unmodified form. This involved the following changes to the aircraft.

All bomb armament was deleted. The crew of the Tu-16KS was increased to seven, the bomb bay housing the WSO's pressurised workstation located between fuselage frames 37-44 – a capsule with its own pressurisation/air conditioning system featuring a cooling turbine, an air/air heat exchanger and temperature controls. At altitudes up to 2,000 m (6,560 ft) the pressurisation air was supplied by a ram air intake on the starboard side; at higher altitudes it was taken from the pipeline supplying air to the rear pressure cabin. The capsule, which had a ventral access hatch with a forward-opening door, was provided with an ejection seat and accommodated some components of the K-3 subsystem, including parts of the K-1M Kobal't-1M radar (*modifitseerovannyy* – modified), aka Kobal't-P. The D-1 antenna module and the radar set of the K-1M radar were likewise housed in the former bomb bay (outside the pressurised capsule). The revolving antenna was enclosed by a semi-retractable radome which could be fully raised when not in use, fully extended for action, or fixed in an intermediate position.

Two BD-187 missile pylons (***bahlochnyy derzhatel'*** – beam-type rack) were installed under the wings 7.05 m (23 ft 1³⁵⁄₆₄ in) from the centreline; some sources call them BD-E because they were specially designed for *izdeliye* E. The pylons featured two pairs of folding sway braces fore and aft of the single shackle, fixtures for hand-cranked hoists used for hooking up the missile, and electrical and fuel connectors for the missiles. The missiles could be carried with an incidence of 0° to 3°30' with respect to the aircraft's fuselage waterline (FWL). The pylons necessitated reinforcement of the wing centre section. Cut-outs were made in the outer flap sections to prevent them from striking the missiles' fins when deployed; they were closed from above by fixed metal strips with stiffening ribs. flap deflection with the missiles in place was restricted to 25°. The D-1M antenna module of the K-1M radar was

Heave-ho! Soviet Navy 'black men' in winter attire prepare to attach a KS-1 to Tu-16KS '24 Red' (c/n 7203818). The additional number 7163 underneath the c/n may signify the 163rd Tu-16 equipped as a missile carrier. Note the clamps securing the missile's control surfaces and the different colour of its nose and tail radomes.

built into the underside of the starboard wing; large dipole aerials (called modules D15 and D16) were mounted under the wingtips.

Changes were made to the fuel system, which included six additional wing tanks (Nos. 17-19L and 17-19R). These were isolated from the main fuel system, being used for starting up the missiles' engines and replenishing the missiles' fuel supply while the missiles were on the wing with engines running prior to launch; special fuel lines ran from them to the pylons. (Confusingly, some sources state that the missiles' engines were fed from the No.1 fuselage tank, with fuel lines running inside the wing leading edge from it to ribs 13L and 13R.) The Nos. 14L and 14R tanks were modified to accommodate the pylon attachment fittings.

The standard bomb bay doors were replaced with three-section doors, the front and centre sections featuring cut-outs for the radome and the WSO's entry hatch respectively. A dorsal emergency exit for the WSO incorporating two windows was provided aft of the pressurised capsule (which had a manhole in the rear pressure dome) in the event of a belly landing or ditching.

The captain's instrument panel featured a course indicator and missile release buttons. The missile engine starting panel was added to the co-pilot's instrument panel, with missile engine monitoring gauges on the centre portion of the main instrument panel;

Top: The missile is positioned below the port wing pylon and ready for hooking up; the folding sway braces are still retracted, but a technician prepares to open the cover on the pylon and extend them.

Above: The missile is in place on the port pylon.

the flight deck and the navigator's station featured additional circuit breakers associated with missile launch and guidance, and there was a new D-29M sight and D-6 guidance system display in the navigator's station. Electrical equipment associated with the missiles was housed in the centre fuselage and the tail cones of the main gear fairings.

Manufacturer's flight tests were held successfully between August and November 1954, with Yuriy T. Alasheyev as project test pilot; the aircraft logged a total of 9 hours 14 minutes in 12 test flights. All mission equipment worked as it should, and the equipment in the WSO's cabin was convenient to use. With two missiles under the wings the handling did not differ from that of the bomber. During tests the Tu-16KS prototype occasionally flew with weight equivalents of the KS-1 missile looking like large torpedoes.

The KS-1 was released at altitudes between 3,500 and 4,000 m (11,480-13,120 ft) and indicated airspeeds up to 370 km/h (229 mph) without any detrimental effect on the aircraft's handling; the aircraft's all-up weight was 58,000-59,000 kg (127,865-130,070 lb). With two missiles the Tu-16KS clocked a maximum speed of 575 km/h (357 mph) without any vibration generated by the external stores. The take-off run with two missiles and an AUW of 54,000 kg (119,050 lb) was 1,240 m (4,070 ft) – the same as for the bomber version. In fact, handling during take-off or landing was barely affected at all, though the landing speed with both missiles in place and a 47,000-kg (103,615-lb) landing weight was 10-15 km/h (6.2-9.3 mph) higher, reaching 245-250 km/h (152-155 mph). When landing with one missile in a 6 to 8-m/sec (12 to 16-kt) crosswind, it was recommended to choose the heading so that the missile was on the upwind side.

Tested at altitudes of 4,000 m, 6,000 m and 8,000 m (13,120 ft, 19,685 ft and 26,250 ft), the K-1M radar had a detection range of 160 km (99 miles), the radarscope's image quality was satisfactory and lock-on and automatic target tracking were stable and consistent. When a single missile was carried, it was recommended to carry it under the port wing; in that case stability could be maintained by transferring 1,400 kg (3,090 lb) of fuel to the starboard wing. When the radome of the K-1M was extended the resulting drag reduced the speed by 15-20 km/h (9.3-12.4 mph) and the maximum indicated airspeed was not to exceed 520-550 km/h (323-341 mph) to prevent vibration of the radome.

Upon completion of the manufacturer's flight tests Tu-16KS c/n 4200305 was ferried to the 71st Test Range at Bagerovo AB in the Crimea, passing further tests at the special target range located there in early 1955. Interestingly, the missile was referred to in the trials report simply as 'KS', not KS-1. After these tests the aircraft was recommended for production and AVMF service. Between 1954 and 1958, a total of 107 examples was built at plant No.22 in Kazan' in parallel with the Tu-16A bomber; since the missile's product code was *izdeliye* E, by extension this code was sometimes applied to the Tu-16KS aircraft at the Kazan' factory. Late production examples had updated avionics, including an R-807 radio with a wire aerial and an SRZO-2M IFF interrogator/transponder.

About forty second-hand Tu-16KSs were supplied to Indonesia and Egypt in the early 1960s. A further 65 were subsequently upgraded to carry KSR-2 and KSR-11 air-to-surface missiles as the Tu-16KSR-2 and Tu-16K-11-16 respectively (see below).

The Tu-16KS prototype's radome of the Kobal't radar had the same shape as that of the Tu-4, having a hemispherical bottom. Production examples had an improved Kobal't-P radar whose radome had a different shape, featuring a flattened bottom; this was meant to eliminate the vibration experienced on the prototype at 520 km/h when the radome was extended.

The Tu-16KS missile system was intended for attacking maritime and ground targets with a high radar signature within a maximum combat radius of 1,800 km (1,118 miles). The production Tu-16KS had an all-up weight of 72,000 kg (158,730 lb) with two missiles and a cruising speed of 800-850 km/h (496-527 mph).

The operational procedure was as follows. The Tu-16KS flew towards the target at up to 10,000 m (32,810 ft); in search mode the Kobal't-P radar acquired the target at a distance of 150-180 km (93-118 miles), whereupon the WSO switched it to tracking mode, the radar generating a high-power directional beam which was scanned in a cone. The aircraft then descended to a launch altitude of 3,500-4,000 m (11,480-13,120 ft) with the engines running at idle; the descent from 10,000 m took seven minutes. The missile's engine was started up a few minutes before launch, and the KS-1 was released at 70-90 km (43.5-55 miles) range, depending on the launch altitude; as the missile was released its engine switched to internal fuel and automatically went to full power. The launch took place at a speed of at least 370 km/h (229 mph).

After launch the missile accelerated in level flight in autonomous control mode, controlled by the APK-5B autopilot, until it entered the radar beam and headed towards the target at 1,060 km/h (658 mph). If the missile strayed outside the radar beam at this stage, the aircraft made a horizontal manoeuvre to get it back 'on track'.

40 seconds after release the Kobal't-P radar transmitted a command switching the missile's autopilot to remote control mode, using the triangulation method, and the KS-1 changed its flight path, following the radar beam's equisignal line to the target. The missile's flight level varied at this stage. When the radar echo from the target picked up by the K-1 radar seeker head reached a preset level, the guidance system switched to homing mode for terminal guidance; this was necessary because, as the distance between the aircraft and the missile increased, so did the width of the aircraft's radar beam cone and hence the error margin. When the KS-1 came within 15-20 km (9.3-12.4 miles) of the target, a second command was transmitted and the K-1 seeker head achieved a lock-on, guiding the missile all the way in; when the range decreased to 500-700 m (1,640-2,300 ft) the autopilot put the missile into a terminal dive onto the target.

The Tu-16KS received the NATO reporting name *Badger-B*.

Tu-16KS (ZA) missile strike aircraft

The final 59 examples of the Tu-16KS built in 1958 were IFR-capable. Such aircraft were known as the Tu-16KS (ZA).

Tu-16KSR development aircraft ('order 245')

A short while after the Tu-16KS entered service the 90-km (43.5-mile) range of the KS-1 and its subsonic speed could no longer meet the requirements of the Soviet military, which needed a new supersonic missile with a range of up to 150 km (93 miles). Consequently, in the mid-1950s OKB-2-155 set about improving the KS-1, working in two directions – using an improved control and guidance system and replacing the turbojet with a liquid-propellant rocket motor. On 29th April 1957, MAP issued order No.169 tasking OKB-283 with developing the Rubicon guidance system for the KS and its rocket-powered derivative, the KSR (*krylahtyy snaryad raketnyy* – rocket-propelled winged missile); the system was built around the then-latest Rubin-1 aircraft radar. A prototype of the system was to be ready for tests by the third quarter of 1957, Tupolev's OKB-156 being tasked with preparing the technical documents for an adaptation of the Tu-16KS by July.

Meanwhile, OKB-2-155 was working on the new rocket-propelled air-to-surface missile. The KSR was designed around an S2.721V single-chamber liquid-fuel rocket motor specially developed for it by Aleksey M. Isayev's OKB-2. The rocket motor had two operating modes selected by a fuel feed valve, providing an initial thrust of 1,200 kgp (2,650 lbst) in launch mode and 600 kgp (1,320 lbst) in cruise mode. It ran on special TG-02 fuel (*toplivo ghipergolicheskoye* – hypergolic or self-igniting fuel), also known under the unclassified name *Samin* – a 50/50 mixture of xylidine and triethylamine which self-combusted when combined with AK-20F oxidiser (AK = *azotnaya kislota* – nitric acid, '20' means 20% nitrogen tetroxide added to give a 5% power boost, F = *fosfornaya kislota* – a small amount of phosphoric acid added as a corrosion inhibitor). The fuel was identical to the German Tonka-250 rocket fuel used in the Second World War; and indeed, some sources decipher TG as *trofeynoye goryucheye* – war booty propellant. A turbo pump running on grade T hydrogen peroxide fed the fuel and oxidiser to the rocket motor; it was started by a cartridge starter, exhausting below the rocket motor nozzle.

Like the KS-1, the KSR had mid-set swept wings swept back 55° at quarter-chord and a cruciform tail unit. The cigar-shaped fuselage had a smaller diameter – 1.0 m (3 ft 3⅜ in) – thanks to the absence of the bulky centrifugal-flow turbojet and its inlet duct, and the entire fuselage nose was occupied by a large parabolic radome housing a new KS-PM radar seeker head. The corrosive oxidiser necessitated the use of stainless steel for the oxidiser tank, but otherwise the airframe was of conventional duralumin construction. The missiles were carried in the same fashion as the KS-1 on wing pylons, but the latter were of a different type (BD-245s instead of BD-187s).

In the autumn of 1958 two Tu-16s were fitted with the Rubicon system under the terms of 'order 245', one to carry the KS-1 missile and the other the KSR; hence the latter aircraft – according to some sources, an uncoded production Tu-16KS (c/n 7203608, tail number 7124) retaining the Rubidiy-MM2 and Kobal't-P radars and the WSO's workstation – was designated Tu-16KSR. During the trials held at the Bagerovo test range between 1st July and 15th November the experimental Tu-16KSR launched 11 KSR missiles – six against target vessels and five against ground targets with radar reflectors. Out of the six launches against targets ships over a range of 90-96 km (43.5-59 miles) there were four hits, one miss and one discounted launch due to a failure of the guidance system. The rocket motor worked well, igniting reliably after release at altitudes of 4,000-10,000 m (13,120-32,810 ft) and speeds of 400-500 km/h (248-310 mph). It had two operating modes, delivering a thrust of 1,200-1,220 kgp (2,650-2,690 lbst) in maximum power mode or 680-700 kgp (1,500-1,540 lbst) in cruise mode.

Tests at the altitudes stated above showed that the radar seeker head could detect a ground target at up to 200 km (124 miles) and provide stable tracking over distances of 160-180 km (99-118 miles). Automatic tracking was disabled at a distance of 13-15 km (8-9.3 miles). In the case of maritime targets, detection and acquisition depended on several factors, including the type of target and the target approach angle. The results of these tests formed the basis for the development of the K-11 and K-16 air-to-surface missile systems (K = *kompleks [vo'oruzheniya]* – integrated weapons system) differing only in their guidance algorithm.

K-16 weapons system
Tu-16KSR-2 (Tu-16K-16) missile strike aircraft ('order 352E'; *izdeliye* NKSR-2, *izdeliye* NK-3)

Although it remained in prototype form, the KSR served as the basis for the KSR-2 missile, which was designed to be carried by the Tu-16 as part of the K-16 weapons system for use against surface ships and ground targets of importance, such as bridges, dams, power stations, factories, railroad junctions, airfields and so on. Like its experimental precursor, the KSR-2 had a mid-wing layout with wings swept back 55° at quarter-chord and two boundary layer fences on each side but the tail surfaces were conventional (with low-set stabilisers), not cruciform; vertical and horizontal tail sweep at quarter-chord was 62° and 55° respectively. Another difference was the new Isayev S5.6.0000 liquid-propellant rocket motor – a derivative of the S2.721V which had slightly different ratings, delivering 1,213 kgp (2,674 lbst) at full thrust and 707 kgp (1,558 lbst) in cruise mode.

The prototypes were manufactured by plant No.256 in Doobna, but subsequently the KSR-2 entered full-scale production at aircraft factory No.475 in Smolensk, western Russia. The production missile was 8.647 m (28 ft 4⁷⁄₁₆ in) long, with a wing span of 4.522 m (14 ft 10 in) and a launch weight of 4,077-4,100 kg (8,988-9,040 lb), including a warhead weight of 840-850 kg (1,850-1,870 lb). As standard the KSR-2 had an FK-2 conventional warhead (*foogahsno-kumulyativnaya [boyevaya chast']* – high-explosive/shaped-charge armour-piercing warhead) for use against ships or an FK-2N HE/SCAP/fragmentation warhead with a so-called active liner made of aluminium for use against ground

targets (N = *nazemnaya tsel'* – ground target). Provision was made for fitting a nuclear warhead with a yield of 1 megaton. The missile could be launched at an altitude of 4,000-10,000 m (13,120-32,810 ft), having a maximum speed of 1,250 km/h (776 mph) and a flight range of up to 160 km (99 miles), though some sources state 120-140 km (74.5-87 miles).

In May-July 1957 the former Tu-16KSR (c/n 7203608, tail number 7124) was converted into the first experimental platform for the K-16 system, becoming the prototype of a new version designated Tu-16KSR-2. This involved removing the entire K-II guidance system, including the semi-retractable radome amidships

The Tu-16KSR-2 prototype.

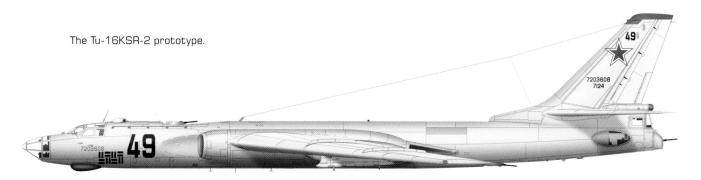

Left and above left: The Tu-16KSR-2 prototype, '49 Black' (c/n 7203608) with the tail number 7124 and photo calibration markings on the nose. Two red-painted KSR-2 missiles are suspended.

Above: The same aircraft in earlier guise (with no code) as the sole Tu-16KSR. A prototype KSR missile is on the starboard pylon; the 'wingless missile' on the port side is a ZDV camera pod.

Right: Close-up of the KSR missile, showing the cruciform tail surfaces (compare this to the low-set stabilisers of the KSR-2).

and the WSO's pressurised cabin associated with the KSR-1 missiles (the Rubicon automated guidance system made the provision of a WSO unnecessary); accordingly the large cut-outs in the bomb bay doors for the Kobal't-1M radome and the WSO's entry hatch were faired over, the patches overlapping the weapons bay door joint line. The starter fuel system for the KSR-1 missiles was also deleted as unnecessary, as was the marker bomb rack. The BD-187 missile pylons were replaced by BD-245s designed for the new missile; the RBP-4 radar was substituted by a Rubin-1 radar (which fitted neatly into the existing chin radome), the OPB-11RM optical bombsight was replaced by the OPB-112 model. Some other avionics items were removed or replaced (including an AP-6E autopilot instead of the AP-5-2M, an RV-UM low-range radio altimeter instead of the RV-2 and the like).

The Tu-16KSR-2 prototype gained the tactical code '49 Black' and photo calibration markings on both sides of the nose looking like eight pairs of vertical and horizontal black stripes. It also featured a data link antenna replacing the cannons in the tail turret. During tests in 1957-58, the aircraft occasionally flew with a test pod enigmatically designated 'ZDV', which looked like a wingless black/yellow chequered KSR-2 missile with no radome (the latter was replaced by a camera port in a 'hog nose').

One or two KSR-2s could be carried; in the latter case they were launched simultaneously or individually. Preparations for launch were the responsibility of the navigator; the high degree of automation allowed him to complete the pre-launch procedures in

less than one minute. Emergency jettison of the missiles could be performed by the captain or the navigator.

Joint state acceptance trials of the K-16 weapons system were held between 25th October 1960, and 30th March 1961, involving the State Committee for Aviation Hardware (GKAT – *Gosudarstvennyy komitet po aviatsionnoy tekhnike*), the State Committee for Electronics (GKRE – *Gosudarstvennyy komitet po rahdioelektronike*) and the State Committee for Defence Technology (GKOT – *Gosudarstvennyy komitet po oboronnoy tekhnike*). Upon completion of the trials the K-16 system was accepted for operational service once the problems discovered in the course of the trials had been resolved. (Incidentally, at this point the Soviet term for cruise missiles was changed from *samolyot-snaryad* ('missile aircraft' or aircraft-type missile) to *krylahtaya raketa* (winged rocket) pursuant to an order signed by Minister of Defence Marshal Rodion Ya. Malinovskiy in 1960.)

(Note: In December 1957, MAP was 'demoted' to a State Committee along with several other ministries due to changing government policies during the Khrushchov era. The unlucky ones included the Ministry of Radio Industry (MRP – *Ministerstvo rahdiotekhnicheskoy promyshlennosti*) and the Ministry of Defence Industry (MOP). In 1965, however, their names and status were restored after Nikita S. Khruschchov had been unseated

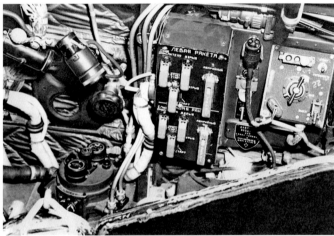

Top: The captain's instrument panel of the Tu-16KSR-2.

Above: The missile control panel on the captain's left console, with separate switches for the port and starboard missiles (marked 'Oxidiser dump', 'Launch/Abort launch', 'Detonation/Non-detonation' and 'Emergency jettison').

Below: A production Smolensk-built KSR-2 on the port pylon, with the hoist in place and the radome of the KS-PM seeker removed. The chequered paint job indicates this is an inert practice round.

Top: The co-pilot's instrument panel of the Tu-16KSR-2.

Above: The wing trailing edge had special cut-outs in the flaps in line with the BD-352 missile pylons to stop the flaps from striking the missiles' tails.

Below: A KSR-2 missile on the starboard pylon of a Tu-16KSR-2.

Opposite page: Tu-16KSR-2 '65 Red' (c/n 7203820/tail number 7164) at GK NII VVS during check-up tests.

and replaced by Leonid I. Brezhnev as the new Soviet leader in 1964.)

Since the K-16 weapons system was making good progress, GKAT proposed to the Soviet Ministry of Defence that 100 Tu-16KS missile carriers and 300 Tu-16A bombers should be converted to carry the KSR-2 and equipped with the Rubicon guidance system. GKAT further suggested that the viability of adapting the Tu-22 supersonic bomber to carry the KSR-2 be explored; in the event such an adaptation was not made, the *Blinder* receiving a very different missile.

On 4th February 1961, the Council of Ministers issued directive No.117-49 spelling out revised performance figures for the K-16 weapons system. This document ordered additional development work and testing to be carried out on the guidance system – particularly the KSR-2's KS-PM radar seeker head, whose antenna dish diameter was increased from 400 to 520 mm (from 1 ft 3¾ in to 1 ft 8¹⁵⁄₃₂ in). After passing state acceptance trials in July-August 1961 the K-16 system was cleared for service with the DA and the AVMF pursuant to CofM directive No.1184-514 dated 30th December 1961.

In 1962 Long-Range Aviation and Naval Aviation maintenance units began converting Tu-16KSs to carry two KSR-2 missiles. Such aircraft were known as 'order 352E' in production, the E suffix denoting a modified Tu-16KS which, as mentioned earlier, was the delivery vehicle for the KS-1 (*izdeliye* E). The service designation was Tu-16KSR-2 or *izdeliye* NKSR-2; sometimes this version was referred to as the Tu-16K-16 or *izdeliye* NK-3 (although some documents feature the rather clumsy designation Tu-16KS-KSR-2, as a reference to the pre-conversion model). The total was much smaller than envisioned originally – only 50 examples were refitted with the K-16 system.

Also in 1962, the first two operational Tu-16KSR-2s, '65 Red' (converted from Tu-16KS c/n 7203820, tail number 7164) and '66 Red' (converted from Tu-16A c/n 5202010), underwent combined check-up tests at GK NII VVS pursuant to the abovementioned CofM directive No.117-49. Lt.-Col. N. N. Sorokin was the engineer in charge of the tests.

These two aircraft differed from the prototypes tested in 1960 in having an updated Rubin-1K version of the radar (featuring a new command link system for working with the missile's seeker head), an AP-6E autopilot replacing the standard AP-5-2M, an OPB-112 bombsight replacing the OPB-11RM, an RV-UM low-range radio altimeter replacing the RV-2, a DISS-1 Doppler ground speed and drift sensor and so on. The Rubin-1K, DISS-1 and PRS-1 gun ranging radar modules had a common pressurisation system. New BD-352 missile pylons were fitted, replacing the earlier BD-245s; this necessitated changes to the Nos. 14L/14R fuel tanks and the IFR system pipeline in the port wing leading edge. The same 25° limit on flap setting applied when the missiles were carried. Further changes to the fuel system included a new No.1 fuel tank with a separate filler cap, which was connected to the No.2 tank; fuel from these could be transferred to the Group 3 tanks (Nos.7-11). Manual controls enabling asymmetric usage from the port and starboard Group 4 wing tanks (Nos. 12-16L/12-16R) were introduced in order to maintain balance when only one missile was carried. Additionally, Tu-16KSR-2 '66 Red' was fitted

with test equipment recording the flight parameters (speed, altitude, pitch/yaw/roll rates, G loads and field performance), control surface travel, fuel usage and vibration levels.

For the first time in Soviet practice, the K-16 system implemented the long-range homing principle. The Rubin-1K radar could detect and select a target at a range of 300-350 km (186-217 miles). It then passed the target co-ordinates to the missile's KS-PM radar seeker head which had achieved a target lock-on while the missile was still on the pylon. 40 seconds after launch the missile's AP-72-4 autopilot was connected to the aircraft's command link system for initial guidance. Once the KS-PM was receiving a clear signal from the target, the navigator sent a command switching the missile to homing mode, the autopilot now receiving commands from the seeker head which guided the missile towards the target. The missiles were launched at an altitude of 4,000-10,000 m (13,120-32,810 ft) and a speed of 700-800 km/h (435-496 mph). After launching its missiles the Tu-16KSR-2 was able to turn away from the target, thus reducing its vulnerability to enemy air defences.

21 inert/instrumented and live KSR-2 missiles were assigned to the tests, with a complement of conventional warheads in maritime (FK-2) and land (FK-2N) versions. The missiles had a revised seeker head, a heated warhead bay and EMVU-525 detonators (*elektromekhanicheskoye vzryvahtel'noye oostroystvo* – electromechanical fuse) replacing the earlier EMVU-514; two of the missiles had electronic counter-countermeasures (ECCM) modules for testing the guidance system for ECM resistance. Additionally, there were three dummy missiles with operational fuel and pneumatic systems rigged with sensors for measuring temperature and vibration parameters and for determining the aircraft's flight performance with the missiles in place.

Among other things, the purpose of the tests was to verify the KSR-2's new experimental nuclear warhead detonation system. This part of the tests proceeded in two stages. The first was the manufacturer's tests undertaken by the Ministry of Medium Machinery (MSM), with Air Force support; the second was the acceptance tests undertaken jointly by MSM and the military.

The combined check-up tests began on 10th September 1962, continuing until 30th June 1964. There was a six-month pause in the tests from 11th October 1962, to April 1963, due to the need to modify the K-16 weapons system; the first missile launch under the test programme did not take place until 18th April 1963.

The tests continued until the summer of 1964 with pauses for alterations and adjustments, but their successful outcome confirmed the viability of the system and allowed the ways of future development to be outlined. All in all, the two aircraft made 110 flights with a total time of 339 hours (Tu-16KSR-2 c/n 7203820, 53 flights/162 hours; Tu-16KSR-2 c/n 5202010, 57 flights/177 hours) and launched 21 KSR-2 missiles.

The Tu-16KSR-2 had the NATO reporting name *Badger-G*. The KSR-2 missile was codenamed AS-5A *Kelt*.

Tu-16KSR-2 (ZA) missile strike aircraft

At first the Tu-16KSR-2 had no IFR capability. When some aircraft were retrofitted with an IFR receptacle, the designation was changed to Tu-16KSR-2 (ZA). Some sources, however, claim this update did not lead to any change in the designation.

Tu-16KSR-2A (Tu-16A-KSR-2) bomber/missile strike aircraft ('order 352A'; *izdeliye* NKSR-2, *izdeliye* NK-3)

In parallel with the modification of Tu-16KS and Tu-16KS (ZA) dedicated missile carriers to Tu-16KSR-2 standard, similar refits of the Tu-16A and Tu-16 (ZA) were also carried out but their nuclear bomber capability was retained. Consequently such aircraft had a slightly different designation, Tu-16KSR-2A, and were known in production as 'order 352A' (the A referring to the conversion from the Tu-16A); they were sometimes referred to in documents as the Tu-16A-KSR-2. The product code was originally *izdeliye* NKSR-2 but was later changed to the less cumbersome *izdeliye* NK-3.

The first Tu-16A to be refitted in this way was the aforementioned '66 Red' (c/n 5202010) which took part in the check-up state acceptance trials in 1962. A total of 155 Tu-16As were modified as Tu-16KSR-2As under the terms of 'order 352A'. Subsequently this difference disappeared when the Tu-16KSR-2 was modified to carry bombs. The K-16 system was the first composite strike weapons system able to carry both free-fall bombs and stand-off missiles.

Relatively few Tu-16As and Tu-16KSs were converted to Tu-16KSR-2 (or Tu-16KSR-2A) configuration in the first half of the 1960s. This was due to a decision to develop the K-11-16 combined weapons system able to use both the KSR-2 active radar homing missile and the KSR-11 passive radar homing missile. In the 1970s the Tu-16KSR-2s and Tu-16KSR-2As were further upgraded to Tu-16KSR-2-5 standard.

Performance of the K-16 air-to-surface missile system	
Combat radius with two missiles and a 75,800-kg (167,110-lb) AUW, without in-flight refuelling and with 5% fuel reserves	1,900 km (1,180 miles)
Missile launch altitude	4,000-11,000 m (13,120-36,090 ft)
Cruising speed with missiles at 10,000 m (32,810 ft)	750-800 km/h (465-496 mph)
Target detection range:	
towns and large targets	320-340 km (198-211 miles)
large bridges	250-290 km (155-180 miles)
large surface ships (cruiser-sized targets)	200-220 km (124-136 miles)
Range of the KSR-2 missile:	
normal	120-140 km (74.5-87.0 miles)
maximum (launch at 10,000 m with the aircraft turning away from the target)	140-150 km (87.0-93.2 miles)
Proximity of the aircraft to the target at the moment of launch	110-130 km (68.3-80.7 miles)
'Kill' probability	80%

Performance of the Tu-16KSR-2	
Empty weight	39,200-39,500 kg (86,420-87,080 lb)
Maximum take-off weight with two KSR-2 missiles	79,000 kg (174,170 lb)
Fuel load	29,500-30,300 kg (65,040-66,800 lb)
Maximum operational range with 5% fuel reserves on landing and with launch of both missiles at mid-range	3,900 km (2,422 miles)
Endurance at maximum range	5 hrs 20 min
Service ceiling with two missiles, a 56,000-kg (123,460-lb) AUW and a 62,000-kg (13,670-lb) TOW	11,900 m (39,040 ft)
Time to service ceiling with a 62,000-kg take-off weight	37 minutes
Time to 10,000 m with a 62,000-kg take-off weight	21 minutes
Take-off run with two KSR-2s:	
with a 75,800-kg (167,110-lb) take-off weight	2,200 m (7,220 ft)
with a 79,000-kg take-off weight	2,400 m (7,870 ft)
Landing run with a 48,000-kg (105,820-lb) landing weight (with both missiles launched):	
with brake parachute	1,200 m (3,940 ft)
without brake parachute	1,600 m (5,250 ft)
Landing run with a 57,000-kg (126,760-lb) landing weight (with both missiles on the wing):	
with brake parachute	1,450 m (4,760 ft)
without brake parachute	1,900 m (6,230 ft)

Tu-16KSR-2 bomber/missile strike aircraft (modified, 'order 684/2' update)

As mentioned above, initially the Tu-16KSR-2 could not carry bombs. However, after modifications under 'order 684/2', free-fall bombs could be carried in the bomb bay as on the Tu-16KSR-2A and the two sub-variants became identical in their capabilities.

Tu-16KSR-2A bomber/missile strike aircraft (modified, 'order 684/1' update)

The Tu-16KSR-2A was able carry a limited bomb load internally, but it was further modified under the terms of 'order 684/1' to carry additional bombs externally, bringing its maximum bomb load to 13,000 kg (28,660 lb). The bombs were carried in two rows on special BD3-16K multiple racks attached to the wing pylons; the K stood for *kryl'yevoy* (wing-mounted) and the '16' was a reference to the aircraft type. The racks developed by OKB-134 could take eight 100-kg/250-kg (220-lb/551-lb) bombs or four 500-kg (1,102-lb) bombs each; their distinctive shape in side view earned them the slang name *shtany* ('breeches' or 'pants'). Special switches were added to the flap control circuitry to disable the 25° flap setting limit imposed by the missiles. In addition to the wing racks, the aircraft was fitted with two standard KD3-416 bomb cassettes in the bomb bay.

The new racks were tested on a Tu-16KSR-2A coded '25 Blue' (c/n 5201604) between 23rd March, and 22nd June 1970; Lt.-Col. Viktor V. Oosenko was project test pilot, with V. V. Zakharenko as engineer in charge. With an AUW of 60,000 kg (132,280 lb) the bomber had a service ceiling of 11,000 m (36,090 ft); the maximum speed at 7,550 m (24,770 ft) with the loaded racks was 820 km/h (509 mph) but the indicated airspeed at up to 10,000 m (32,810 ft) was restricted to 550 km/h (341 mph) due to the risk of wing flutter. Range with a 13,000-kg bomb load in a 'hi-hi-hi' mission with a 75,800-kg (167,110-lb) AUW was reduced by 1,430 km (88 miles) as compared to the two-missile payload option due to the higher fuel burn and reduced fuel supply.

The test report pointed out that the BD3-16K racks met the specifications as regards strength, safety and reliability, but not as regards drag and electrical insulation parameters. All the same, they were recommended for service after the defects had been eliminated.

Top and above: Tu-16KSR-2 '66 Red' at GK NII VVS during the same tests. Unlike '65 Red', which was converted from a Tu-16KS (hence the tail number), this is a converted Tu-16A and therefore retains the 'anti-flash' white paint on the undersides.

This page and below left: Referred to in the test report as a 'Tu-16A-KSR-2' (though Tu-16KSR-2A is more correct), this aircraft ('25 Blue', c/n 5201604) was modified under 'order 684/1' and tested in March-June 1970, with BD3-16K bomb racks on the wing pylons.

Above: A live KSR-2 missile on the starboard pylon of Tu-16KSR-2 '14 Blue' (c/n 5201810). Note the tail number 72.

Above left: A KSR-2 with the tail number 78 on its ground handling dolly, with the wings folded to save space during storage.

Left: Close-up of the port BD-352 pylon of a Tu-16KSR-2 (with sway braces extended) and the modified flap.

Below left and bottom left: A KSR-2 is launched from the port pylon of a Tu-16KSR-2-11. The exhaust of the turbo pump is visible under the rocket motor nozzle. Note the stiffening ribs on the upper side of the wing near the cut-out in the flap.

Tu-16KSR-IS missile strike aircraft

In the early 1970s a number of Tu-16KSR-2s were fitted with ECM equipment to prevent detection by enemy radars – the SPS-5 Fasol' jammer for self-protection, with swept blade aerials below the centre fuselage near the engine air intakes, and the SPS-100 Rezeda-AK jammer in a large parabolic tail fairing instead of the tail turret for operations in a group. Such aircraft were designated Tu-16KSR-IS.

K-11 long-range stand-off weapons system
Tu-16K-11 missile strike (SEAD) aircraft ('order 285')

Development of the K-11 weapons system tailored for the suppression of enemy air defences (SEAD) role – known as 'Wild Weasel' in US Air Force parlance – proceeded in parallel with the K-16. This involved creating a passive radar homing version of the KSR-2 – the KSR-11 anti-radar missile (ARM). Preliminary design work on the K-11 system was initiated by Council of Ministers directive No.902-411 on 20th July 1957, followed up by MAP order No.288 to the same effect on 31st July. According to these, the project completion deadline was early 1958, with manufacturer's tests scheduled to take place in the spring of 1959, and state acceptance trials of the whole weapons system in the autumn of 1959. The directive also contained a clause about the possibility of updating the K-10 weapons system (see below) with passive radar homing capability. OKB-156 was responsible for the Tu-16 missile platform, the MoD's Central Research Institute No.108 (TsNII-108) for the search and targeting system, OKB-2-155 for the missile itself and NII-648 for the guidance and passive homing system.

The KSR-11 (AS-5B *Kelt*) was the first Soviet passive radar homing air-to-surface missile for use against enemy ground or shipboard radars, radar-controlled AAA and SAM sites. It was dimensionally identical to the KSR-2 but featured a 2PRG-11 passive radar seeker head instead of the KS-PM active radar seeker and an AP-72-11 autopilot instead of the AP-72-4, and came strictly with a conventional (high-explosive or HE/fragmentation) warhead. At 4,000 kg (8,820 lb) its all-up weight was 100 kg (220 lb) less than the KSR-2's due to its lighter guidance system which maintained course between launch and impact. Searching for the target radars, determining their operating frequencies and tuning the missiles' radar seeker heads to these frequencies was the responsibility of the Nav/Op whose workstation featured appropriate control panels.

Like the Tu-16KSR-2, the Tu-16K-11 converted from standard Tu-16A and Tu-16 (ZA) bombers could also be used as a bomber. It was outwardly identifiable by a modified navigator's station glazing whose foremost transparency was replaced by an identically shaped metal fairing mounting the direction finder antenna array of the *Ritsa* radar detection/homing system (named after the famous scenic Lake Ritsa in the mountains of Abkhazia, in the Caucasus). This array had a very distinctive appearance, with nine circular antennas in an inverted-T arrangement. Hence the dipole antenna of the GRP-2 glideslope beacon receiver (*glissahdnyy rahdiopriyomnik*), which was normally housed inside the said transparency, was relocated to a ventral position immediately aft of the navigator's station glazing, assuming an inverted-T shape. In order to accommodate the Ritsa system, save weight and avoid a forward shift of the CG the NU-88 fixed forward-firing cannon installation and the associated PKI gunsight were removed (the recess for the cannon was closed by a flush plate).

The missile was launched once its radar seeker head had achieved a lock-on. After launch, the KSR-11 climbed to the same altitude as the Tu-16 and maintained that altitude before finally entering a 30° dive to impact. The Tu-16 could carry out any manoeuvre after launch, including U-turns; the target tracking information was retained by the KSR-11.

The design work on the K-11 system took two years to complete. By the end of 1959, the basic issues of radar detection and target indication (served by the Ritsa system), as well as passive radar homing, had been resolved and the first models of the entire system were ready for testing. Two examples of the Tu-16 were modified at the Kazan' aircraft factory and designated Tu-16K-11 (the conversion job was referred to as 'order 285'). The first prototype Tu-16K-11 made its first flight from Kazan'-Borisoglebskoye in January 1960 and arrived at Zhukovskiy for testing on 12th February. On 1st April, it was joined by the second prototype, and manufacturer's tests of the K-11 system began in May. Despite the fundamental design complexity of the system's components, the tests were concluded successfully in the spring of 1962 and on 13th April that year the Council of Ministers issued directive No.314-157 clearing the Tu-16K-11 for service.

The K-11 system had a 2,000-km (1,242-mile) combat radius with the aircraft flying at altitudes between 4,000 and 11,000 m (13,120-36,090 ft). Missile launch at 10,000 m (32,810 ft) was performed at a cruising speed of 750-800 km/h (465-496 mph). The radar detection range was 270-350 km (167-217 miles), with the KSR-11 possessing a range of 160 km (99 miles) and a 'kill' probability of 80-90% (the heading memory feature meant that the hostile radar would in all probability be destroyed even if the operator switched it off).

Although the K-11 weapons system was accepted, it was decided to use the combined K-11 and K-16 for operational use, which led to the development of the Tu-16K-11-16.

K-11-16 long-range stand-off weapons system
Tu-16K-11-16 missile strike aircraft (Tu-16K-11-16KS, 'order 497E'; *izdeliye* NK-11-16, *izdeliye* NK-2)

The high degree of commonality between the KSR-2 and KSR-11 missiles suggested they could be fitted to the same aircraft. Therefore, in 1961 the K-11-16 weapons system was developed, its missile platform being equipped with the Ritsa radar detection system and the Rubicon guidance system (the latter based on the Rubin-1K radar). Designated Tu-16K-11-16, the aircraft was to carry either two KSR-2s or two KSR-11s, or one of each type (payload options 1, 2 and 3); the existing pylons were replaced with updated BD-352-11 pylons to enable this. The maximum range of the KSR-11 was 85 km (52 miles) if launched from 4,000 m and 120 km if launched from 10,000 m, with detonation between 4 and 12 m (13-39 ft) above the target. The KSR-2 (with a choice of HE or nuclear warheads) had a maximum range of 150 km (93.1 miles) if launched from 10,000 m and a minimum range of 70 km (43.5 miles).

A standard Tu-16A coded '14 Red' (c/n 5202908), which was grounded after a flying accident in 1956, served as a full-size mock-up of the Tu-16K-11-16, with wooden dummy versions of the new equipment modules being fitted in the flight deck and the avionics bay as appropriate. The missile pylons were not fitted; nor were mock-ups of the KSR-2 and KSR-11 missiles presented together with the aircraft. The mock-up review commission worked on 11th-14th December 1961, and gave a thumbs-up to the project, the Air Force C-in-C Air Chief Marshal Konstantin A. Vershinin endorsing the commission's report on 25th January 1962. The report stated that such a conversion significantly enhanced the Tu-16A's combat capabilities, transforming it into a multi-role aircraft. At that point it was planned to convert two Tu-16A (ZA) IFR-capable bombers as pattern aircraft for the new version, with conversion of operational aircraft taking place at Air Force and Naval Aviation aircraft repair plants. Navy representatives objected to the suggestion that only Tu-16A bombers (which the Navy did not have) be converted, stating that Tu-16KS missile carriers should be upgraded as well; AVMF Commander Col.-Gen. Yevgeniy N. Preobrazhenskiy stated this on 20th January.

In 1962 the K-11-16 weapons system was accepted for operational use. 15 Tu-16KSs and a number of Tu-16KSR-2s, as well as a few Tu-16S SAR aircraft (see Chapter 5), were modified to Tu-16K-11-16 standard under the terms of 'order 497' (or 'order 497E' if they carried KS-1 missiles). In service the aircraft was known as *izdeliye* NK-11-16 or, later, *izdeliye* NK-2. Initially it lacked bomber capability (even though the latter was envisaged by the project as payload option 4), but this was subsequently restored on many Tu-16K-11-16s; in such cases the undersides received a

Specifications of the K-11-16 weapons system (as per mock-up review commission report)		
	K-11 system	**K-16 system**
Maximum take-off weight with 2 missiles, kg (lb)	75,800 (167,110)	75,800 (167,110)
Landing weight, kg (lb):		
normal	n.a	47,150 (103,950)
maximum	n.a	52,000 (114,640)
for exceptional cases	n.a.	57,000 (125,660)
Maximum speed at 10,500 m (34,450 ft) with a 60,000-kg (132,280-lb) TOW at maximum continuous thrust, km/h (mph)	885 (549)	885 (549)
Aircraft speed during missile launch		
at 10,000 m (32,810 ft), km/h (mph)	750-800 (465-496)	700-800 (435-496)
Service ceiling, m (ft):		
with a 75,800-kg TOW	n.a.	10,350 (33,960)
with a 72,000-kg (158,730-lb) TOW	n.a.	10,700 (35,100)*
with a 60,000-kg TOW	n.a.	11,200 (36,745)*
Effective range with 2 missiles and a 75,800-kg TOW, 27,000 kg (59,520 lb) of fuel and 5% fuel reserves, km (miles)	n.a.	3,780 (2,347)†
Maximum combat radius with 2 missiles and a 75,800-kg TOW, on internal fuel only with 5% fuel reserves, km (miles)	2,050 (1,273)	1,900 (1,180)
Hostile radar detection range at 10,000 m	270-350 (167-217)	–
Maximum launch range, km (miles)	170 (105)	140-150 (87-93)
Minimum launch range, km (miles)	50 (31)	–
Minimum distance from aircraft to target, km (miles):		
at maximum launch range	160 (99)	120-140 (74.5-87)
at minimum launch range	40 (24.8)	
Take-off run with a 75,800-kg TOW, m (ft)	2,305 (7,560)	2,305 (7,560)
Unstick speed, km/h (mph)	297 (184)	297 (184)
Landing run with a 47,150-kg landing weight, m (ft)	2,305 (7,560)	2,305 (7,560)
Landing speed, km/h (mph)	n.a.	229 (142)

* K-11-16 system
† 3,800 km (2,360 miles) for the K-11-16 system

full or partial 'anti-flash' white paint job. Conversion of the Tu-16KSR-2 into the Tu-16K-11-16 involved installation of the Ritsa radar homing system and removal of the nose cannon and gunsight.

Outwardly the Tu-16K-11-16 differed from the Tu-16KSR-2 in having the tell-tale patches on the centreline where the entry hatch of the WSO's station and the cut-out for the Kobal't-P radar had been on the Tu-16KS. In addition, the undersurfaces of the machines lacking bomber capability were natural metal, not white. The designation Tu-16K-11-16KS was also used occasionally if the original aircraft had been a Tu-16KS.

A total of 441 Tu-16A, Tu-16 (ZA), Tu-16KS and Tu-16S aircraft were refitted to take the K-16 and K-11-16 weapons systems. Of these, 211 aircraft served with the Air Force and 230 with the Navy. The main delivery vehicle was the Tu-16K-11-16 which was equipped with SPS-5 and SPS-100 active jammers. Refits were done at maintenance factories in the 1960s. Later, in the 1970s, the Tu-16K-11-16 was modified yet again to Tu-16K-26 standard.

A small number of Tu-16K-11-16s was supplied to Egypt and Iraq, taking part in the armed conflicts in the Middle East – the Arab-Israeli war of 1973 (the Yom Kippur War) and the Iran-Iraq War of 1980-88.

The performance of the Tu-16K-11-16 barely differed from the Tu-16KSR-2, although the need to carry two guidance systems increased the former aircraft's empty weight to 40,600 kg (89,510 lb), with an attendant reduction of the fuel load to 29,000 kg (63,930 lb). This explains the reduction of the combat radius as compared to the Tu-16K-11 to 1,900 km (1,180 miles). Again, both types of missile were launched at 4,000-11,000 m and 750-800 km/h; target detection range was 270-350 km against radars, 250-290 km (155-180 miles) against ground targets and 200 km (124 miles) against cruiser-sized surface ships.

Tu-16KSR-2-11 bomber/missile strike aircraft ('order 497A'; *izdeliye* NK-11-16, *izdeliye* NK-2)

Under the terms of 'order 497A' 155 Tu-16A and Tu-16A (ZA) bombers were converted to Tu-16KSR-2-11 configuration and the Tu-16KSR-2As were modified. Once again, the product code was originally *izdeliye* NK-11-16 and subsequently *izdeliye* NK-2. The Tu-16KSR-2-11 had an operational radius of 2,050 km (1,273 miles).

Like the Tu-16KSR-2, the Tu-16K-11-16 and Tu-16KSR-2-11 had the NATO reporting name *Badger-G*.

Tu-16K-11-16 bomber/missile strike aircraft (modified, 'order 684/2' update)

At first the Tu-16K-11-16 lacked bomber capability, but after modification under the terms of 'order 684/2' it could carry a full bomb load of up to 13,000 kg (28,660 lb) comprising forty FAB-100 or FAB-250 bombs, or twenty-six FAB-500s, or four FAB-1500s, or two FAB-3000s, or eight torpedoes (four in the bomb bay and four on the wing pylons).

Tu-16K-11-16 missile strike aircraft (modified; 'order 2624' update?)

At least one Tu-16K-11-16 was retrofitted with an SPS-100 Rezeda-AK jammer in a large parabolic tail fairing replacing the DK-7 tail turret and the PRS-1 gun-laying radar; also, an SPS-5 Fasol' jammer was installed in the forward avionics bay. Apparently this was done under the terms of the same 'order 2624' as the modified Tu-16A mentioned earlier. The aircraft ('28 Blue', c/n 5202501) was test flown from Kazan'-Borisoglebskoye on 10th January – 4th April 1968, and underwent check-up tests on 18th May – 29th August 1968, together with this Tu-16A and two more similarly equipped *Badgers* (see Chapter 5/Tu-16 Yolka).

K-26 long-range stand-off weapons system

On 11th August 1962, the Council of Ministers issued directive No.838-357 initiating development of the new K-26 air-to-surface missile system. Developed in accordance with a specific operational requirement (SOR) endorsed by the Air Force C-in-C on 12th March 1963, the system was to comprise either the Tu-16K-26 or Tu-16KSR-2-5 or Tu-16KSR-2-5-11 as a missile platform, two new KSR-5 supersonic ASMs (with conventional or nuclear warheads), with the older KSR-2 or KSR-11 missiles as optional weapons, and the Vzlyot (Take-off) guidance system built around the improved Rubin-1KV radar (the V was a reference to the Vzlyot system) – an upgraded version of the Rubin-1K with alterations allowing it to communicate with the missile's VS-K radar seeker head. It was designed for use against surface ships and radar-defined ground targets (such as dams or bridges) alike. (Oddly enough, some documents state the CofM directive in question as No.552-229 dated 23rd June 1964!)

Development of the KSR-5 had begun at what was then OKB-2-155 (the weapons design section of the Mikoyan OKB) in 1960; its design benefited from the experience gained with the subsonic KS-1, KSR-2 and KSR-11 missiles, as well as with the supersonic Kh-22 (D-2; NATO codename AS-4 *Kitchen*) developed by the same OKB for the Tu-22K *Blinder-B*. Also known as the D-5 (the D probably stood for Doobna where the design office was based), the KSR-5 resembled a scaled-down version of the Kh-22, to which it was similar both aerodynamically and in structural design. It had a conventional mid-wing layout with delta

Top left: The flight deck of a Tu-16K-11-16 showing the IFR control panel (1), the IKO-42 course indicator (2), an extra bank of warning lights (3) and the missile warhead temperature gauges (4).

Top: The modified Nav/Op's workstation of the same aircraft.

Above: The navigator's station of the same aircraft with an RN-6B display (1) and missile launch control panels (2, 3).

Below: The Tu-16K-11-16's distinctive inverted-T antenna array of the Ritsa radar homing system; note the lack of the nose cannon.

Tu-16K-11-16 '28 Blue' (c/n 5202501) with an SPS-100 jammer replacing the tail turret. It underwent check-up tests in May-June 1968. Interestingly, despite being labelled as a Tu-16K-11-16 in the test report, it lacks the Ritsa radar homing system!

wings having 75° leading-edge sweep and cruciform trapezoidal tail surfaces arranged in the vertical and horizontal planes; the tail unit consisted of slab stabilisers (stabilators), an all-movable dorsal fin and a fixed ventral fin which folded to port to facilitate ground handling, deploying after launch. The airframe was mostly made of aluminium alloys, with stainless steel used for the oxidiser tank. The circular-section fuselage was tipped by an ogival radome of glassfibre honeycomb construction. The powerplant was the same as on the Kh-22 – an S5.33 twin-chamber three-mode liquid-propellant rocket motor (aka R201-300) developed by the Moscow-based OKB-300 under Sergey K. Tumanskiy (better known for its turbojet engines). It ran on TG-02 fuel and AK-27P oxidiser; a single turbo pump served both combustion chambers. The booster chamber had one operating mode, the cruise chamber located below it having two modes. At full thrust (with both chambers running) the S5.33 delivered 8,350 kgp (18,410 lbst); with only the smaller chamber running it was 1,400 kgp (3,090 lbst) at intermediate thrust and 650 kgp (1,430 lbst) at cruise thrust.

'14 Red' (c/n 6401208) was one of the missile carriers that were tested at GNIKI VVS. The colour scheme shows it was converted from a Tu-16A and retained the ability to carry nuclear bombs.

The KSR-5 was 10.6 m (34 ft 9^{21}/$_{64}$ in) long, with a wing span of 2.606 m (8 ft 6^{19}/$_{32}$ in) and a body diameter of 0.92 m (3 ft 0^{7}/$_{32}$ in). The launch weight varied from 3,850 to 3,930 kg (8,490-8,660 lb), including a 900-kg (1,980-lb) warhead; the latter could be a shaped-charge/high-explosive warhead ('version M') for use against a pinpoint target (such as a large surface ship) or a TK40-1 thermonuclear warhead ('version N') for use against a large target (such as a group of ships).

The KSR-5 was devised as a highly accurate 'fire-and-forget' missile for use against ground or maritime targets. The missile had a VS-K active radar seeker head, a BSU-7 autopilot (*bortovaya sistema oopravleniya* – on-board control system), a command link system for mid-course guidance, an altimeter and a speed sensor. The seeker head and the autopilot were also components of the Vzlyot guidance system. The VS-K acquired the target while the missile was still on the wing, using target information supplied by the aircraft's radar. In an ECM environment, the guidance system made use of the target co-ordinates stored in its memory; should the ECM become really severe and prolonged, the system switched to another operating frequency which hopefully was not yet jammed.

The KSR-5 was launched at an altitude of 9,000-11,000 m (29,530-36,090 ft) after the aircraft's radar had acquired the target and achieved a lock-on. The launch range was 200-240 km (124-149 miles). As its rocket motor fired three seconds after release and went to full thrust, the missile accelerated to a maximum speed of 2,500-3,000 km/h (1,552-1,863 mph) and pulled up into a climb, cruising at an altitude of 22,500 m (73,820 ft) and receiving mid-course guidance from the aircraft. At a certain range from the target the KSR-5's radar seeker head also achieved a lock-on; the missile still received course updates from the aircraft as required. When the target was 60 km (37.25 miles) away the missile entered a 30° dive; the aircraft was then free to manoeuvre at will or return to base. The radar seeker was turned off 1 km (0.62 miles) from the target. Detonation was performed by an impact fuse if a conventional warhead fitted or by a radio altimeter set for a predetermined height if a nuclear warhead was fitted.

The K-26 weapons system also included ground test equipment for the KSR-5 missiles, including a special VNK-10 device emulating the missile's VS-K radar seeker head.

Here it should be noted that the K-26 weapons system was a blanket designation; it covered any of three missile platforms based on the Tu-16, which had different designations, depending on which version they had been converted from. These aircraft were designated Tu-16K-26, Tu-16KSR-2-5 and Tu-16KSR-2-5-11; details of each version are given below as appropriate. Still, they all looked almost identical and hence were known by the common NATO reporting name *Badger-G Mod*, as the new missiles were the most obvious difference from the 'pure' *Badger-G*.

Manufacturer's flight tests of the K-26 weapons system (known as Stage A) began in October 1964, involving two machines in different versions – Tu-16K-26 '54 Red' (converted from Tu-16K-11-16 c/n 8204022, tail number 8191) and Tu-16KSR-2-5 '66 Red' (converted from Tu-16KSR-2A c/n 5202010). 82 flights were made at this stage, involving ten launches of prototype KSR-5 missiles; five of these were in unguided mode, while the other five were meant to test the missile's homing system.

On 31st January 1967, the K-26 weapons system was submitted for Stage B (the state acceptance trials) but not accepted because the missiles had failed to score a hit on a maritime target. Yet the testing was continued in keeping with the state commission's decisions dated 7th February and 27th June 1967.

Stage A was completed in December 1967. It showed that the K-26 system had an operational radius of 2,100 km (1,304 miles) with two KSR-5 missiles. The missiles were launched with the aircraft cruising at 750-800 km/h (465-496 mph) at an altitude of 10,000 m (32,810 ft). The maximum range of the KSR-5 was between 200 and 240 km.

An additional round of tests involving 13 flights and five more missile launches was held, the missiles being drawn from those earmarked for Stage B. This time hits were achieved on ground and maritime targets.

The system was not formally accepted for state acceptance trials until 25th April 1968 (although the acceptance procedures had taken place on 16th January – 5th February). Since five missiles assigned for the trials had been used up, plant No.256 supplied an additional five KSR-5s. Stage B began on 5th January 1968 and went on until 30th November. In order to speed up the trials the Tu-16K-26 and Tu-16KSR-2-5 prototypes were joined by a second Tu-16K-26 (c/n 4200703) and the first prototype Tu-16K-10-26 ('15 Blue', c/n 1793014); the latter version is described separately. Within this 11-month time frame the four aircraft made 87 flights between them, logging a total of 288 hours (Tu-16K-26 c/n 8204022, 50 flights/185 hours 24 minutes; Tu-16KSR-2-5, 17 flights/55 hours 53 minutes; Tu-16K-26 c/n 4200703, 8 flights/ 34 hours 36 minutes; Tu-16K-10-26, 12 flights/12 hours 7 minutes).

Thirteen KSR-5s were launched at this stage, including two from the Tu-16K-10-26; the ground target was a 1,800-m (5,910-ft) string of radar reflectors emulating a railway bridge, while the maritime target was the decommissioned freighter S/S *Shevchenko* posing as a cruiser. Still, the results were not entirely satisfactory, and three more missiles were delivered for additional launches against the maritime target; this, and the need to make revisions to the missile, accounted for the delay in the trials' completion.

Finally, on 12th November 1969, the Council of Ministers issued directive No.882-315 officially clearing the K-26 weapons system for service with the Long Range Aviation and the Naval Aviation. The system achieved initial operational capability in 1970. The KSR-5 missile entered full-scale production at the Doobna Machinery Plant (DMZ – *Doobnenskiy mashinostroitel'nyy zavod*, formerly plant No.256) in 1966, receiving the NATO codename AS-6A *Kingfish*.

Tu-16K-26 bomber/missile strike aircraft ('order 386'; *izdeliye* NK-26, *izdeliye* NK-4)

This first version of the missile carrier compatible with the KSR-5 missile was based on the Tu-16K-11-16. It differed from the latter in having an upgraded weapons control system based on the Rubin-1KV radar. The existing BD-352 missile pylons were replaced with the BD-352-11-5 version compatible with three missile types, and the missile launch control equipment was modified

Top and above: The Tu-16K-26 prototype ('54 Red', c/n 8204022, tail number 8191) at GNIKI VVS during trials. Note the antenna array of the Ritsa system which was used for launching KSR-5P anti-radar missiles. Note the folded ventral fins of the missiles which are deployed after launch.

to enable carriage of KSR-5 missiles. A special subsystem was introduced for pressurising the KSR-5's avionics bay prior to launch.

The avionics suite included an A-711 LORAN with an A-713 receiver, an RSBN-2S SHORAN, a DISS-1 Doppler radar, an RV-17 high-range radio altimeter and an RV-UM low-range radio altimeter, a KI-12 magnetic compass, a GPK-52 directional gyro, a DIK-46M remote flux-gate compass. Celestial navigation was enabled by an AK-53P celestial compass, a DAK-50M remote celestial compass and an IAS-1M astrosextant. The communications suite included RSIU-5V and R-832M command radios and a 1-RSB-70 communications radio with a US-9 receiver. An SPS-5

jammer was provided for self-protection. The A-326 Rogovitsa formation-keeping system was installed on some aircraft; on the other hand, no ILS was fitted.

The Tu-16K-26 prototype was converted from the abovementioned Tu-16K-11-16 coded '54 Red' (c/n 8204022, tail number 8191). Conversion work in VVS and AVMF repair and maintenance units began in 1969; fifteen Tu-16K-11-16KS missile carriers were modified to Tu-16K-26 standard. In service they were referred to as *izdeliye* NK-26 (this was later changed to *izdeliye* NK-4) and during conversion as 'order 386'. A peculiarity of these aircraft was the patches on the bomb bay doors where the original Tu-16KS's K-1M radome and WSO's entry hatch had

Top and above: Two more views of the Tu-16K-26 prototype with a pair of KSR-5 missiles. Note the nose-down angle of the missiles assisting their separation during launch.

been. Some Tu-16K-26s, however, were converted from Tu-16As and thus retained bomber capability.

The Tu-16K-26 could carry one or two KSR-2, KSR-5 or KSR-11 missiles. One more option was a mixed weapons load comprising a single missile under the port wing plus up to 4,000 kg (8,820 lb) of conventional or nuclear bombs (the *izdeliye* 246T thermonuclear bomb).

Some Tu-16K-26s were equipped with an SPS-151D, SPS-152D or SPS-153D Siren'-D jammer having a receiver antenna in a distinctive thimble-shaped fairing on the navigator's station glazing (which necessitated relocation of the glideslope beacon receiver aerial to an undernose position) and transmitter antennas in egg-shaped pods on short struts near the engine air intakes to cover the forward hemisphere. Others additionally had an SPS-151ZhK, SPS-152ZhK or SPS-153ZhK Siren'-MD jammer in an ogival tail fairing (replacing the tail turret and the bulletproof rear glazing) and an SPS-5 Fasol' jammer with blade aerials flanking the nosewheel well, giving full 360° coverage. This tail fairing was smaller than that of the SPS-100 jammer and had a different shape, with a perceptible step between the top and the tail gunner's station roof. It was also used on other Tupolev types (the Tu-95K-22 *Bear-G* and some versions of the Tu-22). Hence it was known as UKhO (*oonifitseerovannyy khvostovoy otsek* – standardised tail compartment), and the spelling of the Russian acronym coincided with the Russian word *ookho* (ear).

Left: The nose of Tu-16K-26 '54 Red' which was tested at GNIKI VVS.

Below left: A schematic drawing of the flight deck of the Tu-16K-26, with the captain's right control console to the left of the passage leading to the navigator's station.

Right: A KSR-5 missile on the port pylon of a Tu-16K-26 in cruise flight.

Below right: A steamy wake streams from the missile's turbo pump nozzle immediately before launch.

Bottom right: The KSR-5 falls away from the pylon, the ventral fin unfolding as it does.

Bottom, far right: A KSR-5 missile belches flames as it accelerates to cruising speed.

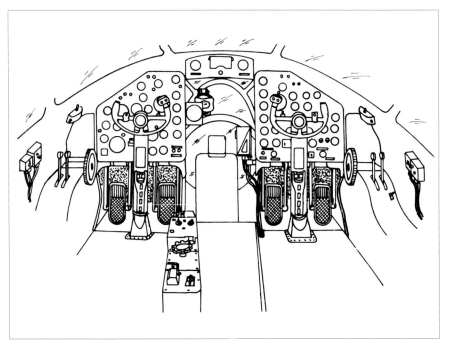

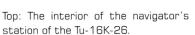

Top: The interior of the navigator's station of the Tu-16K-26.

Above: The Nav/Op's workstation of a Tu-16K-26.

Left: A red-painted prototype KSR-5 missile on its ground handling dolly with the ventral fin folded.

Performance of the Tu-16K-26	
Empty weight	39,480 kg (87,040 lb)
Take-off weight:	
normal	75,800 kg (167,110 lb)
maximum (exceptional combat conditions)	79,000 kg (174,170 lb)
Fuel capacity	43,800 litres (9,636 Imp gal)
Maximum true airspeed at full engine power, with one or two missiles:	
at up to 500 m (1,640 ft)	550 km/h (341 mph)
at 6,000 m (19,685 ft)	720 km/h (447 mph)
at 8,000 m (26,250 ft)	820 km/h (509 mph)
at 10,000 m (32,810 ft)	900 km/h (559 mph)
Maximum permissible Mach number with one or two missiles	0.88
Service ceiling with one or two ASMs, a 62,000-kg (136,680-lb) TOW and engines at nominal power	12,300 m (40,350 ft)
Operational range at optimum altitude with a normal AUW, one ASM launched at midpoint and landing with 5% fuel reserves	4,800 km (2,981 miles)
Combat radius at Mach 0.72	2,150-2,180 km (1,335-1,354 miles)
Ordnance load:	
one KSR-11 missile	4,000 kg (8,820 lb)
two KSR-11 missiles	8,000 kg (17,640 lb)
one KSR-5 missile	3,900 kg (8,600 lb)
two KSR-5 missiles	7,800 kg (17,200 lb)
one KSR-2 missile	4,100 kg (9,040 lb)
two KSR-2 missiles	8,200 kg (18,080 lb)

Tu-16KSR-2-5 bomber/missile strike aircraft ('order 386A'; *izdeliye* NKSR-2-5, *izdeliye* NK-5)

110 examples of the Tu-16KSR-2 missile strike aircraft and Tu-16KSR-2A bomber/missile strike aircraft were also converted for the K-26 system under the terms of 'order 386A', similarly to the conversions of the Tu-16K-11-16KS into the Tu-16K-26 and the Tu-16KSR-2-11 into the Tu-16KSR-2-5-11. The product code was initially *izdeliye* NKSR-2-5 but was later shortened to *izdeliye* NK-5.

The Tu-16KSR-2-5 could be used as a bomber and carried two KSR-2 or KSR-5 missiles of various subtypes (including the KSR-5NM target drone). Unlike the two preceding modifications, the Tu-16K-26 and Tu-16KSR-2-5-11, the Rubin-Ritsa link equipment was not installed and the aircraft was not able to carry the KSR-11 or KSR-5P anti-shipping missiles. The aircraft had an empty weight of 41,020 kg (90,430 lb), a normal take-off weight of 75,800 kg (167,110 lb) and a maximum TOW of 79,000 kg (174,170 lb).

The equipment fitted to the Tu-16KSR-2-5 differed from that of the Tu-16K-26 in that it included an SP-50 ILS, and later an active ECM capability provided by SPS-5M and interchangeable SPS-151/-152/-153 Siren' jammers. The reconnaissance and target-indicating equipment was omitted, as was the bomb-

Above: The Tu-16KSR-2-5 prototype, '16 Red' (c/n 8204111/tail number 8211), seen during trials carrying two KSR-2s.

Below and bottom: An operational Tu-16KSR-2-5 coded '10 Red' carrying KSR-5s. The aircraft is fitted with an SRO-1P Parol' IFF transponder (note the triangular blade aerial on the nose).

sight (although some Tu-16KSR-2-5s retained their OPB-112 bombsight which came into use once more when they were reconverted to bomber capability under the terms of 'order 684/2'). The version had the same defensive armament as the Tu-16A.

The Tu-16KSR-2-5 retained the forward-firing cannon on the starboard side of the nose and hence the PKI reflector gunsight. Outwardly it differed from the Tu-16K-26 in lacking the abovementioned patches on the bomb bay doors; it also had a different kind of aerial on the flight deck roof as compared to the Tu-16KSR-2A.

Top: This Tu-16KSR-2-5 has an identity crisis, being coded '16 Red' on the nose gear doors and '18 Blue' on the fin. The code was changed on the nose after transfer to another unit but no one remembered to change the one on the tail!

Above: Like the aircraft on the left, this Tu-16KSR-2-5 has a Siren'-D jammer (note the antenna fairings on the nose and under the air intakes).

Right: A Tu-16KSR-2-5 wearing the 'anti-flash' colour scheme and the huge code '01 Blue' on the fin.

Above left: In the course of service some Tu-16s were retrofitted with the A-326 Rogovitsa formation keeping system. Its display is visible above the passage to the navigator's station.

Below: A drawing from a Tupolev OKB album showing the performance of the Tu-16 with the K-11, K-16 and K-26 weapons systems. The blanket designation Tu-16K was sometimes used for them.

The prototype was coded '16 Red' (c/n 8204111, tail number 8211) and featured pairs of ring-shaped aerials on the tail cannons (presumably for a data link system which was part of the test equipment). After completing manufacturer's tests and state acceptance trials the Tu-16KSR-2-5 was officially cleared for service by Council of Ministers directive No.1118-514 issued on 30th December 1961.

СИСТЕМЫ Ту-16к

ВАРИАНТЫ БОЕВОЙ ЗАГРУЗКИ
1. По две ракеты „Воздух-Земля" КСР-11 (система К-11)
    КСР-2 (система К-16)
    К-5 (система К-26)
2. Спецбомбы изделия №-246 и 7V
3. Авиабомбы калибра от 100 до 9000кг

ПРИМЕЧАНИЕ : СИСТЕМЫ К-11 И К-16 РАЗМЕЩАЮТСЯ НА ОДНОМ И ТОМ ЖЕ САМОЛЕТЕ ПОД ШИФРОМ ТУ-16К 11-16

		СИСТЕМА К-11	СИСТЕМА К-16	СИСТЕМА К-26
РАДИУС ДЕЙСТВИЯ СИСТЕМЫ С ДВУМЯ РАКЕТАМИ	[КМ]	2000	1900	2100
КРЕЙСЕРСКАЯ СКОРОСТЬ ПОЛЕТА САМОЛЕТА-НОСИТЕЛЯ				
ПРИ ПУСКЕ РАКЕТ НА Н-10000М	[КМ/ЧАС]	750-800	750-800	750-800
МАКСИМАЛЬНАЯ ДАЛЬНОСТЬ ПУСКА РАКЕТ	[КМ]	170	140-150	200-240
ВЫСОТА ПУСКА РАКЕТ	[М]	4000-10000	4000-10000	900-11000
ВЗЛЕТНЫЙ ВЕС САМОЛЕТА	[Т]	75,8	75,8	75,8
ДАННЫЕ РАКЕТ:		КСР-11	КСР-2	КСР-5
МАКСИМАЛЬНАЯ СКОРОСТЬ ПОЛЕТА	[КМ/ЧАС]	1150-1260	1200-1250	2500-3000
ВЫСОТА ПОЛЕТА	[М]			22000-25000
СТАРТОВЫЙ ВЕС	[КГ]	4100	4100	3500

ГЕОМЕТРИЧЕСКИЕ РАЗМЕРЫ

РАЗМАХ _____ 34,0 м
ДЛИНА _____ 35,2 м
ВЫСОТА _____ 9,95 м
КОЛЕЯ ШАССИ ____ 9,78 м

Left (opposite page) and right: The external features of the A-326 system were the antennas on the flight deck roof and low on the port side of the nose.

Far right: The control panel of the Rogovitsa system. When in use, this panel and the display obstructed the passage to the navigator's station.

Below: A Tu-16KSR-2-5 refitted with a Rubin-1M radar.

A performance comparison of the K-26 weapons system (Tu-16K-26 or Tu-16KSR-2-5-11) with the three compatible missiles			
	KSR-11	**KSR-2**	**KSR-5**
Combat radius with two missiles, km (miles)	2,000 (1,242)	1,900 (1,180)	2,100 (1,304)
Cruising speed during missile launch at 10,000 m (32,810 ft), km/h (mph)	750-800 (465-496)	750-800 (465-496)	750-800 (465-496)
Maximum launch range, km (miles)	170 (105)	140-150 (87-93)	200-240 (124-149)
Launch altitude, m (ft)	4,000-10,000 (13,120-32,810)	4,000-10,000 (13,120-32,810)	900-11,000 (2,950-36,090)
Take-off weight, kg (lb)	75,800 (167,110)	75,800 (167,110)	75,800 (167,110)
Missile's maximum speed, km/h (mph)	1,150-1,260 (714-782)	1,200-1,250 (745-776)	2,300-3,000 (1,428-1,963)
Missile cruise altitude, m (ft)	9,700 (31,820)	n.a.	22,000-25,000 (72,180-82,020)

Tu-16KSR-2-5-11 bomber/missile strike aircraft ('order 386A'; izdeliye NKSR-2-5-11, izdeliye NK-5)

Under the terms of the same 'order 386A' 125 examples of the Tu-16KSR-2-11 (which retained bomber capability) were also re-equipped with the K-26 weapons system in similar manner to the Tu-16K-26, carrying a pair of KSR-2, KSR-11 or KSR-5 missiles of various subtypes (excluding the KSR-5P). Such aircraft bore the cumbersome service designation Tu-16KSR-2-5-11 and the product code izdeliye NKSR-2-5-11 (which, again, was later simplified to izdeliye NK-5).

Outwardly the Tu-16KSR-2-5-11s differed from the Tu-16K-26 in lacking the patches on the bomb bay doors and the partial 'anti-flash' white colour scheme. Aircraft thus modified became one of the standard missile-carrying versions of the Tu-16. They also differed from the Tu-16KSR-2-5 in retaining the distinctive inverted-

T aerial array of the Ritsa radar homing system on the navigator's station glazing from pre-conversion times and, accordingly, lacking the NU-88 nose cannon installation. Some examples were retrofitted with the SPS-5 Fasol' jammer.

Tu-16K-26 missile strike aircraft with Berkut radar

One source mentions that 14 examples of the Tu-16K-26 were refitted with the **Berkut** (Golden Eagle) 360° search radar – the same model as fitted to the Il-38 ASW aircraft. The Berkut had a larger antenna, necessitating installation of a larger radome. These 14 aircraft saw service with the Baltic Fleet Air Arm.

Tu-16K-26 missile strike aircraft with Rubin-1M radar

From 1973 onwards some Tu-16K-26s were fitted with the Rubin-1M radar developed in 1973. This was an upgraded version of the

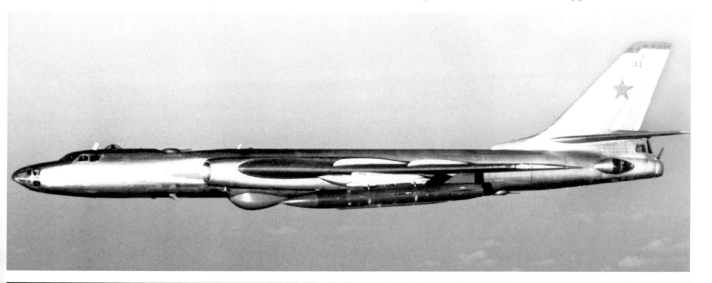

Left: The Rubin-1M radar was bulkier and heavier than the Rubin-1KV and thus had to be relocated to a position amidships, the former position of the radar being faired over. This aircraft carries an interesting mix of missiles – a KSR-2 to port and a KSR-5 to starboard.

Below: Another Tu-16K-26 refitted with a Rubin-1M radar. The aircraft was photographed from a Swedish Air Force fighter; the red-painted trim tabs identify it as a Navy aircraft. When one missile was carried, it was always on the port pylon due to peculiarities of the landing approach.

Rubin-1KV (hence M for *modernizeerovannyy* – updated) offering greater detection range – up to 450 km (279 miles) – and higher resolution. The Rubin-1M had a much larger antenna giving a higher amplification coefficient and a 33% narrower beam. However, the new antenna and the bulkier and heavier radar set proved impossible to accommodate in the usual chin position for space and CG reasons; hence the radar was moved aft to a position below the wing centre section. As a result, the refitted aircraft was quite different in appearance from the other Tu-16 missile strike versions, being readily identifiable by the enlarged and reshaped teardrop radome under the centre fuselage and the lack of the standard flattened chin radome whose position was faired over. Oddly enough, this did not bring about any changes to the NATO reporting name.

The new radar installation necessitated the removal of the No.3 fuel tank located below the wing centre section, reducing the fuel capacity by 3,150 litres (693 Imp gal). The NU-88 nose cannon installation was deleted as a weight-saving measure.

Tu-16KSR-2-5 missile strike aircraft with Rubin-1M radar
From 1973 onwards some Tu-16KSR-2-5s were likewise fitted with the Rubin-1M radar in a relocated and enlarged radome. This version lacked the Ritsa radar homing system and therefore could not carry anti-radar missiles. Outwardly it differed from the version detailed above in lacking the distinctive aerial array on the nose glazing. Like the Tu-16K-26 with the Rubin-1M, it lacked the nose cannon. This version subsequently served as the basis for the Tu-16 Tsiklon-N weather research aircraft (see Chapter 5).

Tu-16K-26M missile strike aircraft (*izdeliye* NK-26M)
In the late 1970s the KSR-5 ASM was updated as the KSR-5B with a new VS-KM seeker head and a new BSU-7M autopilot allowing them to strike at smaller and more difficult targets. Several Tu-16K-26 were modified for this weapons system, known as the K-26M (*modernizeerovannaya*); accordingly the designation was amended to Tu-16K-26M.

K-26N long-range stand-off weapons system
Tu-16K-26N missile strike aircraft
('order 2226', *izdeliye* NK-26N)

The K-26N system (*nizkovysotnaya* – low-altitude) was based on the KSR-5N air-to-surface missile, which had a VS-KN radar seeker and a new APR-5N autopilot (*avtopeelot rakety* – missile autopilot). Hence aircraft equipped to carry this version had a Rubin-1M radar with modifications for low-level operations under the centre fuselage instead of the chin-mounted Rubin-1KV radar and were redesignated Tu-16K-26N. The product code was izdeliye NK-26N.

A small number of Tu-16K-26s, Tu-16K-26Ps, Tu-16KSR-2-5s and Tu-16KSR-2-5-11s were updated to Tu-16-26N configuration in accordance with 'order 2226' and served with the Naval Aviation in the 1980s. If the KSR-5N was used by the already mentioned versions without modification, it was launched at the same altitude as the KSR-5, subsequently descending to its designated flight altitude to enable stealthy approach to the target.

K-26P long-range stand-off weapons system
Tu-16K-26P bomber/missile strike (SEAD) aircraft
('order 397', *izdeliye* NK-26P)

A passive radar homing version of the *Kingfish* was developed in due course. Designated KSR-5P (*protivorahdiolokatsionnaya [raketa]* – ARM). This missile differed from the regular KSR-5 in having a VS-P passive radar seeker head (some sources call it 2PRG-10) and was designed for destroying shore-based and shipboard radars working in search or tracking mode – both stable-frequency units and those whose operating parameters change smoothly or incrementally. Outwardly the KSR-5P was identifiable by the black circle markings of 200 mm (7⅞ in) diameter painted on above the fuselage waterline at the forward/centre fuselage joint.

Hence the K-26P weapons system based on this missile was developed in accordance with Council of Ministers directive No.123-43 of 7th February 1964, although some documents confusingly state its development was triggered by ruling No.14 issued by the CofM Presidium's Commission on Defence Industry Matters (VPK – *Voyenno-promyshlennaya komissiya*) on 21st June 1976. The system's other main component was the Tu-16K-26P aircraft – a 'Wild Weasel' version of the Tu-16KSR-2-5-11 refitted with the Plot (Raft) passive radar detection/guidance system compatible with the new missile; the P again stood for *protivorahdiolokatsionnyy* (anti-radar, used attributively). The Plot system comprised the ANP-K display showing the location of the hostile radars (which was linked to the Ritsa radar detection system), the missile's VSP-K guidance system and its BSU-7N autopilot.

The two missiles could be launched against the same target or different targets without manoeuvring the aircraft (in the latter case, however, one of the targets had to be in line with the aircraft's flight path and the other within a ±7° sector). After launching the missiles the aircraft was able to turn away. Again, it was possible to carry a mixed complement of weapons – one missile and up to 4,000 kg (8,820 lb) of bombs.

The standard K-26 equipment fit was retained so that KSR-5, KSR-2 or KSR-11 missiles could be carried; only the Siren' jam-

mer was omitted (probably because it would interfere with the mission avionics). On the other hand, the aircraft had an SP-50 ILS.

The Tu-16K-26P prototype was modified under the terms of 'order 397', commencing its manufacturer's flight tests in the summer of 1967. State acceptance trials began in April 1972. On 4th September 1973, the K-26P system was cleared for Soviet Navy service by Council of Ministers directive No.643-205. Conversions of Tu-16KSR-2-5-11s to Tu-16K-26P standard were carried out at Naval Aviation repair and maintenance bases. Outwardly such aircraft differed from the Tu-16KSR-2-5-11 in lacking the Siren' ECM antennas, and from the 'pure' Tu-16K-26 in lacking the patches on the bomb bay doors as well.

A tragic accident occurred in the course of the state acceptance trials. The Tu-16K-26P prototype, which had taken off from Akhtoobinsk, was to destroy a low-powered radar acting as a practice target at a test range near the city of Goor'yev (now called Atyrau) on the Caspian Sea coast in western Kazakhstan. During the first pass, which was a 'dry run', the guidance system detected the target and achieved a lock-on; the launch took place on the second pass. As the Tu-16 approached the target, the WSO noticed that the target blip on his radarscope was brighter and farther to the right than before; yet he didn't give it much thought because the blip had been to the right of the aircraft's flight path on the first run, too. However, the crew was unaware that the aircraft had strayed to the south within the confines of the target approach corridor and, by the greatest bad luck, the guidance system had locked on to the ATC radar at Goor'yev airport. Normally a blanket ban on radar operations in the area would be imposed before such a test; however, due to the negligence of some officer in the General Staff the banning order had not reached Goor'yev on time. The radar was on, and of course the KSR-5P went for the stronger signal of this radar instead of the proper target.

All at once the aghast WSO saw a second blip to the left on the radarscope and realised what had happened. Just then, however, the banning order belatedly reached Goor'yev airport; the radar was shut down, and the missile, which had already begun its terminal dive, went ballistic after losing the signal. The missile came

Specifications of the K-26P missile system	
Maximum operational range of the Tu-16K-26P carrying two ASMs at optimum altitudes, without IFR, with missile launch at a distance of 330 km (205 miles) from the target:	
with 5% of fuel remaining on landing:	
with a 75,800-kg (167,110-lb) take-off weight	2,240 km (1,391 miles)
with a 79,000-kg (174,170-lb) take-off weight	2,400 km (1,490 miles)
with 10% of fuel remaining on landing:	
with a 75,800-kg take-off weight	2,130 km (1,323 miles)
with a 79,000-kg take-off weight	2,330 km (1,447 miles)
Missile launch altitude	9,000–11,000 m (29,530–36,090 ft)
Range of the KSR-5P missile:	
maximum (with launch at 11,000 m/36,090 ft)	330 km (205 miles)
minimum (with launch at 9,000 m/29,530 ft)	100 km (62.1 miles)
Average speed of the KSR-5P in cruise flight	3,000 km/h (1,863 mph)
The missile's impact speed	450 m/sec (1,476 ft/sec)

down in a residential area next to the airport; luckily it was an instrumented test round with no warhead, still it destroyed several houses, killing eight civilians. A huge investigation was mounted; the luckless crew was fired from the Air Force but escaped prosecution, and the entire command staff of GNIKI VVS received disciplinary punishment. It is not known whether the main culprit – the General Staff officer responsible for the untimely order – was punished.

Left: Tu-16K-26P '06 Red' showing the Ritsa system allowing it to carry KSR-5P ARMs.

Below left and bottom left: Two views of Tu-16K-26P '72 Red'. Like '06 Red', it also has the A-326 system and an SPS-5 Fasol' jammer with blade aerials flanking the nosewheel well.

Below: Upper view of a Tu-16K-26P. The empty missile pylons are not visible from this angle but the fixed strips closing the cut-outs in the flaps are visible. Note the engine turbostarter exhaust ports.

Tu-16K-26PM missile strike aircraft (*izdeliye* NK-26PM)

All KSR-5s in operational service had their guidance systems progressively updated to KSR-5N standard to achieve fleetwide maintenance and performance commonality; the missiles thus upgraded were known as KSR-5Bs. Eventually most KSR-5s *sans suffixe* and KSR-5Bs were further upgraded to full KSR-5N standard, receiving the designation KSR-5M (*modernizeerovannaya* – updated). Hence some Tu-16K-26s were equipped for carrying KSR-5M and KSR-11 missiles as part of the K-26PM long-range weapons system. Such aircraft were designated Tu-16K-26PM (*izdeliye* NK-26PM) and were equipped with the ANP-K communicator linking the aircraft and missile radars.

Tu-16K-26B bomber/missile strike aircraft ('order 684/2', *izdeliye* NK-26B)

This was a sub-variant of the Tu-16K-26 modified under the terms of 'order 684/2' to carry a greater load of bombs or mines carried both internally and externally. The B referred to the bomb arma-

ment (*bombardirovochnoye vo'oruzheniye*). Part of the ordnance load was carried on BD3-16K bomb racks attached to the BD-352-11-5 missile pylons.

Tu-16K-26-07 missile strike aircraft
One more sub-variant of the Tu-16K-26 fitted with an L007 active jammer for individual protection was designated Tu-16K-26-07.

Tu-16K-22 development aircraft ('order 294/3')
When the Council of Ministers issued directive No.426-201 concerning the development of the Tu-105A (Tu-22) on 17th April 1958, the document contained an item requiring the development of the K-22 long-range weapons system. The latter comprised the Tu-22K missile strike aircraft, the aforementioned Kh-22 air-to-surface missile and the appropriate guidance system (likewise referred to as K-22).

As part of the K-22 weapons system's development programme a single Tu-16 ASM carrier loaned from a first-line Air Force unit was fitted with test instrumentation under the terms of 'order 294/3', acting as a weapons testbed for the Kh-22. Known as the Tu-16K-22, it served successfully for several years during the development of the Kh-22 and its Tu-22K *Blinder-B*, Tu-22M

Backfire and Tu-95K-22 *Bear-G* missile platforms. Some sources, though, say that only the missile's seeker head was fitted in the form of a fixed acquisition round, making the aircraft an avionics testbed.

Tu-16 missile carriers with restored and increased bombing capability
(Tu-16KSR-2, Tu-16KSR-2A, Tu-16K-11-16, Tu-16K-26 and Tu-16KSR-2-5 modified under the terms of 'order 684/1' and 'order 684/2')
In 1969 it was decided to expand the Tu-16's tactical capabilities by refitting some of the missile-toting versions with restored and increased capability to carry bombs or naval mines. In early 1970 Tu-16KSR-2-5 c/n 6203130 was modified in accordance with specifications passed by the Naval Aviation's Engineering Service on 16th March (the bomb racks and the hydraulic bomb bay door actuation system were reinstated); the conversion was carried out by the AVMF's ARZ No.20 (*aviaremontnyy zavod* – aircraft repair plant) in Pushkin, Leningrad Region. Check-up tests were held by the 33rd TsBP I PLS in Nikolayev on 8th June – 1st July 1970, with Lt.-Col. S. P. Dombrovskiy as project test pilot and Lt.-Col. N. V. Rostovskiy as engineer in charge.

With restored bombing capability the machine could carry a normal internal load of 3,000 kg (6,610 lb) and a maximum load of 9,000 kg (19,840 lb) as an alternative to ASMs; provision was made for carrying part of the bombs externally on BD3-16K multiple racks attached to the wing pylons, thereby increasing the maximum bomb load to 13,000 kg (28,660 lb). The maximum number of free-fall bombs carried was two FAB-3000 M-46 or FAB-3000 M-54 bombs; six FAB-1500 M-46 or FAB-1500 M-54 bombs; 18 FAB-500 M-46/FAB-500 M-54 high-drag bombs or twelve 500-kg M-62 series low-drag bombs with longer bodies, with the exception of the IAB-500 practice bombs emulating a nuclear explosion (*imitatsionnaya aviabomba* – 'simulation bomb'); 24 FAB-250 M-46/FAB-250 M-54 high-drag bombs or eighteen FAB-250 M-62 low-drag bombs; and 24 OFAB-100 bombs (*oskolochno-foogahsnaya aviabomba* – HE/fragmentation bomb). Parachute-retarded bombs could be carried for low-level strike missions; in this case the number was reduced to 16 OFAB-100NVs (*nizkovysotnaya* – low-altitude), OFAB-100-120s, OFAB-250-270s or OFAB-250 M-54s, or 12 FAB-500 M-46s retrofitted with TU-500 M-46 parabrakes (*tormoznoye oostroystvo* – braking device). Up to eight mines similar in size to 500-kg (1,102-lb) bombs or 12 mines similar in size to 1,500-kg (3,306-lb) bombs could be carried.

The aircraft made two flights totalling 5 hours 1 minute, dropping a total of 28 P-50-75 practice bombs; the results were good and the modification was approved. The following table shows the aircraft's weight data as recorded during the tests.

Almost simultaneously, between March and June 1970, GNIKI VVS carried out trials on Tu-16KSR-2A c/n 5201604 refitted at plant No.22 in Kazan' (referred to as the Tu-16A-KSR-2 in documents) with increased bomb loads of up to 13,000 kg (28,660 lb), including 4,000 kg (8,820 lb) carried externally. The aircraft attained a maximum speed of 820 km/h (509 mph) at 7,550 m (24,770 ft) and had a service ceiling of 11,100 m (36,420 ft), with a take-off weight of 60,000 kg (132,280 lb). At optimum altitudes and with a 13,000 kg bomb load the aircraft had a maximum operational range of 2,820 km (1,751 miles) with a maximum take-off weight of 79,000 kg (174,170 lb) and 2,400 km (1,4191 miles) with a take-off of 75,800 kg (167,110 lb).

In comparison with the original Tu-16KSR-2 carrying two KSR-2 missiles, the range with a 13,000-kg bomb load and with a 75,800-kg TOW was reduced by 1,430 km (888 miles) due to the smaller fuel load and increased fuel consumption.

The tests carried out on these two aircraft gave good results. Therefore repair and maintenance factories carried out work on restoring the bomber capability (as per 'order 684/2') on the Tu-16KSR-2, Tu-16K-11-16, Tu-16K-26 and Tu-16KSR-2-5, and on increasing this capability (as per 'order 684/1') on the Tu-16A, Tu-16KSR-2A and Tu-16KSR-2-11.

Weights of Tu-16KSR-2-5 c/n 6203130 with restored bombing capability	
Take-off weight:	
normal	75,800 kg (167,110 lb)
maximum	79,000 kg (174,170 lb)
Payload for normal TOW:	
crew (six)	600 kg (1,320 lb)
cannon ammunition (1,800 rounds)	700 kg (1,543 lb)
bombs	2,400-13,000 kg (5,290-28,660 lb)
fuel	31,475-24,875 kg (69,390-54,840 lb)
engine starter fuel and oil	50 kg (110 lb)
oxygen	60 kg (132 lb)
Landing weight:	
normal	48,000 kg (105,820 lb)
maximum	52,000 kg (114,640 lb)
maximum (exceptional cases)	57,000 kg (125,660 lb)
Payload for normal landing weight:	
crew (six)	600 kg (1,320 lb)
cannon ammunition (50% remaining)	350 kg (771 lb)
fuel	6,455 kg (14,230 lb)
engine starter fuel and oil	25 kg (55 lb)
oxygen	30 kg (66 lb)
CG position:	
at normal TOW	21.3-23.7% MAC
at maximum TOW	21 0-23.3% MAC
at normal landing weight	23.9% MAC

K-10 long-range anti-shipping strike weapons system
Tu-16K-10 missile strike aircraft
('order 238'; *izdeliye* NK-10, *izdeliye* NK-1)

The co-operation between the Mikoyan and Tupolev design bureaux in the development of air-to-surface missile system

Above left: A Tu-16K-26B missile strike aircraft with increased bomb carrying capability. The BD3-16K multiple racks are half empty here.

Left: Close-up of the starboard BD3-16K rack on a Tu-16K-26B fully loaded with eight FAB-250 M-54 high-drag bombs. Note the special projections at the top matching the BD-352-11-5 pylon's sway braces.

Right: Heave-ho, part 2: four men can act as a substitute for a bomb hoist if needs must! Here a Tu-16K-26B is being loaded with FAB-250 M-62 low-drag bombs.

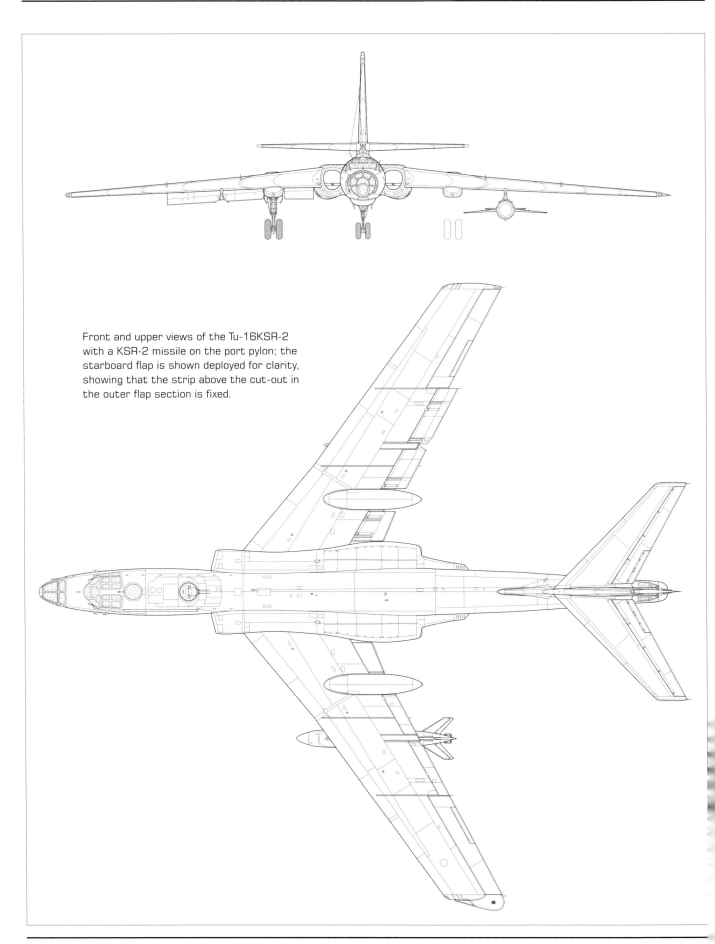

Front and upper views of the Tu-16KSR-2
with a KSR-2 missile on the port pylon; the
starboard flap is shown deployed for clarity,
showing that the strip above the cut-out in
the outer flap section is fixed.

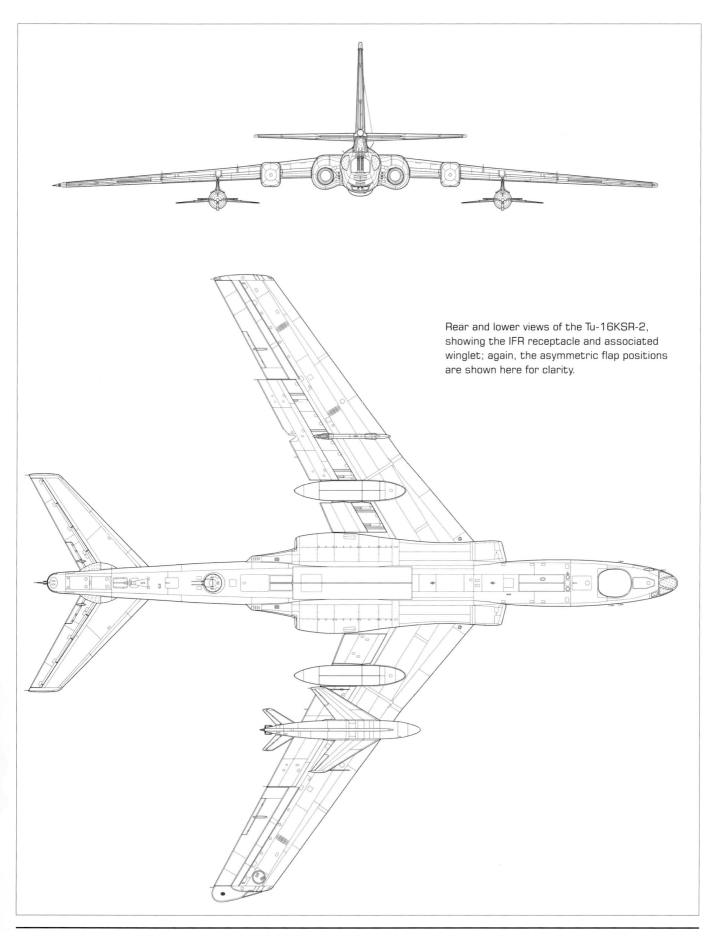

Rear and lower views of the Tu-16KSR-2, showing the IFR receptacle and associated winglet; again, the asymmetric flap positions are shown here for clarity.

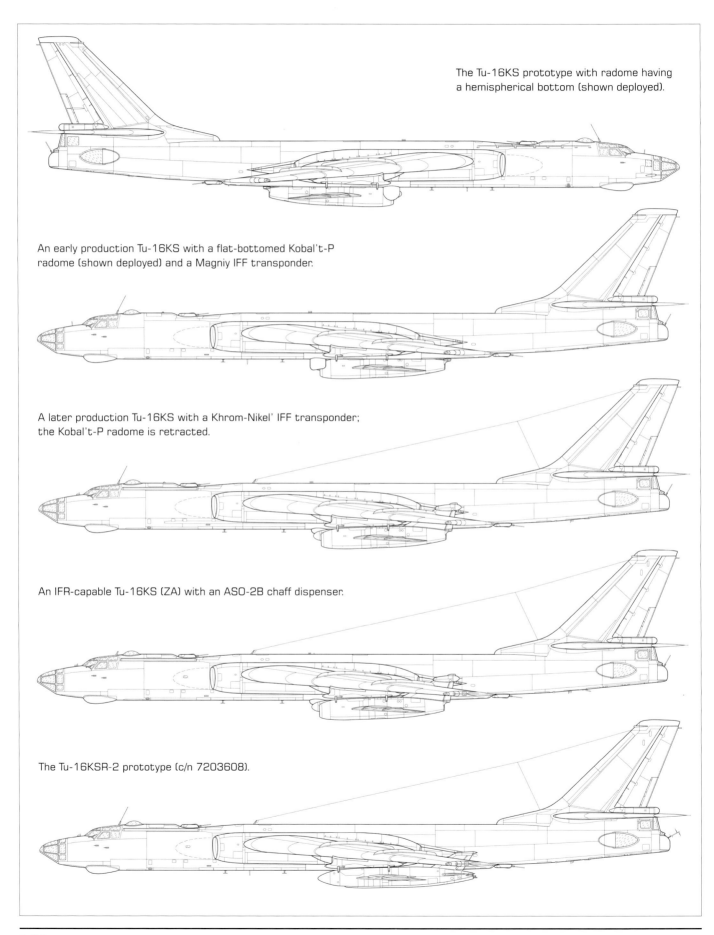

The Tu-16KS prototype with radome having a hemispherical bottom (shown deployed).

An early production Tu-16KS with a flat-bottomed Kobal't-P radome (shown deployed) and a Magniy IFF transponder.

A later production Tu-16KS with a Khrom-Nikel' IFF transponder; the Kobal't-P radome is retracted.

An IFR-capable Tu-16KS (ZA) with an ASO-2B chaff dispenser.

The Tu-16KSR-2 prototype (c/n 7203608).

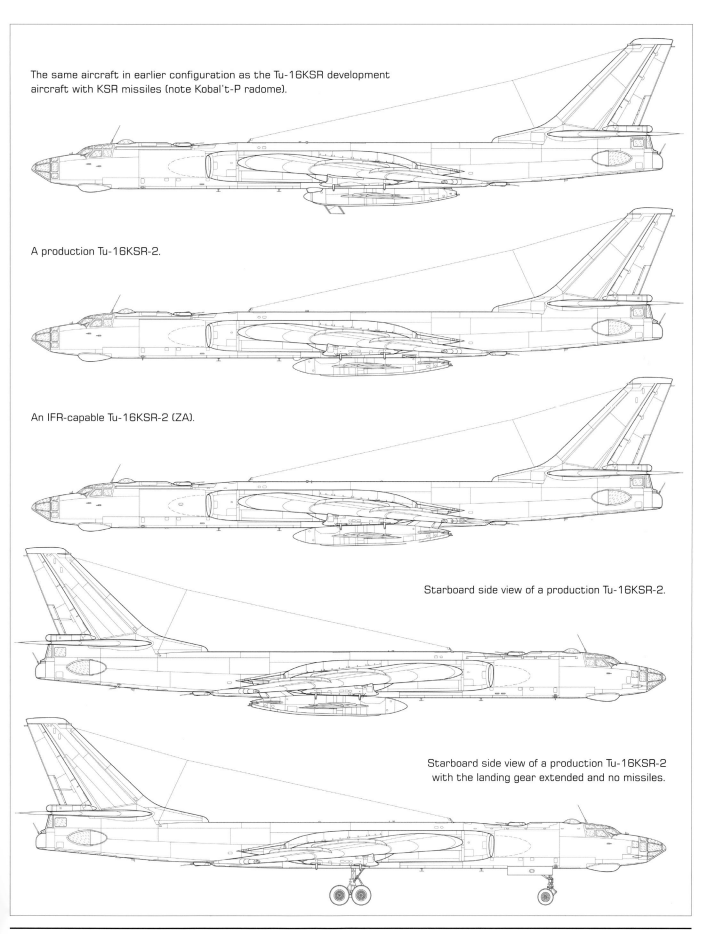

The same aircraft in earlier configuration as the Tu-16KSR development aircraft with KSR missiles (note Kobal't-P radome).

A production Tu-16KSR-2.

An IFR-capable Tu-16KSR-2 (ZA).

Starboard side view of a production Tu-16KSR-2.

Starboard side view of a production Tu-16KSR-2 with the landing gear extended and no missiles.

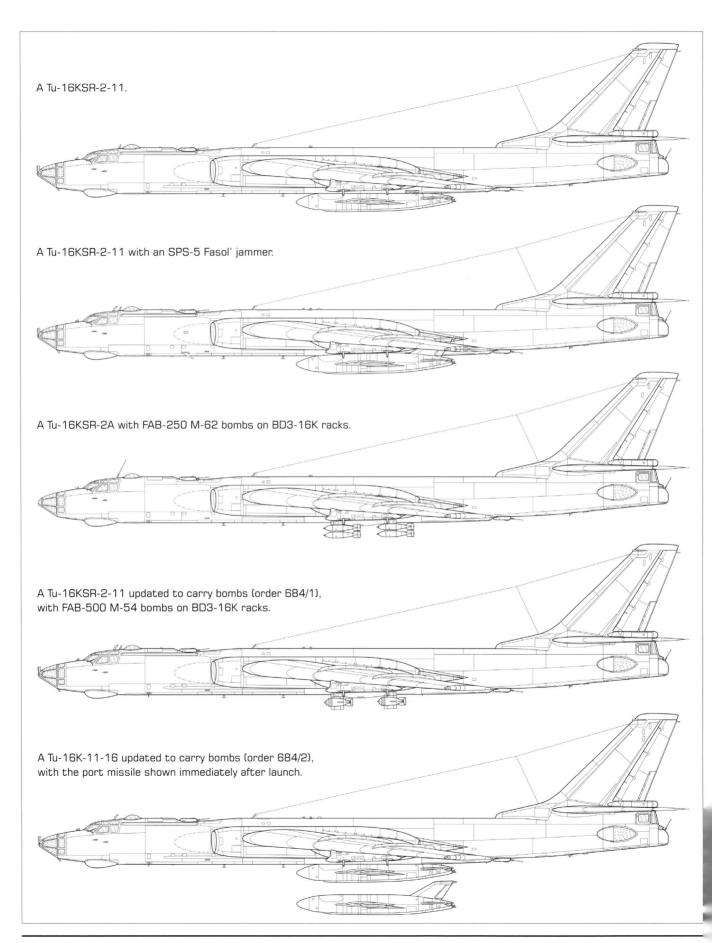

A Tu-16KSR-2-11.

A Tu-16KSR-2-11 with an SPS-5 Fasol' jammer.

A Tu-16KSR-2A with FAB-250 M-62 bombs on BD3-16K racks.

A Tu-16KSR-2-11 updated to carry bombs (order 684/1),
with FAB-500 M-54 bombs on BD3-16K racks.

A Tu-16K-11-16 updated to carry bombs (order 684/2),
with the port missile shown immediately after launch.

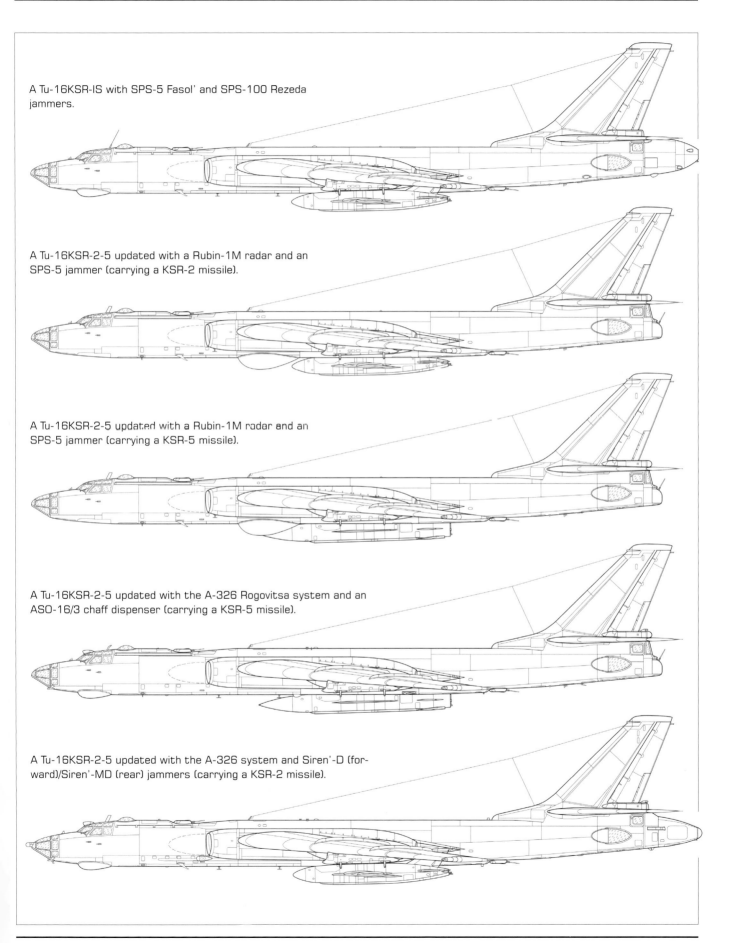

A Tu-16KSR-IS with SPS-5 Fasol' and SPS-100 Rezeda jammers.

A Tu-16KSR-2-5 updated with a Rubin-1M radar and an SPS-5 jammer (carrying a KSR-2 missile).

A Tu-16KSR-2-5 updated with a Rubin-1M radar and an SPS-5 jammer (carrying a KSR-5 missile).

A Tu-16KSR-2-5 updated with the A-326 Rogovitsa system and an ASO-16/3 chaff dispenser (carrying a KSR-5 missile).

A Tu-16KSR-2-5 updated with the A-326 system and Siren'-D (forward)/Siren'-MD (rear) jammers (carrying a KSR-2 missile).

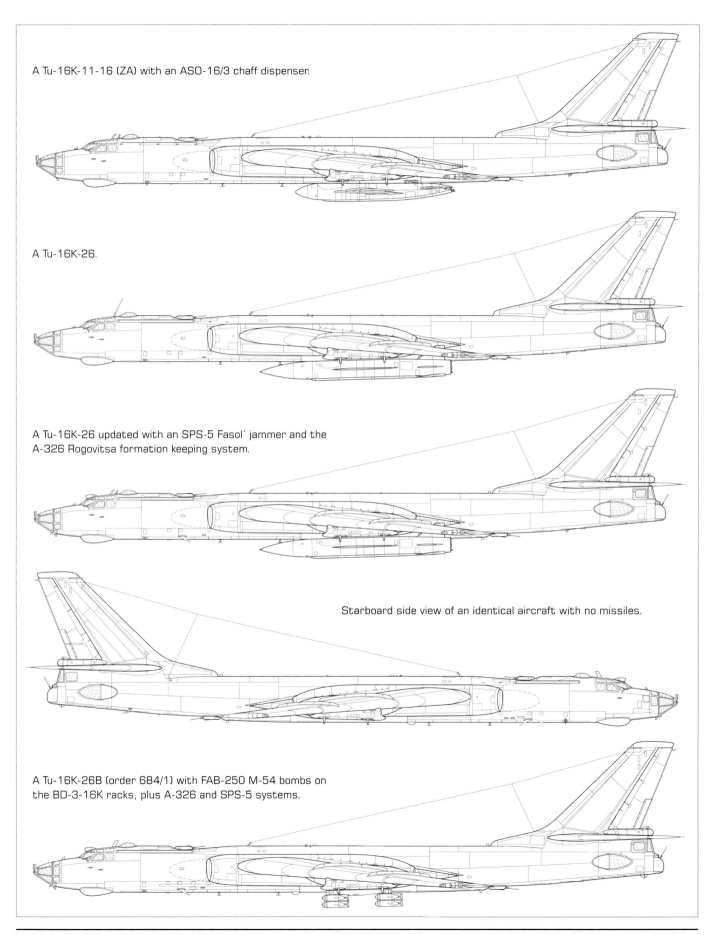

A Tu-16K-11-16 (ZA) with an ASO-16/3 chaff dispenser.

A Tu-16K-26.

A Tu-16K-26 updated with an SPS-5 Fasol' jammer and the A-326 Rogovitsa formation keeping system.

Starboard side view of an identical aircraft with no missiles.

A Tu-16K-26B (order 684/1) with FAB-250 M-54 bombs on the BD-3-16K racks, plus A-326 and SPS-5 systems.

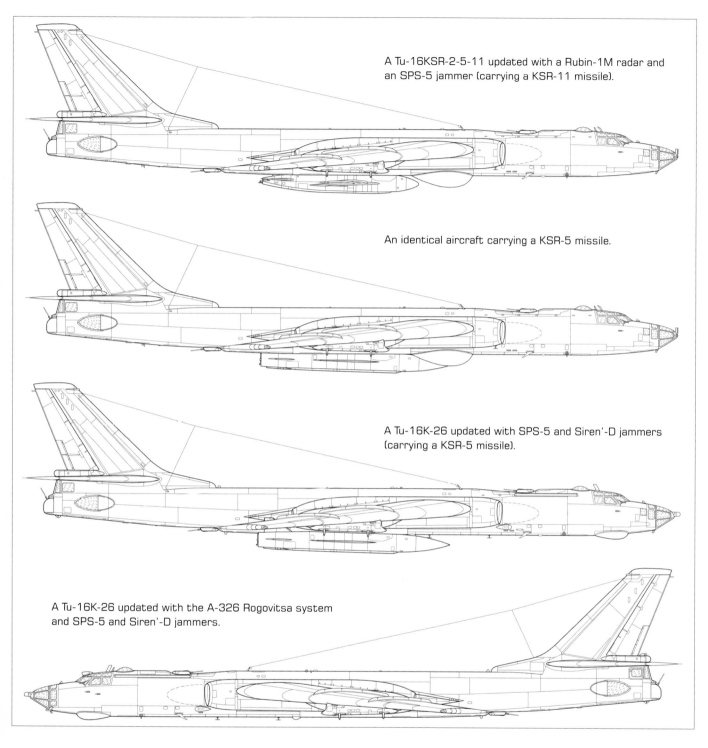

A Tu-16KSR-2-5-11 updated with a Rubin-1M radar and an SPS-5 jammer (carrying a KSR-11 missile).

An identical aircraft carrying a KSR-5 missile.

A Tu-16K-26 updated with SPS-5 and Siren'-D jammers (carrying a KSR-5 missile).

A Tu-16K-26 updated with the A-326 Rogovitsa system and SPS-5 and Siren'-D jammers.

received a new impetus when on 3rd February 1955, the Council of Ministers issued directive No.178-110 kicking off development of the K-10 (Kometa-10) long-range stand-off weapons system for the AVMF. This was to be used primarily against large surface ships with a displacement in excess of 10,000 tons, such as aircraft carriers. Mikoyan's OKB-155 was to create the anti-shipping cruise missile and Tupolev's OKB-156 was to provide the weapons platform – again based on the Tu-16. 16th November 1955, saw the issuance of a further CofM directive, No.1946-1045, whereby plant No.22 in Kazan' was tasked with modifying a Tu-16 into the

prototype of a new missile strike aircraft by 1st March 1957, using drawings supplied by OKB-156; the aircraft was designated Tu-16K-10.

Despite the similar name of the weapons system, the K-10 missile designed by OKB-2-155 had little in common with the KS-1, apart from being turbojet-powered; in fact, it was closer to the rocket-powered KSR-2. It was a supersonic missile which would offer a significantly greater 'kill' range and a 150% improvement in accuracy over the KS-1. The missile had a mid-wing layout with a slender circular-section fuselage whose forward section tipped

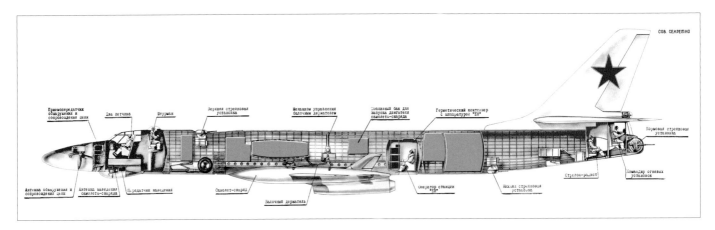

with a large ogival radome incorporated a pressurised and heat-insulated bay housing the guidance system. Aft of it was the warhead bay followed by the fuel tank, which was the main structural element and was made of steel. The wings having 55° sweep at quarter-chord could fold upwards vertically for ease of ground handling. The conventional tail surfaces consisted of stabilators with 55° leading-edge sweep and a fin-and-rudder assembly swept back 55°30' at quarter-chord; the vertical tail was detachable, and the tail surfaces were of cast magnesium alloy construction.

The powerplant was a 3,250-kgp (7,160-lbst) Mikulin M-9FK axial-flow afterburning turbojet produced by engine plant No.26 in Ufa. It was a disposable single-mode version of the RD-9B powering the Mikoyan/Gurevich MiG-19 *Farmer* supersonic tactical fighter (hence, again, the K for *korotkoresoorsnyy* – short-life). The engine was installed in a conformal nacelle under the rear fuselage section, breathing through a quasi-elliptical intake; the afterburner section extended beyond the fuselage tailcone, which mounted a mid-course guidance system aerial.

СИСТЕМА Ту-16К-10

ГЕОМЕТРИЧЕСКИЕ РАЗМЕРЫ:

РАЗМАХ_____ 34,0 м

ДЛИНА_____ 35,2 м

ВЫСОТА_____ 9,95 м

КОЛЕЯ ШАССИ_____ 9,78 м

Left: A drawing from the ADP documents showing the internal layout of the Tu-16K-10.

Below left: A drawing from a Tupolev OKB album showing the dimensions of the Tu-16K-10.

Right: A pre-production Tu-16K-10 in the final assembly shop of the Kazan' aircraft factory.

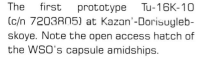

The first prototype Tu-16K-10 (c/n 7203805) at Kazan'-Borisuglebskoye. Note the open access hatch of the WSO's capsule amidships.

The missile came with a choice of conventional or nuclear warheads. The conventional ones were the FK-10 or FK-1M, the latter model being designed for striking large vessels below the waterline; a TK34 nuclear warhead could also be used. The missile was 9.75 m (31 ft 11⅞ in) long, with a wing span of 4.18 m (13 ft 8⁹⁄₁₆ in), a height of 2.27 m (7 ft 4³⁵⁄₆₄ in) and a body diameter of 1.0 m (3 ft 3⅜ in). The launch weight was 4,418-4,555 kg (9,740-10,040 lb), including 850-940 kg (1,870-2,070 lb) for the warhead.

The all-new K-10U guidance system devised by a team led by S. F. Matveyevskiy comprised two subsystems. The aircraft's on-board component was the purpose-built YeN navigation/attack radar developed by OKB-283, an avionics house which later became LNPO **Leninets** (*Leningrahdskoye naoochno-proizvodst-vennoye obyedineniye* – 'Leninist' Leningrad Scientific & Production Association) and then the Leninets Holding Co. The missile itself was fitted with the YeS-1 active radar seeker head used for terminal guidance, the YeS-2D mid-course guidance module picking up signals transmitted by the aircraft's radar and making altitude corrections, and the YeS-3A autopilot. (In the above designations, N stands for *nositel'* – carrier [aircraft] or missile platform and S for *snaryad* – missile.) The K-10U system featured high-powered communications channels and incorporated ECCM features – coded and carefully timed guidance commands, minimising the radar seeker head's operation time and so on). To thwart jamming each aircraft's guidance system worked in several frequencies at once, one of which (the actual control frequency) was stabilised.

The Tupolev OKB began designing the Tu-16K-10 missile platform to Naval Aviation requirements in December 1956, drawing on the experience acquired with the Tu-16KS. The YeN radar was not only powerful but exceedingly bulky; the radar set occupied all of the former navigator's station, with maintenance access hatches on both sides. The radar had two antennas – one for the search/target illumination channel and one for the missile's command link channel. While the command link antenna could be readily accommodated in the usual chin position in a neat teardrop-shaped radome, the main antenna supplanting the navigator's station glazing was too large to fit inside the fuselage diameter. As a result, the Tu-16K-10 received a distinctive nose that was quite unlike any other version of the *Badger*, with a huge

Top: Head-on view of the first prototype at Zhukovskiy during manufacturer's flight tests. A semi-recessed K-10 missile is barely visible.

Above: Tu-16K-10 c/n 7203805 (with no missile) shows its characteristic 'duck bill' nose with twin radomes.

Left: The K-10 missile lowered into pre-launch position.

Top right: This side view of the first prototype shows the ventral fairing tail aerials and wingtip camera fairing associated with test equipment.

Above right and right: The same aircraft with the K-10 missile in cruise and pre-launch positions.

Top and above: The second prototype Tu-16K-10 (c/n 7203806) with the K-10 missile in semi-recessed position. The aircraft has the same fairing replacing the ventral barbette and the same aft-mounted loop aerials but lacks the cine camera recording missile launches.

'duck bill' radome that was wider than the fuselage (in similar manner to the Tu-95K *Bear-B* missile carrier) and had a V-shaped joint line with the top of the nose. This increased the fuselage length and overall length slightly.

The navigator was relocated to the flight deck, occupying the usual position of the Nav/Op under the dorsal blister (above the entry hatch); a pair of small windows in tandem was provided in the port side to admit more light into his workstation. In turn, the WSO was banished to a separate pressurised cabin with a ventral entry/ejection hatch and a dorsal emergency exit, which was located at the rear end of the weapons bay, not in the middle of it as on the Tu-16KS; this also housed guidance system modules and recording equipment.

Accommodating the radar was not the only problem. The K-10 was comparable in length and wing span to the other missiles carried by the Tu-16, but the underslung engine offered insufficient ground clearance if the missile was carried under the wing, entailing the danger of a tailstrike. The only option was to carry the missile on the centreline in a semi-recessed position – just like on the Tu-95K; unfortunately this restricted the offensive weapons load to just one missile. Hence the weapons bay aperture had the same shape as the K-10's fuselage in plan view and was closed by three-section doors which had an ingenious design. The doors' insides were carefully shaped and their rotation axles were positioned inside the fuselage close to the centreline; when the doors rotated outwards, they slid inside the fuselage and its underside along the cut-out became strongly concave instead of convex, accepting the missile. Unlike the bomber variants, the doors were actuated pneumatically, not hydraulically. The missile was carried on a purpose-built BD-238 centreline pylon with a pantographic mechanism which lowered it 550 mm (1 ft $9^{21}/_{32}$ in) prior to engine start-up and release, so that the missile was clear of the fuselage; after the launch

Two more views of the second prototype with the missile raised and lowered. Note how small the missile's ground clearance is in the latter case.

the pylon was raised and the doors closed flush with the fuselage underside. The work on integrating the YeN radar with the airframe and modifying the weapons bay was carried out by the Tupolev OKB's Section V headed by Aleksandr V. Nadashkevich.

Hooking up the missile was a complex affair. The K-10 placed on its ground handling dolly was too tall to pass under the *Badger*'s fuselage. Hence the vertical tail had to be detached before the dolly was wheeled in; it was then inserted into the weapons bay and reinstalled, which was quite tricky because of the limited space.

The special door/pylon design meant that the Tu-16K-10 could not carry bombs or mines internally, and no strike cameras were fitted (there were provisions for installing an AFA-BAM/21R or AFA-BAM/40S camera recording the missile launch). Moreover, it necessitated the removal of the No.3 fuel tank located under the wing centre section, reducing the fuel supply to 32,650 kg (71,980 lb) carried in 26 bag-type tanks. On the other hand, a spe-

cial tank (No.20) holding 500 kg (1,102 lb) of fuel was installed above the missile pylon for starting and running the missile's engine prior to launch.

The new avionics required changes to the electric system, which included a more powerful 6-kVA PO-6000 AC converter (*preobrazovahtel' odnofahznyy* – single-phase [AC] converter) replacing one of the two 4.5-kVA PO-4500 converters. An RSIU-5 communications radio replaced the earlier RSIU-3M, and an R-832M command radio was also fitted. The forward-firing cannon was deleted to save weight – the bulged nose radome covered its location anyway.

The mission profile was as follows. The YeN radar detected a cruiser-sized target at 240-360 km (149-223 miles) range. Once target lock-on had been achieved, the automatic tracking system was activated, with missile launch taking place at a range of 170-200 km (107-124 miles). The K-10 was released at 5,000-11,000 m

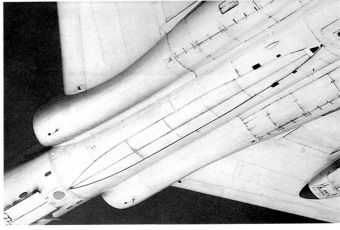

Left: Lower view of an operational Tu-16K-10 with a semi-recessed K-10S missile photographed from an intercepting NATO fighter. The deflected position of the missile's ailerons is noteworthy.

Above: The closed weapons bay doors of a Tu-16K-10.

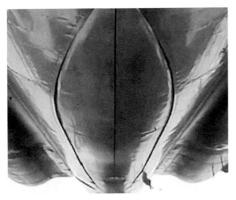

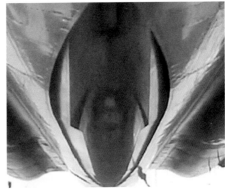

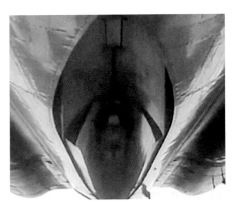

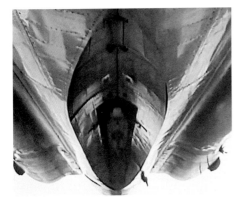

Top left, above left and above: This sequence shows how the three pairs of weapons bay doors open consecutively, rotating outward and sliding inside the fuselage.

Far left: The doors are shaped to form a concave surface when open, the centre pair featuring cut-outs for the missile pylon which is raised here.

Left: The BD-238 missile pylon in lowered position, showing the lock and the sway braces.

(16,400-36,090 ft), dipping below the aircraft's flight level until the engine went to full afterburning thrust and the missile accelerated to 2,030 km/h (1,260 mph). After that, the missile entered the radar beam and was guided by it, accelerating to 1,700-2,000 km/h (1,055-1,242 mph). After launch the Tu-16K-10 was able to make an 80° turn away from the target at a distance of 130-150 km (80-93 miles) from it; the missile then followed a horizontally curved flight path. This considerably increased the minimum distance between the aircraft and the target, minimising the risk of coming within range of the enemy air defences.

A peculiarity of the K-10 was that it manoeuvred in both horizontal and vertical planes en route to the target. First, the missile cruised towards the target at a constant altitude up to 9,000-10,000 m (29,530-32,810 ft). At a distance of 100-110 km (62-68 miles) – some sources say 150 km (93 miles) – a command transmitted from the Tu-16K-10 put the missile into a 14-16° dive; a second command was transmitted when the missile was at 2,400 m (7,870 ft), reducing the dive angle to 6-8°, and then the K-10 recovered to level flight 60-70 km (37-43 miles) from the target, flying at 800-1,000 m (2,620-3,280 ft). At a range of some

10-16 km (6.2-10 miles) the radar seeker head achieved a lock-on for terminal guidance. At the final stage of the flight the missile descended to a few feet above the water, impacting the target above or below the waterline if a conventional warhead was fitted; a nuclear warhead obviated the need for a direct hit, of course. This technique, together with the missile's high speed, relatively small radar signature and the brief period in which the seeker head could be jammed, made it less vulnerable to anti-aircraft defences.

Apart from the radar, the Tu-16K-10's avionics and equipment were virtually the same as for the other missile carriers. The aircraft had an AP-6E autopilot, an ABVU navigation display complementing the usual NI-50BM, an ARK-UVK direction finder complementing the ARK-5U ADF, RV-17M and RV-5 radio altimeters, an RSBN-2S SHORAN, an SP-50 ILS and the like.

In September 1957, the K-10 missile passed its mock-up review commission; a month later the first missile to be assembled was delivered to GK NII VVS for tests. Meanwhile, in 1957 the Tupolev OKB supplied a set of manufacturing documents to plant No.22 in Kazan' for the conversion of two Tu-16K-10 prototypes from brand-new Tu-16s. The first prototype (c/n 7203805) was completed in November, the second aircraft (c/n 7203806) following in December; the conversion job was known as 'order 238'. Both

Above: The flight deck of a Tu-16K-10. Note the circuit breaker panel located where the passage to the navigator's station is on 'glass-nosed' versions.

Right: A production K-10S missile on its AT-10 ground handling dolly. The chequerboard markings and vertical stripe identify it as an inert test or practice round.

The same missile in position under a Tu-16K-10, with the open hatch of the WSO's cabin immediately aft of it. Note the strake added under the engine nacelle to improve directional stability; with it, the ground clearance when the missile is lowered is barely a couple of inches. The missile's vertical tail needs to be detached before hooking the K-10S up to the pylon and reinstalled afterwards!

Above: An armourer watches the K-10S missile being loaded.

Above left: The same missile is lowered into pre-launch position...

Left: ...and released by a Kuibyshev-built Tu-16K-10.

Right and below right: An operational Soviet Navy Tu-16K-10 (ZA) with the flaps set for take-off. Note the navigator's station windows aft of the captain's side windows. The window in the extreme nose is for a wing illumination light used during night in-flight refuelling.

machines wore no tactical codes, and both of them had a non-standard teardrop fairing with an excrescence at the rear replacing the ventral cannon barbette and ring-shaped aerials mounted on the tail cannons in figure-eight fashion, probably serving a data link system. The main external difference was that the first prototype featured a cine camera in a teardrop fairing under the starboard wingtip to record missile launches, whereas the second prototype had none.

In January 1958, the Tu-16K-10 prototypes were ready for manufacturer's flight tests; the first flight took place on 4th January, and the tests continued until 29th September. Tupolev OKB test pilot Mikhail V. Kozlov was one of the pilots involved. Part of the programme was performed with the Air Force's participation at GK NII VVS's facility in Akhtoobinsk. Prior to the state acceptance trials the YeN radar was put through its paces on the two prototypes, while the YeS-2 system was tested on two specially modified MiG-19S *Farmer-C* day fighters built by plant No.21 in Gor'kiy; these were designated MiG-19SMK/1 (serialled '418 Red', c/n N61210418) and MiG-19SMK/2 ('419 Red', c/n N61210419). The first test launch of a K-10S in autonomous mode (without using the guidance and homing systems) took place on 28th May 1958.

On 21st November 1958, the Tu-16K-10 prototypes were submitted for joint state acceptance trials. The trials of the aircraft, the missile and the K-10 system as a whole were conducted by GK NII VVS and took nearly three years to complete, with pauses for modifications and testing of the system's components. The final phase involved operations in an active ECM environment. After the first test launch in May, five more were made between June and September 1958, against small radar-reflecting ground targets over a range of 96 km (59 miles) by a test crew headed by Lt.-Col Vladimir V. Zentsov, Hero of the Soviet Union. Four hits were achieved. Overall, six missiles were fired in 1958 during manufacturer's tests and joint state acceptance trials; four of them hit their targets, making for a 'kill' probability of 80%.

Ten more K-10S were launched in 1959 as the joint state acceptance trials continued. These confirmed the safety of missile separation; the ability of the aircraft to land with the missile still in place was also verified.

The trials also revealed the impossibility of achieving any substantial increase in the missile's range (compared to the KS-1) due to defects in the guidance system. Constant problems with the YeN radar and YeS seeker head, as well as with the missile's engine, resulted in all five test launches at 130-150 km (80-93 miles) range ending in failure. There were also problems with the aircraft's fuel system when subjected to G loads for prolonged periods. Thus, by early 1960, only six hits had been recorded.

Council of Ministers directive No.1475-685 ordering the K-10 system into production was issued on 31st December 1958; aircraft factory No.31 in Tbilisi, Georgia, which normally built fighters, was tasked with building the missile. The production-standard missile was designated K-10S, the suffix being variously deciphered as *sereeynaya* (production, used attributively) or **spets-boyepripahs** ('special munition', that is, nuclear munition). It featured additional heat insulation in the warhead bay, since nuclear munitions are sensitive to temperature fluctuations. Also, the nose radome, the rear portion of the engine nacelle and the fillet between it and the fuselage were altered; late-production K-10S missiles had a shallow strake added under the engine nacelle to improve directional stability.

However, by then the aforementioned K-22 weapons system based on the supersonic Tu-22 and the Kh-22 ASM appeared to hold more promise. The K-10S was thus intended mainly for the obsolescent Tu-16 whose production was due to be terminated soon in favour of the Tu-22 in Kazan' and the Antonov An-10 *Ookraïna* (the Ukraine; NATO reporting name *Cat*) four-turbo-prop medium-haul airliner in Voronezh. (Interestingly, the afore-mentioned Council of Ministers directive No.426-201 and the appropriate GKAT order dated 28th April 1958, contained a provision about arming the Tu-22K with the K-10 missile and commencing state acceptance trials in the first quarter of 1960; however, this variant was never proceeded with.)

Nevertheless, series production of the Tu-16K-10 was initiated at plant No.22. The first pre-production Tu-16K-10 (c/n 8204010) was rolled out there in April 1958; however, the Kazan' plant completed (or rather converted) a mere five Tu-16K-10 (ZA) aircraft

featuring the wing-to-wing IFR system in 1958-59 before halting Tu-16 production to free up the assembly line for the *Blinder*.

Nikita S. Khrushchov's preoccupation with replacing strategic bombers by ICBMs, together with the unsuccessful test launches of the K-10 missile, raised questions whether persevering with the K-10 system was worthwhile. Hence the Kuibyshev aircraft factory No.1 was instructed to terminate Tu-16 production and switch to producing the aforementioned R-7 ICBM designed by OKB-1 under Sergey P. Korolyov. However, in June 1959, the CofM Vice-Chairmen Dmitriy F. Ustinov and Boris M. Ryabikov, GKAT Chairman Pyotr V. Dement'yev and Soviet Air Force C-in-C Air Chief Marshal Konstantin A. Vershinin wrote a joint letter to the Communist Party Central Committee, pointing out that killing off the Tu-16 would be a premature decision. They cited the inadequacy of the USSR's air-to-surface missile carrier fleet (a mere 90 Tu-16KSs at the time) and the obsolescence of its weaponry. Even more to the point, the testing of the R-7 missile was taking longer than anticipated. Hence the instruction was revoked and an order for another 173 Tu-16s placed. In accordance with Council of Ministers directive No.709-337 of 2nd July 1958, in October 1959, the Tu-16K-10 entered production at plant No.1 in Kuibyshev. This factory managed to complete and deliver 59 such aircraft by July 1960, when it was ultimately transferred to the MOM framework and switched to building ballistic missiles and space launch vehicles. During production the Tu-16K-10 was designated 'order 238' and was known in operational service as *izdeliye* NK-10 (this was subsequently shortened to *izdeliye* NK-1).

In 1959, the K-10 achieved initial operational capability with the Soviet Navy as its first highly effective supersonic air-to-surface missile system. Meanwhile, the trials continued. Between September 1959, and November 1960, both simulated and actual launches of the K-10S were practised; in the former case Black Sea Fleet ships served as notional targets, while actual launches were carried out against special target vessels. In particular, the decommissioned freighter S/S *Valeriy Chkalov* (some sources call her a tanker) with a displacement of 9,052 tons was anchored at the Boozachi target range (aka Range No.77) in the Caspian Sea to represent a cruiser-sized target. She was 111.3 m (365 ft 1^{57}/$_{64}$ in) long, with a freeboard of 4 m (13 ft 1^{31}/$_{64}$ in), and was fitted with a tall wire mesh contraption by way of a superstructure; if a missile pierced the wire mesh, this was considered a 'kill'. In July 1960 Naval Aviation crews from the North Fleet's 5th MTAD (***minnotorpednaya aviadiveeziya*** – minelayer and torpedo-bomber division) made their first practice launches of K-10S missiles at the Boozachi range, flying from Vodopoy airfield (the name means 'watering hole') operated by the AVMF's 33rd Training Centre. The first crew captained by Col. Myznikov messed up the launch – the missile fell 40 km (24.85 miles) short of the target; however, the second crew headed by Lt.-Col. Kovalyov achieved a direct hit.

The trials programme involved both prototypes of the Tu-16K-10, the two MiG-19SMK 'missile simulator' testbeds and 34 K-10S missiles, including three live ones. Accuracy was poor; out of the twenty missiles launched, only ten hit their targets. Faulty operation of the YeN radar was to blame for most of the misses; others (one each) were due to crew error (the missile hit an ice floe instead of the target vessel), failures of the YeS-1 seeker head, the YeS-2

module, the YeS-3A autopilot and the missile's engine. According to GKAT and GKRE representatives, design flaws were responsible for half of the failed launches; these flaws were eventually corrected.

In the course of the joint state acceptance trials the Tu-16K-10s made 184 flights. Due to various problems the official completion deadline was postponed until the second quarter of 1960, although in reality the trials were not completed until the end of the year. 25 launches were made in 1960.

According to the system's designers the K-10S had a 71.4% 'kill' probability against a surface target; in the opinion of the Naval Aviation command it was only 62.4%, the military having different views of what should count as a system failure. Either way, it was much lower than the figure stipulated by the CofM directive.

Another unpleasant fact emerged during the trials. The weapons systems operator's pressurised cabin was located in the rear part of the former bomb bay – in other words, between the engines, where the air temperature was higher than elsewhere in the aircraft. This meant that the WSO had to endure temperatures over 40°C (104°F) in the summer.

However, the trials also yielded some encouraging results; some parameters (target detection range, missile launch range and the missile's cruising speed) were better than the figures stipulated by the CofM directive. Large ships could be detected at distances close to the theoretical radar horizon and a lock-on was achieved after closing by a further 50-60 km (31.5-37.2 miles). Although special maximum-range tests on the missile had not been performed, a wayward K-10S carried on to cover a distance of 245 km (152 miles) in 10 minutes 10 seconds after missing the target and splashed down with some fuel still left.

In June 1961, plant No.22 picked up the ball, reinstating series production of the Tu-16K-10 to meet the Navy's demand. As already mentioned in Chapter 3, the new production Kazan'-built examples had a totally different construction number system than hitherto; unfortunately few Tu-16K-10 c/ns under this system are known. Changes to the systems and equipment were made in the course of production. For example, Tu-16K-10s in the first six Kazan'-built batches (up to and including f/n 5605 built in December 1961) had the old NI-50BM navigation display and DAK-B remote celestial compass; from Batch 57 onwards (f/n 5701, the first example built in 1962) they were replaced by the ANU-1A navigation computer (*avtomaticheskoye navigatsionnoye oostroystvo* – automatic navigation device) and DAK-DB-5 respectively. The DISS-1 Doppler radar was also introduced on this particular aircraft.

If we include the seven prototypes and pre-production examples converted from Tu-16A bombers, the Kazan' factory completed 157 Tu-16K-10s by December 1963, when the *Badger* was finally phased out of production. This brought the Tu-16K-10's total production run to 216.

Because of the aforementioned 'kill' probability issues the leaders of GKAT and GKOT were not in a hurry to finalise the trials report; the latter was signed by Lt.-Gen. Ivan I. Borzov, who chaired the State commission, in mid-March 1961 and endorsed by Air Force C-in-C Air Chief Marshal Konstantin A. Vershinin and

Basic performance of the Tu-16K-10

Length overall	36.2 m (118 ft 9¹³⁄₆₄ in)
Fuselage length	35.7 m (117 ft 1³⁄₆₄ in)
Height on ground	9.95 m (32 ft 7⁷⁄₆₄ in)
Wing span	32.989 m (108 ft 2⁵⁄₃₂ in)
Wing area	164.65 m² (1,772.28 sq ft)
Empty weight	39,600 kg (87,300 lb)*
Empty weight with trapped fuel	40,380 kg (89,020 lb)
Take-off weight:	
maximum †	75,800 kg (167,110 lb)
maximum (exceptional conditions)	79,000 kg (174,170 lb)
Fuel load	39,700 kg (87,520 lb)
Fuel capacity	32,150 litres (7,073 Imp gal)
Weapons load (one K-10S ASM)	4,400 kg (9,700 lb)
Maximum speed at full power with missile	
and a 60,000-kg (132,280-lb) AUW:	
up to an altitude of 500 m (1,640 ft)	670 km/h (416 mph)
at 6,250 m (20,510 ft)	890 km/h (551 mph)
at 10,000 m (32,810 ft)	930 km/h (577 mph)
Cruising speed	800 km/h (496 mph)
Maximum Mach number	0.88
Service ceiling with a 62,000-kg (136,690-lb) AUW:	
at nominal power with missile attached	12,300 m (40,350 ft)
with no missile	12,800 m (41,990 ft)
Missile launch altitude	5,000-11,000 m (16,400-36,090 ft)
Climb time:	
to 10,000 m with a 62,000-kg AUW	15 minutes
to service ceiling	33 minutes
Range with a 75,800-kg TOW, a 'hi-hi-hi' mission profile	
and missile launch at midpoint, with 5% fuel reserves	4,850 km (3,012 miles)
Maximum combat radius	2,400 km (1,491 miles)
Take-off run:	
with a 75,800-kg take-off weight	1,900 m (6,230 ft)
with a 79,000-kg take-off weight	2,200 m (7,220 ft)
Landing run:	
with a 48,000-kg (105,820-lb) landing weight,	
brake parachute deployed	1,100 m (3,610 ft)
ditto, brake parachute not used	1,300 m (4,270 ft)
with a 57,000-kg (125,660-lb) landing weight,	
brake parachute deployed	1,300 m (4,270 ft)
ditto, brake parachute not used	1,750 m (5,740 ft)
Required runway length	2,500 m (8,200 ft)
CG position at empty weight	33.6% MAC

* On late production batches the empty weight with 130 kg (286 lb) of trapped fuel was 40,380 kg (89,020 lb)

† Also reported as the normal take-off weight

Soviet Navy C-in-C Fleet Adm. Sergey G. Gorshkov in mid-May. On 12th August 1961, the Council of Ministers issued directive No.742-315 clearing the K-10 weapons system for Soviet Navy service. In the summer of that year production examples of the Tu-16K-10 with missiles attached were shown to the general public for the first time, taking part in the annual Aviation Day flypast over Moscow-Tushino airfield. The foreign military attachés attending the event were quick to take note of the new version,

whereupon the Tu-16K-10 received the reporting name *Badger-C* and the K-10S ASM was codenamed *Kipper*.

In 1962, the possibility of operating the Tu-16K-10 from unpaved airfields was explored, but it was not pursued in practice. On 22nd August 1962, a North Fleet Air Arm/924th GvMRAP (*Gvardeyskiy morskoy raketonosnyy aviapolk* – Guards naval missile strike air regiment) Tu-16K-10 captained by the regiment's CO Col. Vladimir F. Kroopyakov launched a K-10S missile with a 6-kiloton nuclear warhead against a target (a barge fitted with radar reflectors) at the nuclear proving ground on the Novaya Zemlya ('New Land') archipelago during Exercise *Shkval* (Squall). The huge responsibility associated with this important mission weighed so heavily on the WSO that he messed up the pre-launch procedure, managing to complete it correctly only on the second try. This was the only case when a Soviet Naval Aviation aircraft actually used nuclear weapons.

Check-up tests of the K-10 weapons system were held by the 2nd Research and Test Directorate of GK NII VVS in Akhtoobinsk (responsible for testing the Long-Range Aviation's weapons systems) and the 71st Test Range at Bagerovo AB on 10th September – 2nd November 1963, and 7th-24th January 1964. Lt.-Col. V. Ye. Mal'tsev was the project test pilot, with Lt.-Col. V. T. Korobochka as engineer in charge. The purpose of the tests was to check the conformity of production K-10S missiles built in 1963 to production standards, assess the efficacy of the design changes made in the course of production and check the missile's targeting accuracy.

Two Kazan'-built Tu-16K-10s – c/n 4652042 (f/n 6504) in the first round and c/n 2551023 (f/n 5502) in the second round – participated in the tests, making a total of 13 flights and launching a total of five missiles from batches 30, 33, 34 and 39. Four of these were instrumented test rounds in the so-called 'check version M', one of them additionally lacking some avionics modules. These were launched at the abovementioned freighter S/S *Valeriy Chkalov* anchored at the Boozachi target range in the Caspian Sea. The fifth missile was live ('version N') with a reduced-power practice warhead. It was launched at the target vessel S/S *Andrey Zhdanov*, a decommissioned Type 410 (*Lenin* class) tanker with a displacement of 13,334 tons, a length of 132.6 m (435 ft 0³¹⁄₆₄ in) and a freeboard of 16.8 m (55 ft 1²⁷⁄₆₄ in) anchored at the same range.

Tu-16K-10 missile strike aircraft with ECM equipment ('order 2624')

Some Tu-16K-10s were retrofitted with an SPS-100 Rezeda jammer in a large parabolic tail fairing replacing the tail turret plus an SPS-5 Fasol' jammer in the avionics bay. Again, they were probably modified under the terms of 'order 2624'; the first such aircraft was a Kazan'-built machine coded '12 Blue' (c/n 2632024, f/n 6302), which was test flown from Kazan'-Borisoglebskoye on 10th January – 4th April 1968, and underwent check-up tests on 18th May – 29th August 1968, together with three similarly equipped Tu-16s (see Chapter 5/Tu-16 Yolka for more details).

Other *Badger-Cs* featured an SPS-151D, SPS-152D or SPS-153D Siren'-D jammer covering the forward hemisphere and an SPS-151ZhK, SPS-152ZhK or SPS-153ZhK Siren'-MD jammer in an UKhO tail fairing (likewise replacing the tail turret).

Passive ECM equipment consisted of an ASO-2B chaff dispenser with an outlet on the rear fuselage underside. Some Tu-16K-10s were retrofitted with ASO-2A-E7R IRCM flare dispensers.

Tu-16K-10 (ZA) missile strike aircraft (Tu-16K-10ZA, 'order 238'; *izdeliye* NK-10ZA, *izdeliye* NK-1)

A version of the Tu-16K-10 equipped with a refuelling receptacle under the port wingtip was brought out as the Tu-16K-10 (ZA). All Kuibyshev-built Tu-16K-10s had IFR capability, but for some reason most of the Kazan'-built examples did not; only five aircraft were completed in this configuration by plant No.22. This is where the controversy lies. The Kazan' factory's production statistics show all five IFR-capable Tu-16K-10s as pre-production machines converted from 'glass-nosed' bombers in 1958-59, with c/ns under System 1 (including 8204029, 8204103, 8204216 and 8204222). However, one source also mentions the first new-build Kazan'-

built *Badger-C* manufactured in 1961 with a c/n under System 2 (c/n 1511012, f/n 5101) as a Tu-16K-10 (ZA).

As already noted, the fuel system of the Tu-16K-10 (ZA) – later rendered as Tu-16K-10ZA – differed from that of other IFR-capable versions. Not only did it lack the No.3 fuel tank (which was normal for the *Badger-C*) but the No.4 tank in the wing centre section could not be replenished in flight; hence the pipeline from the IFR receptacle was connected only to the Group 1 tanks (Nos. 2 and 5). There were also minor changes in the fuel jettison system, and the navigator did not have the manually trained searchlight present on the 'glass-nosed' versions. Finally, the Tu-16K-10 (ZA) had a customised SETS-300 fuel sequencing system.

Tu-16K development aircraft

Between 1959 and 1961 GK NII VVS tested three prototypes of the Tu-16K – a version of the Tu-16K-10 re-engined with Zoobets

Above: This Kazan'-built Tu-16K-10 tested in 1968 ('12 Red', c/n 2632024) was retrofitted with an SPS-100 jammer in a tail fairing under the terms of 'order 2624'.

Left: Kuibyshev-built Tu-16K-10 '16 Red' makes a low pass with the missile attached. The large tactical code on the nose indicates this was in the early days of the type's operations.

Right: A Tu-16K-10 over international waters in the 1980s. The bold tactical codes on the nose have been replaced by a smaller version on the nose gear doors and the c/n is no longer worn visibly.

RD16-15 turbojets (the same as on the experimental Tu-16B bomber). Apart from structural modifications, the electric starters of the new engines required additional DC batteries to be provided.

The Tu-16K was intended for use by the Naval Aviation and differed little from the Tu-16K-10, apart from its longer range thanks to the more fuel-efficient new engines. Although the tests were successful the Tu-16K did not enter production.

It may be mentioned that concurrently Aeroflot Soviet Airlines tested two prototypes of the Tu-104E – a derivative of the Tu-104B fitted with the same RD16-15 engines. This aircraft likewise remained in prototype form.

K-10D and K-10DV long-range anti-shipping strike weapons systems
Tu-16K-10D missile strike aircraft
(*izdeliye* NK-10D, *izdeliye* NK-1D)

The abovementioned Council of Ministers directive No.742-315 of 12th August 1961 clearing the Tu-16K-10 for service contained a clause requiring the K-10 system as a whole to be updated; within three months the organisations involved were to suggest ways of extending the K-10 missile's range to 300-350 km (186-217 miles). Studies carried out by the Naval Aviation's 33rd TsBP i PLS at Kul'bakino AB in Nikolayev indicated the possibility of launching the K-10S from an altitude as low as 600 m (1,970 ft) over a range of up to 325 km (202 miles).

Work on an improved system initially known as the K-10M (*modernizeerovannaya* – updated) but then redesignated K-10D (*dahl'nodeystvuyushchaya* – long-range) began in 1961, but was hampered by the simultaneous requirements to increase the system's 'kill' range and reduce the altitude at which the missile was launched. The resulting missile was the K-10SD with a greater fuel load, while OKB-283 developed an upgraded YeN-D radar having a detection range of 400-450 km (248-279 miles); the aircraft thus equipped was designated Tu-16K-10D. In both cases, D stands for *dahl'nodeystvuyushchiy*. This version was not built as such, but many *Badger-Cs* were updated to Tu-16K-10D standard by the Navy's aircraft repair plants.

The K-10D weapons system with its longer-range K-10SD missile had obvious advantages when compared to the K-10; however, by the end of the 1960s the Western navies' shipborne anti-aircraft

defences had greatly improved. A carrier task force (CTF) had little difficulty in detecting a large subsonic enemy aircraft flying at cruise altitude 500 km (310 miles) away. It was therefore decided to expand the K-10SD's altitude envelope from 5,000-11,000 m (16,400-36,090 ft) to 1,500-11,000 m (4,920-36,090 ft) by modifying the aircraft's radar and the missile's guidance system; a low-level launch would make early detection by enemy radars less likely. The resulting K-10DV weapons system was based on an appropriately modified YeN-D radar and the K-10SDV missile which had a modified YeS-1DV radar seeker head and a modified YeS-2DV mid-course guidance module, increasing the missile's effectiveness and making the aircraft less vulnerable. The V suffix referred to the programme's codename *Vysotnost'* – [low-]altitude capability. The new launch mode was enabled by a different algorithm of generating or transmitting certain control commands.

First, theoretical research was undertaken by MKB Raduga and MKB *Strela* (Arrow), the latter organisation specialising in air defence systems (it is now known as the Almaz-Antey Aerospace Defence Concern). Next, in October-November 1969, the 2nd Research and Test Directorate of GK NII VVS held a test programme to explore the possibility of launching K-10SDV missiles at low altitude. The tests involving a modified Kuibyshev-built Tu-16K-10D (c/n 1883905) were performed with the participation of the 33rd TsBP i PLS; AVMF test pilot G. G. Kuznetsov was the project test pilot, with V. N. Belousov and L. A. Soorovtsev as engineers in charge.

In the course of nine flights the aircraft launched four K-10SDV missiles from medium altitude at two radar-defined ground targets (clusters of K-2.4 angle reflectors) located 16 km (9.94 miles) apart at the GK NII VVS instrumented test range. Three of these were inert test rounds ('version T', for *telemetricheskaya* – telemetry-equipped) with an RTS-8A data link system (*rahdiotekhnicheskaya sistema* – radio technical system). The fourth was a live missile ('version BM') with a TK34-TB warhead. The launches were filmed from a Tu-104 airliner acting as a camera ship. Three of the launch attempts had to be aborted – twice due to poor weather and once due to a malfunction of the missile's seeker head. In the actual launches, Nos. 2 and 3 scored direct hits on targets 406 and 402 respectively; No.1 failed to home in due to a timing error in the setting of a guidance command, while No.4

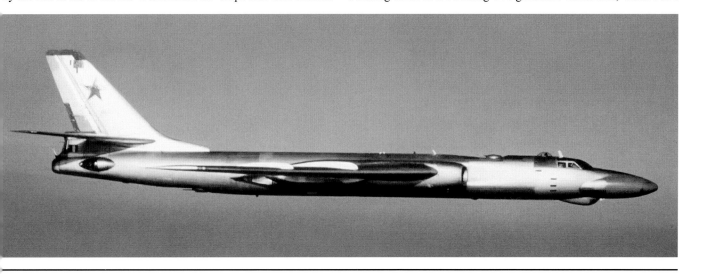

(the live missile) strayed off course when the WSO made an error and a self-destruct command had to be transmitted.

Tests of the K-10DV weapons system confirmed its value and viability; according to the test report, which was endorsed in March 1970, the modifications reduced the effectiveness of the CTF's SAM systems and shipboard fighters against the Tu-16K-10D and its K-10SDV missile by 50%. Hence some of the Tu-16K-10Ds were again modified by AVMF maintenance bases; these machines could carry K-10SD and K-10SDV missiles, as well as the older K-10S and the K-10SN/K-10SNB (see below), although in these cases the attack range was reduced. The latter two versions could likewise be launched at altitudes down to 1,500 m (4,920 ft).

K-10N long-range anti-shipping strike weapons system
Tu-16K-10N missile strike aircraft (*izdeliye* NK-10N, *izdeliye* NK-1N)

The growing potency of the NATO's shipborne anti-aircraft defences prompted another upgrade of the K-10 system enabling the missile to be launched at low level. Estimates suggested that decreasing the altitude at which the missile was launched would reduce its vulnerability to anti-aircraft fire and fighter interdiction by as much as 50%.

Therefore two new versions of the missile were brought out. The K-10SN (*nizkovysotnaya* – low-altitude) was optimised for low-altitude launches in order to maximise the chances of air defence penetration; a further version with a nuclear warhead was designated K-10SNB. (There have been claims that the latter version was optimised for combating large ships with armour protection, hence the B stood for *[dlya porazheniya] bronirovannykh [korabley]* – for destroying armoured ships.)

Both versions were carried by an updated version of the *Badger-C* featuring a modified YeN-2-6 radar to enable launch from an altitude of 500-600 m (1,640-1,970 ft); the aircraft was designated Tu-16K-10N (*izdeliye* NK-10N), the N suffix standing for *nizkovysotnyy*. During the terminal guidance phase the missile flew only a few metres above the water. The range at which a cruiser-type target could be engaged with the K-10SNB was 350-420 km (217-261 miles).

The Tu-16K-10N could also carry a standard K-10S, but this had to be launched at altitudes between 5,000 and 11,000 m (16,400-36,090 ft). Similarly, the K-10SN and K-10SNB could be used by the unmodified Tu-16K-10 or Tu-16K-10D, but in this case the missiles could only be launched at the aircraft's normal operating altitudes.

Top and above: A Kuibyshev-built Tu-16K-10 converted to a Tu-16K-10-26 pictured during trials.

K-10P long-range ECM system
Tu-16K-10P missile strike aircraft

Between 1972 and 1979, development work was carried out on converting the K-10SN missile into an ECM drone fitted with an Azaliya active jammer in lieu of a warhead. According to other sources, the drone was equipped with a *Ryabina* (Rowan) active jammer. Designated K-10SP (*pomekhovaya* – ECM, used attributively), it was to be used to cover the launch of ordinary live missiles and carried by an aircraft designated Tu-16K-10P. The weapons system was designated K-10P.

Since the modifications described above did not cause any changes in the aircraft's appearance, the Tu-16K-10ZA, Tu-16K-10D, Tu-16K-10N and Tu-16K-10P were still known to NATO as the *Badger-C*.

K-10-26 long-range anti-shipping strike weapons system
Tu-16K-10-26 missile strike aircraft
('order 644'; *izdeliye* NK-10-26, *izdeliye* NK-6)

The K-26 weapons system was incorporated not only on the Air Force's Tu-16 missile carriers used against ground targets but on anti-shipping versions as well. On 23rd June 1964, the Council of Ministers let loose with directive No.552-229 requiring the system

to be adapted to the Tu-16K-10; this was to be done in accordance with an SOR endorsed by the Air Force C-in-C on 19th November 1964.

The 'navalised' weapons system was intended for engaging radar-defined ground and maritime targets with KSR-5 missiles, or maritime targets only with K-10SD missiles. It bore the designation K-10-26, the aircraft being accordingly designated Tu-16K-10-26. (The provisional designations K-36 and Tu-16K-36 – generated by adding up 'K-10' and 'K-26' – were in use at the design stage but were soon dropped.)

The Tu-16K-10-26 was retrofitted with the same BD-352-11-5 missile pylons at wing ribs 9-11 as the *Badger-G Mod* for carrying two KSR-5s under the wings. This necessitated local reinforcement of the wing structure and changes to the flaps, which had a 25° limit when missiles were suspended under the wings. A guidance system called VN, or *Venets* (Crown), was installed, allowing the YeN-D radar to work with the missiles' VS-K seeker heads and BSU-7 autopilots; changes were made to the 115 V AC electric system to cater for the missiles' control system. Appropriate equipment was fitted for heating the KSR-5's warhead and pressurising its avionics bay. Additionally, the fuel system was modified, permitting asymmetric fuel usage from the port and starboard

Two more views of the same aircraft with a K-10S missile on the centreline and KSR-5 missiles under the wings.

Group 4 wing tanks in order to maintain balance with one KSR-5 missile and permitting fuel transfer from the No.1 fuselage tank to the Group 3 wing tanks (see Chapter 6/Fuel system).

A single K-10SD missile could be carried on the centreline as usual. Thus, the Tu-16K-10-26 was the first version of the *Badger*

Above: Tu-16K-10-26 '08 Red' carries two inert KSR-5s.

Below: An upper view of a Tu-16K-10-26. The fixed metal strips extending across the flaps just outboard of the inner wing fences are a giveaway that BD-352-11-5 wing pylons are fitted.

Right: A rare shot of an operational Tu-16K-20-26 with three live missiles taxying at an AVMF base in a winter setting. The KSR-5s are painted dark green.

Below right: In contrast, here a Tu-16K-10-26 takes off with a K-10S and red-painted inert KSR-5s, probably for an exercise. Note the weathered paintwork on the radome of the YeN radar.

Below: A Tu-16K-10-26 coded '10 Black' is refuelled in an earthen revetment before a sortie an two inert KSR-5. Note the green radome.

able to carry three air-to-surface missiles at a time. The standard ground test equipment for the K-10 missile was complemented by that developed for the K-26 system, including the VNK-10 device emulating the KSR-5's radar seeker head, and by a special VNK-11 device emulating the YeN-D radar which was unique to the K-10-26 system. The new equipment caused a slight forward shift in the aircraft's CG and increased the normal landing weight above the usual 48,000 kg (105,820 lb).

The two prototypes were converted by aircraft factory No.22 from standard Kazan'-built Tu-16K-10Ds (c/ns 1793014 and 2743054); as mentioned earlier, the former aircraft coded '15 Blue' was involved in the state acceptance trials of the K-26 weapons system as such in January-November 1968. Ground checks and manufacturer's flight tests were held between November 1966, and March 1967, in Kazan'. On 24th April 1967, the Tu-16K-10-26 was submitted for joint state acceptance trials; however, acceptance was postponed until 24th May 1968, due to development

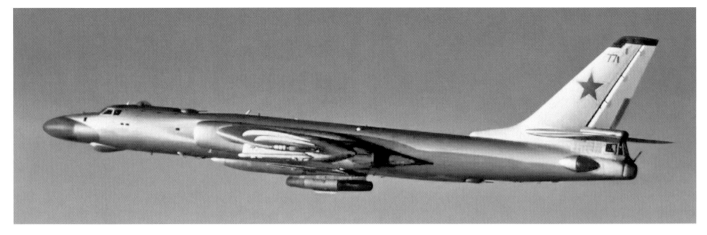

Basic performance of the Tu-16K-10-26 (recorded for c/n 2743054)	
Empty weight with trapped fuel (130 kg/286 lb)	42,160 kg (92,950 lb)*
Payload:	
crew (six)	600 kg (1,320 lb)
cannon ammunition (1,700 rounds)	660 kg (1,455 lb)
two KSR-5 missiles	7,800 kg (17,380 lb)
one K-10SD missile	4,400 kg (9,700 lb)
oxygen	60 kg (132 lb)
Fuel load:	
with two KSR-5s and one K-10SD	19,530 kg (43,060 lb)
with two KSR-5 missiles	24,450 kg (53,900 lb)
with one K-10SD missile	27,300 kg (60,190 lb)
engine starter fuel and oil	50 kg (110 lb)
starting fuel for K-10SD missile in tank No.20	500 kg (1,102 lb)
Weapons load options:	
one K-10SD missile	4,400 kg (9,700 lb)
two KSR-5 missiles	7,600 kg (16,760 lb)
one KSR-5 missile	3,800 kg (8,380 lb)
two KSR-5s and one K-10SD	12,000 kg (26,455 lb)
one KSR-5 and one K-10SD	8,200 kg (18,080 lb)
Normal landing weight:	49,640 kg (109,440 lb)
crew (six)	600 kg (1,320 lb)
cannon ammunition (50% remaining)	330 kg (730 lb)
fuel (20% of full capacity remaining)	6,500 kg (14,330 lb)
engine starter fuel and oil	25 kg (55 lb)
oxygen	30 kg (66 lb)
Fuel capacity	39,700 litres (8,734 Imp gal)
Maximum true airspeed at full engine power,	
with one K-10SD missile:	
at up to 500 m (1,640 ft)	670 km/h (416 mph)
at 6,050 m (19,850 ft)	890 km/h (552 mph)
at 10,000 m (32,810 ft)	930 km/h (577 mph)
Service range at optimum altitude with a K-10SD and	
a 75,800-kg (167,110-lb) take-off weight, with 5% fuel	
reserves and missile launch at midpoint	4,700 km (2,919 miles)
CG position at empty weight	32.5% MAC

* also reported as 41,850 kg (92,260 lb)

problems with the K-26 weapons system as a whole, and the trials did not commence in earnest until late 1968, continuing until the spring of 1969. Only two KSR-5s and two K-10SDs (all of them instrumented test rounds) were allocated for the state acceptance trials, which involved 28 flights totalling 110 hours 22 minutes; in one of the flights the Tu-16K-10-26 launched two missiles (a K-10SD and a KSR-5) at the same target. The target, in all cases, was S/S *Shevchenko* (maritime target No.707).

During the same time frame Tu-16K-10-26 '15 Red' made six launches of updated K-10SD missiles built in 1968 under a check-up test programme to assess the effect of the changes made after the K-10D weapons system's tests in 1967. The results were also used to check the Tu-16K-10-26 aircraft's conformity to the K-10D system's specifications. The performance was almost identical to that of late-production Tu-16K-10s, with a few exceptions as detailed in the table on this page.

The state acceptance trials report was endorsed by MAP, MRP, the Air Force and the Navy in February-March 1969. On 12th November 1969, the K-10-26 system was cleared for service with the Naval Aviation by Council of Ministers directive No.882-315, with the ensuing conversion of 85 Tu-16K-10Ds to Tu-16K-10-26 standard. The modifications, including wing reinforcement, revisions to the flap controls and fuel system, were carried out under the terms of 'order 644' at AVMF maintenance factories in the 1970s. Some of the 85 examples were fitted with a Siren'-D jammer (having antenna pods near the engine air intakes to cover the

Left: Tu-16K-10-26 '77 Black' with only a K-10S on the centreline is photographed over the Baltic Sea from a Swedish Air Force interceptor.

Below left: A closer look at the missile suspended under the same aircraft.

Below: A Tu-16K-10-26B takes off, carrying two different types of naval mines on the fuselage and wing hardpoints.

forward hemisphere) and/or an SPS-5 Fasol' jammer with blade aerials flanking the nosewheel well; moreover, a few carried a Siren'-MD jammer in an UKhO tail fairing while others retained the tail gunner's position.

The combination of the 'duck bill' nose and the underwing missile pylons was an obvious external identification feature of the Tu-16K-10-26, and to distinguish it from 'regular' Tu-16K-10s the new version was given the NATO reporting name *Badger-C Mod*.

Tu-16K-10-26N missile strike aircraft (*izdeliye* NK-10-26N, *izdeliye* NK-6N)

Examples of the Tu-16K-10N modified to take the K-26 weapons system as described above were similarly redesignated Tu-16K-10-26N (*izdeliye* NK-10-26N). The simultaneous use of two high-speed, high-altitude KSR-5 missiles with a low-altitude K-10S missile put the enemy anti-aircraft defences in a much tougher situation.

Tu-16K-10-26P missile strike aircraft ('order 2303', 'order 644P'; *izdeliye* NK-10-26P, *izdeliye* NK-6P)

In keeping with the abovementioned VPK ruling No.14 issued on 21st January 1976, and pursuant to MAP order No.56 dated 9th February 1976, in the late 1970s a small number of Tu-16K-10-26s with SPS-100 jammers in ECM tail fairings were given SEAD

capability by equipping them with the ANP-K system for locating active enemy radars. Designated Tu-16K-26P (again, the P stood for *protivorahdiolokatsionnyy* – anti-radar), such aircraft could carry KSR-5 missiles with active radar homing or KSR-5P ARMs, as well as normal attack missiles (one K-10S and two KSR-5s or KSR-2s of various versions). The revised weapons system was given the designation K-10-26P; the original product code *izdeliye* NK-10-26P was later shortened to *izdeliye* NK-6P. The conversion jobs were known either as 'order 2303' or as 'order 644P'.

Tu-16K-10-26B bomber/missile strike aircraft ('order 2644B'; *izdeliye* NK-10-26B, *izdeliye* NK-6B)

As mentioned earlier, because of its special BD-238 centreline pylon and weapons bay door design the Tu-16K-10 was unable to carry free-fall weapons internally. The issue of enhancing the tactical and strategic potential of the *Badger-C* by adding bomber and mine-laying/torpedo-bomber capabilities was raised several times by the Soviet MoD. As early as 1958, Council of Ministers directive No.709-337 of 2nd July 1958, ordered the Tupolev OKB to explore the possibility of using the Tu-16K-10 for delivering conventional and nuclear free-fall bombs by 1st August.

However, it was not until the 1970s that some Tu-16K-10-26s underwent such a modification at Naval Aviation maintenance facilities in accordance with Tupolev OKB drawings. Such aircraft were designated Tu-16K-10-26B (*izdeliye* NK-10-26B, later shortened to *izdeliye* NK-6B) in service, the B standing for *bombardirovshchik* (bomber); the conversion jobs were referred to as 'order 2644B'. They were fitted with two pairs of detachable BD4-16-52 bomb racks (beam-type [weapons] rack for Group 4 ordnance, developed for the Tu-16, 1952 model) or MBDU-46-68N multiple ejector racks (MERs) under the centre fuselage near the engine nacelles (between frames 26-28 and 35-37). Together with BD3-16K bomb racks attached to the BD-352-11-5 wing pylons, this enabled the aircraft to carry a 4,000-kg (8,820-lb)

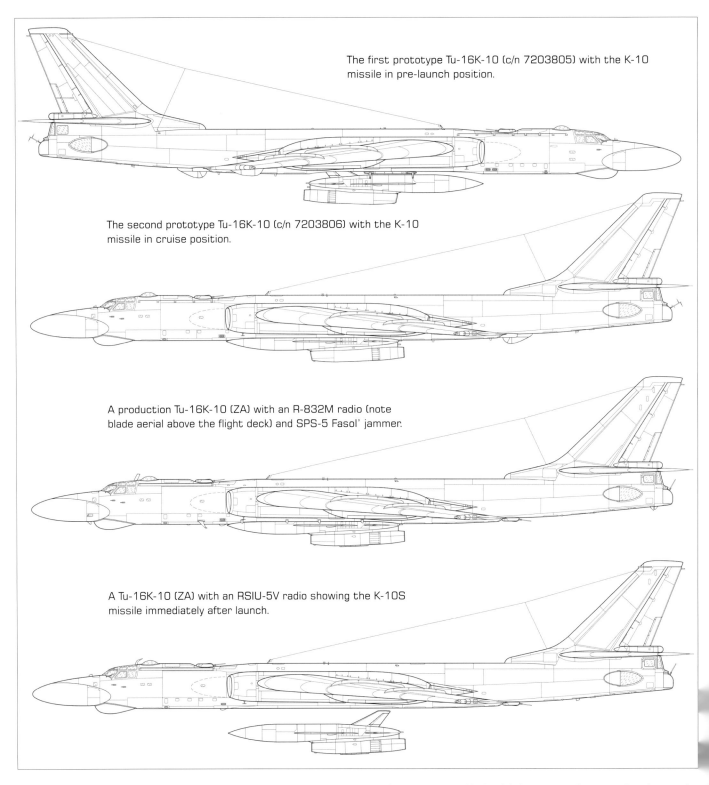

The first prototype Tu-16K-10 (c/n 7203805) with the K-10 missile in pre-launch position.

The second prototype Tu-16K-10 (c/n 7203806) with the K-10 missile in cruise position.

A production Tu-16K-10 (ZA) with an R-832M radio (note blade aerial above the flight deck) and SPS-5 Fasol' jammer.

A Tu-16K-10 (ZA) with an RSIU-5V radio showing the K-10S missile immediately after launch.

bomb or mine load under the wings and a further 4,000 kg of the same under the fuselage.

Typical ordnance loads when configured as a bomber were eight FAB-500 bombs (or sixteen FAB-250 or FAB-100 bombs) or four 650-kg (1,430-lb) torpedoes under the wings plus four FAB-500s (or 16-24 FAB-250s or FAB-100s) or four torpedoes under the fuselage. The smaller bombs were carried on rather untidy-looking MBD3-U6-68 MERs (*mnogozamkovyy bahloch-*

nyy derzhatel' – multi-shackle beam-type [weapons] rack, *oonifit-seerovannyy* – standardised, for Group 3 ordnance, 1968 model) attached to the fuselage-mounted BD4-16-52 racks and carrying 100- or 250-kg bombs in two rows of three. Bomb-aiming was done by means of the radar. The aircraft retained missile strike capability, of course.

The Tu-16K-10-26B and Tu-16K-10-26P likewise had the NATO reporting name *Badger-C Mod.*

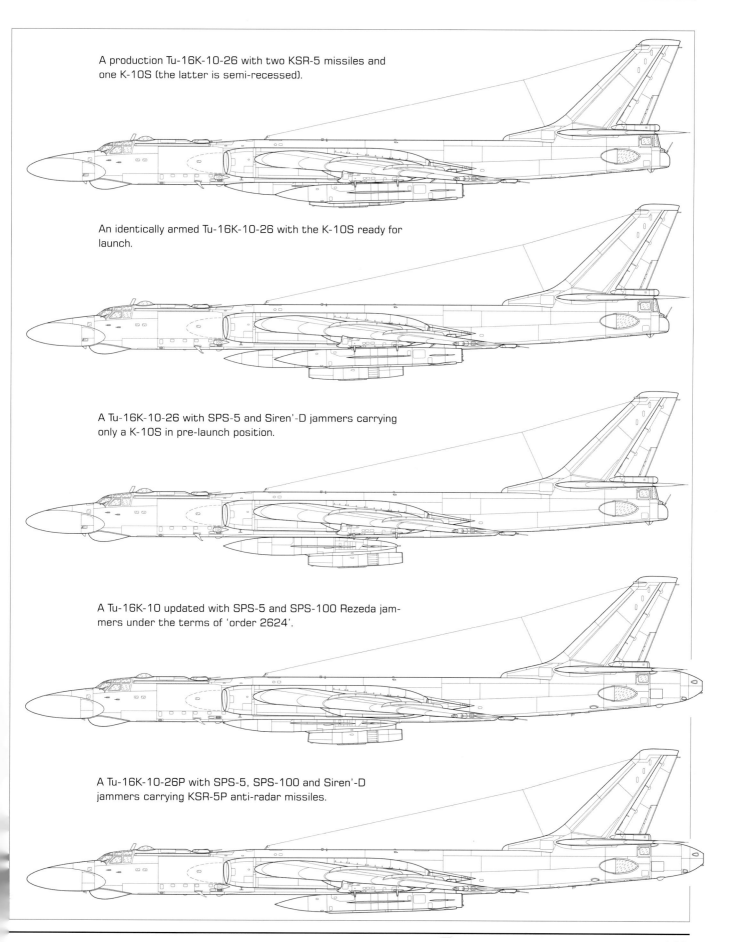

A production Tu-16K-10-26 with two KSR-5 missiles and one K-10S (the latter is semi-recessed).

An identically armed Tu-16K-10-26 with the K-10S ready for launch.

A Tu-16K-10-26 with SPS-5 and Siren'-D jammers carrying only a K-10S in pre-launch position.

A Tu-16K-10 updated with SPS-5 and SPS-100 Rezeda jammers under the terms of 'order 2624'.

A Tu-16K-10-26P with SPS-5, SPS-100 and Siren'-D jammers carrying KSR-5P anti-radar missiles.

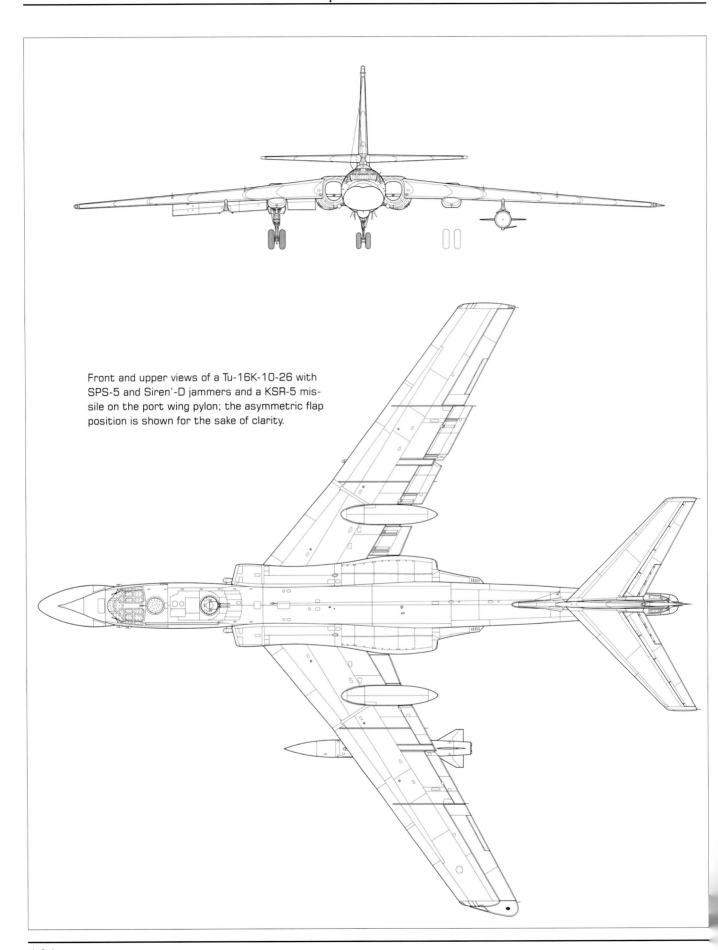

Front and upper views of a Tu-16K-10-26 with
SPS-5 and Siren'-D jammers and a KSR-5 missile on the port wing pylon; the asymmetric flap
position is shown for the sake of clarity.

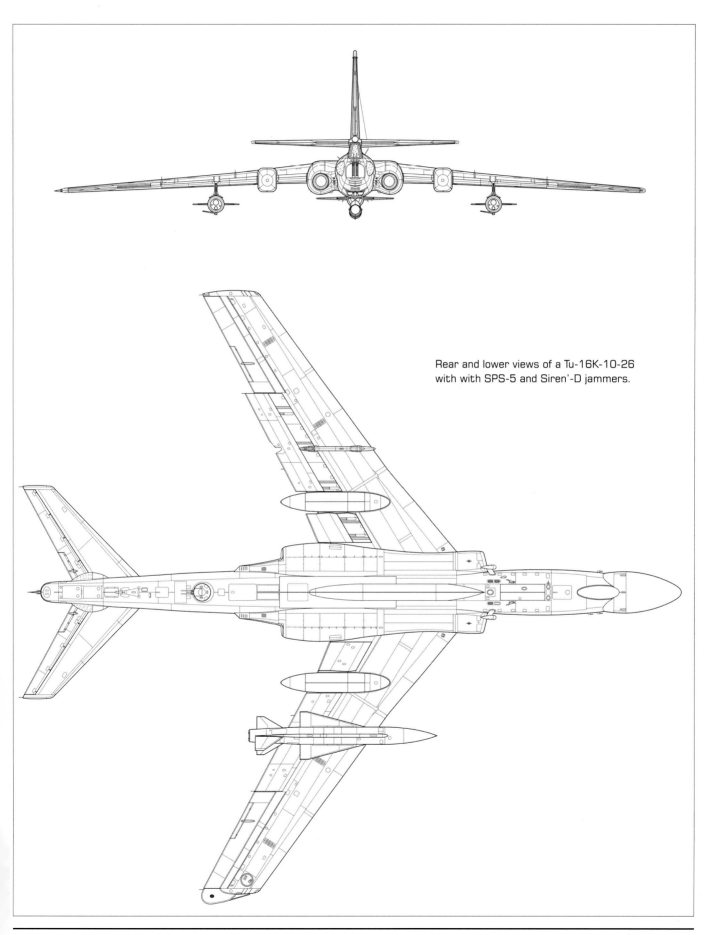

Rear and lower views of a Tu-16K-10-26 with with SPS-5 and Siren'-D jammers.

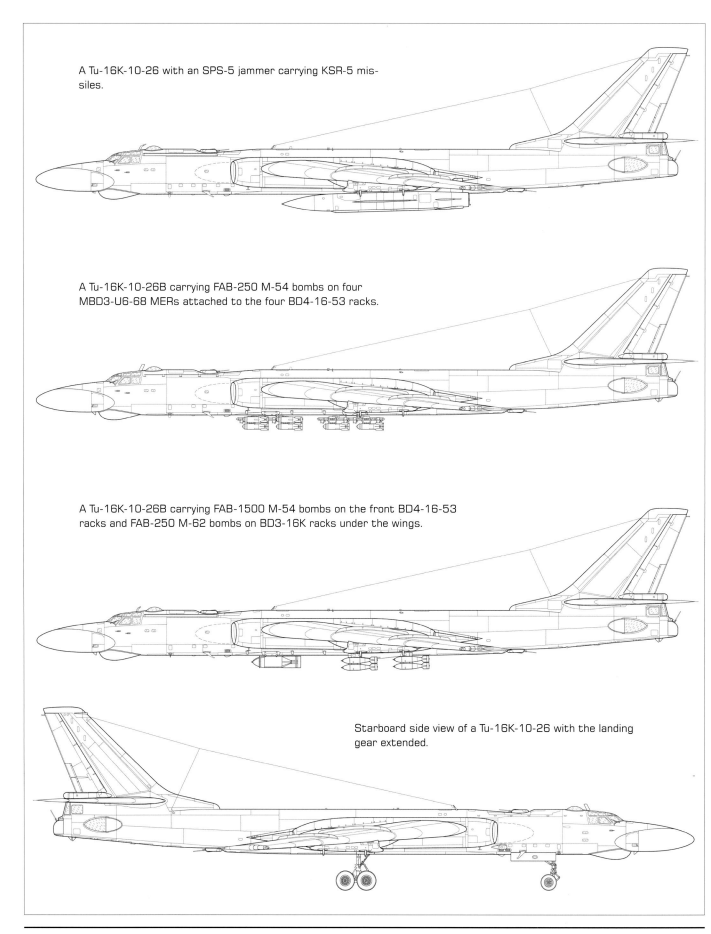

A Tu-16K-10-26 with an SPS-5 jammer carrying KSR-5 missiles.

A Tu-16K-10-26B carrying FAB-250 M-54 bombs on four MBD3-U6-68 MERs attached to the four BD4-16-53 racks.

A Tu-16K-10-26B carrying FAB-1500 M-54 bombs on the front BD4-16-53 racks and FAB-250 M-62 bombs on BD3-16K racks under the wings.

Starboard side view of a Tu-16K-10-26 with the landing gear extended.

Chapter 5

The Tu-16 Family: The Other Soviet Versions

In addition to its primary bomber role (and subsequently missile strike role) the Tu-16 performed a variety of other tasks. The remaining combat and support versions (including some non-military ones) are described in this chapter.

III. The reconnaissance versions

Tu-16R and Tu-16RN (aircraft '92') reconnaissance aircraft (project)

OKB-156 started work on a reconnaissance version of the Tu-16 bomber in 1953. From the outset, the resulting aircraft was conceived as combining photographic reconnaissance (PHOTINT), electronic intelligence (ELINT) gathering and the ability to jam enemy air defence radars. Much depended on the design and production of the crucial electronic equipment.

The Council of Ministers directive No.1659-657 issued on 3rd July 1953, and the corresponding MOP order No.521 dated 18th July called for the creation of the following:

• a new RBP-6 *Lyustra* (Chandelier) bomb-aiming radar derived from the production Rubidiy-MM2 and able to overcome enemy ECM by means of an ECM-resistant high-frequency head, a 2-cm waveband antenna/feeder array and an antenna with a wider scanning arc. Two sets of the new equipment were to be provided by TsNII-108 and OKB-253 by 1954; OKB-156 was to install one such set in a production Tu-16 in the autumn of that year.

• a new *Silikaht* (Silicate) active jammer with a 21.8-30.5 cm waveband for use against enemy ground and shipborne air defence and fighter control radars. This was to be supplied by TsNII-108 which was to co-operate with OKB-156 in installing the set in a Tu-16 in the late spring and early summer of 1955.

Tu-16R *Badger-E* '24 Blue' (c/n 1883207) is intercepted by a US Navy Grumman A-6E Intruder (BuNo 161230/'NH-506') of VA-95 'Green Lizards' operating from USS *Enterprise* in June 1982.

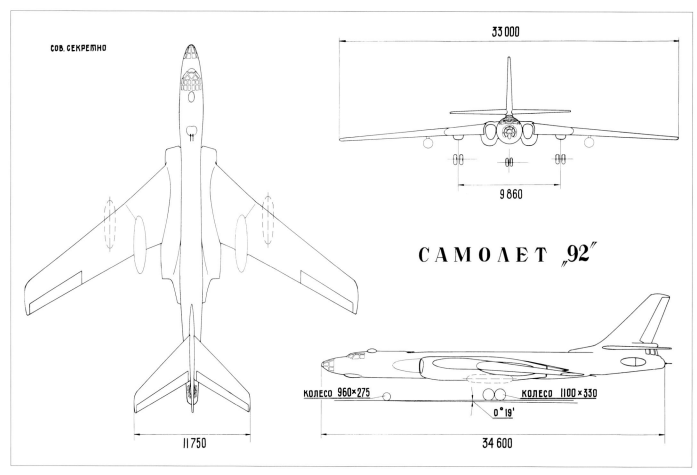

СОВ. СЕКРЕТНО

33 000

9 860

С А М О Л Е Т „92″

КОЛЕСО 960×275   КОЛЕСО 1100×330

0°19'

11 750   34 600

Above: A three-view drawing from the ADP documents of the 'aircraft 92' reconnaissance version showing the SRS-3 ELINT pods under the wings.

Below: The fuselage layouts of the Tu-16R in day reconnaissance (upper) and night reconnaissance configurations, showing the cameras, the flash bombs and the RSO's pressurised capsule.

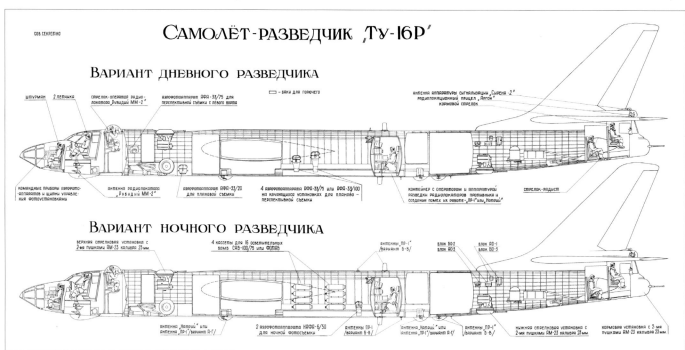

СОВ СЕКРЕТНО

САМОЛЁТ-РАЗВЕДЧИК „ТУ-16Р″

ВАРИАНТ ДНЕВНОГО РАЗВЕДЧИКА

ВАРИАНТ НОЧНОГО РАЗВЕДЧИКА

• a new *Apatit* (Apatite) active jammer with a 2-10 cm wave-band for use against enemy ground and shipborne detection, guidance and target marking radars. This was again the responsibility of TsNII-108 which was to co-operate with OKB-156 in installing this on a Tu-16 during the autumn of 1954.

• a new ASO-2B Avtomat-2 (KDS-16GM) automatic chaff dispenser to scatter radar-reflecting strips of metal-coated glassfibre (chaff) at three- to five-second intervals, working in the 0.6-12 cm waveband. The equipment was to be developed by OKB-134 under Chief Designer Ivan I. Toropov and ready for state acceptance trials on a Tu-16 in the late summer and autumn of 1954.

• a new SRS-3 Romb-1 (Rhombus, or Diamond) automatic ELINT set (SRS = *stahntsiya razvedki svyazi* – communications intelligence set) for use against enemy ground, shipborne and aircraft radars which registered the working frequencies of the radars it detected in the 2.9-30 cm waveband. This was to be supplied by MAP's OKB-483 based in Kiev and by TsNII-108; OKB-156 was to assist with the installation of the SRS-3 in a Tu-16.

• a new ECCM high-frequency head and array developed under the *Planeta* (Planet) programme to protect the RP-1 *Izumrood* (Emerald) airborne intercept radar developed for the MiG-17P *Fresco-B* interceptor (RP = *rahdiopritsel* – 'radio sight', the Soviet term for fire control radars) and the Tu-16's PRS-1 Argon gun-laying radar with a 3-cm waveband against unsynchronised pulse interference. MRP's NII-17 headed by Chief Designer Viktor V. Tikhomirov was to team up with OKB-156 in fitting this ECCM kit to a Tu-16 in the spring of 1954.

In addition to these projects, work was under way on other equipment more resistant to ECM: the Rubin bomb-aiming radar (a joint effort of OKB-283, NII-17 and MOP's Moscow-based TsKB-589), the Topaz radar created by NII-17 and the *Ksenon* (Xenon) radar created by OKB-373, the SRZO-2 Khrom-Nikel' IFF interrogator/transponder. Prototypes of the PR-1 combined ELINT/ECM equipment (*pomekhovo-razvedyvatel'naya [appa-ratoora]*) and the *Natriy* (Sodium) ECM set passed their tests; meanwhile, OKB-134 was completing development of an automatic chaff dispenser intended for the Tu-4, Il-28 and Tu-16.

The camera fit for the reconnaissance version was based on the standard AFA-33 daylight cameras and NAFA-6 night cameras, with the future intention of using the AFA-40 high-altitude camera.

The design and development of this new equipment involved close co-operation with the aircraft designers, who had to work out the best and most compact ways of installing it. On 24th June 1953, MAP issued order No.405, followed by Air Force Operational Requirement No.1197989 which was received by OKB-156 on 9th July; these documents instructed the Tupolev OKB to fit the PR-1 and Natriy sets to production Tu-16 bombers. After making preliminary assessments the OKB considered it more expedient to develop a dedicated reconnaissance version equipped for PHOTINT and ELINT – the Tu-16R (*[samolyot-]razvedchik* – reconnaissance aircraft). This idea was accepted by the Air Force, and a year later, on 23rd June 1954, the Council of Ministers issued

directive No.1249-558 followed by MAP order No.408 on 29th June. These documents tasked the Tupolev OKB with building the Tu-16R powered by two modernised AM-3M-200 engines delivering 9,500 kgp (20,940 lbst) for take-off and 7,650 kgp (16,870 lbst) at nominal power, giving a range of 6,000-6,200 km (3,726-3,850 miles). The Air Force was to place one of its Tu-16s at the disposal of the Tupolev OKB in July 1954, and supply the necessary radio and photographic equipment. The Tu-16R was to be ready for state acceptance trials in March 1955.

The advanced development project of the Tu-16R (initially known in house as 'aircraft 92') was approved on 23rd November 1954, envisaging two versions – the Tu-16R daylight reconnaissance version and a night reconnaissance version designated Tu-16RN (*razvedchik nochnoy*). Since most early Soviet ELINT and ECM systems were not automated, the Tu-16R was to have a special pressurised capsule for their operator (similar to that on the Tu-16KS), bringing the number of crewmembers to seven. The reconnaissance systems operator (RSO) was likewise provided with a downward-firing ejection seat; he shared his quarters with some modules of the PR-1 (or, alternatively, Natriy) equipment. The capsule had its own an air conditioning system to ensure comfortable conditions for the RSO and the equipment. The antennas for the PR-1 (or Natriy) equipment were housed in fairings above and below the RSO's station, as well as in ventral dielectric blisters aft of the RSO's station and under the wing centre section. Additionally, the Tu-16R was to carry the SRS-3 ELINT equipment in underwing pylon-mounted pods. In the aircraft's tail section an antenna for the Sirena-2 radar warning receiver (RWR) was to be fitted above the radome of the Argon gun-laying radar. The standard Rubidiy-MM2 radar was provided with a special FA-RL-1 camera for capturing the images on the radar screen (*fotoapparaht rahdiolokatora* – 'camera for the radar').

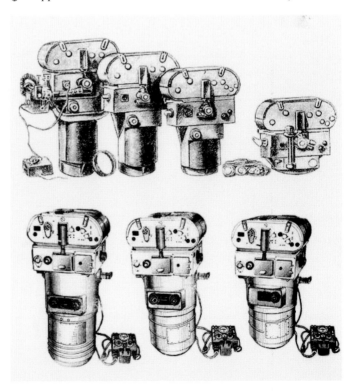

Two types of day cameras with different lenses fitted to the Tu-16R. Upper row, left to right: AFA-33/100, AFA-33/75, AFA-33/50 and AFA-33/20; lower row: AFA-42/100, AFA-42/75 and AFA-42/50.

ADP specifications of the Tu-16R/Tu-16RN ('aircraft 92')		
	Tu-16R	**Tu-16RN**
Empty weight, kg (lb):		
without Romb-1 ELINT set	37,765 (83,260)	37,506 (82,690)
with Romb-1 ELINT set	38,906 (85,771)	38,056 (83,897)
Maximum take-off weight, kg (lb):		
without Romb-1 ELINT set	74,215 (163,610)	75,150 (165,670)
with Romb-1 ELINT set	74,765 (164,825)	75,700 (166,890)
Maximum fuel load, kg (lb)	35,100 (77,380)	35,100 (77,380)
Service ceiling with 55,000-kg (121,250-lb)		
all-up weight, m (ft)	12,800 (41,990)	12,800 (41,990)
Effective range, km (miles)	6,000-6,200	6,000-6,200
	(3,726-3,850)	(3,726-3,850)
Technical range with a 800-km/h (496-mph)		
cruising speed, km (miles)	6,377 (3,960)	6,377 (3,960)
Take-off run with a 75,000-kg (165,350-lb) TOW, m (ft)	1,900 (6,230)	1,900 (6,230)
Landing run with a 41,000-kg (90,390-lb) TOW, m (ft):		
without brake parachutes	1,430 (4,690)	1,430 (4,690)
with brake parachutes	810 (2,660)	810 (2,660)

Performance of the Tu-16R-1 (manufacturer's flight tests)	
Empty weight	38,436 kg (84,735 lb)
Maximum take-off weight	75,370 kg (166,160 lb)
Maximum speed with a 62,000-kg (136,690-lb)	
take-off weight at an altitude of 6,200 m (20,340 ft)	1,000-1,100 km/h (621-683 mph)
Service ceiling	12,400 m (40,680 ft)
Climb time to 10,000 m (32,810 ft):	
with a take-off weight of 62,000 kg	15.1 minutes
with a take-off weight of 75,400 kg (166,230 lb)	24.5 minutes
Operational range	6,300 km (3,913 miles)
Take-off run	2,290-3,275 m (7,510-10,740 ft)

The Tu-16R day reconnaissance version was to carry four AFA-33/75 or AFA-33/100 cameras on AKAFU pivoting mounts (*avtomaticheskaya kachayushchaya aerofotoustanovka* – automatic tilting mount for aircraft cameras) permitting two-strip or four-strip high/medium-altitude photography in its bomb bay, which became a camera bay. An AFA-33/20 vertical camera was also carried for 'opportunity en route' photography. An AFA-33/75 oblique camera was installed in the forward equipment bay, shooting through a camera window on the port side.

Instead of these, the Tu-16RN was to carry two NAFA-6/50 night cameras and 16 SAB-100-75 flare bombs or FotAB-100-80 or FotAB-250-215AM flash bombs (*fotograficheskaya aviabomba* – lit. 'photo bomb') on four cassettes, the flash triggering the camera's shutter via an optical sensor. Both versions had provision for installing the ASO-16/3 chaff dispenser in place of the PR-1 and its operator's capsule.

Tu-16R-1 reconnaissance aircraft prototype

A production Kuibyshev-built Tu-16 bomber (c/n 1880302) manufactured in December 1954, was earmarked for conversion into the reconnaissance prototype, which was performed by plant No.22, with assistance from the local branch office of the Tupolev OKB. Redesignated Tu-16R-1 (the '-1' presumably stood for Version 1 in anticipation of this being the first of several production reconnaissance versions), the aircraft carried a single AFA-33/20M vertical camera, two AFA-33/75M oblique cameras and two AFA-33/10M cameras for photographing targets of opportunity en route. An SPS-1 active jammer was also provided. The aircraft had a crew of seven, the RSO (using the aircraft's radar for reconnaissance) sitting in a Tu-16KS-style pressurised capsule at the rear of the mission equipment bay – that is, the former bomb bay.

Manufacturer's flight tests began on 30th November 1955, and were completed by mid-May 1955. Sixteen flights were made totalling 26 hours 16 minutes.

Equipment changes were made in the course of the tests. SRS-3 (Romb-1) general-purpose signals intelligence (SIGINT) equipment was to be installed in oval-shaped pods mounted on forward-swept pylons under the wings and augmented by an SPS-1AG detailed SIGINT set installed in the fuselage. Delays in the flight tests and the late delivery of electronic equipment caused the Council of Ministers to postpone the state acceptance trials in accord-

A Tu-16R *Badger-E* coded '30 Blue' is escorted by US Navy McDonnell Douglas F-4B-10-MC Phantom II BuNo 149435/'NH-402' of VF-114 'Aardvarks' as it photographs the aircraft carrier USS *Kitty Hawk* in 1963. Note the open camera port of the oblique camera in the zero of the tactical code.

Performance of the Tu-16R-1 (state acceptance trials)				
	without SRS-3 day version	night version	with SRS-3* day version	night version
Empty weight, kg (lb)	38,222 (84,263)	38,041 (83,864)	38,729 (85,381)	35,548 (78,368)
Maximum take-off weight, kg (lb)	75,800 (167,110)	75,800 (167,110)	75,800 (167,110)	75,800 (167,110)
Fuel load, kg (lb)	35,162 (77,517)	35,223 (77,652)	35,655 (78,604)	34,548 (76,164)
Max speed with a 55,000-kg (121,250-lb) TOW, km/h (mph):				
at 6,200 m (20,340 ft)	1,016 (631)	1,016 (631)	1,006 (624)	1,006 (624)
at 10,000 m (32,810 ft)	951 (590)	951 (590)	941 (584)	941 (584)
Service ceiling with a 59,000-kg (130,070-lb) AUW, m (ft)	13,000 (42,650)	13,000 (42,650)	12,900 (42,320)	12,900 (42,320)
Climb time with a 59,000-kg AUW, minutes:				
to 6,000 m (19,685 ft)	6.8	6.8	7.0	7.0
to 10,000 m	14.3	14.3	14.6	14.6
Effective range in a 'hi-hi-hi' mission, km (miles)	6,260 (3,888)	6,080 (3,776)	5,980 (3,714)	5,810 (3,608)
Take-off run with maximum take-off weight, m (ft)	1,960 (6,430)	1,960 (6,430)	–	–
Take-off distance to h=25 m (82 ft) with maximum TOW, m (ft)	3,160 (10,370)	3,160 (10,370)	–	–

* The figures for the version with SRS-3 pods fitted were estimated (obtained by extrapolation)

ance with directive No.424-261 of 26th March 1956 (followed up by MAP order No.194 on 6th April). The trials took place on 19th June – 17th August 1956, involving 27 flights with 97 hours' total time.

The Tu-16R-1 became the prototype for the production Tu-16R, which was to feature SRS-1AG and SRS-3 SIGINT sets, SPS-1 and SPS-3 jammers, and cameras. In reality, however, at the time of the state acceptance trials the prototype had only the SRS-1AG and four AFA-33/75M and AFA-33/100M cameras for two-/four-strip photography, the bomb bay doors featuring two pairs of camera ports with protective shutters for the latter. The Tu-16R-1 also had provisions for twin NAFA-6/50 cameras for night photography at the rear of the bomb bay and a camera port on the port side of the forward fuselage for an AFA-33M/75 oblique camera. Although the wings incorporated hardpoints for the SRS-3 pods, neither the pods nor even the pylons for these were ever fitted to this particular aircraft because ongoing development problems with the SRS-3 prevented its submission for state acceptance trials. The results of the latter are given in the table above.

The Tu-16R-1 was also tested with various loads of flare bombs for night photography (14 FotAB-250-215AMs, or 14 FotAB-100-80s, or eight SAB-250-180MFs). When the cameras were removed from the equipment bay, the machine could be converted to bomber configuration, carrying 14 FAB-250M-50s or ten FAB-500M-50s or two FAB-1500M-50s; bomb-aiming was done by means of the RBP-4 radar and/or the OPB-11R optical bombsight.

The positive results of the state acceptance trials prompted a decision to launch production which was made official by Council of Ministers directive No.1545-777 of 3rd December 1956, and MAP order No.601 of 10th December. The production Tu-16R was to be powered by two AM-3M engines, and plant No.1 was instructed to build 44 examples patterned on the prototype in 1957 after the defects and shortcomings noted during the trials had been rectified. The aircraft was to be manufactured with optional AFA-34-LK/100, AFA-34-LK/75 and NAFA-MK/75 cameras.

The features tested on Tu-16R-1 would later be incorporated in a series of reconnaissance and ECM versions of the *Badger*, including the Tu-16SPS, Tu-16P, Tu-16 Yolka and so on.

Tu-16 Romb reconnaissance aircraft ('order 261')

Although the SRS-3 Romb-1 was not available in time for the manufacturer's tests or state acceptance trials, it was still planned to fit it to the Tu-16R-1 once it became available. However, tests with the intended underwing pods showed that the drag generated by them caused some deterioration in the aircraft's performance. It was therefore decided to accommodate the SRS-3 in the fuselage, the antenna being housed in a ventral fairing.

The urgent need for this long-range reconnaissance aircraft led plant No.1 in Kuibyshev to produce the first five aircraft equipped with the buried SRS-3 set and no SRS-1 set in 1956; such aircraft were officially designated Tu-16 Romb. Later, all five of these aircraft were retrofitted with the SRS-1 ELINT system. In production they were referred to as 'order 261', and they are sometimes called Tu-16R 'Romb' or simply Tu-16R. There was, however, little reduction in drag and subsequent production examples had the SRS-3 equipment housed in underwing pods as originally planned.

Tu-16R reconnaissance aircraft ('order 361', *izdeliye* NR)

In 1957 plant No.1 produced 44 Tu-16Rs and a further 26 in 1958 with various reconnaissance equipment fits in accordance with the abovementioned directive No.1545-777. Of this total of 70 aircraft patterned on the Tu-16R-1 prototype (with provisions for the SRS-3 underwing pods), production was distributed as follows:

• version 1 – 18 aircraft with the SRS-1 (bands A/B/C) and SRS-6 SIGINT sets;

• version 2 – 18 aircraft with the SRS-1 (bands D/E) and SRS-3 SIGINT sets;

• version 3 – 34 aircraft with the SRS-1 (bands D/E) only.

(Note: 'Version 1/2/3' are used here purely for the sake of convenience and are not actual designations. Likewise, the above 'bands A-B-C-D-E' – or 'A-B-V-G-D' in Cyrillic alphabetical sequence – are purely conventional designations for wavebands whose frequencies are not known; this should not be confused with familiar terms like 'J-band' or 'S-band'. The SRS-1 could be tuned to this or that range of wavebands.)

Tu-16Rs with the SRS-3 were built under the terms of 'order 361' and were known in service as *izdeliye* NR. The equipment bays housed the ASO-16/3 Avtomat-1 and ASO-2B Avtomat-2 chaff dispensers. In service the Tu-16R could carry any of four sets of cameras, depending on the mission.

The production Tu-16R differed from the baseline bomber in the following aspects. To enable operation of the daylight vertical cameras, which were operated without opening the bomb bay doors, the latter featured two 280x467 mm ($11^1/_{32}$ in x 1 ft $6^{25}/_{64}$ in) camera ports each, with inward-opening protective shutters; these were located between frames 34-36 for the two AFA-42/75 cameras and between frames 36-38 for the two AFA-34-OK cameras. As mentioned earlier, an AFA-33/75 oblique camera was installed on a tilting mount in the forward equipment bay (just aft of the flight deck's rear pressure dome), shooting through a rectangular camera window between frames 13-15 on the port side closed by horizontally split doors; the camera's axis could be adjusted between –6° and –45° to the horizontal plane.

When the Tu-16R was configured for night PHOTINT with two NAFA-MK-75 cameras, which required the bomb bay doors to be opened, a boxy structure made of duralumin sheet with two glazed camera ports was installed between frames 42-45 to enclose the cameras, protecting them from the slipstream and preventing camera shake. In this case, flare bombs were carried on standard KD3-488 cassettes in the rear part of the bomb bay and dropped automatically by a timer. The RBP-4 radar could also be used for reconnaissance, the image on the radarscope being photographed by a FARM-2 camera. Working with the cameras was the responsibility of the navigator.

As mentioned earlier, the rear part of the bomb bay accommodated a pressurised capsule for the RSO located between frames 45-48A. Hence the Tu-16R's bomb bay doors featured a cut-out on the centreline in this area for the RSO's entry hatch; a dorsal emergency exit was also provided. An instrument panel on the port side featured basic flight instruments and controls for the SIGINT equipment. The capsule's pressurisation and air conditioning system was the same as for other versions with such a workstation.

Apart from the camera ports and the RSO's hatches, which were not very conspicuous when closed, the Tu-16R's main external identification feature – in the absence of the SRS-3 pods, that is – was the two teardrop-shaped GRP fairings fore and aft of the bomb bay. These were of unequal size; the smaller forward blister located between frames 26-27 was slightly offset to port, incorporating a maintenance access panel, and required a recess to be made in the No.3 fuselage fuel tank to accommodate the antenna inside. The large rear blister, which was located between frames 49-52, was mounted on a panel supplanting the clamshell doors of the marker/flare bomb compartment. On versions 2 and 3 above, the forward blister housed the 'band D' antenna of the SRS-1GD set and the rear blister housed the 'band E' antenna of the same. Version 1 was equipped with the SRS-1ABV variety of the same set, and the modified rear blister housed its ventral 'band A/B/C' antennas; two unswept blade aerials covering the same bands were located dorsally fore and aft of the RSO's emergency exit. In this case the forward blister was said to house simply the forward antenna of the SRS-1, with no indication of the waveband.

The hardpoints for the pylons carrying the SRS-3 pods were located at ribs 9-11 and positioned 7.85 m (25 ft $9^3/_{64}$ in) from the centreline. The front spar was reinforced and the Nos. 14 and 15 fuel tanks in each wing were modified accordingly. Each pod had nine frames, the large nosecone and the smaller tailcone being dielectric; four lateral and three ventral detachable panels were provided for access to the equipment inside.

At first the Tu-16R had only passive ECM capability. In common with upgraded bombers an ASO-16/3 chaff dispenser was installed in the bomb bay, with an outlet in the port door aft of the camera ports, and an ASO-2B chaff dispenser was housed in the rear avionics/equipment bay, with an outlet between frames 63-64. The ASO-16/3 was controlled by the Nav/Op, while the ASO-2B was operated by the tail gunner (defensive fire commander). A Sirena-2 radar warning receiver was fitted, with an aft-looking aerial at the tip of the port stabiliser.

As mentioned earlier, the Tu-16R was produced in two versions (for day and night photography). In the daytime PHOTINT configuration there were typically two options. Option 1 comprised an AFA-33/75M oblique camera with a 75-cm focal length and an AFA-33/20 fixed vertical camera with a 20-cm focal length in the forward avionics/equipment bay, plus two AKAFU mounts in the bomb bay, each tilting through 6.3-18.3° to the vertical and mounting two AFA-33/100M cameras with a 100-cm focal length for two-strip/four-strip photography. Option 2 consisted of an AFA-42/100 oblique camera and an AFA-42/20 vertical camera in the avionics bay plus four more AFA-42/100s on the AKAFU mounts. The cameras in the bomb bay covered a strip whose length was 46 times the flight altitude. In the night PHOTINT configuration there was only one camera option (two NAFA-MK-75s) but there was a choice of sixteen FotAB-250-215 flash bombs or 24 FotAB-100-80 flash bombs.

The day version fitted with SRS-1 and SRS-3 SIGINT sets had an empty weight of 39,140 kg (86,290 lb); for the night version carrying a load of 16 FotAB-100 flash bombs it was 39,870 kg (87,900 lb).

Some early-production examples left the factory with AFA-34LK/100 cameras. A few others were completed with a mixed complement of mission equipment, carrying both cameras and the SRS-1 SIGINT set.

By the early 1960s the Tu-16R was in large-scale service with the Soviet Air Force and the Soviet Navy alike, being regarded as a high-speed long-range PHOTINT/ELINT aircraft intended for operations in the enemy's theatre-strategic areas on land and maritime theatres of operations. Four interchangeable standardised sets of equipment were used to suit typical missions.

The Tu-16R lacking the underwing ELINT pods (with ventral blisters only) received the NATO reporting name *Badger-E*. The variety equipped with the SRS-3 pods took a little longer to be detected by the West and thus became known as the *Badger-F*.

In the course of its service career the Tu-16R was fitted with more modern cameras. Other avionics and equipment were updated as well. For example, during maintenance work some Tu-16Rs had the more sophisticated SRS-4 *Kvadraht* (Square) SIGINT system installed in place of the SRS-1; the teardrop fairing for the SRS-4 was slightly bigger than for the SRS-1. Some

Performance of the Tu-16R with the SRS-1 set (without the SRS-3 pods)	
Maximum take-off weight	75,300 kg (166,010 lb)
Maximum speed:	
at 6,250 m (20,510 ft)	1,000 km/h (621 mph)
at 10,000 m (32,810 ft)	930 km/h (577 mph)
Operational range with 5% fuel reserves	6,300 km (3,913 miles)
Service ceiling	13,100 m (42,980 ft)
Take-off run	1,800 m (5,910 ft)
Length and width of camera coverage	600 x 13 km (372 x 8 miles)

Badger-Es had the A-326 Rogovitsa formation keeping system retrofitted. After the infamous defection of Lt. Viktor I. Belenko, a fighter pilot of the 530th IAP stationed at Chugooyevka AB in the Soviet Far East, to Japan in a Mikoyan/Gurevich MiG-25P *Foxbat-A* interceptor on 6th September 1976, the Soviet Air Force and Air Defence Force were compelled to field a new IFF system aptly called *Parol'* (password), and Tu-16Rs remaining in service by then were updated accordingly, having the SRO-2 IFF transponder replaced with the latest SRO-1P transponder. This was revealed by the distinctive triangular blade aerials replacing the earlier sys-tem's equally characteristic triple rod aerials of unequal length that had given rise to the *Odd Rods* codename.

Tu-16R-2 experimental reconnaissance aircraft ('order 455')

On 11th June 1956, the Council of Ministers came up with directive No.788-437 followed by MAP order No.343 on 23rd June. The directive required MAP to make sure all new bomber types had a reconnaissance version from the outset and tasked MAP to begin production of up-to-date reconnaissance aircraft to MoD specifications on 1st January 1957. Among other things, the Tupolev OKB was required to equip a Tu-16 with two AFA-40 high-altitude cameras, two AFA-33/20M cameras and an AFA-37 wide-angle camera, submitting it for check-up trials in January 1957.

Conversion of the original Tu-16R-1 prototype (c/n 1880302) started at plant No.22 in November 1956, under the terms of 'order 455' immediately after the aircraft had completed its state acceptance trials, the mock-up review commission assessing the project of the new version designated Tu-16R-2 that same month. However, the prototype of the new version was not completed until the summer of 1957.

Above and above right: The underwing SRS-3 ELINT pods of the Tu-16R *Badger-F*. The front dielectric portions are larger than the rear ones; note the shape of the pylons.
Below: '23 Red' (c/n 1883314), a production Tu-16R (ZA) with SRS-3 pods.

Top, above and left: This Tu-16R (ZA) *Badger-F* equipped with SRS-3 pods ('05 Blue', c/n 1883405) has been updated with a comprehensive ECM suite, featuring a Siren'-D jammer to cover the front hemisphere (with antennas on the nose glazing and under the air intakes) and a Siren'-MD jammer in a UKhO fairing replacing the tail turret – a late addition.

Above right: Tu-16R *Badger-E* with the SRS-1 system ('29 Red', c/n 1883511) underwent check-up tests with a different tail fairing housing an SPS-100M Mal'va jammer.

Right, centre right and far right: Close-ups of the fairing for the SPS-100 jammer showing the two pairs of emitter antenna blisters, the cooling air scoops and the cooling air outlet at the rear.

On 16th August 1957, the Tu-16R-2 was ferried from Kazan'-Borisoglebskoye to the GK NII VVS base at Chkalovskaya AB near Moscow, but problems with the camera system delayed the start of check-up trials by a full year. These eventually took place between 20th August 1958, and 23rd February 1959. Yet, series production was not recommended – again due to problems with the cameras installed.

Among other things, the aircraft was fitted with an AFA-42/75 oblique camera on a new mount designed by the Tupolev OKB, which underwent state acceptance trials on 18th July – 30th August 1958. This mount had slightly different tilt angles as compared to the production model (–10° to –45°) but, whereas the standard mount was ground-adjustable, the new model had a servo drive and a synchro system. It was slaved to a special sight at the navigator's station, allowing the navigator to tilt the camera in flight. Apart from the cameras, the Tu-16R-2 featured SRS-3 ELINT equipment in underwing pods.

Coded '50 Red' and stripped of the ELINT pods, the Tu-16R-2 finally ended up as an exhibit at the Soviet Air Force Museum (now Central Russian Air Force Museum) in Monino, Moscow Region, where it remains on display to this day.

Tu-16R (ZA) reconnaissance aircraft

Most of the production Tu-16Rs were fitted with a refuelling receptacle under the port wingtip. Accordingly such aircraft were given the designation Tu-16R (ZA).

Tu-16RP reconnaissance aircraft ('order 697')

A few Tu-16Rs – both with and without the podded SRS-3 ELINT system – had additional ECM gear. These were given the designation Tu-16RP, the P referring to *pomekhi* – interference, or ECM. The type of equipment varied. Some *Badger-Es* and *-Fs* were retrofitted with the SPS-5 Fasol' jammer for self-protection, sporting the distinctive blade aerials near the nosewheel well. Others received a more comprehensive ECM suite, featuring the SPS-5, the Siren'-D jammer covering the forward hemisphere (with the thimble fairing on the navigator's station glazing and egg-shaped fairings below the air intakes) and the Siren'-MD jammer in a UKhO tail fairing covering the rear hemisphere.

Tu-16RE reconnaissance aircraft

Some Tu-16Rs had their SRS-1 ELINT equipment replaced by the SPS-2 active jammer. Such aircraft were designated Tu-16RE; the meaning of the E suffix is unknown.

Tu-16R with SPS-100M Mal'va jammer

A single Tu-16R *Badger-E* with the SRS-1 ELINT set ('29 Red', c/n 1883511) was retrofitted with an updated SPS-100M *Mal'va* (Mallow) jammer, which was developed in accordance with Council of Ministers directive No.1008-341 dated 31st October 1967 and the Air Force's SOR dated 27th February 1968. The jammer was housed in the same type of tail fairing supplanting the tail turret as used for the SPS-100 Rezeda, with minor differences.

The aircraft underwent check-up tests at GNIKI VVS on 5th-20th November 1969, with A. S. Konev as project test pilot and Engineer-Maj. K. I. Babunov as engineer in charge. The purpose was to examine the new jammer's performance and check it for electromagnetic compatibility (EMC) with the aircraft's systems. The aircraft made 12 flights, logging 51 hours 21 minutes; the jammer's total operation time was 90 hours, including 47 hours 56 minutes in flight. During this time the SPS-100M was in action against the SON-15 AAA gun-laying radar (*stahntsiya oroodiynoy navodki*) and SNR-125 surface-to-air missile guidance radar (*stah-ntsiya navedeniya raket*) that was part of the S-125 *Neva* (a Russian river; NATO codename SA-3 *Goa*) SAM system, as well as the Sukhoi Su-15 *Flagon-A* interceptor equipped with an *Oryol-D58M* (Eagle) radar and the Mikoyan/Gurevich Ye-155P (the MiG-25P prototype) equipped with a Smerch-A (Tornado) fire control radar.

Tu-16R with RBP-6 Lyustra radar

A small number of Tu-16Rs were fitted with the new RBP-6 Lyustra ground-mapping radar. These were given the NATO reporting name *Badger-K*.

Left: The prototype of the Tu-16RR RINT aircraft with RR8311-100 air sampling pods under the wings

Below left: An operational Tu-16RR is refuelled by a Tu-16Z tanker.

Right: A Tu-16RR is prepared for a sortie. The vehicle on the left is an APA-80 GPU on a ZiL-131 6x6 army lorry chassis.

Below right: A crewman poses with a Tu-16RR; note the hatch of the RSO's capsule and the open bomb bay doors with cut-outs for the hatch.

Tu-16RR RINT aircraft (Tu-16RZA, 'order 2694')

On 22nd November 1967, the Council of Ministers issued directive No.1081-370 requiring the Tupolev OKB to create a radiation intelligence (RINT) version of the Tu-16R capable of sampling the atmosphere and recording radioactive contamination levels. Hence in October-November 1969, a production Kuibyshev-built Tu-16R (ZA) coded '27 Blue' (c/n 1883305) was equipped with two standardised RR8311-100 air sampling pods (*radiatsionnaya razvedka* – RINT). Originally developed in 1964 by the Yakovlev OKB for the Yak-28RR *Brewer-D* tactical reconnaissance aircraft, these compact cylindrical pods had a nose intake closed by a translating cone and a rear shutter turning through 90° to permit straight-through airflow. A paper filter inside arrested dust particles for subsequent analysis on the ground, allowing radiation levels at specific altitudes to be measured; it was also suitable for checking for chemical and biological contamination. Such pods were also carried by several other types – the Antonov An-12RR *Cub*, An-24RR *Coke* and An-30R *Clank* RINT aircraft, the Yakovlev Yak-25RR *Mandrake* high-altitude reconnaissance aircraft and occasionally even the Tu-95K-22 *Bear-G* missile strike aircraft.

In the case of the Tu-16R the pods were mounted under the wings on special pylons at ribs 9-11, replacing the SRS-3 ELINT pods. The SRS-1 SIGINT pack and camera equipment were retained so that the machine could be used as a conventional reconnaissance aircraft. Appropriate controls at the navigator's workstation were also fitted, but the prescribed DP-25 dosimeter was missing because the Air Force did not have them in stock!

The prototype of the RINT version underwent special tests between 23rd December 1969, and 7th January 1970; G. I. Bagayev was the engineer in charge. The testing took place at Khvalynka AB near Spassk-Dal'niy (Primor'ye Territory) in the Soviet Far East, which hosted the 219th ODRAP (*otdel'nyy dahl'niy razvedyvatel'nyy aviapolk* – Independent Long-Range Reconnaissance Air Regiment), but the 71st Test Range at Bagerovo AB closely associated with Soviet nuclear tests was actively involved. The test report calls the aircraft Tu-16RZA – with no parentheses. This has led some researchers to decipher ZA as *zondirovshchik atmosfery* (atmosphere sampler), rather than *zapravlyayemyy [samolyot]* (receiver aircraft) as is usually the case with Tu-16 versions – possibly by analogy with the Antonov An-2ZA (An-6) *Colt*

biplane and the Il-28ZA, although these served a different purpose, being civil weather reconnaissance aircraft. However, the new variant is more commonly called Tu-16RR (*radiatsionnyy razvedchik* – RINT aircraft).

Three flights totalling 9 hours 45 minutes, including one from a dirt airstrip, were made during the tests to assess the aircraft's stability and handling with the pods in place, check if they were attached firmly enough and check the possibility of air sampling; the results were positive. The test report endorsed in May 1970, was signed by Long-Range Aviation Deputy Commander Lt.-Gen. Aleksey A. Plokhov, Commander of the DA's 6th Independent Heavy Bomber Corps Maj.-Gen. Vladimir P. Dragomiretskiy, chief of the MoD 12th Main Directorate's Special Monitoring Service Maj.-Gen. Aleksandr I. Ustyumenko (this service was/is responsible for monitoring nuclear tests) and the Tupolev OKB's Deputy General Designer Aleksandr A. Arkhangel'skiy.

During the early 1970s eight operational Tu-16R (ZA)s were converted to Tu-16RRs under the terms of 'order 2694'. They were used to monitor Chinese nuclear tests at the Lop Nor Proving Ground; flying at high altitude, they also collected data from Soviet nuclear weapons tests to determine how much radioactive contamination resulted from an underground nuclear explosion. Each of these sorties counted as an operational mission for the aircraft's crew.

In the course of operation some Tu-16RRs were fitted with the A-326 Rogovitsa formation-keeping system and an SPS-152 Siren'-D jammer covering the forward hemisphere; its antennas were mounted in a small thimble fairing on the navigator's station glazing and in small teardrop-shaped pods pylon-mounted below the air intakes.

The Tu-16RR had the NATO reporting name *Badger-L*.

Tu-16RM reconnaissance aircraft

In the late 1970s and early 1980s a number of Tu-16Rs was re-equipped as the Tu-16RM (*razvedchik modernizeerovannyy* – reconnaissance aircraft, upgraded). The Tu-16RM carried the more sophisticated AFA-41/20, AFA-42/20, AFA-42/75, AFA-42/100 and NAFA-MK-75 cameras, the SRS-4 Kvadrat ELINT set and the RBP-4 radar was replaced by the Rubin-1K which offered better target resolution. The SRS-1 and SRS-3 SIGINT sets were removed. Externally the Tu-16RM differed from the Tu-16R in lacking the latter's underwing SRS-3 pods and having different dielectric fairings for the Rubin-1K radar and SRS-4 antennas.

Tu-16RM-1 maritime reconnaissance aircraft

The need for a more specialised maritime reconnaissance version of the Tu-16R arose in the late 1950s and early 1960s, and a spin-off of the Tu-16K-10 ASM carrier was chosen as the most suitable option for Naval Aviation needs. Two examples of the Tu-16K-10 nearing the end of their service lives were chosen for conversion as the Tu-16RM-1 prototypes (in this case the RM stood for *razvedchik morskoy* – reconnaissance aircraft, naval), the work being carried out by the Navy's maintenance services under the supervision of Tupolev's OKB-156. The BD-238 missile pylon and launch equipment were removed, the weapons bay doors were locked shut and a specialised YeN-R version of the radar was fitted.

Outwardly the Tu-16RM-1 differed from the Tu-16K-10 in having a slightly deeper chin radome (a feature of the YeN-R radar) and three teardrop-shaped ventral dielectric blisters amidships. The front (big) and rear (small) blisters housed the antennas of the SRS-1 or SRS-1M general-purpose SIGINT set while the centre blister, which was the largest of the three, housed the antenna of the SRS-4 detailed SIGINT set; some examples had dorsal 'band A/B/C' blade aerials for the SRS-1 set. Conventional AFA-33/20M (vertical) and AFA-42/75 (oblique) cameras were also carried, and

Above left: The nose of a Tu-16RM-1 reconnaissance aircraft showing the enlarged lower radome of the specialised YeN-R radar.

Above: The centreline ELINT blisters of a Tu-16RM-1. The non-functional missile bay doors are visible.

Opposite: Tu-16RM-1 '20 Blue' is intercepted by Douglas A-4E Skyhawk BuNo 152012/'AU-662' of CVS-11/Det 1 from USS *Intrepid*.

some Tu-16RM-1s carried SPS-1 and SPS-2 ECM sets. The mission equipment was operated by the RSO sitting in a pressurised capsule which remained at the same location as on the Tu-16K-10.

The 'duck-billed' maritime reconnaissance version was accepted for service in the early 1960s; since series production of the Tu-16 ended in 1963 and no new-build aircraft were available, 11 (12 or 14, according to some sources) Tu-16K-10s were converted to Tu-16RM-1 configuration.

Aside from reconnaissance, the Tu-16RM-1 could also provide mid-course guidance for K-10 ASMs launched by Tu-16K-10 and Tu-16K-10-26 aircraft. The NATO reporting name was *Badger-D*.

Tu-16RM-2 maritime reconnaissance aircraft

The Tu-16RM-2 was a 'glass-nosed' version equipped with an SRS-4 SIGINT set identifiable by the two widely spaced ventral dielectric teardrop fairings of equal size. The bomb bay of such aircraft housed a long-range tank holding 7,000 litres (1,540 Imp gal) located between frames 35-42; the nose cannon was removed.

However, some sources describe the Tu-16RM-2 as 12 (or 11) Tu-16K-10Ds converted to carry the same equipment as the Tu-16RM-1. The reasoning is not clear, since the Tu-16K-10D differed from the Tu-16K-10 in having upgraded missile guidance equipment which would be removed anyway during conversion.

Tu-16RTs experimental maritime reconnaissance/ OTH targeting aircraft

In 1956 OKB-52 headed by Vladimir N. Chelomey began preliminary design studies for the P-6 anti-shipping cruise missile – a submarine-launched derivative of the P-35 (NATO codename SS-N-3A *Shaddock*) surface-to-surface naval missile. The P-6 was developed in 1962-63, successfully passing its state acceptance trials, and was accepted for use with Type 651 (NATO codename *Juliette* class) diesel-electric submarines and Type 675

Above: An interesting top view of a Tu-16RM-1 photographed over a blanket of overcast. The shadow from the dorsal blade aerial of the SRS-4 SIGINT system between the engines shows this is not a Tu-16K-10.

Above right: The same aircraft ('68 Blue') seen from below; here the radomes leave no doubt as to the version.

Left and right: Tu-16RM-1s of the North Fleet's 967th ODRAP parked in the dispersal area at Severomorsk-1 AB.

Top: Tu-16RM-2 '90 Red' shows the widely spaced ELINT blisters of equal size.
Above: TU-16RM-2 '45 Blue' photographed as it overflies the carrier USS *Midway* on 15th March 1983.
Below: The rarely seen Tu-16RTs reconnaissance/OTH targeting aircraft escorted by a Japanese Air Self-Defence Force McDonnell Douglas F-15J Eagle. The lack of missile pylons shows this is not a *Badger-G-Mod* refitted with a Rubin-1M radar.

NATO codename *Echo II* class) nuclear-powered submarines. The missile could be launched while the submarine was submerged. Work proceeded in parallel on an airborne target detection and over-the-horizon (OTH) targeting system able to transmit target data directly to the submarine. After the missile had been launched, the aircraft would provide mid-course guidance.

As part of the P-6 programme three *Badgers* were converted into the prototypes of a maritime version designated Tu-16RTs

(*razvedchik-tseleookazatel'* – reconnaissance/OTH targeting aircraft). Their Rubin-1 radar was replaced by an *Oospekh* (Success) radar whose antenna was housed in a large teardrop radome near the bomb bay.

The P-6 was accepted for service with the Soviet Navy in 1965, but the Tu-16RTs was not. It did, however, take part in tests of the reconnaissance and target designator equipment fitted to the production Tu-95RTs *Bear-D* filling the same role.

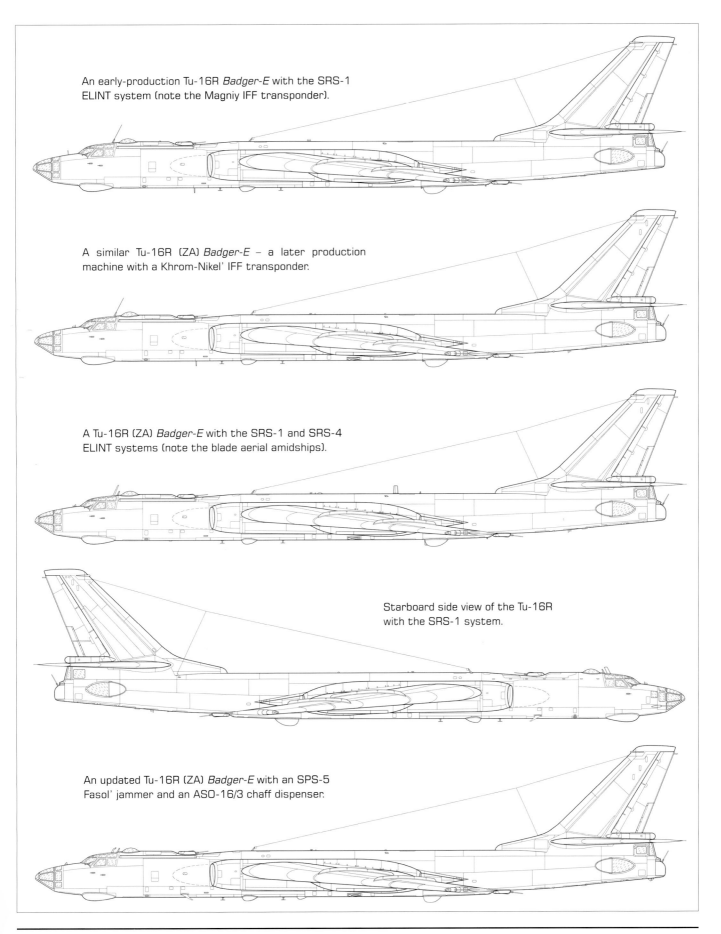

An early-production Tu-16R *Badger-E* with the SRS-1 ELINT system (note the Magniy IFF transponder).

A similar Tu-16R (ZA) *Badger-E* – a later production machine with a Khrom-Nikel' IFF transponder.

A Tu-16R (ZA) *Badger-E* with the SRS-1 and SRS-4 ELINT systems (note the blade aerial amidships).

Starboard side view of the Tu-16R with the SRS-1 system.

An updated Tu-16R (ZA) *Badger-E* with an SPS-5 Fasol' jammer and an ASO-16/3 chaff dispenser.

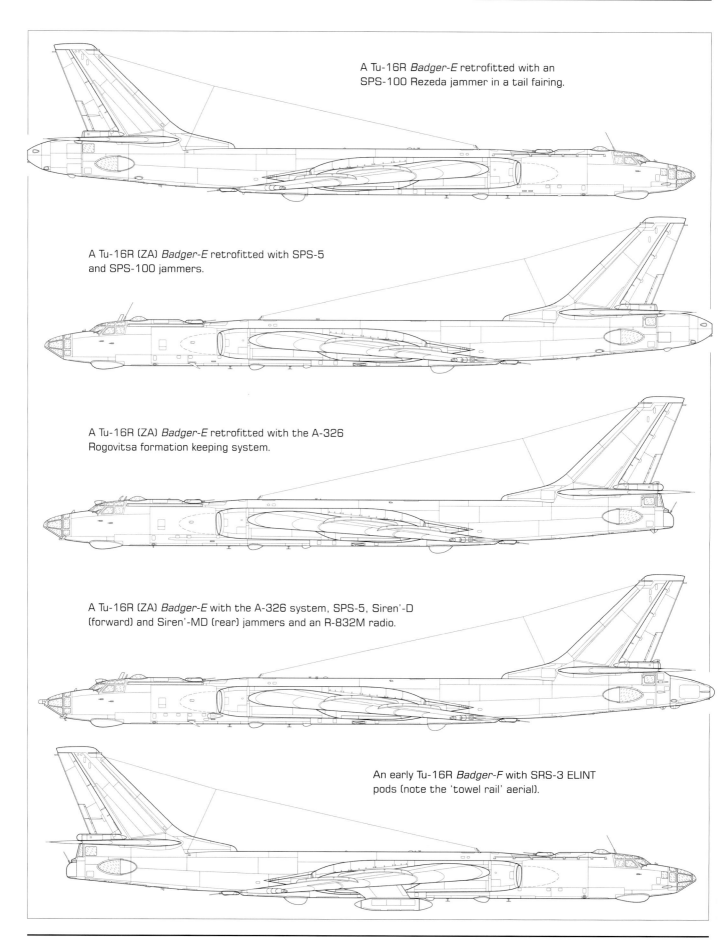

A Tu-16R *Badger-E* retrofitted with an
SPS-100 Rezeda jammer in a tail fairing.

A Tu-16R (ZA) *Badger-E* retrofitted with SPS-5
and SPS-100 jammers.

A Tu-16R (ZA) *Badger-E* retrofitted with the A-326
Rogovitsa formation keeping system.

A Tu-16R (ZA) *Badger-E* with the A-326 system, SPS-5, Siren'-D
(forward) and Siren'-MD (rear) jammers and an R-832M radio.

An early Tu-16R *Badger-F* with SRS-3 ELINT
pods (note the 'towel rail' aerial).

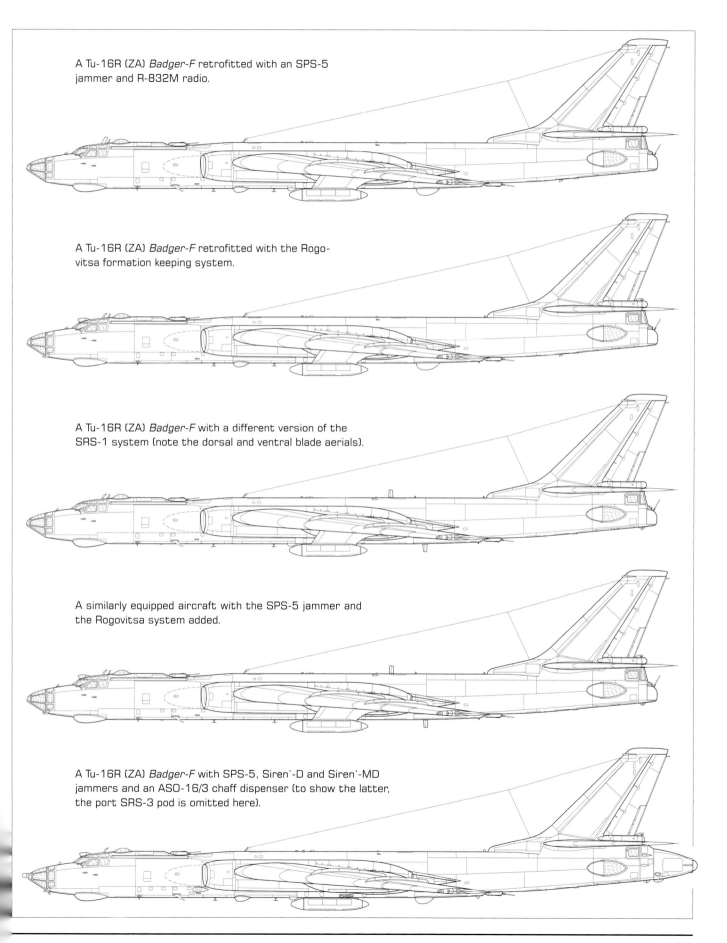

A Tu-16R (ZA) *Badger-F* retrofitted with an SPS-5
jammer and R-832M radio.

A Tu-16R (ZA) *Badger-F* retrofitted with the Rogovitsa formation keeping system.

A Tu-16R (ZA) *Badger-F* with a different version of the
SRS-1 system (note the dorsal and ventral blade aerials).

A similarly equipped aircraft with the SPS-5 jammer and
the Rogovitsa system added.

A Tu-16R (ZA) *Badger-F* with SPS-5, Siren'-D and Siren'-MD
jammers and an ASO-16/3 chaff dispenser (to show the latter,
the port SRS-3 pod is omitted here).

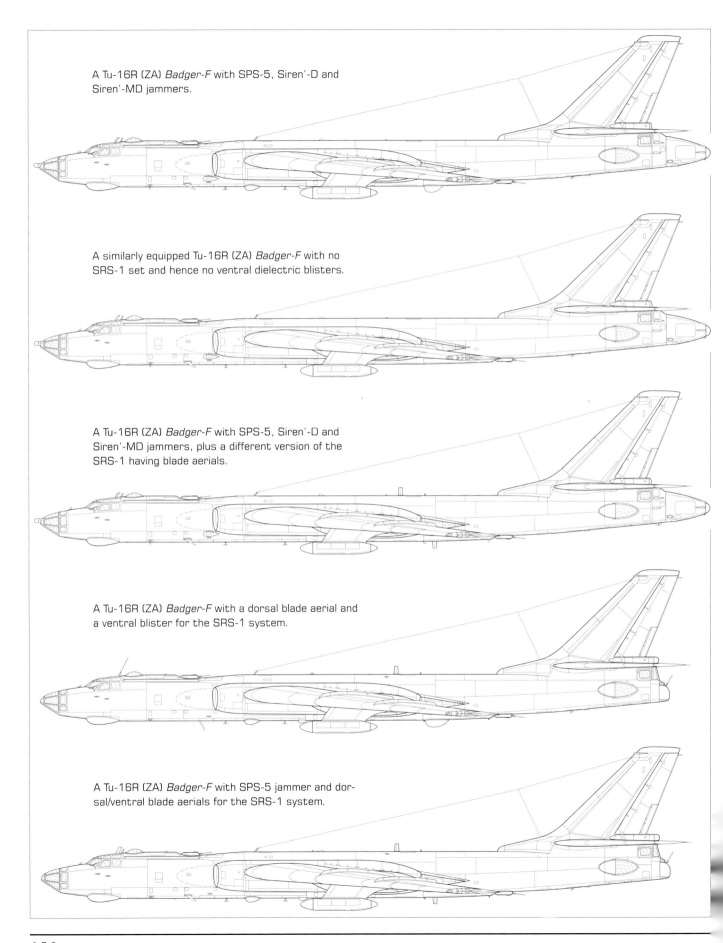

A Tu-16R (ZA) *Badger-F* with SPS-5, Siren'-D and
Siren'-MD jammers.

A similarly equipped Tu-16R (ZA) *Badger-F* with no
SRS-1 set and hence no ventral dielectric blisters.

A Tu-16R (ZA) *Badger-F* with SPS-5, Siren'-D and
Siren'-MD jammers, plus a different version of the
SRS-1 having blade aerials.

A Tu-16R (ZA) *Badger-F* with a dorsal blade aerial and
a ventral blister for the SRS-1 system.

A Tu-16R (ZA) *Badger-F* with SPS-5 jammer and dor-
sal/ventral blade aerials for the SRS-1 system.

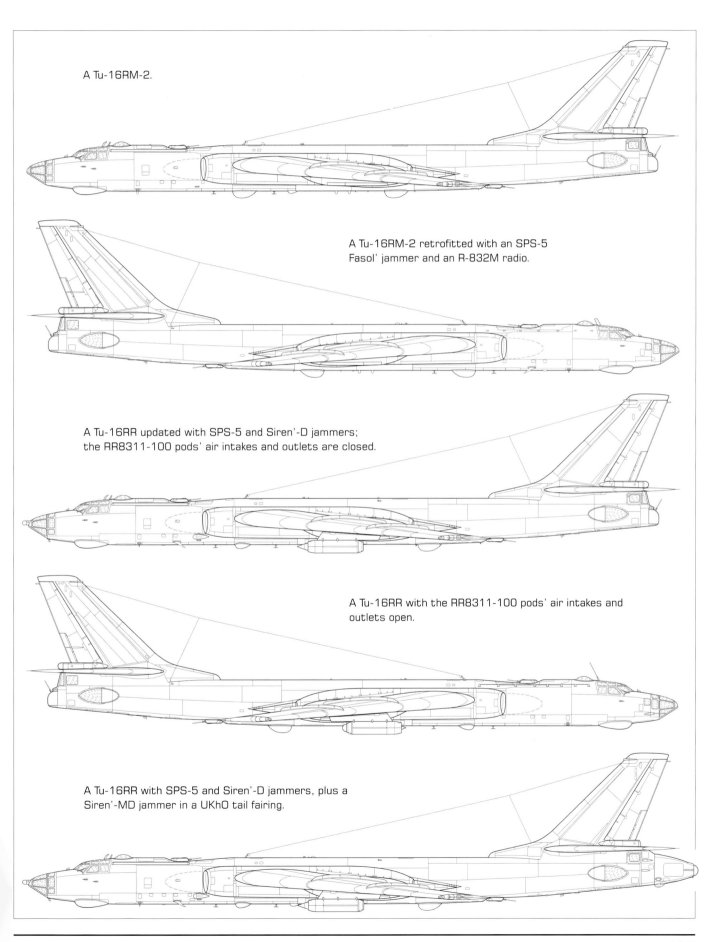

A Tu-16RM-2.

A Tu-16RM-2 retrofitted with an SPS-5 Fasol' jammer and an R-832M radio.

A Tu-16RR updated with SPS-5 and Siren'-D jammers; the RR8311-100 pods' air intakes and outlets are closed.

A Tu-16RR with the RR8311-100 pods' air intakes and outlets open.

A Tu-16RR with SPS-5 and Siren'-D jammers, plus a Siren'-MD jammer in a UKhO tail fairing.

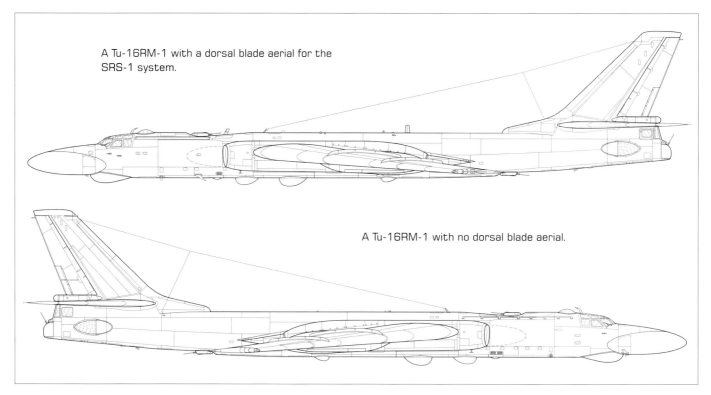

A Tu-16RM-1 with a dorsal blade aerial for the SRS-1 system.

A Tu-16RM-1 with no dorsal blade aerial.

IV. The ECM versions

Tu-16SPS ECM aircraft

The first specialised ECM version of the Tu-16 entered production at plant No.1 in 1955. Designated Tu-16SPS (*stahntsiya pomekhovykh signalov* = active jammer), it was fitted with the SPS-1 and SPS-2 active jammers. During 1955-56 plant No.1 in Kuibyshev produced 42 Tu-16s with SPS-1 sets, plus another 102 machines with the SPS-2 in 1955-57.

The SPS-1 and SPS-2 first-generation jammers developed in the 1950s were designed for group protection of strike aircraft formations. Basically, they were intended to jam ground-based and shipborne AAA radars and airborne intercept radars produced in the 1940s. They were relatively unsophisticated, with low emission power; to make matters worse, they were bulky and heavy. The SPS-1 and SPS-2 required an additional crewmember to operate them – the electronic warfare officer (EWO), who had to detect the enemy radar first, then establish its frequency and tune his ECM set accordingly. All this could take even a well-trained operator three minutes – too long if the aircraft was flying at low altitude. Added to this was the inability of the SPS-1 and SPS-2 to jam multi-channel and tuneable radars effectively.

In common with the Tu-16KS and the Tu-16R, the Tu-16SPS had a removable pressurised capsule suspended in the rear part of the bomb bay between frames 45-48A, with a ventral entry/ejection hatch and a dorsal emergency exit; it accommodated the EWO and part of the special equipment. The two antennas of the SPS-2 jammer covered by fairly small teardrop fairings were located ventrally (the receiver antenna ahead of the bomb bay and the transmitter antenna aft of the bomb bay); as distinct from the Tu-16R, these fairings were of the same size. The rear fairing had

a quarter-spherical metal sheath at the front – presumably to prevent the jammer from affecting the aircraft's own radar. The whip aerials for the SPS-1 could be sited either dorsally (aft of the Nav/Op's observation/sighting blister) or ventrally (ahead of the bomb bay). Aircraft fitted with the SPS-1 and SPS-2 were sometimes referred to as the Tu-16P – which is misleading, as this designation usually refers to a different ECM version described later.

At first the Tu-16SPS was not equipped with a chaff dispenser, and the absence of chaff outlets in the bomb bay doors distinguished it from the later Tu-16Ye. Later, however, ASO-16/3 dispensers were fitted to the Tu-16SPS and the difference disappeared. During the 1960s, nearly all Tu-16SPSs still in service were converted to Tu-16Ps (see below).

In spite of the EWO's cabin, the Tu-16SPS retained a measure of bomber capability – one pair of KD4-316 bomb cassettes or two pairs of KD3-416 bomb cassettes could be installed in the forward section of the bomb bay. On 23rd-27th March 1970, a standard Tu-16SPS operated by the Black Sea Fleet (c/n 8204210) underwent special tests together with a naval Tu-16R (c/n 1883414) for the purpose of checking their ability to carry and deploy naval mines like the Tu-16T. The tests were held by the 3rd Research and Test Directorate of GNIKI VVS located in Feodosiya on the Crimea Peninsula. Various types of mines were used – the AMD-500M, IGDM-500, UDM-500, IGDM, AMD-2M, Lira, Serpey, APM, RM-1 and UDM. The maximum number carried was six for the first three models and four for the others, although the test report surprisingly states '12 live mines or six practice mines' for the IGDM-500 and UDM-500. The results were good, but the report pointed out the need for modifications to ensure correct loading of the Lira, APM and RM-1 mines, as on the Tu-16T.

Above: The equipment modules and aerials of the SRS-1 ELINT set (the version covering the so-called bands A, B and C).

Above right: The equipment modules and movable antennas of the SPS-2 jammer.

Tu-16SPS (ZA) ECM aircraft

The final four Tu-16SPSs with the SPS-2 jammer built in 1957 were IFR-capable. These aircraft were designated Tu-16SPS (ZA).

Tu-16P Buket ECM aircraft (*izdeliye* NP)

The Buket family of active jammers was developed in the late 1950s. Unlike the SPS-1 and SPS-2, these new sets were automated and could jam several radars at a time, including multi-channel and tuneable radars. The family comprised four sets, each covering a certain waveband – the Buket-2 (or B-2 for short) with a wavelength of 21.5-30 cm, the Buket-3 (B-3, 12.5-21.5 cm), the Buket-4 (B-4, 9.8-12.5 cm) and the Buket-5 (B-5, 8.6-9.8 cm). In its day the Buket was the world's most powerful ECM suite, and existing ECCM means were powerless against it. To maintain its function, the enemy radar could only change its operating frequency, but even then one of the four Buket systems would have it covered.

In turn, each of the four Buket systems had four transmitters working in different wavelengths (except the B-3, which had six), enabling it to cover the entire spectrum of wavelengths. The four Buket sets (B-2, B-3, B-4 and B-5) each had their own range of reception channels (18, 45, 30 and 30 respectively) and the power output was 340-1,000 W, 500-100 W, 440-680 W and 400-860 W respectively. The weight was 854 kg (1,882 lb) for the B-2 set, 870 kg (1,918 lb) for the B-3 set, 722 kg (1,591 lb) for the B-4 set and 755 kg (1,664 lb) for the B-5. Ground radars were jammed with full 360° coverage, and the Buket sets could function either automatically or semi-automatically. This automatic capability meant that an additional crewmember (the EWO) was not required; the jammers were operated by the Nav/Op from his workstation.

Special versions of the Buket-2, Buket-3, Buket-4 and Buket-5 optimised for installation in the Tu-16 were developed as the SPS-22N, the SPS-33N, the SPS-44N and the SPS-55N respectively. The N suffix indicated that they were intended for the Tu-16 which, as we remember, had the product code *izdeliye* N.

The Buket sets were first fitted to the Tu-16 in 1962, passing state acceptance trials in 1963; a P-90 Pamir three-co-ordinate air defence radar (aka 1RL115) posed as the 'hostile' radar. The aircraft thus equipped were designated Tu-16P (*postanovshchik pomekh* – ECM aircraft), or Tu-16P Buket, and bore the product code *izdeliye* NP. They were intended to counteract enemy long-range air defence radars and SAM sites.

The jammer suite was housed in the bomb bay between frames 34-48; it was placed in a pressurised container and the latter's design differed, depending on the model of the Buket suite. This

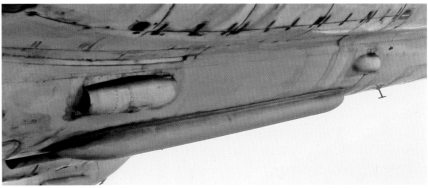

Above: The centreline dielectric canoe fairing of the Tu-16P Buket ECM aircraft.

Left: This view shows the cooling air intakes and the liquid cooling system's heat exchanger fairings of the Tu-16P's ECM suite, as well as the absence of the bomb bay doors.

meant that the bomb armament had to be deleted; so were the bomb bay doors, which were replaced by a special pallet mounting the jammer and its power supply system. The latter comprised four 6-kVA PO-6000 single-phase AC converters and one PT-6000 three-phase AC converter (*preobrazovahtel' tryokhfahznyy*) – the aircraft's standard engine-driven generators could not provide enough power.

Left, below left and bottom left: Tu-16P 'Buket' '29 Red' (c/n 1883606) equipped with the SPS-22N jammer suite; this aircraft passed check-up tests at GNIKI VVS in 1969.

Below: A Tu-16P 'Buket' coded '33 Blue' operated by the North Fleet's 924th GvMRAP and featuring an SPS-5 jammer.

Bottom: Wearing a huge code '10 Blue', this Tu-16P 'Buket' (c/n 1881602) has the Rogovitsa system and the SPS-5 jammer.

The external identification feature of the Tu-16P Buket equipped with the SPS-22N suite was a narrow dielectric canoe fairing on the centreline occupying three-quarter of the bomb bay's length which housed tandem pairs of emitter antennas, with a receiver antenna in between. It was flanked by two pairs of mission avionics cooling air scoops/heat exchanger fairings on the bomb bay doors near its front and rear ends – the Buket suite had a combined air/liquid cooling system.

In the course of the 1960s, 34 aircraft had the decimetre-waveband SPS-22N installed, nine aircraft received the SPS-33N, a further 28 the SPS-44N and 20 aircraft the SPS-55N. Not only the Tu-16SPS but also the Tu-16 Yolka was modified to carry the Buket system; so were several other versions. If the aircraft undergoing conversion had a mission equipment operator's pressurised cabin in the weapons bay, this was deleted – the Tu-16P with the Buket suite had the *Badger*'s normal complement of six crewmembers.

Top left and above left: Tu-16P 'Buket' '42 Red' (c/n 1881305) is retrofitted with the Rogovitsa system, additional SPS-5 and Siren'-D jammers in front, and a Siren'-MD jammer in a UKhO tail fairing. Note the 'anti-flash' white undersides.

Above: A fine upper view of the same aircraft.

Left and right: Tu-16P 'Buket' '34 Red' (c/n 1881410) has the Rogovitsa system but features additional jammers for the front hemisphere only. Also, it has an overall natural metal finish.

The Tu-16P operational in the 1960s had a maximum take-off weight of 75,800 kg (167,110 lb), a top speed of 1,000 km/h (621 mph) at an altitude of 6,250 m (20,510 ft) and 980 km/h (608 mph) at 10,000 m (32,810 ft), a service ceiling of 13,100 m (42,980 ft), an operational range of 5,800 km (3,602 miles) with 5% fuel reserves and a take-off run of 1,800 m (5,910 ft). A single Tu-16P cruising at 10,000-11,000 m (32,810-36,090 ft) in the midst of a bomber formation fitting into a circle of 3-5 km (1.86-3.1 miles) diameter could disrupt the operation of radars and other equipment on the ground within a radius of 300-350 km (186-217 miles).

With the transition to low-level operations several Tu-16Ps were re-equipped with the SPS-77 jammer optimised for these conditions. During the 1970s and 1980s the ECM equipment was constantly updated. For individual and group protection the Tu-16P carried jammers of the Siren' family (SPS-151, SPS-152 or SPS-153). These were housed in the forward equipment bay and, occasionally, in an UKhO ECM fairing replacing the tail turret. The transmitter antennas covering the front hemisphere were mounted low on the centre fuselage sides near the engine air intakes, and the receiver antenna on the navigator's station glazing.

Operating the Buket suite had a few peculiarities. The maintenance personnel on the ground had to observe rigorous safety measures when the jammers were switched on. When the Buket suite was switched on in flight, it was forbidden to use the defensive armament (the electric system would suffer an overload, not coping with the demand) or the Siren' jammers – the big Buket jammer would jam the 'small fry'!

In 1969, a Tu-16P coded '29 Red' (the c/n 1883606 was not worn visibly) and fitted with an SPS-22N jammer set underwent check-up tests at GK NII VVS together with a Tu-16T torpedo-bomber equipped with the same set (c/n 7401706). Both machines were modified in accordance with the aforementioned VPK ruling No.230 issued on 16th September 1964. The jammer installations were almost identical, except that a new PMS-10 cooling agent was used in the liquid cooling system of '29 Red'.

Air Force test pilot Ivan I. Bachoorin and AVMF test pilot Ye. P. Roobtsov were assigned to these aircraft as project test pilots; Engineer-Lt.-Col. N. A. Tumanyan and Engineer-Maj. K. I. Babunov were the engineers in charge. The test programme continued from 14th January, to 10th July 1969, involving 30 flights (the Tu-16P made 17 flights with a total time of 62 hours 6 minutes, while the Tu-16T made 13 flights totalling 48 hours 35 minutes). The jammer fitted to the Tu-16P had a total operating time of 100 hours, including 53 hours in flight; the one installed on the Tu-16T logged 76 hours, including 45 hours in the air.

The testing was complicated by several factors. For one thing, neither aircraft was fitted with test equipment, making it hard to assess the results; for another, the enterprises developing and manufacturing the jammer had neglected to supply ground support equipment for it. Nor were the specifications for the conversion job supplied, making it impossible to check the machines' conformity to the specs.

The Tu-16P had the NATO reporting name *Badger-J.*

Tu-16P Ficus ECM aircraft ('order 2231')

Experience with the Tu-16P Buket revealed that when aircraft were flying in close formation the Buket suite not only jammed enemy ground radars but disrupted the operation of the bombers' own radars. It was therefore necessary to modify the Buket in order to narrow the angle of its powerful jamming signal. A crash programme to resolve this problem resulted in ten Tu-16Ps with the Buket system (more precisely, with SPS-22N and SPS-44N jammers) being modified from 1970 onwards to work with the Ficus array ('order 2231').

The Ficus was intended to increase the energy potential of the Buket suite by narrowing its directional angle in both the vertical and horizontal planes and directing its jamming signal either to port or starboard. The apparatus was operated by the Nav/Op, weighed 232 kg (511 lb) and consisted of five revolving directional antennas with a drive mechanism. Hence the Tu-16P Ficus, as the new version was known, differed outwardly from the Tu-16P Buket in having a much larger square-section ventral 'bathtub' incorporating two dielectric sections over the emitter antennas and maintenance access panels in the metal portions.

Tests were carried out using two Tu-16Ps (c/ns 1882409 and 1883117). The Tu-16P Ficus provided more effective protection for a formation of aircraft than the previous version.

Some Tu-16P Ficus aircraft were additionally fitted with SPS-151/-152/-153 Siren'-D jammers covering the front hemisphere and SPS-5 Fasol' jammers. The latter' aerials were relocated aft to a position near the engine nacelles' rear ends.

Tu-16P Cactus ECM aircraft

Some Tu-16Ps were re-equipped to carry the SPS-120 Cactus jammer on a platform in the former bomb bay, with a large antenna

This modified Tu-16P 'Buket' ('35 Red') photographed by a Swedish Air Force fighter over the Baltic Sea combines the usual canoe fairing with Tu-16RM-style ventral teardrop fairings and chaff outlets on the starboard side of the rear fuselage.

under the platform itself. Access to the equipment was via two hatches in the platform and in the antenna fairing. The SPS-120 was handled by the navigator-operator and thus the number of crew members was unchanged.

Tu-16P (modified) ECM aircraft

A single Tu-16P coded '35 Red' and operated by the AVMF has been seen in a very unusual configuration. Two large teardrop fairings of the same shape and size as seen on Tu-16RM-2s were mounted in tandem between the nosewheel well and the normal canoe fairing of the SPS-22 Buket jammer; a third identical teardrop fairing was located aft of it. Three chaff outlets were located in the rear fuselage ahead of the GRO's starboard observation blister, two of them being vertically paired and provided with a deflector shaped like a half-cone. An SPS-5 Fasol' jammer was also fitted. The aircraft was apparently a one-off, since no other *Badgers* have been seen in this configuration.

Tu-16P Rezeda experimental ECM aircraft

In the second half of the 1960s a production Tu-16P Buket coded '17 Red' (c/n 5202907) was fitted with an SPS-100 Rezeda-AK jammer. The DK-7 tail turret and PRS-1 gun-laying radar were removed and replaced by a large parabolic fairing housing the SPS-100. The aircraft was also equipped with an SPO-3 Sirena-3 RWR which was part of the SPS-100 package. The weight of the jammer and its fairing was equal to the aggregate weight of the deleted turret and radar; therefore the modification did not entail a change of the CG position and hence impair the aircraft's stability and handling.

Tests of the SPS-100 proved successful, but operational Tu-16Ps were not re-equipped with it, although several combat and specialised versions of the Tu-16 were fitted with the Rezeda-AK from 1969 onwards. The prototype ended its days as an M-16 remote-controlled target drone (see below) at GNIKI VVS in Akhtoobinsk.

Far left: The Tu-16P 'Ficus' has a much larger ventral canoe fairing – a real bathtub.

Left: The same fairing of the Tu-16P 'Ficus' seen from the other side.

Right: The ASO-16/3 automatic chaff dispenser with three cassettes of chaff.

Far right: The outlet of the ASO-16/3 on the port bomb bay door.

Above left: Photographed on 26th March 1985, Tu-16 Yolka '71 Red' displays the triple outlets of the ASO-16/7 chaff dispensers, as well as the twin ventral ECM blisters and SPS-5 jammer aerials.

Left: Tu-16 Yolka '53 Red', a Navy aircraft, has the SRS-1 ELINT set with dorsal/ventral blade aerials additionally installed.

Below left: In addition to the SRS-1 set, Tu-16 Yolka '09 Red' (c/n 1882306) is equipped with the Rogovitsa system and an SPS-5 jammer with aft-mounted aerials.

Above: This Tu-16 Yolka intercepted on 11th August 1986, featured a dorsal blade aerial and a ventral blister for the SRS-1 system.

Tu-16 Silikat and Tu-16 Fonar' experimental ECM aircraft
According to Council of Ministers directive No.1659-657 of 3rd July 1953 and MOP order No.521 of 18th July, the Silikat ECM set designed for jamming ground and shipborne radars working in the 21.8-30.5 cm waveband was to be installed in a Kuibyshev-built Tu-16 (c/n 1882106) for testing in the late spring or early summer of 1955. However, this was never done; instead, the new Fonar' ECM set was fitted later. Neither system was put into production.

Some sources, though, claim this particular Tu-16 was indeed completed with the Silikat jammer and was later refitted with the Fonar' jammer. Though not officially a production example, this aircraft was nevertheless purpose-built, not a conversion; it remained a one-off. The designation of the mission equipment was applied to the aircraft itself, which was known as the Tu-16 Silikat, later becoming the Tu-16 Fonar' after the refit.

Tu-16 Yolka active/passive ECM aircraft ('order 214')
In parallel with the development of the Tu-16SPS active ECM aircraft, OKB-156 worked on a passive ECM version designated

Tu-16 Yolka which was produced at the Kuibyshev and Voronezh factories from 1957 onwards in accordance with 'order 214'. This aircraft carried seven ASO-16 Avtomat-1 automatic chaff dispensers (or, as some documents put it, an ASO-16/7 dispenser system with seven KDL-16 chaff cassettes) in its bomb bay, which was provided with chaff outlets – three on the port door and four on the starboard door. The remaining section of the bomb bay was available for bomb carriage.

In addition to the chaff dispensers, an SPS-4 Modulyatsiya radar jamming set was installed under a pair of small blister fairings forward of the bomb bay. The antenna of the SD-1 *Shipovnik* (Dog Rose) distance measuring equipment (DME) was housed in the bomb bay, and a special cover protected its forward section from being damaged by the ejected chaff.

When the ASO-16 chaff dispensers were not installed the entire bay was available for carrying bombs, but in the 1950s the seven ASO-16s were augmented by two APP-22 chaff dispensers (*avtomaht passivnykh pomekh* – automatic passive ECM device). In this case no bombs could be carried. Some machines were fitted with the ASO-2B and ASO-2I-Ye7R chaff/flare dispensers in the tailcones of the main gear fairings. The latter type had been developed for the Mikoyan/Gurevich MiG-21R *Fishbed-H* tactical reconnaissance aircraft, hence *apparaht sbrosa [dipol'nykh] otrazhateley, istrebitel'nyy* ('dipole reflector [that is, chaff] dispenser', fighter type, designed for the Ye-7R – the manufacturer's designation of the MiG-21R). Outwardly the Tu-16 Yolka could be distinguished from the bomber version by the teardrop fairing for the SPS-4 forward of the bomb bay and by the chaff outlets along the bomb bay doors. The chaff outlets were positioned at an angle to the centreline, evoking associations with a simplified rendering of a Christmas tree, which may account for the name Yolka (Spruce – or Christmas tree).

In 1957 plant No.1 produced 42 Tu-16 Yolkas equipped for in-flight refuelling, and a further ten were produced that year by plant No.64. This version was not built at plant No.22 in Kazan', although 19 of the 44 Tu-16 *sans suffixe* bombers built here were modified to 'Yolka' configuration (all possessing IFR capability). Thus, altogether, the Soviet Air Force took delivery of 71 examples of the Tu-16 Yolka which were later updated and modified more than once so that they resembled the Tu-16P in their mix of passive and active ECM equipment.

During production the Tu-16 Yolka was referred to as 'order 214'. Later some of these aircraft were modified under the terms of 'order 212'.

Tu-16 Yolka ECM aircraft with active ECM equipment
The Kazan' factory experimentally fitted a single Tu-16 Yolka coded '19 Red' (c/n 8204213) with an SPS-100 Rezeda-AK jammer in a large parabolic tail fairing and an SPS-5 Fasol' jammer in the avionics bay – apparently again under the terms of 'order 2624'. This aircraft, as well as Tu-16A c/n 7203514, Tu-16K-11-16 c/n 5202501 and Tu-16K-10 c/n 2632024, was modified pursuant to the abovementioned VPK ruling No.230 issued on 16th September 1964.

The ECM installation was almost identical on all four machines. The only difference was that on the three 'glass-nosed' aircraft the jammer control panels were installed between frames 2-3, while on the Tu-16K-10 it was between frames 9-10.

Above: Tu-16 Yolka '19 Red' (c/n 8204213) tested at GNIKI VVS in 1964 had an SPS-100 jammer in a tail fairing, Fasol' and Modulyatsiya jammers with swept ventral blade aerials, and an SPS-1 or SPS-2 jammer with a ventral teardrop fairing.

Left and below left: A Tu-16Ye ECM aircraft with the twin swept blade aerials of the Modulyatsiya jammer flanking the fairing of the SPS-1 or SPS-2 jammer.

Right: The lower fuselage of a Tu-16Ye, showing the ventral antennas of the SRS-1 ELINT set and SPS-1 and Modulyatsiya jammers. The entry hatch of the electronic warfare officer's capsule is visible ahead of them.

Far right: The EWO's capsule of the Tu-16Ye.

Together with the other three aircraft, Tu-16 Yolka c/n 8204213 underwent a common two-stage test programme. The project test pilot team comprised Lt.-Col. Vyacheskav N. Bogatyryov, Lt.-Col. Valentin I. Tsoovaryov, Lt.-Col. Leonid M. Kungoorov and Lt.-Col. A. V. Romanov. The engineers in charge were Engineer-Lt.-Col. S. A. Koodlik, Engineer-Lt.-Col. N. A. Tumanyan and Engineer-Lt.-Col. P. I. Sedelkin (the latter was responsible for the ECM equipment).

First, the four *Badgers* made 13 flights from Kazan'-Borisoglebskoye between 10th January, and 4th April 1968, operating against an SON-15 AAA gun ranging radar located at a GNIKI VVS test range. This mobile radar had a target detection range of

50 km (31 miles) and a target tracking range of 35 km (21.75 miles). The purpose of these flights was to verify the SPS-100 jammer and eliminate any bugs that were discovered.

Check-up tests at GNIKI VVS followed on 18th May – 29th August 1968. The purpose was to check the conformity of the aircraft in general, and their ECM equipment in particular, to the specifications and the performance figures obtained in the course of state acceptance trials, as well as to assess the mission equipment's EMC with the aircraft's systems and its ease of operation. At this stage the Tu-16A made 14 flights with a total time of 53 hours, the Tu-16 Yolka made nine flights totalling 36 hours 48 minutes, the Tu-16K-10 made 13 flights totalling 47 hours, and the

Above: Tu-16Ye '10 Red' (c/n 1883702) has the antenna fairings of the Siren'-D jammer located unusually far forward, looking like a 'bone through the nose'.

Overleaf: Five views of Tu-16Ye '26 Red' (c/n 1882710). The aircraft is fitted with tandem blister fairings for the SPS-1, SPS-2 or SPS-2K jammer (the rear one featuring a shield to stop it from jamming the aircraft's own avionics), plus an SPS-5 jammer with blade aerials at the usual forward location.

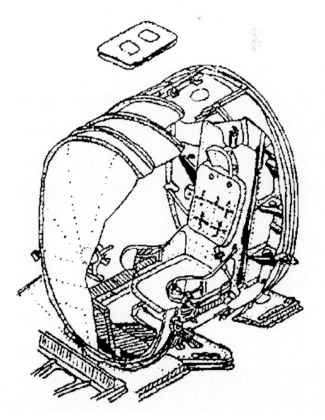

Tu-16K-11-16 made 12 flights totalling 47 hours 56 minutes. The effect of the SPS-100 jammer on the seeker head of the KSR-11 anti-radar missile could not be assessed because the Tu-16K-11-16 lacked some of the avionics. The efficacy of the jammers' protection was not evaluated on this occasion.

The aircraft were also used in support of the check-up tests of a production Su-15 interceptor, checking the ECM resistance of its Oryol-D58M radar (aka RP-15M).

Tu-16Ye ECM aircraft (*izdeliye* NYe)

Another passive ECM version designated Tu-16Ye or *izdeliye* NYe (in Soviet Air Force units it, too, was known as the Tu-16 Yolka) resembled the Tu-16R in its equipment. As on the reconnaissance version, a pressurised capsule was installed in the rear section of the bomb bay for the EWO operating the SPS-1, SPS-2 or SPS-2K jammer (the latter model was called *Pion* – Peony) with its antenna mounted under the EWO's station. The bomb bay also featured mounting racks for two ASO-16 chaff dispensers. Bombs could be carried in its forward section. Later, additional ASO-16 chaff dis-

pensers were housed in the forward section, as well as two APP-22 chaff dispensers, with appropriate modifications to the bomb bay doors; this greatly improved the aircraft's ECM capability at the expense of the offensive armament.

Between 1957 and 1959, 51 examples of the Tu-16Ye were produced at plant No.1; another 38 were built by plant No.22 in 1958. All of these 89 aircraft were IFR-capable. The Tu-16Ye differed externally from the Tu-16 Yolka in having an access hatch for the EWO's cabin in the bomb bay doors.

The Tu-16Ye was given the NATO reporting name *Badger-H*.

Tu-16Ye Azaliya ECM aircraft

During the 1970s a number of Tu-16 Yolka and Tu-16Ye ECM aircraft were modified *in situ* to carry any one of several jammers which formed the Azaliya family – the SPS-61, SPS-62, SPS-63, SPS-64, SPS-65 or SPS-66. such aircraft were accordingly known as the Tu-16Ye Azaliya. As a rule, the SPS-63 or SPS-66 was fitted. Many Tu-16Ye Azaliya aircraft also had jammers of the Siren' family fitted.

Opposite page, top and above: Four aspects of another Tu-16Ye ('45 Red', c/n 1882411) having an identical antenna complement.

Below: A fine study of a Naval Aviation Tu-16Ye coded '50 Red' which has the aerials of the SPS-5 jammer mounted well aft (on both sides of the rear blister fairing for the SPS-1 or SPS-2 jammer).

According to MAP order No.121 of 19th April 1972, the Tu-16Ye had the DK-7 tail turret, PRS-1 Argon gun ranging radar, ASO-16 chaff dispenser, SPO-2 RWR and SPS-2 jammer removed. These were replaced by one of the Azaliya-U series jammers, an SPS-151 Siren'-1 jammer, an SPS-151M Siren'-1M jammer, two SPS-152 Siren'-2 jammers, two SPS-153 Siren'-3 jammers, an SPO-15 *Beryoza-P* (Birch) radar homing and warning system (RHAWS) and an ASO-2I chaff/flare dispenser.

The Siren' sets were installed in the familiar UKhO fairing replacing the tail turret. Aircraft with the SPS-61, SPS-62 and SPS-63 also carried an SPS-6 Los' (Moose) jammer for collective protection, while those with the SPS-64, SPS-65 and SPS-66 had the SPS-5 Fasol' (String Bean). The antennas for the Azaliya were housed in small hemispherical fairings under the fuselage in the forward or aft section of the bomb bay, the remainder of the bay being used to carry bombs or ASO-16 and APP-22 chaff dispensers. When the Azaliya was installed on the Tu-16 Yolka, the antennas were located in the forward section of the weapons bay; on the Tu-16Ye they replaced the entry hatch of the EWO's cabin (the latter was removed). An equally characteristic feature was the dorsal air intake (close to the centreline) and air outlets (port and starboard) for the ECM equipment's heat exchanger located near the wing trailing edge.

Some examples of the Tu-16Ye had the pylon-mounted teardrop antenna pods of the Siren'-D jammer mounted on the sides of the navigator's station rather than below the air intakes, and these were rather larger than usual. The result looked rather bizarre,

Opposite page and below: '69 Red' (c/n 8204214) exemplifies the Tu-16 Ye Azaliya version featuring an Azaliya jammer with two hemi-spherical ventral antenna blisters amidships, as well as SPS-5, Siren'-D/Siren'-MD jammers and the A-326 system. Note also the mission equipment heat exchanger air intakes and outlets located dorsally amidships.

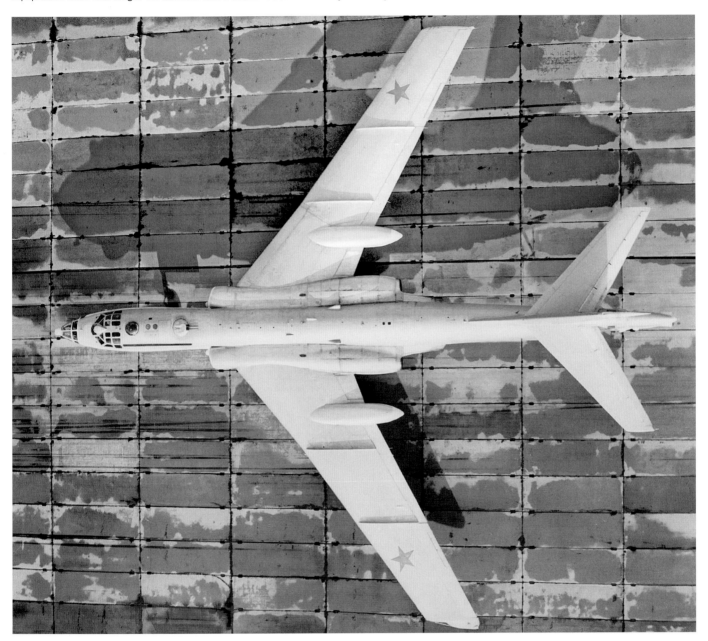

evoking images of a caveman or cannibal with a bone through the nose as portrayed in old cartoons!

Some examples of the Tu-16 Yolka and Tu-16Ye Azaliya had active jammers of the SPS-100, SPS-100A and SPS-100M type, and at least some had the SPO-15 RHAWS. During their service life the aircraft were constantly modified and updated in line with other versions of the Tu-16.

Tu-16YeR reconnaissance/ECM aircraft

Some Tu-16Ye ECM aircraft had the SPS-2 jammer replaced by an SRS-1 ELINT system. This dual-role ECM/ELINT version was designated Tu-16YeR, the R denoting *razvedchik*, and had a distinctive appearance with its whip aerials for the SPS-1 and SRS-1 sets.

Tu-16Ye (Tu-16Ye-KhR) NBC reconnaissance/ ECM aircraft

Yet another ECM version is again officially referred to as the Tu-16Ye, but more commonly known as the Tu-16Ye-KhR (*khim-icheskaya razvedka* – chemical reconnaissance). Its equipment suite permitted photographic, electronic and nuclear/biological/chemical (NBC) reconnaissance, and it closely resembled the Tu-16RR. Its ECM equipment merely facilitated its reconnaissance functions. A crew of seven was carried.

The forward section of the bomb bay bay accommodated an AKAFU tilting mount with two AFA-42/100 cameras, and a pressurised cabin for the EWO occupied the rear section. The central section of the bay could be used to carry bombs or up to four

Above: Tu-16 '47 Red' (c/n 8204130) was used by GK NII VVS to test an internal launcher for RPZ-59 ECM rockets.

Right row: Several versions of the RPZ-59 were tested.

Below: The retracted DPU-RPZ six-rail launcher for the rockets in the bomb bay of Tu-16 '47 Red'. Note the pantographic mechanism.

Right: Two dollies loaded with different versions of the RPZ-59 rocket. The RPZ-59 had a bifurcated nozzle located amidships, leaving the rear half of the body free for bundles of chaff which were ejected in a programmed sequence.

Below: A different installation was tried on Tu-16P c/n 6400903, with two six-round launchers for RPZ-59 rockets mounted on pylons under the wings. Here one of the rockets in the front row is winched into position by means of a hand-cranked hoist.

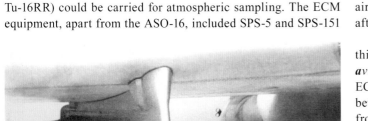

ASO-16 chaff dispensers. The wing structure was reinforced so that two pylon-mounted RR8311-100 pods (the same as on the Tu-16RR) could be carried for atmospheric sampling. The ECM equipment, apart from the ASO-16, included SPS-5 and SPS-151 sets and two SPS-1s. The aerials of the SPS-5 were mounted beside the nosewheel well, the antennas for the SPS-151 beside the engine air intakes and those for the SPS-1s above and below the fuselage aft of the EWO's cabin.

Two aircraft built by plant No.1 in Kuibyshev were refitted in this way. One of them served with the 226th OAPREP (*otdel'nyy aviapolk rahdioelektronnovo protivodeystviya* – Independent ECM Air Regiment) based initially at Poltava in the Ukraine, between 1978 and 1980 at Priluki (also in the Ukraine) and then from 1980 at Spassk-Dal'niy in the Russian Far East. The second aircraft was based at Spassk-Dal'niy from the start. At Poltava and Priluki these aircraft were referred to as the Tu-16Ye-KhR. During maintenance work in 1979-1980 the aircraft were fitted with the Rogovitsa formation keeping system and the SPS-152 Siren'-D jammer covering the forward hemisphere.

Tu-16P with RPZ-59 ECM rockets
On 21st July 1959, the Council of Ministers issued directive No.832-372 envisaging provision of a new individual passive ECM system for the Tu-16. Therefore Ivan I. Toropov's OKB-134, which also developed air-to-air missiles, modified its production RS-1-U beam-riding AAM (alias K-5 or *izdeliye* 1; NATO AA-1 *Alkali*) co-developed with OKB-2 under Pavel D. Grooshin for the MiG-17PFU *Fresco-D* interceptor. The resulting rocket projectile developed under the codename *Avtostrada-1* (Highway-1) was designated RPZ-59 (*raketa protivorahdiolokatsionnoy zashchity* – anti-radar protection rocket). Basically it retained the RS-1-U's tail-first layout with cruciform wings set at 45° to the horizontal plane and a body of 200 mm (7⅞ in) diameter with the angled lateral nozzles of the solid-fuel rocket motor located amidships. However, the guidance system and the cruciform rudders used for pitch and directional control were deleted, as were the stabilising ailerons at the root sections of the trapezoidal wings, and the 9.2-kg (20.3-lb) HE/fragmentation warhead was replaced by bundles of chaff at the rear end of the body, which were ejected in a programmed sequence triggered by a clockwork mechanism.

The RPZ-59 was to be fired by the Tu-16P, ejecting a cloud of chaff some way ahead of the aircraft to (hopefully) jam AAA gun-laying radars, SAM guidance radars and AAM radar seeker heads working in a 3-10 cm waveband in the aircraft's forward hemi-

Top, above and opposite page: Tu-16P '12 Red' (c/n 6400903) with the underwing launchers for RPZ-59 rockets seen during state acceptance trials. Note the wingtip-mounted cine cameras recording rocket launches.

Left: Close-up of the starboard launcher with a load of six rockets.

Below: The empty port rocket launcher.

Below left: Rear view of the launcher. The legend on the rockets' back plates reads 'Remove cover before flight'.

sphere. Rather misleadingly, the weapon was referred to in test reports as an 'anti-radar missile' (*protivorahdiolokatsionnaya raketa*), like such weapons as the Kh-28 and Kh-58 (AS-11 *Kilter*) passive radar homing missiles. Actually, however, it was not an ARM – it was designed to disrupt the operation of enemy radars, not destroy them.

Originally the rockets were to be carried in the weapons bay on a special DPU-RPZ launcher (*derzhatel' pooskovykh oostroystv dlya raket protivorahdiolokatsionnoy zashchity* – [weapons] rack for anti-radar protection rocket launcher) which was lowered clear of the fuselage contour by a hydraulic ram for loading and firing, moving on two pairs of trailing arms. The launcher had two rows of launch rails three-abreast, the centre rail being mounted lower than the outer ones; it featured an emergency jettison system which automatically released the rail together with the rocket if the latter failed to come off the rail. The rockets could be fired singly or in a series (automatically at preset intervals of 30, 60, 90 or 180 seconds). Interestingly, most sources (including the test report) say six RPZ-59 rockets were to be carried. However, a photo in the state acceptance trials report is captioned *'Fig. 1: The Tu-16P aircraft with the **front** DPU-RPZ launcher extended, carrying RPZ-59 rockets'* (our highlighting – Auth.), which implies that there was also a *rear* launcher and the total

number of rockets was 12; and indeed, the position of the launcher in the weapons bay seems to support this. In addition to the launchers, the aircraft was fitted with an ASO-16/3 chaff dispenser.

After preliminary ground tests of the system at the PVO's Anti-Aircraft Artillery Research and Test Range (NIZAP – *Naoochno-ispytahtel'nyy zenitno-artillereeyskiy poligon*) in Dongooz (Orenburg Region), manufacturer's flight tests combined with the joint state acceptance trials were held by GK NII VVS, involving OKB-134, OKB-156 and the Air Force. The aircraft used for the trials was a modified Tu-16 built by plant No.22 in 1958 ('47 Red', c/n 8204130). The trials report endorsed in December 1963/January 1964, calls it a Tu-16P; however, '47 Red' lacked the distinctive canoe fairing of the Buket jammer and associated cooling air scoops, looking more like a Tu-16Ye. The engineers in charge were Lt.-Col. N. V. Rostovskiy from GK NII VVS and A. A. Volkov and A. S. Boobchikov from OKB-134.

The trials began on 2nd April 1962; in some flights a Mikoyan/ Gurevich UTI MiG-15 *Midget* trainer acted as a chase plane from which the launches were filmed. The results proved unsatisfactory; the first launches at 11,700 m (38,390 ft) showed the RPZ-59 to be unstable in flight, which put the aircraft and its crew at risk. On 18th May 1962 the trials were interrupted and the rockets were modified by adding 7.5 kg (16.53 lb) of ballast in the nose to make

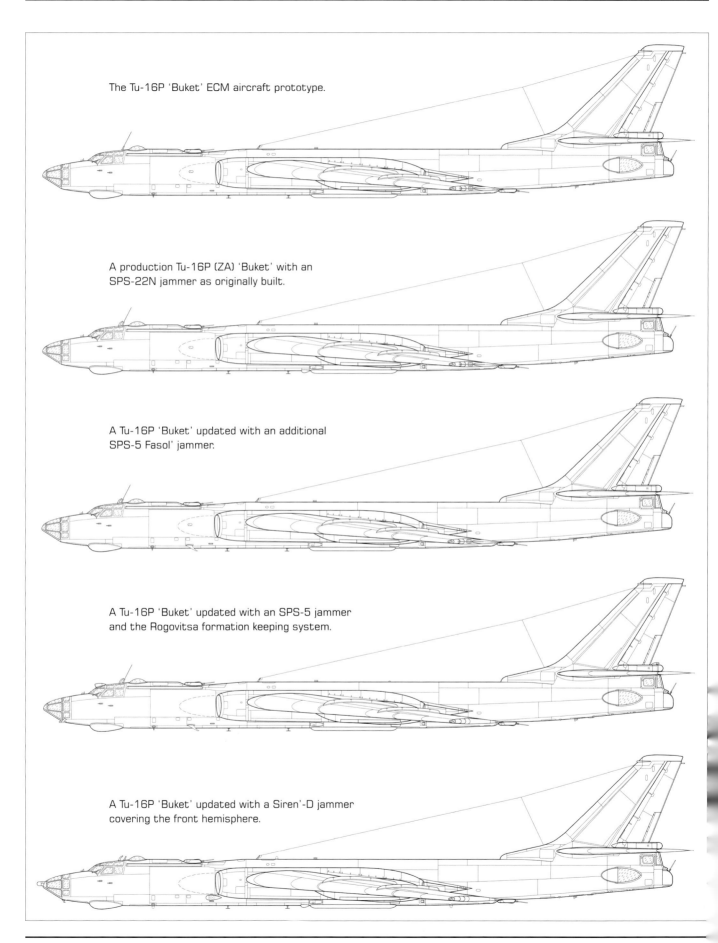

The Tu-16P 'Buket' ECM aircraft prototype.

A production Tu-16P (ZA) 'Buket' with an
SPS-22N jammer as originally built.

A Tu-16P 'Buket' updated with an additional
SPS-5 Fasol' jammer.

A Tu-16P 'Buket' updated with an SPS-5 jammer
and the Rogovitsa formation keeping system.

A Tu-16P 'Buket' updated with a Siren'-D jammer
covering the front hemisphere.

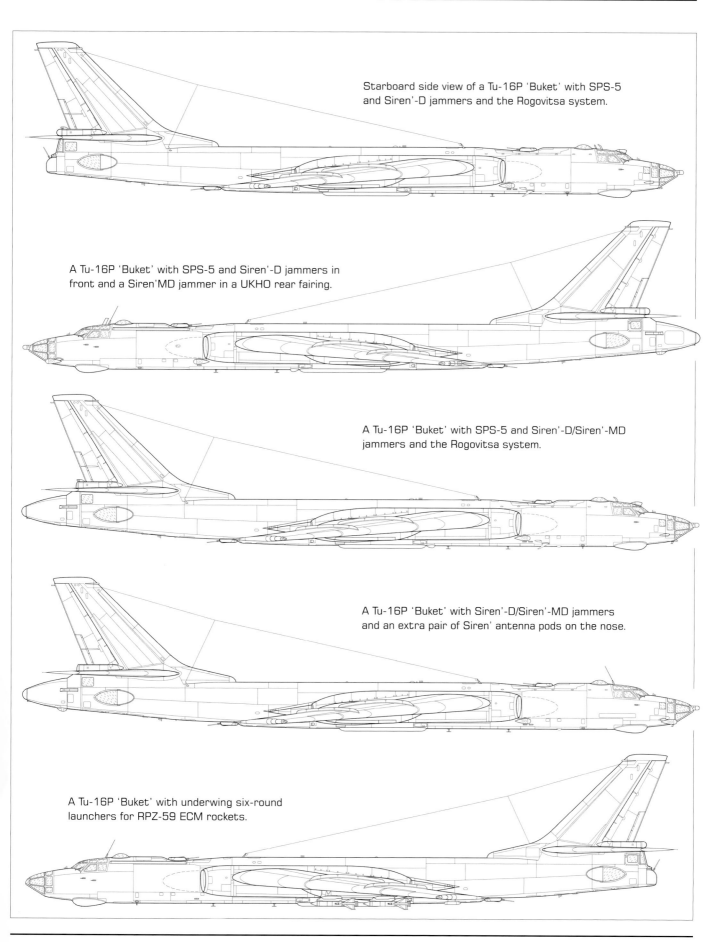

Starboard side view of a Tu-16P 'Buket' with SPS-5 and Siren'-D jammers and the Rogovitsa system.

A Tu-16P 'Buket' with SPS-5 and Siren'-D jammers in front and a Siren'MD jammer in a UKHO rear fairing.

A Tu-16P 'Buket' with SPS-5 and Siren'-D/Siren'-MD jammers and the Rogovitsa system.

A Tu-16P 'Buket' with Siren'-D/Siren'-MD jammers and an extra pair of Siren' antenna pods on the nose.

A Tu-16P 'Buket' with underwing six-round launchers for RPZ-59 ECM rockets.

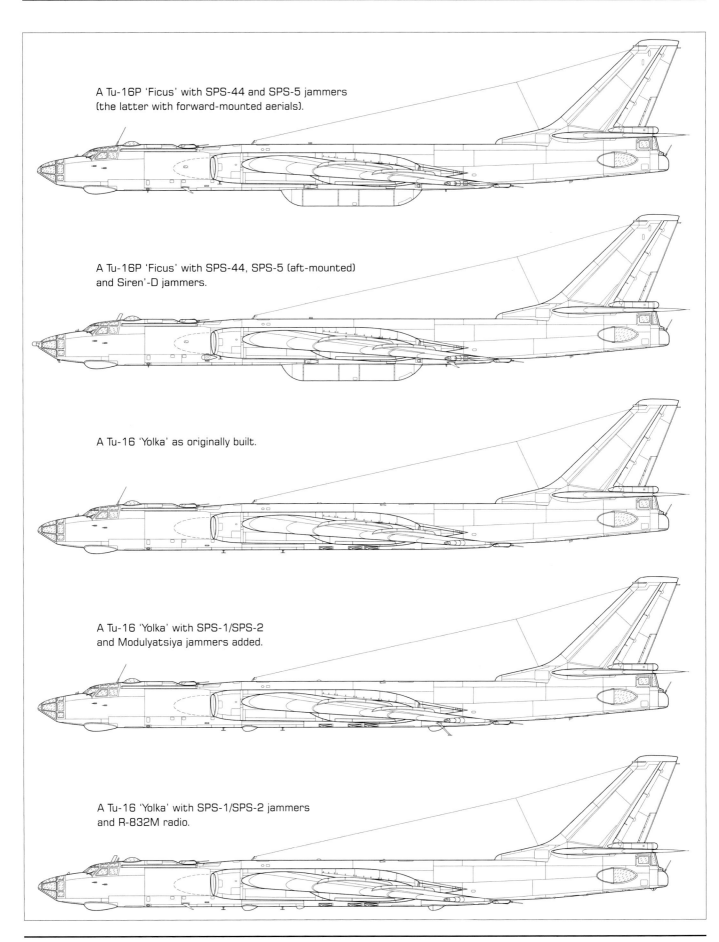

A Tu-16P 'Ficus' with SPS-44 and SPS-5 jammers
(the latter with forward-mounted aerials).

A Tu-16P 'Ficus' with SPS-44, SPS-5 (aft-mounted)
and Siren'-D jammers.

A Tu-16 'Yolka' as originally built.

A Tu-16 'Yolka' with SPS-1/SPS-2
and Modulyatsiya jammers added.

A Tu-16 'Yolka' with SPS-1/SPS-2 jammers
and R-832M radio.

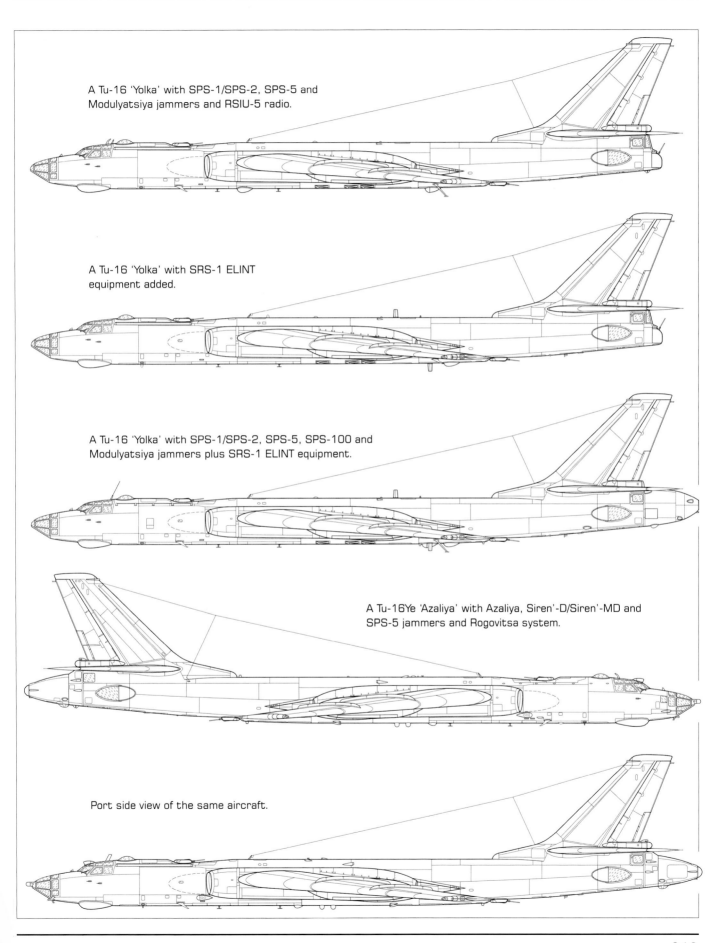

A Tu-16 'Yolka' with SPS-1/SPS-2, SPS-5 and Modulyatsiya jammers and RSIU-5 radio.

A Tu-16 'Yolka' with SRS-1 ELINT equipment added.

A Tu-16 'Yolka' with SPS-1/SPS-2, SPS-5, SPS-100 and Modulyatsiya jammers plus SRS-1 ELINT equipment.

A Tu-16Ye 'Azaliya' with Azaliya, Siren'-D/Siren'-MD and SPS-5 jammers and Rogovitsa system.

Port side view of the same aircraft.

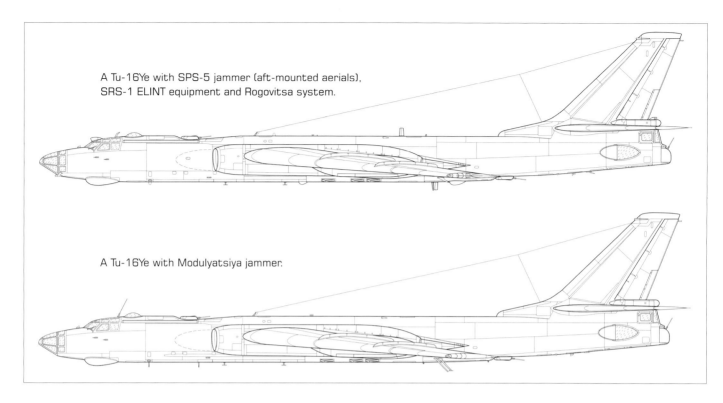

A Tu-16Ye with SPS-5 jammer (aft-mounted aerials), SRS-1 ELINT equipment and Rogovitsa system.

A Tu-16Ye with Modulyatsiya jammer.

them more stable (without success), whereupon three launches took place between 25th May and 8th June 1962. There was another pause from 16th June to 26th July 1962 when the aircraft was undergoing maintenance. During this time OKB-134 made further changes to the launch control circuitry.

Trials resumed on 10th August 1962, but the problems persisted. The trials were suspended again on 2nd September 1962, resuming on 15th February 1963. More changes were made during this pause (the launch rails were made longer, duralumin was substituted by steel in some parts, a new control panel was developed, the circuitry was revised again and so on); also, an AKS-5 cine camera was fitted under the port wingtip to record the launches. Still, the rockets' stability at altitudes above 10,000 m (32,810 ft) remained as poor as ever and operation of the ASO-16/3 was unreliable. In one test flight in 1963 a rocket launched at 8,000 m (26,250 ft) struck the radome of the RBP-6 Lyustra radar, destroying it. Also, a number of uncommanded launches and failed launches occurred. Moreover, the dissemination of chaff by the rockets was unreliable, making it impossible to assess their efficacy against radars.

There was a third pause in the trials between 17th April, and 31st May 1963, when OKB-134 made more revisions. Now the rockets were ejecting chaff as they should. However, on 14th June, an explosive bolt in the launch rail jettison system blew coincidentally with the rocket launch, tilting the rail nose-up; as a result, the rocket struck the fuselage, wiping out the radio altimeter aerial and making a big dent in the skin. Finally, the Air Force ran out of patience and cancelled further testing on 1st July 1963, owing to the Avtostrada-1 system's unreliability. All in all, Tu-16 '47 Red' made 41 flights during the trials, logging 82 hours 18 minutes. In addition, a Sukhoi 'T-3 interceptor with a TsD-30T fire control radar' (*sic*) made four flights totalling 3.5 hours in support of the

programme, posing as a hostile fighter whose radar was to be jammed. (In reality the T-3 *Fishpot-A* prototype had an *Almaz* (Diamond) radar with twin radomes; the TsD-30 radar was fitted to its production derivative, the T-43, better known as the Su-9 *Fishpot-B*, which had a different nose with a single radome.)

Learning from this unfortunate experience, the Air Force and the aircraft industry devised a new system codenamed *Pilon* (Pylon) in 1964; this time it was indeed based on the Tu-16P *Badger-J* with the Buket ECM suite (though the normal SPS-44 jammer was replaced by an SPS-55 jammer). The latter was augmented by 12 RPZ-59 rockets carried on P8700-0 'six-shooter' launchers (almost identical to the DPU-RPZ) with tandem groups of three P8700-10 launch rails; the launchers were attached to suitably modified BD-352 underwing pylons, hence the system's name. This increased the aircraft's empty weight to 41,000 kg (90,390 lb), and a full load of rockets weighed 1,000 kg (2,205 lb).

A Voronezh-built Tu-16P ('12 Red', c/n 6400903) was modified by the AVMF's ARZ No.20 in Pushkin, receiving the underwing rocket launchers which were fitted in accordance with OKB-134 drawings approved by the Tupolev OKB. Further trials were held on this aircraft between September 1968 and May 1969, using an improved version of the RPZ-59 which had worked up an acceptable reliability level. GNIKI VVS pilot Lt.-Col. V. M. Komov was project test pilot; the engineers in charge were Yu. P. Tsaplin (GNIKI VVS) and Valentin P. Glushko (OKB-134).

The aircraft logged 39 hours 49 minutes in 19 test flights between 9th September 1968, and 3rd May 1969 during stage A of the state acceptance trials. These involved ten flights in which 25 rockets were fired to jam SON-15 and SON-30 ground radars, two flights in which six dummy rockets were jettisoned, and four flights to jam the Smerch-A fire control radar fitted to the MiG-25P interceptor prototype, which was then in the midst of its own state acceptance trials. On the other hand, it was impossible to check the efficacy of the experimental SPS-55 jammer because its operating frequencies did not match those of the radars! Stage A and the ensuing stage B of the trials proved successful and the Pilon system was cleared for service use with the Tu-16P. From 1972 onwards a small number of ECM aircraft were adapted to carry the RPZ-59, using the Pilon system.

Before firing the rockets the crew of the Tu-16P had to don oxygen masks and protective goggles and keep them on until the aircraft had passed the cloud of chaff. With the missiles expended, the centre of gravity shifted forward by 0.5% MAC; therefore, to maintain a safe CG position after firing the missiles the Tu-16 had to land with a fuel load of at least 2,000 kg (4,410 lb).

Tu-16PN ECM aircraft (?)
The Long-Range Aviation's equipment and re-equipment plan for 1989 giving numbers of various aircraft in service with specific units (see page 369) mentions ten *Badgers* in service with the 1225th TBAP as ECM aircraft under the designation Tu-16PN. However, this designation was not encountered anywhere else and no details are known.

* * *

The overall number of Tu-16 versions, including the Tu-16P, is remarkable for the numerous combinations and types of ECM equipment fitted. For example, the 226th Independent ECM Air Regiment based at Poltava had 30 Tu-16s with active ECM equipment, and no two were identical. The new ***Klyukva*** (Cranberry) active jammer with improved performance was installed, and several machines had the SPS-4M jammer fitted under the terms of 'order 2615'.

The introduction of infra-red seekers on surface-to-air and air-to-air missiles and the experience gained in local wars compelled the installation of infra-red countermeasures (IRCM) equipment on some versions of the Tu-16, including the Tu-16P. These aircraft had ASO-2I-Ye7R chaff/flare dispensers in the tailcones of the main gear fairings and in the rear fuselage.

V. The auxiliary versions

Tu-16 Zapravshchik (Tu-16Z, Tu-16Yu) in-flight refuelling tanker ('order 198', *izdeliye* NZ)
Even at the project stage the Tupolev OKB explored ways of extending the Tu-16's combat radius, which was no more than 2,500 km (1,552 miles). One of these was the wingtip-to-wingtip in-flight refuelling method developed by LII test pilots Igor' I. Shelest and Viktor S. Vasyanin back in 1948; it involved unreeling a hose from an outlet at the wingtip of one aircraft, the hose then being engaged by a receptacle at the other aircraft's opposite wingtip. First used operationally on the Tu-4 in the early 1950s, it was practiced on a very limited scale by the Soviet Air Force; no more than ten *Bulls* were modified as tankers or receiver aircraft with the Shelest/Vasyanin system. However, the experience gained with the Tu-4 convinced OKB-156 that the technique was viable and applicable for jet bombers as well.

In the autumn of 1953 the Tupolev OKB called a contest for the best design of the wingtip-to-wingtip IFR system intended for the Tu-16, believing that such a system could be developed rapidly.

Providing that two production Tu-16s were delivered in May 1954, for conversion as the tanker and receiver prototypes, manufacturer's flight tests of the system could begin in August and the system could be submitted for state acceptance trials in January 1955. However, this presupposed the active co-operation of OKB-918 under Chief Designer Semyon M. Alekseyev (which assisted in bringing the Shelest/Vasyanin system up to scratch), the test pilots involved in the Tu-4's IFR tests, LII, and the Soviet Air Force.

On 17th September 1953, MAP issued order No.44 giving specific instructions for the development of the IFR system; all new bombers developed henceforth were to have provisions for in-flight refuelling. In particular, the Kazan' factory was to modify the tanker and the receiver aircraft in accordance with Tupolev OKB drawings. OKB-918 was instructed to keep on developing a standardised IFR system for the Tu-16. This was to have a fuel transfer rate of at least 3,000 litres (660 Imp gal) per minute, and refuelling was to take place at 450-500 km/h (279-310 mph) indicated airspeed and 8,000-10,000 m (26,250-32,810 ft). As was the case with the Tu-4, only one bomber could be refuelled at a time.

In order to save weight the Tupolev OKB reversed the design used on the Tu-4 – now it was the tanker, not the receiver aircraft, which deployed the hose. In the course of development work the system's specifications were revised, and so was the schedule. On 26th May 1954, the Council of Ministers issued directive No.1013-438 to this effect, followed by MAP order No.354 of 3rd June, which specified a fuel transfer rate of 2,000 litres (440 Imp gal) per minute and set the state acceptance deadline at the third quarter of 1954. Three Tu-16s were to be delivered for conversion as the tanker prototypes; moreover, it was envisaged that the Tu-16 tanker would refuel not only bombers but also their escort fighters.

The tanker prototypes were, in fact, not Kazan'-built aircraft but the first pre-production and production examples from Kuibyshev (c/ns 1880001 and 1880101). Later, Tu-16 c/n 1880301 was also modified as a tanker to investigate IFR techniques for the MiG-19 tactical fighter.

The KAZ hose drum unit of the Tu-16N refuelling tanker (minus hose and drogue). The hydraulic drive is on the left side.

The first Tu-16 single-point tanker began an almost eighteen-month test programme in 1955 with the participation of LII test pilots Aleksey P. Yakimov and Sultan Amet-Khan. Taking due note of the criticisms made, OKB-156 made the necessary revisions and prepared the technical documents for the production factories. On 15th February 1956 the Council of Ministers issued another directive No.247-159 (backed up by MAP order No.111 of 23rd February), requiring thirty Tu-16s to be modified at the Kazan' plant for service trials with the Air Force (ten as tankers and twenty as receivers), with a deadline of 1st October 1956. The service evaluation was held successfully in late 1956. From early 1957 onwards all three factories building the type began incorporating IFR capability on the Tu-16 bomber as standard while carrying out modification and refit work.

Originally the wingtip-to-wingtip tanker was known in service simply as Tu-16 *Zaprahvshchik* (refuelling tanker) or *izdeliye*

Above: A Tu-16Z wing-to-wing tanker caught by the camera just after lift-off, showing the hose guide tube protruding from the starboard wingtip.

Left: This lower view of a naval Tu-16Z shows the horizontal flat-plate winglets. The starboard one is meant to reduce the snaking of the hose caused by the wingtip vortex, while the port winglet is for the sake of aerodynamic symmetry.

Above right: The drogue parachute appears out of the hose guide tube as the hose starts to unwind. Note the zebra-striped wingtip and chequered guide tube, as well as the red-painted rear portions of the wing fences.

Right: Maj.-Gen. Aleksandr A. Balenko famously commented that refuelling from the Tu-16Z was 'akin to holding a tiger by the tail'. Behold – the Tiger and His Tail! The fuel transfer hose is striped to show how much of it has been paid out.

NZ, but this was soon changed to Tu-16 (Z) and, shortly afterwards, to Tu-16Z. Later on, the tanker's designation was changed to Tu-16Yu – either for security reasons or to prevent a misread as 'Tu-163' due to the similarity of the Cyrillic 'Z' and the numeral 3; the new suffix (Ю, the last-but-one letter of the Cyrillic alphabet) did not signify anything. In production the tanker was referred to as 'order 198'. As already mentioned, receiver aircraft working with such tankers had the ZA suffix at first, but this lapsed with time, as almost all Tu-16s remaining in service were IFR-capable.

The IFR system fitted to the Tu-16 differed somewhat from the version fitted to the Tu-4. The Tu-16Z featured connection equipment and fuel transfer equipment. The former subsystem included a hose 37 m (121 ft 4⁴⁵⁄₆₄ in) long which was stowed in a tube running the full length of the starboard wing's front spar and passing through the wing centre section. The hose had an outer diameter of 88 mm (3¹⁵⁄₃₂ in) and an inner diameter of 76 mm (3 in), featuring 12 integral copper wires serving as electric conductors and steel fittings at both ends. It was deployed from the starboard wingtip by means of an LBZ-6A electric winch (*lebyodka bortovaya zap-rahvshchika* – on-board winch for tanker) with a 46-m (150 ft 11 in) steel cable (replaced from 1958 onwards by the higher-powered LBZ-6B version); the winch was housed inside the starboard wing torsion box. A movable roller adjusted the tension of the cable; a cable cutter was provided, allowing the hose to be jettisoned in an emergency. The so-called main mechanism in the starboard wingtip hermetically connected a fitting at the front end of the hose to the tanker's fuel transfer line. A special electropneumatic mechanism ejected the hose from the wingtip, which was provided with a guide tube protruding 1.8 m (5 ft 10⁵⁵⁄₆₄ in) beyond the trailing edge; this tube housed a stabilising drogue parachute at the rear end of the hose.

The fuel transfer equipment proper comprised a service tank (divided by a partition into two halves), an electric fuel transfer

pump (with a cooling system for the electric motor), a fuel transfer cock, bypass and safety valves, a separate RTS-150 or RTS-150A fuel flow meter (*raskhodomer topliva samolyotnyy*) and the fuel transfer line connecting the service tank to the main mechanism. The tank was suspended in the bomb bay in a rigid metal container attached to the bomb cassettes on the sidewalls and to a shackle on the centreline beam; it featured three electric pumps – two booster pumps and one feed pump. The connection system's control panel was located at the GRO's workstation, the GRO thus acting in part as the refuelling system operator.

There were other differences from the basic bomber's fuel system. The Nos. 1, 2 and 5 fuel tanks were separated from the rest of the fuel system, being connected to the service tank in the bomb bay; however, the tanker's engines could still draw fuel from all of these tanks if necessary. The maximum transferable fuel amount was 24,500 litres (5,390 Imp gal). The fuel metering and sequencing system was revised, the tanker featuring a special SETS-60-MZ version of the automatic fuel sequencing system (the Z stood for *zaprahvshchik*). Changes were also made to the fuel tanks' inert

gas pressurisation system, the pneumatic system, the fire suppression system and the engine nacelles' de-icing system.

Two flat-plate horizontal winglets of trapezoidal planform with no incidence were installed at the wingtips; their shape was slightly different from that on the receiver aircraft. The starboard winglet served to reduce the width of the wingtip vortex and move it outward, minimising its influence on the hose; thereby the swaying of the hose as it left the wingtip was greatly reduced. The other winglet was fitted for the sake of aerodynamic symmetry. These winglets and the tubular hose guide were the Tu-16Z's main external identification features. The starboard wingtip and winglet were painted with black zebra stripes and the hose guide tube was chequered as a visual reference for the crew of the receiver aircraft; a white rectangle – another feature unique to the tanker – was sometimes painted on the rear fuselage ahead of the GRO's starboard blister, serving the same purpose, while the hose had white/red/white bands applied to it at regular intervals to show how much had been paid out.

As on the receiver aircraft, additional lighting equipment was fitted to enable contact at night. It included a light in the starboard main gear fairing illuminating the rear fuselage and fin, a light illuminating the starboard winglet, two lights illuminating the upper and lower surfaces of the starboard wing, and a manually trained searchlight at the GRO's starboard blister. Finally, local reinforcement of the airframe was made as required. According to the project the tanker had an empty weight of 38,800 kg (85,540 lb) and carried 19,000 kg (41,890 lb) of transferable fuel.

The avionics and equipment were similar to those of the bomber versions (with all due updates in the course of service). Unlike the latter, the Tu-16Z had neither active nor passive ECM equipment, yet the Sirena-2 RHAWS was a standard fit.

The IFR operation involved the captains, co-pilots and GROs of both aircraft. The receiver aircraft approached the Tu-16Z, which deployed the hose from its starboard wing, the hose trailing completely behind the aircraft on the cable. The receiver aircraft then placed its port wing on the hose about 2 m (6 ft 6 in) from its end and moved outward so that the hose slid along the wing underside until it was stopped by a restraint under the wingtip. The cable was then rewound until the rear end of the hose automatically locked into the receiver aircraft's receptacle. When this had been done, the cable was rewound further until the front end of the hose locked into the tanker's main mechanism; the two aircraft assumed close echelon starboard formation with the tanker slightly ahead, the hose forming a loop and rotating the receptacle through 180°, whereupon fuel transfer could begin. Decoupling could be made instantly at any stage in the process, either by the GRO or automatically if the two aircraft drew apart. Supervision and control of the fuel transfer was the responsibility of the co-pilot in each aircraft while the captain manoeuvred and then maintained formation; the GRO took care of the connection and (in the case of the receiver aircraft) corrected the captain's actions.

In its final form the tanker had a normal take-off weight of 75,800 kg (167,110 lb) and carried a maximum of 24,500 litres (5,390 Imp gal) of transferable fuel. IFR was practiced intensively over the sea during training, reconnaissance and patrol flights both by the DA and the AVMF. Refuelling could be made in a climb at indicated airspeeds of 480-510 km/h (298-316 mph). One fuel top-up on the outbound leg increased the Tu-16's range by almost 2,000 km (1,242 miles), and a second refuelling on the return leg raised this to almost 3,500 km (2,173 miles), with 5% fuel reserves in each case.

The wingtip-to-wingtip refuelling method had its advantages in that the aircraft being refuelled was not in the tanker's wake vortex, there was room for manoeuvring (a tight formation was not essential), and the system was relatively straightforward, with few components. On the down side, there was the need to manoeuvre when making contact, the risk of damage to the wing skin if the initial contact was made clumsily, and no option for a second coupling if the drogue parachute stabilising the hose was lost.

An added bonus was that the Tu-16 was able to operate from shorter and less heavily concreted runways by taking off with a substantially lower fuel load – that is, a take-off weight of 60,000 kg (132,270 lb), giving a take-off run of 1,200 m (3,940 ft) – and then topping up the tanks immediately afterwards. The range in this case could be slightly greater than if the aircraft had taken off with a full fuel load. Experience also proved that it was easier to carry out IFR at altitudes lower than the cruise altitude, since the engines had a bigger power reserve and piloting was easier.

The parameters of the Tu-16's wingtip-to-wingtip IFR system (final version)

Indicated airspeed	480-510 km/h (298-316 mph)
Maximum flight level	9,000 m (29,530 ft)
Maximum climb/sink rate during refuelling	3 m/sec (590 ft/min)
Fuel quantity in the Tu-16Z's service tank	10,500-10,700 litres (2,310-2,354 Imp gal)
Transferable fuel	19,000-20,000 litres (4,180-4,400 Imp gal)
Duration of procedure (from wing-to-hose contact)	12-15 minutes
Disengagement time	2-3 minutes
Fuel transfer rate	2,000 litres/min (440 Imp gal/min)
Pump pressure	6.5 kg/cm² (92.85 psi)
Winch cable pay out/rewind speed	1.2 m/sec (3.9 ft/sec)
Cable length	112 m (367 ft 5 in)
Hose length	37 m (121 ft 4⁴⁵⁄₆₄ in)

Performance of the Tu-16Z at the end of its service career

Empty weight	38,515 kg (84,910 lb)
Take-off weight:	
normal	75,800 kg (167,110 lb)
maximum (combat conditions and	
exceptional training conditions)	79,000 kg (174,160 lb)
Overall fuel capacity	54,300 litres (11,946 Imp gal)
Maximum transferable fuel	24,500 litres (5,390 Imp gal)
Maximum speed at max continuous power and	
an AUW of 55,000-70,000 kg (121,250-154,320 lb):	
at up to 500 m (1,640 ft)	670 km/h (416 mph)
at 6,250 m (20,500 ft)	890 km/h (552 mph)
at 10,000 m (32,810 ft)	960 km/h (596 mph)
Maximum permissible Mach number	0.9
Service ceiling with a take-off weight of 62,000 kg (136,690 lb)	12,800 m (41,990 ft)
Service range with a take-off weight of 75,800 kg	6,000 km (3,726 miles)

Tu-16Z '30 Blue', apparently an Air Force machine, has been fitted with an SPS-5 jammer for self-protection.

The Tu-16Z (Tu-16Yu) tanker was modified in the course of service. For example, the original Y-shaped attachment yoke of the drogue parachute was replaced with a single cable. The 'towel rail' aerial of the R-807 command radio on the upper starboard side of the forward fuselage was deleted, giving way to the L-shaped aerials of the R-832 radio on the flight deck roof and low on the starboard side of the forward fuselage, and the wire aerial running from the mast amidships to the fin served an R-808 communications radio instead of the original R-807.

In the autumn of 1955 IFR experiments were made in accordance with the aforementioned Council of Ministers directive No.1013-438 and MAP order No.354, involving two MiG-19 *sans suffixe* (*Farmer-A*) day fighters specially modified for using the wingtip-to-wingtip method (Mikoyan OKB designation *izdeliye* SM-10). The requirements were as follows: the fuel transfer rate was to be 1,000-1,200 litres (220-264 Imp gal) per minute, the refuelling taking place at indicated airspeeds of 450-500 km/h (279-310 mph) and altitudes of 9,000-10,000 m (29,530-32,810 ft). The system was to be ready for state acceptance trials in the third quarter of 1955.

The two fighters built by the Gor'kiy aircraft factory No.21 and serialled '316 Red' (c/n N59210316) and '415 Red' (c/n N59210415) were modified by OKB-155 (the Mikoyan design bureau), being fitted with a receptacle under the port wingtip. The Tu-16 tanker (c/n 1880301) was modified by OKB-156 and OKB-918; its refuelling equipment remained virtually unchanged, apart from the replacement of the normal 88-mm hose by one of 50 mm (1^{31}/$_{32}$ in) diameter. The technique of making contact was also virtually identical.

Stage A of the tests took place in the autumn of 1955; A. Komissarov was the chief engineer for the project, with Igor' I. Shelest as LII's project test pilot. Some 3,000 litres (660 Imp gal) of fuel could be transferred at a rate of 1,000 litres per minute – half the transfer rate for *Badger*-to-*Badger* refuelling. On one occasion the SM-10 was refuelled twice in one mission, staying airborne for six hours. Refuelling could be done several times during a mission – both in the daytime and at night, unless impeded by cloud.

The Tu-16's wingtip vortex caused problems, but after initial manufacturer's flight tests in 1956 the SM-10 and the Tu-16Z tanker were handed over to LII for further testing with a revised hose. This was shorter, had a more reliable attachment mechanism, was less prone to folding and was less affected by the tanker's wingtip vortex. Manufacturer's flight tests of the new fuel hose proved favourable, but the verdict of the ensuing state acceptance trials was that the method was too difficult. Work on IFR systems for fighters was therefore shelved, resuming only in the 1970s.

According to the Tupolev OKB, a total of 114 Tu-16 bombers were converted to Tu-16Z wingtip-to-wingtip tankers at the production factories in the mid-1950s (other sources give a figure of only 46), and 571 aircraft – over a third of all Tu-16s built – were equipped as receivers. Originally the tankers could be reconfigured back to bombers by field maintenance units by removing the extra fuel tanks from the weapons bay, although later the OPB-11R bombsight was removed, making reversion impossible.

Tu-16N in-flight refuelling tanker ('order 358', *izdeliye* NN)
The conversion of the Tu-16 into a probe-and-drogue tanker came into consideration when the Tu-22RD *Blinder-C* reconnaissance

Top and above: '02 Red' (c/n 7203428), a Tu-16N hose-and-drogue tanker, wears an 'anti-flash' colour scheme from its days as a Tu-16A. The aircraft is equipped with an SPS-5 jammer and the Rogovitsa formation keeping system.

aircraft, Tu-22KD *Blinder-B* missile strike aircraft, Tu-22PD *Blinder-E1/Blinder-E2* ECM aircraft and Tu-22UD *Blinder-D* conversion trainer equipped with telescopic IFR probes (D = ***dahl'niy*** – long-range) entered Long-Range Aviation and Naval Aviation service in the 1960s. Initially the DA's IFR-capable Tu-22s had worked with Myasishchev M-4-2 *Bison-A* and 3MS-2 *Bison-B* tankers, but after several years of operations the drawbacks of this combination became apparent; the 3M had a take-off run of 1,700 m (5,580 ft) and a landing run of 2,800 m (9,190 ft) which restricted it to only a few airbases. It was deemed advisable to use a lighter tanker able to operate from the same (or similar) airfields as the Tu-22 with shorter runways. Being based solely at Engels-2 AB in the Saratov Region of southern central Russia, the 3MS-2s had to fly across almost the whole extent of European Russia to reach the rendezvous zone. Conversely, though carrying less fuel than the

Bison, the Tu-16 tankers could operate from airfields in the Ukraine or Belorussia which were close to the bombers' home bases.

For starters, the Tupolev OKB and LII performed a special test programme in 1960 to determine the parameters of the line astern formation the aircraft would assume during refuelling. Tu-16 c/n 1882314 (which later was actually converted as a hose-and-drogue tanker) was the lead aircraft, a second Tu-16 (c/n 1880101) posing as the receiver aircraft; along with other pilots, they were flown by Tupolev OKB test pilots Mikhail V. Kozlov and Nikolay N. Kharitonov. A series of six flights were made at altitudes of 7,000-9,000 m (22,965-29,530 ft) and 550-650 km/h (341-403 mph), the 'receiver' approaching as close as 75 to 10 m (250 to 33 ft) behind and 2 m (6 ft 6 in) below the 'tanker' to explore the latter's wake turbulence. Vibrations of the receiver aircraft's tail unit caused by wake turbulence were noted; although not critical,

An upper view of the same aircraft. Note the white tips of the main gear fairings.

they demanded extra attention and some physical exertion on the part of the pilots. Also, if the receiver aircraft strayed to the left or to the right from directly line astern, it tended to roll because of the tanker's wingtip vortices. In the fourth flight the receiver aircraft's starboard engine flamed out when the pilots inadvertently took the machine right up to the tanker's flight level and hit wake turbulence. The receiver aircraft could manoeuvre safely within 2.5 m (8 ft 2 in) to the left/right of the tanker if flying 5 m (16 ft) below it and within 5 m if flying 10 m (33 ft) below it. It was recommended that the closing rate on approach to the tanker be 0.5-1 m/sec (1.6-3.3 ft/sec).

Next, the probe-and-drogue IFR system in use on the 3MS-2 was suitably adapted to the *Badger*, passing its tests on modified Tu-16 c/n 1882401. From 1963 onwards several Tu-16 were similarly converted at the Kazan' factory under the terms of 'order

358', receiving the service designation Tu-16N (*izdeliye* NN); again, the suffix did not denote anything specific. The IFR system had the codename **Konus** (Cone) referring to the conical shape of the drogue; hence the tanker equipped with it is occasionally referred to as the Tu-16N Konus.

The Tu-16N was equipped with a hose drum unit (HDU) developed by OKB-918. Designated KAZ (*kombineerovannyy agregaht zaprahvki* – combined refuelling module), this item was taken straight from the 3MS-2 – even though fitting it into the smaller bomb bay of the Tu-16 was a tight squeeze. The HDU was attached to beams on the bay sidewalls and deployed a hose terminating in a rigid metal drogue after the bay doors had been opened. The hose drum and the fuel transfer pump were hydraulically powered. The service tank holding 5,000 kg (11,020 lb) of fuel was located in the bomb bay aft of the HDU. On the Tu-16N the fuel

Top: A Tu-16N refuels a Tu-22RD (equipped with an UKhO rear ECM fairing) over thick overcast.

Above: A Tu-22UD trainer prepares to make contact with a Tu-16N. As often as not such contacts with the trainer were 'dry runs' without actual fuel transfer because on many Tu-22UDs the IFR probe was not connected to the fuel tanks.

delivery rate of the KAZ had to be reduced from 2,000 to 1,600 litres (from 440 to 352 Imp gal) per minute.

The aircraft was equipped with an ARK-UM *Istok* (Source of a river) ADF to ensure rendezvous with the bomber; its aerials were located on the rear fuselage and on the navigator's station glazing. A red stripe was painted along the centreline on the rear fuselage to assist the bomber's pilot in keeping formation. To enable night operations the drogue was fitted with FR-100 lights (*fara roolyozhnaya* – taxi light, which is what the thing originally was);

one more FR-100 light was installed on the outboard side of the starboard main gear fairing. Appropriate changes were made to the tanker's hydraulics and electrics. The forward-firing cannon and its NU-88 mount were deleted, as was the dorsal OSS-61 anti-collision light. An AKS-2 cine camera (*apparaht kinosyomochnyy*) was fitted to record the contact with the bomber. The avionics were similar to those of the standard Tu-16 bomber.

During refuelling the Tu-22 would assume a position 16-17 m (52-55 ft) below the tanker's flight level in order to stay clear of its wake vortex. The Tu-16N deployed the drogue, which would be 8-12 m (26-39 ft) below its fuselage axis and 25-30 m (82-100 ft) aft of it; the bomber then moved in close and 'speared' the drogue, whereupon fuel transfer could begin. The HDU mechanism maintained a constant tension of the hose to prevent a whiplash which could break the bomber's probe.

In mid-1966 Tu-16N c/n 1882314 underwent state acceptance trials, a production Tu-22RD (c/n 3083012, f/n 08-01) acting as the receiver aircraft; the results were good, and the system was recommended for service by a joint Air Force/MAP resolution. In keeping with the latter a total of 23 Tu-16 bombers were converted to Tu-16N standard at the Kazan' factory between 1968 and 1970. Like the Tu-16Z, they could revert to bomber configuration if necessary.

With a single top-up from the Tu-16N the Tu-22 had a range of 7,200 km (4,472 miles), increasing to 8,000 km (4,968 miles) with two top-ups on the outbound leg. Using a different technique (one top-up on the outbound leg and one on the return leg) further extended the range to 8,500 km (5,279 miles). Refuelling took place at a speed of 600 km/h (372 mph) and an altitude of 8,000 m (26,250 ft); a maximum of 15,800 kg (34,830 lb) of fuel could be transferred at a rate of 1,600-1,800 litres (352-396 Imp gal) per minute.

Operational experience with the Tu-16N revealed a number of shortcomings and prompted an upgrade programme agreed upon by the Air Force and MAP on 15th-16th October 1970. Modifications were made to the valve of the drogue and the hose shut-off valve in the HDU; the single light on the starboard main gear fairing was replaced by two faired FR-100 lights located low on the centre fuselage sides to illuminate the rear fuselage. The tanker was retrofitted with an updated RSBN-2SV *Svod-Vstrecha* (Dome-Rendezvous) SHORAN to ensure rendezvous with the bomber.

From 20th January, to 16th February 1971, a production Tu-16N (c/n 1882202) incorporating these changes passed check-up tests at GNIKI VVS. The aircraft came from the 251st GvTBAP (*Gvardeyskiy tyazholyy bombardirovochnyy aviapolk* – Guards Heavy Bomber Regiment) based at Belaya Tserkov' AB ('White Church') in the Kiev Region of the Ukraine. This time the receiver aircraft were a Tu-22KD ('53 Red', c/n ...53704..., f/n 53-04) and a Tu-22UD trainer ('40 Red', c/n 2568034, f/n 56-03) from the 15th TBAD (*tyazholaya bombardirovochnaya aviadiveeziya* – Heavy Bomber Division)/341st TBAP at Ozyornoye AB near Zhitomir, a regional centre in western Ukraine. The project test pilots were Col. Valentin F. Ivanov (GNIKI VVS), who flew the tanker, and V. G. Loman (the Long-Range Aviation Command), who flew the *Blinders*.

In addition to checking the efficacy of the changes, the crews explored the limits of the zone within which the receiver aircraft could manoeuvre during the contact with the tanker and assessed the peculiarities of the Tu-22's IFR procedures. The Tu-16N logged 6 hours 52 minutes in five flights; the Tu-22KD made two flights totalling 2 hours 28 minutes, while the Tu-22UD made three flights totalling 4 hours 1 minute. An additional two flights with the trainer involved 'dry' contacts in which no fuel was transferred.

The results of the check-up tests were positive and the changes were incorporated on other in-service Tu-16Ns. Furthermore,

Performance of the Tu-16N	
Empty weight	39,720-41,130 kg (87,570-90,670 lb)
Take-off weight:	
normal	76,670 kg (169,025 lb)
maximum (combat conditions and exceptional training conditions)	79,000 kg (174,160 lb)
Overall fuel capacity	48,900 litres (10,758 Imp gal)
Maximum transferable fuel	19,500 litres (4,290 Imp gal)
Maximum speed at max continuous power and an AUW of 55,000-70,000 kg (121,250-154,320 lb):	
at up to 500 m (1,640 ft)	670 km/h (416 mph)
at 6,250 m (20,500 ft)	890 km/h (552 mph)
at 10,000 m (32,810 ft)	960 km/h (596 mph)
Maximum permissible Mach number	0.9
Service ceiling with a take-off weight of 62,000 kg (136,690 lb)	12,800 m (41,990 ft)
Service range with a take-off weight of 76,670 kg	6,200-6,400 km (3,850-3,975 miles)

Note: According to some documents, the full fuel load was 19,740 kg (43,520 lb) including 11,580 kg (25,530 lb) of transferable fuel. Refuelling took place at a speed of 600 km/h (391 mph) and an altitude of 6,000 m (19,685 ft).

while initially the Tu-16N lacked ECM gear, some tankers had the Rogovitsa formation keeping system and the SPS-5 Fasol' jammer added. With these improvements the Tu-16Ns served on into the 1980s, when they were progressively retired after reaching the end of their service lives. After that, the Air Force was stuck again with the heavy 3MS-2 tankers, which soldiered on until 1996.

The Tu-16N again had the NATO reporting name *Badger-A*.

Tu-16NN in-flight refuelling tanker

A total of 20 standard Tu-16Z tankers were converted to probe-and-drogue tankers in 1969 along the lines of the bombers converted to Tu-16N standard. Such aircraft were designated Tu-16NN to discern them from bombers originally converted to probe-and-drogue tankers; outwardly they differed from the latter in retaining the horizontal winglets and in having duralumin patches riveted on where superfluous equipment from the Tu-16Z had been removed. However, they were so similar to the Tu-16N that they were likewise referred to as Tu-16Ns in Soviet Air Force service.

Tu-16D (?) experimental probe-and-drogue refuelling receiver

In the late 1950s a single Tu-16 was converted into a receiver aircraft using the probe-and-drogue IFR technique. The IFR probe was installed on the centreline above the navigator's station, necessitating changes to the latter's glazing. A similar combination of the glazed nose and the IFR probe was later seen on the Tu-95M *Bear-A* bomber and the Tu-95RTs maritime reconnaissance/OTH targeting aircraft. The fuel line from the probe ran to the Nos. 2-5 fuel tanks; modifications were made to the pneumatic system for operating the telescopic probe and a new fuel metering and usage system was fitted. Two retractable FPSh-5 lights (*fara podsveta shtahngi* – [IFR] probe illumination light) were buried in the upper side of the nose on both sides of the probe; a green signal light was built into the fin leading edge, illuminating when

Three aspects of a Tu-16NN hose-and-drogue tanker ('45 Blue', c/n 1882503) showing the rear fuselage illumination lights and the probe aerial on the navigator's station glazing associated with the SHORAN system ensuring rendezvous with the receiver aircraft.

Top: Upper view of the same tanker.
Above: Another Tu-16NN ('41 Blue', c/n 1882302) which additionally features the Rogovitsa formation keeping system.

contact with the drogue had been made to tell the tanker's refuelling system operator that fuel transfer could begin.

Although the trials were successful, the system was not adopted for in-service Tu-16s. Instead, this modified Tu-16 served as an IFR system testbed developing IFR equipment for the Tu-95KD *Bear-B* and Tu-22KD long-range ASM carriers. Some documents refer to this one-off aircraft as the Tu-16D (obviously again standing for *dahl'niy* – long-range), although the designation was not officially used during the trials.

Tu-16S maritime search and rescue aircraft ('order 454', *izdeliye* NS)

In the mid-1950s the Soviet Navy perceived a need for a search and rescue (SAR) aircraft capable of delivering a lifeboat or life rafts rapidly to the crew of a ditched aircraft (or an aircraft shot down into the sea) or a vessel in distress. By the time a ship reached the scene it might be too late for the rescuees – especially in the cold northern seas. This work was long overdue; after all, the USA had been operating specialised air-sea rescue aircraft since 1945 – initially the Boeing B-17H (aka SB-17G or PB-1G) Flying Fortress, nicknamed 'Dumbo', which carried a Higgins A-1 paradroppable lifeboat, and later the Boeing SB-29 'Super Dumbo' with the Higgins A-3 lifeboat, which saw action in the Korean War.

Work on an SAR version of the *Badger* for the AVMF began pursuant to Council of Ministers directive No.1952-1047 issued on 26th December 1955. This tasked MAP with equipping the Tu-16

to carry a self-propelled lifeboat; the prototype was to be completed in the third quarter of 1956 and submitted for state acceptance trials in the first quarter of 1957.

The programme bore the codename 'Arkhangel'sk' (which was rather appropriate because this city hosts a major Soviet Navy base). It proceeded under the overall guidance of Iosif F. Nezval', who in 1957 was appointed head of a different branch of OKB-156 in the town of Tomilino (Moscow Region).

Designated Tu-16S (*spasahtel'nyy* – rescue, used attributively) or *izdeliye* NS, the aircraft was based on the RD-3M-powered Tu-16 *sans suffixe* bomber or the Tu-16T torpedo-bomber and was to carry a remote-controlled powered lifeboat under the centre fuselage. The boat, the first of its kind in the Soviet Union, was designed to MoD specifications by TsKB-5 of the Ministry of Shipbuilding (MSP – *Ministerstvo soodostroitel'noy promyshlennosti*) under the guidance of project chief N. A. Makarov, initially bearing the project designation Type 347. Having no prior experience with paradroppable lifeboats, which would be subjected to considerable aerodynamic loads, TsKB-5 had to rely heavily on assistance from the Tupolev OKB in matters concerning aerodynamics, structural strength and manufacturing technology. A research and development programme was undertaken, including wind tunnel tests of scale models and drop tests to verify the boat's aerodynamics during separation from the aircraft and its strength during splashdown. A full-size-mock-up of the Type 347 boat was built in the southern Ukrainian city of Kherson by plant No.831 of

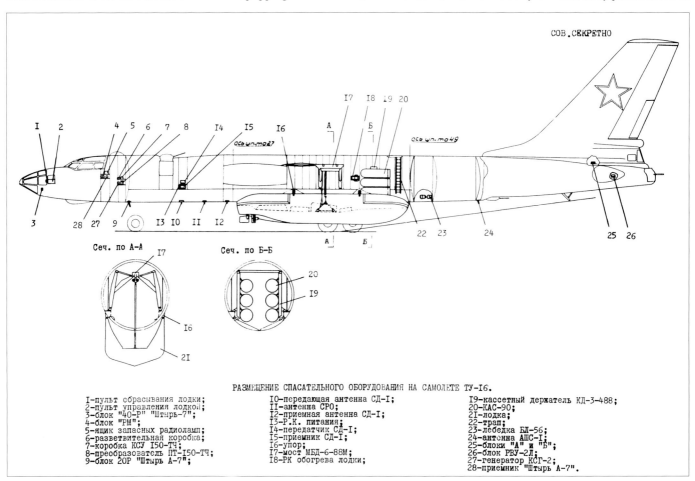

СОВ.СЕКРЕТНО

РАЗМЕЩЕНИЕ СПАСАТЕЛЬНОГО ОБОРУДОВАНИЯ НА САМОЛЕТЕ ТУ-16.

1-пульт сбрасывания лодки;
2-пульт управления лодкой;
3-блок "40-Р" "Штырь-7";
4-блок "РМ";
5-ящик запасных радиоламп;
6-разветвительная коробка;
7-коробка КСУ I50-ТЧ;
8-преобразователь ПТ-I50-ТЧ;
9-блок 20Р "Штырь А-7";

I0-передающая антенна СД-I;
II-антенна СРО;
I2-приемная антенна СД-I;
I3-Р.К. питания;
I4-передатчик СД-I;
I5-приемник СД-I;
I6-упор;
I7-мост МБД-6-88М;
I8-РК обогрева лодки;

I9-кассетный держатель КД-3-488;
20-КАС-90;
2I-лодка;
22-трап;
23-лебедка БЛ-56;
24-антонна АШС-I;
25-блоки "А" и "Б";
26-блок РВУ-2Л;
27-генератор КСГ-2;
28-приемник "Штырь А-7".

Below left: A drawing from the ADP documents of 'Project *Arkhangel'sk*' showing the mission equipment placement on the Tu-16S air-sea rescue aircraft. In addition to the lifeboat, the aircraft was to carry six KAS-90 pods with rescue materiel.

Right: A full-size mock-up of the Type 347 lifeboat submitted to the mock-up review commission. The boat has its beaching/ground handling gear attached, the mast erected and and the sail hoisted. Note the canopy over the helmsman's station, with an aerial for the communications radio and the Soviet Navy flag flying from the flagstaff.

Below: The Tu-16S demonstrator ('19 Blue', c/n 5400801) with the lifeboat mock-up attached. The boat was carried back to front.

the Kherson Regional Economic Council (*sovnarkhoz*, a type of regional authority reintroduced by Khrushchov in 1957 as part of an economic reform); it was fitted to a Tu-16 coded '19 Blue' (c/n 5400801) to check if the attachment fittings were OK and how the boat's gunwales adhered to the fuselage sides. All of this made it possible to select the optimum size, shape and structural design of the lifeboat.

According to the project, the Type 347 lifeboat was 9.3 m (30 ft 6⁹⁄₆₄ in) long and 1.6 m (5 ft 3 in) high, with a beam of 2.3 m (7 ft 6³⁵⁄₆₄ in), a freeboard of 1.2 m (3 ft 11¼ in) at the bows and 1.07 m (3 ft 6⅛ in) at the stern, and an average draught of 0.52 m (1 ft 8¹⁵⁄₃₂ in); the displacement loaded was 4.48 tons. The boat was

of riveted duralumin construction, with unsinkability features, and designed to operate in rough seas (sea state 5) with wave heights up to 3.5 m (11 ft 5 in). The boat could accommodate 20 persons, with enough food and water to last them for four days. To protect the rescuees from the environment the foredeck and quarterdeck featured domed metal covers, with a rubberised fabric tent between them; these were collapsed while the boat was attached to the aircraft, popping up pneumatically after splashdown. The helmsman's station near the stern was provided with a pop-up glazed canopy. Propulsion was by means of a 40-hp 1,220-cc AM402-SR3 petrol engine adapted from a Moskvich-402 saloon car, which gave a maximum speed of 15 km/h (8.1 kts) and a max-

Two more views of the Tu-16S demonstrator with the Type 347 lifeboat mock-up.

imum range of 1,500 km (931 miles or 810 nm), but a mast with a square sail could be erected if the engine broke down or ran out of fuel.

The Type 347 lifeboat was equipped with a PG-3715-54 parachute system (*parashoot groozovoy* – cargo parachute) stowed at the bows, enabling delivery at indicated airspeeds up to 500 km/h (310 mph) and various altitudes. This was developed by NIEI PDS and comprised an extractor parachute, a stabilising drogue parachute, a brake parachute and a single main canopy with an area of 1,580 m² (17,007 sq ft). The boat, complete with parachute system and emergency supplies, was to weigh 3,580 kg (7,890 lb).

The lifeboat was suspended under the bomb bay between fuselage frames 27-49, back to front (with the bows facing aft). It was attached by a special yoke to a standard MBD6-88M centreline bomb cradle with a Der6-5 bomb shackle, as used for carrying the Tu-16's biggest bombs (the '88' is a reference to 'aircraft 88'). Ver-

tically adjustable restraints were mounted on the lower fuselage sides at frames 34 and 43 to stop the boat from rocking. To enable access to the bomb bay when the boat was in place, a dorsal hatch measuring 0.37x0.75 m (1 ft 2⁹⁄₁₆ in x 2 ft 5¹⁷⁄₃₂ in) was added between frames 47-48A, in similar manner to the WSO's capsule escape hatch of the Tu-16KS, with a ladder on the starboard side.

In addition to the lifeboat, the Tu-16S carried six KAS-90 pods (*konteyner aviatsionnyy spasahtel'nyy* – air-delivered rescue equipment container) on standard KD3-488 bomb cassettes in the rear section of the bomb bay. Developed and manufactured by plant No.468 in Moscow, which specialised in paradropping equipment, the KAS-90 (manufacturer's designation P-89) had been added to the AVMF inventory in 1954, finding use on such types as the Beriyev Be-6 *Madge* flying boat, the Be-12 amphibian and the Tu-14. It was a paradroppable cylindrical metal capsule containing rescue materiel – an LAS-5M dinghy (**lodka avar-**

Rear and three-quarters rear views of the same aircraft.

eeyno-spasahtel'naya) plus an emergency radio, or an SP-12 inflatable raft (*spasahtel'nyy plot* – rescue raft for 12 persons), or food and clothing. Of course the pods could only be dropped after the lifeboat had been released. The pods were loaded and the lifeboat was lifted into position by means of standard clip-on BL-56 electric hoists (***bombovaya lebyodka*** – bomb hoist, 1956 model).

The Tu-16S had mission avionics unique to it – the ***Lodka-M*** (Boat-M) radio remote control equipment allowing the crew to control the lifeboat after splashdown, the *Pritok* (Tributary) receiver and the *Shtyr'* (Rod) direction finder. The latter was linked to the Rubidiy MM-2 radar and allowed the aircraft to zero in on the signals of the rescuees' ELT, making it easier to find the rescuees in adverse weather; the reception range was 60-100 km (37-62 miles). The Lodka-M system could transmit the following commands: 'start engine', 'full speed ahead', 'half speed ahead' and 'stop' (throttling back to idle rpm).

On 20th-28th June 1958, the project materials and the Tu-16S demonstrator with the mock-up of the lifeboat were examined by the mock-up review commission. A month later, on 31st July, its chairman, Deputy Commander-in-Chief (Experimental Aircraft Construction) of the Soviet Air Force Lt.-Gen. Aleksandr N. Ponomaryov, signed the commission's protocol; the latter was endorsed by representatives of the Tupolev OKB, NIEI PDS, TsKB-5 of what was now the State Committee for Shipbuilding (GKSP – *Gosudarstvennyy komitet po soodostroitel'noy promyshlennosti*) and plant No.831. The protocol gave a generally positive appraisal of the project; however, it also contained a long list of shortcomings to be eliminated, mostly concerning the lifeboat's aerodynamics, propulsion and equipment. Also, the mock-up lacked the abovementioned pop-up protective covers and tent, which were not ready yet; these were to be examined by the mock-up review commission later.

Design maximum speed of the Tu-16S with the Type 347 lifeboat*

Altitude, m (ft)	Sea level	2,000 (6,560)	4,000 (13,120)	6,000 (19,685)	8,000 (26,250)	10,000 (32,810)	12,000 (39,370)
Speed, km/h (mph):							
at maximum continuous power	692 (429)	765 (475)	847 (526)	962 (597)	940 (583)	916 (568)	886 (550)
at nominal power	692 (429)	765 (475)	847 (526)	920 (571)	912 (566)	888 (551)	836 (519)

* All-up weight 55,000 kg (121,250 lb), lifeboat fitted

Some project specifications of the Tu-16S with the Type 347 lifeboat

Empty weight	37,670 kg (83,050 lb)
Take-off weight	75,800 kg (167,110 lb)
Landing weight	39,920 kg (88,010 lb)
Fuel load	32,680 kg (72,050 lb)
Range with the above TOW and fuel load, with lifeboat and six KAS-90 pods, boat dropped/boat not dropped:	
'hi-hi-hi' flight profile	5,498/5,238 km (3,416/3,254 miles)
at 10,000 m (32,810 ft)	5,193/4,973 km (3,226/3,090 miles)
at 8,000 m (26,250 ft)	4,786/4,586 km (2,973/2,849 miles)
at 4,000 m (13,120 ft)	3,348/3,188 km (2,080/1,981 miles)

TsKB-5 set to work again, but for various reasons it was not until 1964 that the definitive version of the lifeboat designated Type 347A *Fregaht* (Frigate) was ready for testing. Apparently the military were forced to curb their appetite – the definitive version was designed to accommodate only 15 rescuees, with emergency supplies for only three days instead of four. The boat had an equipped weight of 3,300-3,570 kg (7,280-7,870 lb) and a displacement of 4.2 tons. Performance was also reduced – the Type 347A boat had a maximum speed of 13.9 km/h (7.5 kts) and a range of 1,480 km (920 miles or 800 nm), but this was still enough to reach the nearest shore within a reasonable time.

There were structural differences as well. In particular, the engine was enclosed by a watertight cowling and provided with electric heaters connected to the aircraft's electric system. The propeller featured a protective housing to prevent being fouled by the parachute lines.

The aircraft, too, had a slightly different equipment fit. The definitive Tu-16S had an RPM-S direction finder (*rahdiopelengahtor mayakov samolyotnyy* – aircraft-mounted locator for [emergency] beacons) picking up the signals of *Opushka* (Edge of the forest) individual ELTs; it was linked to the RBP-4 radar, and its aerial was mounted on the starboard nose gear door. An ARK-U2 *Istok* ADF with an aerial mounted on the centreline ahead of the nosewheel well between frames 12-13 was fitted for homing in on the signals of the R-855U ELT fitted as standard to many Soviet military aircraft; it also facilitated rendezvous with the Tu-16Z tanker. The remote control equipment consisted of a *Reya-S* (Yardarm) transmitter with an AShS-1 swept blade aerial (*antenna shtyrevaya strelovidnaya*) on the rear fuselage underside between frames 56-57, whose signals were picked up by a Reya-L receiver on the lifeboat; the S and L suffixes stood for *samolyot* (aircraft) and *lodka* (boat) respectively.

Oddly, most sources claim the KAS-90 pods could be carried only as an alternative to the Type 347A boat, not together with it.

The *modus operandi* was as follows. Once the SOS signal of the vessel or aircraft in distress had been relayed to the fleet headquarters, a Tu-16S standing on ready alert at one of the fleet's airbases would scramble and be directed towards the disaster area. En route the crew would pre-heat the lifeboat's engine by means of the electric heaters to ensure reliable start-up which might otherwise be foiled by a cold soak at high altitude. If the people in distress had an emergency locator beacon, the aircraft would zero in on its signals when it came within reception range; if not, the search would be performed by means of the aircraft's radar or visually.

After locating the area and spotting the survivors (if any) the Tu-16S dropped the lifeboat, the parachute system being jettisoned automatically on splashdown. After that, the aircraft's navigator started the boat's engine by radio and steered the boat was towards the rescue area, guiding it to within 2-5 m (6-16 ft) of the rescuees, who would then swim up and climb aboard. Using the boat's radio, the first rescuee(s) was/were to establish radio contact with the aircraft and confirm that he/they was/were aboard; the crew would advise them of any other people who were still overboard. If any of the rescuees knew how to manage the boat, he would steer it manually; if not, it was up to the aircraft's navigator to steer it by radio. However, once all the rescuees were safely aboard one of them had to steer the boat anyway because the aircraft could not loiter in the area too long. Before returning to base the crew of the Tu-16S was to determine the boat's course towards the shore (or the nearest ship) and advise the boat's captain of it, alert ships in the area or shore command posts of the boat's whereabouts and organise radio communication between them. A second sortie could be required to check on the boat if it was at sea for an extended time.

Two prototypes of the Type 347A lifeboat were built by the *Mor'e* (Sea) shipyard in Feodosiya on the Crimea Peninsula, passing initial tests in November 1965. After that, the air-sea rescue system based on the Tu-16S was successfully tested by the Black Sea Fleet Air Arm and approved for service with the AVMF.

About 50 production Type 347A lifeboats were built by the Mor'e shipyard in 1965-68. Starting in 1965, the production factories building the *Badger* converted a number of Tu-16T torpedo-bombers remaining in service to Tu-16S standard as 'order 454'. Most of these aircraft were delivered to the North Fleet where they saw service until the late 1980s; however, they were never used in an actual emergency. Regrettably, the last examples were retired just before the tragic loss of the Soviet Navy/North Fleet Type 685 (NATO reporting name *Mike* class) nuclear-powered submarine K-278, better known as SNS *Komsomolets* (Member of the Young Communist League), which sank in the Norwegian Sea on 7th April 1989 after an on-board fire. 42 of the 69 crewmembers lost their lives, mostly succumbing to hypothermia in the ice cold

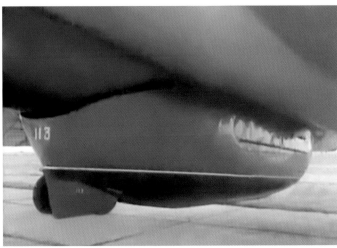

Top left: An actual Tu-16S during tests at GNIKI VVS with a production Type 347A Fregat lifeboat attached.

Above left: Close-up of the lifeboat.

Left: A still from a GNIKI VVS documentary showing a Type 347A lifeboat being dropped. The drogue parachute extracting the parachute system (which is stowed in the bows) is deployed.

Top and above: More stills from the same film showing a Tu-16S taking off with a different example of the lifeboat.

impossible to climb aboard unassisted. As a result, the next model of paradroppable lifeboat developed by TsKB-5, the rather different Type 347M, was designed to be dropped with a crew of two in special shock-absorbing seats so that they could help the rescuees.

Tu-16KRM target drone carrier ('order 299')

A special version of the Tu-16 was created to assist the Air Defence Force (PVO) in the development of missiles capable of engaging high-flying supersonic aircraft. It carried two MV-1 supersonic target drones (*mishen' vysotnaya* – high-altitude target drone) on the existing wing pylons; the drones were also known as KRM-2

water; had the Tu-16S been available to fly a rescue mission, the number of survivors could have been much higher.

Yet, quite apart from the Tu-16S's inadequate operational radius of some 2,000 km (1,242 miles), the Type 347A unmanned paradroppable lifeboat had an inherent shortcoming: people weakened by exposure to cold water could find it difficult or even

Above: A Tu-16KRM target drone carrier aircraft taking off.

Above right: This shot of the same aircraft with the landing gear in mid-retraction gives a better view of the targets suspended on the wing pylons. These appear to be not KRM rocket-powered drones based on missiles but rather PM-6 diving targets with parachute recovery, as carried by appropriately modified IL-28 bombers.

Below and bottom: A Tu-16 Yolka ECM aircraft (c/n 1883704) seen in the process of conversion to a Tu-16KRME drone launcher. The chaff outlets of the ASO-16/7 dispenser and the EWO's entry hatch (with associated cut-outs in the bomb bay doors) are evident.

(*krylahtaya raketa-mishen'* – cruise missile used as target), hence the drone carriers received the service designation Tu-16KRM. The drones were used in the development of the Tu-128S-4 long-range air defence system comprising the Tu-128 *Fiddler* twin-turbojet heavy interceptor, which first flew on 18th March 1961, and its R-4 (NATO AA-5 *Ash*) medium-range AAM developed by OKB-293 under Matus R. Bisnovat – the semi-active radar homing R-4R (*izdeliye* 36R) and the infrared-homing R-4T (*izdeliye* 36T).

The MV-1 was a derivative of the KSR-2 cruise missile; it had a launch weight of 4,000 kg (8,820 lb), a top speed of 2,760 km/h (1,714 mph) at an altitude of 22,500 m (73,820 ft), and a maximum range of 376 km (233 miles). After launch it climbed to a cruise altitude of 20,000-25,000 m (65,620-82,020 ft); the flight time was limited to 7.2 minutes.

The conversion to Tu-16KRM standard involved changes to the flap actuation system (flap deflection was restricted to 25° when the drones were carried) and reinforcement of the wing spars. The fuel system was altered (there were provisions for transferring fuel from the No.1 tank to the Nos. 7-11 tanks and a ground-controllable cock was introduced in the pipeline between the Nos. 1 and 2 tanks); special equipment for launching the drones was fitted. The RBP-4 radar was retained. The aircraft had a maximum speed of 885 km/h (549 mph), a service ceiling of 10,000-11,000 m (32,810-36,090 ft) and a range of 3,800 km (2,360 miles) with two drones.

Two Tu-16KRM prototypes were converted by plant No.22 in 1962 from Tu-16 c/n 8204026 (original version and tactical code unknown) and Tu-16K-11-16 '16 Red' (c/n 8204111, tail number 8211). 'Production' drone carriers were converted from Tu-16KS and Tu-16KSR missile strike aircraft under the terms of 'order 299' in the late 1960s.

Tu-16KRME target drone carrier ('order 299E')

A variant of the Tu-16Ye ECM aircraft adapted to carry MV-1 target drones but retaining its SPS-1/SPS-2/Siren' jammers and ASO-16/3 chaff dispenser was designated Tu-16KRME. When the drones were launched, the aircraft could simulate enemy ECM, creating additional complications for the PVO's SAM crews. Like the Tu-16Ye, it had a crew of seven.

Tu-16NKRM target drone carrier ('order 332')

A further drone carrier version developed in 1964 under the terms of 'order 332' was designated Tu-16NKRM (*nositel' krylahtykh*

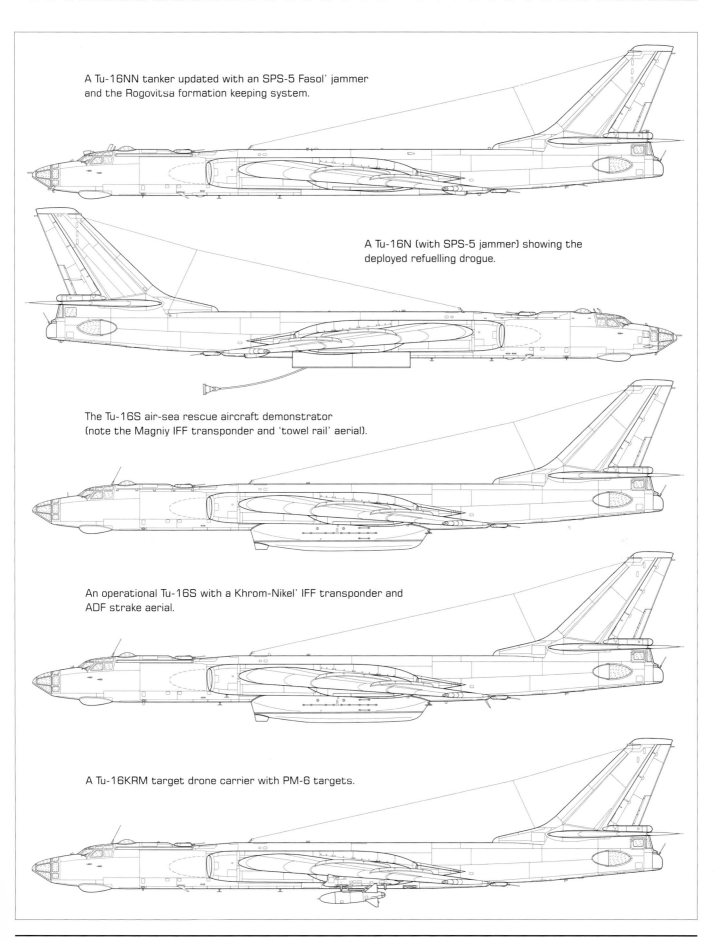

A Tu-16NN tanker updated with an SPS-5 Fasol' jammer
and the Rogovitsa formation keeping system.

A Tu-16N (with SPS-5 jammer) showing the
deployed refuelling drogue.

The Tu-16S air-sea rescue aircraft demonstrator
(note the Magniy IFF transponder and 'towel rail' aerial).

An operational Tu-16S with a Khrom-Nikel' IFF transponder and
ADF strake aerial.

A Tu-16KRM target drone carrier with PM-6 targets.

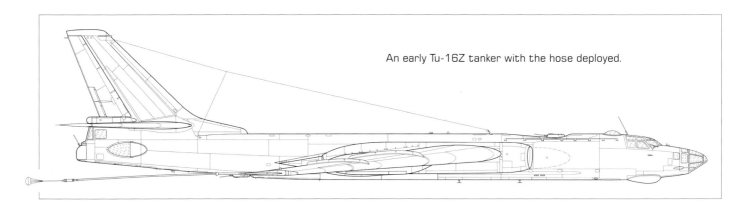

An early Tu-16Z tanker with the hose deployed.

raket-misheney – carrier of cruise missiles used as targets). It carried two 540-kg 1,190-lb) ITs-59 *Olen'* (Deer) high-speed, high-altitude drones (ITs = *imitahtor tseli* – simulated target) powered by liquid-fuel rocket motors. In 1980 the improved 1,052-kg (2,319-lb) ITs-59V *Magnit* (Magnet) drone with a liquid-fuel sustainer and two solid-fuel rocket boosters became available and was likewise carried by the Tu-16NKRM. Both types of drones were used by the PVO for SAM development and troop training.

Tu-16NM target drone carrier
The KSR-5NM low-altitude target drone (alias D-5NM, *nizkovysotnaya mishen'*) and the KSR-5MV high-altitude target drone (D-5MV, *mishen' vysotnaya*) were evolved by MKB Raduga from the KSR-5N cruise missile in the early 1990s. Both drones simulated air-to-surface and anti-shipping air-launched missiles and were used in the development of new SAM systems. The drones could be programmed to simulate high-altitude missiles, strategic or tactical bombers or low-altitude missiles. Depending on the programme, the drone could have a top speed of Mach 4.2, a maximum range of 400 km (248 miles) and a maximum flight altitude of 40,000 m (131,230 ft). Both drones had a launch weight of 3,944 kg (8,695 lb) and could be launched at altitudes from 500 to 11,000 m (1,640-36,090 ft). They were able to carry additional equipment, either in single items or as a set, for measuring the trajectory, transmitting data to measuring stations via data link, recording a miss by an attacking missile and automatically assessing the launch results.

The KSR-5NM and KSR-5MV drones were carried by a version of the *Badger* designated Tu-16NM (*nositel' misheney* – target drone carrier) modified in similar manner to the Tu-16K-26 missile strike aircraft. The modifications included strengthening the wing spars and installing BD-352-11-5 pylons, altering the flap operating system to restrict flap deflection to 25° when the drones were carried, altering the fuel system and adding a system for pressurising the drones' avionics compartments. The KSR-5NM was launched at an altitude of 450-550 m (1,480-1,800 ft) with the aircraft flying at 500-550 km/h. The drone's powered flight time was between 75.7 and 379.4 seconds, giving it a maximum range of 110.4 km (68.6 miles).

In addition to the Tu-16NM, the KSR-5NM and KSR-5MV drones could also be launched by ordinary Tu-16K-26s, Tu-16KSR-2-5s and Tu-16KSR-2-5-11s without requiring any modifications to the aircraft.

Tu-16 target tug
The Tu-16 was also used in a rather unusual capacity – as a target tug for training AAA crews and fighter pilots in the interests of the PVO. To this end the DK-7 tail turret was removed to make room for a towing winch and associated gear. The aircraft worked with a PM-3Zh target (*plahner-mishen'* – glider-type target) developed by OKB-487 under Grigoriy I. Bakshayev. The PM-3Zh, which was normally towed by suitably modified Il-28s, had a wide-chord tail swept back 45°, narrow-chord unswept wings placed well aft and a tricycle landing gear with small wheels. The towing cable was paid out to the required length before the aircraft flew over the gunnery range to preclude 'friendly fire' incidents and rewound before landing. The 'aircraft plus target' combination was known in Russian terminology as *aeropoyezd* (air train)!

Tu-16 remote-controlled target drones
As early as 1956 the Tupolev OKB was tasked with developing a large target drone based on the Tu-16 to be used for testing anti-aircraft weapons and conducting Air Defence Force exercises. On 23rd November 1956, the Council of Ministers issued directive No.1528-768 followed by MAP order No.592 on 3rd December, both concerning development of the Tu-16M (*mishen'* – practice target or, in his case, target drone). The aircraft was to retain the flight performance of the production Tu-16 and the first three examples were to be ready for joint OKB/Air Force trials during the second quarter of 1958. Development was to proceed jointly with the Ministry of Radio Industry (MRP).

Due to delays caused by development problems the first three experimental Tu-16M drones did not reach the Tupolev OKB's flight test facility in Zhukovskiy until the end of 1958, allowing tests of the remote control system to begin. Hence on 16th April 1958 the Council of Ministers followed up with directive No.419-198 (and MAP with order No.131 of 24th April), postponing the beginning of the trials until the second quarter of 1959.

While the research and development work was under way, during the first six months of 1959 the Kuibyshev aircraft factory No.1 built 13 Tu-16s *sans suffixe* (c/ns 1883701 through 1883713) which were earmarked for conversion into drones for the PVO. However, again progress was hindered by the problems engendered by the creation of a reliable and effective radio control system (the abovementioned 13 *Badger-As* were eventually completed as Tu-16Ye ECM aircraft and delivered to the VVS, not the PVO), and in 1960 the Tupolev OKB transferred all further work on tar-

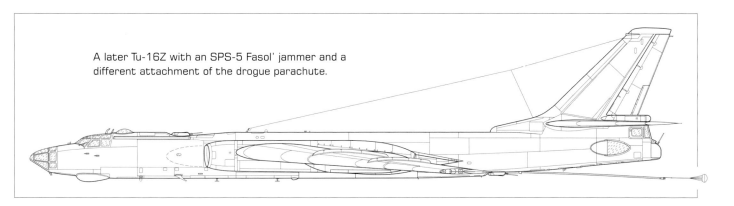

A later Tu-16Z with an SPS-5 Fasol' jammer and a different attachment of the drogue parachute.

get drone versions of the Tu-16 to its Tomilino branch headed by Iosif F. Nezval'.

The Air Defence Force required the Tu-16M to be controlled by radio commands transmitted from either a ground command post or a drone director aircraft. The drone was to have both active and passive ECM equipment, as well as data link to transmit the required information on systems status to the command post. Originally, in accordance with PVO specifications, the Tu-16M was conceived as a pilotless disposable drone. It was to take off with a normal crew who would eject after taking the aircraft to the required altitude, whereupon the drone was to be fired upon by PVO assets, with the option of self-destruction if they missed. However, apparently the specialists at OKB-156 and LII thought this was wasteful, so they devised a system enabling the Tu-16M to take off and land under radio control; this allowed recovery of the drone for re-use if it survived the attack and obviated the need for unnecessary ejections (with potential injuries). Importantly, the Tu-16M differed from other types of target drones converted from aircraft in being able to accommodate a large amount of ECM equipment

After further development work, the Tu-16M target drone was accepted for service on 17th April 1965, under the designation M-16. This was normal practice in the PVO – the manufacturer prefix was substituted with an M when this or that aircraft type was converted to target drones in considerable numbers; cf. M-17 based on the MiG-17 (not to be confused with the Myasishchev M-17 *Mystic-A* high-altitude aircraft), M-21 based on the MiG-21 *Fishbed*, M-28 based on the Il-28 and so on. The designation Tu-16M was only applied (and then only briefly) to those drones modified by plant No.22 in Kazan'. By then a considerable number of Tu-16s were reaching the end of their service lives, and many of them were converted to M-16 drones.

The demand for the drones was small at first, with the Kazan' factory carrying out the modifications in parallel with series production of the Tu-22 (and later Tu-22M) supersonic bombers, but the early 1980s saw the *en masse* retirement of the Tu-16 and the re-equipment of the Long-Range Aviation with the Tu-22M2 and Tu-22M3. As the scope of conversion work increased, the Kazan' factory could no longer cope and the drone modification job was taken on by the Air Force's ARZ No.12 in Khabarovsk. The aircraft converted there still had some airframe life remaining, allowing them to be used as proficiency trainers for a while.

The conversion involved removing all offensive and defensive armament, the associated targeting and control equipment and

(initially) the ECM equipment; in the case of the Tu-16P the jammer suite's heat exchangers remained, even though the dielectric canoe fairing between them was gone. The deletion of the equipment not only reduced weight but caused a forward shift of the CG, so ballast had to be installed in the rear avionics/equipment bay to restore the CG position.

The equipment interpreting the guidance commands and feeding them to the control system servos was located on the starboard side of the flight deck between the seats of the co-pilot and the Nav/Op. The automated flight control system comprised three electric programmed control mechanisms (for take-off/climb, landing approach and landing respectively), an automatic tracking mechanism, an RA-144-7 control servo (*roolevoy agregaht*), the AP-6E autopilot, the RV-2 or RV-5 radio altimeter, an automatic wheel brake control module and interfaces; an electric servo drive was installed on the captain's side console to move both throttles by means of a push-pull rod.

The crew was reduced to five, there being no tail gunner and the GRO being 'demoted' to a simple radio operator. The navigator's instrument set was reduced to the barest minimum.

Thus, regardless of the original version, the M-16 drones could be identified by the absence of the cannon installations (the locations of the dorsal and ventral barbettes were faired over, while the tail turret was replaced by a hemispherical metal fairing similar to that of some demilitarised An-12 transports transferred to Aeroflot) and by the forward- and aft-pointing probe aerials of the command link system. The forward pair of aerials was mounted on triangular metal panels supplanting part of the navigator's station glazing, and the rear pair was located on the sides of the tail fairing or, occasionally, at the tips of the horizontal tail. L-shaped loop aerials serving the data link system were mounted in the area of the weapons bay. Some M-16s had three tracer flares on short pylons under each outer wing to facilitate visual observation from the ground during night sorties.

Soon the military had second thoughts about the ECM equipment; a target drone fitted with such equipment would make for a more realistic scenario. The drones converted by the two plants had some fundamental differences; for instance, the Tu-16Ms converted in Kazan' usually had passive ECM gear, while the M-16s converted by ARZ No.12 had active jammers.

After conversion the aircraft were delivered to first-line regiments for crew training, their last flights usually taking place over a practice range in Kazakhstan as targets for SAM systems. In the

Left: An M-16 target drone equipped with a Siren'-D jammer covering the front hemisphere and cine camera pods under the wings. The metal panels replacing part of the nose glazing carry the forward pair of remote control aerials. The aircraft was probably modified by plant No.22.

Below: Similarly configured M-16 '31 Red' (c/n 6203326) taxies out for take-off, showing the distinctive dished rear fairing with the rear pair of remote control aerials. Note the ECM antenna pods on top of the wing-tips.

early 1990s a few M-16s were also operated by the GNIKI VVS facility at Vladimirovka AB in Akhtoobinsk, making their last flights from there.

Before the (theoretically) last flight the crew started the engines, taxied the M-16 to the holding point, armed the automatic flight control system, then climbed out and shut the entry hatches; everything else proceeded in remote control mode. When the take-off command was transmitted the PME-1-16 electric programmed control mechanism (*programmnyy mekhanizm elektricheskiy*) revved up the engines to full thrust, released the brakes and initiated rotation and climb at the proper moment, the elevators being controlled by the autopilot; then it retracted the landing gear and flaps and throttled back the engines to 80% of the nominal thrust for the climb. After reaching the preset altitude the aircraft maintained altitude and speed, changing course at the autopilot's commands; engine speed was controlled by the

RA-144-7 servo. If the missile was not fired for some reason (or missed the target), the drone could be guided back to base and land in radio control mode. The landing gear was extended and the flaps deployed automatically when the radio altimeter and speed sensor gave appropriate readings. When the M-16 descended to 20 m (65 ft), the PME-2-19 programmed control mechanism took charge, throttling back the engines at the moment of flareout; upon touchdown the brake parachutes were deployed automatically and oleo compression triggered the PME-3-16 programmed control mechanism, which activated the wheel brakes, maintained a straight course on the runway and released the brake parachutes at the proper moment.

The Tu-16 was a tough aircraft, and at times the drone survived a direct hit of a missile and flew on; in this case a second missile had to be fired. If the automatic flight control system malfunctioned, making a landing impossible, a self-destruct command

Above and right: Shown here at the 929th GLITs in Akhtoobinsk in the early 1990s, '77 Red' is an M-16-2 drone featuring 360° ECM capability. The rear control aerials are mounted on the UKhO fairing housing a Siren'-MD jammer; the Siren'-D jammer is mounted in the nose. The air intakes and outlets on top of the centre fuselage show this aircraft to be a former Tu-16Ye Azaliya.

Below: '80 Red' seen at Akhtoobinsk around the same time is an M-16-3 drone with only a Siren'-D jammer covering the front hemisphere. The triple tracer flare holders are just visible under the wings.

The one-off M-16 Orbita target drone showing the large fairings housing IRCM flare dispensers and the trapezoidal aerials replacing the dorsal and ventral cannon barbettes.

Below and below left: Stills from video footage through a fighter's head-up display capturing the final moments of an M-16 as the missile hits and the drone erupts in flames.

was transmitted. This did not mean blowing the aircraft up – the control surfaces were deflected to initiate a right-hand spin and then a vertical dive, the aircraft breaking up in mid-air after exceeding the dynamic pressure limit.

In unmanned configuration the M-16 had a take-off weight of 70,000 kg (154,320 lb). The drone flew at a speed of about 890 km/h (553 mph) and altitudes up to 11,000 m (36,090 ft); range was only about 300 km (186 miles), being restricted by the remote control system's reception range, but the endurance was up to four hours.

Tu-16M (M-16) target drone (*izdeliye* NM; 'order 212', 'order 2212')

As mentioned above, Tu-16s converted to drones at the Kazan' plant No.22 under the terms of 'order 212' were initially known by the service designation Tu-16M (*izdeliye* NM); subsequently, in common with the conversions carried out at Khabarovsk, they were called M-16. At Kazan' most conversions were from Tu-16A bombers; those examples which had 12 ASO-2B Avtomat-2 chaff dispensers installed in the bomb bay during conversion were known as 'order 2212'. Later it was the turn of Tu-16Ye and Tu-16P

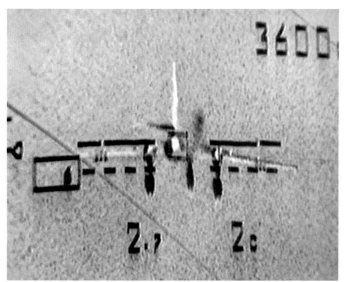

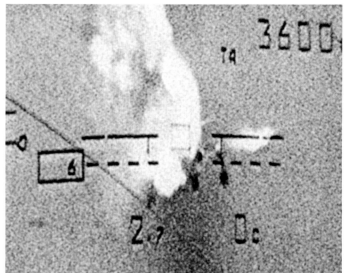

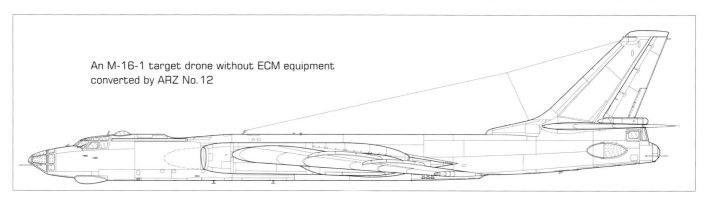

An M-16-1 target drone without ECM equipment converted by ARZ No. 12

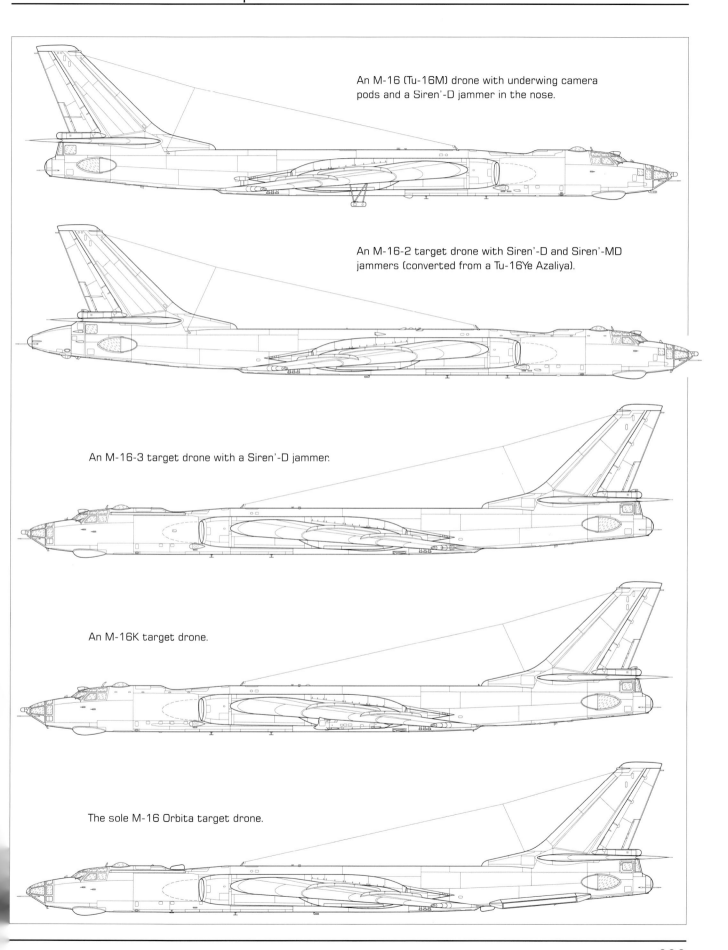

An M-16 (Tu-16M) drone with underwing camera pods and a Siren'-D jammer in the nose.

An M-16-2 target drone with Siren'-D and Siren'-MD jammers (converted from a Tu-16Ye Azaliya).

An M-16-3 target drone with a Siren'-D jammer.

An M-16K target drone.

The sole M-16 Orbita target drone.

ECM aircraft to be converted; missile strike versions rarely ended up this way. They were intended for use in the development of SAMs and AAMs, four flights being made with a crew on board and a fifth as a pilotless target.

M-16-1 target drone

In Khabarovsk various versions of the Tu-16 underwent conversion into drones. Tu-16A bomber conversions with no active ECM equipment were designated M-16-1.

M-16-2 target drone

Tu-16 drones fitted with Siren'-D and Siren'-MD active jammers giving full 360° coverage were designated M-16-2. These conversions were mainly carried out in Khabarovsk and based on Tu-16A bombers and Tu-16Ye ECM aircraft which already had an UKhO rear ECM fairing. In this case the rear pair of command link aerials was mounted on the halves of the UKhO fairing. The antennas of the Siren'-D were located in the usual manner – a 'thimble' on the navigator's station glazing and two 'eggs on legs' below the engine air intakes.

M-16-3 target drone ('order 254'?)

Some drones with a Siren'-D jammer covering only the forward hemisphere were designated M-16-3. Various versions of the Tu-16, including those fitted with the Azaliya, Buket and Ficus ECM systems, underwent this conversion at ARZ No.12 – reportedly under the terms of 'order 254'. In this case the ECM antennas could be located on the navigator's station glazing and below the air intakes in the same fashion as on the M-16-2, but some examples had larger egg-shaped ECM antenna fairings on the sides of the navigator's station in the same 'bone through the nose' arrangement as seen on some Tu-16Ye aircraft.

Some M-16-3s carried small cine camera pods under the wings on tripod-like supports. The cameras apparently recorded the distance by which the incoming missile missed the target. This was obviously only possible with inert test or training rounds (since modern AAMs and SAMs have proximity fuses and do not need to score a direct hit, such cine film footage could help to determine whether a launch could count as a hit – that is, whether the missile was close enough to detonate.

(It should be noted there is some controversy as to what 'order 254' really was. Some sources claim this order applied to outfitting operational Tu-16s – that is, *not* M-16 drones – with the Buket jammer, including Naval Aviation Tu-16RMs.)

M-16K target drone ('order 254K')

Drones converted at Khabarovsk from 'glass-nosed' missile-carrying versions of the Tu-16 with forward-looking Siren' jammers, as on the M-16-3, were known as 'order 254K' during conversion and as the M-16K in service, the K suffix referring to their previous missile strike role. The BD-352 missile pylons were retained.

M-16 Orbita target drone ('order 254 Orbita')

In 1990 a retired Tu-16 ('32 Red', c/n 7203616) was converted into the M-16 *Orbita* (Orbit) experimental target drone (referred to during conversion as 'order 254 Orbita'). It differed from the other M-16 drones in having strake-like trapezoidal aerials replacing the dorsal and ventral cannon barbettes and sporting large boxy fairings low on the rear fuselage sides. The fairings housed APP-50 *Avtomaht-F* (aka L029) chaff/flare dispensers (*avtomaht postanovki [passivnykh] pomekh* – automatic passive ECM/IRCM device) firing 50-mm PPI-50 magnesium flares (*peeropatron infrakrasnyy* – infrared flare) or chaff packs downward/to the sides to decoy incoming missiles. This version failed its state acceptance trials and remained a one-off.

M-16 drone launcher/target drone ('order 285K')

An unconventional version of the target drone was developed by a certain R&D establishment under the aegis of the PVO and converted from a drone carrier in 1991 under the terms of 'order 285K', retaining the wing pylons and the Rubin-1K radar. It was given a three-year service life extension and was still used to carry target drones until it reached the end of its service life when it became a target drone itself. Outwardly the aircraft could be recognised by the trapezoidal command link aerials at the wingtips. Unlike other drone versions, the cannon armament was retained and the crew comprised six persons.

Tu-16KP airborne command post

On 20th May 1954, the Council of Ministers issued a directive ordering the development of unmanned strike systems capable of delivering a nuclear warhead over a range of 8,000 km (4,970 miles). In keeping with this directive Semyon A. Lavochkin's OKB-301, best known for its wartime piston-engined fighters, started work on the **Boorya** (Storm) supersonic ground-launched cruise missile (GLCM), also known as *izdeliye* 350 – the world's first intercontinental cruise missile. The Boorya had a two-stage design. The main stage featuring cropped-delta wings and cruciform tail surfaces was powered by a 7,650-kgp (16,865-lbst) RD-012U ramjet sustainer designed by OKB-670 under Mikhail M. Bondaryuk; it was flanked by two boosters with 68,400-kgp (150,790-lbst) S2.1150 liquid-propellant rocket motors designed by Aleksey M. Isayev's OKB-2. The missile was designed to cruise at Mach 3.2-3.3 at altitudes of 17,000-25,000 m (55,770-82,020 ft); it had a monstrous launch weight of 94,860 kg (209,130 lb), including 40,860 kg (90,080 lb) for the main stage, and was to carry a 2,350-kg (5,180-lb) nuclear warhead over a range of 8,500 km (5,280 miles).

Flight tests began in July 1957 at the Kapustin Yar missile test centre in the Astrakhan' Region of southern central Russia; the first successful launch took place on 22nd May 1958. Further launches were made from Vladimirovka (Astrakhan' Region) where GK NII VVS had one of its facilities. In its 18th and final launch on 16th December 1960 the missile covered a distance of 6,500 km (4,038 miles).

Because of the Boorya's long range, tests of the missile necessitated several command posts along its flight path for tracking its flight and making whatever course corrections were necessary. Airborne command posts (ABCPs) able to fly at high altitude and cover a wide radius, as well as accompanying the missile for some time, were clearly preferable to ground installations; therefore a few Tu-16s were suitably converted. Known as the Tu-16KP

Above: This aircraft coded '10 Blue' has been reported as a Tu-16RT telemetry pick-up aircraft.

Right: The dorsal pair of aerials on Tu-16 '10 Blue'.

(*komahndnyy poonkt* – command post), such aircraft carried special missile control equipment in the equipment bay and in the bomb bay, with a pressurised cabin for the operator in the aft section of the bomb bay, as on the Tu-16R. These specially converted *Badgers* were stationed at DA bases along the missile's flight path along with normal Tu-16s; after the missile's launch they were able to take off and track it.

However, the Boorya was, so to say, facing a storm more potent than itself. Back in 1957 the aforementioned R-7 ICBM had been fielded; as a point of interest, shortly afterwards this missile would be developed into the famous *Soyooz* (Union) space launch vehicle which has been the staple of the Soviet/Russian manned space programme. ICBMs were perceived as being more immune against the potential adversary's air defences; hence Nikita S. Khrushchov declared the Boorya missile system 'unnecessary'. And that's all there was to it – he could not be persuaded otherwise. Also, General Designer Semyon A. Lavochkin passed away on 9th June 1960, and after his death there was no one to stand up for the Boorya. When further work on the missile was discontinued, the Tu-16KPs reverted to their original form.

Tu-16RT telemetry pick-up aircraft
Another special version of the *Badger* involved in the testing of the Boorya GLCM was the Tu-16RT (*retranslyator* – signal relay station) developed in 1956. Its mission was to pick up the telemetry transmitted by the missile as it flew towards the Koora target range on the Kamchatka Peninsula. This was the first Soviet aircraft of the kind, and its existence was due to the fact that building ten to fifteen ground-based telemetry pick-up stations quickly along the route from Vladimirovka to Kamchatka was not feasible.

A fleet of nine telemetry pick-up aircraft based on the Tu-16 and the Antonov An-2 *Colt* utility biplane was outfitted within a

short time; all of them carried the purpose-built RTS-8S data link system (*rahdiotekhnicheskaya sistema, samolyotnaya* – airborne radio technical system). The system had 64 analogue channels with pulse-time modulation, registering 64 parameters of the flight and recording them on magnetic tape for later deciphering and analysis. The six Tu-16RTs were responsible for the main part of the Boorya's trajectory, while the three An-2RTs took over at the terminal phase of the missile's flight.

The Tu-16RT carried the mission equipment in pressurised containers in the bomb bay. Outwardly it differed from a standard *Badger* in having probe aerials in the nose and tail, as on Tu-16M drone, and tandem pairs of L-shaped loop aerials above and below the centre fuselage. The telemetry pick-up aircraft operated from Vladimirovka AB, Belaya AB near Irkutsk and Ookraïnka AB (aka Seryshevo AB) in the Amur Region, loitering in designated areas to cover the missile's entire route.

After the demise of the Boorya programme the telemetry pick-up aircraft were stripped of their mission equipment. Only one Tu-16RT coded '10 Blue' (c/n 6401607) is known; it apparently ended its days as an M-16 target drone, as suggested by the triple tracer holders under the wings visible in a photo.

Tu-16 – unidentified version 1
In the 1990s a Voronezh-built Tu-16 coded '14 Red' (c/n 6401208) in service with the Russian Air Force's 929th GLITs (*Gosudarstvennyy lyotno-ispytahtel'nyy tsentr* – State Flight Test Centre named after Valeriy P. Chkalov, formerly GNIKI VVS) was noted at Vladimirovka AB in Akhtoobinsk, sporting five non-standard

Opposite page and right: Although it may appear at a glance to be an M-16K, a closer look at Tu-16 '14 Red' (c/n 6401208) shows it is not a drone after all – not yet, at any rate. The aircraft still has the cannon barbettes (albeit without cannons) and lacks the M-16's characteristic remote control aerials and tracer flare holders. On the other hand, non-standard loop aerials are mounted above and below the centre fuselage and on the starboard side of the nose.

loop aerials of trapezoidal shape which were oriented lengthwise. Four of them were arranged in tandem pairs above and below the centre fuselage, while the fifth aerial was located low on the starboard side of the nose where the forward-firing cannon should have been. The aircraft still had BD-352-11-5 missile pylons from its days as a *Badger-G Mod*, but the absence of the probe aerials associated with remote control and of the tracer flare holders under the outer wings showed this was not an M-16K target drone, even though the aircraft was parked together with several M-16s. Possibly '14 Red' was an avionics testbed of some sort.

Tu-16 – unidentified version 2

Another Tu-16 operated by the 929th GLITs and seen at Vladimirovka around the same time – a Kazan'-built *Badger-A* coded '15 Red' (c/n 5202506) – was even more unusual, being fitted with narrow slab-sided fairings under the wings. The fairings, whose function is unknown, had a trapezoidal shape in side elevation and were located at about the same positions as the missile pylons. The aircraft – again probably a testbed – was out of service by then, sitting on the same hardstand and possibly being earmarked for conversion as an M-16 drone.

Tu-16K-10 'camera ship' version

Two examples of the Tu-16K-10 transferred from a first-line AVMF unit were converted for air-to-air filming during the testing and development of the Tu-16's in-flight refuelling system. All equipment associated with the former missile carrier role was removed, as was the defensive armament, and remote-controlled cine cameras on special mounts were installed in the dorsal and tail turrets. Both aircraft served for a long time in a number of flight test programmes.

Tu-16N 'sky cleaner' adaptation

Two Tu-16N tankers were used for spraying liquid carbon dioxide in the late 1970s as part of the *Tsiklon* (Cyclone) weather research programme. They were used for 'sky cleaning' (dispersing rain

clouds to prevent rain from ruining a public holiday). The aircraft were based at Chkalovskaya AB.

Tu-16AFS photo survey aircraft

In the early 1970s a Kuibyshev-built Tu-16 *Badger-A* coded '69 Red' (c/n 1883601) in service with one of the Soviet Air Force units was re-equipped to perform aerial photography along the Baikal-Amur Railway. Designated Tu-16AFS (*aerofoto-syomshchik* – photo survey aircraft), it operated from various civilian airports, although it was 'registered' to LII and officially based at Zhukovskiy. The aircraft could still be seen derelict at the LII airfield in the 1990s, sitting on the grass between the old runway 08/26 (at present used as an aircraft parking area) and the active runway 12/30 together with several other dumped aircraft.

Tu-16U (Tu-16U-1, Tu-16U-2, Tu-16U-3, Tu-16U-4) bomber trainer (project)

Being the standard bomber of the Long-Range Aviation (DA) and Naval Aviation (AVMF) in the 1950s and 1960s, the Tu-16 was also used for conversion training of aircrews. The bomber was on strength with the training regiments at the Tambov Military Pilot College named after Marina Raskova (TVVAUL – *Tambovskoye vyssheye voyennoye aviatsionnoye oochilischche lyotchikov*) at Tambov-Vostochyy AB in central Russia, the Chelyabinsk Military Navigator College (ChVVAUSh) and two Combat Training & Aircrew Conversion Centres – the DA's 43rd TsBP i PLS at Dyagilevo AB and the AVMF's 33rd TsBP i PLS at Kul'bakino AB on the south-eastern limits of Nikolayev, southern Ukraine. At first machines of the first production batches were relegated for training, but they were joined later by examples of the Tu-16A bomber and even, in small numbers, by the Tu-16K-something-or-other missile-toting versions.

When the Soviet Union became a signatory to arms limitation treaties, the need arose for aircraft which could be used for training the crews of strategic bombers but would not rate as strategic aircraft themselves in the eyes of the law. *Badgers* retired from

Left and below left: Another unidentified special version at Akhtoobinsk converted from Tu-16 '15 Red' (c/n 5202508). The aircraft features trapezoidal underwing fairings of uncertain purpose.

As this photo shows, '15 Red' retains the cannon barbettes (albeit minus cannons) and lacks the remote control aerials typical of an M-16. The position of the underwing fairings is more clear in this view.

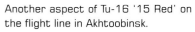

Another aspect of Tu-16 '15 Red' on the flight line in Akhtoobinsk.

operational service appeared to be ideally suited for this, with the proviso that armament, ECM equipment and other mission equipment were removed. Such aircraft were to be redesignated Tu-16U (*oochebnyy [samolyot]* – trainer) and have a red band painted on the rear fuselage to mark them as non-combat aircraft for arms reduction monitoring purposes. The crew would be reduced to five, there being no tail gunner.

Various versions of the Tu-16U were planned. The Tu-16U-1 was to be a dedicated aircrew trainer version for mastering piloting and navigation techniques; all of its armament was to be removed and the bomb bay faired over. The Tu-16U-2 was envisaged as a bomber trainer; hence the bomb armament was to be retained. The Tu-16U-3 would be used for ASM launch training, while the Tu-16U-4 was to be a similar trainer version of the Tu-16K-10-26.

For political reasons none of these versions materialised. Firstly, the Tu-16 fell outside the strategic weapons category covered by the SALT I and SALT II strategic arms limitation treaties; secondly, as the *Badger* was being phased out, many Tu-16s were already being converted as M-16 drones. It was therefore decided to combine two functions in the M-16 target drone: as mentioned earlier, the aircraft would serve as a bomber trainer until it reached the end of its useful life and flew its final mission as a target. For that reason the *Badgers* being converted to M-16 drones in Khabarovsk were refurbished to give them a three-year service life extension, allowing them to be used as trainers for a considerable time. As for the training roles described above, they were assigned to the Tu-95U and Tu-95KU – decommissioned versions of the Tu-95 *Bear-A* bomber and the Tu-95K missile strike aircraft respectively.

However, the aforementioned Long-Range Aviation's equipment and re-equipment plan for 1989 (see page 369) states that one DA regiment (the 203rd TBAP) had several Tu-16Us. Perhaps this was merely a bit of 'artistic licence' and the aircraft were ordinary bombers used for proficiency training.

Tu-16 'Sokol' record-breaking aircraft (skydiving aircraft)
In 1957 a Tu-16 coded '61 Red' and presumably operated by GK NII VVS was used for a series of record-breaking stratospheric parachute jumps. The bomber, which was known as the Tu-16 *Sokol* (Falcon), was suitably lightened by removing non-essential items, including the armament, and equipped with seats in the bomb bay. On 20th-21st August 1957, the aircraft made two flights from Chkalovskaya AB where GK NII VVS was located; it was captained by Lt.-Col. Bobrov. On the first occasion only a single test parachutist, Lt.-Col. Nikolay K. Nikitin, made a jump after the Tu-16 had climbed to 15,650 m (51,350 ft), which is way above the *Badger's* normal service ceiling. Some sources, though, state that Nikitin made the jump at 15,383 m (50,469 ft) and fell 14,620 m (47,965 ft) before opening his parachute. Either way, he set both a national record and a world record.

On the second occasion the Tu-16 'Sokol' carried a team of six parachutists – Vasiliy G. Romanyuk, Gleb Nikolayev, Aleksandr Savin, Nikolay Zhukov, Yevgeniy N. Andreyev and Anatoliy Vanyarkho. Because of the extreme altitude, as had been the case with Nikitin, the skydivers wore pressure helmets and protective suits similar to the first-generation space suits of future Soviet cosmonauts. The jump was performed at 15,200 m (49,870 ft); however, again Romanyuk himself gave different figures – the six parachutists left the Tu-16's bomb bay at 14,811 m (48,592 ft) and opened their parachutes after falling 14,045 m (46,079 ft). The free fall lasted about four minutes.

Tu-16G (Tu-104G) mailplane and civil aircrew conversion trainer
Apart from serving as the basis for the Tu-104 airliner, the *Badger* was involved quite directly in the development of civil jet aviation in the Soviet Union. Before the Tu-104 entered service with Aeroflot Soviet Airlines, three production Tu-16 bombers were transferred to Aeroflot to facilitate aircrew conversion training. Starting in 1954, Aeroflot similarly used a small number of demilitarised Il-28 bombers under the designation Il-20 (the second aircraft thus designated) for lead-in jet training; however, the Tu-16 was obviously much closer to the real thing.

The bombers had all offensive and defensive armament and other military equipment removed (except maybe the radar, which

Right: The record-breaking team of skydivers in the bomb bay of the Tu-16 'Sokol'.

Below: Nikolay K. Nikitin makes the jump from the Tu-16 'Sokol'.

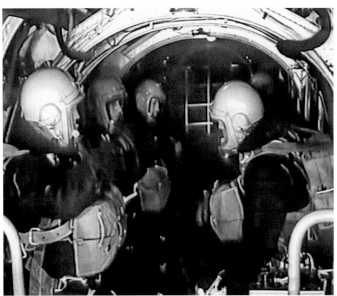

Above and left: CCCP-L5411, one of the Tu-16G mailplanes and civil aircrew trainers, at the KIIGA training facility after being withdrawn from use, with a second Tu-16 to keep it company. The aircraft carried Aeroflot titles and logo but not the Soviet flag, which should have been painted on the tail.

could be used for navigation). In addition to their training role, they were used as high-speed mailplanes, delivering matrices of the main Soviet daily newspapers *Pravda* (Truth) and *Izvestiya* (News) from Moscow to regional centres, such as Irkutsk, where both papers had additional print shops. (If the papers were delivered to the eastern regions of the Soviet Union all the way from Moscow, they would be one day old by the time they were on the street, and who wants yesterday's news?) The matrices were carried in special containers in the bomb bay.

Designated Tu-16G (*grazhdahnskiy* – civil) or, rather misleadingly, Tu-104G (*groozovoy* – cargo, used attributively), the *Badgers* received civil registrations, wearing small Aeroflot titles and the airline's winged hammer-and-sickle logo (irreverently

called *kooritsa*, 'chicken', in slang) on the forward fuselage. Only one aircraft registered CCCP-Л5415 (that is, SSSR-L5415 in Cyrillic characters; c/n 1881301) has been positively identified; however, c/ns 1881302 through 1881304 have also been reported as Tu-104Gs. (Under the Soviet civil aircraft registration system used in 1922-1958 the CCCP- country prefix was followed by a code letter denoting the aircraft's owner plus up to four digits. The code L stood for *leeneynyy [samolyot]* (aircraft in regular airline service), denoting the Main Directorate of the Civil Air Fleet (GU GVF – *Glahvnoye oopravleniye Grazhdahnskovo vozdooshnovo flota*).)

When sufficient numbers of the 'true' Tu-104 became available, it was possible to use the airliners for crew training between

Tu-16G SSSR-L5411

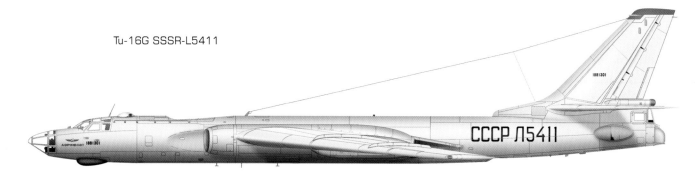

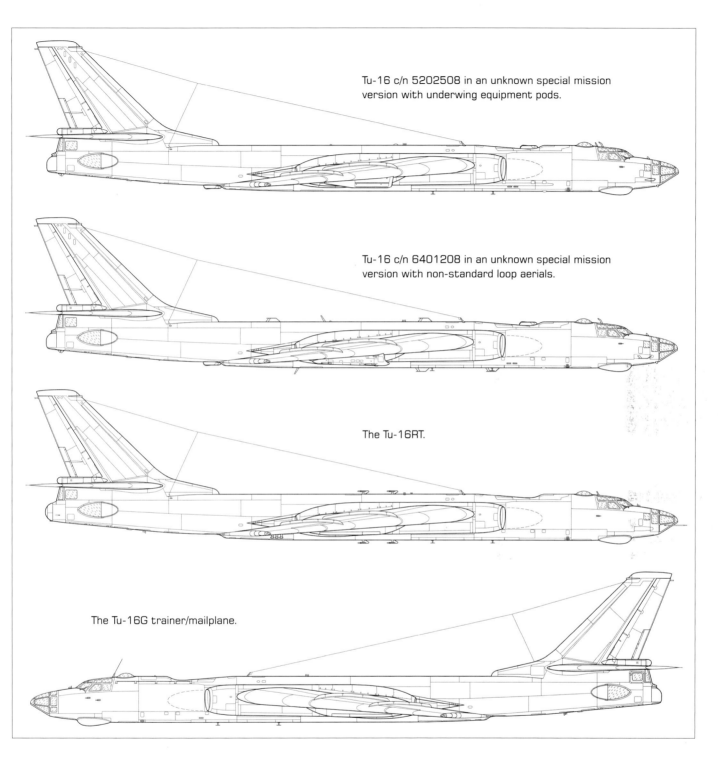

Tu-16 c/n 5202508 in an unknown special mission version with underwing equipment pods.

Tu-16 c/n 6401208 in an unknown special mission version with non-standard loop aerials.

The Tu-16RT.

The Tu-16G trainer/mailplane.

scheduled flights. Also, new methods of data transmission rendered the Tu-16G unnecessary as a mailplane. Hence the Tu-16Gs were returned to the Soviet Air Force and 'remilitarised'.

VI. The testbeds and research aircraft
Starting as early as 1954, the Tu-16 was used on a wide scale for testing new jet engines, structural components, assemblies, avionics, equipment and armament. Such aircraft were usually called Tu-16LL (*letayushchaya laboratoriya* – lit. 'flying laboratory'), regardless of the nature of their testbed role.

Tu-16LL engine testbeds ('order 226')
Most often, however, the designation Tu-16LL is applied to the nine engine testbeds operated by LII from Zhukovskiy. These aircraft were standard bombers with the radar and all armament removed, carrying the experimental turbojet or turbofan in a special nacelle under the fuselage. Several types of these engine pods were used, but most had either a cylindrical (or teardrop) shape or a curious shape resembling a reversed bottle.

The engine pod was semi-recessed in the bomb bay during take-off/landing to provide adequate ground clearance; before

The first of the nine Tu-16LL engine testbeds operated by LII wore the highly unusual alphanumeric code 'ЛЗ' (L3 in Cyrillic characters). It is shown here taxying with the development engine semi-recessed in the bomb bay and its intake shutter deployed. Note that the radar is still in place.

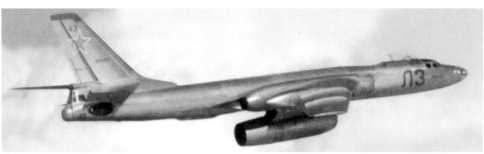

The same aircraft in flight with the Lyul'ka AL-7F development engine extended and running. Judging by the absence of the radar, the photo was taken at a later date. Note also that the smaller tactical code on the fin is different, '43 Blue' (derived from the aircraft's c/n 1880403).

Above left: The bomb bay of a Tu-16LL, looking aft, showing the heavy-duty pylon for the development engine and its pantographic retraction mechanism. Note also the fuel line and the many electrical connectors dangling from the pylon.

Above: Another view inside the Tu-16LL's bomb bay, showing the development engine's air intake shutter in retracted position.

Left: Tu-16LL '01 Blue' is jacked up for maintenance in one of LII's hangars pending installation of the development engine. The air intake cover is marked '501', indicating c/n 6401501. Note the reinforcement plate low on the forward fuselage – a way of addressing the Tu-16's initial structural strength problem.

Above: The detached development engine nacelle of a Tu-16LL (minus rear fairing) on a ground handling dolly in one of LII's hangars, showing the numerous access panels and the four cooling air intakes in a square arrangement at the front end. LII's An-12BK 'Tanker' de-icing systems testbed (CCCP-48974) is parked in the background.

Above right: The detachable tail fairing of the development engine nacelle on a dolly alongside Tu-16LL '02 Blue' (c/n 4201002).

Right: The compressor face of a development engine installed in a fully extended nacelle. For ground runs the air intake features a built-in foreign object damage (FOD) prevention grille.

Right: A Lyul'ka AL-7F runs in full afterburner during a ground test on the Tu-16LL. The aircraft is parked on sloping concrete ramps to increase the engine's ground clearance and the wings and main gear bogies are under wraps to protect them from snowfall.

Below: A fighter engine (the convergent-divergent afterburner nozzle is clearly visible) is prepared for a ground run beneath a Tu-16LL. The rear fuselage underside has heat-resistant steel plates riveted on to protect the skin from the jet blast. Note the tarpaulins covering the main gear bogies, the pan collecting any oil dripping from the engine and the safety barrier erected in front of it. Many of the hatches on the development engine nacelle have been left open to facilitate adjustments in case of need.

start-up the pod was lowered clear of the fuselage by a special pantographic mechanism with a hydraulic actuator to prevent the turbulent boundary layer from affecting engine operation. A hinged circular cover closed the air intake when the engine was stowed to prevent windmilling when not in use and preclude foreign object damage; it tilted forward to lie flat against the aircraft's belly before the engine pod was lowered. The nacelle featured an emergency jettison mechanism (in case it failed to retract before landing or the development engine caught fire). Heat-resistant steel panels were riveted to the underside of the rear fuselage to protect it from the development engine's exhaust. All this necessitated changes to the centre fuselage structure which were made by the manufacturing plant(s), and the conversion job was known as 'order 226'.

Some 30 engines – nearly all Soviet second-/third-generation jet engines – were tested on the Tu-16LLs in the course of some 30 years. The first *Badger* to be converted for engine testing was

Above: Here, Tu-16LL '02 Blue' (c/n 4201002) sits parked in front of one of the purpose-built ramps at Zhukovskiy in the 1990s. The development engine is stowed but the intake shutter remains open. A common feature of the Tu-16LL testbeds was the absence of the radar and the armament.

Left and above left: The same aircraft in a later configuration taxies at Zhukovskiy, the development engine's intake firmly closed by the shutter. The retractable nacelle has a larger diameter and a different shape. Note the difference in the presentation and location of both the tactical code and c/n which had been altered during the course of an overhaul.

a Kuibyshev-built example manufactured in 1954 (c/n 1880403), which was coded '43 Blue' on the tail and wore the unusual alphanumeric code 'ЛЗ' ('L3' in Cyrillic) on the nose. (Some sources mistakenly report it as a Voronezh-built aircraft, c/n 6401403.) This aircraft was used for testing the Lyul'ka AL-7F-1 afterburning turbojet developed for the Sukhoi Su-7 *Fitter-A* fighter-bomber which was rated at 6,240 kgp (13,760 lbst) at full military power and 9,600 kgp (20,280 lbst) in full afterburner.

Kazan'-built Tu-16 c/n 4201002 (which, as mentioned earlier, was the pattern aircraft for 1955 production) became the second Tu-16LL; the conversion was begun by plant No.22 in October

1955 and the aircraft was redelivered in 1956. In keeping with LII's practice it was coded '02 Blue', the tactical code matching the last digits of the c/n. The first engine tested on this particular aircraft was the afterburning turbojet that started life as the Mikulin AM-11 and was eventually built as the Tumanskiy R11-300 after Aleksandr A. Mikulin's removal from office. It was rated at 4,200 kgp (9,260 lbst) dry and 5,110 kg (11,270 lbst) reheat in the initial R11A-300 version powering the Yakovlev Yak-28 *Brewer* supersonic twinjet tactical bomber prototypes.

The other seven Tu-16LL engine testbeds were Voronezh-built '01 Blue' (c/n 6401401), '08' (c/n 6401408), '41 Blue'

One of the Tu-16LL engine testbeds – presumably '01 Red' (c/n 6401501) – with a large turbofan engine lowered into running position. Note the test equipment heat exchangers mounted in prominent fairings directly on the development engine nacelle.

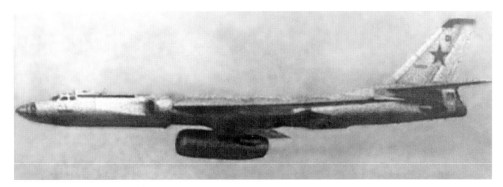

A different Tu-16LL, '01 Blue' (c/n 6401401; note the differently applied tactical code), with a very similar development engine nacelle – right down to the test equipment heat exchanger placement. Here, the test engine nacelle has a 'reversed bottle' shape with a lengthened rear end.

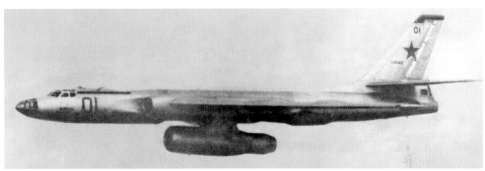

Right, below and below right: The same Tu-16LL in action, in this case with a different development engine nacelle identical to the one shown at the top of page 249.

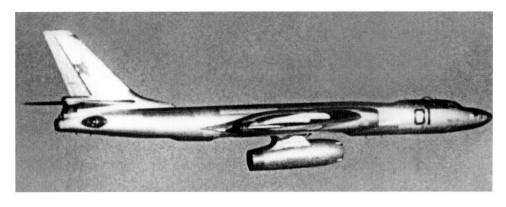

(c/n 6401410) and '01 Red' (c/n 6401501), Kazan'-built '05 Blue' (c/n 8204105) and 'Tu-16 No.117' (c/n 8204117) which could be coded '17', and Kuibyshev-built '10 Blue' (c/n 1881110). '01 Blue' was flown with at least two versions of the engine pod – a big cylindrical nacelle with four small scoops at the front or a 'reversed bottle' nacelle with test equipment heat exchangers in teardrop fairings on both sides. '01 Red' similarly carried two dif- ferent types of big cylindrical engine nacelle with lateral heat exchangers (one had a protective mesh on the inlet and a pitot head on the starboard side). '02 Blue' flew with a big cylindrical engine nacelle with lateral fairings, a smaller cylindrical nacelle (housing an afterburning turbojet) or a small 'reversed bottle' nacelle; '05 Blue' had a smaller engine in a cylindrical nacelle. '41 Blue' carried a big cylindrical nacelle with heat exchangers, then another

Left and below left: Tu-16LL '01 Blue' (c/n 6401401) makes a low pass during the Aviation Day flypast at Zhukovskiy on 16th August 1990. The unidentified development engine is in running position; the shape of its nozzle is noteworthy. LII's airfield was still off limits to the general public then, so the demo flights were staged over specially built public grandstands on the bank of the Moskva River.

Bottom left: The same aircraft comes in to land; the development engine is stowed and the intake shutter closed. Note how the 'ears' of the test equipment heat exchangers almost touch the aircraft's engine nacelles.

Above right: Tu-16LL '41 Blue' (c/n 6401410) sits on elevated concrete ramps for ground runs of the development engine. Note the open crew entry hatch.

Right: At one stage of its career '41 Blue' carried a Lotarev D-36 turbofan in a standard Yak-42 engine nacelle. The test equipment heat exchangers were mounted dorsally because it was impossible to mount them on the test engine nacelle. The picture was taken from the prototype of the Yak-40K convertible feederliner (CCCP-87490) used as a chase plane.

Below right: Another excellent air-to-air of Tu-16LL '41 Blue' with the D-36 engine running.

without heat exchangers; at LII this aircraft was known as the Tu-16LL-410 (after the last three digits of the c/n).

In the late 1950s and early 1960s two of the Tu-16LLs (Nos. 3 and 4), which were converted by the Kazan' plant in late 1956, served as testbeds for the massive Tumanskiy KR15-300 afterburning turbojet having a maximum afterburner rating of 15,000 kgp (33,070 lbst), a continuous afterburner rating of 10,000 kgp (22,045 lbst) and an engine life of 50 hours (hence the K for *korotkoresoorsnyy* – short-life). The engine was developed for the Tupolev '121' supersonic GLCM, which remained in prototype form, and its production reconnaissance drone derivatives –

the semi-expendable Tu-123, aka DBR-1 *Yastreb-1* (Hawk; DBR = *dahl'niy bespilotnyy razvedchik* – long-range reconnaissance UAV) and the fully recoverable Tu-139 (DBR-2 Yastreb-2). The engine later evolved into a long-life version – the R15-300 powering the MiG-25 interceptor and reconnaissance/strike aircraft, and the R15B-300 was also tested on the Tu-16LL.

Later one of these aircraft was used for testing the 18,500-kgp (40,790-lbst) Zoobets RD-16-17 afterburning turbojet. This engine intended for the Myasishchev M-50B *Bounder* supersonic strategic bomber was not yet fully developed when the M-50 programme was cancelled and Myasishchev's OKB-23 was dissolved.

In the 1970s and 1980s Tu-16LL '41 Blue' was used in the extensive trials of the Lotarev D-36 turbofan with a take-off rating of 6,500 kgp (14,330 lbst) and a cruise rating of 1,600 kgp (3,530 lbst) which was developed for the Yakovlev Yak-42 *Clobber* short-haul airliner. D-36 c/n 3612 was fitted to this aircraft; this time a standard Yak-42 engine nacelle was used, therefore the test equipment heat exchangers were mounted atop the centre fuselage.

At this time, too, the Tu-16LLs found use for testing full-size airframe assemblies together with their engines. Thus, '02 Blue' and '41 Blue' took turns carrying a complete fuselage of the Yak-36M *Forger* shipboard vertical/short take-off and landing (V/STOL) attack aircraft with a 6,900-kgp (15,210-lbst) Khachatoorov R27V-300 thrust-vectoring turbojet and two 2,350-kgp (5,180-lbst) Kolesov RD36-35V lift turbojets. A version of these lift-jets with a maximum continuous operation time extended to five minutes was tested on the Tu-16LL between 11th May, and 6th June 1972.

One Tu-16LL reportedly carried a complete fuselage of the Yak-141 *Freestyle* shipboard V/STOL supersonic fighter with the Khachatoorov R79V-300 thrust-vectoring afterburning turbofan rated at 10,500 kgp (23,150 lbst) dry and 15,500 kgp (34,170 lbst) reheat plus two 4,100-kgp (9,040-lbst) Kolesov RD-41 lift turbojets. '10 Blue' (called Tu-16LL-110 at LII) and '02 Blue' carried a complete fuselage of the Czech Aero L-39 Albatros advanced trainer with a 1,720-kgp (3,790-lbst) Ivchenko AI-25TL turbofan. These tests allowed the effect of the air intake design on the engine's operation to be studied and engine operation at various angles of attack to be verified. As in the case of the engines alone, the aircraft assemblies were housed in the former bomb bay and lowered clear before engine starting.

One Tu-16LL was used in 1976-78 to test the Izotov RD-33 afterburning turbofan developed for the

Above: This Tu-16LL coded '01 Blue' (c/n 6401401) was part of a static display staged at Zhukovskiy in May 1991 on the occasion of LII's 50th birthday. Note that the design of the nacelle's intake shutter varied on individual aircraft, depending on the type of engine fitted (or, to be precise, its intake diameter).

Left and below left: Close-up of the last engine tested on '01 Blue'.

Right: Another Tu-16LL, '10 Blue' (c/n 1881110), sits on a rain-soaked hardstand. With no development engine installed, the door-less bomb bay creating a concave lower fuselage contour is readily apparent.

Above: Three-quarters rear view of Tu-16LL '01 Blue', showing the fairing supplanting the DK-7 tail turret. It replicates the turret's shape and is different from that used on M-16 drones.

Right: Engines and other parts missing, time-expired Tu-16LL '05 Blue' (c/n 8204105) sits forlorn on a hardstand opposite LII's hangars in the 2000s. Note the development engine intake shutter dangling from the bomb bay.

Above and above right: The end of the road for Tu-16LL '41 Blue'. The retired aircraft sits on the grass next to Tu-154LL CCCP-85024 (one of the three used in the Buran space shuttle development programme), awaiting disposal.

Left: Another view of the retired Tu-16LL '05 Blue' after it had been towed from the hardstand to the grass area.

The bomb bay of Tu-16LL '41 Blue'; the development engine pylon is in the extended position and the retracted intake shutter is just visible.

Above: A fine view of Tu-16LL '01 Blue' parked at Zhukovskiy. Though seemingly intact, this aircraft is also out of service.

Right: The lowered development engine pylon of '01 Blue'.

Above: At one point Tu-16LL '41 Blue' carried a full-size fuselage of the Yak-36M V/STOL shipboard attack aircraft, being used for testing the *Forger's* R27V-300 lift/cruise engine and RD36-35V lift-jets. The short parabolic nose of the fuselage matches that originally envisaged for the Yak-36M (it was reshaped on the definitive Yak-38).

Left and above left: Tu-16LL '02 Blue' (c/n 4201002) also carried the Yak-36M fuselage for a while. The dark-coloured heat shield on the rear fuselage underside is clearly visible. Note that the RBP-4 radar was still in place at that stage.

MiG-29 *Fulcrum* tactical fighter, with a rating of 5,040 kgp (11,110 lbst) dry and 8,300 kgp (18,300 lbst) reheat. This particular testbed is sometimes referred to as LL-88, the number obviously denoting 'aircraft 88'.

Other engines tested on the Tu-16LL included the following:

• the RKBM (Dobrynin) VD-7M afterburning turbojet created for the Tu-22 rated at 10,580 kgp (23,325 lbst) dry and 15,690 kgp (34,590 lbst) reheat;

• the 13,000-kgp (28,660-lbst) RKBM (Dobrynin) VD-19 afterburning turbojet tested in 1963 as the intended powerplant of the Tu-138 heavy interceptor (a projected successor to the Tu-128);

• the 11,000-kgp (24,250-lbst) Zoobets M-16-15 turbojet powering the Tu-16B, Tu-16K and Tu-104E;

• the 16,000-kgp (35,270 lbst) RKBM (Kolesov) RD36-41 afterburning turbojet powering the Sukhoi T-4 ('aircraft 100') supersonic missile strike aircraft;

• the RKBM (Kolesov) RD36-51 turbojet powering the Myasishchev M-17 (see 17LL-1 below);

• the 10,500-kgp (23,150-lbst) Kuznetsov NK-8-2 and NK-8-4 turbofans powering the Tu-154 *sans suffixe*/Tu-154A/Tu-154B *Careless* medium-haul airliner and the Il-62 *sans suffixe* (*Classic*) long-haul airliner;

Right: At one time Tu-16LL '10 Blue' (c/n 1881110) was used for testing the Ivchenko AI-25TL turbofan optimised for the Aero L-39 trainer. In order to check the interaction between the engine and the lateral air intakes the engine was installed in a full-size L-39 fuselage. It is seen here in Czechoslovakia with the L-39 fuselage raised. Note that the engine covers are marked '110', hence this aircraft's designation Tu-16LL-110.

Below: The same aircraft taxies out for a test mission.

Bottom and bottom right: Tu-16LL '10 Blue' with the L-39 fuselage lowered clear of the bomb bay and the test engine running.

Above: The ER-8 two-stage research rocket suspended under the fuselage of Tu-16 '01 Blue' (c/n 6401401). Note the large diameter of the booster stage and the shape of its tail surfaces.
Above right: The ER-8 accelerates away after launch.

• the 5,400-kgp (11,900-lbst) Solov'yov D-20P commercial turbofan created for the Tu-124 *Cookpot* short-haul airliner;

• the 6,800-kgp (14,990-lbst) Solov'yov D-30 commercial turbofan created for the Tu-134 *Crusty* short-haul airliner;

• the 11,500-kgp (25,350-lbst) Solov'yov D-30K turbofan which, in its D-30KU version, powers the Il-62M and Tu-154M;

• the 12,000-kgp (26,455-lbst) D-30KP turbofan powering the Il-76 transport;

• the Solov'yov D-30F-6 afterburning turbofan created for the Mikoyan MiG-31 *Foxhound* heavy interceptor, rated at 9,140-9,270 kgp (20,400-20,690 lbst) dry and 14,965-15,510 kgp (33,400-34,620 lbst) reheat;

• the 5,750-kgp (12,680-lbst) Tumanskiy R11AF-300 afterburning turbojet fitted to early production Yak-28 *Brewer-As* and the 6,100-kgp (13,450-lbst) R11AF2-300 powering most of the *Brewer*'s versions, the Yak-28U *Maestro* trainer and Yak-28P *Firebar* interceptor;

• the Tumanskiy R13-300 afterburning turbojet powering the second-generation versions of the MiG-21 fighter and the Su-15T/Su-15TM/Su-15UM *Flagon-E/F/G*, rated at 4,100 kgp (9,040 lbst) dry and 6,600 kgp (14,550 lbst) reheat;

• the 10,200-kgp (22,490-lbst) Tumanskiy R27F2S-300 afterburning turbojet powering the MiG-23S;

• the Tumanskiy R29-300 afterburning turbojet rated at 4,200 kgp (9,260 lbst) dry and 11,500 kg reheat which powers the MiG-23M/MF/MS *Flogger-B/E* fighters, MiG-23UB *Flogger-C* trainer and MiG-23BN *Flogger-H*, MiG-27 *Flogger-D/J*, Su-20 *Fitter-C* and Su-22/22M *Fitter-E/F/J* fighter-bombers;

• the Lyul'ka AL-7F-2 and AL-7F-4 afterburning turbojets, the latter being rated at 11,200 kgp (24,690 lbst);

• the Lyul'ka AL-21F afterburning turbojet rated at 7,800 kgp (17,195 lbst) dry and 11,215 kgp (24,720 lbst) reheat powering the Sukhoi Su-17/Su-22 *Fitter-C/D/E/G/H/K* fighter-bomber family and the Su-24 *Fencer* tactical bomber;

• the Lyul'ka AL-31F afterburning turbofan rated at 7,850 kgp (17,305 lbst) dry and 12,500 kgp (27,560 lbst) reheat powering the Su-27/Su-30 *Flanker* fighter family and the Su-34 *Fullback* fighter-bomber;

• the Lyul'ka AL-41F afterburning turbofan which powered the Mikoyan '1.44' fifth-generation fighter demonstrator;

• the 4,100-kgp (9,040-lbst) Gavrilov R-95Sh turbojet powering the Sukhoi Su-25 *Frogfoot* attack aircraft;

• the Aerosila TA-12 APU fitted to the Tu-204 and Tu-214 medium-haul airliners and the Antonov An-124 Ruslan (*Condor*) heavy transport.

Unfortunately the tests did not always go well. One Tu-16LL was lost when the development engine caught fire (some sources say the test engineer mistook the glow of the setting sun on the development engine's nacelle for a fire!) and the entire crew captained by Sergey N. Anokhin ejected. Another example crashed on 1st February 1971, killing the crew of five captained by Sultan Amet-Khan (HSU); the cause was never established because the aircraft had hit the ground in a dive and was totally destroyed.

By the turn of the century the remaining Tu-16LLs had been retired as time-expired. '41 Blue' was the last of the kind, remaining operational as late as 2001.

17LL-1 engine testbed
In 1978 one of the Tu-16LLs listed above was supplied to the Myasishchev Experimental Machinery Factory (EMZ – *Eksperimentahl'nyy mashinostroitel'nyy zavod*, as the former OKB-23 was known after its resurgence) for testing the 7,000-kgp (15,430-lbst) Kolesov RD36-51V non-afterburning turbofan developed for the Myasishchev M-17 high-altitude aircraft. The aircraft stood out among the other Tu-16LLs in that, in keeping with Myasishchev OKB tradition, it had an additional designation – 17LL-1, which denoted the first testbed created under the M-17's development programme.

Tu-16 development aircraft with RD-3MR engines and 'hushkit'
In 1957-59 LII carried out ground and flight tests of a Kuibyshev-built Tu-16 ('08 Red', c/n 1882808) fitted with new RD-3MR engines featuring cascade-type thrust reversers (hence the R for *revers tyagi* – reverse thrust). The reversers had a rather unusual design. As a rule, cascade-type thrust reversers have a fixed jet-pipe with outlet grilles closed by two internal blocker doors, the latter rotating aft on axles close to the engine axis to obstruct the nozzle and open the grilles at the same time – or, on modern tur-

bofans, a sliding cowl which moves aft, exposing the grilles inside while the multiple blocker petals close the bypass duct. Instead, the RD-3MR had a telescopic jetpipe, its aft-sliding outer section incorporating the grilles which were obstructed by the inner section in forward thrust mode. Two movable airfoil-section vanes were mounted close together in a 'biplane' arrangement inside the jetpipe. When the outer section moved aft hydraulically, opening the grilles, the vanes rotated through 40° toward each other in a V arrangement to direct part of the exhaust flow up and down through the grilles, which directed it forward. This necessitated modifications to the rear ends of the engine nacelles. The reverser added 310 kg (683 lb) to the engine's weight – the RD-3MR weighed 3,410 kg (7,517 lb); the engine's length increased from 5.38 m (17 ft 7¹³⁄₁₆ in) to 5.884 m (19 ft 3²¹⁄₃₂ in) in forward thrust mode and 6.484 m (≈ 21 ft 3⁹⁄₆₄ in) with the reverser deployed.

The reversers reduced the landing run by some 30-35% – from 1,500 to 950 m (from 4,920 to 3,120 ft). On the down side, when the reversers were in operation, the engines were prone to exhaust

gas ingestion and surging when the aircraft slowed down to a certain speed. Moreover, the take-off run was much longer than the landing run anyway; all this eventually led OKB-300 and LII to abandon these tests. A lighter version of the thrust reversers was developed for the Tu-104 airliner in 1959 but not introduced on the production model.

In 1961 the same Tu-16 was used to test noise-suppression engine nozzles (or, to use a commercial aviation term, a 'hushkit'). Two models were tested – a multi-lobe air-exhaust mixer (similar to that fitted to the Rolls-Royce Spey turbofans of 'hushkitted' BAC 111 airliners) and an annular noise attenuator. Again, the 'hushkits' were tested on the Tu-104B in 1961-62. The new nozzles were not adopted for production and service on either type because they led to an increase in fuel consumption.

Tu-16LL research rocket launch platform

In addition to testing engines, Tu-16LL '01 Blue' (c/n 6401401, or 'Tu-16LL No.401') was used at one point in time for launching an

Below: For a while Tu-16 '10 Blue' (c/n 1881110) was an avionics testbed used by LII. Note the long pitot installed on the fin.

Bottom and bottom right: Special antennas were installed in lieu of the ventral barbette and below the rudder on '10 Blue'.

Top: Tu-16 '57 Red' (c/n 1880101) was a testbed for a missile's radar seeker head. Note the retaining braces and the cine camera 'egg' aft of the flight deck.

Left: The same testbed at a later date, recoded '24 Red'.

Above and above left: The braced test article mount on the nose of Tu-16 '24 Red'; the test articles are different and the braces' layout has been changed over time.

unmanned aerial vehicle called ER-8 (*eksperimentahl'naya raketa* – experimental rocket). The two-stage rocket had a slim main stage with cruciform wings and a fat booster with wings in a squashed-X arrangement connected by vertical endplates. The thing was carried under the centre fuselage on a set of struts, the aperture of the bomb bay being faired over.

Tu-16 avionics and equipment testbeds

• Among other things, the fifth production machine serialled '1 Black' (c/n 3200105) was used by LII to test long-range radio communications system for ECM resistance.

• In 1955 Tu-16 c/n 1880202 served as a testbed for unspecified SIGINT equipment.

Above: A view of Tu-16A '30 Blue' (c/n 7203630), a testbed of unknown purpose, in one of LII's hangars. A fairing with experimental equipment replaces the DT-7V dorsal barbette.

Right: A different angle on the same aircraft, showing the experimental installation and the tandem loop aerials on the centreline associated with data link.

Below right: Close-up of the experimental installation. It appears to have an optical seeker with a strongly convex lens.

• In the late 1950s and early 1960s OKB-156 modified a Tu-16 as a testbed for the data link system of the Tu-123 (DBR-1 Yastreb) reconnaissance drone.

• Tu-16 c/n 1880202 became a testbed for the RBP-6 Lyustra radar and later the SRS-3 Romb-1 ELINT system, both of which were used on the Tu-16R.

• Before being further modified as an engine testbed, Tu-16LL '10 Blue' (c/n 1881110) served with LII as an avionics testbed of unknown purpose. It had an oblong magnetoelectric antenna on the starboard side of the tail (at the base of the rudder) and a flush circular antenna supplanting the DT-N7S ventral barbette. A long pitot was mounted on the fin leading edge at the top. All armament was removed.

• Tu-16 c/n 7203513 served as a testbed for new ECM equipment.

• The Flight Research Institute also converted the first Kuibyshev-built production Tu-16 (originally coded '24 Red', later recoded '57 Red', c/n 1880101) for testing missile guidance systems for ECM resistance. A missile seeker head in a conical metal fairing tipped by a dielectric radome was installed at the extremity of the nose (on the navigator's station glazing); to prevent the heavy assembly from breaking loose it was firmly secured to the forward fuselage structure by four pairs of sloping bracing struts and a horizontal beam ahead of the flight deck windscreen. A cine camera in an egg-shaped fairing was fitted aft of the flight deck when the aircraft was coded '57 Red'.

• Kazan'-built Tu-16KS '30 Red' or '30 Blue' (c/n 7203630) was modified for exploring the heat signature of various targets. It was outfitted with optical sensors on the DT-7V dorsal turret and L-shaped loop aerials for data link mounted in pairs above and below the centre fuselage. All cannons were removed.

Tu-16 control system testbeds

In 1954-55 an unidentified Tu-16 served for verifying certain features of the control system developed for the aforementioned Boorya intercontinental GLCM developed by the Lavochkin OKB.

Another Tu-16 served as an altogether different control system testbed for verifying an automatic take-off system developed for the Tu-16M (M-16) target drone.

Tu-16 landing gear testbed

In the late 1950s the Myasishchev OKB (OKB-23) adapted a late-production Kazan'-built Tu-16 coded '56 Red' (c/n 7203724) on loan from the Air Force for verifying the ingenious nose gear bogie mechanism devised for its M-50 supersonic heavy bomber. The latter had a bicycle landing gear, and because the normal ground angle was insufficient for 'automatic' take-off (as in the case of the M-4/3M *Bison* bombers, which 'took off by themselves') a special actuator tilted the four-wheel nose gear bogie on achieving rotation speed to provide the required angle of attack on take-off.

A telescopic twin-wheel 'jump strut' with the same size of wheels was mounted immediately aft of the Tu-16's standard nose gear unit, emulating the M-50's four-wheel nose gear bogie. A pair of small wheels was mounted on the tail bumper to prevent a tail-strike. The experimental landing gear was non-retractable. Later the aircraft was reconverted to standard configuration and returned to the Air Force, gaining the new code '07 Red'.

Left and below left: Tu-16 '56 Red' (c/n 7203724) was converted by the Myasishchev OKB into a testbed for the nose bogie tilting mechanism of the M-50 bomber. The nose gear unit was fitted experimentally with a telescopic second strut emulating the tilting mechanism. Here it is seen in the tilted position (at the M-50's envisaged rotation angle), the 'jump strut' lifting the Tu-16's normal nosewheels off the ground.

Above right: The tail bumper of '56 Red' had a pair of wheels from a Tu-95's tail bumper added as an extra protection in the event of over-rotation. The strake is a fairing enclosing the rear aerials of the SRZO-2 IFF transponder.

Right and far right: Close-ups of the non-retractable modified nose gear unit, showing the plethora of braces and the twin actuation rams of the 'jump strut', which had no shock absorber or torque link. It appears that the 'jump strut' could be remote-controlled via a cable from the ground when the aircraft was motionless.

Above: Tu-16 '56 Red' taxies with both pairs of nosewheels resting on the ground.

Right: Here the 'jump strut' comes into play, initiating rotation, and the normal nosewheels come off the ground.

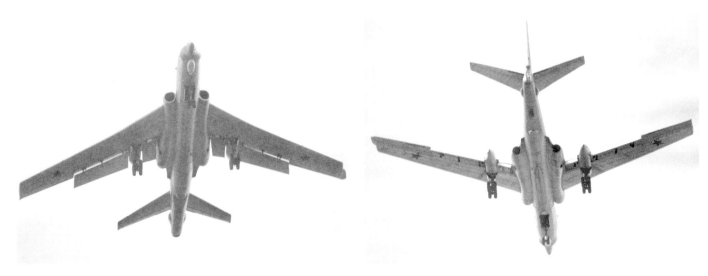

Above and above right: The 17LL-2 avionics/weapons testbed, a much-modified Tu-16K ('57 Red'), on short finals to Zhukovskiy.

Above and above right: The 'Saigak', as the 17LL-2 testbed was dubbed, sits on the Myasishchev apron at Zhukovskiy following retirement. Note the fairing supplanting the lower radome of the YeN radar and the ILS aerial above the now-empty sensor window.

Another view of the 17LL-2 targeting system testbed for the M-17 parked in the Myasishchev compound at Zhukovskiy.

Tu-16 weapons testbeds

• In April-May 1957, Tu-16 c/n 1881304 was for manufacturer's flight tests of new bomb fuses with an electropyrotechnical arming system. Actually two systems were tested on this aircraft – the PU-16S electropyrotechnical arming system and the PU-16PM electropyrotechnical/mechanical arming system; both were developed by Ivan I. Toropov's OKB-134. The need for such systems was caused by the fact that the conventional mechanical arming system then in use was not safe enough – in certain conditions the bomb fuses could get armed before release, creating the danger of an explosion inside the aircraft.

After the shortcomings noted by the military had been rectified, the PU-16S system was fitted to another Kuibyshev-built Tu-16 (c/n 1882102), which was submitted to GK NII VVS for state acceptance trials in July 1957. The tests were carried out with various types of bombs – SAB-250-150MF and SAB-100-90 flare bombs, SMAB-100-90P and SMAB-100-70P marker flare bombs, FAB-1500-2600TS HE bombs (*tolstostennaya* – thick-walled version with a reinforced body for greater penetrating power), KhAB-1500-900SM-46 chemical warfare bombs (*khimicheskaya aviabomba*), FZAB-500 HE/incendiary bombs (*foogahsno-zazhigahtel'naya aviabomba*) and IAB-3000 practice bombs (*imitatsionnaya aviabomba* – 'simulation bomb') emulating the flash and the mushroom cloud of a nuclear explosion.

• A single Tu-16 was converted into a weapons testbed as part of the Tu-22's development programme, having the standard DK-7 twin-cannon tail turret replaced with a DK-20 (*izdeliye* 9-A-243) single-cannon tail turret developed for the *Blinder*. The remote-controlled turret was electrohydraulically powered, mounting a 23-mm Rikhter R-23 cannon.

17LL-2 avionics/weapons testbed

Best known as a peaceful ozone layer research aircraft, the Myasishchev M-17 had in fact been conceived as a specialised high-altitude interceptor for use against drifting reconnaissance balloons which were launched *en masse* from the West. These were a real menace right up to the end of the 1970s – a type of target that existing Soviet interceptors were finding it hard to cope with. Hence a special search and targeting system (STS) and gun turret developed for the M-17, and a Tu-16K-10 (ZA) transferred to the Myasishchev EMZ from the Soviet Navy was converted for testing them. At the Myasishchev EMZ the aircraft was known as the 17LL-2 (the second testbed under the M-17 programme).

Coded '57 Red' (c/n 4652042, f/n 6504), the aircraft had the twin radomes of the YeN radar and the supporting structure cut away and replaced by the M-17's extreme nose incorporating sighting window; the standard DT-7V turret was likewise replaced by the one developed for the high-flyer. The distinctive nose profile made the 17LL-2 look uncannily like a saiga antelope, and that was exactly the nickname bestowed upon it – *Saigak*.

The aircraft was based at the Myasishchev flight test facility on the south side of the LII airfield. Live weapons trials were carried out on this aircraft, using real balloons as targets. In the 1990s the 17LL-2 could still be seen (minus cannons) at Zhukovskiy, sitting under a shed protecting it from the lenses of US surveillance satellites.

Tu-16 aerodynamics testbeds (laminar flow research aircraft)

• A Tu-16 *sans suffixe* coded '44 Red' (c/n 4200404) was used in several test and research programmes by LII. In particular, in 1963-70 it served for laminar flow tests at subsonic speeds with airfoil-section test articles mounted vertically above the centre fuselage. Several versions were tested, including an unswept airfoil section with an endplate and with pressure sensors on an inverted-U shaped frame behind it; this test article manufactured in 1957 was called UPS-1 (*oopravleniye pogranichnym sloyem* – boundary layer control). It had a TsAGI SR-5S-12 airfoil and a chord of 1.5 m (4 ft 11³⁄₆₄ in). The UPS-1 was tested in 1963-65 at speeds of Mach 0.5-0.85 and altitudes of 4,000-12,000 m (13,120-39,370 ft). An open-ended tubular thingamajig was installed on a short pylon over the centre fuselage to starboard of this test article.

Later, '44 Red' was fitted with a test article called LK-2 (*laminarnoye krylo* – laminar-flow wing) which replicated the outer wing portion of the Tu-134 *Crusty* short-haul airliner. The LK-2 was swept back 35° at quarter-chord, having a length of 2.3 m (7 ft 6³⁵⁄₆₄ in), a root chord of 1.4 m (4 ft 7⁷⁄₆₄ in), a tip chord of 0.7 m (2 ft 9³⁄₆₄ in), an area of 2.42 m² (26.05 sq ft) and a TsAGI P35-12M airfoil. It featured a boundary layer suction system with 103 slits 0.1 mm wide. This time a braced vertical rack with pressure sensors was installed over the centre fuselage to starboard of the test article. This configuration was tested in late 1966 (stage 1) and early 1967 (stage 2), flights being made at Mach 0.4-0.75 and 5,000-10,000 m (16,400-32,810 ft). With boundary layer suction the drag on the tip portion of the test article was reduced by 55-62%; however, attempts to obtain a laminar flow over the root portion in the same manner failed – the flow remained turbulent over more than one-third of the area. During stage 2 the LK-2 test article was installed at 3° to the aircraft's centreline to emulate the wing incidence in cruise flight which had a considerable effect on the airflow parameters. The results were used in refining the Tu-134, which had first flown in 1963.

• Another Tu-16 operated by LII ('09 Blue', c/n 6401309) was used in 1959 for testing the ASKR-1 automatic critical flight mode warning device (*avtomaticheskiy signalizahtor kriticheskikh rezhimov*) and the ASUA automatic angle of attack warning device (*avtomaticheskiy signalizahtor ooglov ataki*). It was fitted with a stick-shaker, critical AOA warning lights, three air data booms with DUAS-15 pitch/yaw sensor vanes (*dahtchik oogla ataki i skol'zheniya*) on the starboard side of the nose (replacing the nose cannon) and on the starboard wing leading edge, plus an extra pitch sensor vane to starboard aft of the flight deck serving the ASUA. Vasiliy A. Komarov was the project test pilot, with I. L. Strizhevskiy as engineer in charge.

The aircraft made ten flights under this programme with an all-up weight of 50,000-70,000 kg (110,230-154,320 lb), the critical modes being initiated at speeds of Mach 0.45-0.9 and altitudes of 10,000-11,000 m (32,810-36,090 ft) to make sure there was ample room for spin recovery. A special button was fitted to the captain's control wheel which the pilot could push to indicate the onset of vibration or instability on the test equipment recording. Upon completion of the test programme Tu-16 c/n 6401309 was reconverted to standard configuration and returned to the Air Force.

Top: Tu-16 '44 Red' (c/n 4200404) was an aerodynamics testbed used by LII for researching laminar airfoils.
Above: Close-up of the UPS-1 test article on '44 Red' with a pressure probe array aft of it; the role of the tubular object is unknown.
Above right: Tu-16 '44 Red' in a test flight with the UPS-1 test article.

Tu-16 ejection seat testbed

The fifth production Kazan'-built Tu-16 *sans suffixe* ('1 Black', c/n 3200105) was used for testing the *Badger*'s crew escape system with its purpose-built ejection seats, so it may be regarded as an ejection seat testbed. The seats had passed preliminary tests on a Tu-2 piston-engined tactical bomber converted into the Tu-2K testbed by LII, but now was the time to check their operation on the real thing – all the more so because only ground tests of the ejection system were performed on the prototypes.

The aircraft sported photo calibration markings used when it was filmed from a chase plane – vertical black stripes on the nose and rear fuselage plus L-shaped markings on the tail. Inward-looking cine cameras were installed under the wingtips to capture the ejection sequence.

Manufacturer's tests of the crew escape system began in accordance with to MAP order No.738 dated 15th December 1954; the engineers in charge at this stage were G. Sh. Meyerovich (representing LII) and Capt. A. K. Pavlenko (representing GK NII VVS). The state acceptance trials came next. The flights were performed by LII test pilot Stepan F. Mashkovskiy on 2nd July – 10th September 1955; the engineers in charge were V. I. Khlimanov (LII), I. N. Bazlov (GK NII VVS) and G. I. Skryl'nikov (Tupolev OKB). The aircraft made a total of 32 flights, including 17 in which dummies and LII test parachutists V. S. Kochetkov, V. I. Golovin and N. S. Alekseyev were ejected. Five more flights were made to test the escape hatch jettison system and a further two to assess the time needed by the crewmembers to prepare for ejection. The remaining eight flights were made to explore the Tu-16's flyability with the escape hatch covers gone, when the turbulent slipstream entered the flight deck. The tests were successful, albeit there were a few minor defects to be rectified.

Upon completion of the tests Tu-16 c/n 3200105 was returned to normal configuration and delivered to one of the first Air Force units to operate the type – the 402nd TBAP (see Chapter 7).

Tu-16 parachute testbeds

• A Voronezh-built Tu-16 coded '04' (most probably '04 Blue', c/n 6401404) was fitted experimentally with a spin recovery para-

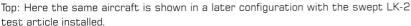

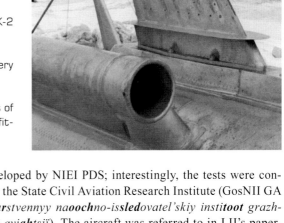

Top: Here the same aircraft is shown in a later configuration with the swept LK-2 test article installed.

Right: Close-up of the LK-2, showing the boundary layer suction holes and the very different pressure probe array aft of it.

Above: Tu-16 '09 Blue' (c/n 6401309) was used by LII for verifying new positions of the pitot heads and air data system vanes. An experimental air data boom was fitted instead of the nose cannon for these tests.

chute instead of the tail turret. The parachute canister was closed by a jettisonable hemispherical cover, in similar manner to such aircraft as the first prototype Ilyushin Il-86 *Camber* wide-body medium-haul airliner, the first prototype Tu-204 medium-haul airliner or the Il-76K and Il-76MDK zero-G trainers used in the Soviet/Russian space programme. The port wing's upper surface was covered with wool tufts to visualise the airflow at high angles of attack; a cine camera 'egg' was mounted on a lattice-like structure above the fuselage to record this, and a pitot was installed on the fin leading edge near the top.

• A different *Badger-A* – the abovementioned '08 Red' (c/n 1882808) – was used in 1972 for testing multi-canopy brake parachute systems (MKS – *mnogokoopol'naya sistema*), appar-

ently developed by NIEI PDS; interestingly, the tests were conducted by the State Civil Aviation Research Institute (GosNII GA – *Gosudarstvennyy naoochno-issledovatel'skiy institoot grazhdahnskoy aviahtsiï*). The aircraft was referred to in LII's paperwork as 'Tu-16 No.808'.

The parachutes were stowed in a bay on the rear fuselage underside. In the first version of the system each cruciform parachute canopy had an area of 13 m² (139.9 sq ft). The following versions were tested, all with a small drogue chute:
  • three-canopy system on an 8 m (26 ft 3 in) long line;
  • four-canopy system on a 12 m (39 ft 4⁷⁄₁₆ in) long line;
  • five-canopy system on an 8 m long line;
  • six-canopy system on an 8 m long line.

Above: Tu-16 '04 Red' (c/n 6401404) was modified for exploring the airflow patterns at high angles of attack; the wings were covered with wool tufts and a pod with cine cameras was installed above the fuselage to record the airflow patterns. Note the extra pitot mounted on the fin.

Left, centre left and far left: The tail turret of Tu-16 '04 Red' was replaced by a spin recovery parachute container. These photos show the empty container, the packed parachute attached to the low-mounted lock, and the jettisonable hemispherical cover installed.

Tu-16 '04 Red' in flight with the spin recovery parachute deployed.

The second version with one to four 25-m² (269.1 sq ft) cruciform parachutes was also tested. In some versions the parachute line was 4 m (13 ft 1³¹⁄₆₄ in) long.

The reason for this programme was that at the time the Soviet aircraft industry was producing a huge nomenclature of ribbon-type and cruciform brake parachutes for various types of aircraft, which was costly and difficult. It was deemed expedient to develop a standardised model of brake parachute and obtain the braking power appropriate for a specific aircraft by using the proper number of canopies.

Tu-16 as a 'mother ship'

Well, actually this 'mother ship' was a fake, but nevertheless it deserves to be mentioned here because the aircraft was certainly modified. During 1960 or 1961 a Kuibyshev-built Tu-16 coded '46 Red' (c/n 1881907) was used for filming certain ground scenes of the Soviet science fiction film *Bar'yer neizvesnosti* (The Barrier of Uncertainty) directed by Nikita F. Kurikhin and released by Lenfilm Studios, Leningrad, in 1961. The *Badger* posed as a 'mother ship' for an experimental rocket-powered hypersonic aircraft designated Ts-1 and called *Tsiklon* (Cyclone). A wooden mock-up of the Ts-1 was suspended on airfoil-shaped struts under the Tu-16's belly, which obviously required the bomber to be modified. The aircraft taxied and made high-speed runs with the mock-up in place but did not become airborne because the mock-up was not strong enough to withstand the dynamic pressure; in-flight scenes were filmed using scale models.

Right: Tu-16 '08 Red' (c/n 1882808) was used by LII for testing multi-canopy brake parachute systems composed of cruciform canopies with an area of 13 m² each connected by lines 8 m long. The parachutes were housed in the regular brake parachute container. In this case the system has three canopies.

Below right: A test of the four-canopy version.

Above: Here we have the five-canopy version. Note the twin drogue parachutes extracting the main canopies.

Right: The biggest version tested with the small canopies was this six-canopy version.

A different multi-canopy brake parachute system tested on the same Tu-16 had 25-m² cruciform canopies attached by 12-m lines. The three-canopy version is shown here.

A version with four 25-m² cruciform canopies was also tested.

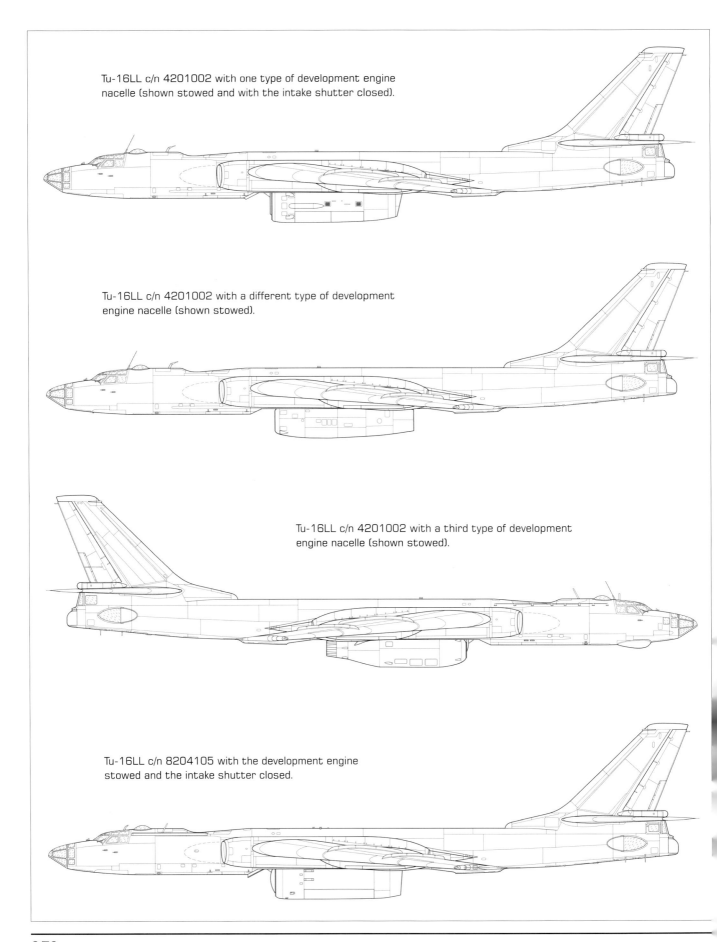

Tu-16LL c/n 4201002 with one type of development engine
nacelle (shown stowed and with the intake shutter closed).

Tu-16LL c/n 4201002 with a different type of development
engine nacelle (shown stowed).

Tu-16LL c/n 4201002 with a third type of development
engine nacelle (shown stowed).

Tu-16LL c/n 8204105 with the development engine
stowed and the intake shutter closed.

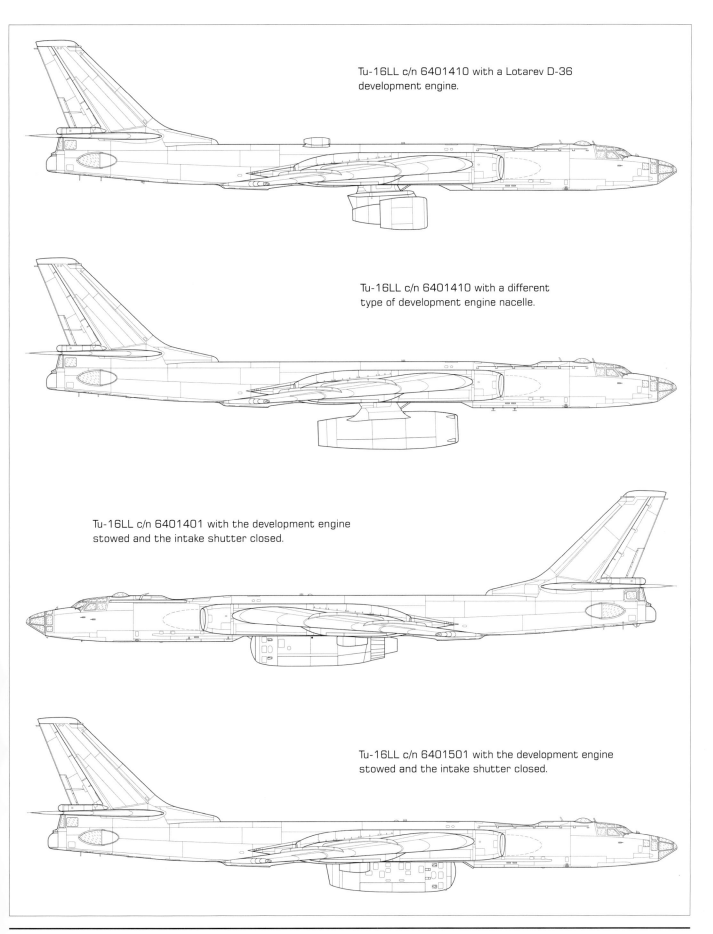

Tu-16LL c/n 6401410 with a Lotarev D-36 development engine.

Tu-16LL c/n 6401410 with a different type of development engine nacelle.

Tu-16LL c/n 6401401 with the development engine stowed and the intake shutter closed.

Tu-16LL c/n 6401501 with the development engine stowed and the intake shutter closed.

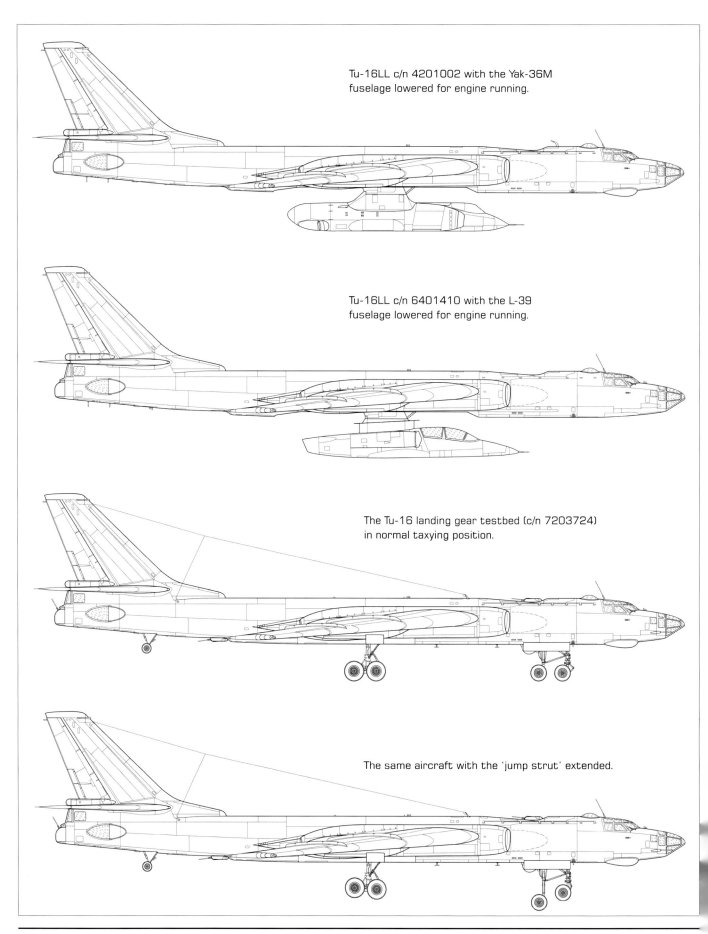

Tu-16LL c/n 4201002 with the Yak-36M
fuselage lowered for engine running.

Tu-16LL c/n 6401410 with the L-39
fuselage lowered for engine running.

The Tu-16 landing gear testbed (c/n 7203724)
in normal taxying position.

The same aircraft with the 'jump strut' extended.

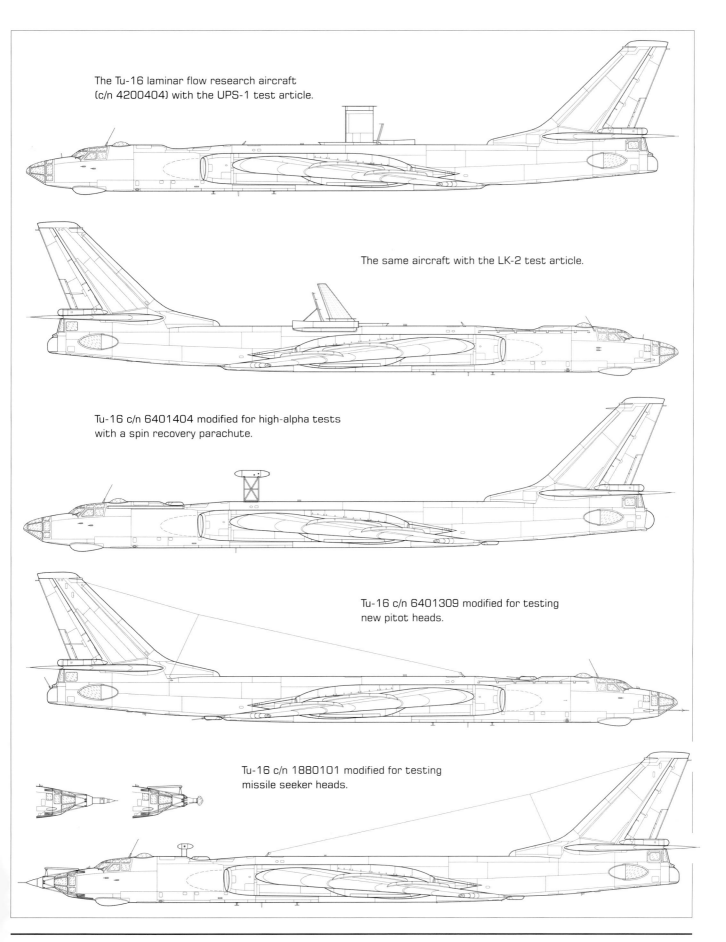

The Tu-16 laminar flow research aircraft
(c/n 4200404) with the UPS-1 test article.

The same aircraft with the LK-2 test article.

Tu-16 c/n 6401404 modified for high-alpha tests
with a spin recovery parachute.

Tu-16 c/n 6401309 modified for testing
new pitot heads.

Tu-16 c/n 1880101 modified for testing
missile seeker heads.

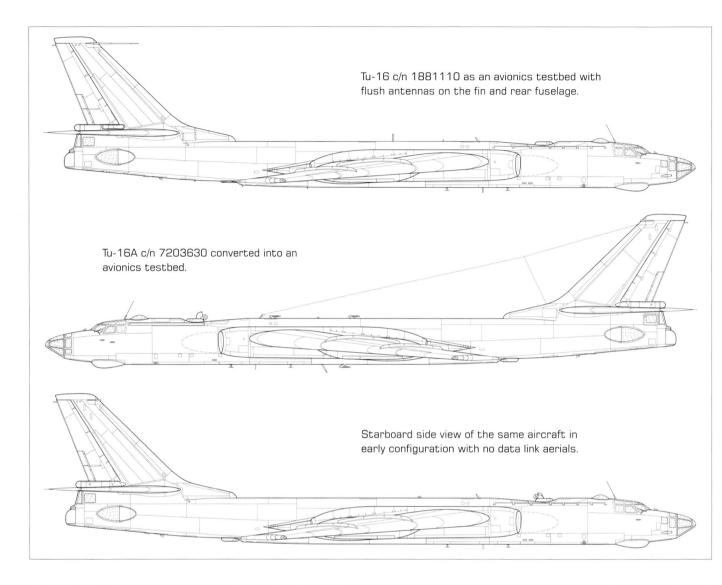

Tu-16 c/n 1881110 as an avionics testbed with flush antennas on the fin and rear fuselage.

Tu-16A c/n 7203630 converted into an avionics testbed.

Starboard side view of the same aircraft in early configuration with no data link aerials.

Tu-16 Tsiklon-N weather research aircraft ('order 386')

Speaking of cyclones, in the early 1970s several Soviet aircraft, including Tu-104A CCCP-42454, Il-18D CCCP-75442, two An-12BPs (CCCP-11530 and CCCP-11531) and An-26B *Curl* CCCP-26209, were modified for use in the Tsiklon programme for atmospheric research under the auspices of the Central Aerological Observatory (TsAO – *Tsentrahl'naya aerologicheskaya observatoriya*), a division of the Soviet Union's State Committee for Hydrometeorology and Environmental Control (*Goskomghidromet*). On 4th April 1976, MAP issued instruction No.810, which was followed on 25th April by order No.176 envisaging the conversion of several Tu-16s into Tu-16 Tsiklon-N weather research aircraft and specifying the performance targets and the conversion method. The N was a reference to the basic aircraft's product code (*izdeliye* N). The Tupolev OKB was to prepare the manufacturing drawings and send them to the Soviet Navy's ARZ No.20 at Pushkin, Leningrad Region, in the fourth quarter of 1976. By the end of the third quarter of 1977 both aircraft were to be ready for delivery.

The Tupolev OKB approached the Naval Aviation, which transferred two Tu-16K-26 (or Tu-16KSR-2-5) missile carriers

built in Kazan' in 1956 – c/ns 6203203 (coded '19') and 6203208 (tactical code unknown). The two aircraft were converted for the weather research role at ARZ No.20 in 1977 as planned and delivered to the Soviet Air Force.

The Tu-16 Tsiklon-N was intended for studying the principal thermodynamic and electric parameters of the atmosphere and cloud formations, as well as for cloud-seeding in order to make rain (for instance, when it was necessary to prevent an impending hailstorm which could destroy crops, or to prevent a downpour on a public holiday). Accordingly all armament and military equipment (except for the missile pylons) was removed and replaced by R-802V and R-802GM radios, a Rubin-1M wide-scan weather radar (which was housed in a teardrop radome amidships), a time synchronisation system, an RV-18Zh radio altimeter, an AKS-2 cine camera, K-10-51 and K-20-22 oscillographs and other special equipment.

The weapons bay initially housed special 'weather bombs' filled with rainmaking chemicals (such as silver iodide), which were eventually rejected; instead, KDS-150 dispensers firing PV-50 flares filled with rainmaking chemicals (silver iodide) were used. The wing hardpoints were used for carrying special K-76(L)

A scene from the feature film *Bar'yer neizvesnosti* (The Barrier of Uncertainty) showing a mock-up of the Ts-1 Tsiklon aerospaceplane under a Tu-16 'mother ship'.

A GAZ-69A jeep with a 1950s military number plate (V4-46-45) tows a dolly with the Ts-1 mock-up prior to attaching the latter to the Tu-16.

Tu-16 '46 Red' (c/n 1881907) with the mock-up in place taxies out for a high-speed run. The struts attaching the Ts-1 to the bomber are visible.

The actual high-speed run. The tail of the Ts-1 had to be made exceedingly short to fit under the bomber without requiring a cut-out in the belly; still, rotation would be difficult!

One of the few known photos of Tu-16 Tsiklon-N CCCP-42484. Note the attached KMGU-1 dispensers filled with rainmaking chemicals.

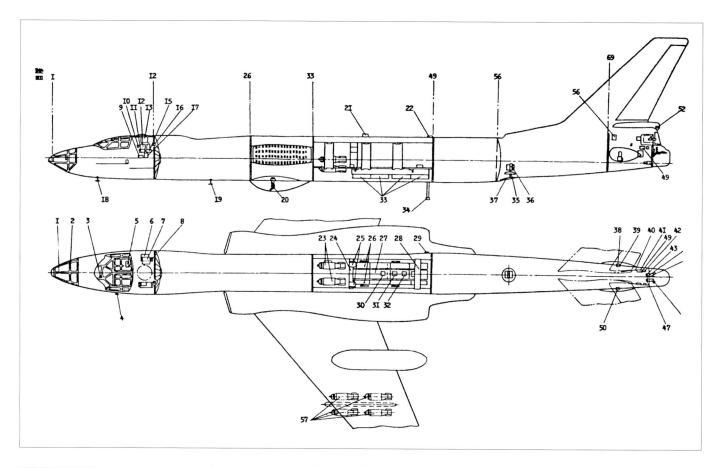

Above: A drawing showing the location of the mission equipment on the Tu-16 Tsiklon-N weather research aircraft.

Left: A rare photo of Tu-16 Tsiklon-N CCCP-42484 in flight. The 'smoke trail' is the powdered rainmaking chemicals being dumped from the KMGU-1 dispensers.

Below left: The other Tu-16 Tsiklon-N, CCCP-42355, at Pushkin airfield. The photo was taken from a hot-air balloon during an air rally!

Below: The nose of CCCP-42355 with the Tsiklon logo.

Tu-16 Tsiklon-N CCCP-42484.

Tu-16 Tsiklon-NM CCCP-42355.

Above: The Tu-16 Tsiklon-NM sits on the grass at Chkalovskaya AB in the late 1990s after being withdrawn from use.
Below: CCCP-42355 at the same base at an earlier date when it was still parked on the flight line. The dorsal sensors are clearly visible.

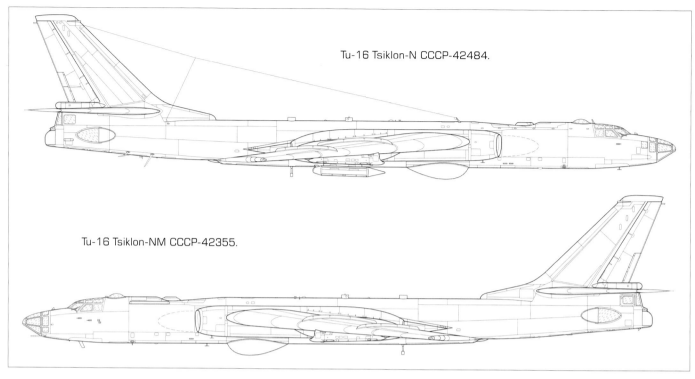

Tu-16 Tsiklon-N CCCP-42484.

Tu-16 Tsiklon-NM CCCP-42355.

For a while the Soviet Air Force considered equipping its IL-28 tactical bombers with a probe-and-drogue IFR system. This still from a cine film shows IL-28 '211 Blue' flying in formation with a Tu-16 posing as a tanker in early 1954. The purpose of the flights was to establish how close the IL-28 could get to the tanker without being affected by its wake turbulence.

Another view of IL-28 '211 Blue' formating with the Tu-16. The flight level is the same and the horizontal separation is 8.5 m. The IL-28 appears to have forward-swept wings but it is merely an optical illusion created by the shadow cast by the bomber's wing!

Right: When no engines were due for testing, the Tu-16LLs (minus development engine pod) were sometimes used by LII pilots for proficiency training on heavy aircraft. Here, '01 Blue' streams its brake parachutes on landing at Zhukovskiy.

pods or stock KMGU-1 submunitions dispensers (*konteyner dlya malogabaritnykh groozov ooniversahl'nyy* – versatile small items container) loaded with cement powder or chemicals for causing precipitation. The crew included two meteorologists occupying the workstations of the Nav/Op and the tail gunner.

The acceptance procedures at GK NII VVS and TsAO lasted from November 1977, to April 1978, being hampered by the lack of the mission equipment. Trials began next, continuing from August 1978 to April 1980, whereupon both aircraft were placed on the Soviet civil register as CCCP-42355 (the first aircraft thus registered, c/n 6203203) and CCCP-42484 (c/n 6203208). In spite of this, they were still operated by the military – specifically, GNIKI VVS, being home-based at Chkalovskaya AB east of Moscow where the institute's branch tasked with testing transport aircraft was located.

As an aside, under the Soviet civil aircraft registration system introduced in 1958 (which is still in use today) the first two digits of the five-digit registration are a sort of code which is usually allocated to a specific type. This was done to promote flight safety, so that air traffic controllers can instantly identify the aircraft type on hearing the registration (which was used in air-to-ground radio communication in lieu of flight numbers in the USSR) and thus do not pose unreasonable demands which the pilots cannot comply with because of the aircraft's performance limits. The 42xxx registration block was initially reserved for the Tu-104, and it was rather appropriate that the 'civil' Tu-16s should be registered in this block because the *Badger* was the Tu-104's direct ancestor! The odd bit is that, while Soviet civil registrations were often allocated in large batches in the aircraft's production order, CCCP-42355 had somehow dropped out of the sequence for Tu-104As built by the Omsk aircraft factory No.166 back in 1958 (c/n 86600801 was CCCP-42354 while c/n 86600802 was CCCP-42356). Similarly, according to the registration sequence CCCP-42484 should have been allocated to a Kazan'-built Tu-104B manufactured in 1960 (c/n 021502) – which instead received the totally out-of-sequence registration CCCP-06195 in a 'mixed bag' block allocated to MAP!

In keeping with their new mission and quasi-civil status the 'Cyclones' gained the 1973-standard blue/white Aeroflot livery – save that the type was marked on the nose simply as 'Tu'. Like the other research aircraft in the Tsiklon series, the Tu-16s sported the eye-catching Tsiklon emblem to clarify their 'storm chaser' role.

The aircraft's performance was similar to that of missile-carrying versions. The Tu-16 Tsiklon-N had an empty weight of 41,763 kg (92,071 lb), a maximum take-off weight ranging from 76,631 to 79,000 kg (168,942-174,165 lb) and a fuel load of 33,160 kg (73,105 lb).

The two Tu-16 Tsiklon-Ns served for more than ten years in a variety of scenarios over central Russia and the Ukraine, including 'sky cleaning' missions during the XXII Summer Olympics in Moscow in 1980 and monitoring radiation levels in the area of the Chernobyl' Nuclear Power Station in the wake of the Chernobyl' nuclear disaster on 26th April 1986. CCCP-42484 was used for the latter mission, operating from Belaya Tserkov' ('White Church') AB south of Kiev in the Ukraine.

Tu-16 Tsiklon-NM weather research aircraft

On 19th November 1986, the Council of Ministers ordered that both Tu-16 Tsiklon-N aircraft should be re-equipped to enable them to participate in international weather research programmes. This included installation of an A-723 LORAN system, a Koors-MP-70 (Heading) compass system replacing the SP-50 ILS, a new ARK-15 ADF replacing the ARK-5, a new DISS-013 Doppler radar replacing the DISS-1, new A-063 (high-range) and RV-5M (low-range) radio altimeters replacing the RV-17 and RV-UM respectively, an SO-72M ATC transponder, a *Mikron-3A* (Micron) radio replacing the 1RSB-70 and R-862 and so on. Furthermore, new oxygen equipment was fitted and a single-point pressure refuelling connector was installed.

Actually only CCCP-42355 was upgraded, becoming the Tu-16 Tsiklon-NM (*modernizeerovannyy* – updated) in so doing. The reason was that unfortunately CCCP-42484 had accumulated such a dose of radiation during the Chernobyl' damage control opera-

tion that it defied decontamination. After two weeks of scouring and scrubbing at Belaya Tserkov' AB in April 1987, the aircraft had to be struck off charge; it was eventually scrapped in 1995.

Tests of the Tu-16 Tsiklon-NM began in 1991 but were interrupted by the collapse of the USSR at the end of the year. The Tu-16 Tsiklon-NM was reportedly to be used operationally for the last time during the First Chechen War in 1995-96 – apparently for 'sky cleaning', because the typically bad weather over Chechnya in the winter hampered the operations of Russian aviation against the Chechen guerrillas. In fact, the aircraft did not take part in the campaign and was retired by 1997. Regrettably, after sitting in storage at Chkalovskaya AB for several years (in reasonably good condition) the Tu-16 Tsiklon-NM was broken up in 2005; this aircraft should have found a place in a museum. Curiously, in late December 1987, the registration CCCP-42355 was reused for a Yakovlev Yak-42 *Codling* short-haul airliner (c/n 4520424711399, f/n 1308) delivered to Aeroflot's Lithuanian Civil Aviation Directorate; thus, contrary to all rules there were two aircraft with the same registration in service at the same time!

* * *

In describing the variants of the Tu-16, initially IFR-capable aircraft were denoted by the letters ZA in parentheses: Tu-16(ZA), Tu-16A(ZA), Tu-16KS(ZA), Tu-16K-10(ZA) and so on. Later the parentheses were omitted and the rendering changed to Tu-16ZA, Tu-16AZA, Tu-16KSZA, Tu-16K-10ZA, Tu-16RZA and so on. Occasionally the letters 'za' in lower case were used in documents – Tu-16za, Tu-16Rza and so on. Once the IFR system had become an almost standard feature of the aircraft and most Tu-16s possessed IFR capability, the letters 'ZA' were no longer used and the designation reverted to its original form. To determine whether a particular example was IFR-capable or not you needed to see its record card where the ZA suffix was retained.

There were subtleties in the designation of the missile carriers, and various versions were often 'grouped together' under a common designation in Soviet Air Force service. Thus the Tu-16KSR-2, Tu-16KSR-2A and Tu-16KSR-IS were generally given the common designation Tu-16KSR-2, while the Tu-16K-11-16 and Tu-16KSR-2-11 were both referred to as the Tu-16K-11-16. The largest single grouping was K-26, where the designation Tu-16K-26 might refer to a Tu-16K-26, a Tu-16K-26-07, a Tu-16K-26V, a Tu-16K-26 with a Rubin-1M radar, a Tu-16KSR-2-5, a Tu-16K-26-2-5 with a Rubin-1M radar or a Tu-16KSR-2-5-11. Only the Tu-16K-26P SEAD version armed with anti-radar missiles retained its own individual designation in squadron service.

The specialised naval missile strike versions were treated in the same fashion. In squadron service the Tu-16K-10, Tu-16K-10D, Tu-16K-10N and Tu-16K-10P had the common designation Tu-16K-10. Sometimes the Tu-16K-10D was given its own individual designation. Similarly, the Tu-16K-10-26, Tu-16K-10-26D and Tu-16K-10-26N were referred to by the designation Tu-16K-10-26. The exceptions were the Tu-16K-10-26P SEAD version and the Tu-16K-10-26B, the only version of the *Badger-C* with bombing capability.

Sometimes the Tu-16KS was referred to by the alternative designations Tu-16KS 'E' or Tu-16KS (E), the letter 'E' indicating

that the aircraft was armed with the Kometa ASM which was given the production designation '*izdeliye* E' for security reasons. For this reason a series of orders for the Tu-16 to be converted from one version to another had only letter suffixes to differentiate them – for instance, 352A and 352E, 497A and 497E, depending on the original version from which the modification had been made (Tu-16A bomber or Tu-16KS missile carrier). For that reason too the Tu-16KSR-2 is sometimes referred to as the Tu-16KSR-2E, and the Tu-16K-11-16 as the Tu-16K-11-16E.

In service manuals the Long-Range Aviation's Tu-16 missile strike versions (and sometimes the naval versions as well) are given the common designation Tu-16K (for *kompleks [vo'oruzheniya]* – weapons system), although it actually applied to an experimental version of the Tu-16K-10 developed in the late 1950s.

In squadron service barely any differentiation was made between the Tu-16RE, Tu-16RR, Tu-16RM and Tu-16 'Romb' which were all referred to as the Tu-16R. Similarly, no differentiation was made between Tu-16P aircraft fitted with the Buket, Kaktus and Fikus ECM systems or those armed with the RPZ-59 'anti-radar' rockets; they were all referred to as the Tu-16P. On the other hand, the Tu-16Ye was almost invariably referred to as the 'Yolka', although this particular designation was borne by a different version. The Tu-16YeR was referred to simply as Tu-16Ye, while the Tu-16Ye's chemical reconnaissance version was given the unofficial designation Tu-16Ye-KhR.

In Soviet Air Force service no distinction was made between the Tu-16NN and Tu-16N tankers, only the latter designation being used. Target drones also bore the common designation M-16, and Tu-16M was rarely used. The Tu-16PLO is sometimes referred to as the Tu-16PL in documents, and the Tu-16Z tanker (rather misleadingly) as the Tu-16T (for 'tanker')!

Special attention was given to increasing the bomb-carrying capacity (under the terms of 'order 684') and at the Tupolev OKB such modifications were given the 'B' suffix. But even within the design bureau itself the designations Tu-16AB, Tu-16KSR-2B, Tu-16K-11-16B, Tu-16KSR-2-5B and Tu-16KSR-2-11B were hardly ever used, nor were they used in service. Even the aircraft record cards showed no change in designation, with just a note made to the effect that the machine had been modified to carry a greater bomb load. Exceptions to this were the Tu-16K-26B and Tu-16K-10-26B whose designations rarely appear in special documents. In service these designations were hardly ever used.

'Order 684' for the increase in bomb-carrying capacity was especially unusual in that several versions of the Tu-16 were affected. Some versions merely had their capabilities as bombers enhanced, while others received a bombing capability they had not had before. Refits under the terms of 'order 684' began in 1972 and involved aircraft previously modified in accordance with 'order 657'. Aircraft which had hitherto lacked bomber capability could be affected by both orders. These orders brought no change in the aircraft's designation. Only the Tu-16K-11-16 was redesignated Tu-16K-26B when it was equipped with the K-26 ASM and received an increased bomb load. Similar work was carried out in the Naval Aviation when the Tu-16K-10-26 was modified to carry bombs. Originally these machines lacked bombing capability and were redesignated Tu-16K-10-26B after modification.

Chapter 6

The Tu-16 in Detail

The following structural description applies to the baseline production Tu-16 *sans suffixe* conventional bomber ('order 882', *izdeliye* N) built in the mid-1950s and unaffected by subsequent modification bulletins concerning the aircraft's systems, armament and equipment.

Type: Twin-engined high-speed long-range medium bomber designed for operation in VMC and IMC, in daytime or at night, delivering strikes on ground or maritime targets of strategic importance singly or as part of a group. The aircraft has a crew of six: captain, co-pilot, navigator/bomb aimer, navigator/operator (who also acts as flight engineer), gunner/radio operator (defensive stations commander) and tail gunner.

The airframe is of all-metal riveted construction, with D16 series duralumin as the primary structural material. Other structural materials are MA8 and ML5-T4 magnesium alloys (ML = *magniy litey-*

nyy – magnesium optimised for casting; the T4 is a reference to the thermal treatment mode), V95 series aluminium alloys; AK6 and AK8 aluminium alloys, various grades of steel used for the attachment fittings and the crew stations' armour protection, glassfibre Textolite composite, polystyrene, and even wood.

Fuselage: Semi-monocoque stressed-skin structure of basically circular cross-section changing to a pear-shaped cross-section at the rear extremity. Maximum diameter 2.5 m (8 ft 2²⁷⁄₆₄ in), fineness ratio 13.9.

The fuselage has a smooth skin supported by 82 frames and a set of stringers manufactured from extruded and formed components. The spacing of the fuselage frames varies from 260 to 570 mm (from 10¹⁵⁄₆₄ in to 1 ft 10⁷⁄₁₆ in); the portion of the fuselage located between frames 12 and 46 has a cylindrical shape. The stringers are placed around the fuselage circumference at 10° inter-

A typical production Tu-16 in the baseline bomber version.

Exploded view of the Tu-16

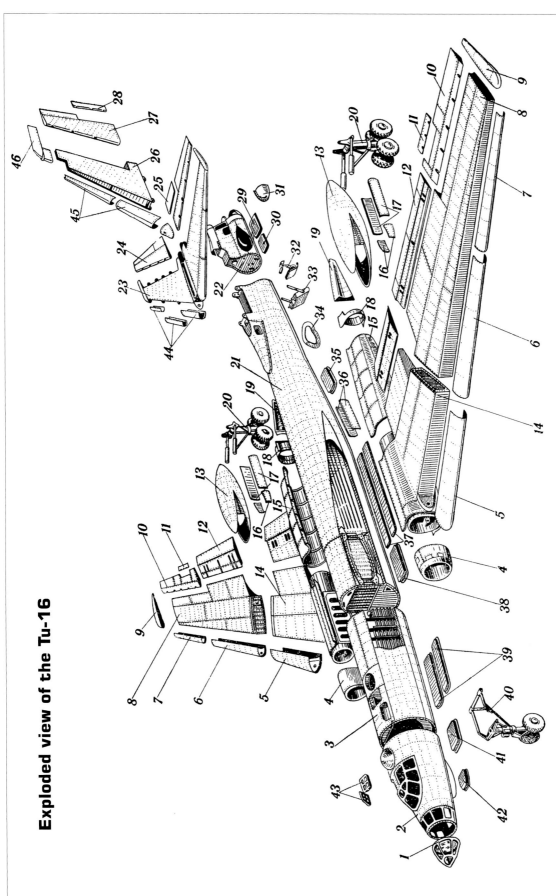

1. Navigator's station glazing framework (Section F-1); 2. Front pressure cabin (Section F-2); 3. Centre fuselage (Section F-3); 4. Air intake assembly; 5. Detachable inner wing section leading edge; 6, 7. Detachable outer wing section leading edge; 8. Outer wing section; 9. Detachable wingtip fairing; 10. Aileron; 11. Aileron trim tab/geared tab; 12. Outer flap section; 13. Main landing gear fairing; 14. Inner wing section; 15. Rear portion of engine nacelle with hinged cowlings; 16. Forward (small) mainwheel well doors; 17. Rear (large) mainwheel well doors; 18. Engine jetpipe fairing; 19. Nacelle-to-fuselage fairing; 20. Main gear struts; 21. Rear fuselage (Section F-4); 22. Rear pressure cabin (Section F-6); 23. Stabiliser; 24. Elevator; 25. Elevator trim tab; 26. Fin; 27. Rudder; 28. Rudder trim tab/geared tab; 29. Rear pressure cabin entry door; 30. Gunner/radio operator's ejection hatch cover; 31. GRO's blister fairing; 32. Retractable tail bumper; 33. Rear avionics/equipment bay access door; 34. Ventral barbette fairing; 35, 38. Fuel tank container access cover; 36. Marker bomb compartment doors; 37. Weapons bay doors; 39. Nosewheel well door; 40. Nose gear strut; 41. Front pressure cabin entry door; 42. Navigator/bomb-aimer's ejection hatch cover; 43. Pilots' ejection hatch covers; 44. Detachable stabiliser leading edge; 45. Detachable fin leading edge; 46. Fin tip fairing.

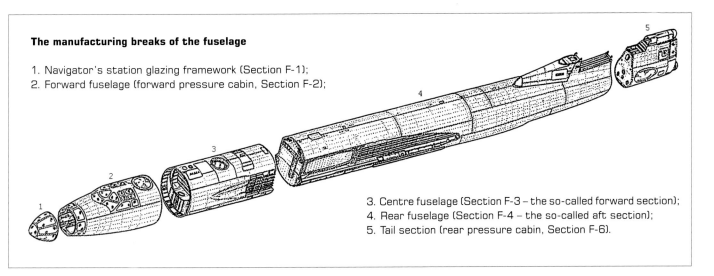

The manufacturing breaks of the fuselage

1. Navigator's station glazing framework (Section F-1);
2. Forward fuselage (forward pressure cabin, Section F-2);

3. Centre fuselage (Section F-3 – the so-called forward section);
4. Rear fuselage (Section F-4 – the so-called aft section);
5. Tail section (rear pressure cabin, Section F-6).

vals; auxiliary stringers are used in some places to reinforce the skin in the gaps between the regular stringers. The overall number of regular stringers in the forward section of the fuselage is 36, with fewer in the rear section. Where the structure is weakened by cut-outs (the nosewheel well and the bomb bay), transverse and longitudinal reinforcing beams are provided to absorb the loads from the airframe's load-bearing elements, equipment and armament.

The skin is mostly 1-2 mm ($\approx 0^3/_{64}$ in to $0^5/_{64}$ in) thick, the skin thickness increasing to 3 mm ($\approx 0^7/_{64}$ in) in the most highly stressed areas. The skin and the internal structure are mostly made of D16ATV and D16ATNV duralumin and their varieties; MA8 magnesium alloy sheet is used for some non-stressed parts of the fuselage. The skin panels are attached to the internal structure by double rows of rivets; flush riveting is used on all exterior surfaces except in highly stressed locations (such as the areas near the gun barbettes), where brazier-head rivets are used. Roundhead rivets are used in areas not exposed to the airflow. The skin is electro-chemically coated to improve corrosion resistance and additionally sprayed with clear varnish after assembly.

For ease of assembly the fuselage is divided by manufacturing breaks into five sections: the navigator's station glazing framework (Section F-1), the forward fuselage (Section F-2), the centre fuselage (Section F-3 – the so-called forward section), the rear fuselage (Section F-4 – the so-called aft section), and the tail section (Section F-6). For some obscure reason there is no Section F-5. The fuselage sections are bolted together by means of flanges.

The *navigator's station glazing framework* (Section F-1, frames 0-2) is a one-piece casting having a modified parabolic shape. The glazing panels are attached to the cast framework made of ML5-T4 magnesium alloy by duralumin strips and screws. The lower centre pane of quasi-oval shape tapering towards the rear is an optically flat window made of Triplex silicate glass to avoid distortions of the view during bomb-aiming. The rest of the glazing is moulded birdproof Plexiglas, with a single strongly convex crescent-shaped transparency at the tip and six panes (four trapezoidal ones and two triangular ones) in the second row. Part of the navigator's station glazing is actually located on Section F-2.

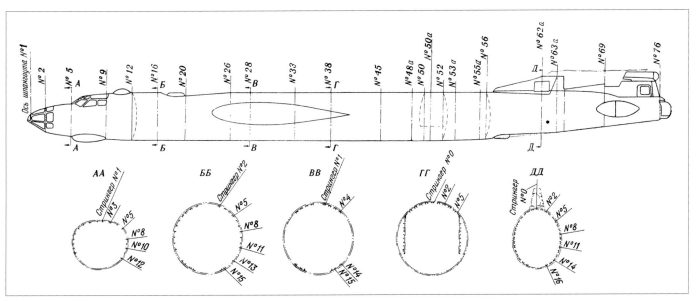

A drawing showing the fuselage cross-section and stringer positions at various frames.

The *forward fuselage* (Section F-2, frames 2-12) comprises the navigator's station and the flight deck; together with Section F-1 it forms the forward pressure cabin. Two types of frames are used – regular and reinforced (mainframes). Pressurisation is ensured by placing special sealing tape between the skin and the internal structure before riveting. The pressure cabin walls are lined with quilted heat- and soundproofing mats made of ATIM-1 (*aviatsionnyy teplo'izolyatsionnyy materiahl* – aviation-specific thermal insulation material) and ANZM (*aviatsionnyy nevosplamenyayemyy zvooko'izolyatsionnyy materiahl* – aviation-specific non-combustible soundproofing material).

The forward pressure cabin accommodates four of the six crew members – the captain on the left, the co-pilot on the right, the navigator/bomb-aimer ahead of and below them, and the aft-facing navigator/operator (who works the radar and the dorsal cannon barbette) behind and above them. The navigator's station (frames 2-5) features two more rows of glazing panels which are located asymmetrically, with three panes to port/two to starboard in the third row (frames 2-3; the lower starboard pane is omitted because the barrel of the forward-firing cannon is located there) and a single pane in the fourth row on the starboard side between frames 3-4. The navigator/bomb-aimer's ejection hatch with a jettisonable cover is located on the forward fuselage underside (frames 2-5).

A recess for the forward-firing cannon is located low on the starboard side of the nose between frames 2-5. It is formed by a massive cast metal part riveted to the fuselage frames and incorporating fixtures for the cannon; the recess is closed by detachable cover plates and a cannon barrel fairing.

The flight deck (frames 5-12) is extensively glazed, with a framework made of duralumin profiles (frames 5-9) whose rear end is flush with the top of the fuselage. It features a three-piece windscreen (with trapezoidal optically-flat outer panes and a rectangular centre pane), three triangular (port/starboard) or trapezoidal (centre) eyebrow windows, four trapezoidal side windows (the forward two are aft-sliding direct vision windows) and eight rectangular or trapezoidal upper windows. The left and right windscreen panes in front of the pilots are made of Triplex silicate glass, all other panes are Plexiglas. A dorsal sighting blister/astrodome is located immediately aft of the flight deck glazing between frames 9-12; it is made of 10-mm (0^{25}/$_{64}$ in) Plexiglas.

The flight deck's pressure floor is located between frames 5-9, featuring longitudinal and transverse beams, frame webs and duralumin skin. Underneath it is an unpressurised bay for the navigation/bomb-aiming radar antenna (frames 5-8), which is closed by a detachable radome made of glassfibre Textolite composite (frames 5-9). Further aft is the entrance hatch under the Nav/Op's seat (frames 9-12) with a forward-hinged cover incorporating boarding steps. The hatch covers and the frames of these hatches are made of cast ML5-T4 magnesium alloy. The flight deck roof features two jettisonable covers (with four windows each) over the pilots' seats enabling ejection in an emergency; they can be detached to allow the seats to be removed for maintenance. All hatches have inflatable perimeter seals. The crew stations have armour protection (see Crew protection and crew rescue system).

Section F-2 terminates in a strongly convex rear pressure dome (frame 12). The dome incorporates a circular hatch in the centre for access to the forward avionics/equipment bay at the front of Section F-3.

The unpressurised *centre fuselage* (Section F-3, frames 12-26) is 'pinched' at the sides in the rear portion where it is flanked by the engine air intakes, having an 'hourglass' cross-section, and flattened at the top near the middle, where it the dorsal cannon barbette is located (frames 17-20). The structure includes seven mainframes and eight regular frames. The nosewheel well flanked by beams is located between frames 13-20, giving access to the forward equipment bay aft of it (among other things, the latter houses a vertical camera and features a camera port). Two containers for the Nos. 1 and 2 fuel tanks are located fore and aft of the cannon barbette between frames 15-17 (above the nosewheel well) and 22-26; their walls are lined with glassfibre Textolite composite sheets and the access panels are secured by screws. A container with a hinged cover above the equipment bay houses a rescue dinghy for the aircrew in the forward cabin. Blast plates made of heat-resistant steel are riveted to the upper fuselage skin aft of the cannon barbette to protect the duralumin skin from the flames of the muzzle flash.

The unpressurised *rear fuselage* (Section F-4, frames 26-69) – actually more like the centre/rear fuselage – accounts for more than 57% of the fuselage length, being 20 m (65 ft 7^{13}⁄$_{32}$ in) long. Its forward section is flanked by the engine nacelles. Section F-4 remains more or less cylindrical up to frame 46 (the wing/fuselage/engine nacelle junction is designed in accordance with the area rule); further aft it tapers off gradually and assumes an elliptical section with the larger axis vertical. It has seven mainframes, 19 regular frames and six auxiliary frames (Nos. 48A, 50A, 53A, 55A, 62A and 63A).

Section F-4 may be subdivided into two portions; the front portion incorporates the wing centre section (frames 26-33, see Wings section) and the weapons bay (frames 33-49). A container for the No.3 fuel tank is located beneath the wing centre section, with an access hatch between frames 27-30. The fuselage skin in this area is supported by stringers and Z-section formers; the structure is mostly made of MA8 magnesium alloy, except the

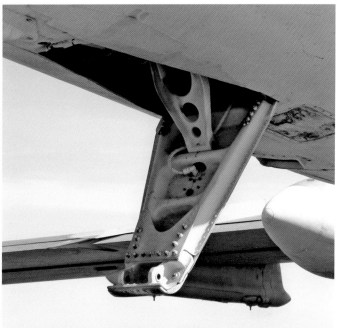

Top left and above left: The navigator's station and flight deck of Tu-16KSR-2-5 '10 Red' preserved in the Technical Museum of AvtoVAZ (the Lada car factory) in Togliatti (Samara Region) with the fake c/n 5207981.

Left: The navigator/bomb-aimer of a Tu-16 working the OPB-11R bombsight. Note the GRP-2 glideslope receiver dipole antenna at the top.

Top right: The dorsal sighting blister.

Above right: The retractable tail bumper. The wire is for the rear IFF aerial.

Right: The centre fuselage of a Tu-16K-26P with the bomb bay doors open. Note the steel-skinned nacelle tail fairing.

stringers and the frame around the cut-out for the aerial of the original Bariy-M IFF transponder, which are made of duralumin.

The weapons bay is 6.702 m (21 ft 11^{55}⁄$_{64}$ in) long; it is closed by large clamshell doors. The doors are actuated hydraulically; if the hydraulic system fails they can be opened by a spring-loaded mechanism. The opening and closing of the bomb bay doors is electrically controlled by the navigator/bomb-aimer. All fuselage frames in the weapons bay area are formers, with the exception of frame 49, which is a bulkhead. The skin thickness in this area gradually lessens from 3 mm to 2.5 mm (from ≈ 0^7⁄$_{64}$ in to 0^3⁄$_{32}$ in). The structure around the bay is reinforced by two hefty triangular-section beams flanking the aperture (running all the way from frame 26 to frame 52) and two beams inside the bay below stringers 5L and 5R; they serve as attachment points for the weapons bay doors and the bomb cassettes. During redeployments to other bases the bomb bay can house a cargo container for the ground support equipment.

The skin of the fuselage sides between frames 33-49 is formed by flat vertical panels which are a continuation of the wing centre section's tip ribs and feature attachment fittings for the engine nacelles; the stringers are located externally in this area. Frames 43 and 46 feature four attachment fittings for the engines; the ones on frame 46 convey the thrust generated by the engines.

The rear portion of Section F-4 (frames 49-69) has no manufacturing break (otherwise it could have been the missing Section F-5!). It has 26 frames, two T-section longerons forming a continuation of the bomb bay beams, and a set of full-length channel-section stringers riveted to the skin. The skin thickness decreases towards the tail from 2 mm to 1.8 mm to 1.5 mm (≈ 0^5⁄$_{64}$ in, 0^1⁄$_{16}$ in and 0^3⁄$_{64}$ in). Frames 50, 52 and 56 are bulkheads delimiting the containers for the Nos. 4 and 5 fuel tanks; a compartment for flare bombs/marker bombs is located between frames 49-52 and closed by clamshell doors, the bomb cassette being attached to a transverse beam and frame 52. Aft of the tanks is the rear equipment bay housing the ventral cannon barbette, the LOX converter for the rear cabin and other equipment. Again, steel blast plates are riveted on aft of the cannon barbette to protect the skin. The equipment bay is accessible via a ventral hatch (frames 62-63); further aft are a recess for the retractable tail bumper (frames 64-66) and the brake parachute container (frames 67-69; see Landing gear). The front ends of the protective metal fairings of the GRO's observation blisters are located on the rear fuselage sides between frames 68-69.

The rear portion of Section F-4 also carries the fin fillet (frames 57-63A; see Tail unit); underneath it is a supporting structure made of 2-mm duralumin sheet with longitudinal stiffeners located between frames 64-69. The fillet has duralumin skin 0.8 mm (0^1⁄$_{32}$ in) thick. A container with a hinged cover on the port side is built into the fillet between frames 62-63, housing the rescue dinghy for the aircrew in the rear cabin.

The *tail section* (Section F-6, frames 69-76) is the rear pressure cabin accommodating the gunner/radio operator (working the ventral cannon barbette) and the tail gunner (defensive fire commander). The latter normally operates the tail cannon barbette and the gun ranging radar but is able to control and fire all other cannons except the nose cannon in case of need.

The rear cabin has two lateral blisters at the GRO's station located between frames 69-73; their front portions up to frame 70 are made of metal and the glazing is 10-mm (0^{25}⁄$_{64}$ in) Plexiglas. The glazing of the tail gunner's station comprises two side windows (with double Plexiglas panes) and three rear windows made of bulletproof Triplex silicate glass in a cast ML5-T4 magnesium alloy framework. A fairing for the gun ranging radar terminating in a hemispherical radome made of polystyrene is positioned above the cabin.

Access to the rear cabin is via a ventral hatch under the tail gunner's seat (frames 72-74) with a forward-hinged cover incorporating steps. The GRO's ejection hatch with a jettisonable cover is located immediately ahead of it (frames 69-72); the frames of these hatches are made of cast ML5-T4 magnesium alloy, while the hatch covers have a cast magnesium alloy liner and duralumin armour skin. The tail gunner's port side window is an inward-opening emergency exit to be used in the event of ditching or a belly landing when the ventral hatch is unusable.

The rear pressure cabin is sealed and heat-insulated/soundproofed in the same way as the front one. Apart from frames and stringers, the structure includes a flat forward pressure bulkhead (frame 69) reinforces by vertical and horizontal beams, which is attached to longerons. Frame 72 has an unusual design, consisting of two lateral duralumin armour plates connected by a transverse beam at the top and by the gunners' entry and ejection hatch frames. Frame 75 is a variable-thickness armour-plated rear pressure bulkhead to which the tail turret is bolted; it has apertures for the tail turret's ammunition belt sleeves.

Wings: Cantilever mid-wing monoplane; sweepback at quarter-chord 35°, leading-edge sweep 37° from root to ribs 7L/7R and 36° outboard of these. Anhedral 3° from root to tip, incidence 1°, aspect ratio 6.627, taper 2.416.

To improve the aerodynamic characteristics at high subsonic speeds, the wings are composed of special high-speed aerofoil sections with a low thickness/chord ratio which vary along the span. A TsAGI PR-S-10S-9 symmetrical aerofoil with a thickness/chord ratio of 15.7% was used at the roots, changing to a TsAGI SR-11-12 aerofoil with a thickness/chord ratio of 15% at ribs 7L/7R and a TsAGI SR-11-12 aerofoil with a thickness/chord ratio of 12% at the tips.

The wings are of two-spar stressed-skin riveted construction with 53 ribs. The main structural materials are D16T, D16AT and

Left: The rear equipment bay access hatch, with the tail bumper visible in the foreground.

Right: The starboard wingtip, aileron and winglet of a retired Tu-16Z tanker; the hose guide tube is missing. De-icing system air outlet slits are visible ahead of the winglet; the projection ahead of them houses a wing leading edge illumination light.

D16ATNV duralumin, AK6, AK8 and V95 aluminium alloys; flush riveting is used throughout, and bolt joints are used where the loads are highest. The wing torsion box absorbing the structural loads has thick skin panels reinforced by stringers.

The wings are built in five pieces: the centre section, inner (first) and outer (second) detachable sections, which are held together by bolts. The *centre section* is integral with the fuselage and equal in span to the fuselage width; its front and rear spars made of D16T, D16AT and D16ATNV are mated to fuselage mainframes 26 and 33 respectively, running at 90° to the fuselage axis. It has three ribs which are parallel to the centreline – two end ribs made of 3.5-mm (≈ 0⁹⁄₆₄ in) D16ATNV sheet with wing/fuselage attachment fittings and one centreline rib). The upper and lower skin panels are smooth and composed of aluminium alloy sheets 3-5 mm (≈ 0⁷⁄₆₄ to ≈ 0¹³⁄₆₄ in) thick; they are reinforced with stringers made of V95 alloy. The centreline rib divides the centre section into two bays housing fuel tanks; the insides of the bays (except the front walls and upper panels) are lined with glassfibre Textolite composite sheets. The upper skin panel has a fitting for the brace of the centreline bomb rack in the weapons bay.

The *inner wing sections* are joined to the centre section along the fuselage sides and have eight ribs each – Nos. 1, 2, 2A (a false rib) and 3-7; these are at 90° to the front spar, except ribs 1 and 2, which are parallel to the centreline. In addition to the materials mentioned above, grade 30KhGSA, 30KhGSNA and 30KhNMA steel forgings and cast magnesium alloy parts are used.

The inner wings are built integrally with the engine nacelles' centre portions (that is, except for the cowling sections enclosing the engines proper, which are attached to the fuselage). Hence the root portions of the spars are manufactured as one-piece extruded oval frames made of AK8 alloy; the remaining parts of the spars are constructed from spar caps, solid webs and struts made of AK8, D16T and D16ATN. The wing skins are made of V95ATNV alloy. The upper skins are one-piece parts reinforced by nine stringers; the lower ones are split chordwise into four panels with a total of ten stringers, one of the panels being detachable for access to the bays in the torsion box accommodating the fuel tanks. Again, these bays (located between ribs 2A/3, 3/4, 4/5 and 5/7) are lined with glassfibre Textolite composite and additionally sealed with rubber or rubberised fabric strips.

Ribs 6 and 7 feature steel attachment fittings for the main gear struts. The leading edge consists of four detachable sections. The leading-edge and trailing-edge portions outside the torsion box have no stringers; adequate rigidity is provided by the closely spaced ribs.

The *outer wing sections* are mated to the inner ones at ribs 7L/7R. They have 18 ribs each (Nos. 8-25); all of them except the tip ribs are at 90° to the front spar. The design is similar to that of the inner wings, except that the spars are strictly conventional. The primary materials are D16ATNV and V95 alloys; D16ATUP duralumin with a thicker electrochemical coating layer (hence the UP for *ootolshchonnaya plakirovka*) is used in the leading-edge section. Again, the outer wings have one-piece upper skins and multiple lower skin panels, one of which is detachable. Each outer wing houses five fuel tanks between ribs 7-12; provisions are made for installing three more tanks in each wing up to rib 15. Each outer wing has two boundary layer fences; the inboard pair is located near the inner/outer wing section joint and the outboard pair is in line with the ailerons' inboard ends. The two-piece leading-edge sections are detachable, as are the wingtip fairings.

The elements of the wing structure are electrochemically coated and sprayed with clear varnish after assembly. The internal structure is coated with ALG-1 yellow primer (*aviatsionnyy lahkovyy groont* – aviation-specific varnish-type primer) to prevent corrosion.

The wings carry the main landing gear fairings, which overlap the inner/outer wing joints. Their axes are parallel to the centreline; the cross-section is close to square with rounded corners,

Left: The tail unit of a Tu-16Ye showing the triple flush antennas of the RSBN-2S SHORAN system and the wire aerial of the RSIU-5V communications radio (the rear aerial mast is visible ahead of the starboard stabiliser). Note how the 'anti-flash' paint on the vertical tail is applied to the rudder only (unlike the horizontal tail whose entire underside is white).

Below left: This view shows the 'horseshoe' aerial of the KRP-F localiser receiver on the fin cap, the tail gunner's station glazing and the ammo belt sleeves inside the partly dismantled DK-7 tail turret.

changing to circular at the rear ends. The fairings are of riveted duralumin construction with 14 ribs/formers, an upper beam and two lower beams to which the wheel well doors are attached; the front ends are forked to fit around the wing torsion box. On early Tu-16s the front ends of the lower portions were dielectric (made of glassfibre Textolite composite), enclosing IFF aerials; this was changed to an all-metal design when a different IFF system was introduced and the aerials were relocated.

There are no leading-edge devices (the detachable leading-edge sections act as de-icers). The trailing edge is occupied along the entire span by flaps (up to ribs 16L/16R) and ailerons. The slotted Fowler flaps of single-spar riveted construction are built in two sections divided by the main landing gear fairings. The flaps are electromechanically operated by an MPZ-3M actuator (*mekhanizm privoda zakrylkov* – flap drive mechanism) with twin electric motors and common reduction gear via drive shafts and angle drives; each flap section is actuated by two screw jacks. The inboard sections have two flap tracks each and are about three times shorter than the outboard ones, which move on three flap tracks each. Flap settings are 20° for take-off and 35° for landing.

The one-piece ailerons are of single-spar riveted construction. They are aerodynamically balanced and mass-balanced and are carried on two brackets each (at ribs 19 and 23); the travel limits are ±15°. Each aileron incorporates an inset trim tab (terminating some way short of the inboard end) carried on three brackets; the travel limits are ±5°.

Tail unit: Conventional cantilever swept tail surfaces utilising symmetrical aerofoil sections. The tail assembly is of riveted duralumin construction, except for the attachment fittings and the wooden fairing at the tip of the fin. All duralumin parts are electrochemically coated, the steel parts primed, and the wooden part is coated with VIAM-B3 bonding agent to prevent decay (VIAM = *Vsesoyooznyy institoot aviatsionnykh materiahlov* – the All-Union Institute of Aviation Materials).

The *vertical tail* with 42° sweepback at quarter-chord and a leading-edge sweep of 46° comprises a detachable fin, a large fin root fillet built integrally with the rear fuselage and a one-piece rudder. The fin is a two-spar structure with 22 ribs (Nos. 0-21). It is attached to fuselage frames 64 and 69 by bolts at four points (two fittings made of grade 30KhGSA steel at each frame); the fin/fuselage joint is sealed by shaped metal strips attached by screws. Rib 0 (the attachment rib) is parallel to the fuselage waterline, the others are at 90° to the front spar and spaced at 300 mm (11¹³⁄₁₆ in); ribs 11, 16 and 21 are reinforced, carrying the rudder mounting brackets made of AK6 alloy. The fin has one-piece port and starboard skins reinforced by 11 stringers, a two-piece detachable leading-edge section doubling as a de-icer, and a trailing-edge section with multiple webs. The tip fairing has a mostly wooden structure with a few metal parts and a skin made of birch veneer; it incorporates communications radio and ILS aerials.

The rudder is of single-spar construction with 34 ribs (Nos. 0-33, including four reinforced ribs). It is hinged on three brackets at ribs 9, 19 and 29 and a lower support; the rudder travel limits are ±25°. The rudder is aerodynamically balanced and features a trim tab at the root hinged on four brackets; the travel limits are ±7°.

The *horizontal tail* also has 42° sweepback at quarter-chord; leading-edge sweep is slightly less at 45°. There is no dihedral. Tailplane incidence is normally –1°30' and can be adjusted on the ground between 0° and –2°30' at 0.5° increments, using the holes in the attachment fittings on the fuselage. The tailplane/fuselage junction is again sealed by metal fairings attached by screws to the lower stabiliser skin and to the fuselage sides. The stabilisers are of similar two-spar design, having 16 ribs each (Nos. 0-15) and upper/lower skins reinforced by 12 stringers each; they are bolted together on the centreline and likewise attached to fuselage frames 64 and 69 by bolts at four points (two fittings made of grade 30KhGSA steel at each frame). Rib 0 (the attachment rib) is parallel to the centreline and located 250 mm (9^{27}/$_{32}$ in) from the centreline. The others are at 90° to the front spar and are spaced at 500 mm (1 ft 7^{11}/$_{16}$ in); ribs 6, 9, 12 and 15 are reinforced, carrying the elevator mounting brackets made of AK6 alloy. The three-piece leading-edge sections doubling as de-icers are detachable but the metal tip fairings are not; the trailing-edge sections have 40 webs each.

The one-piece elevators are of single-spar construction with 44 ribs (Nos. 0-43, including five reinforced ribs) and are connected on the centreline by a shaft with a universal joint ensuring simultaneous deflection. They are aerodynamically balanced and mass-balanced; the travel limits are 12° down and 26° up. Each

elevator is carried on four brackets and incorporates a trim tab at the root; the travel limits are ±12°.

Landing gear: Hydraulically retractable tricycle type; all three units retract aft. All three units have oleo-pneumatic shock absorbers and scissor links, uplocks and downlocks.

The steerable nose unit attached to fuselage frames 13-14 has jury struts and an aft-mounted breaker strut with a single hydraulic ram. It is fitted with twin 900 x 275 mm (35.43 x 10.82 in) K2-86 non-braking wheels, two main and one auxiliary shimmy dampers, and a steering mechanism operated by the rudder pedals.

The port and starboard main units attached to inner wing ribs 5 and 7 are identical. They feature four-wheel bogies with KT-16, KT-16/2, KT-16/2M, KT-16/2U or KT-16/2D wheels equipped with hydraulic brakes (KT = *koleso tormoznoye* – brake-equipped wheel), all measuring 1,100 x 330 mm (43.3 x 12.99 in). When

Above right: The nose gear unit in no-load condition. The jury struts are just visible. Note the 'spoked' design of the K2-86 nosewheels.

Right: The starboard main gear unit of an early-production Tu-16 *sans suffixe* showing the original one-piece forward-hinged door design, with a window for the taxi light attached to the oleo strut. The inclined strut at the front is connected to the bogie's rocking damper and tilts the bogie during retraction.

Far right: The definitive main gear door design with two pairs of clamshell doors.

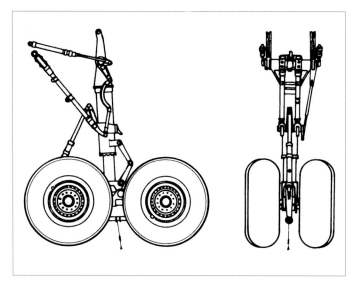

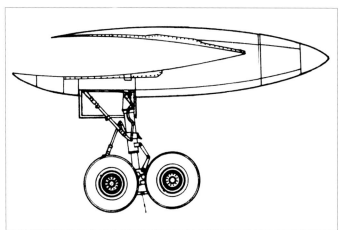

extended, the main gear struts are almost vertical; the bogies assume a slightly nose-down attitude in no-load condition. During retraction the struts are tilted aft by twin hydraulic rams; in so doing a system of linkages and rocking dampers rotates the bogies aft through 180° with respect to the ground position, the bogies stowing inverted in the streamlined fairings protruding beyond the wing trailing edge.

The nosewheel well is closed by two lateral doors; the latter remain open when the gear is down, closing by means of mechanical linkages as the strut retracts. Each main unit has two large main doors (bulged to accommodate the wheels) and, on early-production aircraft, a one-piece forward-hinged door with a glazed window for the taxi light, which was replaced by small clamshell doors in line with the gear fulcrum (mechanically linked to the strut) on later aircraft. The main doors are hydraulically actuated, opening only when the gear is in transit. The nose unit retracts much quicker than the main ones.

A retractable tail bumper with a shock absorber is provided to protect the rear fuselage in the event of overrotation or a tail-down landing. It is located between frames 64-66 and operated by an MP-250 electric drive (*mekhanizm privoda* – actuating mechanism), retracting/extending simultaneously with the landing gear.

A PT-16 twin-canopy brake-parachute system (*parashoot tormoznoy* – brake parachute for the Tu-16) is provided to reduce the landing run on a waterlogged or short runway, an unpaved airstrip, after an incorrectly executed landing approach or in the event of brake failure. The circular parachutes with a total area of 40 m² (430.56 sq ft) are housed in a detachable container with clamshell doors in the rear fuselage underside. The parachutes are deployed and released electrically. They reduce the landing run to no more than 1,535 m (5,040 ft) on a dry concrete runway with automatic wheel braking applied and the parachutes deployed after touching

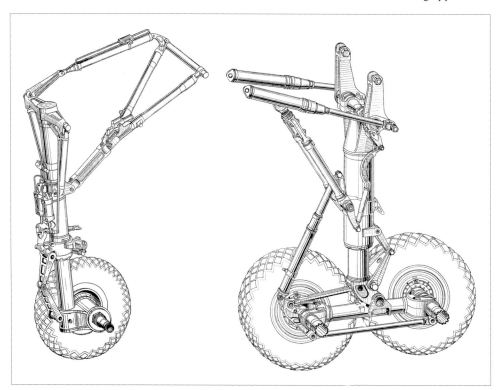

Above right: The Mikulin AM-3 engine. Note the air intake slit for the S300-75 turbostarter housed in the parabolic intake centrebody, with the exhaust at the front.

Top left: Side and front views of a Tu-16 main gear unit. Note the earth connection/static discharge wick.

Above left: The starboard main gear unit and fairing seen from the inboard side One of the smaller clamshell doors is omitted here.

Far left: The nose gear strut complete with actuation ram and drag strut/breaker strut.

Left: One of the main gear units, showing the twin actuation rams, the rocking damper/tilting mechanism and the push-pull rods connecting the front and rear wheel brake mechanisms.

down at a speed no greater than 270 km/h (167 mph), with a landing weight up to 47,000 kg (103,620 lb).

Powerplant: Early-production Tu-16s were powered by two Mikulin AM-3 (RD-3) non-afterburning turbojets with a take-off thrust of 8,750 kgp (19,290 lbst) and a cruise thrust of 6,200 kgp (13,670 lbst). Later aircraft had RD-3M (RD-3M-200) engines with a take-off thrust increased to 9,500 kgp (20,940 lbst), a cruise thrust increased to 7,650 kgp (16,865 lbst). and a two-minute contingency rating of 10,608 kgp (23,386 lbst); from 1961 onwards these were replaced by identically rated RD-3M-500s having an increased time between overhauls and higher reliability. Operation time at take-off power is limited to eight minutes.

The AM-3 (RD-3) is a single-spool axial-flow turbojet having a fixed-area subsonic air intake with a large fixed parabolic centrebody supported by six radial struts, an eight-stage compressor, an annular combustion chamber with 14 straight-through flame tubes housed in a common shroud, a two-stage turbine and a fixed-area subsonic nozzle. The spool rotates in three supports with

roller bearings in the first two and dual ball bearings in the third one. The compressor casing is divided into three sections; the front and rear sections are annular, while the centre section is made up of eight segments. The third compressor stage features an automatic anti-surge air bleed valve; further bleed valves are provided at the seventh stage (for the air conditioning system and the engine/air intake de-icers) and the eighth stage (for the wing de-icers). Only about one-third of the air passing through the compressor is mixed with fuel in the combustion chamber; the rest is used to cool the chamber and the turbine. The combustion chamber features four SPN-4-3 igniters energised from a KP14-2R1 ignition coil.

Three accessory gearboxes (left, right and lower) are located on the centre portion of the engine, being driven by a vertical shaft with angle drives in the front part of the compressor casing. The left gearbox mounts two GSR-180000 generators, a Model 453V hydraulic pump and a centrifugal breather; the right one mounts an AK-150 air compressor, a PN-28B (or, on the AM-3, PN-28-15) fuel control unit (FCU; PN = *ploonzhernyy nasos* – piston-type pump) and a TsD-1 centrifugal engine speed sensor (*tsentrobezh-*

Above: The starboard engine air intake. Note the accessory cooling air intake in the horizontal splitter.
Above right: The rear portion of the starboard nacelle, showing the cowling and the turbostarter intake door.

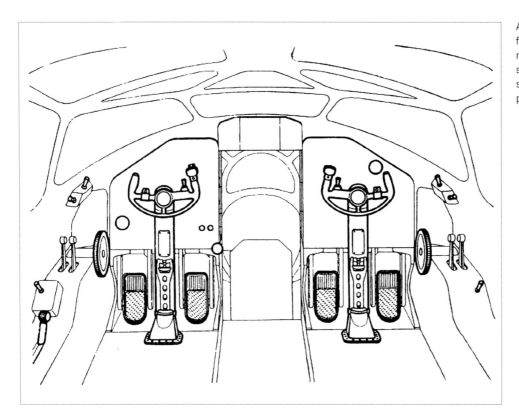

A schematic drawing of the Tu-16's flight deck with the control yokes and rudder pedals and the pilots' side consoles; the interior of the navigator's station is partly visible through the passage leading to it.

nyy **dahtchik**) controlling the anti-surge valve. The lower one mounts the engine oil pumps (two feed pumps and a scavenging pump) and the TsN-1D fuel feed pump (*tsentrobezhnyy nasos* – centrifugal pump).

Starting is by means of an S300-75 turbostarter (that is, starter, developed by OKB-300, power output 75 shp) on the AM-3 or the S300M version on the RD-3M et seq. This is a small centrifugal-flow gas turbine engine driving the spool directly via a clutch; the term 'jet fuel starter' is not applicable, since the S300-75 runs on aviation gasoline. The turbostarter is, in turn, started by a 1.2-kilowatt SA-189B electric starter and has its own PNR10-3M fuel pump (*pooskovoy nasos-regoolyator* – starter FCU); it runs at 31,000-35,000 rpm. The S300-75 (S300M) is housed in the air intake centrebody, back to front, breathing through slits in the centrebody. The starter air intake is located low on the side of the engine nacelle and closed by twin doors rotating on longitudinal axles; the dog-leg exhaust pipe runs from the tip of the intake centrebody to a dorsal outlet. The engine starting procedure is automated.

SFC 1.0 kg/kgp·hr (lb/lbst·hr) at take-off power and 0.931 kg/kgp·hr at cruise power. Engine speed 4,650 rpm at take-off power and 4,350 rpm at nominal power. Mass flow at take-off power 150 kg/sec (331 lb/sec), engine pressure ratio 6.2 at take-off power and 7.2 at the contingency rating; turbine temperature at take-off power 1,130°K. Length overall 5.38 m (17 ft 7¹³⁄₁₆ in), casing diameter 1.4 m (4 ft 7⁷⁄₆₄ in), dry weight 3,100 kg (6,830 lb).

The engines are housed in area-ruled nacelles adhering to the centre fuselage, being located behind the wings' rear spar. The front portions of the nacelles are detachable structures with four frames and a detachable leading edge; they are made of AMTsM magnesium alloy and D16T duralumin. The centre portions are integral with the inner wing sections and are constructed from multiple panels. The engines breathe through air intakes of quasi-triangular cross-section located well forward of the wing leading edge and set apart from the fuselage sides to prevent boundary layer ingestion. The inlet ducts bifurcate ahead of the wing torsion box, the oval-section main duct passing through the wing spars and the auxiliary duct passing below them; the two ducts merge ahead of the engine. Thus each inlet duct is built in four sections (front, upper, lower and rear). The horizontal air intake splitter features a ram air intake for cooling the engine accessories and the engine bays, the cooling air being ejected together with the engine efflux.

Each engine is attached to fuselage frames 43 and 46 by six adjustable rods and an auxiliary strut made of grade 30KhGSA steel. The engines are set at a small toe-in angle to stop the jet efflux from impinging on the fuselage. This is assisted by the specially shaped tail sections of the nacelle/fuselage fairings with heat-resistant stainless steel skins which make sure that there is a gap between the fuselage and the exhaust jet when the engines run at full power. The rear portions of the nacelles incorporate longitudinal and transverse (front and rear) firewalls. Maintenance access is provided by 20 dorsal and ventral detachable covers and hinged cowling panels secured by tension locks.

The engine controls (throttles and fuel shut-off cocks) are connected to the throttles located on the port and starboard consoles in the flight deck by means of a system of cables and pulleys.

Control system: Conventional mechanical flight control system with full dual controls, the control columns featuring U-shaped control wheels. The flight controls are manual (that is, unpowered); all control surfaces are aerodynamically balanced to reduce the control forces.

The system includes an AP-5-2M or (on aircraft built from 1959 onwards) AP-6E electric autopilot with servos providing stabilisation in all three control channels. The autopilot incorporates a longitudinal and lateral stabiliser, a course stabiliser, a course indicator, servos, an amplifier, a unit of precession gyros, and PAG-1F and PO-45 AC converters providing electric power. It automatically maintains straight and level flight, controls the aircraft by means of the autopilot servos, using the remote control handles; it also allows the navigator/bomb-aimer to adjust the heading during the bombing run with the aid of the optical bomb sight and stabilises the optical bomb sight in azimuth.

Roll control is by means of ailerons, which are connected to the control wheels by a combination of tubular push-pull rods and bellcranks (in most areas) and cables in the mechanism where the control runs from the captain's and co-pilot's wheels are combined. KSAN ultra-pliant steel cables are used (*kanaht stal'noy aviatsionnyy neraskroochivayushchiysya* – aviation-specific steel cable resistant to unravelling). The aileron control rods inside the wings run along the back of the rear spar up to rib 15 and enter the torsion box between ribs 15-16 (just inboard of the ailerons and outside the area reserved for extra fuel tanks). Both ailerons feature trim tabs which double as geared servo tabs, with MP-100A-60 electric actuators on the wings' rear spar.

Pitch control is by means of elevators, the elevator control circuit featuring push-pull rods throughout. The elevator trim tabs are mechanically operated by means of a handwheel on the port cockpit console via a system of cables; a UT-11 electric actuator (*oopravleniye trimmerom* – trim tab control) is fitted as a back-up.

Directional control is by means of a rudder which utilises rigid linkages to the rudder pedals. The rudder trim tab has an MP-100-36 electric actuator located on the fin's rear spar and again doubles as a servo tab.

A gust lock is provided to prevent damage to the controls on the ground; it is operated by cables, with a locking handle on the captain's console.

Fuel system: The primary fuel system comprises 27 bag-type tanks (fuel cells) made of kerosene-proof rubber. The tanks are divided into ten groups (five for each engine); if necessary, both halves of the system can be connected via a cross-feed valve, allowing any engine to draw fuel from any group of tanks. The tanks within each group are interconnected; each group includes a service tank from which the fuel is drawn.

The maximum fuel capacity is 43,800 litres (9,636 Imp gal). At the normal all-up weight of 72,000 kg (158,730 lb) the maximum fuel load is 34,360 kg (75,750 lb). This equals 41,400 litres (9,108 Imp gal) if the Tu-16's primary fuel grade – T-1 kerosene with a specific gravity of 0.83 – is used, or 43,750 litres (9,625 Imp gal) if the alternative fuel grade – TS-1 kerosene with a specific gravity of 0.78 – is used.

Tanks Nos. 1-5 are housed in the fuselage (Nos. 1 and 2 ahead of the wings, No.3 below the wing centre section, Nos. 4 and 5 aft of the wings). The others are accommodated in the wing torsion box – two in the centre section, five in each inner wing section and five in each outer wing section. Their distribution between the groups is as follows. For the port engine, Group 1 comprises tanks

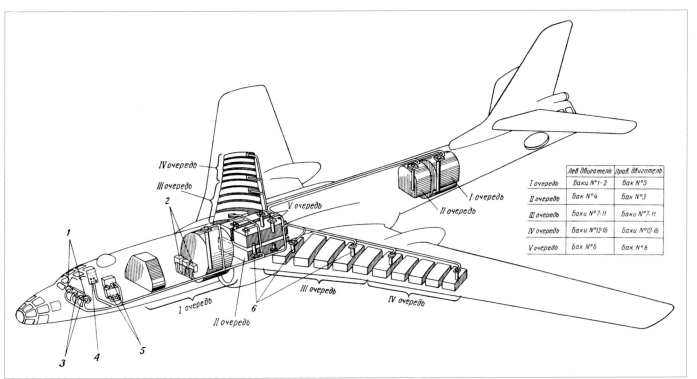

	Лев двигатель	Прав. двигатель
I очередь	Баки N°1-2	Бак N°5
II очередь	Бак N°4	Бак N°3
III очередь	Баки N°7-11	Баки N°7-11
IV очередь	Баки N°12-16	Баки N°12-16
V очередь	Бак N°6	Бак N°6

Location of the SETS-60D fuel metering/fuel management system components. 1. Fuel gauges; 2. Automatic fuel management system amplifiers; 3. Circuit breakers; 4. Fuel system control panel; 5. Fuel metering system amplifiers; 6. Fuel quantity sensors. The Roman numerals show the groups of fuel tanks numbered in the fuel usage sequence; the table shows these groups for the port and starboard engines.

1-2, Group 2 is tank 4, Group 3 is inner wing tanks 7L-11L, group 4 is outer wing tanks 12L-16L, and Group 5 is the wing centre section tank 6. For the starboard engine, Group 1 is tank 5, Group 2 is tank 3, Group 3 is inner wing tanks 7R-11R, group 4 is outer wing tanks 12R-16R, and Group 5 is again tank 6.

The system features 12 ETsN-T booster pumps (*elektricheskiy tsentrobezhnyy nasos* – electric centrifugal pump) – one in each group's service tank, except Groups 2 and 5, which have two such pumps each for added reliability; however, fuel feed by gravity is possible at altitudes up to 12,000 m (39,370 ft). From the service tanks the fuel is fed via the check valves (of which there are 16) and the shut-off cocks to the TsN-1D engine-driven fuel feed pumps, then passes through RTS-16 fuel flow meters (*raskhodomer topliva samolyotnyy*), Model 62 fuel/oil heat exchangers and fuel filters – one for each engine in all cases – before entering the FCUs.

Ground refuelling is by gravity; each group of tanks has a single filler cap and has to be filled separately. The Tu-16 (ZA) version has an in-flight refuelling receptacle under the port wingtip. Fuel usage is automatically sequenced by the SETS-60D system (or, on aircraft with IFR capability, the SETS-60M system).

All tanks are self-sealing, except Nos. 1, 2 and 5, the fuel from which is consumed first (and thus they are likely to be empty if hit by enemy fire, which means no leak will ensue). An inert gas pressurisation system using carbon dioxide (CO_2) is provided to minimise the risk of fire and explosion if hit by incendiary rounds. It features six OSU-3NG or, on later aircraft, OSU-5 spherical bottles (*ognetooshitel' stationarnyy ooglekislotnyy* – stationary fire extinguisher charged with [liquid] CO_2), a filter, reduction valves and manifolds.

The fuel tanks have a common vent system. An emergency fuel jettison system is provided; it is connected to the Group 1, 3 and 4 tanks. The fuel jettison pipe is located in the port wingtip fairing to minimise the risk of fire.

The engines' turbostarters have a separate fuel system (the so-called starter fuel system). This uses 70-octane B-70 aviation gasoline with 1% of engine oil added; the starters are fed from a common Avgas tank with a capacity of 21 litres (4.62 Imp gal). The first Kazan'-built batch (c/ns 3200101 to 4200105) had independent starter fuel systems for the port and starboard engines.

Oil system: The engines and their turbine starters have separate lubrication systems, both of which use MK-8P grade mineral oil or transformer oil; each engine's oil tank has a capacity of 40 litres (8.8 Imp gal). The engine oil is cooled in the fuel/oil heat exchangers mounted on the airframe.

Hydraulics: Two separate hydraulic systems, each with its own reservoir, filter and controls. The main system is powered by two engine-driven Model 435V piston-type pumps. It operates the landing gear and weapons bay doors in normal mode, as well as the nosewheel steering mechanism and the pilots' windshield wipers. An NRO-1 emergency pump (NR = *nasos roochnoy* – hand-driven pump) can be connected to the system in case of need to perform certain in-flight and ground operations.

The brake system originally had an NSh-29 electric pump (*nasos shesteryonchatyy* – gear-type pump) which was later replaced by a Model 465K electric pump; it features a hydraulic accumulator. In addition to operating the wheel brakes in normal and emergency modes, it is used for emergency landing gear retraction/extension and emergency closure of the weapons bay doors.

Both systems use AMG-10 mineral oil-type hydraulic fluid (*aviatsionnoye mahslo ghidravlicheskoye* – 'aviation-specific hydraulic oil'); total capacity is 120 litres (26.4 Imp gal). Nominal pressure for both systems is 150 kg/cm² (2,140 psi); an SPME-130 sensor gives warning of low pressure. The systems feature both rigid pipelines and rubber hoses; they feature a common pressurisation and venting system.

Electrics: The electric system caters for the armament, avionics, engine starting system, fuel system, lighting equipment, indication and warning systems, and part of the de-icing system. With all electric equipment in operation at once, the maximum current is 1,700 A, which equals 70% of the electric system's total capacity; thus, there is a power reserve for added reliability.

Primary 28-28.5 V DC power is supplied by four 18-kW GSR-18000 (or GSR-18000M) generators connected in parallel to power a common circuit, each engine driving two generators to provide a total power capacity of 72 kW. Each generator works with a RUG-82 carbon voltage regulator (*regoolyator oogol'nyy*), a DMR-600 differential minimum relay and a BS-1800 ballast resistor (*ballastnoye soprotivleniye*); the latter maintains the voltage of the generator, protecting it against reverse currents and permitting operation in parallel with the other generator. Back-up DC power is provided by two 12SAM-53 or 12SAM-55 lead-acid batteries (*startyornaya, aviatsionnaya, monoblochnaya [akkumulyatornaya batareya]* – aircraft-type monobloc starter battery) accessible via the nosewheel well.

As a safety measure, DC power is delivered through three circuits:
• the primary circuit drawing on all four generators in any combination and both DC batteries;
• an emergency circuit which draws on only one generator (No.2 or No.3) and one DC battery;
• a dual-feed circuit which automatically switches between the primary circuit (if the latter is power-on) and emergency supply (if the primary circuit fails).

Accordingly there are three sets of power distribution buses. The normal feed buses are connected full time to the primary circuit, supplying power to equipment which is normally in use but can be dispensed with if the primary circuit dies, such as the autopilot or the tail unit de-icers. Dual-feed buses are connected full time to the dual-feed circuit; they cater for essential items which make it possible to complete the objective and return to base even with a failed primary circuit, such as the fuel pumps, the flight instruments and the armament. It also caters for the emergency bomb release and IFF transponder self-destruct functions. Finally, a triple-feed bus is connected full time to the dual-feed circuit. If both the latter and the primary circuit are disabled it can be connected manually to the DC batteries to power vital equipment enabling an emergency landing – the back-up artificial horizon, the turn and bank indicator, the pitot head heaters (making sure that barometric instruments are serviceable), the intercom and emergency flight deck lighting. Maximum operating time in this mode is two hours.

Ground AC power can be supplied via a RAP (*razyom aerodromnovo pitahniya* – ground power receptacle) or ShRA-400LK connector located on the port side of the fuselage at frame 16. The operation of the electric power sources is monitored by means of four type A-3 ammeters, a type A-2 (or A-1) ammeter and a switchable V-1 voltmeter.

115 V/400 Hz single-phase AC power is provided by two 4.5-kVA PO-4500 AC converters, each of which works with an R-25V carbon voltage regulator and an RS-4M rheostat. One converter is used at any one time while the other is a back-up; they alternate between active and back-up modes with the purpose of equalising the wear on the carbon brushes and using the converters' service life equally. Operation of the AC subsystem is checked by means of a VF-150 voltmeter.

In addition to the main power sources, the Tu-16 has various autonomous power sources catering for specific equipment items to provide electric power for the control, navigation and communications systems. These are the PAG-1F AC converter providing 36 V/400 Hz three-phase AC for the artificial horizon (hence PAG for *preobrazovahtel' aviagorizonta*), PT-125Ts three-phase AC converters (later replaced by the PT-200Ts model), MA-1 single-phase AC converters (later replaced by the PO-500 model), and U-500 and RU-11AM dynamotors/converters.

The electric circuitry uses mainly BPVL and MGShV copper wire and BPVLA aluminium wire, the airframe acting as the 'earth' electrode. To reduce radio interference, part of the copper wiring is shielded BPVLE wire (*ekraneerovannyy* – shielded) or the wiring bundles are enclosed in a common sheath.

Exterior lighting equipment includes tandem pairs of port (red) and starboard (green) BANO-45 navigation lights (*bortovoy aeronavigatsionnyy ogon'*) enclosed by flush Plexiglas fairings at the wingtips, a white KhS-39 or KhS-57 tail navigation light (*khvostovoy signahl*) atop the housing of the gun ranging radar, two retractable LFSV-45 landing lights (*lampa-fara samolyotnaya vydvizhnaya* – aircraft-type retractable sealed-beam lamp, 1945 model) or, on late-production aircraft, FRS-200 landing lights side by side immediately ahead of the nosewheel well between frames 12-13, and two FR-100 taxi lights (*fara roolyozhnaya*) mounted on the main gear struts. For night operations in a group, PSSO-45 formation lights (*plafon siniy stroyevykh ogney* – blue formation light, 1945 model) are mounted flush with the upper and lower surfaces in several places. Kazan'-built Tu-16s up to and including c/n 5201801 had FBV-45 lights (*fara dlya bombometahniya 'po vedooshchemu'* – [signal] light for 'follow-the-leader' bombing) enclosed by domed transparencies in the tips of the main gear fairings, allowing the flight leader to tell his wingmen when to drop the bombs while maintaining radio silence. Late-production aircraft feature red OSS-61 revolving anti-collision beacons (*ogon' svetosignahl'nyy* – signal light) in teardrop-shaped Plexiglas fairings on the starboard nose gear door and on top of the centre fuselage near frame 37. The Tu-16 (ZA) has an SMF-1 lamp installed behind a small window on the port side between frames 18-19 for illuminating the tanker's hose at night and a signal light in the port wingtip telling the tanker crew that fuel transfer can begin.

Interior lighting equipment comprises PS-45 and PSM-51 overhead lights (*plafon samolyotnyy* – aircraft-type lighting fixture), KLSRK-45 movable white lights, ARUFOSh-45 ultra-violet lamps (*armatoora ool'trafioletovovo osveshcheniya sharneernaya* – articulated UV lighting fixture, 1945 model) to make the instrument dials glow in the dark without revealing the aircraft's position to enemy fighter pilots, and PL-10-36 portable lamps (*perenosnaya lampa*).

Pneumatic system: The pneumatic system operates the fuel jettison valves, the IFR receptacle on the Tu-16 (ZA), the cannons' cocking mechanisms, the flare/marker bomb bay doors, the cabin pressurisation system valves, the de-icing system valves, the inflatable perimeter seals of the entry and ejection hatches, and the pilots' ejection hatch jettison mechanisms. It also pressurises the radar sets of the RBP-4 navigation/bomb-aiming radar and the PRS-1 gun ranging radar. Compressed air is supplied by the AK-150 engine-driven compressors. Nominal pressure is 150 kg/cm² (2,142 psi); reduction valves are provided to reduce it where necessary to as low 1.2 kg/cm² (17.14 psi).

Pressurisation and air conditioning system: To enable high-altitude operations the Tu-16 has ventilation-type pressurised cabins; their entry and ejection hatches have inflatable perimeter seals.

At altitudes up to 2,000 m (6,560 ft) the cockpits are pressurised and ventilated by ram air supplied by air scoops on the starboard side of the fuselage at frame 13 for the front cabin and in the fin leading edge for the rear cabin. This is mainly used in hot weather when the cabin temperature on the ground can be anywhere between +20°C and +40°C (68-104°F). At higher altitude the system automatically switches to air bled from the seventh compressor stage of both engines; the maximum possible flow of air through each of the two cabins is 500 m³ (17,567 cu ft) per hour. The quantity of air supplied to the two cabins from both engines is 2,000 m³ (70,629 cu ft) per hour, which allows the pressurisation/air conditioning system to work adequately on one engine.

In so doing the cabin pressure exceeds the ambient pressure, decreasing slowly as the aircraft climbs. Up to an altitude of 7,250 m (23,790 ft) the cabin pressure is equal to 2,000 m above sea level; above that altitude a constant pressure differential of 0.4 kg/cm² (5.7 psi) is maintained by ARD-50 or ARD-54 automatic pressure governors (*avtomaticheskiy regoolyator davleniya*), one in each cabin.

In the event that the ARD-54 is inoperative in both cabins, the pressure differential can be maintained manually at 0.05-0.43 kg/cm² (0.71-6.14 psi), using KKD valves (*klapan kontrolya davleniya* – pressure control valve). On entering an area where anti-aircraft fire or combat with enemy fighters (and hence damage to the pressure cabins) is likely, the pressure differential is reduced to 0.2 kg/cm² (2.85 psi) – either by the ARD-54 or by the KKD valves – in order to avoid a sudden abrupt decompression if the aircraft's skin is pierced.

Before entering the pressure cabins the engine bleed air is cooled by a TKhU-128 cooling turbine (*toorbokholodil'naya oostanovka*). The air temperature is maintained automatically by TRTVK-45 (*termostaht-regoolyator temperatoory vozdukha v kabine*) or TRTVK-45M cabin air temperature regulators within set limits between +15.5° and +26.5°C (59.9-79.7°F), or manually between +10° and +30°C (50-86°F).

Oxygen system: The Tu-16 was the first Soviet aircraft to carry oxygen in liquid form which was then converted to gaseous form. The use of liquid oxygen (LOX) achieved a weight and volume saving six or seven times greater than that obtained with gaseous oxygen.

The oxygen enables flight at high altitudes and ensures survival after ejection at high altitudes. The crew station oxygen equipment, which was used in normal flight, consists of two KPZh-30 LOX converters (*kislorodnyy pribor zhidkosnyy* – liquid oxygen apparatus) in the front and rear equipment bays, serving the front and rear pressure cabins respectively, as well as six KP-24 breathing apparatus (or KP-16 on early production aircraft) with KM-24 oxygen masks (*kislorodnaya mahska*), fixtures, manometers and charging connectors.

The emergency oxygen equipment of each crewmember (used when ejecting from the aircraft) is a KP-23 breathing apparatus as part of his parachute pack.

De-icing system: Hot air de-icing for the wing leading edges and the engines. The hot air de-icing system comprises two separate subsystems: one for the wings and another for the engines. The wing de-icing subsystem uses bleed air from the eighth compressor stage; the hot air passes through gaps between the leading-edge skin and the corrugated internal liner before escaping through slits in the wingtip fairings. The port and starboard wings are served by the respective engines, but there is a cross-feed valve so that if one engine fails the system can still be supplied by the other engine.

The other subsystem caters for the air intake leading edges, the splitters in the engines' inlet ducts, the inlet guide vanes and the turbostarter exhaust pipes. Air for this subsystem is bled from the seventh compressor stages.

Electric de-icing for the fin and stabiliser leading edges, the pitot heads (115 V AC), the pilots' windscreens and the optically flat lower sighting window of the navigator's station (27 V DC). The heated panes are provided with an AOS-81M temperature regulator (*avtomaht obogreva styokol* – automatic glazing heating regulator) to prevent the glass from overheating and cracking.

Additionally, all other glazing panels in the navigator's station and flight deck, as well as the dorsal and lateral blisters for the optical sighting stations and the tail gunner's station glazing, are de-iced and demisted by warm air from the air conditioning system.

Fire suppression system: OSU-3P stationary fire extinguisher bottles charged with CO_2 for fighting fires in the engine bays and the fuel tank containers; several OU-2 portable fire extinguishers in the crew cabins. An SSP-2A fire warning system (*sistema signalizahtsiï pozhara*) with DPS-1AG flame sensors (*dahtchik pozharnoy signalizahtsiï*) and new OS-8M stationary fire extinguisher bottles charged with grade '3.5' or $11V_2$ chlorofluorocarbon extinguishing agent were retrofitted as part of a mid-life update.

Avionics and equipment: The Tu-16 is fully equipped for day/night operation in VMC and IMC, including automatic flight assisted by an autopilot.

a) navigation and piloting equipment: The Tu-16's navigation and piloting suite includes an AK-53P celestial compass; a DAK-50M remote celestial compass (on Kazan'-built Tu-16s c/ns 3200101 to 4200105, replaced later by the DAK-2 and later still by the DAK-DB or DAK-DB-5); a DIK-46M remote flux-gate compass, replaced later by the DGMK-7 (*distantsionnyy gheeromagnitnyy kompas*) with a flush sensor in the port wing underside between ribs 21L/22L and a VK-53RB correction switch (*vyklyuchatel' korrektsiï*); a KI-12 magnetic compass (replaced later by the KI-13); a GPK-48 directional gyro (replaced later by the GPK-52); an NI-50B navigation display; an SPI-1 or SPI-3M aircraft receiver-indicator device (*samolyotnyy priyomoindikahtor*) as part of the RSDN-1 Meridian LORAN system.

Main and back-up ARK-5 automatic direction finders are fitted, with a whip aerial immediately aft of the flight deck glazing and a flush aerial glued to the Nav/Op's dorsal blister; both ADFs can be used simultaneously by tuning them to different transmitters. An RV-17M high-altitude radio altimeter and an RV-2 low-altitude radio altimeter are installed, both of them using the same tandem dipole aerials on the centreline ahead of the weapons bay. An SP-50 Materik ILS is fitted, comprising a KRP-F localiser receiver with a horseshoe-shaped aerial on the leading edge of the wooden fin tip fairing, a GRP-2 glideslope receiver with a dipole aerial inside the navigator's station glazing, an SD-1 or SD-1M distance measuring equipment kit with tandem rod aerials on the rear fuselage underside and an MRP-48P marker beacon receiver whose antenna is flush with the rear fuselage underside.

Subsequently, in the course of production and service, the radio navigation equipment was updated more than once and by the end of the Tu-16's operational life it differed slightly on different variants. On some aircraft the ARK-5 ADF was replaced by the ARK-11; others had an ARK-U2 direction finder was fitted. Some Tu-16s had the RV-2 altimeter replaced by the RV-UM. A DISS-1 Doppler ground speed and drift angle sensor system was fitted; the MRP-48P marker beacon receiver was replaced by the MRP-56P; an A-711 LORAN system and the associated A-713M receiver was fitted. Some Tu-16s had the RSBN-2S Svod SHORAN system added; finally, an A-326 Rogovitsa formation flight system was fitted.

To facilitate piloting and ease the workload on the pilots and navigator during long flights and while bombing, an AP-5-2M autopilot was fitted initially. From 1959 onwards it was replaced by the AP-6E autopilot.

b) communications equipment: The Tu-16 originally had a 1-RSB-70M (aka R-807) high-frequency (HF) communications radio with a US-9 receiver (served by a 'towel rail' aerial low on the starboard side of the rear fuselage), a 1-RSB-70M (aka R-808) HF command radio with a US-9DM receiver (served by a 'towel rail' aerial high on the starboard side of the forward fuselage), and an RSIU-3M VHF command radio with two receivers and a wire mesh antenna integrated into the skin of the wooden fin cap. Later the RSIU-5V communications radio with a wire aerial running from an aerial mast amidships to the fin and R-832M Evkalipt VHF command radio with L-shaped aerials above and below the

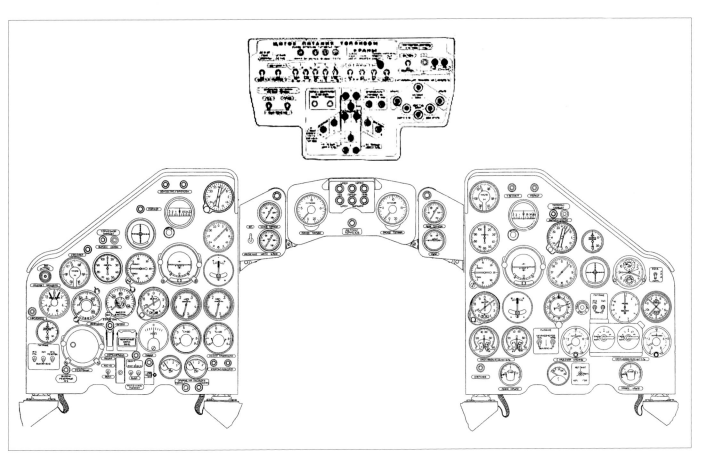

forward fuselage were installed. An SPU-10 intercom (*samolyot-noye peregovornoye oostroystvo*) provides crew communication.

In the course of operation an R-851 emergency locator transmitter was fitted; there was also an AVRA-45 emergency radio, later replaced by the R-861.

For air-to-ground communication in radio silence mode (for example, in the event of a radio failure) two EKSP-39 electric signal flare launchers (*elektricheskaya kasseta signahl'nykh patronov*) are installed in tandem low on the starboard side of the forward fuselage immediately aft of the nosewheel well. Each launcher fires four 26-mm (1.02-in) flares of different colours (red, green, yellow and white).

c) radar equipment: The basic Tu-16 bomber features a Rubidiy-MM-2 navigation/bomb-aiming radar capable of detecting large ground targets at no less than 140 km (87 miles) range, which works in conjunction with the OPB-11R optical bombsight. The radar displays are installed at the navigator/bomb-aimer's and navigator/operator's stations. Later Tu-16 bombers have the improved RBP-4 navigation/bomb-aiming radar. In the late 1950s a small number of Tu-16s were built with the RBP-6 Lyustra navigation/bomb-aiming radar in an identical chin radome which had improved performance and worked with the OPB-112 optical sight. Some Tu-16 were built or retrofitted with the R-1 bombing system (the Rubin radar plus OPB-112 optical sight).

Above: The captain's and co-pilot's main instrument panels, the centre instrument panel and the overhead circuit breaker panel.

Right, clockwise from top: The radio operator's instrument panel, the navigator's instrument panel (on 'glass-nosed' versions) and the navigator/operator's instrument panel.

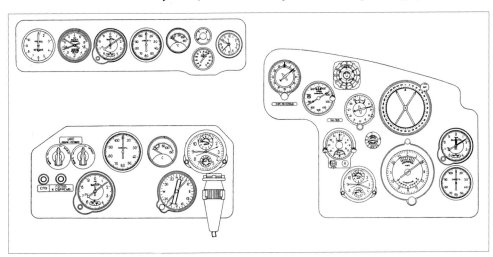

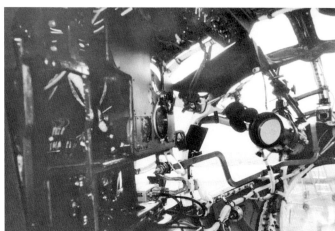
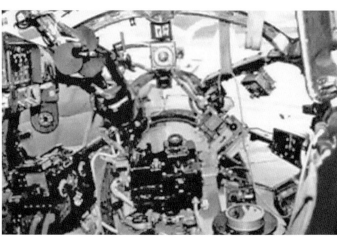
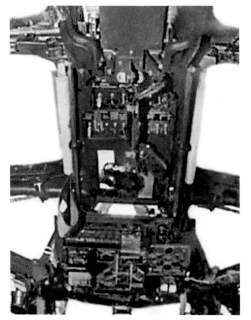

Top left: The captain's workstation on a Tu-16. The large circle on the left is the elevator trim tab handwheel on the side console.

Top right: The co-pilot's workstation on a Tu-16. The aircraft type is marked on the hubs of the aileron control wheels, as was often the case on Soviet aircraft – not only Tupolev types.

Above and above right: The navigator's station of a Tu-16A, with the OPB-11R optical bombsight occupying centre place. Note the instrument panel on the port side, the radar display and the rubber-bladed cooling fan.

Left: The overhead circuit breaker panel between the jettisonable hatches above the pilots' seats.

Above right: Parts of the flight deck instrumentation and the control yokes of a Tu-16 preserved in a museum.

Right: The captain's instrument panel. The placard reads 'Warning! In case of sudden decompression descend to 12,000 m'.

Far right: The co-pilot's instrument panel.

A PRS-1 Argon gun ranging radar is installed above the tail gunner's station.

d) IFF equipment: Early Tu-16s had a Magniy-M IFF radar interrogator with a range of 30-40 km (18.6-24.5 miles) fitted as part of an autonomous identification system for recognition of 'friendly' aircraft or vessels fitted with SRO or *Fakel-MO* (Torch-MO) transponders and for short-range radio navigation. Its rod aerials were located above the navigator's station and under the front ends of the main gear fairings. A Bariy-M IFF transponder with an operating range of 35 km (21.75 miles) was also fitted, with a rod aerial under the centre fuselage. On later aircraft these

were replaced by the SRZO-2 Khrom-Nikel' combined interrogator/transponder with triple rod aerials above the navigator's station and under the rear fuselage. Some aircraft were updated with the SRO-1P Parol' transponder with triangular aerials at the same locations. The IFF transponder can be destroyed by a built-in explosive charge at the push of a button to prevent the secret IFF codes from falling into enemy hands in the event of capture or a shootdown.

e) ECM and ESM equipment: In the course of several refits and upgrades while in service, the Tu-16 had various types of active and passive ECM equipment and radar warning receivers fitted which differed on various versions of the aircraft and was constantly updated. Some production Tu-16s had ASO-16/3 Avto-

mat-1 chaff dispensers in the weapons bay between frames 46-48, with an attendant reduction in the bomb load; earlier production examples of the Tu-16, Tu-16A and Tu-16 (ZA) were modified to incorporate this system. Towards the end of their service lives, the bomber versions had the SPS-5 (SPS-5M) active jammer and the Sirena-2 RWR fitted.

Also in the 1970s some Tu-16s were retrofitted with ASO-2I flare dispensers for releasing infrared countermeasures flares. Three sets (six 32-round units) were installed in the rear fuselage underside and in the tailcones of the main gear fairings.

f) flight instrumentation: The pilots' and navigator's instrument panels featured AGB-1 artificial horizons (*aviagorizont bombardirovochnyy* – artificial horizon for bombers; replaced

Left: The interior of a Tu-16's bomb bay, looking rearward. Bomb casettes are installed on the sidewalls. Note the pressurisation system pipelines running along the ceiling of the bay to the rear pressure cabin.

Below left: Close-up of one of the KD3-488 bomb cassettes, with guide rods forming part of the bomb fuse arming system installed beside it.

Opposite page: Various types of bombs carried in a Tu-16's bomb bay on KD3-488 bomb cassettes. Note how the front and rear fuses are connected by arming cables to the guide rods, removing the safety pins at the moment of bomb release.

progressively by the AGB-2, then by the AGB-3 and finally the AGD-1), KUS-1200 airspeed indicators (*kombineerovannyy ookazahtel' skorosti* – combined ASI), a VD-17 (later VD-20) two-needle barometric altimeter (*vysotomer dvookhstrelochnyy*), a VAR-30-3 vertical speed indicator (*variometr* – VSI), an SSN-3 dynamic pressure indicator (*signalizahtor skorosnovo napora*), a BSPK-1 comparator and bank angle limit indicator (*blok sravneniya i predel'novo krena*) installed as a mid-life update, EUP-46 (later EUP-53) turn and bank indicators (*elektricheskiy ookazahtel' povorota*), an MS-1 Mach meter, an AM-10 accelerometer, an IAS-51 aircraft sextant; AChKhO and AVR-M chronometers, later replaced by the AChS-1 (*aviatsionnyye chasy strelochnyye*); a UVPD-15 cabin altitude and pressure differential indicator (*ookazahtel' vysoty i perepada davleniya*), a VS-46 high-altitude pressure warning indicator (*vysotnyy signalizahtor*) telling the crew when it's time to don the oxygen masks, and a TUE-48 thermometer (*termometr ooniversahl'nyy elektricheskiy* – multi-purpose electric thermometer).

The following engine instruments are installed: TE5-2 remote-sensing rpm gauges (*takhometr elektricheskiy* – electric tachometer) for the engines and TE-45 rpm gauges for the turbostarters, TVG-11 and TVG-29 exhaust gas temperature gauges (*termometr vykhodyashchikh gahzov*), a TTsT-13 thermometer; an EMI-3R three-needle electric indicator (*elektricheskiy motornyy indikahtor*) showing fuel pressure, oil pressure and oil temperature; an EDMU-3 electric remote standardised pressure gauge (*elektricheskiy distantsionnyy manometr oonifitseerovannyy*); DIM-80T induction-type remote pressure gauge (*distantsionnyy indooktsionnyy manometr*); RTS-16 (later RTS-16A) fuel flow meters, and fuel gauges making up part of the SETS-60D fuel metering kit.

g) photo equipment: To carry out the limited range of reconnaissance duties (photographing targets of opportunity and performing bomb damage assessment), the Tu-16 bomber can carry the following photo equipment:

• a set of AFA-33/50M (low-altitude), AFA-33/75M and AFA-33/100M cameras for daylight photography;

• a set of NAFA-3S/50 or NAFA-6/50 cameras for night photography;

• a FA-RL-1 camera for recording the image on the display of the RBP-4 radar;

• an AKAFU-156N automatic swivelling camera mount (for all types of daylight cameras listed above) which enables two-strip vertical and oblique photography; a mount for night cameras; a camera hatch and a control panel for the hatch and the AKAFU camera mount.

Only one camera can be installed at any one time (excluding the FA-RL-1 which is always fitted) and only one camera mount. The photographic equipment is housed in the fuselage (section F-3) aft of the nosewheel well.

The bomb bay can house 24 FotAB flash bombs for reconnaissance missions flown by night.

Starting with c/n 6203401, the Tu-16 was fitted with a swivelling mount permitting installation of the AFA-34-OK and AFA-42/75 cameras and the AFA-BAF-40R training camera. Aircraft from c/n 7203509 onwards were fitted with an NAFA-MK/75 camera for night photography.

Until 1957 the set of cameras fitted to a specific aircraft was decided in squadron service, depending on the needs of the particular unit. However, that year the following photo equipment became standard for the Tu-16. One aircraft in every three was fitted with the AFA-34-OK, AFA-BAF-40R and NAFA-6/50 cameras. From July 1957, onwards all Tu-16 bombers had an AFA-34-OK camera and an AFA-42/75 camera as standard, while one aircraft in every three had an AFA-BAF-40R and an NAFA-MK/75. At the end of the 1950s the FARL-1 was replaced by the FARM-2 camera (*fotoapparaht rahdiolokatora modernizeerovannyy* – updated camera for the radar), and a PAU-457-4 gun camera was fitted to record the display of the PRS-1 gun ranging radar.

h) data recording equipment: In squadron service the Tu-16 was retrofitted with the MSRP-12 crashworthy flight data recorder (FDR; MSRP = *magnitnyy samopisets rezhimov polyota* – magnetic flight mode recorder) for mission debriefing or accident investigation. It captures 12 parameters, including barometric altitude, indicated airspeed, roll rates, vertical and lateral G forces, control surface deflection and throttle settings, as well as gear/flap transition and the like. Some examples had a K-3-63 backup FDR fitted; unlike the primary FDR, it records only altitude, IAS and vertical G forces.

An MS-61 cockpit voice recorder (CVR; MS = *magnitofon samolyotnyy* – aircraft-specific tape recorder) was retrofitted in service; it uses magnetised steel wire instead of tape, making sure it won't melt in a post-crash fire. Some machines had an MIZ-9 CVR.

Armament: The Tu-16 has a full set of offensive and defensive armament.

a) offensive armament: The Tu-16's bomb armament was standard for Soviet heavy bombers of the day. The bomb racks, bomb hoists and the release and locking mechanisms for the bomb load are housed in the bomb bay between fuselage frames Nos. 33 and 49. The bombsight, release mechanisms and bomb bay door control panels are located in the forward pressurised cabin. Depending on the composition of the bomb load, the following interchangeable racks can be fitted in the bomb bay:

• six KD3-488 four-shackle bomb cassettes with Der3-48 shackles;

• four KD4-388 two-shackle bomb cassettes with Der4-49 shackles;

• an MBD6-16 or MBD6-16M beam-type rack with a Der6-5 shackle.

The bomb release control system is electrically operated and comprises normal and emergency subsystems, each of which has is own independent electrical wiring to the release mechanism. The basic subsystem is the normal (so-called combat) bomb release control which functions in conjunction with the bombsight, electric release mechanisms, and the bomb release mode relay used for selecting the bomb release sequence and intervals at which the bombs are dropped.

The loading of bombs (and unloading, in the event they remained unused) was originally carried out by means of detachable BL-47EM hoists (*bombovaya lebyodka elektromekhanicheskaya* – electromechanical bomb hoist, 1947 model) bomb hoists with the aid of cables, belts, pulleys and crosspieces. They were later replaced by the BL-56 model. Control of the bomb hoists was effected using a special mobile control panel which was part of the ground equipment.

The normal bomb load is 3,000 kg (6,610 lb) and the maximum bomb load 9,000 kg (19,840 lb); in maritime strike configuration the maximum naval mine of torpedo load is 8,700 kg (19,180 lb). Bombs of 5,000 kg (11,020-lb), 6,000 kg (13,120-lb) and 9,000 kg calibre are suspended on the MBD6-16 centreline rack; smaller bombs are carried on KD3-488 and KD4-388 bomb cassettes attached to the bomb bay sidewalls. When the Tu-16T torpedo-bomber was used on naval theatres of operations, carrying mines and torpedoes, the latter were suspended from the KD3 and KD4 cassettes. The maximum load of mines and torpedoes was 8,700 kg (19,180 lb). The aircraft is fitted with an ESBR-49A electric release mechanism (*elektrosbrasyvatel'*) enabling single weapons or 'sticks' of bombs, mines or torpedoes to be dropped throughout the Tu-16's altitude and speed envelope. For greater reliability the bombing system is energised from two electric power circuits.

Bomb-aiming is performed by means of an OPB-11R vector-synchronised optical sight with automatic drift correction located in the navigator's station in the extreme nose. It is linked to the AP-5-2M autopilot, which allows the navigator/bomb-aimer to maintain the aircraft's course automatically during bomb-aiming. Some Tu-16s had an OPB-112 bombsight working in conjunction with the RPB-6 Lyustra or R-1 (Rubin-1) radar.

If the target is not visible (when bombing through overcast or at night), bomb-aiming can be carried out using the radar (Rubidiy-MM2, RBP-4, RBP-6 or R-1). In this case bombing accuracy is increased since the OPB-11R (or OPB-112) is linked to the radar,

Types of bombs carried by the Tu-16

Type	Quantity	Total weight
SAB-100-75 flare bomb	16	1,152 kg (2,539 lb)
FotAB-100-80 flash bomb	24	1,920 kg (4,232 lb)
FAB-250 M46 high-explosive bomb	24	5,253 kg (11,580 lb)
FAB-250 M54	24	5,660 kg (12,478 lb)
FAB-500 M46	18	7,686 kg (16,944 lb)
FAB-500 M54	18	8,386 kg (18,487 lb)
FAB-1500 M46	6	8,871 kg (19,556 lb)
FAB-1500 M54	6	9,324 kg (20,555 lb)
FAB-3000 M46	2	5,963 kg (13,146 lb)
FAB-3000 M54	2	6,116 kg (13,483 lb)
FAB-5000 M54	1	5,220 kg (11,508 lb)
FAB-9000 M54	1	9,290 kg (20,480 lb)
FAB-250 M43	16	4,000 kg (8,818 lb)
FAB-500 M43	12	5,706 kg (12,579 lb)
FAB-1000 M43	4	4,380 kg (9,656 lb)
FAB-2000 M43	4	8,260 kg (18,210 lb)
BrAB-6000 armour-piercing bomb	1	n.a.

Naval mines and torpedoes carried by the Tu-16

Type	Quantity
AMD-500 mine	4 or 12
AMD-1000 mine	4
AMD-2M mine	6 or 8
IGDM mine	8
Serpey mine	6
Desna mine	8
Lira mine	8
RAT-52 torpedo	4
45-36MAV torpedo	6

Below: A diagram showing the fields of fire of the Tu-16's DT-V7 dorsal barbette, DT-N7S ventral barbette and DK-7 tail turret.

Bottom: A diagram showing the fields of view of the Tu-16's PS-53VK dorsal PS-53BL (port) and PS-53BP (starboard) lateral sighting stations, PS-53K rear sighting station and PRS-1 gun-laying radar.

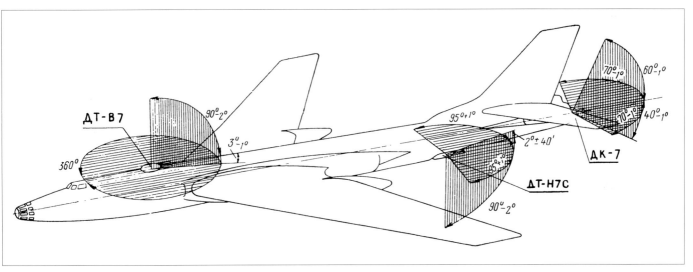

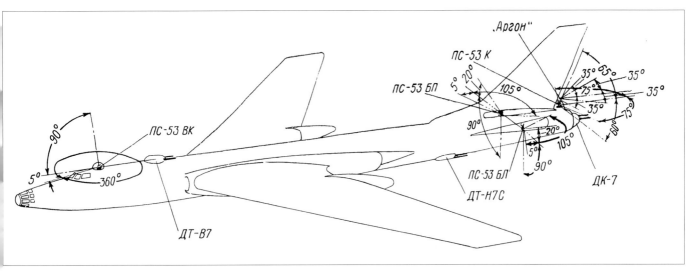

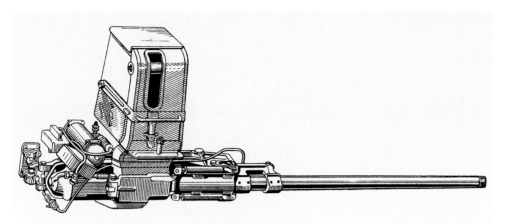

Right: The NU-88 cannon installation (the AM-23L3 forward-firing cannon and its ammunition box). The muzzle brake is not shown.

Below left: The DT-N7S ventral barbette and its ammunition box.

Below: The DT-7V dorsal barbette and its ammunition box.

computing the necessary parameters for the latter: the slant range, the lateral stabilisation angle and the azimuth stabilisation angle.

The dropping of bombs, mines and torpedoes is normally carried out by the navigator/bomb-aimer, but can also be done by the Nav/Op whose workstation features a weapons release switch. In this case all parameters for the drop must be set by the navigator/bomb-aimer. The latter opens and closes the weapons bay doors in manual bomb release mode by means of an electric switch. In automatic bomb release mode the bay doors are controlled by the bombsight, which opens them immediately before bomb release. Emergency opening of the weapons bay doors, as part of the emergency bomb jettison procedure, is carried out by the navigator/bomb-aimer and the co-pilot. The pilots operate the secondary weapons bay door closing system.

In addition, two DYa-SS racks (*derzhatel' yashchichnyy signahl'nykh sredstv* – box-type rack for signal means) were installed a special compartment, carrying twelve TsOSAB-10 coloured marker/signal flare bombs or OMAB maritime marker bombs (*oriyenteerno-morskaya aviabomba*). These were released by the navigator/bomb-aimer.

b) defensive armament: For defence against fighter attacks the Tu-16 features the PV-23 cannon system which comprises seven 23-mm Afanas'yev/Makarov AM-23 cannons. The AM-23 weighs 43 kg (94.8 lb). It is belt-fed and fires 200-gram (7.05-oz) projectiles; the muzzle velocity is 690 m/sec (2,263 ft/sec) and the rate of fire is 1,300 rounds per minute.

The cannons are installed in four positions, three of which are movable. A single forward-firing cannon in the AM-23L3 version

Right: The barrel of the AM-23L3 forward-firing cannon equipped with a muzzle brake/flame damper.

Below right: The DT-7V dorsal barbette with the barrels pointed forward. Note the gun blast plates riveted on aft of it.

Centre right: The DT-N7S ventral barbette.

Bottom right: The DK-7 tail turret with the cannons at maximum elevation.

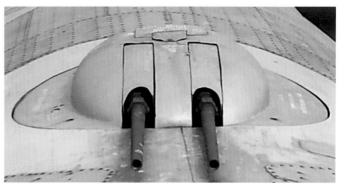

with 100 rounds of ammunition is installed on a fixed NU-88 mount on the starboard side of the nose. It is aimed by the captain, using a PKI collimator gunsight. Unlike the other cannons, the forward-firing cannon features a muzzle brake/flame damper to avoid dazzling the pilots and the navigator/bomb-aimer.

The other positions are twin-cannon remote-controlled powered turrets – the DT-7V dorsal barbette, DT-N7S ventral barbette and DK-7 tail turret. They provide coverage of the rear hemisphere, the upper hemisphere and the rear part of the lower hemisphere. Kazan'-built aircraft up to and including c/n 4200603 (except c/n 4200401) had PS-48MM optical sighting stations with a ballistic computer unit providing the target lead angle. From c/n 4200604 onwards these were replaced by the more advanced PS-53 optical sighting stations (as detailed below) with new PVB-53 ballistic computers.

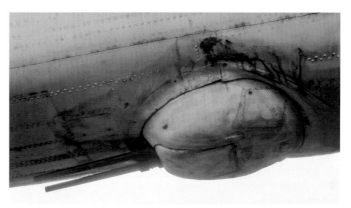

The DT-7V dorsal barbette is enclosed by a flattened circular fairing and has an ammunition supply of 500 rounds (250 rpg). The field of fire in azimuth is 360°, while the elevation limits depend on the direction of fire because of the barbette's low-drag depressed installation, being +13°/+90° forward, +4°/+90° rearward and –3°/+90° to the sides. Primary control is exercised by the Nav/Op, using the PS-53-VK dorsal sighting station, but the dorsal barbette can also be controlled by the tail gunner (defensive fire commander) from the rear cabin.

The DT-N7S ventral barbette is enclosed by a similar fairing and has an ammunition supply of 350 rpg. Its field of fire is ±95° in azimuth in the rear hemisphere, 2°40' up and 90° down. Primary control is exercised by the gunner/radio-operator by means of the PS-53-BL (port) and PS-53-BP (starboard) sighting stations located at the lateral blisters. Auxiliary control can be exercised by the tail gunner from the rear sighting station.

The DK-7 tail turret is enclosed by a four-piece fairing whose lateral parts are detachable for maintenance access. It has a ±70° field of fire in azimuth, an elevation of 60° and a depression of 40°. The full ammunition supply is 1,000 rpg. Primary control is exercised by the tail gunner using the PS-53K rear sighting station. Auxiliary control can be exercised by the Nav/Op from the dorsal sighting station, or by the GRO from the lateral sighting stations. Unlike the other cannons, spent cases and belt links are ejected, not collected in special bays.

A remote control system synchronises the cannons' movement with that of the optical sighting stations. It includes the AVS-53 automatic gunnery computer (*avtomaticheskiy vychislitel' strel'byy*), the DSP-53 speed and density sensor (*dahtchik skorosti i plotnosti*), the VSP-53 speed and density computing module (*vychislitel' skorosti i plotnosti*) and the ADP-53 automatic auxil-

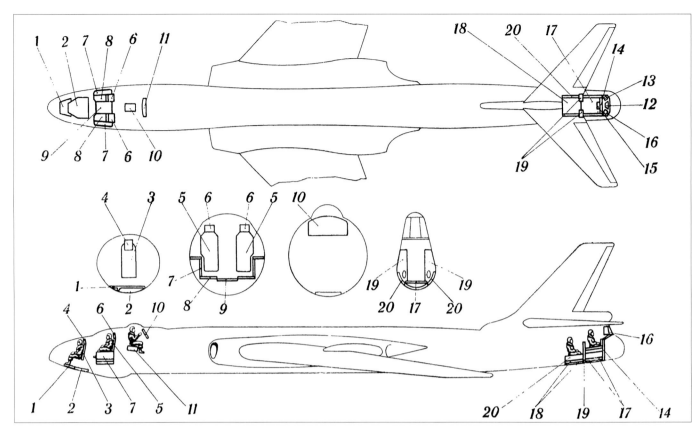

The Tu-16's armour protection

Structural element	Description
a) Front cabin:	
Navigator/bomb-aimer's station floor	8-mm (0⁵/₁₆ in) APBA-1
Navigator/bomb-aimer's station ejection hatch cover	24-mm (≈ 0¹⁵/₁₆ in) APBA-1
Navigator/bomb-aimer's seat backrest	24-mm APBA-1
Navigator/bomb-aimer's seat headrest	10-mm (0²⁵/₆₄ in) KVK-2/5Ts
Pilots' seat backrests	20-mm (0²⁵/₃₂ in) KVK-2/5Ts
Pilots' seat headrests	25-mm (0⁶³/₆₄ in) KVK-2/5Ts *
Flight deck side armour	2 x 6-mm (0¹⁵/₆₄ in) APBA-1
Flight deck floor	2 x 8-mm APBA-1
	1 x 15-mm (0¹⁹/₃₂ in) glassfibre
	Textolite composite
Navigator/operator's upper rear armour	10-mm KVK-2/5Ts
Navigator/operator's seat pan	8-mm APBA-1
b) Rear cabin:	
Rear bulletproof glass pane	135-mm (5⁵/₁₆ in) Triplex glass
Lateral bulletproof glass panes	2 x 105-mm (≈ 4⅛ in) Triplex glass
Tail gunner's armour	24-mm KVK-2/5Ts †
Podium for PS-53K sighting station	10-mm KVK-2/5Ts
Tail gunner's station glazing framework	10-mm ML5-T4
Rear cabin entry hatch cover	5-mm (0¹³/₆₄ in) ML5-T4 + 5-mm APBA-1
GRO's station ejection hatch cover	5-mm ML5-T4 + 5-mm APBA-1
GRO's armour	2 x 14-mm (0³⁵/₆₄ in) APBA-1
GRO's and tail gunner's side armour	2 x 5-mm APBA-1
Tail gunner's rear armour at frame 75	10-mm KVK-2/5Ts

* From c/n Kazan'-built c/n 4200601; it was 20 mm thick up to and including c/n 4200505
† From c/n 4201201 onwards; up to and including c/n 4201110 it was made of variable-thickness APBA-1L24

The Tu-16's armour protection.
1. Navigator/bomb-aimer's station floor; 2. Navigator/bomb-aimer's ejection hatch cover; 3. Navigator/bomb-aimer's seat backrest; 4. Navigator/bomb-aimer's seat headrest; 5. Pilots' seat backrests; 6. Pilots' seat headrests; 7. Flight deck side armour; 8, 9. Flight deck floor; 10. Navigator/operator's armour plate; 11. Navigator/operator's seat pan; 12. Rear bulletproof glass pane; 13. Tail gunner's lateral bulletproof glass panes; 14. Tail gunner's rear armour plate; 15. Podium for PS-53K sighting station; 16. Tail gunner's station glazing framework; 17. Rear cabin entry hatch (tail gunner's ejection hatch) cover; 18. GRO's ejection hatch cover; 19. GRO's rear armour; 20. GRO's and tail gunner's side armour.

iary parallax computing module (*avtomaht dopolnitel'novo parallaksa*). Other components are an MA-500 converter, KS-3 and KS-4 synchro-sensors and receivers, SU-3R and EMU U-700 servo-amplifiers, DV-1100A drive motors and control panels.

All cannons are equipped with electropneumatically operated AP-10 automatic cocking mechanisms (*avtomaht perezaryadki* – automatic reloading device), using the main pneumatic system. The rounds are counted by USB-1 counters (*oonifitseerovannyy shchotchik boyepripahsov*), one for each cannon. An S-13 gun camera is provided for the forward-firing cannon.

The PRS-1 Argon gun ranging radar enables gunnery in the rear hemisphere under all visibility conditions. It scans a cone of ±35° in azimuth and elevation.

Crew protection and crew rescue system: All crew stations are provided with armour protection against cannon shell fragments as detailed in the table on this page. Three types of armour

<table>
<tr><td colspan="2">Performance of the Tu-16 sans suffixe (1956 production)</td></tr>
</table>

Length overall	35.2 m (115 ft 5⁵⁄₆₄ in)
Fuselage length	34.8 m (114 ft 2⁵⁄₆₄ in)
Wing span	32.989 m (108 ft 2²⁵⁄₃₂ in)
Wing mean aerodynamic chord (MAC)	5.021 m (16 ft 5⁴³⁄₆₄ in)
Aileron span (each)	5.3 m (17 ft 4²¹⁄₃₂ in)
Flap span (each)	6.87 m (22 ft 6¹⁵⁄₃₂ in)
Height:	
theoretical (landing gear in no-load condition)	10.355 m (33 ft 11⁴³⁄₆₄ in)
practical (height on ground)	9.85 m (32 ft 3⁵¹⁄₆₄ in)
Horizontal tail span	11.75 m (38 ft 6¹⁹⁄₃₂ in)
Landing gear track	9.775 m (32 ft 0²⁷⁄₃₂ in)
Landing gear wheelbase	10.913 m (35 ft 9⁴¹⁄₆₄ in)
Fuselage cross-section area	4.9 m² (52.74 sq ft)
Wing area	164.65 m² (1,772.28 sq ft)
Aileron area (total)	14.77 m² (158.98 sq ft)
Vertical tail area	23.305 m² (250.85 sq ft)
Rudder area	5.213 m² (56.11 sq ft)
Horizontal tail area	34.452 m² (370.83 sq ft)
Elevator area (total)	8.646 m² (93.06 sq ft)
Dry weight	36,600 kg (80,690 lb)
Empty weight (with trapped fuel, starter fuel and oil)	37,040 kg (81,660 lb)
Take-off weight:	
normal (in maximum-range flight)	55,000 kg (121,250 lb) [1]
maximum	72,000 kg (158,730 lb) [1]
Fuel load:	
normal	13,660 kg (30,115 lb)
in overload configuration	30,220 kg (66,620 lb)
maximum for exceptional occasions	30,660 kg (67,590 lb)
Crew weight	600 kg (1,320 lb)
Normal bomb load	3,000 kg (6,610 lb)
Weight of cannon ammunition (1,800 rounds)	700 kg (1,540 lb)
Landing weight:	
normal	48,000 kg (105,820 lb)
maximum (exceptional conditions)	55,000 kg (121,250 lb)
Unstick speed:	
with a 57,000-kg (125,660-lb) take-off weight	250 km/h (155 mph)
with a 71,560-kg (157,760-lb) take-off weight	280 km/h (174 mph)
Maximum landing gear transition speed	375-400 km/h (233-248 mph)
Maximum permitted indicated airspeed with flaps down:	
20° flap	400 km/h (248 mph)
above 25° flap	340 km/h (211 mph)
Maximum speed at take-off power	
with a 55,000 kg all-up weight:	
at 6,250 m (20,500 ft)	992 km/h (616 mph)
at 10,000 m (32,810 ft)	938 km/h (582 mph)
Maximum speed at nominal power	
with a 55,000 kg AUW:	
at 6,250 m	958 km/h (595 mph)
at 10,000 m	915 km/h (568 mph)
Maximum Mach number	0.9
Landing speed	
with a 44,000-kg (97,000-lb) landing weight	223km/h (138 mph)

Dynamic pressure limit at an AUW	
of 55,000-72,000 kg (121,250-158,730 lb):	
in level flight	2,200 kg/m² (451.0 lb/sq ft) [2]
in a descent	2,800 kg/m² (574.0 lb/sq ft) [3]
Dynamic pressure limit at an AUW up to 55,000 kg:	
in level flight	2,300 kg/m² (471.56 lb/sq ft) [4]
in a descent	2,800 kg/m² (574.0 lb/sq ft) [3]
Service ceiling at nominal power:	
with a 57,000-kg take-off weight	12,800 m (41,990 ft)
with a 71,560-kg take-off weight	11,300 m (37,070 ft)
Time to reach service ceiling:	
with a 57,000-kg TOW	31 minutes
with a 71,560-kg TOW	38 minutes
Maximum technical range ('hi-hi-hi' flight profile)	
with a 3,000-kg (6,610-lb) bomb load:	
with a 71,560-kg TOW	5,640 km (3,503 miles)
with a 72,000-kg TOW	5,760 km (3,577 miles)
Take-off run at take-off power with 20° flap:	
with a 57,000-kg take-off weight	1,140 m (3,740 ft)
with a 71,560-kg take-off weight	1,900 m (6,230 ft)
Take-off distance to h=25 m (82 ft) at take-off	
power with 20° flap:	
with a 57,000-kg take-off weight	1,885 m (6,180 ft)
with a 71,560-kg take-off weight	3,165 m (10,380 ft)
Landing run with a 44,000-kg	
landing weight and 35° flap:	
without brake parachute	1,655 m (5,430 ft)
with brake parachute	1,050 m (3,440 ft)
Landing distance from h=25 m with a 44,000-kg	
landing weight and 35° flap:	
without brake parachute	2,785 m (9,140 ft)
with brake parachute	2,180 m (7,150 ft)
Time from brake release to unstick:	
with 57,000-kg TOW	28.7 sec
with a 71,560-kg TOW	45.0 sec
Time from touchdown to standstill with a 44,000-kg	
landing weight:	
without brake parachute	34.5 sec
with brake parachute	28.5 sec
CG position:	
empty aircraft, gear down	34.3% MAC
with a 72,000 -kg take-off weight	22.6-25.4% MAC
with a 55,000-kg all-up weight	24.7-25.4% MAC
with a 44,000-kg landing weight and 6,750 kg	
(14,880 lb) of fuel remaining	24.5-24.8% MAC

Notes:

1. Different pages in the same structural manual give contradictory information, variously stating 72,000 kg as the maximum TOW or the normal TOW (in the latter case 55,000 kg is stated as the normal AUW)

2. Up to an altitude of 6,250 m (20,510 ft) at 675 km/h (419 mph) IAS

3. At 760 km/h (472 mph) IAS

4. Up to an altitude of 6,000 m (19,685 ft) at 690 km/h (428 mph) IAS

are used: cast APBA-1L24 duralumin (*aviatsionnaya pro-tivo'oskolochnaya bronya alyuminiyevaya* – aviation-specific aluminium armour for protection against shell fragments), cast ML5-T4 magnesium alloy and KVK-2/5Ts steel.

In the event of an in-flight emergency or a shootdown, all crewmembers are provided with PLK-45 seat-type parachutes (*parashoot lyotchika, kvadrahtnyy* – pilot's parachute with square canopy, 1945 model) and cartridge-fired ejection seats developed

The Tu-16's speed performance

Altitude, m (ft)	True airspeed, km/h (mph)	Indicated airspeed, km/h (mph)	Mach number
a) at take-off power (4,650 rpm)			
sea level (0 m)	675 (419)	688 (427)	0.787
1,000 (3,280)	708 (439)	690 (428)	0.790
2,000 (6,560)	745 (462)	694 (431)	0.794
3,000 (9,840)	784 (487)	698 (433)	0.798
4,000 (13,120)	828 (514)	703 (436)	0.803
5,000 (16,400)	873 (542)	709 (440)	0.808
6,250 (20,510)	992 (616)	762 (473)	0.872
7,000 (22,965)	983 (610)	730 (453)	0.874
8,000 (26,250)	970 (602)	685 (425)	0.876
9,000 (29,530)	955 (593)	640 (397)	0.875
10,000 (32,810)	938 (582)	594 (368)	0.870
11,000 (36,090)	919 (570)	547 (339)	0.863
12,000 (39,370)	897 (557)	493 (306)	0.843
b) at nominal power (4,350 rpm)			
sea level (0 m)	675 (419)	688 (427)	0.787
1,000 (3,280)	708 (439)	690 (428)	0.790
2,000 (6,560)	745 (462)	694 (431)	0.794
3,000 (9,840)	780 (484)	698 (433)	0.798
4,000 (13,120)	828 (514)	703 (436)	0.803
5,000 (16,400)	873 (542)	709 (440)	0.808
6,250 (20,510)	958 (595)	735 (456)	0.844
7,000 (22,965)	952 (591)	706 (440)	0.848
8,000 (26,250)	942 (585)	665 (413)	0.852
9,000 (29,530)	930 (577)	620 (385)	0.855
10,000 (32,810)	915 (568)	575 (357)	0.850
11,000 (36,090)	895 (556)	528 (328)	0.843
12,000 (39,370)	872 (541)	480 (298)	0.820

The Tu-16's time-to-height performance at nominal power

Altitude, m (ft)	Rate of climb, m/sec (ft/min)	Time, minutes
a) with a 57,000-kg (125,660-lb) take-off weight		
sea level (0 m)	22.0 (4,330)	–
1,000 (3,280)	20.4 (4,015)	0.8
2,000 (6,560)	19.0 (3,740)	1.7
3,000 (9,840)	17.4 (3,425)	2.5
4,000 (13,120)	15.8 (3,110)	3.5
5,000 (16,400)	14.2 (2,795)	4.5
6,000 (19,685)	12.6 (2,480)	5.9
7,000 (22,965)	11.0 (2,165)	7.4
8,000 (26,250)	9.6 (1,889)	9.0
9,000 (29,530)	8.0 (1,574)	10.8
10,000 (32,810)	6.4 (1,259)	13.1
11,000 (36,090)	4.8 (944)	16.0
11,300 (37,070)	4.0 (787)	17.2
12,000 (39,370)	2.4 (472	21.0
12,800 (41,990)	0.5 (98)	31.0
b) with a 71,560-kg (157,760-lb) take-off weight		
sea level (0 m)	18.0 (3,543)	–
1,000 (3,280)	15.0 (2,952)	1.0
2,000 (6,560)	13.4 (2,637)	2.2
3,000 (9,840)	12.0 (2,362)	3.7
4,000 (13,120)	10.7 (2,106)	5.0
5,000 (16,400)	9.4 (1,850)	5.6
6,000 (19,685)	8.0 (1,574)	8.6
7,000 (22,965)	6.7 (1,318)	11.0
8,000 (26,250)	5.3 (1,043)	13.8
9,000 (29,530)	4.0 (787)	17.3
10,000 (32,810)	2.6 (511)	22.5
11,000 (36,090)	1.2 (236)	31.0
11,300 (37,070)	0.5 (98)	38.0
12,000 (39,370)	–	–
12,800 (41,990)	–	–

by the Tupolev OKB specifically for the Tu-16. The pilots eject upwards; before ejection their seats are forcibly slid into the extreme aft position, whereupon the flight deck roof hatches are jettisoned pneumatically and the control columns folded away to prevent injury. The G force on ejection is 15-18 Gs, lasting 0.2-0.3 seconds; the initial ejection speed is 20-22 m/sec (65-72 ft/sec) to ensure that the pilots' seats clear the vertical tail.

The other crewmembers (navigator/bomb-aimer, Nav/Op, gunner/radio-operator and tail gunner) eject downwards after jettisoning the entry or escape hatch covers below the seats. The G force for those ejecting downwards is much lower (3-5 Gs).

Each seat has a dished pan to take a seat-type parachute; the pan is attached to a lightweight frame on which it moves along guide rails firmly secured to the fuselage structure. The seat has a base, a back, a headrest and grips on the sides of the seat pan. The piston of the ejection gun is rigidly attached to the seat frame, and its cylinder to the fuselage structure. The head of the piston is packed with a cartridge which explodes when the firing pin is pulled by means of a handle on the right-hand grip, the pressure ejecting the piston together with the seat.

In the event of a belly landing or ditching, the crew can escape from the front cabin through the pilots' ejection hatches and from the rear cabin through the emergency exit in the tail gunner's sta-

tion glazing. The aircraft is able to remain afloat long enough for the crew to use the life rafts, and flotation can be significantly enhanced by dumping the fuel before ditching.

Two LAS-5M five-man inflatable life rafts are carried. They are stored in special boxes in the upper part of the fuselage on the port side between frames 12-15 (for the crew members in the front cabin) and in the fin fillet between frames 62-63 (for those in the rear cabin). The raft bay covers cane be opened both from inside the cabins and from the outside; upon release the rafts are automatically inflated by CO_2 from the two bottles they are equipped with. Each crew member had his own first-aid kit, thermos flask and emergency rations. When the crew abandoned the aircraft they took with them the emergency and emergency SOS radios. In the 1980s the Soviet Air Force and Soviet Navy started providing the Tu-16s with radio beacons working with the KOSPAS search and rescue satellite system (*kosmicheskaya sistema poiska avareeynykh soodov* – space system for locating vessels in distress).

Each crewmember is supplied with a personal first-aid kit, a thermos flask, in-flight rations, an emergency radio and emergency rations.

Chapter 7

In Action

The baseline Tu-16 bomber achieved initial operational capability with the Soviet Air Force in February-March 1954. As already mentioned, the type made its public debut during the 1954 May Day parade in Moscow when a formation of nine Tu-16s passed over Red Square.

The western military districts (MDs) of the USSR were the first to receive the Tu-16, being closest to the potential adversary; this was normal practice when fielding new combat materiel. As had been the case with the Tu-4, the first Long-Range Aviation unit to receive the type in early 1954 was the 45th *Gomel'skaya* TBAD of the 50th VA (*vozdooshnaya armiya* – Air Army); the division was headquartered at Bolbasovo AB near Orsha (Vitebsk Region, northern Belorussia) and assigned to the Belorussian MD. The 45th Division's 203rd *Orlovskiy* GvTBAP, which was then based at Bolbasovo AB but moved to Baranovichi in the Brest Region of western Belorussia in 1955, led the way. This regiment

was something of a 'showcase unit' which was the first to receive new combat hardware in the DA. The honorary appellation *Orlovskiy* had been conferred on this unit for its part in liberating the Russian city of Oryol during the Great Patriotic War; the 45th Division had received its honorary appellation for its part in liberating the city of Gomel' in south-eastern Belorussia. The 203rd Regiment was followed in short order by the division's other two regiments – the 402nd TBAP at Bolbasovo and the 52nd GvTBAP, then based at Machoolishchi AB a short way south of Minsk.

Service tests of the Tu-16 were conducted in the 45th TBAD and were complicated quite a bit by the bomber's teething troubles. At times the special teams from the OKB and the factories making modifications to the bombers would replace the units' own tech staff completely on the flight lines. Suffice it to say that the list of defects discovered and complaints voiced during the Tu-16's evaluation period filled 12 hefty volumes!

A Tu-16 missile carrier equipped with a Siren'-D jammer and the Rogovitsa formation keeping system on the 929th GLITs flight line at Vladimirovka AB, Akhtoobinsk.

Above: The Soviet Air Force's 'sunburst' flag.

Above left: A pristine Tu-16A coded '35 Red' is readied for a sortie on a winter night.

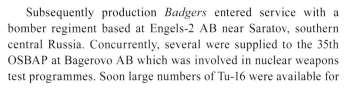

Left: A pair of Tu-16s make a low-level pass. The aircraft coded '10' is a missile carrier while the lead aircraft ('08') has no pylons and may be a Tu-16Z tanker.

Below left: An IAB-3000 practice bomb is ready for loading into a Tu-16's bomb bay.

Above right: A Tu-16 is being refuelled. The *Badger* did not have single-point pressure refuelling, and filling the tanks was a laborious procedure that involved crawling all over the aircraft.

Right: A technician uses a tall ladder to check the rudder of a Tu-16, while another is at work on the equipment in the rear pressure cabin.

Subsequently production *Badgers* entered service with a bomber regiment based at Engels-2 AB near Saratov, southern central Russia. Concurrently, several were supplied to the 35th OSBAP at Bagerovo AB which was involved in nuclear weapons test programmes. Soon large numbers of Tu-16 were available for service with the DA units and then with the AVMF (naval operations are described separately).

Tu-16R reconnaissance aircraft began to enter service with the DA in the mid-1950s. The first unit to receive them in October 1956, was the 199th **Brest***skiy* GvODRAP at Nezhin in the Chernigov Region, central Ukraine (Kiev MD), which operated the type until it re-equipped completely with the Tu-22R in early 1967. The honorary appellation had been given for the unit's part in liberating the city of Brest (Belorussia), which was the first to be attacked during the German invasion of the Soviet Union on 22nd June 1941.

As per 1st January 1955, the Long-Range Aviation had a total of 30 heavy bomber regiments distributed between 12 heavy bomber divisions. Of these, ten divisions were equipped with Tu-4s, operating a full complement of 63 to 94 aircraft each; the remaining two were equipped with Tu-16s – or rather underequipped, having no more than 54 aircraft each instead of the required 130. Of these, one division with 63 Tu-4s and another with 43 Tu-16s were so-called special divisions armed with 'special munitions', that is, nuclear weapons.

At the time the piston-engined Tu-4 was the backbone of the Soviet heavy bomber force. Now, the introduction of an aircraft

belonging to a new generation which took the Long-Range Aviation into the jet age necessitated changes in the DA's order of battle, the fundamentals of its operational training, and radical improvements to its airfield network and logistics system. The significant differences between the Tu-4 and Tu-16, particularly in speed, called for a modernisation of the existing airfields – concrete runways had to be strengthened and extended, taxiways and parking areas reorganised. The switch from Avgas to kerosene required the petrol, oil and lubricant (POL) storage facilities to be rebuilt and expanded to cope with the much larger quantities of fuel for the Tu-16's thirsty engines. Last but not least, the airbases were equipped with new radio communications systems and navigation aids (air traffic control radars and ILS beacons).

Up to then, heavy bombers were parked in long rows on the flight lines, which made them vulnerable in the event of an air raid. The Tu-16 gained the distinction of being the DA's first type to use dispersed parking in earthen revetments (which were sometimes covered with camouflage netting) to minimise vulnerability to air raids and missile strikes. The introduction of the Tu-16 required a complete overhaul of all airfields used by the Long-Range Aviation – they were upgraded to 1st class, which means a runway length of 3,250 m (10,660 ft), and often to an even higher grade – so-called unclassed airfield with a runway in excess of 3,250 m. Such airfields were suitable for practically any type of aircraft, including the main Soviet strategic bomber, the Tu-95. Civil airfields equipped to these standards did not come into being in the Soviet Union until the end of the 1950s.

By the mid-1950s the Tu-16 was in large-scale production, and by the end of the decade it had become the Long-Range Aviation's primary bomber type. By 1st January 1958, the DA's bomber fleet had changed qualitatively – the number of Tu-16s had grown to 1,120 while the Tu-4 fleet had shrunk to 778. Because the new Soviet leader Nikita S. Khrushchov had a predilection towards

missile systems (especially intercontinental ballistic missiles) to the detriment of manned combat aircraft, many bomber regiments were transformed into ICBM units; others became military airlift units. Outlining the Long-Range Aviation's development prospects, Soviet Air Force C-in-C Air Chief Marshal Konstantin A. Vershinin and Long-Range Aviation Commander Air Marshal Vladimir A. Soodets suggested that by 1st January 1961 the DA's bomber fleet should have the following composition:

'- new aircraft types – 405 aircraft (15.5%);
- obsolete Tu-16s – 1,381 aircraft (52.7%);
- Tu-4 piston-engined bombers – 255 aircraft (9.2%);
- shortage of aircraft [versus required full strength] – 578 aircraft (22%).'

The *Badger* retained this position until the mid-1980s when it was gradually replaced by the supersonic Tu-22M2/Tu-22M3 *Backfire-B/C* third-generation long-range bomber. This dominating position also extended to the Soviet Naval Aviation for the same reasons.

The air regiments operating the Tu-16 were usually part of a heavy bomber division (TBAD, roughly equivalent to a Bomb Group (Heavy) in the USAF) but could be independent (that is, direct reporting) units; the latter operated mainly reconnaissance or ECM variants or, in rare cases, bombers. Each TBAD consisted of two or three heavy bomber regiments (TBAP, ≈ Bomb Wing (Heavy)). In the 1950s the Tu-16 was in service with three of the Long-Range Aviation's air armies (VA), roughly equivalent to a numbered air force in the USAF. These were the 5th VA headquartered in Blagoveshchensk (the Soviet Far East), the 43rd VA headquartered in Kirovograd (the Ukraine) and the 50th VA headquartered in Smolensk (European Russia).

The Tu-16 was inducted into squadron service rapidly thanks to the thought which had gone into its design and the shrewd choice of stability and handling properties under different flying conditions. At cruising speeds the gradient of stick forces was within the acceptable limits for heavy aircraft (30-100 kgf/66-220 lbf). At high Mach numbers they increased more steeply and the controls became heavy: when the Tu-16 was doing Mach 0.9 at

The versions of the Tu-16 operated by the Air Force (Long-Range Aviation), the Naval Aviation and the Air Defence Force (PVO)			
Version	**Air Force**	**Naval Aviation**	**Air Defence Force**
Tu-16	yes	yes	no
Tu-16A	yes	yes	no
Tu-16 (Z)	yes	yes	no
Tu-16N	yes	no	no
Tu-16T	no	yes	no
Tu-16S	no	yes	no
Tu-16SP	no	yes	no
Tu-16R	yes	yes	no
Tu-16RP	yes	no	no
Tu-16 'Yolka'	yes	yes	no
Tu-16Ye	yes	yes	no
Tu-16SPS	yes	yes	no
Tu-16P 'Buket'/'Ficus'/'Cactus'	yes	no	no
Tu-16RR	yes	no	no
Tu-16KS	yes	yes	no
Tu-16KSR-2	yes	yes	no
Tu-16KSR-2-11	yes	yes	no
Tu-16K-11-16	yes	yes	no
Tu-16KSR-2-5	yes	yes	no
Tu-16K-26	yes	yes	no
Tu-16K-10	no	yes	no
Tu-16K-10-26	no	yes	no
Tu-16RM	yes	no	no
Tu-16RM-1	no	yes	no
Tu-16RM-2	no	yes	no
Tu-16KRM	yes	yes	yes
M-16	yes	yes	yes

an altitude of 10,000 m (32,810 ft) with the centre of gravity at 21% MAC, the stick forces reached 120-130 kgf (264-286 lbf).

The Tu-16 was stable in the pitch up to Mach 0.83, with some instability appearing at Mach 0.83-0.87 but not causing too much trouble. At Mach 0.87 the aircraft became rock-steady once more

Right: A Tu-16KSR-2-5 at rest. The changing of the guard is in progress – Tu-22M2 bombers can be seen in the revetments beyond.

Below left: A Tu-16R *Badger-E* equipped with an SPS-100 jammer in a large tail fairing completes its landing run.

Below: Tu-16 Yolka '32 Red' is due to depart on a mission shortly, with an APA-2 GPU connected for engine starting.

– in fact, significantly more stable than at lower speeds. As far as roll stability was concerned, the Tu-16 behaved normally at speeds up to Mach 0.8. At higher speeds lateral stability deteriorated sharply until, between Mach 0.87 and 0.9, it became neutral, and was then lost as speed was increased further. This induced a reverse roll reaction to rudder inputs (the aircraft rolled right instead of left when left rudder was applied).

The aircraft's Mach limit determined by its longitudinal stability and controllability was Mach 0.9 at up to 10,000 m; higher speeds below this altitude resulted in an inadmissible increase in all control forces – the machine became to all intents and purposes uncontrollable. The Tu-16 could only exceed Mach 0.9 in a dive from 10,000-13,000 m (32,810-42,650 ft) in order to evade SAMs.

During squadron service, the following indicated airspeed limits were imposed:

• 645 km/h (400 mph) at altitudes up to 7,000 m (22,965 ft) with an all-up weight of 70,000-75,800 kg (154,320-167,110 lb);
• 685 km/h (425 mph) at altitudes up to 6,250 m (20,510 ft) with an all-up weight of 55,000-70,000 kg (121,250-154,320 lb);
• 700 km/h (435 mph) at altitudes up to 6,000 m (19,685 ft) with an all-up weight of 55,000 kg or less;
• 420 km/h (260 mph) at all altitudes with the undercarriage extended.

The maximum permissible IAS with the flaps deployed was 400 km/h (248 mph) with 20° flap and 340 km/h (211 mph) with greater flap settings. The maximum landing gear transition speed was 400 km/h IAS.

The Tu-16 served in roughly equal numbers with the Soviet Air Force (Long-Range Aviation) and the Naval Aviation. By the early 1960s it had completely replaced the Tu-4 in DA service. In AVMF

Above and left: A pair of Tu-16KSR-2s carrying grey-painted live KSR-2 missiles. '10 Red' are fitted with an ASO-16/3 chaff dispenser, while '12 Red' has none.

The unit badge of the 185th GvTBAP based at Poltava, one of the first DA units to receive the Tu-16.

Above right: A Tu-16P 'Buket' 'burns rubber' at the moment of touchdown.

Right: A Tu-16K-26P with a Siren'-MD jammer in a UKhO tail fairing at Akhtoobinsk.

regiments the Tu-16 superseded the Tu-14T torpedo-bomber and, to a certain extent, the Il-28T torpedo-bomber and Il-28R photo reconnaissance aircraft. Most of the many Soviet Air Force and Soviet Navy air regiments equipped with the type had previously operated piston-engined aircraft, but some were newly established as jet bomber units. In the course of the Tu-16's forty years of service some of the units operating it were disbanded, others re-equipped with newer aircraft, and there were some which, after operating more modern types for a while, reverted to the *Badger*.

Special tests were carried out to expand the Tu-16's operational envelope. In 1956 (some sources say 12th July 1955) Lt.-Col. G. S. Yaglov, a wartime bomber pilot with a lot of experience, successfully took off from an unpaved runway in a Tu-16 for the first time, subsequently landing on the same runway; the mission was personally authorised by DA Commander Air Marshal Vladimir A. Soodets. After this, operations from sparsely equipped auxiliary airfields in the tundra and on the Arctic ice were made on a regular basis without any adverse consequences.

By the end of the 1950s the Long-Range Aviation's Tu-16 *sans suffixe* and Tu-16A bombers, Tu-16SPS, Tu-16 'Yolka' and Tu-16Ye ECM aircraft, and Tu-16R reconnaissance aircraft were in service with the heavy bomber regiments and independent long-range

reconnaissance air regiments (ODRAP). The task of the former was to strike at targets deep inside enemy territory and photograph the results of bombing raids, as well as objectives of opportunity en route to and from the target area. The reconnaissance regiments were to carry out PHOTINT and ELINT missions by day or night in their support. Their ECM-equipped aircraft were to be used as required to assist bomber formations in penetrating strong enemy air defences.

Details of Tu-16 allocations before 1960 are rather incomplete. For example, the 13th GvTBAD (then comprising the 184th and 226th GvTBAPs in Poltava and the 202nd GvTBAP in Mirgorod) started converting to the type in January 1955. Sol'tsy AB in the Novgorod Region of north-western Russia hosted two Tu-16 regiments of the 326th TBAD – the 840th TBAP (which converted in 1955) and the 345th TBAP. The latter converted from the Tu-4 in 1956, remaining in existence until 1959 and retaining the Tu-16 even in 'after-life' (of which more will be discussed later). The 1023rd TBAP was established at Uzin AB (pronounced *oozin*), Kiev Region, in February 1956, initially flying six Tu-16s and a single Tu-95; a year later it was up to full strength, with Tu-95s as the principal hardware and the Tu-16s equipping Sqn 4 which was the proficiency training squadron. On 16th-30th December 1958,

The badge of the 444th *Berlinskiy* TBAP.

Above: A KSR-2 missile shortly after being hooked up to a Tu-16KSR-2. Someone had taken the trouble to paint a tomcat on the missile.

Left: Close-up of a slightly different tomcat on another missile – obviously the handiwork of the same artist in the same unit. The drawing is... well, a bit naughty, to say the least!

Below: A Tu-16R *Badger-E* with a Siren'-D jammer in front and a Siren'-MD jammer in a UKhO tail fairing flies a mission in 1987.

Above right: A pair of Tu-16Rs in echelon formation.

Right: A fine study a Tu-16R *Badger-F*.

the unit redeployed to its new home base, Chagan AB near Semipalatinsk in Kazakhstan. There are indications that the 1226th TBAP, which was formed in Belaya Tserkov' in 1959 and redeployed to the same Chagan AB, also started life with the Tu-16 before equipping with Tu-95s.

The units' command staff took conversion training at the factories building the Tu-16, while the rest of the crews were trained on site. The training proceeded at a rapid pace, some crews logging as many as 190-220 flight hours per annum. In the very first year of operations, the most experienced crews started making sorties beyond the Arctic Circle.

The introduction of stand-off air-to-surface missiles in the DA began in 1955, when the 116th TAD (*tyazholaya aviadiveeziya* – Heavy Air Division, without the 'bomber' designator) was formed at Ostrov AB near Pskov, comprising the 12th and 685th TAPs (*tyazholyy aviapolk* – Heavy Air Regiment); they were equipped with Tu-16KS missile carriers and were joined in 1958 by the 132nd TAP. The division also had a squadron flying MiG-17SDK 'missile emulators' (*samolyot-dooblyor Komety* – 'doubler aircraft', that is, analogue, of the Comet missile) for practicing missile launches without wasting KS-1 missiles. The fighters were modified to feature the KS-1's guidance system, including the K-1M radar installed in a large bullet-shaped radome on the air intake upper lip and the aft-looking antenna on top of the fin receiving mid-course guidance signals from the Tu-16KS. The MiG-17SDK rendezvous'd with the Tu-16KS and was guided by it, just like a real KS-1 missile; the *Badger-B's* crew did all the preparations for launch as if they were working with the real thing, with the exception of engine starting as the MiG's engine was already running. The MiG-17SDK's pilot sat back and did not touch the controls until the MiG-17SDK was within 500-600 m (1,640-1,970 ft) from the target; then the pilot took over at and flew the fighter back to base.

Meanwhile, starting in 1956, a number of Tu-16A bombers with nukes loaded were on full-time ready alert. This quick-reaction alert (QRA) duty was abolished in 1961.

A decision taken at the top level in late 1959 signified a downturn of the Long-Range Aviation's fortunes. In spite of all the efforts the Air Force command in general, and the DA command in particular, were making to convince the Soviet government that manned combat aircraft were 'getting second wind' and should not be dismissed so easily, a new service of the Soviet Armed Forces – the Strategic Missile Force (RVSN – *Raketnyye voyska strategicheskovo naznacheniya*) – was established on 17th December 1959. Apparently during the preceding discussions at the Politburo (the Political Bureau of the Communist Party's Central Committee, the top policy making organ of the USSR) Soviet Air Force C-in-C Air Chief Marshal Konstantin A. Vershinin was not argumentative enough to win over his opponents – Marshal Mitrofan I. Nedelin (the first C-in-C of the RVSN) and Marshal Dmitriy F. Ustinov (then Vice-Chairman of the Council of Ministers and Chairman of the VPK) who succeeded in ramming home their idea of a separate service with intercontinental ballistic missiles, impressing the members of the Politburo with the advertised might of this new weapon. By comparison, in the US all ICBMs were

A US Air Force 21st TFW/43rd TFS McDonnell Douglas F-15A Eagle from Elmendorf AFB, Alaska, intercepts a blue-coded Tu-16R (ZA) *Badger-E* which is doing a photo run.

Right: F-14A-135-GR BuNo 162608/ NF-106 of CVW-2/VF-1 'Wolfpack' from USS *Ranger* escorts a pair of Tu-16R *Badger-Fs* reconnoitring the carrier task force.

under the control of the US Air Force's Strategic Air Command (SAC).

As a result, in the course of the military reform that began in 1960 two of the Long-Range Aviation's three air armies were transferred to the RVSN and redesignated as missile armies. Several bomber divisions were similarly transformed into missile divisions. The Air Force's remaining heavy bomber assets were reorganised, with a new order of battle that included three independent heavy bomber corps (OTBAK – *otdel'nyy tyazholyy bombardirovochnyy aviakorpus*) to which the heavy bomber divisions and independent air regiments now reported. Specifically, the remnants of the former 43rd VA became the basis of the 2nd OTBAK headquartered in Vinnitsa (the Ukraine); units of the former 50th

VA were organised into the 6th OTBAK headquartered in Smolensk, while the 8th OTBAK (initially headquartered in Blagoveshchensk and later, from 1965 onwards, in Irkutsk, Eastern Siberia) was fashioned together from elements of the 5th VA and the 19th Far Eastern Air Corps on 13th March 1960. The 8th OTBAK had the honorary appellation *Smolenskiy*, inheriting it from the wartime 8th Long-Range Aviation Corps; the latter had received it for its part in liberating the Russian city of Smolensk.

The three corps reported to the Long-Range Aviation Command. This order of battle (or 'corps system', as it is known) remained in existence for 20 years (until 1980). At the start of its existence, in the early 1960s, the DA's three corps had ten heavy bomber divisions comprising 26 regiments, plus six independent

Left: The crew of a Tu-16R *Badger-F* equipped with a Siren'-D jammer pose with their mount. Although the airmen are wearing life vests indicating overwater missions, the uniforms reveal this is an Air Force unit, not a Navy unit.

Right: Another Tu-16R with SRS-1 and SRS-3 SIGINT systems approaches a NATO naval task force at low level.

bomber and reconnaissance regiments. 18 of the 32 regiments were equipped with various versions of the Tu-16, as were the three independent ELINT/ECM and tanker squadrons – although this changed as the Tu-22 was fielded in growing numbers. In addition, the 43rd TsBP i PLS training centre and the Arctic Special Operations Group (of which more will be said later in the book) reported directly to the DA Command.

By the early 1960s the Air Force regiments operating the Tu-16 were based at the following locations. In the European regions of the USSR, the westernmost Belorussian Military District had Tu-16 units in Baranovichi, Bobruisk (Mogilyov Region, eastern Belorussia), at Machoolishchi AB on the southern outskirts of Minsk and Zyabrovka AB near Gomel'; in the north-west it was Tartu in Estonia (Baltic MD) and Sol'tsy AB in the Novgorod

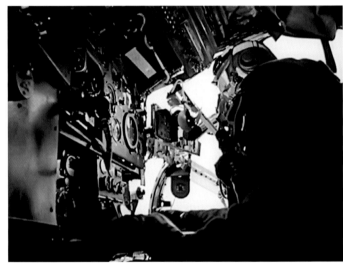

Top: The pilots of a Tu-16 as seen from the navigator's station. The red handles in the foreground are the emergency wheel brake handles.

Centre: The navigator/operator of a Tu-16 at his workstation. Note the radarscope with its rubber sunblind.

Top: The pilots' instrument panels and the passage to the navigator's station.

Centre: The navigator at work, facing the port side.

Above and above left: The captain's workstation. Note the PKI-1 gunsight above the instrument panel shroud indicating that a forward-firing cannon is fitted.

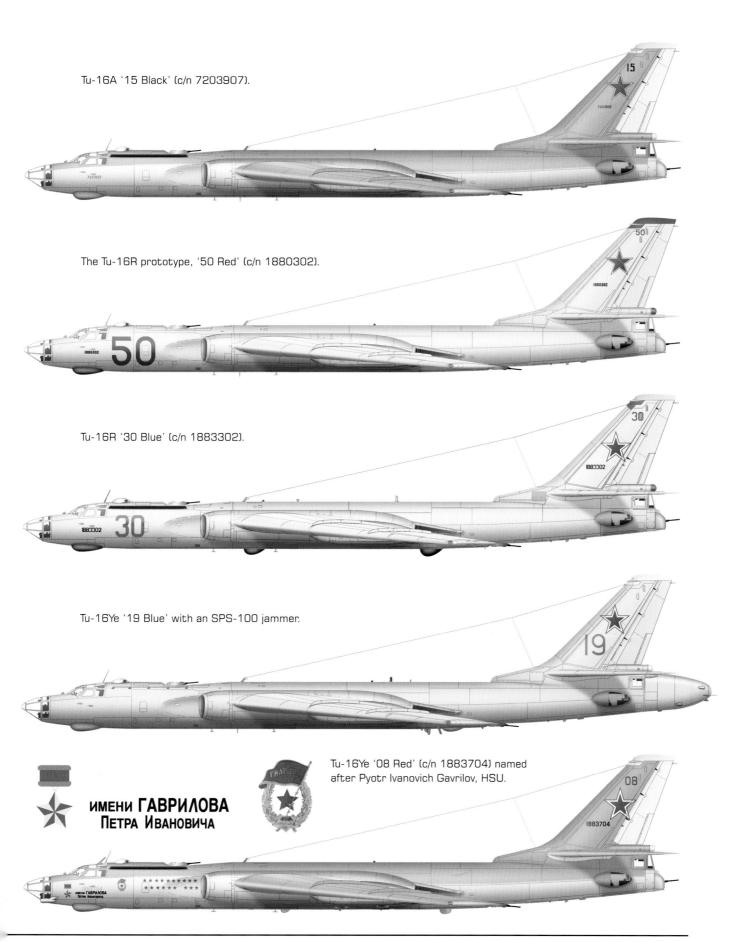

Tu-16A '15 Black' (c/n 7203907).

The Tu-16R prototype, '50 Red' (c/n 1880302).

Tu-16R '30 Blue' (c/n 1883302).

Tu-16Ye '19 Blue' with an SPS-100 jammer.

Tu-16Ye '08 Red' (c/n 1883704) named after Pyotr Ivanovich Gavrilov, HSU.

ИМЕНИ ГАВРИЛОВА
Петра Ивановича

Long-Range Aviation units equipped with the Tu-16 in 1961 (the 'corps system' order of battle)

Unit	Base	Notes
Long-Range Aviation Command, HQ Moscow		
• Direct reporting units:		
43rd TsBP i PLS	Dyagilevo AB, Ryazan'	
Arctic Special Operations Group	HQ Tiksi, Yakutian ASSR	
2nd OTBAK, HQ Vinnitsa *		
• Direct reporting units:		
199th *Brestskiy* GvODRAP	Nezhin, Chernigov Region	Tu-16R introduced 10-1956. Re-equipped with the Tu-22R in 1964-67
477th OAP RTR	Mirgorod, Poltava Region	Equipped with Tu-16Rs. Merged with the 226th GvTBAP in 1969 to form the 226th OAP REB SN
• 13th Dnepropetrovsko-Budapeshtskaya GvTBAD, HQ Poltava, Poltava Region:		
184th GvTBAP	Priluki, Chernigov Region	
185th GvTBAP	Poltava	Re-equipped with the Tu-22M2 in 1974
226th GvTBAP	Poltava	Became the direct reporting 226th OAP REB SN in 1969
• 15th TBAD, HQ Zhitomir: †		
251st GvTBAP	Belaya Tserkov', Kiev Region	Aka. Gayok AB. Tu-16 introduced in 1956.
260th TBAP	Stryy, L'vov Region	
341st TBAP	Ozyornoye AB, Zhitomir	Tu-16 introduced in 1956. Re-equipped with the Tu-22 in 1968
6th OTBAK, HQ Smolensk: ‡		
• Direct reporting units:		
290th GvODRAP	Zyabrovka AB	Equipped with Tu-16Rs. Re-equipped with the Tu-22R in 1965
34th OAE SN i RP	Olen'ya AB, Olenegorsk	Tu-16 ECM variants
179th OTAE SZ	Siauliai, Lithuania	Formerly 345th TBAP at Sol'tsy AB with Tu-16 bombers, reorganised 1959. Tu-16Z tankers and Tu-16 bombers. Bombers withdrawn 1969 when the unit became an ECM regiment (117th OAP REB)
• 22nd TBAD, HQ Bobruisk:		
121st *Sevastopol'skiy* GvTBAP	Machoolishchi AB, Minsk	Tu-16 introduced in 1958. Re-equipped with the Tu-22R in 1964-65 as the 121st GvODRAP
200th TBAP	Bobruisk, Mogilyov Region	
203rd GvTBAP	Baranovichi	Tu-16 introduced in 1954. Became 203rd ODRAP operating Tu-16Rs; re-equipped with the Tu-22R in 1963
• 56th *Breslavl'skaya* TBAD, HQ Kalinin, Kalinin Region:		
45th TBAP	Migalovo AB, Kalinin	Transferred to Chelyabinsk Military Navigator College in 1975 as the 45th UAP
173rd TBAP	Migalovo AB, Kalinin	Disbanded in 1975
52nd GvTBAP	Shaikovka AB, Kaluga Region	Tu-16 introduced in 1954; unit transferred to 13th GvTBAD in 1975
• 326th TBAD, HQ Tartu, Estonia:		
132nd TBAP	Tartu	
402nd TBAP	Bolbasovo AB, Orsha	Tu-16 introduced in 1954
840th TBAP	Sol'tsy AB, Novgorod Region	
8th OTBAK, HQ Blagoveshchensk (later Irkutsk)		
• Direct reporting units:		
1225th OTBAP	Belaya AB, Irkutsk Region	
1229th OTBAP	Belaya AB, Irkutsk Region	
219th ODRAP	Khvalynka AB	Spassk-Dal'niy, Primor'ye Territory. Equipped with Tu-16Rs. Re-equipped with the Tu-22R in 1965
335th OAE RTR	Borzya, Chita Region	Equipped with Tu-16Rs
• 55th TBAD, HQ Ussuriysk, Primor'ye Territory:		
303rd TBAP	Khorol' AB, Amur Region	Also reported as based Zavitinsk, Amur Region
444th TBAP	Vozdvizhenka AB, Ussuriysk	
• 79th TBAD, HQ Semipalatinsk, Kazakhstan: §		
1023rd TBAP/Sqn 4	Chagan AB, Semipalatinsk Region	Training squadron, established 1956. Sqn 4 disbanded in the spring of 1964

Notes:

OAE SN i RP = *otdel'naya aviaeskadril'ya spetsiahl'novo naznacheniya i rahdioelektronnovo protivodeystviya* – independent special mission & ECM air squadron; OTAE SZ = *otdel'naya tyazholaya aviaeskadril'ya samolyotov-zaprahvshchikov* – independent heavy aerial refuelling squadron; UAP = *oochebnyy aviapolk* – training air regiment

* The 2nd OTBAK also included the 106th TBAD with three regiments flying Tu-95s/Tu-95Ks. † According to some sources the 15th TBAD also included the 14th GvTBAP at Belaya Tserkov' which received the Tu-16 in 1956. ‡ The 6th OTBAK also included the 201st TBAD with two regiments flying M-4s/3Ms. § The 79th TBAD had two regiments equipped with Tu-95s

A McDonnell Douglas F-4E-40-MC (68-0473) from the USAF's Pacific Air Force/21st TFW based at Misawa AB, Japan, intercepts a Tu-16R *Badger-F*.

Below: Tu-16R '21 Blue' has just engaged the hose of a Tu-16Z, which is now rewinding the hose cable so that the front end of the hose locks into place as well. Note the striped markings on the hose.

Region (Leningrad MD). In in the Ukraine, units covering the south-western direction were stationed at Belaya Tserkov' (Kiev Region), Nezhin, Priluki (both Chernigov Region, northern Ukraine), Poltava, Ozyornoe AB 15 km (9.3 miles) south-east of Zhitomir, and Stryy AB (L'vov Region, western Ukraine). In central Russia, Tu-16s were based at Shaikovka AB in the Kaluga Region and Migalovo AB near Kalinin (now renamed back to Tver'), both in the Moscow MD. East of the Urals Mountains the type was deployed at Belaya AB in the Irkutsk Region (Transbaikalian MD), Zavitinsk in the Amur Region, Spassk-Dal'niy and Vozdvizhenka AB near Ussuriysk (both in the Primor'ye Territory), all Far Eastern MD. The table on the opposite page lists the DA units equipped with the Tu-16 under this OrBat.

During the 1960s most of the DA's bomber regiments re-equipped with missile strike versions of the Tu-16 and were tasked primarily with striking at hostile surface ships (yes – even though they were Air Force units, not Navy units) and strategic land targets in the European, Asian and Pacific theatres of operations. The introduction of the missile systems in the DA's Tu-16 units proceeded very intensively. In the 6th OTBAK, the 400th and 200th

TBAPs commenced conversion training for the K-16 weapons system in 1961-63 and made the first launches of KSR-2 missiles in 1964. That year the 52nd, 132nd, 840th and 111th TBAPs commenced conversion training for the K-16, the first launches taking place in 1965. In 1966 the 132nd TBAP was the first to commence conversion to the K-11-16 weapons system; the 52nd, 200th, 402nd, 840th and 111th TBAPs followed suit in 1967. In 1969 the 840th TBAP completed the training course for the then-latest K-26 weapons system, making the first launches in 1970. By 1978 the 132nd and 200th TBAP had re-equipped with the Tu-16K-26 and the like.

The introduction of the missile systems, too, was not trouble-free due to the missiles' unreliability in the early days. During one exercise in the mid-1970s, not a single launch of the KSR-2 missiles was successful – often the missiles crashed way short of the target. One such 'miss' ended in a scandal when a KSR-2 launched by a 444th TBAP Tu-16KSR-2 from Vozdvizhenka failed to make the target range on Sakhalin Island and knocked out a major communications cable, severing the link between the island and the mainland. There were cases when KSR-2 missiles fell off sponta-

Tu-16KSR-2 '21 Red' carrying one missile is seen from a Swedish Air Force fighter over the Baltic Sea.

neously, including one episode in the Kherson Region of the Ukraine and another over the suburbs of Kalinin; luckily none of these incidents resulted in loss of life, only collateral damage being caused (and paid for by the MoD). In order to get to the bottom of this trouble several missiles were fitted with test equipment and the data recorders were sent to the Air Force's 13th NII ERAT (*Naoochno-issledovatel'skiy institoot ekspluatahtsiï i remonta aviatsionnoy tekhniki* – Aviation Hardware Operation & Repair Institute) for analysis. This establishment played an important role in improving the missiles' reliability and accuracy.

The later availability of more modern versions of the Tu-16 with more sophisticated and powerful ECM equipment (such as the Tu-16P 'Buket') enabled the Long-Range Aviation to retain an effective strike presence on the key sectors of potential TOs. The Tu-16 maintained this role virtually until the end of the 1980s. However, it proved necessary to upgrade the ECM versions constantly – not least to prevent them from jamming their own radars.

In accordance with the Soviet Minister of Defence's order No.005 dated 5th January 1980, and a General Staff directive dated 13th March 1980, the Soviet Air Force's Long-Range Aviation Command was eliminated. The three corps were reorganised into Air Armies of the Supreme Command – respectively the 24th VA at Vinnitsa, the 46th VA at Smolensk and the 30th VA at Irkutsk. The first of these was a Tactical Aviation air army equipped with Su-24 tactical bombers. The others were still in the DA system and were termed as Strategic Air Armies of the Supreme Command (VA VGK (SN) – *vozdooshnaya armiya Verkhovnovo glavnoko-mahndovaniya strategicheskovo naznacheniya*); so was the newly established 37th VA. This was no mere renumbering – a reshuffle of the constituent air divisions took place to confuse would-be spies. For example, in the former 2nd OTBAK the 13th TBAD, 15th TBAD and 199th GvODRAP passed to the 46th VA while the 106th TBAD and three other divisions taken from the three corps were grouped into the 37th VA, none of them operating Tu-16s.

The Swedish Air Force also had to deal with ECM *Badgers*, such this Tu-16 Yolka ('15 Red', c/n 1882017).

A curious aspect of the new reorganisation was that the 1225th and 1229th Heavy Bomber Regiments were organised into the 31st TBAD. Nevertheless, they were still listed as OTBAPs (that is, direct reporting units) for a while; the 'independent' bit vanished only when the units transitioned to the 'swing-wing' Tu-22M2.

It took the top military authorities eight years to recognise the fallacy of this restructuring whose negative consequences by far outweighed the gains. Hence in accordance with the Minister of Defence's order No.0008 dated 25th February 1988 the headquarters of the 37th VA VGK (SN) was transformed into the reinstated Department of the Commander of the Long-Range Aviation, and the 30th and 46th Air Armies were subordinated to it. (It may be mentioned that in the modern Russian Air Force, the entire Long-Range Aviation was pooled into the 37th VA VGK (SN) in April 1998 during a military reform but re-emerged under its previous name in 2009.)

In addition to the airfields listed in the table on this page, at various times Tu-16 units operated from Mozdok (Ingushetia,

North Caucasian MD), Engels-2 AB and Skomorokhi AB (Zhitomir Region, northern Ukraine). A few *Badgers* were based at Vladimirovka AB near Akhtoobinsk, the main facility of GNIKI VVS (8th GNII VVS), which used them extensively for test and development work (as did LII, the Tupolev OKB and other research and development establishments in the MAP framework).

Apart from the Long-Range Aviation and the Naval Aviation, the *Badger* was operated in small numbers by the air component of the Air Defence Force (PVO). The latter, along with the DA and the AVMF, used Tu-16KRM drone launchers and M-16 target drones for training the air defence assets. A PVO unit operating the type was based at Priozyorsk (Djezkazgan Region, Kazakhstan).

Badgers on ice
In the mid-1950s only a few Soviet airfields beyond the Arctic Circle were suitable for heavy bombers. These included Amderma on the Kara Sea coast (Nenets Autonomous District), Severomorsk on the North Sea (Murmansk Region), Tiksi-Tsentral'nyy on the

Long-Range Aviation units equipped with the Tu-16 in 1982		
Unit	**Base**	**Notes**
30th VA VGK (SN), HQ Irkutsk		
• 31st TBAD, HQ Belaya AB, Irkutsk Region, Russia:		
1225th OTBAP	Belaya AB, Irkutsk Region	Re-equipped with the Tu-22M2 in 1982
1229th OTBAP	Belaya AB, Irkutsk Region	Re-equipped with the Tu-22M2 in 1982
• 55th TBAD, HQ Ussuriysk,		
Primor'ye Territory, Russia:		
303rd TBAP	Vozdvizhenka AB, Ussuriysk; later Zavitinsk, Amur Region	Re-equipped with the Tu-22M3
444th TBAP	Vozdvizhenka AB, Ussuriysk	Tu-16K-26 or similar version. Re-equipped with the Tu-22M3 and Tu-22MR
37th VA VGK (SN), HQ Moscow: *		
• Direct reporting units:		
43rd TsBP i PLS	Dyagilevo AB, Ryazan'	
Arctic Special Operations Group	HQ Tiksi, Yakutian ASSR	
46th VA VGK (SN), HQ Smolensk		
• Direct reporting units:		
226th OAP REB SN	Poltava	
• 13th *Dnepropetrovsko-Budapeshtskaya* GvTBAD,		
HQ Poltava:		
52nd GvTBAP	Shaikovka AB, Kaluga Region, Russia	Tu-16K-... variants. Re-equipped with the Tu-22M2 in 1981-82
184th GvTBAP	Priluki, Chernigov Region, the Ukraine	Tu-16K-... variants. Re-equipped with the Tu-22M3 in 1984-87
• 15th TBAD, HQ Zhitomir, the Ukraine:		
251st GvTBAP	Belaya Tserkov', Kiev Region	Aka. Gayok AB. Later redesignated 251st UTBAP and reporting to the 43rd TsBP i PLS
260th TBAP	Stryy, L'vov Region	Operated Tu-16K-... variants since the 1970s. Re-equipped with the Tu-22M3 and transferred to the 22nd TBAD in 1989
• 22nd *Donbasskaya* TBAD, HQ Bobruisk,		
Mogilyov Region, Belorussia:		
200th Brestskiy TBAP	Bobruisk, Mogilyov Region	Re-equipped with the Tu-22M3 in 1986
• 326th *Tarnopol'skaya* TBAD, HQ Tartu, Estonia:		
132nd TBAP	Tartu	Re-equipped with the Tu-22M3 in 1984
402nd TBAP	Bolbasovo AB, Orsha, Vitebsk Region	Re-equipped with the Tu-22M3 in 1983
840th TBAP	Sol'tsy AB, Novgorod Region	Re-equipped with the Tu-22M2 in 1982

Notes: OAPREB = *otdel'nyy aviapolk rahdioelektronnoy bor'byy* – independent ECM air regiment; UTBAP = *oochebnyy tyazholyy bombardirovochnyy aviapolk* – training heavy bomber regiment
* The 37th Air Army's primary units (the 73rd, 79th, 106th and 201st TBADs) operated Tu-95KD missile carriers and 3MS/3MN *Bison-B* and 3MD *Bison-C* bombers

Above: An enamel badge marking the 70th birthday of the 251st GvTBAP. The badge depicts a Tu-16K-26.

Left and below: Two night shots of a Tu-16K-26 equipped with the Rogovitsa formation keeping system.

Right: A pair of Tu-16Ye ECM aircraft get ready for a night sortie.

Below right: An atmospheric shot of a pair of Tu-16s flying a sortie at sunset; a *Badger-F* is about to refuel from a Tu-16Z.

Laptev Sea coast (Yakutian ASSR), Chekoorovka on the Lena River near where it emptied into the Laptev Sea, Wrangell Island in the Arctic Ocean off the north coast of Chukotka – the one in the Novaya Zemlya ('New Land') Archipelago, not the one in the Alexander Archipelago which is part of Alaska! – and a few others. These airbases, and the military commandant's offices maintaining the auxiliary airstrips in operational condition, were organised into the Long-Range Aviation's Special Operations Group in the Arctic (OGA – *Operativnaya grooppa v Arktike*) headquartered at Tiksi on the Laptev Sea coast, which was formed in 1958 to co-ordinate the work of the sixteen airfields in the High North. In addition to these, forward operating locations (FOLs) with hard-packed dirt runways or ice runways were set up, although these were not intended for heavy bomber operations; on take-off and landing, clods of earth or chunks of ice could be ingested by the aircraft's engines, damaging them.

In the late 1950s Soviet Tu-95 or M-4 strategic bombers operating from Tiksi were able to strike at targets in the USA across the North Pole. However, the USAF was obviously able to strike at Soviet territory in the same fashion; moreover, it was pursuing a 'harassment' tactic, making provocative flights along the Soviet

The Combat Flag of the 184th GvTBAP.

Union's northern borders. Therefore the Soviet MoD decided to build temporary airstrips on ice fields in the Arctic Ocean which would allow the Long-Range Aviation to continue operations if its main bases were bombed. This was no easy task, since the landing weight of the bombed-up strategic aircraft ranged from 70,000 to 95,000 kg (154,320-209,440 lb). While the bomber's weight could not break through the pack ice, which was many metres thick, the aircraft could skid off the runway when it braked on landing. Added to this, the high salinity of the sea water made the ice's surface friable; as a result, the aircraft shook so violently on take-off and landing that it was impossible to read the instruments properly.

In the spring of 1958 Guards Lt.-Col. A. S. Krotov, the then CO of the 52nd GvTBAP, was ordered to prepare his three best aircrews for Arctic flights, which included landing on an *ad hoc* ice airstrip in poor weather. Shortly afterwards more specific orders were issued. Five aircraft were involved – three Tu-16As and two Tu-4R photo reconnaissance aircraft from the 121st *Sevastopol'skiy* GvODRAP at Machoolishchi AB. The destination was Ice Station SP-6 (*Severnyy polyus* – North Pole), the sixth in a long series of Soviet drifting Arctic research stations; it had been inaugurated on 19th April 1956, and was at that time manned by its third crew under the supervision of Sergey T. Serlapov. The station had a runway used by the aircraft bringing supplies; the thickness of the ice floe hosting the station varied from 6 m (19 ft 8 in) in the summer to 13 m (42 ft 8 in) in the winter.

Col. Anton A. Alekhnovich, Deputy CO/Chief of Flight Training of the 45th TBAD which included the 52nd GvTBAP, was chosen to lead the mission. He was a former combat pilot with 205 sorties in the Great Patriotic War and the former CO of what was then the 121st GvTBAP. The fact that he had the HSU title, two Lenin Orders, two Orders of the Red Banner of Combat, the Patriotic War Order and the Red Star Order sure says a thing or two about how he flew and fought.

In April 1958 the 52nd GvTBAP prepared five Tu-16As and six crews, one of which was in hot reserve. (It has to be said that various accounts of the story are rather contradictory; some say there were four aircraft from Baranovichi – which would mean the 203rd TBAP – and two from Machoolishchi.) First, the aircraft redeployed to Tiksi which was the staging point. On 24th April, two days before the actual flight to the Pole, Alekhnovich assembled the crews and briefed them on the mission. The Tu-16As would head for the SP-6, and the first bomber would land on the ice runway, make a U-turn at the end and take off immediately in a reciprocal direction while the others circled, waiting their turn. The procedure would then be repeated by the other two *Badgers* before the trio flew back to Tiksi. Next, the Tu-4Rs would land, offload supplies for the SP-6 and return to Tiksi as well. Only then would it be possible to report to the high command that the objective had been completed and the strategic FOL was in operation.

Yet, the best-laid plans of mice and men go astray. While this was going on, all members of the SP-6 crew not engaged in scientific experiments toiled away, extending and reinforcing the ice runway which had to be huge by local standards. As they shovelled and rolled the snow to create a smooth surface, guessing what sort of aircraft was going to land, someone suggested drilling holes in the ice to admit sea water, which would then freeze, and covering the resulting 'ice arena' with a layer of hard-packed snow. This turned out to be a dumb idea.

26th April 1958, dawned with brilliant sunshine, just as the ice station's weatherman had forecast. One by one the *Badgers* took off from Tiksi-Tsentral'nyy and set course for the SP-6; the lead aircraft coded '04 Red' was captained by Col. Anton A. Alekhnovich himself, with Maj. N. Bazarnyy as co-pilot. The navigators found the ice station without any trouble, and on receiving permission to land from the improvised 'tower' at SP-6 Alekhnovich began the landing approach. The touchdown and the landing run appeared to go OK, everyone cheering as the Tu-16 slowed down and turned in the opposite direction, lining up for take-off. The first-ever landing of a jet bomber on a drifting ice field had been successfully accomplished. The location was 81°15' N, 147°42' E.

Opposite, left: Tu-16A '04 Red' lands on the runway of Ice Station SP-6 on 26th April 1958.
Opposite, right: Col. Anton A. Alekhnovich, the captain of '04 Red' on the fateful mission.

Top and above: A time-expired Tu-16R awaiting disposal.
Below: A pair of fully armed Tu-16K-26s makes a flypast during an 'open house' at Kubinka AB in the early 1990s.

Receiving take-off clearance, Alekhnovich revved up the engines, released the brakes, and the 70-ton (154,320-lb) aircraft rolled forward. Then the catastrophe occurred. It turned out that a pothole filled with salt water had not frozen properly and the runway surface was not firm enough. As luck would have it, the Tu-16's port main gear bogie hit this weak spot and the resulting jerk was enough to throw the accelerating aircraft off course on the slippery surface. Veering off the runway into the snow, the bomber headed straight for a parked civil Ilyushin Il-14T *Crate* transport from Aeroflot's Polar Aviation Directorate which was being used to maintain radio communications with the bombers. (Again, there's some confusion here; one source claims the aircraft was a Lisunov Li-2 *Cab* – the Soviet licence-built derivative

of the Douglas DC-3.) The take-off was aborted and Alekhnovich tried to steer clear, even using differential thrust to help it; still, the bomber clipped the Il-14 with its port wingtip and then hit a stack of 200-litre (55-gallon) fuel drums, sending them flying in all directions. As the Tu-16 came to a halt, fuel poured from the port wing; luckily no fire ensued.

Both aircraft were seriously damaged but thankfully there were no casualties or serious injuries – apart from Maj. Bazarnyy, who had a cut on his forehead which he had hit on the instrument panel shroud, and the navigator, whose legs were badly bruised. On seeing what had happened, the ATC officer forbade the other Tu-16s to land and, after circling the ice station once, the *Badgers* headed back to Tiksi.

Left: A line-up of assorted Tu-16s shortly before an overwater mission (judging by the crews' life jackets), with a Tu-16K-11-16 in the foreground. The differently coloured tactical codes are noteworthy, as are the 'whitewall tires' on the nosewheels of '09 Red'.

Right: A different Tu-16 with the same code '09 Red' flies an overwater sortie on 15th March 1974.

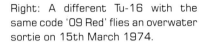

Next, however, the Tu-4Rs (one captained by Guards Maj. Alfyorov, the other by Guards Maj. Aleksey Akoolov) came in and landed safely. Even as they approached the ice station the crews could see that trouble was afoot. When the Tu-4 crews climbed out and surveyed the aftermath of the collision, Col. Alekhnovich slowly walked up, waved a hand in dismay and said in a strangely flat voice: *'That's it, guys. So much for my flying career.'* He was well aware that in the Khrushchov era, the attitude to manned military aviation being the way it was, not even a Hero of the Soviet Union with many awards like himself would be pardoned for a flying accident; it hurt him all the more because this was the sole accident in his distinguished flying career. The crew of Tu-16A '04 Red' were evacuated to the mainland by the Tu-4Rs (though one source claims this was done by another Polar Aviation Il-14 which arrived the next day).

The important mission had been bungled, and now someone would have to pay. The crew were blameless, since the accident had been caused by a poorly prepared runway in combination with a strong crosswind. Yet this fact didn't matter a hoot to Alekhnovich's superiors who were looking for a scapegoat, being more concerned about saving their own asses than anything else. They now did an amazing about-face in their assessment of the pilot; the very same commanders who had previously given Alekhnovich excellent references were now accusing him of incompetence. One general went so far as to claim that the pilot had taken on the mission out of vanity – 'forgetting' the fact that there had been no crowd of volunteers for this dangerous mission. Alekhnovich could be rather irreverent towards the big brass at times, and perhaps some people simply saw the opportunity to get even. After a brief investigation, on 27th August 1958, Col. Anton A. Alekhnovich, who had 3,410 hours total time (including 1,550 hours of night flights), was kicked out of the Air Force on the pretext of 'poor health' (!). He found a job as an air traffic controller at Minsk-1 airport and did his job with distinction.

News of the accident was kept secret; officially the aircraft was 'undergoing repair on the mainland'. The Air Force repair crew which arrived two weeks later was unable to repair the Tu-16's damaged wing on site – in Arctic field conditions the job proved to be beyond their capabilities. For a full year the Tu-16 drifted through the Arctic Ocean, accompanied by the staff of Ice Station SP-6 and the aircraft's chief technician (crew chief) Guards

Lt. (SG) Revmir Kagirov left to guard it. Despite being hidden under camouflage nets, as early as 21st August 1958, the bomber was detected and photographed by a Royal Canadian Air Force reconnaissance aircraft (apparently a Canadair CP-107 Argus, which had just entered service); this was immediately reported all the way up to the Kremlin. The USA filed a formal protest about the setting up of Soviet strategic bases on neutral territory relatively close to the American continent, and the Western press began to make noises. Meanwhile, the ice fields were shifting and crumbling, which created additional problems; a crack appeared across the runway at SP-6, rendering it unusable. Pieces kept breaking away from the ice floe so that by April 1959, it was reduced to half its original size. It was only when the winds and currents began to carry the SP-6 towards the Greenland Sea and the prospects of evacuation loomed large that the decision was taken to destroy the aircraft after all salvageable items had been removed to prevent it from falling into NATO hands.

While stripping the bomber down, the technical crew had to use an LAS-5M inflatable dinghy to reach it due to the melting ice. Once the engines and equipment had been recovered, on 16th April 1959 the airframe was doused with kerosene and set alight. By then the Tu-16 had covered a distance of 3,348 km (2,079 miles) on the ice floe. The ice station was ultimately abandoned on 13th September 1959; the personnel of the SP-6, the technician and the dismantling crew were evacuated to the mainland. For his 'lengthy secondment' Kagirov was given a substantial reward and leave.

After this accident, neither the Soviets nor the Americans tried operating jet bombers from the drifting ice ever again, although jet aircraft operations in support of the Soviet ice stations in the Arctic did take place. These involved the then-latest Antonov An-74 *Coaler* twin-turbofan short take-off and landing (STOL) transport.

In Soviet Navy service
The Soviet Naval Aviation was an equally important operator of the type. In 1956 the then Minister of Defence Marshal Gheorgiy K. Zhukov signed an order by which the AVMF was to re-equip with the Tu-16. Initially these were mainly 'landlubber' versions (that is, not specialised naval versions), with only a few Tu-16KS and Tu-16T aircraft tailored for naval service. Regardless of version, however, they were to be flown by aircrews well versed in overwater operations.

Left: A Naval Aviation crew wearing typically naval white-topped peaked caps pose for a publicity shot with a Tu-16K-10.

Below: An enamel badge marking the 30th birthday of an AVMF unit flying Tu-16K-10s.

Bottom: This shot of Tu-16K-10 (ZA) c/n 1883820 intercepted on 1st October 1985 was one of the first photos of the *Badger-C* published in the West.

The plan envisaged supplying the North Fleet with 85 Tu-16s in 1956, a further 170 going to the Black Sea Fleet and the Pacific Fleet in 1957. Despite being closest to the potential adversary, the Baltic Fleet would be the last to receive the Tu-16, taking delivery of 170 examples in 1958. Thus, over the course of three years, the Naval Aviation would receive 424 Tu-16s – just slightly less than the number supplied to the Long-Range Aviation. In reality, things worked out somewhat differently. The first *Badgers* were in fact supplied to the Baltic Fleet Air Arm. This was because in 1955 the 57th TBAD comprising two regiments of Tu-4s (the 170th TBAP and 240th GvTBAP) based at Bykhov AB (Mogilyov Region, Belorussia) had been transferred from the Air Force to the Naval Aviation – specifically, the Baltic Fleet. The division's aircrews were well trained, but their obsolescent Tu-4 bombers could not meet AVMF requirements. Since the division was stationed in one of the 'hottest' sectors of the Cold War, the MoD decided it should have priority in receiving new aircraft. Some of the Tu-4s were handed down to the Naval Aviation's 33rd TsBP i PLS at Nikolayev-Kul'bakino, others converted into transports, and high-time examples were scrapped. The division's command staff, flight and ground crews were sent to the aircraft factories to take Tu-16 conversion training.

The naval Tu-16 originally saw service with minelayer and torpedo-bomber regiments (MTAP) which were either part of minelayer and torpedo-bomber divisions (MTAD) or direct reporting. These divisions and independent regiments made up the backbone of the Soviet Navy fleets' air arms.

The Naval Aviation took delivery of its first four Tu-16s on 1st June 1955, and as early as 25th June, the Baltic Fleet's 240th GvMTAP DD (*Gvardeyskiy minno-torpednyy aviapolk dahl'nevo deystviya* – Guards Long-Range Minelayer & Torpedo-Bomber Regiment) of the 57th MTAD DD (*Gvardeyskaya minno-torped-naya aviadiveeziya dahl'nevo deystviya* – Guards Long-Range Minelayer & Torpedo-Bomber Division, the former 57th TBAD) flew its first training sorties with the type. The change of 'owner-

Above right: Maintenance in progress on a Tu-16K-10. The shape of the YeN radar's main radome and its V-shaped joint line are clear to see.

Right: A Tu-16K-10 passes low overhead, demonstrating the K-10S missile lowered into pre-launch position.

Overleaf, above: An AVMF armourer refastens the cover on the port missile pylon of a Tu-16KS after attaching a KS-1 missile. Unusually, the latter has red-painted radomes.

Overleaf, below: A fine study of a Tu-16KS carrying a single KS-1 missile, the red colour identifying it as an inert practice round.

ship' and change of name did not mean redeployment – the 170th MTAP DD and 240th GvMTAP DD stayed at Bykhov, quite a long way from the sea.

The crews went through an extensive theoretical training course lasting 400 to 500 hours, and the flight crews were subjected to a rigorous selection process. The Tu-16 was at that time considered the very latest in aviation technology, and the best aircrews were chosen to fly it. In the Naval Aviation, Tu-16 captains were strictly Pilots 1st Class (an official grade reflecting experience and expertise) with at least 600-700 hours on the Il-28 or Tu-14; for co-pilots the 'entry level' was 200 hours.

The first version to see service with the Navy was the baseline bomber, but with the start of Tu-16T production and conversion of bombers to this standard the Baltic Fleet air regiments began getting to grips with the minelayer/torpedo-bomber version. In June-July 1956, the 57th MTAD received the first Tu-16T torpedo-bombers, and by September nine 240th GvMTAP DD crews had carried out five practice torpedo attacks, including two with the inert practice version of the RAT-52 torpedo. After this, the Tu-16T was delivered to other naval units.

In the Black Sea Fleet, the 5th GvMTAP DD of the 88th MTAD DD based at Gvardeyskoe AB near Simferopol' on the Crimea Peninsula (Odessa MD) converted from the Il-28 to the Tu-16T in April 1956, the co-located 124th MTAP DD of the same division following suit in June; the 943rd MTAP of the 141st MTAD (Oktyabr'skoye AB, likewise near Simferopol') did the same in May 1957, and the North Fleet's 574th MTAP at Katoonino AB (Lakhta, Arkhangel'sk Region) in November 1957.

In the Pacific Fleet, the 568th MTAP of the 692nd MTAD at Mongokhto AB (aka Kamennyy Ruchey – 'Stone Brook') near Sovetskaya Gavan' ('Soviet Harbour') in the Khabarovsk Region,

Above: A Tu-16K-10 carrying no missile flies a proficiency training sortie.

Right: An AVMF Tu-16P takes off past an officer in parade dress holding a flag emblazoned 'Glory to the Union of Soviet Socialist Republics!'

The reverse of a Navy medal inscribed 'To a Naval airman, a veteran of the Cold War on the seas'.

Left: An NBC drill is in progress as ground crewmen wearing gas masks and the green trousers and boots from the Soviet Army NBC protection outfit (known as OZK) push a dolly with a KSR-2 missile into position for loading under the port wing of a Soviet Navy Tu-16KSR-2 (ZA). This view gives a close look at the port wingtip with the horizontal winglet (which carries the rear pair of navigation lights) and the signal light ahead of it telling the tanker crew that the fuel transfer hose is locked into place.

Left: Here the same missile is aligned with the port pylon and ready for lifting into position. Of course the armourer on the missile's wing will have to climb down first.

Below: A GAZ-66 4x4 army lorry with a van body (probably housing ground test equipment) tows a dolly with a KSR-5 missile towards a Tu-16K-10-26. The twin nozzles of the missile's S5.33 rocket motor are noteworthy.

Above: A Kazan'-built Tu-16K-10 of the Pacific Fleet coded '50 Red' is shadowed by a US Navy A-4B (BuNo 142132/'NG-1') from VA-93 'Blue Blazers' which was temporarily based aboard the ASW carrier USS *Bennington* (CVS 20) in 1964.

Right: A busy scene on the military side of Vladivostok-Knevichi airport in 1988. Senior Ensign Yelanskiy (foreground), the defensive fire commander of a Pacific Fleet (25th MRAD/183rd MRAP) Tu-16K-something-or-other, loads 23-mm ammunition for the tail cannons via the open hatch of the rear avionics/equipment bay. Meanwhile, an armourer is busy with the DT-N7S ventral barbette. Note the open bomb bay and a second Tu-16 parked in one of the revetments in the background.

began converting from the Il-28T to the Tu-16 in January 1957. Gradually, other units of the Naval Aviation were re-equipped.

Unlike the Il-28T and Tu-14T, which could only carry two torpedoes, the Tu-16T could take up to six torpedoes. Theoretical studies indicated that the probability of hitting a surface ship when four torpedoes were launched was increased by a mere 2-3% when compared with a single-torpedo attack. Experience with the Tu-16T proved that its operational radius was significantly greater and its equipment more sophisticated than that of the Il-28T or Tu-14T, allowing different combat tactics to be used. The Tu-16T was to be used predominantly at night and in daytime adverse weather conditions to strike selected enemy vessels. The 'kill' probability was to be increased by 50-100% by launching the torpedoes in a fan-like

spread, although in practice this method of torpedo attack was not used.

The Tu-16T took part in several exercises held by all four Soviet Navy fleets, the last of these with the Black Sea Fleet in 1959. Four aircraft participated on the latter occasion, each carrying up to six 45-53VT torpedoes optimised for high-altitude attack. During the exercises the aircraft took off from unpaved airfields with their maximum take-off weight. The torpedoes were released in a single pass, using the optical sight.

As a result of Nikita S. Khrushchov's far-reaching cutbacks in Soviet air power, the AVMF's minelayer and torpedo-bomber units were to all intents and purposes eliminated in 1960. Almost all MTAPs operating the Il-28T (the Tu-14T had been phased out by then) were disbanded and their aircraft decommissioned and broken up; In the Pacific Fleet alone some

Opposite page, top: The crew of a Tu-16RM in summer everyday attire pose with their aircraft. Note the differing style of headdress.

Left and far left: The co-pilot and Nav/Op of a naval Tu-16 at their workstations.

Below left: Five out of six members of the same crew. The airmen are wearing VMSK waterproof naval flight suits.

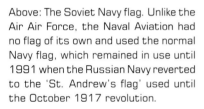

Above: The Soviet Navy flag. Unlike the Air Air Force, the Naval Aviation had no flag of its own and used the normal Navy flag, which remained in use until 1991 when the Russian Navy reverted to the 'St. Andrew's flag' used until the October 1917 revolution.

Above right: A Tu-16K-10 undergoes ground checks. The aircraft is jacked up for a landing gear swing, a UPG-250GM hydraulics test vehicle on a GAZ-51A general-purpose lorry supplying hydraulic power. Note also the device suspended in front of the YeN radar's command link antenna to emulate the missile's seeker head.

Right: A publicity photo of two Naval Aviation Tu-16 crewmen enjoying a break between flights.

Below: An enamel badge marking the 40th birthday of the Pacific Fleet air arm in 1972.

Above: BAe Sea Harrier FRS.1 ZD582/'127' of No.800 Sqn from HMS *Illustrious* escorts a Tu-16RM-1 which is keeping an eye on Exercise *Ocean Safari '87*.

Below: Tu-16K-10-26 '07 Red' wearing an 'Excellent aircraft' badge sits on a hardstand with the positions of support vehicles marked.

Top right: Naval Tu-16KSR-2-5 '55 Blue' intercepted by a Swedish Air Force fighter.

Right: Naval Tu-16P '40 Red' seen in similar circumstances.

Below right: A Tu-16K-10-26 in a revetment with K-10S and KSR-5 missiles ready for loading.

Top left: A naval Tu-16R *Badger-F* seen from the tail gunner's station of a sister ship.

Left and above left: Tu-16K-10-26 '92 Red' wearing the 'Excellent aircraft' badge taxies out for take-off.

Top: Tu-16Ye '10 Black' intercepted by a Swedish Air Force fighter.

Above: An enamel badge with an image of a Tu-16 marking the 40th birthday of the North Fleet air arm's 987th MRAP. Judging by the long nose, it depicts a Tu-16K-10-26.

Above right: '86 Blue', a Tu-16RM-2, as seen by the pilot of an intercepting NATO fighter.

Right: A Tu-16K-10-26 is seen immediately after becoming airborne. The aircraft carries no missiles, indicating this is a practice sortie to polish the pilots' flying techniques.

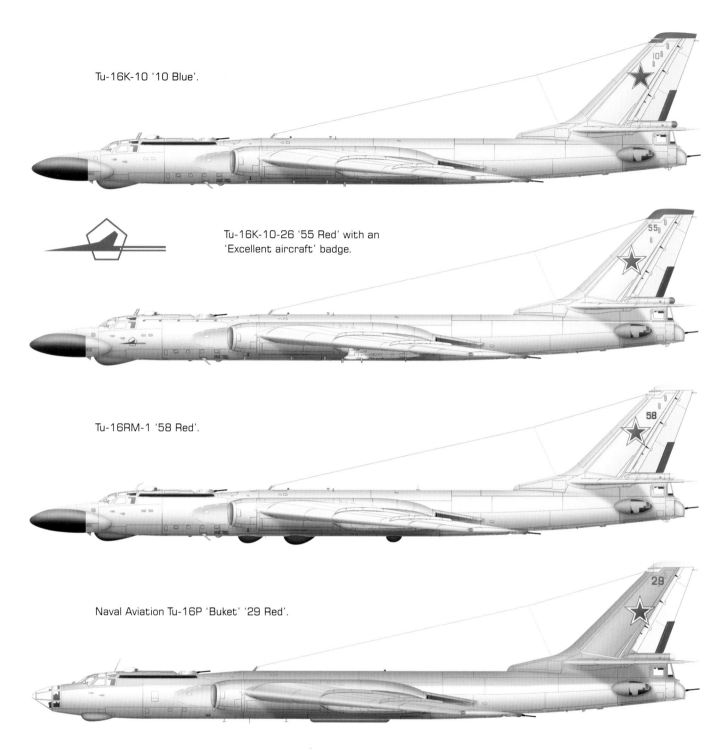

Tu-16K-10 '10 Blue'.

Tu-16K-10-26 '55 Red' with an
'Excellent aircraft' badge.

Tu-16RM-1 '58 Red'.

Naval Aviation Tu-16P 'Buket' '29 Red'.

400 aircraft were scrapped within a short time. The Naval Aviation had not suffered such devastation even in the darkest days of the Great Patriotic War. The Tu-16 in its various versions remained as the sole heavy combat aircraft type in naval service.

The Tu-16KS missile strike variant entered service with the Northern and Pacific Fleets in 1957, augmenting the Tu-4KS and subsequently replacing it. Also, the Tu-16K-10 armed with the K-10S supersonic ASM was officially added to the inventory in 1959, entering service in growing numbers. The first units to operate the Tu-16K-10 were the Baltic Fleet's 170th GvMTAP DD and

the North Fleet's 924th GvMTAP DD and 987th MTAP DD. They were followed by the Baltic Fleet's 240th GvMTAP DD, the Black Sea Fleet's 5th GvMTAP DD and 124th MTAP DD, and the Pacific Fleet's 169th GvMTAP DD of the 3rd MTAD DDat Khorol' AB (Primor'ye Region), which was transferred from the Air Force in 1960, and 570th MTAP DD, which re-equipped with the *Badger-C* in 1960-61. As early as August 1961 individual launches of the K-10S ASM had been carried out by the various fleet air arms. Soon afterwards, exercises involving groups of the new missile carriers against shipping convoys began, and before long many

Right: Some of the ECM versions retained the ability to deliver bombs, as exemplified by this naval Tu-16Ye.

An enamel badge marking the golden jubilee of the North Fleet, showing a Tu-16 silhouette.

naval missile strike air regiments had become familiar with the K-10 weapons system.

At first the delivery of missile strike variants had no immediate effect on the units' designations. However, in line with the general trend towards 'missilisation', on 20th March 1961, the Soviet Minister of Defence Marshal Rodion Ya. Malinovskiy issued an order whereby some of the surviving torpedo-bomber and minelayer air divisions regiments operating the Tu-16 were redesignated naval missile strike air divisions (MRAD – *morskaya raketonosnaya*

aviadiveeziya) and their constituent regiments became naval missile strike air regiments (MRAP). This reflected the actual state of affairs, since by then the units had been re-equipped to a considerable degree with the Tu-16KS. Most of the remaining Tu-16T torpedo-bombers were converted to the Tu-16S search and rescue version which served on with the Soviet Navy for a considerable time. On 26th January 1966 the Council of Ministers authorised the transfer of six Tu-16T aircraft, apparently the last machines of their kind, to the United Arab Republic as part of the Soviet military aid.

Modern-day serpent-bearers: technicians extract the fuel transfer hose from the starboard wing of a Tu-16Z for a check.

In 1962 the AVMF fielded the Tu-16KSR-2 armed with KSR-2 cruise missiles. Its major advantage over the predecessors was that the KSR-2 was a 'fire and forget' weapon – the aircraft was able to turn back after launching the missile, staying out of harm's way. The first units to receive the *Badger-G* were the 540th IIMRAP (*instrooktorsko-issledovatel'skiy morskoy raketonosnyy aviapolk* – instructional & test naval missile strike air regiment) of the AVMF's 33rd Training Centre and the Pacific Fleet's 568th MRAP in 1963; they were followed by the Baltic Fleet's 12th OMRAP (*otdel'nyy morskoy raketonosnyy aviapolk* – independent naval missile strike air regiment) in 1964 and the Pacific Fleet's 49th MRAP in 1967. The service entry of the Tu-16KSR-2 enhanced the Naval Aviation's strike capability considerably; now a mixed formation of Tu-16s could launch two types of missiles with different speed and altitude envelopes, making it harder for the adversary's air defences to neutralise the threat.

The Tu-16K-26 armed with two KSR-5 supersonic cruise missiles entered Naval Aviation service in 1963. Later, some of the older Tu-16K-10s were upgraded to Tu-16K-10-26 standard, being able to carry one K-10S missile on the centreline and two KSR-2s, KSR-5s or KSR-11s under the wings. In the early 1970s the units operating Tu-16K-26s were issued KSR-5P anti-radar missiles which provided a major boost in the AVMF's strike capability without requiring additional missile platforms.

The Navy's reconnaissance units began equipping with the Tu-16 in 1956. In the North Fleet the 967th ORAP converted from the Il-28R to the Tu-16R in 1956, while the 50th GvORAP based at Novorossiya-Zapadnaya AB (= Novorossiya-West), Primor'ye Territory, did the same in 1958.

Above left: An excellent shot of a North Fleet Tu-16K-10 taken from a Swedish Air Force fighter.

Left: Tu-16K-10 '49 Red' is examined by F-4S (former F-4J-34-MC) BuNo 155570/NF-111 of VF-161 'Chargers' from USS *Midway*.

Above: F-14A-80-GR BuNo 159465/'AB-104' of VF-102 'Diamondbacks' escorts an unarmed Tu-16K-10-26 coded '07 Black'.

Right: 'You spy on us, we spy on you' – the tail gunner of a Tu-16 intercepted by a NATO fighter 'returns fire' with his own camera.

Above: A medal commemorating the 50th birthday of the Pacific Fleet air arm, with an aircraft silhouette vaguely resembling a Tu-16.

Above right: A different version of the same medal featuring the Navy's 'Guards ribbon'.

Naval Aviation Tu-16s were reportedly also based at Novofyodorovka AB near Saki (Black Sea Fleet) and near Shevchenko (Mangyshlak Region, Kazakhstan; now renamed Aktau), the Caspian Sea Flotilla.

Most, if not all, Tu-16 missile carriers and Tu-16R reconnaissance aircraft were equipped with the wingtip-to-wingtip in-flight refuelling system for working with Tu-16Z tankers. The AVMF units started practicing IFR procedures in 1958-59. Initially during training sessions the units' deputy COs acted as instructor pilots on the receiver aircraft, while the squadron commanders did the same on the tankers; later, as the pilots grew more familiar with the IFR technique, lower-ranking commanders started performing this function. In-flight refuelling not only extended the *Badger*'s combat radius but also allowed the aircraft to operate from short and unpaved tactical airfields by taking off with a reduced weight and topping up the tanks en route.

Above left: Armourers attach FAB-250 M-54 high-drag bombs to a BD3-16K rack mounted on the port missile pylon of a Tu-16K-10-26B.

Left: A pair of Tu-16K-10-26Bs (the wingman is barely visible behind the lead aircraft) in a strange 'lop-sided' configuration carrying a BD3-16K bomb rack to port and a KSR-5 missile to starboard.

This Tu-16K-10-26B is configured with the forward pair of BD4-16-52 fuselage-mounted bomb racks in between frames 26-28.

A Tu-16KSR-2-5-11 from a Soviet Air Force unit retrofitted with a Rubin-1M radar in an amidships position carries a single live KSR-5 under the port wing. The aerial array of the Ritsa system is visible, indicating the ability to carry anti-radar missiles. The IFR receptacle is also evident.

Right: '20 Blue', another *Badger-G Mod* with the Rubin-1M radar – this time a Naval Aviation example (note the red-painted trim tabs) without the Ritsa system. The aircraft carries a KSR-2 on the port pylon.

Below: A naval Tu-16K-26 coded '02 Blue' carrying a single KSR-5 missile.

Naval Aviation units operating the Tu-16 after 1960

Unit	Base	Notes
Naval Aviation Command		
• **Direct reporting units:**		
33rd TsBP i PLS:		
540th IIMRAP*	Kul'bakino AB, Nikolayev	
Black Sea Fleet (HQ Sevastopol')		
• **Direct reporting units:**		
30th ODRAP	Novofyodorovka AB, Saki	Re-equipped with the Tu-22R
• **2nd MRAD, HQ Gvardeiskoye:**		
5th GvMRAP	Vesyoloye AB, Crimea Region	Re-equipped with the Tu-22M3 in 1985
124th MRAP	Gvardeiskoe AB, Simferopol'	Disbanded 1990
943rd *Konstantsskiy* MRAP	Oktyabr'skoe AB, Simferopol'	Ex-1676th MTAP, redesignated in 1961. Partly re-equipped with the Tu-22M2 in 1974 and fully with the Tu-22M3 in 1987
Baltic Fleet (HQ Kaliningrad)		
• **Direct reporting units:**		
9th GvMRAP *	Ostrov AB, Pskov Region	Equipped with the Tu-16KS. Ex-North Fleet, transferred 7-1971; disbanded 30-12-1974
12th GvOMRAP	Ostrov AB, Pskov Region	Established 1960; disbanded 1989
• **57th MRAD, HQ Bykhov:**		
170th GvMRAP	Bykhov AB, Mogilyov Region	Re-equipped with the Tu-22M2 in 1975
240th GvMRAP	Bykhov AB, Mogilyov Region	Forcer 240th GvMTAP was in the Air Force in 1961-63. Re-equipped with the Tu-22M2 in 1976
342nd AP REB	Ostrov AB, Pskov Region	Tu-16P. Established 1978; became independent (342nd OAP REB). Disbanded 1989
North Fleet (HQ		
• **5th MRAD, HQ Olenegorsk, Murmansk Region:**		
574th MRAP	Katoonino AB	Lakhta, Arkhangel'sk Region
924th MRAP	Olen'ya AB, Olenegorsk	Re-equipped with the Tu-22M2
987th MRAP	Severomorsk-3 AB	Equipped with the Tu-16K-10 (later Tu-16K-10-26). Disbanded 3-1993
Pacific Fleet (HQ Vladivostok)		
• **Direct reporting units:**		
317th OSAP	Petropavlovsk-Kamchatskiy/Yelizovo AP	Included Tu-16Rs
• **143rd MRAD, HQ Mongokhto:**		
568th MRAP	Mongokhto AB	Alias Kamennyy Ruchey AB. Re-equipped with the Tu-22M2
570th MRAP	Khorol' AB	Re-equipped with the Tu-22M2
183rd MRAP	Petropavlovsk-Kamchatskiy/Yelizovo AP	
Caspian Sea Flotilla		
??	Shevchenko	

* Despite not being part of the 57th Air Division, the 9th GvMRAP did not have the 'Independent' prefix to its name, like the 12th GvOMRAP

The Black Sea Fleet units were among the first to master IFR operations by groups of Tu-16KSs; refuelling extended the group's combat radius to 2,600-2,700 km (1,615-1,677 miles). If the tanker and the receiver aircraft took off from the same base, refuelling took place at 800 km (496 miles) from the base. During group operations each Tu-16Z consecutively refuelled two Tu-16KSs at 550-850 km (341-528 miles) range, transferring 10,000 litres (2,200 Imp gal) to each aircraft, and returned to base with at least 6,000 litres (1,320 Imp gal) of fuel remaining. The most compli-cated procedure was refuelling at mid-point on the return leg; this was practiced in emergencies only. By the early 1960s, having mastered the Kometa weapons system and IFR techniques, the Tu-16KS crews started flying maximum-range missions over the seas and oceans.

Naval Aviation Tu-16s were the only Soviet *Badgers* to be deployed overseas. The Soviet Navy had two bases in Vietnam, and the Pacific Fleet's 169th GvSAP (*Gvardeyskiy **smeshannyy aviapolk*** – Guards composite air regiment) deployed to Cam Ranh

AB in southern Vietnam (Da Nang Province) included a missile strike squadron with 16 Tu-16Ks-something-or-other in the 1970s and early 1980s, flying overwater sorties from there. Studies were made at this time on the effects of the prolonged exposure to the hot and humid tropical climate (coupled with the salty ocean air) on the aircraft's airframe, equipment and electrical wiring. On 28th August 1989, however, the Minister of Defence signed an order reducing the 169th GvSAP to an independent composite air squadron with a complement of four Tu-142MK *Bear-F Mod 2* ASW aircraft, four Tu-95RTs maritime reconnaissance/OTH targeting aircraft and two Antonov An-26 *Curl* transports. The regiment's missile strike squadron, the fighter squadron with 14 MiG-23MLD *Flogger-Ks* and the helicopter flight with three Mil' Mi-14 *Haze* amphibious helicopters were all to disband in 1990.

For a while the AVMF also considered deploying Tu-16R ELINT aircraft to Tiyas AB in Syria located north-east of Damascus (also known as T4 airbase) as required, for which special arrangements would be made with the Syrian government. However this never actually happened.

Learning the ropes
A few words must be said about how the men who flew the Tu-16 were picked and trained. At first the conversion training took place directly at the MAP factories producing the type, the factory test pilots acting as instructors, but this situation could not last long. Hence the *Badger* was used by three of the Soviet Air Force's training establishments. One of them (placed under the direct control of the Long-Range Aviation Commander) was the 43rd TsBP i PLS at Dyagilevo AB in Ryazan', which comprised three instructional heavy bomber regiments based at Dyagilevo AB, Shaykovka AB (Kaluga Region) and Belaya Tserkov' (in the Ukraine). By the early 1990s these three regiments operated 27 Tu-16s, 19 Tu-22Ms and 11 Tu-95s (the latter were stripped of armament and converted to trainers). Tu-16 pilots also took conversion training at the DA's Tambov Military Pilot College named after the famous aviatrix Marina M. Raskova (TVVAUL – *Tambovskoye vyssheye voyennoye aviatsionnoye oochilishche lyotchikov*) located at Tambov-Vostochnyy AB (= Tambov-East). These outfits were supplied with early production examples of the Tu-16 for aircrew training.

When units converted to the Tu-16, aircraft captains were selected and trained from the following personnel: Tu-4 captains, Il-28 pilots proficient in all-weather day operations and VMC operations at night, Tu-16 co-pilots with at least 150 hours' total time on the type, and captains of military transport aircraft trained to a set minimum in all-weather flying by day and night. Pilots accepted for conversion training on the Tu-16 as captains had to have at least 800 hours' total flying time, a good or excellent grasp of piloting skills and an unblemished service record. Co-pilots for the Tu-16 were chosen from co-pilots on the Tu-4 and pilots who had qualified on jet aircraft at tactical bomber aviation flying schools.

Tu-16 navigators took their training at the Chelyabinsk Military Navigator College (ChVVAUSh – *Chelyabinskoye vyssheye voyennoye aviatsionnoye oochilishche shtoormanov*), starting in 1957. Though based at Shagol AB on the northern outskirts of the city, the college also had training facilities at other locations;

Tu-16 training was conducted by the 605th UAP (*oochebnyy aviapolk* – training air regiment) at Kamensk-Ural'skiy (Sverdlovsk Region), the 108th UAP at Shadrinsk (Kurgan Region) and the 45th UAP at Kustanai (northern Kazakhstan; now called Kostanai) – the former 45th BAP. The Voroshilovgrad Military Navigator College (VVVAUSh – *Voroshilovgradskoye vyssheye voyennoye aviatsionnoye oochilishche shtoormanov*) at Voroshilovgrad in eastern Ukraine (now renamed back to Lugansk) also did some Tu-16 navigator training at the 457th UAP in Mirgorod, albeit it mostly trained Tactical Aviation personnel.

Navigators/bomb-aimers were selected from the following: Tu-4 navigators with navigational and bombardier experience in VMC/IMC by day and VMC by night at medium/high altitudes, and Tu-16 co-navigators (*sic* – presumably this means navigator-operators) who had successfully carried out live weapons training sorties. Co-navigators (Nav/Ops) were appointed from Tu-4 weapons systems operators with navigational and bombardier experience by day and night at medium/high altitudes, Tu-4 assistant navigators who met the same criteria and had taken conversion training for the Tu-16, and navigators who had qualified at the DA's operational training schools as navigator-operators.

At first the specially converted Tu-4UShS trainers (*oochebno-shtoormanskiy samolyot* – navigator trainer aircraft) – a version of the *Bull* with no cannon armament and with a Rubidiy-MM2 radar and an OPB-11R bombsight as fitted to the Tu-16 (instead of the usual Kobal't radar and OPB-5SN bombsight) – were used for navigator training. Several regiments had these machines, which remained in service until the early 1960s. Later they were replaced by the Tu-124Sh-1 – a purpose-built navigator trainer version of the Tu-124V twin-turbofan short-haul airliner for the Long-Range Aviation. It was fitted with the bomb-aiming and flight instrumentation of the bomber, and later the missile strike versions, of the Tu-16. The Tu-124Sh-1 was used in the training regiments of the Chelyabinsk VVAUSh and also for pilot training at the Tambov VVAUL, since the aircraft was similar to the Tu-16 in its handling characteristics. Later all three colleges, the most important ones for training navigators and pilots for the DA, were supplied with actual examples of the Tu-16 to optimise aircrew training. However, the 457th UAP was disbanded in 1977 as a cost-cutting measure; the 45th UAP followed suit in 1980, ceding its Tu-16s to the 46th UAP of the Voroshilovgrad VVAUSh based at Ostraya Mogila AB immediately south of Voroshilovgrad.

Defensive fire commanders (tail gunners) and senior radio operators were selected from GROs trained for the Tu-16 and possessing a qualification no lower than Gunner 2nd Class (national service and extended service sergeant and warrant officer ranks). GROs for the Tu-16 were picked from non-commissioned officers who had qualified at sergeant schools and received a Radio Operator 3rd Class rating after two flights in the Tu-4UShS. As a rule, these were national service sergeants; until the mid-1950s, the conscription term for enlisted men and NCOs in the Soviet Air Force was five years, which was long enough to allow outstanding aircrew and ground crew members to be trained.

Qualified flying instructors (QFIs) were trained within the operational units under the authority of the regiment CO and the control of the division CO. The task of bomb-aiming and naviga-

Left: A Tu-16R *Badger-F* retrofitted with Siren'-D (front) and Siren'-MD (rear) jammers.

Below: Tu-16Ye Azaliya '23 Blue' – likewise equipped with Siren'-D and Siren'-MD jammers – is caught by the camera immediately after touchdown, as the fully deployed flaps show.

tional instruction was allocated to leading navigation personnel who had gained top grades in navigation and bomb-aiming as navigators or co-navigators.

As the number of aircraft in squadron service increased, so did the need for aircrews. The Soviet Air Force Command decided therefore to give initial training directly to aircrew cadets in mili-

tary schools. The training of navigators was inaugurated at the Chelyabinsk VVAUSh and the training of pilots at the Tambov VVAUL. Those qualifying from their schools were appointed WSOs and co-pilots when they were posted to an air regiment. After obtaining a set skill rating, they became navigators and crew captains.

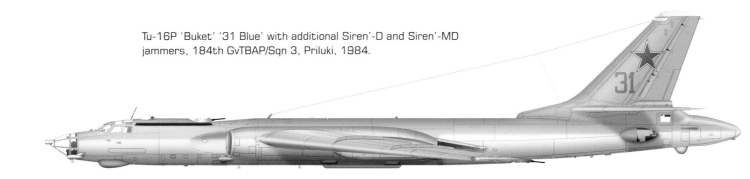

Tu-16P 'Buket' '31 Blue' with additional Siren'-D and Siren'-MD jammers, 184th GvTBAP/Sqn 3, Priluki, 1984.

Naval Aviation pilots flying the Tu-16 were trained by the 540th MTAP of the Nikolayev Minelayer and Torpedo-Bomber Flying School (VMMTAU – *Voyenno-morskoye* **minno-torped-** *noye aviatsionnoye oochilishche*) named after Sigizmund A. Levanevskiy at Nikolayev-Kul'bakino AB. In 1960 it became the AVMF's 33rd Training Centre which, in turn, served as the basis for the 33rd TsBP i PLS named after Yevgeniy N. Preobrazhenskiy (the former AVMF C-in-C) in 1967, the regiment being restyled as the 540th IIMRAP. As for navigator training, the AVMF had no navigator college of its own, and the naval Tu-16 navigators were trained in Chelyabinsk and Voroshilovgrad along with their colleagues from the Air Force.

Ground crews working with the Tu-16 were trained in military aviation technical schools. Specialists on airframes, engines and aviation equipment took their training at the Irkutsk Military Aviation Technical Staff College (IVATU – *Irkootskoye voyennoye aviatsionno-tekhnicheskoye oochilishche*), which had several early Tu-16s, including second pre-production Kuibyshev-built Tu-16 (c/n 1880002), as ground instructional airframes. Technicians specialising in armament were trained at the Achinsk VATU, and radar specialists at the Tambov Military Aviation Technical Staff College (TVVAIU – *Tambovskoye* **vyssheye voyennoye** *avi-atsionnoye inzhenernoye oochilishche*).

Various missions, various problems

As one might expect of a new aircraft, the Tu-16 was beset with many problems at the service entry stage – not least because it had been rushed into production, as was often the case. The Tupolev OKB kept an eye on all Tu-16 aircraft during the early phase of their service. Any defects arising in the airframe, systems or equipment were rectified and, if necessary, the findings applied to aircraft in service and on the production line. The accidents that did occur were investigated and the causes discovered; measures were then taken to ensure that they did not recur in future.

One particular problem was the insufficient strength of the forward fuselage structure on early machines. In a hard landing this could result in structural damage – right down to the flight deck section breaking away. One such accident at Sol'tsy AB involved a resident 840th TBAP aircraft captained by the regiment CO Col. Gheorgiy 'Goga' G. Agamirov (HSU); luckily there was no fire and the entire crew walked away. At first the OKB denied there was something wrong with the aircraft, but eventually admitted the problem was there and set to work resolving it; the fuselage was beefed up, and aircraft already in service were recalled to have reinforcement plates added.

A dangerous and hitherto unknown phenomenon dubbed *pod-khvat* (pick-up, as an action) manifested itself on the Tu-16; on encountering an upward vertical gust of wind the aircraft could pitch up spontaneously, climbing and losing speed until it stalled and entered a spin. The same problem affected the Tu-104 airliner based on the Tu-16, and after one fatal crash of the airliner and several near-accidents in which control was restored, the Tupolev OKB set to work on the problem. The cause was eventually traced to the tail unit design, and on the Tu-104 the problem was cured by altering the stabiliser incidence, modifying the elevators and imposing restrictions on the flight envelope. An equally danger-

ous phenomenon seen on the Tu-16 was the uncommanded movement of the ailerons at high speed and high altitude leading to loss of control. On 27th March 1961, a 56th TBAD Tu-16 captained by Maj. I. Ye. Yupatov got into a most unusual situation – after flicking into a spin the aircraft rolled inverted and both engines flamed out. Luckily the captain managed to relight the engines and recover to straight and level flight (right side up), making a safe landing. After this, changes were introduced into the bomber's design and recommendations on how to act if the aircraft stalled were issued to the aircrews.

A regiment operating the Tu-16 usually consisted of three squadrons, equipped at first with the Tu-16 and Tu-16A. When the Tu-16KS entered service, a regiment could be equipped solely with this version or consist of one Tu-16KS squadron and two squadrons of bombers.

The number of versions in a regiment rose with the advent of in-flight refuelling, which helped to overcome the Tu-16's inadequate range – at 5,800 km (3,603 mile), it was only 400 km (248 miles) greater than that of the Tu-4, with a combat radius of 1,800-2,300 km (1,120-1,430 miles). Normally Squadrons 1 and 2 flew bomber or missile strike versions, including those with IFR capability, while the Sqn 3 operated Tu-16Z tankers (sometimes with limited ECM capability).

In-flight refuelling, particularly with the Tu-16's wing-to-wing system, was a complex procedure that took a heavy toll on the crews' nerves. Maj.-Gen. Aleksandr A. Balenko, CO of the 2nd TBAD, was one of the first service pilots to master the IFR technique; he famously commented that it was *'akin to holding a tiger by the tail – all fear and no fun'* and that refuelling at night was *'just the same, except that you can't see shit'*. During IFR operations the pilot's blood pressure soared and his pulse could go as high as 200; the stress was so severe that pilots could lose about 2 kg (4.4 lb) of body weight in a single sortie. There was a joke in the Air Force that you could identify the pilot of an IFR-capable Tu-16 by the sweat stains on his leather flying jacket!

The refuelling procedure harboured a danger: if the pilot of the receiver aircraft placed his port wing on the tanker's hose too abruptly, the hose could bend over and form a loop, ensnaring the port aileron; the result was inevitably a departure from controlled flight. This phenomenon was dubbed the 'Gibalevich Loop' after a 185th TBAP Tu-16 captain who was the first to crash for this reason. Entering the tanker's wake vortex was likewise fraught with loss of control, the receiver aircraft rolling to port, which resulted in a collision with the tanker.

When in 1956 the 13th GvTBAD – by then composed of the 184th, 185th and 226th GvTBAPs – started getting to grips with IFR, the tankers were concentrated in the 175th TBAP in Mirgorod; additionally, a special IFR procedures training group was set up in the 184th GvTBAP. At first Col. Vladimir D. Ikonnikov (HSU) and Col. Nikolay V. Novozhilov (HSU) from the DA's Flight Safety Inspectorate were assigned to the group as instructors; *Badger* crews from far and wide were seconded to this group to take their training.

The refuelling procedure was filmed from inside the aircraft and the films were used for instructional purposes. By the end of 1960 as many as 70% of the crews in the 226th GvTBAP were

capable of refuelling in daytime and at night; in 1962-63 the unit was 100% rated for night-time IFR. The training was very intensive; for example, the regiment's Deputy CO Col. Gheorgiy T. Goobin made no fewer than 330 contacts with the tanker!

Eventually the wing-to-wing technique was mastered, but at a heavy price. In 1958-64, in two regiments alone (the 184th GvTBAP and the 226th GvTBAP) fifteen Tu-16s were lost with all hands in the course of in-flight refuelling – and that means 90 young and fit airmen who were real pros. Quite apart from the accidents, there was a lot of incidents, such as the tanker's hose breaking or getting ingested by the receiver aircraft's port engine.

Only one specialised aerial refuelling unit equipped with the *Badger* existed in the DA – the 179th *Berlinskaya* OTAE SZ at Siauliai, which was formed in 1959 by reorganising the 345th TBAP. The honorary appellation was inherited from the latter unit which had gained it for participating actively in the Berlin Offensive Operation of 1945. Even so, the 179th OTAE SZ was not an all-*Badger* unit (and not even an all-tanker unit, for that matter) – it operated Tu-16 bombers and Myasishchev M-4-2 *Bison-A*

tankers alongside the Tu-16Z! For whatever reason the 179th Squadron had the unofficial name *Normandiya* (Normandy). However, there were tanker squadrons within several bomber regiments – such as the 1225th TBAP at Belaya AB, the 303rd TBAP at Khorol' AB and the 219th ODRAP at Khvalynka AB (all reporting to the 8th OTBAK).

After March 1964 the Air Force no longer practiced in-flight refuelling with the Tu-16 because ICBMs were being fielded on a growing scale; the Navy, on the other hand, chose to retain this IFR capability. By the early 1970s the number of operational Tu-16Z tankers declined as the requirement for wing-to-wing refuelling changed and the aircraft reached the end of their service lives. Most of the tankers were converted into ASM carriers. A whole series of regiments lost their tankers, despite the fact that almost all combat versions of the Tu-16, as well as reconnaissance and ECM versions, were IFR-capable.

The Tu-16N/Tu-16NN tanker using the probe-and-drogue system was much less widespread. It equipped just a single squadron – namely Sqn 4 of the 200th GvTBAP based at Bobruisk, which

Above: Tu-16R *Badger-F* '05 Black' equipped with Siren'-D and Siren'-MD jammers receives fuel from a Tu-16Z ('30 Black) over the rugged terrain of the Far East.

Left: Silhouetted against the sun, a Tu-16Z tanker is seen from the flight deck of a Tu-16 due to be refuelled.

Right and above right: Two more views of the same pair from a further *Badger-F*, which is probably either due to refuel next or has been refuelled already.

was established in 1972 to cater for the operations of Tu-22K missile carriers based in Belorussia. Later the tankers were transferred to the 251st GvTBAP at Belaya Tserkov'.

With the advent of ECM versions, these were usually flown by a bomber regiment's Sqn 3, the tankers by Sqn 2 and combat versions by Sqn 1. This was not always the case; in the 200th GvTBAP Sqns 1 and 2 were equipped with Tu-16KSR-2 missile carriers, Sqn 3 had Tu-16SPS ECM aircraft, while Sqn 4 was the tanker squadron. One unit at Poltava, the 226th Independent ECM Air Regiment, consisted solely of ECM versions – the Tu-16Ye and various versions of the Tu-16P, including several with the Cactus

system. In 1986 the 226th OAP REB was disbanded, leaving a single ECM squadron. Independent reconnaissance air regiments likewise had a 'mixed bag', operating tankers and ECM versions in addition to reconnaissance machines.

The AVMF's Tu-16 regiments had an even more variegated mix of aircraft. In addition to the versions they shared with the Long-Range Aviation, they also operated purely naval versions: the Tu-16K-10 missile carrier, the Tu-16RM-1 and Tu-16RM-2 spyplanes, the Tu-16T torpedo-bomber, the Tu-16S SAR version and the Tu-16PLO ASW version. The Tu-16T was the basic element of minelayer and torpedo-bomber units and the Tu-16K-10 of the mis-

sile strike units. With the conversion of the Tu-16T into the Tu-16S and Tu-16PLO, these latter versions were operated by independent ASW air regiments.

Combat training on the Tu-16PLO was taken seriously, the ASW version participating in a number of Navy exercises. This, in April 1963 North Fleet air arm Tu-16PLOs searched for their target in an area located 1,200-1,300 km (745-807 miles) from the base, tracking the 'hostile' submarine for 13 hours after detecting it. This involved in-flight refuelling, especially if the Tu-16PLO in 'killer' configuration with a load of AT-1 torpedoes loitered in a designated area, waiting for the orders to attack. Still, using the *Badger* for ASW duties was a stop-gap measure, and in 1969 the squadrons equipped with Tu-16PLOs were stood down after six years of operation when more advanced shore-based and amphibious ASW aircraft came on the scene.

Tu-16R crews started flying reconnaissance missions on a regular basis in mid-1961. In the summer of 1961, a North Fleet Tu-16R captained by Maj. F. V. Oozlov made a flight over the North Pole, refuelling twice en route and staying aloft for an unprecedented 11 hours 48 minutes. In the Far East, Pacific Fleet/317th OSAP Tu-16R crews also began systematically flying sorties over the Sea of Japan and refining aerial reconnaissance techniques. Supported by Tu-16Z tankers, they periodically reconnoitred the approaches to the east coast of Japan with a view to detecting the US Navy carrier task forces heading for the naval base at Yokosuka in timely fashion. The first encounters with a CTF usually involved US Navy fighters scrambling from the carrier to intercept the 'visitors' and escort them away; therefore, Soviet crews would try to escape early detection by coming in at low level, staying below the principal lobe of the ship's radar, until visual contact had been established. The techniques of using the SIGINT equipment were also polished.

Reconnaissance versions of the Tu-16 were used in combined-arms exercises on land and naval exercises, and the Tu-16R was regularly used to follow the movements and exercises of NATO navies in the seas and oceans adjacent to Soviet territorial waters. A pair of Tu-16Rs were normally assigned to this task. There were two reasons why such sorties were invariably flown in pairs. Firstly, one aircraft in the pair was often fitted with the SRS-1 ELINT set and the other with the SRS-3; this was to ensure comprehensive coverage of all possible radar frequencies used by the NATO ships. Secondly, if one aircraft came down in the ocean the crew of the other Tu-16 could report the co-ordinates of the crash site to the base, improving the chances that the downed crew would be rescued before they died of exposure.

When the Tu-16RM-1 and Tu-16RM-2 entered Soviet Navy service they, too, were used in these operations, as monitoring the movements of NATO carrier task forces was a standing assignment. In the 1960s and 1970s Western aviation publications were full of photographs showing Soviet Tu-16Rs and 'RMs flying over the decks of US Navy and Royal Navy aircraft carriers.

It was perhaps the reconnaissance versions that saw the most action in the Cold War. In the course of such sorties the *Badgers* were often intercepted by shore-based or shipboard NATO fighters over international waters. As a precaution against itchy trigger fingers, it was a standing rule that neither side should use the other as a practice target during such intercepts so as to avoid an accidental shootdown, and the tail gunners of the Tu-16s always kept the cannons fully raised to show they had no hostile intentions.

Still, incidents did happen, especially at times when political tensions between the East and the West were high. In October 1973, a Tu-16R captained by A. P. Sviridov was flying a routine surveillance sortie over a US Navy CTF in the Norwegian Sea. Everything was business as usual until the pilot of an intercepting McDonnell Douglas F-4 Phantom II decided to put on a show of force. Manoeuvring sharply next to the *Badger*, he misjudged the distance and caused a collision. Despite the damage, the Soviet crew completed the mission and returned to base; for this sortie Sviridov was awarded the Order of the Red Banner of Combat.

In the early 1980s a Tu-16 on patrol over the Atlantic Ocean was intercepted by three of the latest American carrier-based fighters, the McDonnell Douglas F/A-18A Hornet. Trying to scare the Soviet aircraft off its intended course, the fighters performed dangerous manoeuvres, including head-on passes. Eventually this game of chicken got the better of the players: two of the fighters collided directly above the Tu-16 and exploded; one pilot was killed, the other managed to eject. The *Badger*, too, was struck by flying debris and damaged; luckily the aircraft managed to limp back to base thanks to the courage and skill of its crew.

Conversely, sometimes the US Navy fighters would actually lead the Tu-16s to the CTF. The reason was simple: the fighters always operated in pairs or threes; the crews would take pictures of each other's aircraft and get paid for a properly documented intercept! There seemed to be a tacit understanding between the Soviet and American airmen; like, 'look, we're both pros; we're both doing our job, so we'll let you do your job if you let us do ours'.

The missile strike versions, too, had their share of the Cold War action – though mercifully they did not have to fire in anger. For example, on 21st September 1964 three squadrons of North Fleet air arm Tu-16K-10s managed a low-altitude approach to a group of NATO warships in the North Atlantic participating in Exercise *Team Work '64* and made simulated launches; in a real-life launch scenario the ships would have been sunk.

Major exercises sometimes cause the Tu-16 units to redeploy to unfamiliar bases. For example, on 11th-16th March 1974 two squadrons of the Air Force's 200th GvTBAP redeployed from Bobruisk in Belorussia to Ookrainka AB in the Far East (Amur Region) with refuelling stops at Vorkuta and Tiksi to practice operations on the Far Eastern TO; live weapons training sorties were flown from there to the Litovko target range 50 km (31 miles) north of Khabarovsk. On the way back the Tu-16s staged through Chagan AB near Semipalatinsk, flying further bombing practice sorties as the Nogotai target range (Irkutsk Region) and the Turtkuduk target range in Kazakhstan. In 1975 the unit participated in Exercise *Vesna-75* (Spring-75) which involved a redeployment to Migalovo AB in Kalinin.

So-called 'inter-fleet operations' were practiced during major naval exercises as well. Thus, during the strategic exercise *Okean-70* (Ocean-70, pronounced *okiahn*) ten Tu-16K-10s from the Pacific Fleet's 143rd MRAD redeployed to North Fleet airbases, from where they flew sorties against practice targets on the Kola Peninsula.

An enamel badge of the Black Sea Fleet's 574th MRAP, showing the year when the regiment was established.

Above: Tu-16 crewmen from the 540th IIMRAP of the Naval Aviation's 33rd TsBP i PLS at Nikolayev-Kul'bakino.

Below: A Tu-16Z photographed as it passes over a Soviet Navy missile submarine.

On 9th November 1975, Soviet Navy Tu-16K-10s nearly ended up in a situation of having to attack one of their own ships. The Baltic Fleet's Type 1135.2 (**Bditel'nyy** class; NATO *Krivak* class) ASW cruiser SNS *Storozhevoy*, whose crew had raised mutiny instigated by the ship's chief political officer Lt.-Cdr. Valeriy M. Sablin, left her base at Riga seaport and set course towards Leningrad; Sablin intended to enter the Neva River, cast anchor and address the nation, exposing the follies of the regime headed by Leonid I. Brezhnev. However, the Soviet MoD top brass hastily branded the ship's crew as traitors, suspecting that Sablin intended to defect to Sweden together with the ship, and ordered the cruiser sunk. Several 170th MRAP *Badger-Cs* scrambled from Bykhov AB; luckily they did not have to carry out the attack – the *Storozhevoy* was detected by Yak-28 tactical bombers of the Air Force's 668th BAP which launched from Rumbula AB near Riga. After the Yak-28s had dropped the first bombs behind her stern as a 'warning shot', the cruiser stopped and the crew surrendered.

An embarrassing incident occurred in the Pacific Fleet in 1964. A Japanese ship outbound from the Soviet seaport of Nikolayevsk-on-Amur with a cargo of timber (according to some sources, the Japanese fishing vessel *Shino Maru*) entered a restricted area around the Mys Tyk maritime target range near Sakhalin Island. Just then a Tu-16K-10 was attacking a practice target with a K-10S missile, and the latter locked on to the Japanese ship which had a bigger radar signature. The ship was saved by pure luck: realising at the last moment that the target was a commercial ship, the *Badger*'s crew set the missile to self-destruct, the warhead detonating 400 m (1,310 ft) from the ship. (Another account has it that the missile was preset to detonate a short way from the practice target to save it from excessive damage so that it would last longer – decommissioned ships were not so thick underfoot, after all!) Nevertheless, fragments of the missile riddled the ship's superstructure, seriously injuring one of the crew, and the missile's engine went clean through the hull, punching holes in both sides. The ship called at the Soviet seaport of Kholmsk on Sakhalin Island, where the wounded man received medical treatment. An investigation ensued, and the matter took quite a while

to settle through diplomatic channels. According to unconfirmed reports, the ship's crew had sent a cable to the Soviet authorities, extending condolences 'on the death of a Soviet fighter pilot' – they had allegedly mistaken the missile for a crashed fighter jet.

Occasionally the Tu-16s would pose as 'aggressor' aircraft. Maj. Vladimir M. Yegorov, who served in the 121st GvODRAP when the unit was still operating Tu-16Rs, recalls: *'In July 1961, together with unit CO [Col. Aleksey Ya.] Nekipelov, we flew to Olen'ya AB near Murmansk; from there the regiment staged an "air raid on Moscow", testing the vigilance of the city's air defences. The avenues of approach lay east of the Moscow Region. [...] We took off, flew over Noginsk* (a town in the east of the Moscow Region – Auth.) *at 1,200 m [3,940 ft], and there was not a single fighter to "greet" us. We turned [west] and set course for Moscow. I turned on all the cameras; we passed over the Kremlin and the Lenin Mausoleum, photographing all of city centre and [further west] all the way to Vnukovo [airport]. We landed at Shaikovka [AB] without ever being detected. The Moscow air defences had missed us completely.'* A classic case of some people's professionalism highlighting other people's incompetence.

Unlike Soviet tactical aircraft (fighters, bombers and helicopters), which were deployed outside the USSR full time in large numbers as part of the groups of Soviet forces in Eastern Europe (East Germany, Poland, Hungary and Czechoslovakia) and Mongolia, foreign deployments of the Tu-16 were rare. Occasionally the *Badgers* did fly over Eastern Europe during Warsaw Pact exercises, but landing there was to be avoided by all means – unless an emergency landing was necessary.

L. Z. Petukhov, a pilot who served with the 1023rd TBAP in the 1960s, recalled that in March or April 1965, when Soviet-US relations were severely strained because of the Vietnam War, a large group of Tu-16s unexpectedly deployed to Chagan AB, occupying all available parking space. They were fitted out with nuclear bombs; at the political briefing in the evening the personnel of the resident 1023rd TBAP was told that the Soviet Union was preparing an ultimatum to the USA with a demand to withdraw troops from Vietnam within 48 hours, and in the morning the bombers were to redeploy to forward bases in China from where they would attack American targets if the demands were not met! However, China refused to let the Soviets use its airfields for this;

a few days later the bombers returned, offloaded the unused nukes and left, and life was back to normal.

Speaking of nukes, the Tu-16 was involved in Soviet nuclear tests at Semipalatinsk and Novaya Zemlya (proving grounds No.2 and No.6 respectively) on a regular basis. At Semipalatinsk alone, no fewer than five nuclear bombs were dropped in 1957 (on 8th March, 22nd August, 26th August, 13th September, and 26th September); in 1958 the number rose to eight – on 4th January, 13th March, 14th March, 15th March (two!), 18th March, 20th March, and 22nd March.

In particular, the aircraft of the 1023rd TBAP/Sqn 4 participated in such tests at Semipalatinsk in 1961-63. Vladimir P. Poortov, another veteran of this unit, recalled that the tests took place in September-October. *'A team from Moscow would arrive; we called them the "black patch guys" because they wore uniforms like those of artillery or [military] construction troops instead of Air Force uniforms.* (Sic – this means that the lapel patches and the band on the peaked cap were black as in most branches of the ground forces, not light blue as in the Air Force – Auth.) *Our Sqn 4 would be placed at their disposal right away. [...] The "Muscovites" came with their own Tu-16 that carried the nuke; it was parked over a special trench on a separate hardstand with a barbed wire fence around it. Our Sqn 4 supplied two aircraft which flew as back-ups with conventional 3-ton [6,610-lb] bombs. Taking off after the bomber carrying the nuke, they would take air samples in the mushroom cloud of the nuclear explosion; this was the main task of Sqn 4.*

On one occasion, however, the assignment changed. The aircraft of the Moscow team developed a fuel leak, and it was decided that a Tu-16 coded "17" from Sqn 4 should deliver the [nuclear] bomb. It was then that I had a chance to visit the special hardstand guarded by armed sentries. There was a railroad spur with boxcars behind the HQ of the [1023rd] regiment. [...] When the aircraft had been readied we were ordered to go outside the barbed

A Tu-16KSR-2-11 carrying a single missile is depicted in high-altitude cruise.

wire fence, and we watched the proceedings from there. A dolly with a canvas tent shaped like a peaked roof was wheeled out of the boxcar. They hooked it up to a jeep which slowly towed it to the trench, accompanied by officers. The underside of the aircraft [near the bomb bay] was also concealed by a canvas tent, and we could see nothing. The bomb was loaded by the Moscow team. The aircrew, on the other hand, was from our squadron. After this sortie the squadron's Chief Navigator Maj. Ivan I. Dryomov had to go to hospital for treatment because the blinding flash of the explosion had hurt his eyes.' For this mission, which took place in 1961, Dryomov and the aircraft's captain I. L. Nikolaychuk (the squadron commander) received the Red Star Order and the Order of the Red Banner of Combat respectively in March 1962. That same year the Tu-16 performed the last-ever Soviet nuclear test before the Soviet Union signed the Comprehensive Test Ban treaty.

Occasionally, however, the Tu-16s of the 1023rd TBAP/Sqn 4 would use their bombs for totally unwarlike purposes. Each year the squadron was tasked with bombing ice jams in order to prevent floods; this was known as 'ice alert duty'. The ones on the rivers of Uzbekistan were bombed first (in the early spring); the rivers Lena, Yenisey, Ob' and other Siberian rivers, which thawed later, were also taken care of in due course. Vladimir Poortov recalled that PK-75 bombs (*sic*) were used, and occasionally they failed to explode, sinking to the river bed because the low altitude left insufficient time for the fuses to arm.

Unfortunately no aircraft type is immune to accident attrition, and the Tu-16 is no exception. In the course of the *Badger's* 40-year service career 122 aircraft were lost in accidents; brief details of known accidents are given in Appendix 2. The worst attrition was between 1957 and 1960 when about ten machines were lost each year. The causes varied; some crashes were the result of design defects, such as the insufficiently strong forward fuselage mentioned earlier, or other hardware failures caused by poor workmanship or improper maintenance, such as the loss of a 402nd TBAP Tu-16 on 6th April 1954, due to spontaneous deflection of the elevator trim tab. As often as not, however, the cause was the tell-tale human factor. This was by no means limited to crew error – a mid-air collision between a Tu-16 and a civil Antonov An-24 *Coke* airliner on 24th August 1981, was due to air traffic control incompetence. When a Tu-16R crashed into the Sea of Japan immediately after passing over an American carrier group on 15th July 1964, the cause was never established; to this day there are allegations that the aircraft had been shot down by the US Navy air defences.

Sometimes an order given by command staff on the ground was the potential cause of an accident. Before the 1954 May Day flypast test pilot Mikhail A. Nyukhtikov was ordered to descend after passing over the History Museum at the nothern entrance to Red Square and pass the Lenin Mausoleum at the same height as the saluting stand before climbing away steeply over St Basil's Cathedral. Nyukhtikov saw clearly how impossible this was; yet he had no alternative but to obey the order. He resolved the dilemma by losing height very slightly and then accelerating away at around 1,000 km/h (621 mph) with a roar of engines. The effect was so dramatic that no one remembered to ask why the pilot had not carried out his order to the letter.

The nose of a Tu-16K-10 seen during an intercept on 1st September 1982.

Speaking of parades and flypasts, the Tu-16 was a regular participant in the May Day and 7th November parades in Red Square, as well as the Aviation Day (or Air Fleet Day) flypasts staged on the third Sunday of August. (7th November was the anniversary of the October Revolution, one of the most important public holidays in the Soviet Union. Here it should be explained that on 26th January 1918, three months after the revolution, Soviet Russia switched from the outdated Julian calendar to the Gregorian calendar. Thus 25th October, the 'old style' date of the revolution, equals 7th November according to the current calendar.)

Before the 1956 May Day parade the huge Tu-16 formation – 75 bombers from the 121st, 171st and 203rd TBAPs – practiced daily at Chkalovskaya AB east of Moscow. First, the bombers were lined up on the runway and markers taped on them to help the pilots memorise the correct position in the formation. Next, daily practice flights began to ensure perfect station-keeping and timing. The landing of this armada was a problem in itself; the intervals had to be reduced to 20 seconds because with normal intervals the last of the bombers would have to wait their turn for hours! On one occasion this nearly led to a ground collision when the bomber in front had an engine problem and stopped on the runway.

The practice flights were recorded on cine film from the ground and the films used for debriefing. Occasionally the DA Commander Air Marshal Vladimir A. Soodets would attend the debriefing; he was famous for his hot temper and could mete out punishment promptly. If Soodets noticed something untoward at the debriefing, he would order the 'movie' stopped and demand: *'Aircraft coded such-and-such! Who's the aircraft captain?'* A frightened major would rise and identify himself. Then he would receive the full blast: *'Why didn't you maintain formation [expletive deleted]?'* *'I ran into wake turbulence, Comrade Marshal'* – the culprit would stammer. *'If a Major can't maintain formation, then maybe a Captain can [expletive deleted]!'* – the marshal would comment and the 'movie' would continue.

Came May Day, and the bomber armada led by 45th TBAD CO Col. Vitaliy A Gordilovskiy took off and began the circuitous route to Moscow, assuming close formation before the final turn onto the heading that would take them along Leningradskiy Prospekt avenue, then along Gor'kiy Street and over Red Square. All of a sudden the group flying at 300 m (990 ft) went smack into thick clouds that should not be there at all – the weather reconnais-

The numbers of the Tu-16 versions in service with the Long-Range Aviation as of 1st January 1979								
Year of manufacture	Tu-16	Tu-16A	Tu-16Z	Tu-16N	Tu-16R	Tu-16KSR	Tu-16 'Yolka'	Tu-16P 'Buket'
1954	–	3	–	–	–	17	–	–
1955	8	5	5	–	–	99	8	25
1956	4	9	15	2	–	52	27	44
1957	10	21	–	8	14	38	4	27
1958	1	–	–	–	8	5	29	8
Total	23	38	20	10	22	211	68	104
Grand total	496							

sance flight 90 minutes earlier had shown clear skies. Receiving no orders from the leader or from the ground, the pilots did the only possible thing and moved the bombers apart to avoid a collision in the clouds. When they broke clear of the clouds at 3,000 m (9,840 ft), the beautiful tight formation had gone to the dogs and there was no time to restore it. Someone radioed in clear code, telling the bomber pilots to abort the mission and return to base. The mood was rotten, but at least everyone landed in one piece. At Chkalovskaya the crews waited for the big brass and the inevitable repercussions. At length one of the DA's Deputy Commanders arrived – a level-headed and businesslike man. He summoned the airmen to the officers' mess where the tables had been set for the occasion. *'Well, Comrades pilots –* the general said after accepting a glass of vodka, *– what will we be celebrating? May Day or your birthday?'* Of course everyone said *'Birthday, Comrade General!'* The general drank and went on: *'Happy birthday! Everyone came out of this alive – which means you did the right thing!'* Ironically, the jet fighters that approached Red Square ahead of the bombers followed a different route, taking off from Kubinka AB west of Moscow; they avoided the freak clouds, making the flypast without any trouble.

On one occasion the Tu-16 was called upon to act as a passenger aircraft, carrying some unusual civilian passengers. Nikita S. Khrushchov's style of running the country earned him some bitter enemies, and attempts to depose him were made more than once before he was finally toppled in 1964. In 1957, a situation arose when it was vital to summon the First Secretaries (that is, bosses) of the regional and district Communist Party committees pronto for an extraordinary full party meeting to support Khrushchov against a so-called 'anti-Communist opposition group' within the Soviet government. Using his power as Minister of Defence, Gheorgiy K. Zhukov arranged for the necessary Communist Party bosses to be flown in by Tu-16 bombers. Khrushchov was thus able to convoke a plenum quickly and gain the necessary number of votes. In this way the Tu-16 played a crucial part in the power struggle among the Soviet political leaders in the second half of the 1950s.

The Tu-16 formed the backbone of the Long-Range Aviation for a considerable time. When the Tu-22 supersonic long-range bomber entered service in 1963, several DA regiments at Baranovichi, Machoolishchi, Zyabrovka, Ozyornoe and Nezhin and naval air regiments at Saki, Ostrov and Kaliningrad began converting to the new type. However, the service entry of the Tu-22 bomber hardly diminished the role of the Tu-16 in the nation's defence. Firstly, the *Blinder* was built in much smaller numbers and

equipped far fewer regiments; secondly, the Tu-16 was the more versatile machine with a significantly wider range of applications. Thirdly, at its subsonic cruising speed, with only a supersonic dash over the target, the Tu-22 had no real advantage in performance over the Tu-16; fourth, the K-26 weapons system with the KSR-5 missile was at least equal, and in some aspects superior, to the K-22 system. Finally, the Tu-22 was rather troublesome and accident-prone – at least initially; it was also more complicated to fly because there was no co-pilot. Knowing this, many Tu-16 pilots treated it with distrust and were reluctant to convert to the *Blinder*. In fact, the 444th TBAP at Vozdvizhenka AB took delivery of several new Tu-22 bombers initially, but quickly passed them on to other regiments and reverted to the Tu-16.

During the 1970s more modern types of bombers and missile carriers, the Tu-22M2 and later the Tu-22M3, began to enter service with the DA and the AVMF. In 1972 the 185th GvTBAP at Poltava was the first to receive the Tu-22M2, followed by the 840th TBAP at Sol'tsy, the two regiments at Belaya Tserkov', the 52nd GvTBAP at Shaikovka and so on. The 184th GvTBAP at Priluki was re-equipped with this type in the 1980s. In the Naval Aviation the regiments at Nikolayev, Sovetskaya Gavan', Bykhov and the like were re-equipped. But even when full-scale production and deliveries of the Tu-22M2 and Tu-22M3 got under way in Kazan', the Tu-16 remained in service with the vast majority of Long-Range Aviation and Naval Aviation regiments. In fact, naval units converting to the Tu-22M2 initially retained a single squadron of Tu-16K-26s or Tu-16K-10-26s for proficiency training to save wear and tear on the new bombers.

The table on this page shows the Air Force's *Badger* fleet in 1979. A similar number of Tu-16s (including 209 missile strike aircraft) remained in service with the Naval Aviation. At the end of 1981 the Long-Range Aviation had 487 Tu-16 and the Naval Aviation 474. A further 156 examples were in service with other elements of the Soviet Armed Forces and the defence industry. MAP documents also listed 106 examples as 'not current' by then (this included both aircraft written off due to technical condition and accident attrition). The remaining machines, apart from those exported, do not appear in the statistics for some reason.

According to Soviet practice one or two aircraft repair plants would repair and refurbish all aircraft of a given type, regardless of where they were based (including export aircraft), though occasionally the manufacturer did the job as well. If the aircraft was built and operated in large numbers, several repair plants could be assigned to cope with the workload. This was the case with the

Tu-16. The plants handling the Air Force's *Badgers* were ARZ No.12 in Khabarovsk, ARZ No.148 in Belaya Tserkov', ARZ No.360 in Ryazan' (Dyagilevo AB), ARZ No.558 in Baranovichi, ARZ No.571 in Orsha (Bolbasovo AB). Naval Tu-16s were repaired and refurbished by ARZ No.20 in Pushkin (Leningrad Region), ARZ No.67 at Severomorsk-1 AB, ARZ No.153 on the military side of Vladivostok-Knevichi airport and ARZ No.328 in Nikolayev (Kul'bakino AB; later known as NARP, *Nikolayevskoye aviaremontnoye predpriyatiye* – Nikolayev Aircraft Repair Enterprise). According to some sources, the aircraft repair factories in Tartu (ARZ No.299) and Staraya Roossa (ARZ No.123) were also involved in the repair and maintenance of the type.

In addition to overhauls, the aircraft repair plants carried out more far-reaching work. When series production of the Tu-16 came to an end, the ARZs were assigned responsibility for carrying out modifications to those Tu-16s still in squadron service. Such aircraft were re-equipped in the course of scheduled repairs and heavy maintenance. In this way the Tu-16K-11-16, Tu-16K-26 and Tu-16K-26P missile carriers, the Tu-16RM-1 and Tu-16RM-2 reconnaissance versions, the ECM versions with Azaliya, Ficus and Cactus jammers, the Tu-16N/Tu-16NN tankers, the Tu-16KRM drone launchers, the M-16 target drones and other versions came into being. Repair and maintenance of the Tu-16 at Orsha continued until 1980, at Belaya Tserkov' until 1985 and at Khabarovsk all the way until 1992.

In the late 1980s/early 1990s the Tu-16's designated service life was 35 years, but a decision was then taken to extend this to 38 years. In 1990-91 a number of *Badgers* dating from 1955-56 were refurbished and converted to M-16 target drones by ARZ No.12 in Khabarovsk. The last such conversion took place in 1992 when five Tu-16s built in 1957 were modified as target drones, whereupon all further work on re-equipping and overhauling the *Badger* ended. In the political and economic chaos of the 'wild 1990s' that set in after the dissolution of the USSR, there were no funds available to maintain old hardware, let alone replace it.

We may mention that the Tu-16 figured in at least two Soviet feature films. One was the aforementioned sci-fi movie *Bar'yer neizvesnosti* (see Chapter 5) where the Tu-16 makes a cameo appearance as a 'mother ship' for the Ts-1 Tsiklon experimental rocket-powered hypersonic aircraft. This latter, which had a tail-first layout with mid-set delta wings of remarkably short span and a short, sharply swept vertical tail, was an aerospaceplane designed to reach an altitude of 100 km (328,000 ft) and speeds in excess of 7,200 km/h (4,472 mph). Moreover, it had nuclear-fuelled boosters (!), which were fitted when the aircraft was in place under the 'mother ship', and upon completion of the high-speed run and deceleration/descent the Ts-1 was to rendezvous with the Tu-16 and hook up again for landing – just like the McDonnell XF-85 Goblin parasite fighter!

The other film, ***Sloochay v kvadrate tridtsat' shest' – vosem'desyat*** (Incident at Map Grid 36-80), is a military action movie directed by Mikhail I. Tumanishvili and released by Mosfilm Studios, Moscow, in 1982. In this picture the *Badger* is involved on a much larger scale and in a more life-like manner. One of the main protagonists, Maj. Ghennadiy Volk (starring Boris Shcherbakov), is the captain of a North Fleet Air Arm Tu-16Z tanker. When the North Fleet stages an exercise in the North Atlantic (with the US Navy keeping a close watch), Volk's regiment is involved as well; for Volk this means refuelling other *Badgers*, mostly Tu-16Rs and Tu-16Ps, and engaging in cheerful banter with Maj. Armstrong, the captain of a US Navy Lockheed P-3A Orion (the latter was portrayed by a suitably painted-up Il-38). Everything is pretty much business as usual until a US Navy nuclear-powered missile submarine monitoring the exercise and staging a mock attack on the Soviet carrier task force led by the Type 1143 aircraft carrier SNS *Kiev* develops a malfunction in the reactor's cooling system and has to surface. The Americans assure the Soviets that everything is OK – until one of the sub's crew, who tried unsuccessfully to fix the reactor controls and was exposed to a lethal dose of radiation, sends an SOS, acting against

Several Tu-16s, including '12 Red' (c/n 1881809) shown here parked in front of a jet blast deflector at Vladimirovka AB, were used by the 929th GLITs in various programmes until the mid-1990s.

Left: Still wearing fake Egyptian Air Force insignia left over from their Middle Eastern deployment with the 90th ODRAE ON, North Fleet Tu-16Rs sit in revetments at Severomorsk-3 AB in the spring of 1973.

Below: One of the 'Egyptian' *Badger-Fs* at Severomorsk, with an APA-35-2M GPU on a ZiL-130 lorry providing ground power.

the captain's orders. The sub is too far from other US ships, and US air-sea rescue aircraft stationed on Greenland are grounded by bad weather. The Soviet North Fleet command sends a Tu-16S rescue aircraft carrying a Fregat lifeboat with a rescue crew (*sic* – as noted in Chapter 4, in reality the boat was unmanned); the aircraft is captained by none other than Capt. Leonid Gremyachkin, who used to be Volk's co-pilot.

This is where problems begin. Gremyachkin runs into a stiff headwind which increases his fuel burn; he needs to top up his tanks to reach the stricken submarine, and the only Tu-16Z tanker in the area is Volk's. The tanker loiters, waiting for the Tu-16S and using up costly fuel. Meanwhile, learning of the Soviet rescue operation in progress, the US Navy command does not wish to let the Soviets reach the sub, never mind boarding her. Armstrong, who is still in the area as well, receives orders to prevent the Soviet tanker from refuelling the Tu-16S. He manoeuvres the Orion, trying to foil the refuelling operation, but the Soviet airmen are determined to succeed; it's no time for small talk now, and the tanker's GRO even moves the dorsal cannons, preparing to fire warning shots. Eventually the Tu-16S does receive its load of fuel and presses on towards the disaster scene, dropping the lifeboat close

to the submarine (sure enough, the Soviet rescue crew is denied permission to board her). But now the tanker is left with not enough fuel to reach the base; Volk is ordered to head for the shore and ditch when the aircraft runs out of fuel. Fortunately the navigator remembers there is an abandoned auxiliary airstrip on an island close to the shore that the Luftwaffe had used during the war. When the engines quit due to fuel starvation, Volk manages a perfect dead-stick landing on this airstrip – albeit not without some damage to the aircraft, which rams through an old wooden hangar. In short, all's well that ends well.

As a point of interest, the scenes showing the drop of the lifeboat were not filmed for the movie – Mosfilm used genuine footage of the Tu-16S's tests. Also, the scene where the lifeboat approaches the submarine after splashing down contains a blooper – if you look closely you can see that the beaching gear used for moving the boat about on the shore is in place!

The Tu-16 at war

In addition to the many exercises, reconnaissance flights and other special duties on behalf of the Soviet Armed Forces, the Tu-16 also took part in actual combat in other countries.

The early 1950s were characterised by a boom of national liberation movements and revolutions; this was due in no small part to the spread of socialist ideas. The Soviet leader Nikita S. Khrushchov actively promoted a friendly policy towards Asian, African and Latin American states in the hope of winning them over into the socialist bloc – and often succeeded. Among other things, this policy included the extension of military aid – the armed forces of the 'friendly nations' would be trained by Soviet instructors and equipped with Soviet hardware.

On 23rd July 1952, a military coup took place in Egypt. The king was deposed and the Arab Republic of Egypt was proclaimed; Gamal Abdel Nasser, the leader of the coup, became Egypt's first President. In 1956 the Egyptian government nationalised the Suez Canal, precipitating the Suez Crisis; Great Britain, France and Israel sought to recapture the canal by force. In the ensuing war, Egypt was backed by the Soviet Union, which had started supplying arms and sending military advisors after the revolution.

As part of the Soviet military aid, 15 Tu-16 crews from the Long-Range Aviation's 56th *Breslavl'skaya* TBAD/244th TBAP were on temporary deployment to Egypt in October 1962 – February 1963. The group was commanded by the division's deputy CO Col. Sevast'yanov; the crews were captained by Lt.-Col. A. S. Shmonov, Lt.-Col. Yu. I. Vladimirov, Lt.-Col. Ye. N. Kartunovskiy, Maj. A. N. Volkov, Maj. V. A. Shoyev, Maj. V. F. Laputin, Maj. B. B. Bachoorin, Maj. A. A. Ternovskiy, Maj. P. F. Goodkovskiy, Maj. Yu. P. Zakharov, Capt. A. M. Oseledets, Capt. V. T. Povedeyko *et al.*

The Tu-16s were mostly operated by mixed Soviet-Egyptian crews; sorties were flown in large groups up to the bomber's maximum combat radius of 3,700 km (2,300 miles) and at altitudes up to 16,000 m (52,490 ft), and sometimes even higher. Most of the targets were in South Yemen, with an occasional target in Saudi Arabia. In order to hit the enemy vehicle convoys delivering weapons the bombers often had to descend to low altitude. The sorties were mostly flown at night, and when the Tu-16s returned to base in the early morning their fuel tanks were almost empty. Quite

often the bomber formation was led by Brigadier Col. Hosni Mubarak, who would later become Egypt's third President.

The working conditions in Egypt were tough; quite apart from the hot climate, the crews maintained a 24/7 readiness. In addition to the 244th TBAP, crews from other DA units were seconded to the Soviet detachment. All of the Soviet airmen displayed excellent combat skill and unyielding discipline. After the Egyptian tour of duty the participating aircrews received Soviet and Egyptian military awards.

In 1967 Israel unleashed the Six-Day War (5th-11th June), delivering massive air strikes against Egypt, Syria and Jordan; the air forces of these three nations were largely destroyed. The Soviet Union took the difficult decision to intervene, having economic and military assistance treaties with the three Arab nations. When Israel refused to abide by the UN Security Council resolutions demanding an immediate ceasefire, the Soviet Union broke off diplomatic relations with Israel and started preparing bombing strikes against Tel Aviv and other Israeli targets by DA units. Luckily the raid was called off when Israel chose to halt its offensive.

After the cessation of the hostilities, a group of six Tu-16T torpedo-bombers destined for the Egyptian Air Force arrived

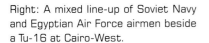

Above right: The Soviet ground crew of a 90th ODRAE ON Tu-16P receive instructions for the day's work at Cairo-West.

Right: A mixed line-up of Soviet Navy and Egyptian Air Force airmen beside a Tu-16 at Cairo-West.

Tu-16KSR-2-5- '71 Red' (c/n 7203804), 251st GvTBAP, on temporary deployment at Maryy-2 AB during the Afghan War, December 1988; note the 30 mission markers.

from the USSR in September 1967, taking up residence at Cairo-West AB, a major EAF base. There, Soviet instructors began training Egyptian crews to fly the type.

When the tension in the Middle East had subsided a little, Egypt began rebuilding its air force. Accordingly in April-May 1968, a group of Soviet airmen headed by A. S. Shmonov (who was by then a colonel and CO of the 45th TBAD) ferried ten brand-new Tu-16s to Egypt; it included Lt.-Col. V. P. Mikhaïlenko, N. Semenchuk, I. Ye. Yupatov, E. Zaïtsev, V. Kurushin and others. Its primary mission was to demonstrate the capabilities of the Tu-16's reconnaissance and strike versions to the Arab nations in the hope of attracting orders. This placed heavy demands on the pilots' skill – most of the Syrian and Egyptian airbases had rather short runways and offered neither the required support equipment nor proper navigation aids. Once the task had been completed, the Soviet crews turned the bombers over to the Egyptians and returned home aboard a Soviet Air Force Antonov An-12 *Cub* transport.

A second deployment of Soviet *Badgers* to Egypt at the request of the Egyptian government came in keeping with an agreement signed in March 1968, due to the deterioration of Arab-Israeli relations. This time it was a Soviet Navy composite detachment called the 90th ODRAE ON (*otdel'naya dahl'nyaya razvedyvatel'naya aviaeskadril'ya osobovo naznacheniya* – Independent Special Mission Long-Range Reconnaissance Squadron) gathering intelligence for both nations and performing ASW duties. Originally the detachment was based at Cairo-West; later some of the aircraft moved to Mersa Matruh AB. The *Badgers* were assigned to the squadron on a rotational basis; North Fleet Tu-16Rs were the first to deploy in 1968, being superseded by Black Sea Fleet aircraft in

Nose art on a 251st GvTBAP Tu-16KSR-2-5 which flew combat sorties in Afghanistan in 1988.

1970, and at least four Tu-16Ps from the Baltic Fleet followed in 1971. Although Soviet-operated, the aircraft of the 90th ODRAE ON wore Egyptian markings and Arabic serials.

The squadron made a total of 354 flights from Egyptian airbases in 1968, including 258 sorties by the Tu-16Rs. The following year North Fleet aircrews flew 667 sorties from Egyptian airbases, 273 of them in the Tu-16. In 1970 Naval Aviation aircraft flew 643 sorties from Egyptian bases. Operations from the Egyptian bases continued until 1973 – that is, until the fourth Arab-Israeli war, known as the Yom Kippur War, broke out on 6th October 1973. In this war EAF Tu-16K-11-16s of the 403rd Bomber Brigade/36th Bomber Sqn launched a total of 25 KSR-2 and KSR-11 missiles at targets in Israel, but only five of them scored hits, destroying two radars and a supply dump; the other 20 were shot down by Israeli air defences.

In 1968 the Tu-16 was involved in another conflict much closer to home. On 21st August that year the Tu-16P was used to provide ECM cover for the deployment of tactical aviation and military airlift formations on the opening day of Operation *Dunaï* (Danube) – the Soviet-led invasion of Czechoslovakia. During the operation, which lasted until 11th September 1968, all Warsaw Pact nations except Romania intervened to stomp out deviations from socialism in Czechoslovakia under President Ludvík Svoboda and Czechoslovak Communist Party Chairman Alexander Dubček. Fortunately, the operation did not escalate into large-scale fighting, as had been the case in Hungary in 1956 under similar circumstances

The only major war in which Soviet Air Force Tu-16s were directly involved was the Afghan War of 1979-89. The type was used in bombing raids against the bases and concentrations of Mujahideen guerrillas opposing the pro-Soviet government in Kabul. Apart from attacking insurgent positions, the Tu-16s carried out bombing raids in the vicinity of the towns of Herat and Kandahar which were controlled by the guerrillas.

The first deployment of the Tu-16 to the Afghan War was in late 1979 when 203rd TBAP *Badgers* from Orsha deployed to Khanabad AB near Karshi, Uzbekistan (not to be confused with the one in Afghanistan) and those of the 184th TBAP relocated to Semipalatinsk (Chagan AB). The intention was to bomb Mujahideen targets on the outskirts of Herat, where a mutiny had erupted; eventually, however, the sortie was called off. Thus, the Tu-16 really saw action in Afghanistan for the first time in 1984 during the Panjsher Offensive. The targets were the rebel forces controlled by Ahmad Shah Massoud, one of the most influential Afghan warlords. The first sortie was flown on 19th April 1984.

The Tu-16 operated over Afghanistan alongside other Long-Range Aviation aircraft from the Tupolev stable – Tu-22PD ECM aircraft from Ozyornoye AB and Tu-22M3s from Poltava, Orsha and Sol'tsy (the *Backfire-Cs* were armed with free-fall bombs). The bomber versions – the Tu-16A, the bomber-capable Tu-16KSR-2-5 and Tu-16KSR-2-5-11 missile strike aircraft – were used on the biggest scale; they were supported by Tu-16R reconnaissance aircraft and Tu-16P ECM aircraft. Other variants rarely saw action in Afghanistan. The *Badger*'s typical bomb load consisted of twelve FAB-500 bombs. Sometimes, in special circumstances, larger or smaller bombs were used – 250-kg (551-lb), 1,000-kg (2,205-lb), 3000-kg (6,610-lb), 5,000-kg (11,020-lb) and even 9,000-kg (19,840-lb) M-54 or M-46 series bombs. On occasion this was simply because the bombs were nearing the end of their shelf life and had to be disposed of.

The primary reason why the 'veteran' Tu-16 was used in this conflict at all was that it was the DA's only aircraft able to carry the FAB-9000 bomb. The latter could give the terrain a 'working over', levelling hills and high ground and producing craters so that the terrain resembled a moonscape. The Tu-16s dropped a total of 289 such bombs during the Afghan War. However, the FAB-9000 was cumbersome and required a special BT-6 dolly (***bombovaya telezhka*** – bomb dolly, Group 6) which required a few dozen men to move it when it was loaded. On one occasion a poorly secured FAB-9000 nearly dropped on the ground, sending the personnel running for cover.

Bombing raids were mostly carried out during daylight hours, using the OPB-11R optical bombsight; the outdated RBP-4 radar was not used, being useless in Afghanistan with its jumbled rocky terrain. The sorties could last as many as 3.5-4 hours. The bombers were supported by Tu-16P 'Buket' ECM aircraft to jam the Pakistani air defence radars, and also to counter the Pakistan Air Force General Dynamics F-16A fighters which often intervened and posed a serious threat to the Soviet bombers. Since the veteran Tu-16s lacked infrared countermeasures equipment, they were always escorted by MiG-29 *Fulcrum-A* fighters or Su-17M3 *Fitter-G* fighter-bombers; on long sorties the fighter escort operated in shifts, with relief fighters (MiG-23MLDs of the 120th IAP) taking off from Bagram in Afghanistan. The reason was not the possibility of ground fire but again the threat posed by Pakistani fighters. The Su-17M3s proved useful in another capacity – during the Tu-16s' rare night sorties the *Fitters* provided target illumination with flare bombs.

Bombing operations over Afghan territory were carried out by almost all air regiments operating the Tu-16 in the European part of the USSR in order to give the crews a taste of real combat. The 251st GvTBAP from Belaya Tserkov' was the most active unit. The missions were flown from bases in the Soviet Central Asian republics located close to the Afghan border, particularly Maryy-2 AB in Turkmenia and Karshi in Uzbekistan. From there the crews made training flights over the desert and practised bombing with the aid of LORAN. The aircraft operated in small groups: a flight of three or four or a squadron of eight to ten machines. Only experienced aircrews trained in formation flying were chosen for the mission, and the aircraft captains and navigators/bomb-aimers had to have at least a Pilot 2nd Class (or Navigator 2nd Class) rating.

One of the biggest raids against a Mujahideen base in Afghanistan took place on 22nd April 1984. Twenty-four Tu-16KSR-2-5s took part in the raid; some of them carried 25 FAB-250 HE bombs internally, while others were fitted with BD3-16K racks on the wing pylons to carry 40 such bombs each. The target was located in a mountain valley near Kandahar. Two squadrons of the 200th TBAP at Bobruisk and one squadron of the 251st GvTBAP were involved; the aircraft flew in echelon formation, one squadron behind the other. The first group of eight machines was led by Guards Col. Ye. A. Pachin, CO of the 200th GvTBAP.

At first it was planned to deliver the bombs from an altitude of 6,000 m (19,685 ft), but the formation flew into cloud on approach to the target, which created the danger of collision, since the aircraft were flying in close formation. In these conditions the group leader took the decision to climb and the target was approached at an altitude between 8,700 and 9,500 m (28,540-31,170 ft). The lack of visibility meant that the bombing had to be carried out using LORAN. The first eight machines were greeted with Mujahideen anti-aircraft fire, although they were out of the air defences' range. The bombs dropped by the leading squadron neutralised the anti-aircraft defences, so that the other two squadrons carried out their attack unmolested. Gaps in the cloud showed explosions testifying to the accuracy of the bombing. On average each squadron dropped 250 bombs into an area measuring 200 x 300 m (660 x 990 ft).

After the Tu-16s had done their bit, the Mujahideen base was hit by Su-24 tactical bombers and Su-25 ground attack aircraft. As the Tu-16, Su-24 and Su-25 formations attacked from different directions, the raid was unofficially dubbed a 'star strike' (*zvyozdnyy nalyot* – an old term for such a tactic dating back to the late 1920s).

On returning to Karshi the Tu-16KSR-2-5s were refuelled and rearmed, and a repeat raid was carried out four hours later. This time each group of aircraft had its own individual objectives in destroying the remains of the Mujahideen gang who were fleeing in all directions from the devastated area. The bombs were dropped from between 1,500 and 2,000 m (4,920-6,560 ft) with the enemy clearly visible against the snowy background.

Post-attack reconnaissance was made by the Tu-16Rs. The photos showed clearly that the air group had carried out their mission perfectly.

One last brief deployment of the *Badger* to the Afghan War was in 1989 with the purpose of covering the Soviet withdrawal from Afghanistan. A special Independent Air Group of the DA was formed, including eleven Tu-16s of the 251st GvTBAP; they were temporarily stationed at Maryy-1 AB in Turkmenistan. Many of the targets lay near Kandahar and Jalalabad which had been vacated by the Soviet forces – just to make sure the Mujahideen would not pursue them.

The aircraft were beginning to show their age, and one sortie from Maryy nearly ended in disaster when a Tu-16 captained by Capt. Ye. Pomorov lost the entire navigator's station glazing at 10,000 m (33,140 ft) and 850 km/h (528 mph). The flight deck decompressed instantly, the crewmen receiving the gale force of the slipstream right in their faces, the navigator (Capt. Lylov) being the worst off; the heavy-duty fur-lined flying outfits and old-fashioned flying goggles saved the day. The manual prescribed an immediate descent in such a situation; yet the target

Seen from a ship, a Tu-16RM-1 flies low over the sea.

was just 15 minutes away, and the captain chose to maintain altitude and course. After dropping the FAB-9000 the Tu-16 returned safely home. For this mission Pomorov was awarded the Red Star Order, the rest of the crew receiving Combat Merit Medals.

Eclipse

The scales began to tip in favour of the Tu-22M in the 1980s when the Tu-16 fleet was shrinking rapidly. By then the Tu-16 was hopelessly outdated, not to mention the fact that most *Badgers* had run out of service life.

In 1990, however, the Tu-16 made an unexpected comeback when the entire *Backfire* fleet had to be grounded pending modifications in the wake of an accident. In the meantime, the aircrews temporarily flew the good old Tu-16s, not all of which had fortunately been scrapped yet.

After their retirement from first-line service, Soviet Air Force Tu-16s were consigned to the aircraft storage depots at Belaya AB in Russia, Belaya Tserkov' AB in the Ukraine and Chagan AB in Kazakhstan. At the latter location no fewer than 190 *Badgers* were assembled from far and wide, starting in October 1989. The origi-

This Tu-16 survives as a gate guard at Vladimirovka AB, Akhtoobinsk.

Regiment	Versions	No. of aircraft: planned	actual	To be transferred (all versions)	To be refurbished
13th TBAD					
52nd GvTBAP	Tu-16P	0	13	1 to be struck off charge; 12 to other units To receive up to 28 Tu-22M3s	3
185th GvTBAP	Tu-16K-...*	0	4	10 to other units	2
	Tu-16P	8	14		
15th TBAD					
251st GvTBAP	Tu-16K-...	19	23	9	6
	Tu-16T †	9	9		
	Tu-16P	0	5		
260th TBAP	Tu-16K-...	8	31	1 to 1229th TBAP; 28 from 200th TBAP! + to receive 4+10 Tu-22M3s	7
	Tu-16P	8	17		
22nd TBAD					
200th TBAP	Tu-16P	8	14	28 (sic) to 260th TBAP	5
203rd TBAP	Tu-16U ‡	3	3		
31st TBAD					
1225th TBAP	Tu-16PN §	8	10	2 to other units	
1229th TBAP	Tu-16P	8	3	1 from 260th TBAP	
55th TBAD					
303rd TBAP	Tu-16K-...	19	28	9 to other units	4
	Tu-16P	9	9		
444th TBAP	Tu-16K-...	19	26	10 to other units	10
	Tu-16P	9	12		
201st TBAD					
184th TBAP	Tu-16P	0	8	4 to other units	
326th TBAD					
132nd TBAP	Tu-16K-...	0	25	28 from 200th TBAP! To receive 1 Tu-22M3	4
	Tu-16P	8	11		
402nd TBAP	Tu-16K-...	0	18	17 to other units	6
	Tu-16P	8	7		
840th TBAP	Tu-16P	8	13	5 to other units	7
Direct reporting units					
219th ODRAP	Tu-16R	19	20	1 received, 1 to other units	10
	Tu-16Z	9	9		
	Tu-16P	0	2		
43rd TsBP i PLS	Tu-16	14	23	9 to other units	3

Notes:

* The original table has 'Tu-16K', which is just a blanket designation for various missile strike variants and is not to be confused with the real (experimental) Tu-16K

† *Sic*; the 'Tu-16T' in the original table is not a torpedo-bomber but a tanker variant – probably the Tu-16N

‡ Apparently an unofficial reference to the Tu-16s used as proficiency trainers

§ *Sic*; no such version exists

nal intention was that they would be placed in long-term flyable storage, but political developments made short work of these plans.

The Tu-16 outlasted the Soviet Union, though not by much. At the end of 1990 a total of 173 Tu-16s remained in the European part of the USSR (81 in the Air Force and 92 in the Naval Aviation). In late 1981 the DA had been operating 487 Tu-16s; by 1991 this number had shrunk to only 81. The DA's Tu-16 served with the 251st UAP at Belaya Tserkov' (40 aircraft), the 260th TBAP at Stryy (23 aircraft) and the 200th TBAP at Bobruisk (18 tankers). The Navy's 33rd TsBP i PLS at Nikolayev had 20 machines, and a further 38 Black Sea Fleet examples, mainly Tu-16K-10-26s, were operating from airfields in the Crimea. In the North Fleet, four examples remained in service with the 924th MRAP at Olen'ya AB and 30 more with the regiment at Severomorsk-3 AB in 1991. About 60 machines remained in service with the Pacific Fleet.

With the collapse of the Soviet Union the property of the former Soviet Armed Forces was up for grabs. After 1991 almost all surviving Tu-16 were withdrawn from use, a handful remaining active with the Russian Navy, the Russian Air Force's GNIKI VVS and LII. The last Long-Range Aviation regiment to fly the Tu-16 was the 219th ODRAP at Spassk-Dal'niy. After the regiment had re-equipped with the Tu-22M, the *Badgers* were ferried to Belaya AB for storage. Alas, they were soon broken up; no funds were

available for even mothballing the aircraft. The last of the naval Tu-16s were retired from North Fleet service in 1993 and relegated to the storage depot at Ostrov AB.

The newly independent Ukraine took possession of whatever military aircraft were based on its soil, including the Tu-16s. The Ukrainian *Badgers* never received the new insignia and virtually ceased to operate at the end of 1995, although 49 examples were stored at air bases and 19 others continued in serve as trainers with the 540th IIMRAP at Nikolayev. By this time not a single active Tu-16 remained in Belarus'.

In May 1992 the Tu-16s stored at Chagan were appropriated by the newly-independent Kazakhstan. Yet, owning is one thing and operating is another; the Kazakhstan Air Force had no use for the bombers, and in 1994 the *Badgers* were reduced to scrap metal in order to make a quick profit. A similar fate befell the Ukrainian machines, which sat rusting away for a long time.

In Russia the Tu-16 was officially phased out in 1994, although there were examples of the Tu-16K-10 built in 1963 which had not reached the end of their 35-year service life. By this time the Tupolev OKB had ceased to work on the Tu-16.

The two Tu-16 Tsiklon-N/Tsiklon-NM weather research aircraft sat idle for a long time. At Zhukovskiy only a single Tu-16LL was kept in flying condition. Apparently this was the last airworthy Tu-16 on Russian soil.

Tu-16 units in the Naval Aviation as of early 1992		
Unit	**Base**	**Quantity**
Direct reporting units		
5501st BRSV*	Ostrov AB, Pskov Region, Russia	Tu-16 (74)
33rd TsBP i PLS (HQ Nikolayev)		
540th IMRAP	Kul'bakino AB, Nikolayev, the Ukraine	Tu-16 (20)
North Fleet		
967th ODRAP	Severomorsk-1 AB, Murmansk Region, Russia	Tu-16R
• 5th *Kirkenesskaya* Red Banner MRAD (HQ Olenegorsk):		
987th MRAP	Severomorsk-1 AB, Murmansk Region, Russia	Tu-16K-10-26 (30)
Black Sea Fleet		
• 2nd MRAD (HQ Gvardeiskoye AB):		
[124th MRAP]	Gvardeiskoye AB, Crimea Region, the Ukraine	Tu-16 (19); in storage (unit disbanded in 1990)
5th GvMRAP	Vesyoloye AB, Crimea Region, the Ukraine	Tu-16 (15)
943rd MRAP	Oktyabr'skoye AB, Crimea Region, the Ukraine	Tu-16 (4)
Pacific Fleet air arm		
304th GvODRAP	Khorol' AB, Primor'ye Territory, Russia	Tu-16K-10-26
134th ODRAE	Russian Federation	Tu-16R/Tu-16RM (12)
317th OSAP	Petropavlovsk-Kamchatskiy (Yelizovo IAP), Kamchatka Region, Russia	Tu-16R
• 25th MRAD (HQ Vladivostok):		
141st GvMRAP	Khorol' AB Primor'ye Territory, Russian Federation	Tu-16
169th GvSAP	Khorol' AB, Primor'ye Territory, Russia;Cam Ranh AB, Da Nang Province, Vietnam	Tu-16K-10-26, Tu-16SPS, Tu-16Z
• 143rd MRAD (HQ Mongokhto):		
570th MRAP	Mongokhto AB, Primor'ye Territory, Russia	Tu-16 (1 squadron)

* BRSV = *bahza rezerva samolyotov i vertolyotov* – Fixed-Wing Aircraft & Helicopter Reserve (that is, storage) Base

Chapter 8

With an Oriental Flavour: The Chinese Versions

In the 1950s and 1960s the USSR readily granted manufacturing licences for its aircraft, albeit not for the latest types, to 'friendly nations' with an aircraft industry of their own. There were two reasons for this. One was that occasionally the Soviet aircraft industry alone could not cope with the demand for a particular aircraft type, and factories in Soviet satellite nations were called upon to bridge the capacity gap. The other reason was economic co-operation and specialisation within the Eastern Bloc; some Soviet aircraft types were 'subcontracted out' to other nations within the framework of the Council for Mutual Economic Assistance (COMECON) – just to give the aircraft industries of those nations some work, and much of their production was exported to the Soviet Union.

The People's Republic of China (PRC), which was originally on very good terms with the Soviet Union, was probably the biggest licensee. The Soviet Union had helped to establish the Chinese People's Liberation Army Air Force (PLAAF) after the 1949 revolution that brought communists to power in China. Initially the aircraft were delivered directly from the Soviet Union, but, considering the size of the PRC and the number of aircraft required by the PLAAF, it was deemed advisable to set up indigenous production. This started on a small scale with fighters and trainers, but soon was expanded to include heavier aircraft.

Harbin FeiLong-201/Xian H-6 medium bomber
In early 1956 the Soviet Union agreed to licence production of the Tu-16 bomber to China. The actual licensing agreement was signed in September 1957. Under the terms of this agreement, in 1958 China received two production Tu-16s as pattern aircraft, a

H-6As '10897 Red' and '10990 Red' cruise high over the mountainous landscape of inland China.

The final assembly shop at the Xian Aircraft Company, with three substantially complete H-6s in the foreground (the third aircraft is just visible on the right) and Y-7H (licence-built An-26) transports at the far end.

Right: The flight line at Leiyang AB crammed with blue-coded H-6As of the PLAAF's 8th Air Division, with a lone Y-7H in between. The 'anti-flash' colour scheme is noteworthy. Note the vertical red stripes facilitating flight in close formation. Oddly, the crews are running away from the bombers, not towards them, as they might in a scramble!

Below right: Blue-coded PLAAF 10th Air Division/28th Air Regiment H-6As at Anqing-North AB. Note the low-visibility version of the Chinese 'stars and bars' insignia.

further two aircraft in the form of semi-knocked-down (SKD) kits and a CKD kit essential for mastering the assembly of the first bombers, a set of blanks and raw materials for parts manufacture, and the necessary technical documents. The latter were supplied by plant No.22 in Kazan', which had ended production of the type in favour of the new Tu-22 supersonic bomber. Conversely, the abovementioned two bombers were Kuibyshev-built; this created additional complications because the production tooling at the Kazan' and Kuibyshev plants was not identical.

The Bureau of Aircraft Industry (BAI), which was set up in 1951 as the first authority supervising aircraft production in China, allocated two factories for Tu-16 production – factory No.1 in Harbin, Heilongjiang Province, in the extreme north-east of China and the new factory in Xian (sometimes spelled Xi'an), Shaanxi Province, in central China. The Harbin factory had started life in 1952 as an aircraft repair facility, but a major reconstruction in order to transform it into a manufacturing plant began in 1958, in the course of which the shop floor area was doubled; the plant received assistance in the form of 200 qualified workers seconded from the Shenyang Aircraft Factory producing Mikoyan/Gurevich UTI MiG-15 *Midget* trainers and MiG-17F *Fresco-C*

fighters under licence. In May 1959, the Harbin Aircraft Factory took delivery of the two pattern aircraft and the CKD kit, the latter being used immediately to assemble a bomber. The first Chinese-assembled Tu-16 was completed in just 67 days (28th June – 3rd September), making its maiden flight from the factory's Pingfang airfield in the southern part of the city on 27th September 1959, and was handed over to the PLAAF that December.

A large Soviet technical team was sent to China in 1959 to assist in setting up series production. It remained in China until the autumn of 1960.

Meanwhile, the large factory at Xian was commissioned in 1958, and the Shenyang Aircraft Factory was obliged to help again, sending 1,040 skilled technical and engineering staff and 1,697 other workers to assist in setting up Tu-16 production there. In 1961 the BAI decided to concentrate licence production of the *Badger* at Xian so that the Harbin factory could concentrate on the Il-28 tactical bomber, a manufacturing licence for which had also been obtained (the *Beagle* was built in China as the Harbin H-5); the transfer of production took place in 1962-64. In 1964 the Xian Aircraft Factory finally began manufacturing the jigs and tooling for series production of the Tu-16. New production methods dif-

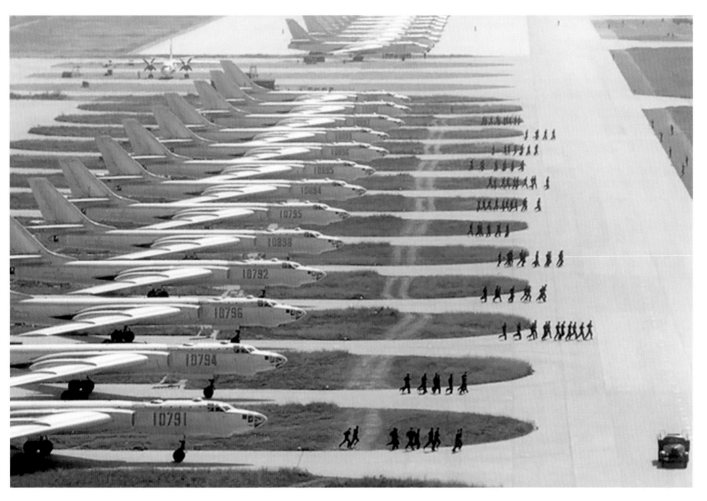

Above: The pilots of an H-6A check the route of the forthcoming flight on a map.

Below: '20615 Red', an overall grey H-6A from the PLAAF's 10th Bomber Division/28th Regiment (Nanjing Military Region).
Bottom: 20712 Red', another H-6A from the same unit.

Above right: Originally the H-6As wore an 'anti-flash' scheme akin to that to the Tu-16A.
Below right: H-6A '20714 Red' comes in to land.

fering from the Soviet ones were used, including explosive forming and epoxy resin male moulds instead of metal ones. The first Tu-16 airframe assembled from Chinese parts was completed in October 1966, one year ahead of schedule; it underwent static tests at the BAI's Aircraft Structure Analysis Research Institute in December 1968.

At the time of its first flight the bomber bore the local designation FeiLong-201 (Flying Dragon-201). The manufacturer's designation system used for Chinese aircraft in the 1950s and early 1960s consisted of a lofty and sometimes ideologically flavoured codename in typical Chinese style and a three-digit number. Each name corresponded to a particular class of aircraft – DongFeng (East Wind) for fighters, FeiLong for bombers, XionYing (Mighty Eagle) for attack aircraft, HongZhuan (Red Craftsman) for trainers and so on. The first digit was again a code for the class (1 = fighter, 2 = bomber, 3 = attack aircraft, 5 = trainer; 4 was probably not used because the Chinese numeral 'four' sounds similar to the Chinese word for 'death') and the other two ran in sequence. Thus, the designation FeiLong-201 identified the licence-built Tu-16 as the first Chinese-made bomber. The military used two-digit service designations matching the year when the type was inducted, with a suffix letter added as required (thus the Dongfeng-102/Dongfeng-103/Dongfeng-105 family based on the MiG-19S supersonic fighter became the Type 59, Type 59A and Type 59B respectively). However, the Tu-16 did not have such a 'type' designation.

In 1964 China switched to a new and more businesslike system used by the manufacturers and the military alike. The Chinese word(s) denoting the aircraft's role were usually abbreviated to a one- or two-letter prefix followed by a sequential number within each class of aircraft. In accordance with this system the Chinese-built Tu-16 received the designation under which it was to enter mass production and service – H-6 (*Hongzhaji* – bomber, Type 6).

Licence production of the RD-3M-500 turbojet was assigned to the Harbin Engine Factory (HEF, now called Dong'an Engine Manufacturing Co.), the Shenyang Engine Factory (SEF, now the Shenyang Liming Motor Co.) and the Xian Engine Factory (XEF, now the Xian Aero-Engine Corporation); the Chinese version was designated WP-8 (*Wopen-8* – turbojet engine, Type 8). The three factories co-produced the engine, and it is hard to say which one was the pilot plant. The S300-75 turbostarter was copied as the WQJ-1.

The Tu-16's avionics, equipment and armament components were also copied and manufactured locally. For example, a clone of the RBP-4 navigation/bomb-aiming radar was produced as the HL-2 (aka Type 241). The Chinese copy of the AM-23 cannon was designated Type 23-2 (the first two digits referring to the calibre); after 1980 its production came under the control of the China North Industries Corporation (Norinco), which produces firearms among other things. (Interestingly, many western sources state that the H-6 had the older NR-23 cannons, which were likewise copied in China as the Type 23-1 and used on the H-5.)

On 24th December 1968 the first Xian-built production H-6 bomber completely manufactured in China (with Chinese-made WP-8 engines) made its first flight from Yanliang AB on the north-eastern outskirts of the city – the factory airfield of the Xian plant. The crew was commanded by test pilot Li Yuanyi, with Xu

Wenhong as co-pilot. After this, full-scale production of the H-6 got under way.

The reason why it took so long to launch production was the disruption of the Chinese aircraft industry caused by domestic and international political developments. In May 1958, inspired by the successful fulfilment of the first five-year economic development plan (1953-58), the Chinese government headed by Mao Zedong grew bullish and launched an ambitious plan of accelerated industrial development known as the 'Great Leap Forward'. In all areas of the economy, quantity was the main priority, whereas quality control and fundamental research (in the case of the aircraft industry, the laws of aerodynamics, knowledge of structural materials and even the basic design principles) were brushed aside. As a result, the aircraft built in 1958-60 were of such poor workmanship that the PLAAF refused to accept them. Politically motivated decisions (such as the transfer of production from one factory to another) were often detrimental to production, and the H-6 was a case in point. Much of the design documentation was lost during the move from Harbin to Xian, and it took forever to restore it.

Even more damaging was the notorious Cultural Revolution – Chairman Mao's last attempt to assert himself over his more pragmatically minded comrades-in-arms and restore his position which was faltering after the failure of the 'Great Leap Forward'. This period, which lasted from 1966 to Mao's death in 1976, was characterised by intensive power struggle in the nation's leadership and ideological purges at all levels, leading to untold chaos in the national economy and the country's life as a whole. The shortage of specialists caused by the repressions was a further blow to the aircraft industry.

Moreover, in 1960 Sino-Soviet relations began deteriorating on ideological grounds, dropping to a freezing point in just five years; the Chinese political leaders accused the Soviet Union of 'revisionism' and 'moving towards imperialism'. As a result, further work on the Tu-16 in China proceeded as a go-it-alone effort.

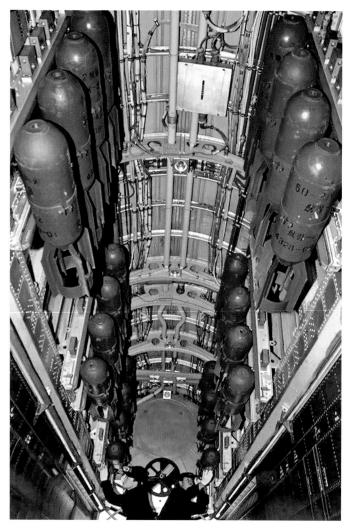

6,250 m (20,500 ft), a cruising speed of 786 km/h (488 mph) or Mach 0.75, a service ceiling of 13,100 m (42,980 ft), a ferry range of 6,000 km (3,728 miles) and a combat radius of 1,800 km (1,120 miles).

The H-6 appears to have two construction number systems. One is a nine-digit system whose meaning is unknown. Only one c/n under this system, 222000159, has been reported to date, referring to an H-6 serialled '4251 Black outline' which is on display in the PLAAF Museum at Datangshan. Indeed, it is not certain that it is really the c/n and not something else – although the middle part does suggest Batch 00, 01st aircraft in the batch. One might be tempted to suppose 59 denotes the year of production, which would make '4251 Black outline' the very first FeiLong-201 assembled from Soviet parts in Harbin; however, it is far from certain that this first aircraft has survived.

The other system used for most H-6s is straightforward, consisting of six digits. For example, an H-6A preserved in the same museum is c/n 052408 – that is, Batch 05, product code 24 (H-6), 08th aircraft in the batch; apparently there was a maximum of ten aircraft in each batch. The c/n is stencilled in small digits on the port side of the fin.

H-6A nuclear-capable bomber
Back in the early 1950s the Soviet Union donated 25 Kazan'-built and Kuibyshev-built Tu-4 nuclear-capable long-range bombers to China (Iosif V. Stalin and Mao Zedong had reached an agreement in principle, providing for a transfer of nuclear weapons technology to China). The PLAAF intended to use the Tu-4s as the delivery vehicles for the Chinese nuclear bomb; the latter, however, took a while to develop. The first Chinese nuclear test (codenamed 'Chic 1' by western intelligence agencies) took place on 16th October 1964 when the 22-kiloton '596' implosion-type nuclear device was detonated at the Lop Nor Proving Ground at Malan, Xinjiang Province, in western China. Thus the PRC joined the 'nuclear club', becoming the world's fifth nuclear power. The '596' was not yet a real bomb – the device was installed on a tall tower to simulate an airburst, not air-dropped.

When the preparations to build the Tu-16 in China began, it seemed that the days of the slow and obsolete Tu-4 were numbered; the H-6 was clearly a better nuclear weapons platform.

The standard H-6 *sans suffixe* was dimensionally identical to the standard Tu-16 *sans suffixe*. Like the latter, it had a normal take-off weight of 72,000 kg (158,730 lb) and a maximum take-off weight of 75,800 kg (167,110 lb); the normal and maximum weapons load was 3,000 kg (6,610 lb) and 9,000 kg (19,840 lb) respectively and the maximum fuel load was 33,000 kg (72,750 lb). The H-6 attained a maximum speed of 1,014 km/h (630 mph) at

Left: Armourers check the load of 50-kg practice bombs on the bomb cassettes of an H-6.

Below, far left: The co-pilot of an H-6. Note that the flight deck is totally devoid of any interior trim.

Below left: 250-kg bombs in the bomb bay of an H-6A.

Right: A publicity shot of a PLAAF H-6A crew discussing the mission details. A GPU on a Yuejin NJ 1041 light truck stands by to start up the engines.

Below: An unserialled HZ-6 reconnaissance aircraft; the ELINT pods are just visible below the wings.

Hence, even before production of the basic H-6 had been fully implemented, the Xian Aircraft Factory started modifying a Harbin-built Tu-16 assembled from Soviet parts as a nuclear weapons platform designated H-6A. This programme bore the codename 'Mission 21-511' and was supervised by Li Xipu. The H-6A was the counterpart of the Soviet Tu-16A. In common with the latter the bomb bay was heat-insulated and air-conditioned to provide the correct environment for the nuke; the bomb release system was modified and, in the case of the prototype, the necessary monitoring and recording equipment for nuclear testing was installed.

On 14th May 1965, captained by H-6 project test pilot Li Yuanyi, the H-6A prototype successfully carried out the second Chinese nuclear test ('Chic 2'), dropping a 20-kiloton atomic bomb – an air-droppable version of the '596' – at Area D of the Lop Nor Proving Ground. The flight crew received a collective government award for this mission. (It should be mentioned that some sources claim the delivery vehicle to be a Tu-4.)

Another controversial claim repeated in several sources is that on 29th September 1969, an H-6 bomber dropped China's first thermonuclear bomb with a yield of 3 megatons. In fact, it involved a warhead developed for the DF-3 (DongFeng-3) ICBM; this was a three-stage device with a boosted uranium-235 primary and a uranium-238 pusher. However, the test carried out on that date ('Chic 10') was not the first; the first Chinese thermonuclear weapon test involving an identical warhead had taken place on 17th June 1967 ('Chic 6'). The delivery vehicle was again an H-6A, the parachute-retarded bomb exploding at an altitude of 2,960 m (9,710 ft), and the yield was even greater at 3.3 megatons.

This wind tunnel model appears to represent the H-6D naval missile strike version, judging by the large radome.

The H-6A entered production at Xian in due course. Outwardly it differed from the conventional version in having a partial 'anti-flash' white colour scheme, just like the Tu-16A.

H-6B (HZ-6?) reconnaissance aircraft

At least one H-6 was converted into an ELINT version with pylon-mounted underwing pods similar to the SRS-3 pods of the Tu-16R and a hemispherical dielectric blister ahead of the bomb bay. The designation H-6B quoted in some sources for a reconnaissance version may apply to this aircraft – unless the Chinese have more than one reconnaissance version. A suggested alternative designation is HZ-6 (*Hongzhaji Zhenchaji* – bomber/reconnaissance aircraft), and the mission equipment reportedly included an HD-42 thermal imager and optical cameras for day/night high-altitude PHOTINT.

H-6C (H-6A II, H-6 III) nuclear-capable bomber

In 1970 the Chinese aircraft industry started work on a second-generation integrated navigation/bomb-aiming system for the H-6A with a high degree of automation. The system comprised an LHS-2 bombing computer, an HL-3 air data navigator, a BDP-1 attitude and heading reference system (AHRS), a DPL-1 (Type 773) Doppler navigation radar with a flush dielectric panel aft of the bomb bay replacing the clamshell doors of the marker bomb compartment, a more refined KJ-3C autopilot, an HZX-1 gyro, a WL-7 ADF and a revised HL-2A (Type 244) bomb-aiming radar. The aircraft also had a WD-3 IFF transponder, a WJ-2A RWR, an HM-3 optical bombsight and a Type 211 gun ranging radar. The system, in many of its essentials, was based on whatever Western components were available.

Tests of an H-6A fitted with the new system took place between 1975 and 1981. Initially the aircraft was designated H-6A II and later H-6 III (it was common practice at the time to designate new versions of Chinese aircraft with Roman numerals); the designation was eventually changed to H-6C. The aircraft could carry both conventional and nuclear bombs, lay anti-shipping mines and drop torpedoes.

Outwardly the H-6C differed from earlier versions in introducing new low-drag curved wingtips which increased the wing span from 32.989 m to 34.19 m (from 108 ft 2²⁵⁄₃₂ in to 112 ft 2¹⁄₁₆ in)

and the wing area from 164.65 m² to 167.55 m² (from 1,772.28 to 1,803.5 sq ft). The new wingtip fairings gave a 350-km (217-mile) increase in the aircraft's range. The air outlets of the wing leading edge de-icers were located on the fairings' underside, not laterally.

The updated version replaced the H-6A on the production line in 1982, starting with Batch 12 (c/n 122401). Most Chinese *Badgers* from the pre-1990 production run were built in this version, serving both with the PLAAF and the People's Liberation Army Naval Air Force (PLANAF).

H-6D (H-6 IV, B-6D) naval missile strike aircraft

The *Badger's* evolution in China paralleled that in the Soviet Union. In 1975 the Chinese aircraft industry began developing a stand-off anti-shipping strike version of the H-6A for the PLANAF. Originally known as the H-6 IV but later redesignated H-6D, the aircraft was armed with two YJ-6L cruise missiles as its primary weapon; YJ (short for YingJi – Eagle Strike) was a generic designation for Chinese air-launched anti-shipping missiles. Interestingly, the YJ-6L (export designation C-601, NATO codename CAS-1 *Kraken*) was not a purpose-built air-to-surface missile but a local adaptation of the HY-2 shipboard/shore-based anti-shipping missile (HY = HaiYing – Sea Eagle; NATO codename CSS-N-2 *Safflower* for the coastal defence version and CSSC-1 *Silkworm* for the shipboard version). The latter, in turn, was a derivative of the Soviet P-15 *Termit* (Termite; *izdeliye* 4K40, NATO codename SS-N-2 *Styx*) developed by MKB Raduga from 1955 onwards and supplied to China at the end of the 1950s. The adaptation was performed by the China HaiYing Electro-Mechanical Technology Academy (CHETA) and the missile was produced by aircraft factory No.320 in Nanchang, Jiangxi Province.

The YJ-6L had mid-set cropped-delta wings and three tail surfaces seat at 120° to each other. It was powered by a liquid-propellant rocket motor; unlike the HY-2, there was no solid-fuel rocket booster. The missile had an inertial guidance system for midcourse guidance and an active radar seeker head for terminal guidance. The YJ-6L was 6.6 m (21 ft 7²⁷⁄₃₂ in) long, with a wing span of 2.4 m (7 ft 10³¹⁄₆₄ in) and a body diameter of 0.76 m (2 ft 5⁵⁹⁄₆₄ in); the launch weight was 2,300 kg (5,070 lb), including a 513-kg (1,131-lb) HE/SCAP warhead. The missile had a maximum range of 120 km (74.5 miles), though some sources give a figure of only 85 km (52 miles), and cruised at 100-300 m (330-980 ft) and a speed of Mach 0.8.

The missiles were carried on large reverse-tapered pylons located just outboard of the inboard wing fences; this necessitated local reinforcement of the wing structure. Unlike the Soviet missile strike versions, there was no need to make cut-outs in the flaps because the latter could not come into contact with the YJ-6's short fins. The H-6D reportedly also retained a level bombing capability, a modified HM-3A optical bombsight being fitted for this purpose. The defensive armament was reduced to six Type 23-2 cannons by deleting the nose cannon – probably for CG reasons.

The H-6D was equipped with an automated navigation system (including a DPL-1 Doppler navigation radar) and a ZJ-6 missile guidance system. The latter was based on a new HL-6D (Type 245) navigation/attack radar developed by the Laiyang Electronics Technology Research Institute (LETRI) and produced by plant No.781. It was installed in the same chin position and housed in a much larger flat-bottomed radome of quasi-elliptical shape in plan view, which was attached to a metal 'skirt' so that its joint line was straight, not curved as on the baseline H-6. The radar, which was linked to the missile guidance system, could work in 360° or sector scan mode. At an altitude of 9,000 m (29,530 ft) it could detect a surface target with a radar cross-section of 7,500 m² (80,645 sq ft) from a maximum range of 150 km (93 miles). A curious side effect of the new radar installation was that the landing lights were moved from their usual position ahead of the nosewheel well to the underside of the engine nacelles just aft of the air intakes because the bulky radome otherwise obstructed them completely. The aircraft had a crew of five – captain, co-pilot, navigator, WSO and radio operator.

Development of the missile and its guidance system was rather protracted. It was not until 29th August 1981, that the H-6 IV pro-

Top right: An H-6D carrying two YJ-6 anti-ship missiles. As a rule, the naval version wore the same 'anti-flash' colour scheme and low-visibility national insignia as the H-6A.

Above right: Various versions of the YJ-6 were carried by PLANAF *Badgers*. This is a prototype example of the YJ-6(Y) with what looks like a ventral air intake for a jet engine at the rear. Note the data link aerial low on the starboard side and the pitch/yaw transducer (with ground cover) at the starboard wingtip.

Right: This H-6D carries two YJ-6(L) missiles; their colour scheme suggests these are dummies or instrumented test rounds. Note the open bomb bay doors.

This page and below right: A demonstrator of the H-6D's export version, the B-6D, wearing a dark green camouflage scheme. Oddly, the aircraft is marked 'RJAF 357', although the Royal Jordanian Air Force never ordered the type.

The B-6D demonstrator with two C-601 missiles on the pylons.

An export B-6D missile strike aircraft.

Above: H-6s share the final assembly shop at Xian with Y7H transports. An H-6D is in the foreground, with a 'solid-nosed' HY-6 tanker on the left.

Left: Production of H-6 bombers and Y7-100 airliners (a licence-built derivative of the An-24B) at the Xian aircraft factory. To prevent scratches the nose glazing is temporarily papered over and the dorsal blister closed by a metal cover.

Above right: Another view of the same final assembly shop, with three H-6Ds (note the deep chin radome and pylons).

Right: A mix of 250-kg and 500-kg bombs that will shortly be loaded into PLAAF 36th Division H-6E bombers at Wugong AB. The national insignia on the fuselage are low-visibility, while those on the wings' upper surface appear to be the standard red version.

totype made its maiden flight with Zhai Xijie in the captain's seat. The first launch of an inert YJ-6L instrumented test round followed on 6th December; all four tests of inert missiles were reportedly successful. The trials of the aircraft and the anti-shipping strike weapons system as a whole were concluded by live missile tests at the end of 1983.

In May 1985, the H-6D and its YJ-6L (C-601) missiles were exhibited statically at the 36th Paris Air Show. In December that year the new anti-shipping strike system officially entered service with the PLANAF. In-service H-6Ds reportedly had the defensive armament removed.

Later, the YJ-6L was replaced by the more modern YJ-61 (C-611) missile which has a range of 200 km (124 miles), a monopulse active radar seeker head and a cruise altitude of less than 20 m (65 ft) making it harder to detect and destroy. The H-6D remained in PLANAF service until at least 2010 when 30 were reportedly still on strength.

An export version of the H-6D was offered as the B-6D (B for bomber). The only overseas customer was Iraq which took delivery of four, together with a supply of C-601 and C-611 missiles.

The H-6D was dimensionally identical to the H-6C bomber, and the flight performance was generally similar. Differences included a service ceiling reduced to 12,000 m (39,370 ft).

H-6E nuclear bomber

The H-6E was a new-build updated version of the H-6A – a dedicated nuclear bomber with upgraded equipment, upgraded engines

A somewhat unusual angle on an H-6E, showing the extended wingtips. Oddly, the insignia are low-visibility but the tactical code is not.

offering slightly higher thrust and a new ECM system with flush antennas built into the wingtips, which had the same shape as on the H-6C. Externally it differed from the H-6A in lacking the latter's nose cannon and in having an overall bluish grey finish which made it less visible from below. Some sources have called it H-6 I – but see page 395.

The H-6E entered PLAAF service in the late 1980s, shortly before production was suspended. However, despite its updated avionics, the aircraft had no stand-off attack capability and therefore was vulnerable to enemy air defences. This led to the development of the H-6G missile strike version.

H-6F bomber

In the early 1990s some H-6A and H-6C bombers received a mid-life update to a standard similar to the H-6E concerning mostly their mission avionics; such aircraft were redesignated H-6F. The most significant improvement was the introduction of an integrated navigation suite comprising an inertial navigation system, satellite navigation and a DPL-1 Doppler navigation radar. The original manually operated bombsight was replaced by an automatic fire control system, enabling the H-6F to perform long-range interdiction and maritime strike missions at low altitude in all-weather, day/night conditions. The forward-firing cannon was

Above: A mix of grey and white H-6Es on the flight line at Lintong AB, with a GPU on a Yuejin NJ 131 chassis beside each aircraft.
Above right: Chinese sources occasionally supply fakes. This is the original photo; the one of the left is a horizontally flipped mirror image with the tactical codes 'correctly' photoshopped in, as revealed by the c/ns on the wrong side!

deleted. Like the H-6E, the bomber wore a light grey colour scheme.

The H-6F was incapable of delivering precision guided munitions (PGMs). Therefore it was to be used mainly as a maritime bomber for conventional level bombing against surface ships if the enemy air defences were relatively weak. Yet modern naval ships are equipped with highly effective anti-aircraft missile systems making the bomber highly vulnerable.

According to the London-based Institute for Strategic Studies, an estimated 120 or so H-6s in various versions had been built up to 1987, when production of the type was suspended for several years.

H-6G missile strike aircraft

In the early 1990s, in a move to bolster the PLAAF's strategic strike potential, China sought to purchase a number of Tu-22M3 *Backfire-C* multi-mode 'swing-wing' supersonic bomber/missile strike aircraft from Russian Air Force stocks. However, the deal fell through; either the parties failed to reach an agreement on the price or the Russians thought better of it, deciding that selling *Backfires* to China was a bad idea. For one thing, the Tu-22M3 was no longer in production, and the Russian Air Force wanted to keep its *Backfires* that were still operational. For another, the Chinese would be very likely to copy the bomber, and intellectual property rights were being taken seriously now.

Hence China had to 'make do and mend', using new technologies – first and foremost 'smart' weapons – to give the venerable H-6 a new lease of life. This helped meet new PLA doctrinal goals by producing a higher technology weapon to win 'local wars in high-tech conditions', such as a hypothetical new war against Taiwan (the Republic of China), but that did not necessarily assume all-out confrontation with the USA.

Top: '089 Black', the H-6G prototype, at Xian-Yanliang AB.

Above: The same aircraft seen departing on a test flight with missiles on the outer pair of pylons.

Below: A still-unpainted H-6G is prepared for a pre-delivery test. The four pylons and the lack of the rear sighting blisters are evident.

Luckily the Xian Aircraft Company (XAC, or *Xian Feiji Gongye Gongsi*), which was by then part of the Aviation Industries of China I (AVIC I) state corporation, had not been in a hurry to throw the tooling away when H-6 production ended in 1987. This allowed it to resume production in the late 1990s in response to the requirements for an aerial platform to deliver new stand-off PGMs.

The first evidence of a new naval ASM carrier version of the H-6 came when a video of the prototype was shown at the fourth Airshow China held in Zhuhai, Guangdong Province, on 3rd-7th November 2002. Designated H-6G, the aircraft has four wing pylons instead of two (the inboard ones are located similarly to the H-6D, while the outer ones are just outboard of the outer wing fences). This allows it to carry four YJ-81 or YJ-83K ASMs. All four pylons are identical and are shorter than those of the H-6D, since the missiles are more compact; they are attached to the pylons via launch rails. Alternatively, the outer pylons can be used for carrying ECM pods.

Developed by CHETA, the YJ-81 powered by a solid-fuel rocket motor is a derivative of the shipboard YJ-8 (CSS-N-4 *Sardine*), the Chinese counterpart of the French AM-39 Exocet ASM. The YJ-83K is a version powered by a small turbojet engine and having an estimated maximum range of 250 km (155 miles).

All defensive armament has been deleted on the assumption that cannons would be useless in a modern combat scenario where a hostile fighter would almost certainly launch a missile without coming within gunnery range. Hence the dorsal barbette is eliminated altogether, as are the GRO's lateral sighting blisters and the rear glazing of the tail gunner's station (the side windows remain), while the ventral barbette and the tail turret are replaced by fairings. This, together with the four pylons and the deep chin radome outwardly identical to that of the H-6D, are the H-6G's main recognition features.

Left: '81214 Red', an operational 1st Bomber Division H-6G, at the moment of rotation.

Centre left: Sister ship '81216 Red' shows the H-6G's lack of tail and ventral cannon barbettes and lateral sighting blisters for the ventral barbette.

Below left: One more H-6G, '81217 Red', takes off, showing the twin wing pylons.

Bottom left: H-6Gs on the flight line at a PLANAF airbase.

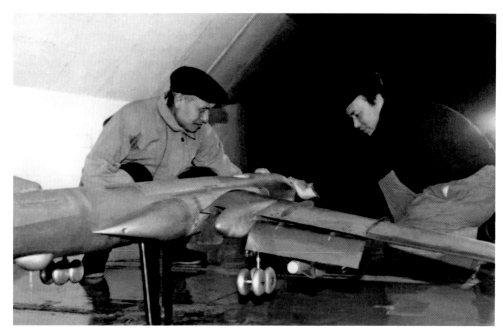

Above right: XAC engineers apply the finishing touches to a metal wind tunnel model of the H-6H missile strike aircraft. The starboard missile can just be seen and the rear radome housing the missile guidance antenna is plainly visible.

Right: Still in primer finish, the H-6H prototype ('02 Blue') is depicted during a test flight with two white-painted KD-63 land attack cruise missiles (probably inert test rounds) under the wings.

The H-6G reportedly entered service with the PLANAF in 2005, replacing the H-6D.

H-6H missile strike aircraft

Another new-build missile strike version was developed for the PLAAF as the H-6H. Again, it featured an H-6D style chin radome and two large pylons under the wings but differed outwardly in lacking defensive armament (except the tail turret, which was retained on some aircraft) and featuring a large teardrop-shaped dielectric fairing supplanting the ventral barbette; the GRO's sighting blisters and the tail gunner's station glazing were retained, even if the tail turret was absent. The lower anti-collision light was relocated from a position ahead of the bomb bay to a position aft of the Doppler radar dielectric panel.

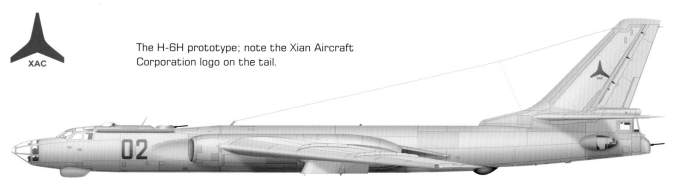

The H-6H prototype; note the Xian Aircraft Corporation logo on the tail.

Left, below and below left: A grey-painted live KD-63 missile is readied for hooking up to H-6H '40176 Red', a 36th Air Division aircraft, with a GPU and a Jiefang CA 141 refuelling bowser in attendance. The ground handling dolly features four hand-cranked hoists with cables and rollers. Note the shape of the missile pylons.

Below, centre: A KD-63 on the starboard pylon of an H-6H. The engine air intake is clearly visible.

Bottom left: Manhandling an identical dolly with a gaudily painted KD-63.

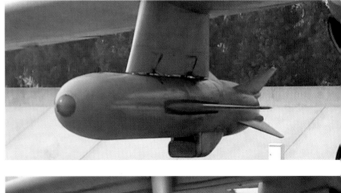

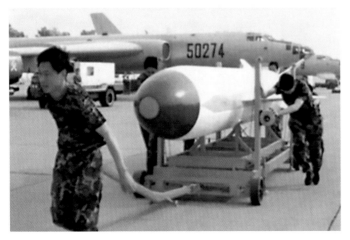

'18598 Red', an H-6H of the 8th Air Division/23rd Regiment, taxies with two differently painted KD-63 LACMs.

A KD-63 missile in the same white/blue/red scheme as the one shown opposite is wheeled away from H-6H '40176 Red'. This is obviously a dummy version, as the missile lacks the prominent ventral air intake.

Right: A publicity shot showing parked blue-coded H-6Hs of the same 36th Air Division with pre-2005 tactical codes.

Left: Here, for a change, a KD-63 is hooked up by means of an ACK-2 self-propelled hydraulic bomb lift. Note the missile's optical guidance system window with the ground cover removed.

Above: '40175 Red', an H-6H of the 36th Division/107th Regiment serialled under the 2005 system, with cannons in the tail turret.

Below: H-6H '40079 Red' shows the aft-mounted missile guidance system radome that distinguishes it from the earlier H-6D.

Above right and far right: Two H-6Hs pass overhead, toting differently painted KD-63s. The white missile is an engineless dummy.

Right: Another 36th Air Division H-6H (40174 Red) with a full load of live missiles. There are no cannons in the tail turret.

The H-6H carries two KongDi-63 (KD-63, or K/AKD-63) land attack cruise missiles (LACMs). This rather bulky weapon – the first such indigenous missile to give the PLAAF a tactical precision strike capability – appears to be based on the airframe of the YJ-6 ASM (which explains the size of the missile pylons), having similar cropped-delta mid-set wings, but the tail surfaces have a squashed-X configuration and the powerplant is a small turbojet engine (reportedly the Williams FW-41B) breathing via a rectan-

gular ventral air intake with an S-duct. The KD-63 reportedly uses inertial/GPS mid-course guidance and has a TV seeker head for terminal guidance; hence the abovementioned dielectric fairing under the aircraft's rear fuselage houses a command link antenna for the missiles. The missile carries a 500-kg (1,100-lb) conventional warhead over a range of 150-200 km (93-124 miles), cruising at Mach 0.9. Some sources claim the KD-63 missile also has naval (anti-shipping) applications and therefore ascribe the alternative

Above: H-6H '40175 Red' breaks formation with sister ship '40076 Red'. Both aircraft, which are carrying two live missiles each, lack cannons.

Left: A full frontal of a taxying H-6H.

Above right: A retouched photo of the H-6M (the code '0001 Red' is fake) with two CJ-10K cruise missiles on the inboard pylons. The port side chaff/flare dispensers are visible ahead of the national insignia.

Right:
An operational H-6M ('40576 Red') arrives at Zhuhai-Sanzao airport for Airshow China 2014 where it was a static exhibit. Note the tail cannons and the different size of the inboard and outboard pylons.

Navy-style designation YJ-63 to it.

The H-6H first flew on 2nd December 1998, and the first successful test launch of a KD-63 took place in November 2002. The aircraft probably entered service in 2004-05. This put the PLAAF into a position to attack small but strategically important targets, like the entrances to the large tunnels near Hualien that Taiwan had built to hide its air forces from initial PLA attack.

An H-6H serialled '18692 Red' was in the static park of the eighth Airshow China at Zhuhai-Sanzao airport (16th-21st November 2010).

H-6M bomber/missile strike aircraft

A further new-build missile strike version for the PLAAF was brought out as the H-6M. It resembles a cross-breed between the H-6G and the H-6H, featuring the former version's four short missile pylons but retaining part of the defensive armament. The tail turret with two cannons is in place, but not the radome of the gun ranging radar, which is replaced by a small hemispherical metal fairing. The GRO's lateral sighting blisters are also retained. A new feature is the addition of IRCM flare launchers built into the rear fuselage sides (six on each side, in three rows of two) for protection against heat-seeking missiles. Two pairs of missile attack warning system (MAWS) sensors are located on

Left: H-6M '40671 Red' demon-strates its conventional bombing capability by dropping a stick of 250-kg HE bombs when combatting ice jams on the Yellow River.

Below and below left: The result of the bombing run.

Bottom: H-6M missile carriers on the flight line. The flight deck and the entire centre fuselage are under heavy wraps.

Top right: The only known photo of the H-6 I experimental version powered by four Rolls-Royce Spey turbofans. Note the reduced size and circular shape of the inboard engines' air intakes. The long pylons and small ground clearance of the outer engines are also noteworthy.

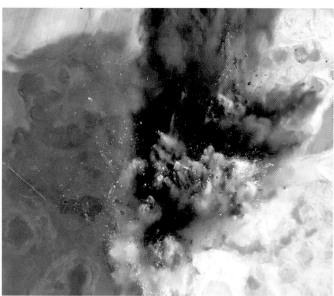

the sides of the nose and on the fairing above the tail gunner's station; two pairs of RWR aerials are mounted on the fin cap to give 360° coverage.

The H-6M carries two CJ-10K LACMs on the inboard pylons and ECM pods on the outboard ones. A small additional pylon is installed on the centreline immediately aft of the Doppler radar's dielectric panel, probably for carrying some sort of equipment pod.

The CJ-10 (*Cháng Jiàn* – Long Sword) is the air-launched version of a tri-service second-generation subsonic cruise missile that also comes in ground-launched and sea-launched versions. It was reportedly developed by the China Aerospace Science and Industry Corporation (CASC) Third Academy and CHETA. The missile apparently draws on the technology of the US Raytheon BGM-109 Tomahawk (captured) and the Soviet MKB Raduga Kh-55 (AS-15 *Kent*, purchased from the Ukraine). It features a slender fuselage with a parabolic nose, mid-set unswept wings folding aft into a recess in the fuselage, and cruciform tail surfaces. The powerplant appears to be a small turbofan buried in the rear fuselage, with a pop-out ventral air intake. Full details are not yet known but the CJ-10 is credited with a range of more than 1,500 km (931 miles), a CEP of 10 m (33 ft) and the ability to carry a conventional or nuclear warhead.

H-6M '40576 Red' (c/n 252401) was displayed statically at the tenth Airshow China (11th-16th November 2014).

H-6 I development aircraft

In the late 1970s, when the PRC was still on reasonably good terms with the western world, an experimental version of the H-6 was developed in an attempt to improve the bomber's range. To this end the Chinese designers replaced the thirsty WP-8 turbojets with four less powerful but more fuel-efficient Rolls-Royce RB.163-25 Spey 512 non-afterburning turbofans. These were rated at 5,416 kgp (11,940 lbst), increasing the overall take-off thrust from 19,000 to 21,664 kgp (from 41,890 to 47,760 lbst). Two engines were installed at the usual locations aft of the rear spar, breathing through smaller intakes of perfectly circular shape, while the other two were installed under the wings at about half-span in nacelles mounted in a slightly nose-up attitude on large, sharply swept pylons. The result looked strikingly similar to the stillborn project version of 'aircraft 88' powered by four AL-5 turbojets.

Known as the H-6 I (the Roman numeral 'one'), the re-engined aircraft – apparently having no serial – was tested and showed promising results; in particular, range was improved from the standard H-6's 5,760 km (3,579 miles) to 8,060 km (5,008 miles). Yet for reasons unknown the H-6 I was abandoned. Some sources claim that attempts to reverse-engineer the Spey failed, leaving the bomber without a powerplant. Others maintain that on the production version the Spey 512 was to have been replaced by the 9,300-kgp (20,500-lbst) RB.168 Spey Mk 202 afterburning turbo-

Above right: A display model of the H-6K (BC-1) showing the restyled nose, the larger air intakes and six missiles on underwing pylons.

Right: An H-6K flight deck section on a rocket-propelled sled is used for testing the HTY-6F zero-zero ejection seat developed for the bomber. Note the forward-mounted high-speed camera.

Left: The first prototype H-6K in zinc chromate primer finish at the Xian factory before the rollout ceremony, hence the 'bouquet' on the nose. The greatly enlarged air intakes and the size of the nose radome are readily apparent. Note the gyrostabilised optronic 'turret' under the nose.

Below: The same aircraft after a visit to the paint shop, sporting the serial '001 Blue'. The AVIC I logo and the export designation BC-1 can be seen on the tail, and the legend in Chinese characters on the nose apparently reads 'Bomber, China'. The six pylons with missile rails are clearly visible.

fan, which was eventually produced under licence as the WS-9 (*WoShan* – turbofan engine), but it transpired that this would require so much time that the idea was dropped.

H-6K (BC-1 God of War) bomber/missile strike aircraft

The failure of the H-6 I did not put XAC off, and two decades later the idea of re-engining the bomber was dusted off. Development

of the *Badger's* latest version probably began in 2000. Designated H-6K, this aircraft incorporates the most radical changes made to the type so far.

The powerplant consists of two non-afterburning turbofans mounted at the usual locations aft of the wing torsion box. Most sources agree that the engines are Russian-made Aviadvigatel' (Solov'yov) D-30KP Srs 2 turbofans rated at 12,000 kgp

Above: One of the H-6K prototypes 'cleans up' as it departs Xian-Yanliang on a test flight, wearing no insignia other than the CFTE test serial '861 Black'. Note the circular black and white photo calibration markings on the fuselage. This view illustrates the absence of the rear glazing and the APU exhaust in the hemispherical tail fairing.

Below left: A look inside the H-6K's flight deck in a test flight.

Below, far left: '861 Black' rests between test flights with the flight deck section under wraps; the open bomb bay doors can be seen.

Below: Another H-6K prototype,'862 Black', with yellow-striped KD-63 missiles o the centre pair of pylons.

(26,445 lbst) for take-off. This engine powers the Il-76TD *Candid-A*/Il-76MD *Candid-B* transports operated by the PLAAF in substantial numbers, as well as the Il-76MD's locally developed KJ-2000 *Mainring* AWACS derivative, and using it for the H-6K makes sense from a spares commonality point of view. This view is supported by the fact that China had taken delivery of 55 D-30KP engines in 2009-11 and placed an order for 184 more in 2011. Some sources, though, claim that the H-6K is powered by the identically rated indigenous WS-18 non-afterburning turbofan developed by the Chengdu Engine Company (CEC, a part of the AVIC II corpo-

ration) since 2009 in order to reduce dependence on deliveries from Russia. Actually the WS-18 is a Chinese (some sources say co-produced) version of the D-30KP Srs 2.

The greater mass flow of the new engines necessitated a redesign of the engine nacelles and air intakes. In order to avoid a redesign of the frames at the roots of the wing spars through which the main inlet ducts pass, the designers at XAC increased the cross-section of the auxiliary ducts passing below the wing torsion box, thereby extending the fatter nacelles downward. The air intakes still have the Tu-16/H-6's distinctive quasi-triangular

shape but are substantially enlarged. Since the D-30KP is started by a high-pressure air starter, the turbostarter inlet and exhaust ports present on all previous versions have been eliminated. The shape of the engine cowlings, however, is similar to the old one and the engines have plain nozzles, without the clamshell thrust reversers normally fitted to the D-30KP (which, in theory, could have been incorporated without major problems).

Speaking of engine starting, the new engines require an auxiliary power unit (APU), which is housed in the former tail gunner's station. The APU exhaust is located at the rear extremity of the fuselage but the location of the air intake, which is closed when the APU is not running, is not obvious.

That is not all, however – the fuselage structure is reinforced and considerably redesigned. The entire forward fuselage is completely new, featuring a 'solid' nose; the extreme nose ahead of the flight deck is slightly drooped, incorporating a new, more powerful multi-function radar in a huge radome and an optoelectronic imaging system in a gyrostabilised 'ball turret' under the nose. Two pairs of 'warts' are positioned aft of the radome, carrying RWR antennas and MAWS sensors. Two avionics bay cooling air scoops and two air outlets are located high on the forward fuselage sides.

The flight deck section is no longer as extensively glazed as on the previous versions, featuring a conventional opaque roof; the glazing is totally different, comprising a V-shaped windshield composed of two panes instead of three and six side windows, the foremost pair being triangular (these are sliding direct vision win-

Left: H-6Ks share the final assembly shop with Xian MA-60 twin-turboprop regional airliners (a much-modified derivative of the An-24). This view shows the bulkier engine nacelles, the avionics bay access covers on the sides of the nose and the crew entry door.

Below left: A 'toad's eye view' of a half-finished H-6K airframe.

Above right: Production H-6Ks in service with a PLAAF unit. The aircraft taxying out in the foreground is an H-6H (note the rear observation blisters and the two pylons).

Right: H-6K '20014 Red' of the 10th Air Division/28th Regiment seen in a practice flight without armament.

A trio of H-6Ks on the flight line at Nanjing, The large number of ground support vehicles suggests a training sortie is due to take place soon.

Above: A fine landing study of H-6K '11196 Red', an 8th Air Division/ 24th Regiment aircraft.

Left: A close up of the H-6K's nose and port wing. Note the 'Danger, air intake' markings introduced on this version and the red undersides of the pylons with no missile rails attached.

Below left. Maintenance in progress on two 24th Regiment H-6Ks. '11092 Red' has the entry door and the engine cowlings open; the APU exhaust on the other aircraft is closed by a canvas cover.

Above right: H-6K '11195 Red' seen from a sister ship during a PLAAF exercise.

H-6K '11194 Red' comes in to land with a CJ-10 missile on the port centre pylon. Note the chrome yellow insides of the engine inlet ducts. The air scoops on the forward fuselage are for avionics cooling.

dows) and the other two rectangular. Instead of a ventral hatch serving for entry/egress and ejection, the H-6K's flight deck is accessed via a large airliner-style rectangular door on the port side opening outward and forward through 180°; somewhat surprisingly, it is not a plug-type door, featuring simple faired hinges.

The H-6K features a 'glass cockpit' with six colour multi-function displays (MFDs). The high degree of automation in the avionics and systems made it possible to reduce the crew to three (two pilots and the WSO). The crew members are provided with new HTY-6F zero-zero ejection seats developed by the Shenyang Aircraft Design Institute (*Shènyáng fēijī shèjì yánjiù suǒ*, aka 601 Aircraft Design Institute); this is a version of the seat fitted to

several Chinese combat aircraft, such as the Xian JH-7 *Flounder* fighter-bomber.

A teardrop-shaped dielectric blister (smaller than that of the H-6H) is installed at the former position of the ventral barbette, probably again having to do with weapons guidance; a second dielectric blister is located dorsally just ahead of it, obviously housing a satellite navigation or communications antenna. The rear cabin glazing is completely eliminated; there are three IRCM flare dispensers on each side of the rear fuselage.

A third pair of missile pylons has been added under the inner wings (inboard of the main gear fairings), bringing the total of missiles carried externally to six; the pylons are of the same short

type as on the H-6G/H-6M. Compatible weapons include the CJ-10 (according to some sources, its newer version, the CJ-20) with a range of 1,500-2,500 km (931-1,552 miles). The bomb bay doors are retained but the bay is reportedly occupied by additional fuel tankage – albeit some sources credit the H-6K with the ability to carry weapons internally. 'Smart bombs' with either laser guidance (using onboard or off-board sensors) or satellite guidance have been stated as possible weapons of the H-6K.

The H-6K prototype was completed and rolled out at Xian-Yanliang in late 2006, making its first flight on 5th January 2007. Initially the aircraft flew in primer finish and with no markings whatever; on one occasion it was seen with a full load of six CJ-10 missiles. Later the H-6K prototype received a grey finish and the serial '001 Blue', sporting the AVIC I logo and the alternative designation BC-1 ('Bomber, China') on the tail. By then the aircraft had received a popular name, 'God of War'. The serial was apparently changed to '861 Black' when the first prototype entered test with the China Flight Test Establishment (CFTE) at Xian-Yanliang – the Chinese counterpart of LII. It was soon joined by a second prototype, '862 Black', and production began soon afterwards.

The type achieved initial operational capability with the PLAAF in 2009 and was fielded in significant numbers in 2011, and deliveries are continuing.

On 17th February 2015, Chinese Communist Party leader and People's Liberation Army Supreme Commander-in-Chief Xi Jin-

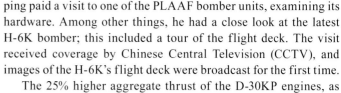

ping paid a visit to one of the PLAAF bomber units, examining its hardware. Among other things, he had a close look at the latest H-6K bomber; this included a tour of the flight deck. The visit received coverage by Chinese Central Television (CCTV), and images of the H-6K's flight deck were broadcast for the first time.

The 25% higher aggregate thrust of the D-30KP engines, as well as their lower SFC, give the H-6K both a greater payload and longer range. The aircraft is now credited with a combat radius of 1,800-2,200 km (1,120-1,370 miles). Extra fuel tanks in the bomb bay reportedly enable a 3,500-km (2,170-mile) combat radius; hence the H-6K is considered to be a strategic aircraft by western analysts.

Western experts assessed the H-6K as putting China into a position to *credibly threaten the U.S. military buildup on Guam*. They went on to say such an aircraft would be able to deliver strikes against Japan, India and Australia, not to mention Taiwan – all of which *are ill-equipped to defend against new PLA LACMs*.

HY-6 (H-6U, HU-6) refuelling tanker

Until the late 1980s, the primary role of the PLAAF was to defend the mainland; hence there was no requirement for in-flight refuelling. Later, however, when China began pursuing a more expansive policy, the PLA launched a modernisation programme to transform itself from a purely defensive force to a force with both offensive and defensive capabilities. This sparked a requirement to expand the reach of the PLAAF and PLANAF to China's peripheral regions, such as the South China Sea and the Taiwan Strait – and hence the need for IFR capability. Such a need first arose in 1988 when China and Vietnam had a territorial dispute; the apple of discord was the Johnson Reef in the Spratly Islands – an archipelago in the South China Sea which is claimed by six nations.

The H-6 was selected as the basis for the PLAAF's first in-flight refuelling tanker designated HY-6 (*Hongzhaji You* – bomber/tanker); it has sometimes been referred to in the press as the H-6U or HU-6. Like most air forces, the PLAAF chose the probe-and-drogue IFR system. Unlike the Soviet tanker variants of the *Badger* (the Tu-16Z and Tu-16N/Tu-16NN), the HY-6 was intended for supporting tactical aircraft (notably the Shenyang J-8D *Finback* interceptor), not heavy bombers; it was therefore a two-point tanker with RDC-1 podded HDUs mounted on pylons under the outer wings.

Top left: The RDC-1 podded hose drum unit as fitted to the HU-6 tankers.

Above left: Crews race towards their HY-6s during a practice alert. The new-build tanker's nose design with that peculiar ring of transparencies is clearly in evidence.

Left: HY-6 '43595 Blue' shows off the low-visibility national insignia.

Right: A publicity photo showing an HY-6 accompanied by J-8D fighters.

Top, top left and above: HY-6s '18897 Red' and '18792 Red' accompanied by Chengdu J-10A fighters during the 60th Anniversary parade in Beijing on 1st October 2009.

Above left: Another view of an HU-6 accompanied by J-8Ds.

The origin of the HDUs merits a comment. At first China approached the UK company Flight Refuelling Ltd. (FRL) for potential purchase or licence production of IFR systems. In keeping with a memorandum of understanding signed in 1988, FRL would supply the HDUs and assist with their integration. However, these plans were foiled by sanctions imposed on China after the 1989 crackdown on student protests in Beijing's Tiananmen Square. In the early 1990s China reportedly obtained some 1960s/70s Western IFR equipment via Israel or Iran; this was later used by China's Institute of Aero Accessories as a pattern for the RDC-1 HDU, which looks suspiciously similar to the FRL Mk 32 pod.

Left: '18792 Red', an 8th Air Division HY-6, 'unbuttoned' for maintenance. Note the asymmetrical navigator's station glazing is (compare this to the photos on page 402) and the small ventral blister fairing ahead of the entry hatch.

Below left and bottom left: The same aircraft taxies at Zhuhai-Sanzao during Airshow China 2008.

Below: '18792 Red' becomes airborne for an airshow routine (an inflight refuelling simulation) at Zhuhai.

Right: '18897 Red' depicted on final approach shows the HY-6's triple red stripes on the underside of the wings which serve as a reference for the pilots of the receiver aircraft. The nose treatment is the same as on '18792 Red'.

The fuel load was 37,000 kg (81,570 lb), including 18,500 kg (40,785 lb) of transferable fuel, part of which was carried in a tank inside the former bomb bay. The refuelling systems operator's station was located in the former tail gunner's station of the H-6.

Changes were made to the avionics. The most obvious change was a reprofiled nose with a weather/navigation radar mounted conventionally in a small parabolic radome ahead of the navigator's station, which had asymmetrical glazing of greatly reduced area; the usual chin radome was replaced by a small blister fairing. Also, the tanker had a duplicated (main and backup) inertial navigation system, plus a duplicated tactical area navigation (TACAN) system ensuring rendezvous with the receiver aircraft, with all-weather day/night mutual detection and approach from distances up to 200 km (124 miles). The HY-6 also had a radio/signal light system for night refuelling operations.

The HY-6 was unveiled in model form during a defence technology exhibition held in Beijing in 1988. The actual prototype was probably completed in 1989, the maiden flight taking place in 1990. The first successful aerial refuelling operation between an HY-6 and a J-8D fighter took place in 1993. Proof of the actual aircraft's existence (in the form of US surveillance satellite imagery) did not come until 1996.

An estimated 24 new-build HY-6s (some of them were from batches 20 and 21) were delivered to the PLAAF's 8th Air Division at Leiyang AB in Guangzhou province. Each tanker is capable of refuelling two J-8D fighters simultaneously, and up to six fighters in one sortie, extending their combat radius from 800 to 1,200 km (from 496 to 745 miles). The HY-6 can also work with the indigenous Chengdu J-10 fighter and possibly the Xian JH-7 fighter-bomber but is incompatible with the PLAAF's Sukhoi Su-30MKK

Above: An HY-6 with entry hatches open and a Yuejin NJ 131 GPU connected. The tactical code '69696 Blue' is fake, having been crudely altered by a censor; the actual code is '43696 Blue'.

Left: Close-up of an HY-6's nose showing the asymmetrical glazing.

Above right: '18893 Red', another HY-6, in landing configuration.

Right: A fine study of sister ship '18897 Red' as the landing gear begins its retraction sequence.

Flanker-G fighter whose IFR probe has a different design. This prompted the PLAAF to order the Il'yushin Il-78MK *Midas-A* tanker/transport from Russia; these aircraft were to cater for the Su-30MKKs but were never delivered because the manufacturer (the Tashkent Aircraft Production Association in Uzbekistan) ran into serious problems and was eventually declared bankrupt.

The HY-6 was displayed publicly for the first time during the National Day military parade held in Beijing on 1st October 1999, when two tankers escorted by four J-8D fighters flew over Tiananmen Square, indicating that the type was already operational. Nine years later an example serialled '18792 Red' participated in the seventh Airshow China at Zhuhai-Sanzao (4th-9th November 2008). The tanker was one of the highlights of the flying display, performing a simulated refuelling of two J-8Ds.

H-6DU refuelling tanker

The PLANAF has a tanker version of its own, and a rather different one at that. Several H-6D missile carriers were converted into two-point hose-and-drogue tankers designated H-6DU. Unlike the PLAAF's HY-6 tankers, they retain a fully glazed navigator's station in the nose and the deep chin radome. The H-6DU was likewise fielded in the mid-1990s with the PLANAF's 9th Divi-

Above: An actual. refuelling of two J-10s by an HY-6. The aircraft's identities have been removed by the military censor.

Left: Front view of an H-6DU tanker based on the H-6D and retaining the latter's glazed nose and deep chin radome. The aircraft appears to be light grey overall.

Below left: An H-6DU in the standard 'anti-flash' colour scheme with low-viz markings and the low-viz code '81228 Blue outline' refuels a PLA-NAF J-8D coded '81290 Red'. Note the reference lines on the tanker's wings.

Top right: This model is the only evidence of the existence of the HD-6 ECM version with a ventral canoe fairing and underwing equipment pods.

Above right: A model of the Air-Launched Launch Vehicle that was to be launched by a suitably modified H-6 to place small commercial satellites into orbit.

Right: H-6 '40672 Red' with the Shenlong experimental suborbital launch spacecraft seen in 2007.

sion at Lingshui, Hainan Province, primarily for supporting the PLANAF's J-8D fighters.

HD-6 ECM aircraft

An ECM version of the H-6 – the Chinese counterpart of the Tu-16P – was also developed. Designated HD-6 (*Hongzhaji Dian* – bomber/electronic warfare aircraft), it has been revealed in model form only. The model shows a large canoe fairing under the centre fuselage similar to that of the Tu-16P Ficus. Unlike the latter, however, the HD-6 has an additional small dielectric blister ahead of this fairing, plus pylon-mounted pods under the wings resembling the SRS-3 ELINT pods of the Tu-16R. Furthermore, the model appears to have a 'solid' nose with a parabolic radome but this may be simply an inaccurate rendering of the nose glazing – especially since an H-6D style chin radome is present.

H-6 drone launcher version

The Xian Aisheng Technical Group of the Northwest Polytechnic University (NPU) developed a high-altitude, high-speed target drone designated Ba-6. This was a derivative of the HQ-2 (HongQi-2 – Red Banner-2) SAM which was a Chinese copy of the Soviet S-75 (NATO codename SA-2 *Guideline*). The Ba-6 was basically the second stage of the SAM equipped with a second engine (possibly a ramjet) in a ventral nacelle).

Accordingly an H-6 bomber was modified for launching the Ba-6 drone. It was able to carry one such drone on the fuselage centreline or two drones under the wings. No exact designation is known.

H-6 suborbital launch vehicle carriers

At the sixth Airshow China in November 2006, the China Aerospace Corporation (CASC) revealed its new Air-Launched Launch Vehicle (ALLV), a solid-fuel rocket launched from an H-6 bomber at an altitude of 11,000 m (36,090 ft). This concept had been under development since 2000. Conceptually and outwardly the ALLV is very similar to its Russian and American counterparts – the *Burlak* suborbital launcher rocket (co-developed by MKB Raduga and the Moscow Energy Institute) and the Pegasus suborbital launcher rocket (developed by the Orbital Sciences Corporation)

respectively, having a cylindrical body with shoulder-mounted cropped-delta wings and three rudders set at 120° to each other. With an advertised payload of 50 kg (110 lb), the ALLV could be used for putting micro-satellites into low Earth orbit (LEO) – or serve as an anti-satellite (ASAT) weapon, a thing that China has already demonstrated its ability to create.

An even more ambitious programme pursued by China since 1986 was to result in the creation of a reusable aerospace plane – the Chinese equivalent of the Space Shuttle. As part of this continually evolving programme, a subscale proof-of-concept vehicle called Shenlong ('Divine Dragon') and codenamed Project 863-706 was built, featuring a circular-section fuselage with a para-

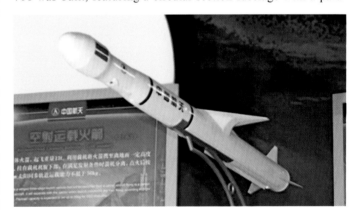

bolic nose and low-set delta wings. It was powered by a single rocket motor with a large exposed bell nozzle. Again, the vehicle was carried aloft by a specially modified H-6.

Pictures have been released showing an H-6A with the Shenlong attached, the fuselage adhering directly to the bomber's belly; apparently the vertical tail was to fit inside the bomb bay having specially modified doors. Interestingly, the aircraft wore an ordinary PLAAF serial ('40672 Red'), not a three-digit test serial. The first launch (or drop test) took place on 11th December 2007.

H-6 engine testbed
In 1986 an H-6 bomber operated by the CFTE with the test serial '086 Blue' (originally '86 Blue') was refitted as a testbed for new jet engines. In similar manner to the Soviet Tu-16LL the development engine was housed in a special nacelle suspended on a pantographic mechanism in the bomb bay; it was semi-recessed on the ground and lowered clear of the fuselage and its turbulent boundary layer before start-up. Unlike the Tu-16LL, the Chinese testbed appeared to have an additional icing test function, with what looked like a water sprinkler grid mounted a short way ahead of the development engine's air intake.

The aircraft remained in operation for 20 years. In 2006 it was retired and replaced in the CFTE test fleet by a modified Il-76MD – to be precise, a conversion of one of the five Ilyushin/Beriyev 'aircraft 976' *Main-*

Far left: '86 Blue', the H-6 engine testbed, with the development engine nacelle lowered. Note the spray rig ahead of it for icing tests.

Below left: The same aircraft in later days as '086 Blue'.

Left: Close-up of the development engine pod on this aircraft.

Right: '40077 Red', the H-6H supposedly used for testing radar-absorbent material coatings. The dark areas are allegedly covered with RAM.

stay-C radar picket aircraft based on the Il-76MD, which had been used by LII in Zhukovskiy during ballistic and cruise missile test launches. This was converted into an engine testbed similar to the Soviet/Russian Il-76LL (*letayuschchaya laboratoriya*).

H-6G weapons testbed

An H-6G missile strike aircraft operated by CFTE found use as a testbed for new air-to-surface missiles. A photo taken in 2013 shows the aircraft, which wears the usual overall grey colour scheme but a three-digit test serial typical of CFTE machines ('872 Black'), carrying a pair of the latest YJ-12 supersonic anti-shipping missiles on the inboard pylons.

The YJ-12 resembles a scaled-up version of the Russian Raduga Kh-31A *Taïfoon* (Typhoon; NATO codename AS-17 *Krypton*), featuring an integrated powerplant comprising a solid-fuel booster and a ramjet sustainer which breathes through four intakes located around the body's circumference in two perpendicular planes (the same planes as the cruciform fins and aft-mounted all-movable cruciform rudders). When the missile is on the pylon the intakes are closed by conical fairings with off-centre tips which are whisked away by the slipstream as the booster fires. To reduce the cross-section area and hence drag the booster is designed to fit

into the ramjet nozzle like a plug and is ejected after burnout. The YJ-12 has an active radar homing system, the seeker head being enclosed by an ogival radome.

The missile was apparently tested against the PLA Navy target ship *Zhenjiang* (hull number 514), a 35-year-old former East Sea Fleet Type 053H (NATO codename *Jianghu-I* class) guided missile frigate decommissioned on 12th May 2013. At an unspecified date the frigate took a direct hit in the superstructure. There was no explosion because the missile was inert, but the impact was so violent that the bridge was wiped out completely and the hull warped, indicating that the missile was large and heavy and was travelling at great speed.

H-6H stealth technology testbed

On 24th September 2015, a PLAAF H-6H coded '40077 Red' was observed flying over China in a rather unusual guise. The extreme nose (the navigator's station glazing framework), the flight deck glazing framework, the underside of the nose immediately ahead of the chin radome, the entire front portions of the engine nacelles, the wing, stabiliser and missile pylon leading edges, the front and rear ends of the main gear fairings, the dorsal fin, a band around the rear fuselage near the ventral dielectric teardrop fairing for the

Left and below left: H-6G '872 Black' was used by the CFTE as a weapons testbed. Here it is seen carrying test examples of the YJ-12 supersonic ASM on the inboard pylons.

Right: '090 Red' is an unidentified special version based on the H-6G's airframe with no rear observation blisters. This view shows the six missile pylons and the long IFR probe on the nose. The latter appears to feature an HY-6 style radome instead of the usual deep chin radome.

missile guidance antennas, the GRO's sighting blister fairings and the fairing replacing the tail turret were painted dark grey, suggesting they were coated with radar absorbing material (RAM). The main gear doors, bomb bay doors, flaps and ailerons were heavily outlined in the same dark grey colour. Moreover, the abovementioned fairing at the rear extremity of the fuselage appeared to be longer and have a different shape.

The aircraft was assumed to be involved in the testing of the RAM. The latter is not necessarily intended for the H-6 itself; it may find application on China's fifth-generation fighters, such as the Chengdu J-20.

H-6… development aircraft (testbed?)
A photo circulated on the Internet in 2015 shows an as-yet unidentified version of the H-6 undergoing tests. The aircraft, which again is painted grey overall and wears the test serial '090 Red' suggesting it is operated by the CFTE, appears to be based on the

H-6G – it has WP-8 engines, the same rear end treatment (with no lateral observation blisters and no ventral radome) and the same type of missile pylons. However, the number of pylons is increased to six, and they are located differently from the H-6K – all six are mounted outboard of the main gear fairings (and spaced equally on each wing), the outer pair being just outboard of the ailerons' inner ends. Moreover, the nose resembles that of the HY-6 tanker, having the same parabolic contour and nose radome, but the navigator's station glazing is completely gone. Finally, a long IFR probe canted slightly downward is mounted on top of the extreme nose, suggesting '090 Red' is being used for testing an IFR system developed for heavy aircraft.

H-8 I bomber (project)
Persisting with the idea of improving the H-6's performance, on 23rd March 1970 the Chinese government tasked Research Institute No.603 with developing a strategic bomber designated H-8.

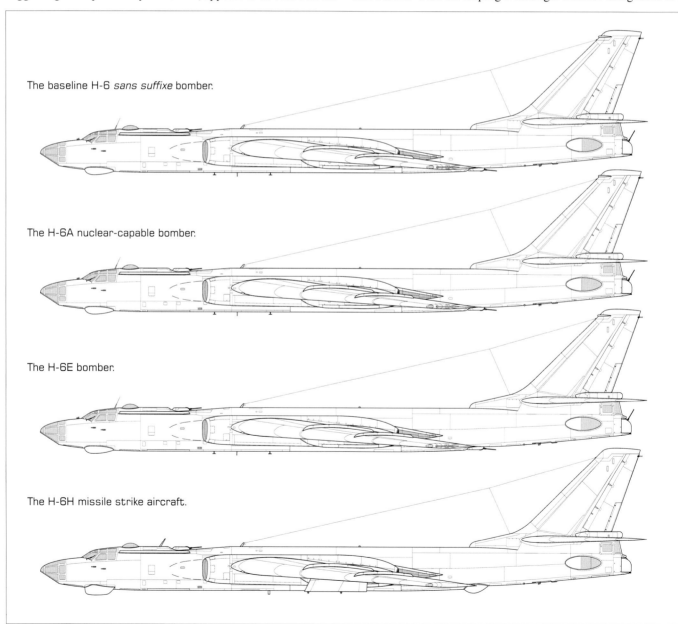

The baseline H-6 *sans suffixe* bomber.

The H-6A nuclear-capable bomber.

The H-6E bomber.

The H-6H missile strike aircraft.

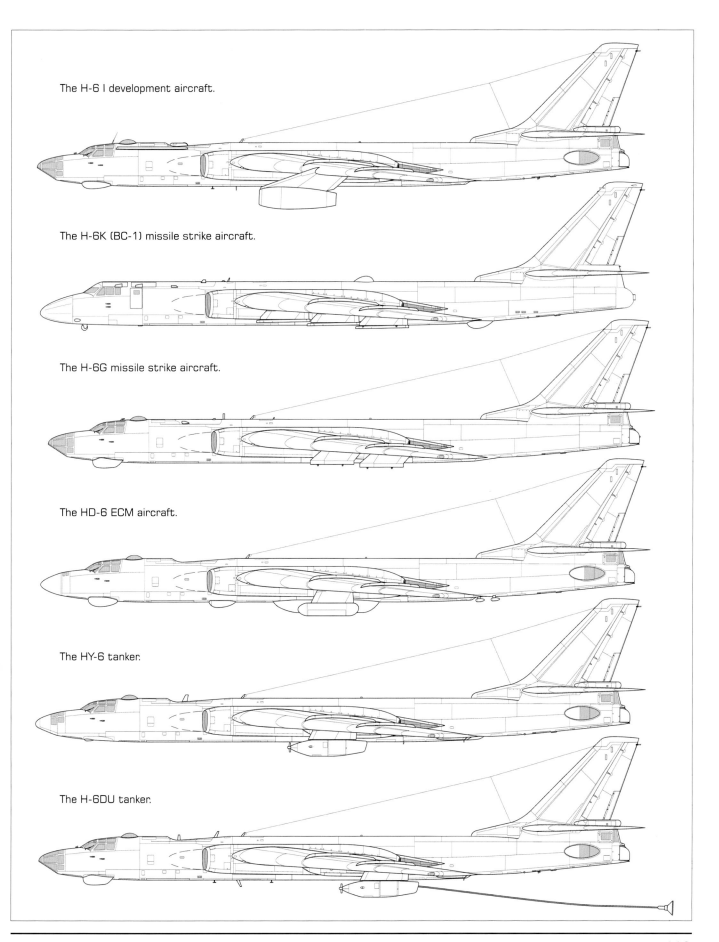

The H-6 I development aircraft.

The H-6K (BC-1) missile strike aircraft.

The H-6G missile strike aircraft.

The HD-6 ECM aircraft.

The HY-6 tanker.

The H-6DU tanker.

A model of the projected H-8 I bomber with four WS-6 turbofans.

The aircraft was to be capable of delivering conventional and nuclear free-fall weapons or air-to-surface missiles over long range, as well as of operating at night and in adverse weather without the assistance of airborne command posts.

The designers chose a 'quick fix' approach, retaining much of the H-6's airframe. The forward and rear fuselage sections were basically unchanged, except that the navigator's station glazing was tipped by a small radome in the manner of the HU-6 tanker (there was no chin radome). The centre fuselage and the wings were new; albeit the basic wing design was the same, the H-8 featured a conventional wing/fuselage joint without the engine housings flanking the fuselage and the inlet ducts passing through the wing torsion box. The centre fuselage section was longer than the

progenitor's, making for a larger bomb bay that was 8.6 m (28 ft 2^{37}/$_{64}$ in) long, 1.8 m (5 ft 10^{55}/$_{64}$ in) wide and 2.72 m (8 ft 11^{3}/$_{32}$ in) deep. The H-6's landing gear and the tail unit were retained.

The powerplant was completely different. The first project version, designated H-8 I, had four 11,026-kgp (24,308-lbst) WS-6 Jia (Type 910) non-afterburning high-bypass turbofans in pylon-mounted nacelles located just outboard of the main gear fairings and just outboard of the ailerons' inboard ends. An alternative version with six 8,175-kgp (18,020-lbst) Pratt & Whitney JT-3D-3B non-afterburning turbofans also came into consideration.

The overall dimensions were increased. The H-8 I was to be 48.5 m (159 ft 1^{29}/$_{64}$ in) long, with a wing span of 46.47 m (152 ft 5^{33}/$_{64}$ in). The maximum ordnance load was to reach 18,000 kg (39,680 lb), half of which was to be carried externally on pylons under the inner wings.

H-8 II bomber (project)

An even more ambitious project was the H-8 II – an even larger bomber powered by six WS-6 Jia turbofans; the engine nacelles were spaced equally along the span, the inboard ones being located inboard of the main gear units. The overall length and wing span were even greater. Some drawings show a redesigned flight deck section with an extended 'solid' nose. Very little information is available about this project; anyway, the H-8 never materialised.

Xian H-6 specifications			
	H-6A	**H-6D**	**H-6H**
Fuselage length	34.8 m (114 ft 2^{5}/$_{64}$ in)	34.8 m (114 ft 2^{5}/$_{64}$ in)	34.8 m (114 ft 2^{5}/$_{64}$ in)
Wing span	32.989 m (108 ft 2^{25}/$_{32}$ in)	34.19 m (112 ft 2^{1}/$_{16}$ in)	34.19 m (112 ft 2^{1}/$_{16}$ in)
Height on ground)	9.85 m (32 ft 3^{51}/$_{64}$ in)	9.85 m (32 ft 3^{51}/$_{64}$ in)	9.85 m (32 ft 3^{51}/$_{64}$ in)
Landing gear track	9.775 m (32 ft 0^{37}/$_{32}$ in)	9.775 m (32 ft 0^{37}/$_{32}$ in)	9.775 m (32 ft 0^{37}/$_{32}$ in)
Landing gear wheelbase	10.913 m (35 ft 9^{41}/$_{64}$ in)	10.913 m (35 ft 9^{41}/$_{64}$ in)	10.913 m (35 ft 9^{41}/$_{64}$ in)
Wing area, m² (sq ft).	164.65 (1,772.28)	167.55 (1,803.5)	167.55 (1,803.5)
Empty weight, kg (lb)	37,729 (83,178)	38,530 (84,944)	n.a.
Take-off weight, kg (lb):			
normal	n.a.	72,000 (158,730)	72,000 (158,730)
maximum	72,000 (158,730)	75,800 (167,110)	75,800 (167,110)
Landing weight, kg (lb):			
normal	48,000 (105,820)	n.a.	n.a.
maximum	55,000 (121,250)	55,000 (121,250)	n.a.
Maximum fuel load, kg (lb)	33,000 (72,750)	33,000 (72,750)	n.a.
Maximum wing loading, kg/m² (lb/sq ft)	437.3 (89.57)	452.4 (92.66)	n.a.
Maximum thrust loading, kg/kgp (lb/lbst)	3.8	4.0	n.a.
Max rate of climb at sea level, m/sec (ft/min)	n.a.	19.0 (3,740)	n.a.
Service ceiling, m (ft)	n.a	12,000 (39,370)	13,100 (42,980)
Unstick speed, km/h (mph)	n.a	302 (188)	n.a
Maximum speed, km/h (mph)	n.a	n.a	1,015 (631)
Cruising speed, km/h (mph)	n.a	785 (488)	n.a
Landing speed, km/h (mph)	n.a.	233 (145	n.a
Stalling speed, km/h (mph)	n.a	n.a	233 (145
Range, km (miles)	n.a	4,300 (2,762)	6,000 (3,728)
Combat radius, km (miles)	n.a	1,800 (1,118)	n.a
Endurance	n.a	5 hrs 41 min	n.a
Take-off run, m (ft)	n.a	2,100 (6,890)	1,670 (5,480)
Landing run, m (ft)	n.a	1,540 (5,050)	1,655 (5,430)

Chapter 9

The Tu-16 Abroad

Unlike Soviet tactical aircraft, which were a big sales success with 'friendly nations', Soviet heavy bombers were not widely exported. The Tu-16 was no exception; only four nations outside the Soviet Union received and operated the type in the 1950s and 1960s. (We say 'obtained' instead of 'purchased' because in at least one case the Tu-16s were supplied free of charge as military aid.) On the other hand, in the first of those four nations descendants of the *Badger* serve on to this day, outlasting both the original Tu-16 and its country of origin.

China (People's Republic of China)

As mentioned in Chapter 8, China was the first Soviet ally to receive the Tu-16, taking delivery of two bombers as pattern aircraft for licence production and a CKD kit in May 1959. China was also the largest foreign operator of the type; some 120 copies of all Xian H-6 versions powered by WP-8 (licence-built RD-3M-500) turbojets were built before production was interrupted.

The H-6 saw service with both the Air Force and the Navy. Initially the **People's Liberation Army Air Force** (PLAAF, or

Blue-coded H-6As of the PLAAF's 8th Air Division taxi out at Leiyang AB for a sortie in squadron strength. The ones parked on the newer hardstand in the foreground are obviously due to follow shortly.

Left: A dozen H-6As queueing for take-off on the main taxiway of a PLAAF base.

Right: H-6As flying in close formation over the Chinese mainland en route to the target range.

Below right: The bombs dropped by an H-6 explode at the target range.

Chung-kuo Shen Min Taie-Fang-Tsun Pu-tai; now rendered as *Zhòngguó Rénmín Jièfàngjùn Kòngjùn*) operated the baseline H-6 *sans suffixe* conventional bomber whose production entirely from locally made parts was not mastered until December 1968. However, several years earlier the Xian aircraft factory began development of a nuclear-capable version similar to the Soviet Tu-16A. Designated H-6A, this aircraft first flew in 1965 and subsequently entered production, serving with the PLAAF in large numbers.

The updated H-6C (H-6 III) bomber with a second-generation navigation/attack suite entered production in 1982. It could carry conventional and nuclear bombs, naval mines and torpedoes. Most H-6s were built in this version, serving with the Air Force and the Navy alike.

The H-6E, a further updated version of the H-6A, entered service in the late 1980s. However, it had no stand-off attack capability and could not deliver precision guided munitions (PGMs).

Several missile strike versions of the H-6 were developed in due course. The PLAAF did not receive such an aircraft until its

attempts to purchase the Tu-22M3 from Russia failed and the Xian Aircraft Company (XAC) resumed H-6 production in the late 1990s to meet a requirement for a land attack cruise missile platform. Designated H-6H, this version was equipped for external carriage of two KD-63 LACMs to give the PLAAF a tactical precision strike capability. The new-build H-6H first flew in December 1998 and probably entered service in 2004-05.

The H-6M version followed suit in 2007. In similar manner to the naval H-6G, the aircraft was armed with two CJ-10K LACMs on wing pylons and could carry underwing ECM pods. Yet the H-6M was apparently a low-cost, stop-gap solution pending the service entry of the latest version – the radically redesigned H-6K featuring a new powerplant (Solov'yov D-30KP turbofans), a completely redesigned flight deck section with a 'glass cockpit' and an electro-optical system to give night capability, and the ability to carry up to six CJ-10K LACMs on wing pylons, or 'smart bombs' with either laser guidance (using onboard or off-board sensors) or navigation satellite guidance. The H-6K achieved IOC with the

Above: The standard (full-colour) version of the PLAAF insignia.

Right: The personnel of a PLAAF bomber regiment operating H-6As lines up under a slogan for a ceremonial occasion. The aircraft have low-visibility tactical codes, with 50776 Blue outline nearest and 50770 Blue outline next. GPUs based on the old Jiefang CA 10 general-purpose lorry (a Chinese copy of the ZiS-150) are parked beside each aircraft.

PLAAF in October 2009, and became fully operational in 2011; the latest known delivery, a batch of 15, was in 2013.

In the late 1980s the People's Liberation Army began a modernisation programme to transform itself from a purely defensive force to a force with both offensive and defensive capabilities. This sparked a requirement to expand the PLAAF's and PLANAF's reach to China's peripheral regions, and hence for in-flight refuelling capability. Hence the H-6 became the basis for the PLAAF's first IFR tanker, the HY-6 two-point probe-and-drogue tanker (also referred to as the H-6U or HU-6); it is intended for supporting tactical aircraft. The HY-6 was tested in the early 1990s before entering service. As mentioned earlier, the tanker is capable of working with the PLAAF's Shenyang J-8D and Chengdu J-10 fighters, but not with the Russian-supplied Su-30MKK *Flanker-G* which has a different IFR probe.

An ECM version of the H-6 was designated HD-6. At least one H-6 was converted into an ELINT version designated HZ-6. One more specialised version was adapted for launching Ba-6 high-speed, high-altitude target drone.

The PLAAF's *Badgers* have been operated by the 8th Bomber Division (comprising the 22nd Regiment at Shaodong/Shadyang-

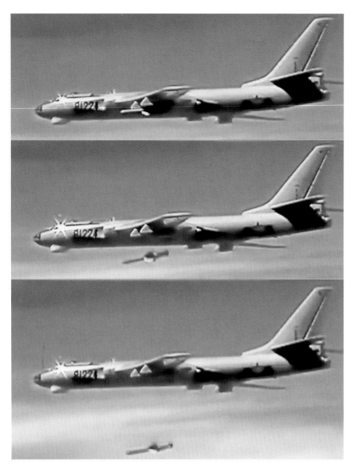

In the early 1990s some PLANAF H-6As and H-6Cs received a mid-life update to permit long-range low-level interdiction and maritime strike missions in any weather, day or night, the resulting version being designated H-6F. Yet again, being intended mainly for conventional bombing attacks against surface ships if the enemy air defences are relatively weak (which is normally not the case), the H-6F was vulnerable to enemy air defences. This led to the development of the H-6G missile strike version at the turn of the century. The new-build H-6G entered PLANAF service in 2005, replacing the H-6D. Based on the H-6H, it features two pylons under each wing, with CJ-10K missiles carried inboard and ECM pods outboard. 36 such aircraft are reportedly in service with the PLANAF.

The Navy has its own tanker version – some H-6Ds were converted into H-6DU two-point tankers. The H-6DU was fielded in 1998 the PLANAF's 9th Division at Lingshui, Hainan Province, primarily for supporting the PLANAF's J-8D fighters. Four are reportedly in service.

Apart from that, several modified H-6s have been used by the **China Flight Test Establishment** (CFTE) at Xian-Yanliang AB in various test programmes. One of them is an engine testbed similar to the Soviet Tu-16LL with the development engine mounted ventrally on the centreline.

The H-6 saw service with all three of the PLA Navy's fleets – the 1st Bomber Division of the East Sea Fleet (the 1st Air Regiment at Jiaoxian), the 2nd Bomber Division of the North Sea Fleet (the 4th Air Regiment at Tuchengzi) and the 3rd Bomber Division of the South Sea Fleet (the 8th Air Regiment at Guiping-Mengshu). Currently the PLANAF operates only the H-6G version which, after a reorganisation of the naval air arm, serves with the 6th Division/17th Regiment at Changzhou-Benniu AB (formerly 1st Air Regiment) and the 8th Division/23rd Regiment at Guiping-Mengshu AB (formerly 8th Air Regiment).

So far the H-6s have not fired in anger. Occasionally, however, the PLAAF is called on for help by the civilian authorities, and one of its unwarlike activities is ice jam busting to prevent disastrous floods. Probably the first case when the Chinese *Badgers* flew actual 'combat' sorties was the bombing of ice jams on the Yangtze, China's longest river, in March 1995.

It is the same story on the Huanghe (Yellow River), China's second-longest river. The 5,464-km (3,395-mile) Huanghe originates in Qinghai Province in the northwest and flows eastward through the Gansu, Ningxia, Inner Mongolia, Shaanxi, Shanxi, Henan and Shandong Provinces before emptying into the Bohai Sea. Different sections of the river freeze and thaw at different times; the upper reaches often thaw first, and when the ice run flows to a still-frozen section further downstream, an ice jam occurs which causes a flood peak, threatening lives and property. The situation in the Inner Mongolian section of the Huanghe is typically the worst.

In the spring of 2009 the situation in northern Inner Mongolia Autonomous Region became threatening. A spokesman for the Inner Mongolia Yellow River Ice Blockage Prevention Headquarters stated that by 1st March, the volume of floodwater conserved in the section of the river from Sanhuhe to Toudaoguai alone had reached an all-time high of 1.22 billion m³ (43,083,893,400 cu ft).

liangshihtang AB with H-6Hs, the 23rd Regiment with H-6Hs/HY-6s and the 24th Regiment with H-6Ks, both at Leiyang AB), Guangzhou Military Region; the 10th Bomber Division (including the 28th Regiment at Anqing and the 29th Regiment at Nanjing-Dajiaochang AB, both with H-6Es), Nanjing MR; and the 36th Bomber Division (comprising the 107th Regiment at Lanzhou-Lintong with H-6Hs and the 108th Regiment at Wugong with H-6Hs/H-6Ms), Lanzhou MR. Currently the type is in service with the 8th Air Division (comprising the same three regiments, except that the 23rd Regiment now reportedly has HU-6 tankers only), the 10th Air Division (the 28th Regiment has re-equipped with H-6Ks, while the 29th Regiment now operates H-6Hs) and the 36th Air Division whose 107th Regiment and 108th Regiment both reportedly operate a mix of H-6Cs/H-6Es/H-6Hs (oddly, no mention is made of the H-6Ms).

The **People's Liberation Army Naval Air Force** (PLANAF, or *Zhōngguó Rénmín Jiěfàngjùn Hǎijùn Hángkōngbīng*) started off with the H-6C bomber and received its first missile strike variant – the H-6D (H-6 IV) – much earlier than the Air Force. First flown in August 1981, the H-6D was the first PLANAF aircraft to have stand-off missile capability, being armed with two YJ-6L anti-shipping cruise missiles on underwing pylons, but reportedly also retained a conventional bombing capability. The H-6D entered service in December 1985, remaining on the inventory all the way until 2006; in the course of service the YJ-6L missiles were replaced by the more modern YJ-61 (C-611) missiles having longer range.

The overall volume of floodwater in the region had reached 1.7 billion m³ (60,034,933,420 cu ft), surpassing that of 2008 and posing a severe challenge to flood prevention.

The administration of the Inner Mongolia Autonomous Region sought assistance from the armed forces. On 8th March 2009 three PLAAF H-6H bombers, including '40671 Red', carried out a trial ice blasting operation, attacking the ice jam with free-fall HE bombs.

On 1st October 2009, the National Day Parade took place in Beijing's Tiananmen Square. This time the military and civil parade was held on an especially grand scale, since the People's Republic of China was celebrating its 60th anniversary in 2009. It deserves mention that the parade

Left: A PLANAF H-6G ('81224 Red') launches an anti-shipping missile.

Above right: A dramatic shot of an H-6A being readied for a night sortie on a moonlit hardstand, with a Yuejin NJ 131 GPU supplying electric power.

Right: Another H-6A being worked upon amid a thicket of work platforms – some of them being there for sheer effect.

Below: An HY-6 tanker in a simulated refuelling formation with two J-8D fighters.

An HY-6 tanker is prepared for a night sortie; the serial has been deleted by the military censor. A pair of fuel bowsers on a Sino Steyr ZZ1166 general-purpose lorry chassis stand by to refill the *Badger's* tanks.

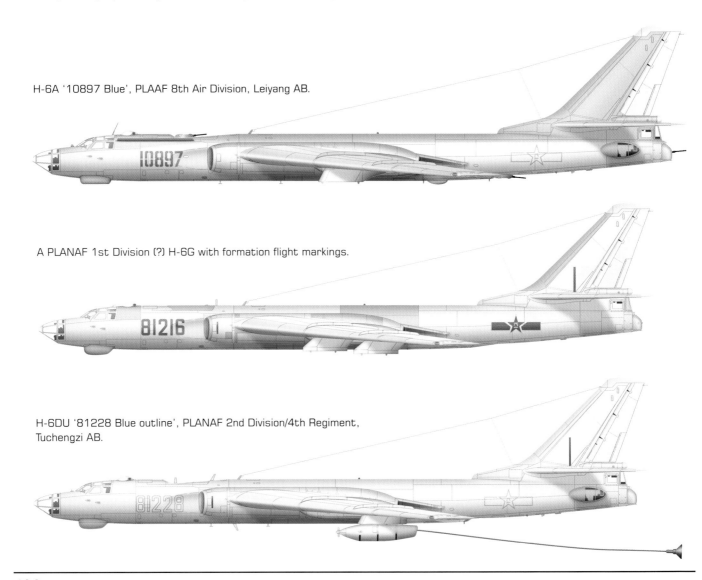

H-6A '10897 Blue', PLAAF 8th Air Division, Leiyang AB.

A PLANAF 1st Division (?) H-6G with formation flight markings.

H-6DU '81228 Blue outline', PLANAF 2nd Division/4th Regiment, Tuchengzi AB.

A row of similarly 'anonymised' HY-6s, with more capacious Sino Steyr ZZ1251 6x4 fuel bowsers waiting to refuel them.

was orchestrated by the internationally acclaimed Chinese film-maker Zhang Yimou (one of the best-known of the Fifth Generation of Chinese film directors, who began making films after the Cultural Revolution).

As usual, the National Day Parade included a large aviation component. Prior to the parade the PLAAF had undertaken a special operation to disperse rain clouds approaching Beijing involving 18 aircraft (the largest-ever operation of the kind), causing heavy showers in Beijing the night before the parade but brilliant sunshine on the day of the event. The latter included a flypast by no fewer than 151 assorted aircraft and helicopters coming in twelve waves. Among other things, Wave 3 consisted of 15 H-6H bombers from the PLAAF's 36th Bomber Division carrying two KD-63 cruise missiles each. Wave 4 was two HY-6 tankers from

the PLAAF's 8th Air Division – one ('18796 Red') accompanied by two PLAAF/9th Air Division Shenyang J-8D fighters and another accompanied by two 44th Air Division Chengdu J-10A fighters in a simulated refuelling formation.

On 27th November 2015, the PLAAF put on a show of force when eight H-6Ks supported by three electronic warfare aircraft participated in an exercise over the East China Sea. Chinese state media quoted a PLAAF spokesman as saying the exercise affirmed China's East China Sea Air Defence Identification Zone (ADIZ), which was declared in December 2013. At first the eight *Badgers* stayed together, with a Shaanxi KJ-200 airborne early warning and control (AEW&C) aircraft based on the Y8F-400 transport providing support for the group. Then, west of Okinawa, the formation split; four of the bombers remained within the East China

An H-6K returns from a practice sortie in the evening light.

Sea ADIZ, while the other four flew on through the Ryukyu Island Chain and over the Miyako Strait near Miyakojima Island. The same PLAAF spokesman was quoted as saying they flew 1,000 km (621 miles) into what is known in current Chinese naval strategy as the Second Island Chain (that is, the Ogasawara Islands and Volcano Islands of Japan, plus the Mariana Islands). These four aircraft were supported by a PLAAF Tu-154M/D (a Chinese-developed ELINT version of the Tu-154M airliner) and a Shaanxi

Y8CB ECM aircraft (a derivative of the Antonov An-12BP *Cub* four-turboprop transport; NATO reporting name *Gaoxin 1*, 'High New 1'). Japan Air Self-Defense Force (JASDF) fighters scrambled from Okinawa to keep an eye on the uninvited guests.

A note must be made on the Chinese military aircraft serials. Actually it is more appropriate to call them tactical codes, since they reflect the unit operating the specific aircraft and its place within the unit, changing if the aircraft is transferred to a different

Known Chinese Tu-16s (H-6s)

Type	Tactical code	C/n	Notes
1. PLAAF			
H-6	86 Blue	**24**	CFTE, engine testbed; serial later changed to 086 Blue
H-6	4251 Blue	222000159	Harbin-built? Preserved PLAAF Museum, later as 4251 Black outline
H-6A	10791 Blue	**24**	8th Div.
H-6A	10792 Blue	**24**	8th Div.
H-6A	10793	**24**	8th Div.
H-6A	10794 Blue	052408	8th Div. Preserved PLAAF Museum
H-6A	10795 Blue	**24**	8th Div.
H-6A	10796 Blue	**24**	8th Div.
H-6A	10797 Blue	**24**	8th Div.
H-6A	10799 Blue	**24**	8th Div.
H-6A	10890 Blue	**24**	8th Div.
H-6A	10891 Blue	**24**	8th Div.
H-6A	10892 Blue	**24**	8th Div.
H-6A	10893	**24**	8th Div.
H-6A	10894 Blue	**24**	8th Div.
H-6A	10895 Blue	**24**	8th Div.
H-6A	10896 Blue	**24**	8th Div.
H-6A	10897 Blue	**24**	8th Div.
H-6A	10898 Blue	**24**	8th Div.
H-6A	10899	**24**	8th Div.
H-6A	10990 Blue	**24**	8th Div.
H-6A	10991	**24**	8th Div.
H-6A	20011 Red	**24**	10th Div./28th Regt.; also reported as H-6H
H-6A	20012 Red	**24**	10th Div./28th Regt.; also reported as H-6H
H-6A	20013 Red (No.1)	**24**	10th Div./28th Regt.
H-6A	20014 Red	**24**	10th Div./28th Regt.; also reported as H-6H
H-6A	20015	**24**	10th Div./28th Regt.
H-6A	20016 (No.1)	**24**	10th Div./28th Regt.; see H-6K below
H-6A	20018 Red	**24**	10th Div./28th Regt.
H-6A	20019 Red	**24**	10th Div./28th Regt.
H-6A	20110 Red	**24**	10th Div./28th Regt.
H-6A	20114	**24**	10th Div./28th Regt.
H-6A	20115	**24**	10th Div./28th Regt.
H-6A	20119 Red	**24**	10th Div./28th Regt.
H-6A	20210 Red	**24**	10th Div./28th Regt.
H-6A	20211	**24**	10th Div./28th Regt.
H-6A	20215 Red	**24**	CFTE, 10th Div./28th Regt.
H-6A	20216	**24**	10th Div./28th Regt.
H-6A	20610	**24**	10th Div./28th Regt.
H-6A	20611	**24**	10th Div./28th Regt.
H-6A	20612 Red	**24**	10th Div./28th Regt.
H-6A	20614	**24**	10th Div./28th Regt.
H-6A	20615 Red	**24**	10th Div./28th Regt.
H-6A	20617 Red	**24**	10th Div./28th Regt.
H-6A	20618 Red	**24**	10th Div./28th Regt.
H-6A	20619	**24**	10th Div./28th Regt.
H-6A	20712 Red	**24**	10th Div./28th Regt.
H-6A	20714 Red	**24**	10th Div./28th Regt.
H-6A	20715 Red	**24**	10th Div./28th Regt.
H-6A	30116	**24**	10th Div./28th Regt.
H-6A	30211 Blue	**24**	10th Div./28th Regt.
H-6A	30218 Blue	**24**	10th Div./28th Regt.
H-6A	30310 Blue	**24**	10th Div./28th Regt.
H-6A	30312 (No.1)	042408	10th Div./28th Regt. Preserved Shanghai City
H-6A	30312 (No.2)	102410	10th Div./28th Regt. Preserved Nanchang
H-6A	30313 Blue	**24**	Preserved Xian Northwest University
H-6A	40672 Red	**24**	36th Div./107th or 108th Regt. Converted to suborbital launch vehicle carrier
H-6A	40895	**24**	
H-6A	50271	**24**	36th Div. (pre-2005 serial)
H-6A	50275	**24**	36th Div.
H-6A	50371	**24**	36th Div.
H-6A	50373	**24**	36th Div.
H-6A	50378	**24**	36th Div.
H-6A	50379	**24**	36th Div.
H-6A	50471	**24**	36th Div.
H-6A	50473	**24**	36th Div.
H-6A	50474	**24**	36th Div.
H-6A	50475	**24**	36th Div.
H-6A	50476	**24**	36th Div.
H-6A	50477	**24**	36th Div.
H-6A	50478	**24**	36th Div.
H-6A	50479	**24**	36th Div.
H-6A	50570	**24**	36th Div.
H-6A	50671	**24**	36th Div.
H-6A	50672	**24**	36th Div.
H-6A	50673	**24**	36th Div.
H-6A	50674 Blue outline	**24**	36th Div.
H-6A	50675 Blue outline	**24**	36th Div.
H-6A	50676 Blue outline	**24**	36th Div.
H-6A	62649	**24**	
H-6A	63019	**24**	
H-6E	50678 Blue	**24**	36th Div. (pre-2005 serial); grey c/s
H-6E	50679 Blue	**24**	36th Div.
H-6E	50770 Blue outline	**24**	36th Div.
H-6E	50772 Blue	**24**	36th Div.
H-6E	50773 Blue	**24**	36th Div.
H-6E	50775 Blue	**24**	36th Div.; grey c/s
H-6E	50776 Blue	**24**	36th Div.; grey c/s
H-6E	50777 Blue outline	**24**	Ex-50777 Blue, 36th Div.; grey c/s

H-6E	50778 Blue	**24**	
H-6G	089 Black	**24**	CFTE, prototype, primer finish
H-6G	872 Black	**24**	CFTE, grey overall, missile testbed
H-6H	02 Black	**24**	Prototype, primer finish
H-6H	18593	**24**	8th Div./23rd Regt.
H-6H	18595	**24**	8th Div./23rd Regt.
H-6H	18598 Red	**24**	8th Div./23rd Regt.
H-6H	18692 Red	222403	8th Div./23rd Regt.
H-6H	20013 Red (No.2)	**24**	10th Div./28th Regt.
H-6H	40071 Red	232405	36th Div./107th Regt
H-6H	40072 Red	**24**	36th Div./107th Regt
H-6H	40073 Red	**24**	36th Div./107th Regt
H-6H	40074	**24**	36th Div./107th Regt
H-6H	40076 Red	**24**	36th Div./107th Regt
H-6H	40077 Red	**24**	36th Div./107th Regt, stealth technology testbed
H-6H	40078	**24**	36th Div./107th Regt
H-6H	40079 Red	**24**	36th Div./107th Regt
H-6H	40171 Red	232401	36th Div./107th Regt
H-6H	40173 Red	**24**	36th Div./107th Regt
H-6H	40174 Red	**24**	36th Div./107th Regt
H-6H	40175 Red	**24**	36th Div./107th Regt
H-6H	40176 Red	**24**	36th Div./107th Regt
H-6H	40177	**24**	36th Div./107th Regt
H-6H	40178	**24**	36th Div./107th Regt
H-6H	40179	**24**	36th Div./107th Regt
H-6H	50171 Blue	**24**	36th Div. (pre-2005 serial)
H-6H	50179 Blue	**24**	36th Div.
H-6H	50274 Blue	**24**	36th Div.
H-6H	50370 Blue	**24**	36th Div.
H-6M	40573	**24**	36th Div./108th Regt
H-6M	40574 Red	**24**	36th Div./108th Regt
H-6M	40575	**24**	36th Div./108th Regt
H-6M	40576 Red	252401	36th Div./108th Regt
H-6M	40577	**24**	36th Div./108th Regt
H-6M	40578	**24**	36th Div./108th Regt
H-6M	40670	**24**	36th Div./108th Regt
H-6M	40671 Red	**24**	36th Div./108th Regt
H-6M	40672	**24**	36th Div./108th Regt
H-6M	40677 Red	**24**	36th Div./108th Regt
H-6M	40679	**24**	36th Div./108th Regt
H-6M	40770 Red	**24**	36th Div./108th Regt
H-6M	40776	**24**	36th Div./108th Regt
HU-6	18790	**24**	8th Div./23rd Regt.
HU-6	18791	**24**	8th Div./23rd Regt.
HU-6	18792 Red	202410	8th Div./23rd Regt.
HU-6	18793	**24**	8th Div./23rd Regt.
HU-6	18796 Red	202405	8th Div./23rd Regt.
HU-6	18890	**24**	8th Div./23rd Regt.
HU-6	18892 Red	212401	8th Div./23rd Regt.
HU-6	18893 Red	**24**	8th Div./23rd Regt.
HU-6	18895	**24**	8th Div./23rd Regt.
HU-6	18897 Red	**24**	8th Div./23rd Regt.
HU-6	43499 Blue	**24**	
HU-6	43592 Blue	**24**	
HU-6	43595 Blue	**24**	
HU-6	43696 Blue	**24**	
HU-6	43697 Blue	**24**	
HU-6	43698 Blue	**24**	
H-6K	001 Blue	?	Prototype, grey overall, BC-1 titles
H-6K	200 Red?	?	Serial may be fake
H-6K	861 Black	?	CFTE, grey overall; ex-001 Blue?
H-6K	862 Black	?	CFTE, grey overall
H-6K	11092 Red	?	8th Div./24th Regt.
H-6K	11094 Red	?	8th Div./24th Regt.
H-6K	11095 Red	?	8th Div./24th Regt.
H-6K	11097 Red	?	8th Div./24th Regt.
H-6K	11190 Red	?	8th Div./24th Regt.
H-6K	11192 Red	?	8th Div./24th Regt.
H-6K	11194 Red	?	8th Div./24th Regt.
H-6K	11195 Red	?	8th Div./24th Regt.
H-6K	11196 Red	?	8th Div./24th Regt.
H-6K	11198 Red	?	8th Div./24th Regt.
H-6K	11199 Red	?	8th Div./24th Regt.
H-6K	20012 Red	?	10th Div./28th Regt.
H-6K	20013 Red (No.3)	?	10th Div./28th Regt.
H-6K	20016 Red	?	10th Div./28th Regt.
H-6K	20113 Red	?	10th Div./28th Regt.
H-6K	20114 Red	?	10th Div./28th Regt.
H-6…	090 Red	**24**	Development aircraft with 6 pylons and IFR probe

2. PLANAF

H-6D	81022 Red	**24**	2nd Bomber Div.
H-6D	81026	**24**	2nd Bomber Div.
H-6D	81123	**24**	2nd Bomber Div.
H-6D	81124	**24**	2nd Bomber Div.
H-6D	81125 Blue outline	**24**	2nd Bomber Div.
H-6D	81223 Blue outline	**24**	2nd Bomber Div.
H-6D	81225 Blue outline	**24**	2nd Bomber Div.
H-6D	81226 Blue outline	**24**	2nd Bomber Div.
H-6D	82031 Blue outline	**24**	3rd Bomber Div.
H-6D	82033	**24**	3rd Bomber Div.
H-6D	82034	**24**	3rd Bomber Div.
H-6D	82035	**24**	3rd Bomber Div.
H-6D	82036	**24**	3rd Bomber Div.
H-6D	82037	**24**	3rd Bomber Div.
H-6D	82038	**24**	3rd Bomber Div.
H-6D	82039	**24**	3rd Bomber Div.
H-6D	82130	**24**	3rd Bomber Div.
H-6D	82131	**24**	3rd Bomber Div.
H-6D	82132	**24**	3rd Bomber Div.
H-6D	82134 Blue outline	**24**	3rd Bomber Div.
H-6G	81211 Red	**24**	1st Bomber Div.
H-6G	81214 Red	**24**	1st Bomber Div.
H-6G	81215 Red	**24**	1st Bomber Div.
H-6G	81216 Red	**24**	1st Bomber Div.
H-6G	81217 Red	**24**	1st Bomber Div.
H-6G	81224 Red	**24**	Reported in error as H-6DU
H-6DU	81220 Blue outline	**24**	2nd Bomber Div.
H-6DU	81222	**24**	2nd Bomber Div.
H-6DU	81228 Blue outline	**24**	2nd Bomber Div.; to 81228 Red
H-6DU	81229	**24**	2nd Bomber Div.
H-6DU	82032	**24**	3rd Bomber Div.
H-6DU	82133	**24**	3rd Bomber Div.
H-6DU	82332 Blue outline	**24**	3rd Bomber Div.

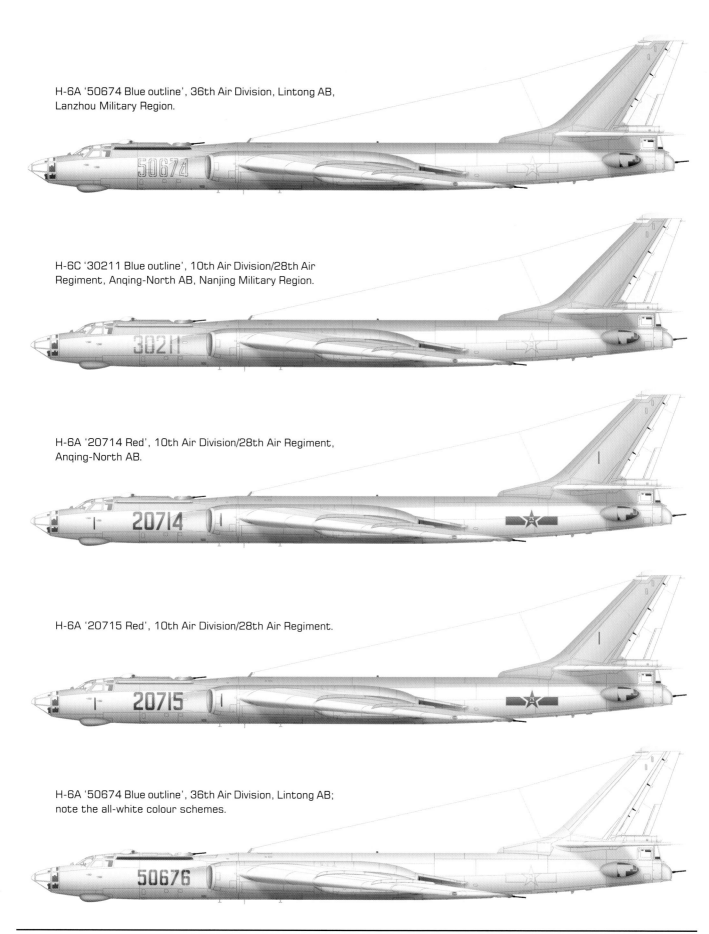

H-6A '50674 Blue outline', 36th Air Division, Lintong AB, Lanzhou Military Region.

H-6C '30211 Blue outline', 10th Air Division/28th Air Regiment, Anqing-North AB, Nanjing Military Region.

H-6A '20714 Red', 10th Air Division/28th Air Regiment, Anqing-North AB.

H-6A '20715 Red', 10th Air Division/28th Air Regiment.

H-6A '50674 Blue outline', 36th Air Division, Lintong AB; note the all-white colour schemes.

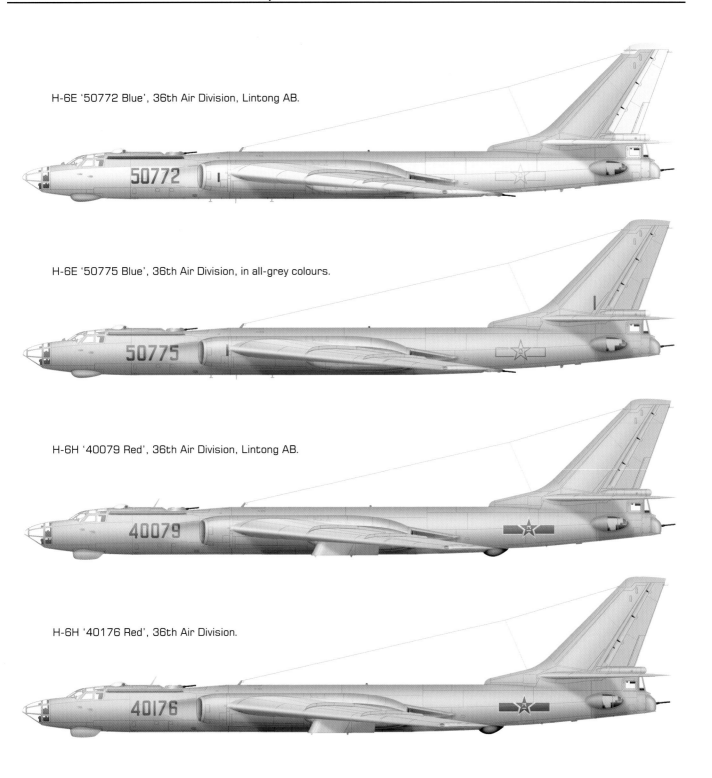

H-6E '50772 Blue', 36th Air Division, Lintong AB.

H-6E '50775 Blue', 36th Air Division, in all-grey colours.

H-6H '40079 Red', 36th Air Division, Lintong AB.

H-6H '40176 Red', 36th Air Division.

unit. In ordinary units (Air Regiments forming part of an Air Division) the tactical codes consist of five digits, following the AB#C# pattern; A and C indicate the division number determined by means of a special coding table with ten columns across and seven rows down. Each division consists of two or three regiments, and B denotes the number of the regiment within the division; this is not the actual number of the regiment. The regiments are numbered consecutively – thus, the 1st Air Division comprises the 1st, 2nd and 3rd Regiments, the 2nd Air Division has the 4th, 5th and

6th Regiments and so on until the 50th Air Division, which has the 148th, 149th and 150th Regiments. ## indicates the number of the aircraft within the regiment, and these digits are often carried in addition to the full code for quick identification; for example, the code 30312 denoted the 10th Air Division (3xx1x), 28th Air Regiment (0), the 32nd aircraft in the regiment.

In June 2005, the system was changed for security reasons by switching the numbering in the 'across' row of the coding table from 1-0 to 0-9. Thus, the aircraft of the same 10th Air Division now carry codes in the 2xx1x block. The codes are usually red or blue, but some H-6s carried a low-visibility outline version of the code (and sometimes a low-visibility version of the PLAAF 'stars and bars' insignia).

PLANAF tactical codes in 'ordinary' units (those forming part of an air division) follow the same pattern, except that the first digit is always an 8. Thus, the pattern is 8A#B#, the B denoting the number of the division and the A denoting the number of the regiment within the division (but not its actual number), while ## again is the aircraft's sequential number in the unit.

Aircraft operated by the CFTE are an exception to the rule. They wear three-digit serials which have no specific meaning; aircraft tested under the same programme receive consecutive codes.

Egypt

Egypt, which had been under British control since 1882 and a British protectorate since 1914, was formally declared an independent kingdom in 1922; the Suez Canal Zone, however, remained under British control. On 2nd November 1930 King Fuad I decreed the formation of an Egyptian Army Air Force which, in 1937, became the autonomous Royal Egyptian Air Force. On 23rd July 1952, King Farouk I was overthrown in a military coup led by Gamal Abdel Nasser. After the declaration of the Arab Republic of Egypt on 18th June 1953, with Nasser as President, the **Egyptian Air Force** (EAF, or *al Quwwat al-Jawwiya al-Jomhouriya il-Misriya*) was created.

The new government's independent political course angered Great Britain, which was the primary arms supplier to Egypt, and

new aircraft deliveries to the EAF dried up. Financial constraints forced Egypt to buy outdated aircraft, such as Gloster Meteors and de Havilland Vampires, and even this was not easy. Hence President Nasser had to seek new arms suppliers, and he quickly found allies in the Eastern Bloc, including the Soviet Union.

On 1st February 1958, Syria and Egypt formed a union called the United Arab Republic (UAR); a month later this was joined by the Kingdom of Yemen (North Yemen) to create the Union of Arab States. Hence the joint Egyptian/Syrian air arm was known as the **United Arab Republic Air Force** (UARAF). The union proved to be short-lived – Syria seceded on 28th September 1961; nevertheless, Egypt persisted with the UAR name until 1971. Accordingly the EAF name was restored in 1971.

In 1963 about 20 Tu-16KS *Badger-B* missile carriers were supplied to the Egyptian Air Force where they formed two squadrons based at Cairo-West AB and Beni Sueif AB. The aircrews were trained in the USSR and Soviet specialists took part in their service induction in Egypt. A while later, on 26th January 1966, the Soviet government approved the delivery of six Tu-16T *Badger-A* torpedo-bombers to Egypt.

This first batch of Tu-16s did not last long. In 1967 the relations between Israel and its Arab neighbours worsened after Egypt compelled the United Nations Emergency Force to leave the Sinai Peninsula, closed the Straits of Tiran to Israeli ships, rendering the port of Eilat unusable, and proposed united Arab action against Israel. The Israeli response was a pre-emptive attack against Egypt, Syria and Iraq (in that order) triggering the third Arab-Israeli war, commonly referred to as the Six-Day War (5th-10th June 1967).

Appearances are deceptive! This Tu-16R Badger-F *wearing Egyptian insignia and the serial 4380 in Arabic characters is actually a Soviet Navy aircraft operated by the 90th ODRAE ON reconnaissance squadron on temporary deployment in Egypt.*

Israel had been planning this war long and carefully – right down to building five mock Egyptian airbases in the Negev Desert where they constantly practiced raids against the real thing. Within a year all Israeli Defence Force/Air Force (IDF/AF) combat squadrons had passed a training course at these facilities. Building on the results of this training, the Israeli high command developed a 'first strike' plan known as Operation *Moked* ('focus' in Hebrew). The combined air forces of the Arab nations outnumbered the IDF/AF almost three times (Egypt, Syria, Jordan, Lebanon and Iraq had some 800 combat aircraft at the start of the war), so it was decided to destroy them on the ground rather than tangle with them in the air; this would ensure air superiority and demoralise the enemy. The 30 Egyptian Tu-16 bombers (plus six in Iraq) were among the priority targets during the planned air strikes.

The first attack was targeted at 19 airfields deep inside Egypt, but it was decided to spare the runways at the four bases on the Sinai Peninsula so that Israeli aircraft could use them, once the peninsula had been occupied. Four waves of strike aircraft were to destroy the greater part of the EAF on the ground by 1400 hrs; after that, the attacks would be redirected at airbases in Syria, Jordan and Iraq.

On the morning of 5th June the IDF/AF launched a massive assault against Arab airbases. The first wave of 170 strike aircraft launched at 0714-0828 hrs Israeli time (0814-0928 hrs Egyptian time) and crossed the Egyptian coastline at low altitude at 0845 hrs ET to attack ten airbases. The timing was chosen because the Egyptian fighters were not expected to be out on combat air patrol and the base commanders were usually not on site that early, which would prevent the Egyptians form organising an effective defence. The Egyptians were taken completely by surprise; no one could even suppose that the Israelis would have the nerve to attack in broad daylight.

The Israelis claimed 196 Egyptian jets destroyed on the ground in this first wave alone. In particular, eight Tu-16s were destroyed at Cairo-West and another 12 at Beni Sueif. In one of the first retaliatory action on the part of the Arabs, a lone Egyptian Tu-16 bombed the Israeli coastal town of Netanya and was shot down by the air defences.

After the war, in the autumn of 1971, the USSR supplied Egypt with about 20 Tu-16KSR-2A and Tu-16KSR-2-11 *Badger-G* mis-

Top: A real EAF Tu-16KS escorted by two MiG-21F-13 fighters during a parade. The last digits of the serial (4108) are repeated in European numerals on the nose.

Above: Tu-16RM-2 '4378' of the 90th ODRAE ON is escorted by F-4B-24-MC BuNo153012/'AB-103' of VF-14 'Top Hatters' in 1973.

Below left: EAF 34 or 35 Sqn crews pose with Tu-16KSR-2 '4405'.

Below: A 90th ODRAE ON Tu-16R with its Soviet crew.

Left: Egyptian Tu-16K-11-16 '4407' (again with the last two digits repeated in European characters on the nose) sits on ready alert with two missiles attached. The aircraft wears a late-style three-tone camouflage. Oddly, the front cabin entry hatch is open for rapid boarding, but not that of the rear cabin.

Below left and bottom left: '4406', another EAF Tu-16K-11-16, parked in the open with no missiles. The Arabic serial is bolder, the last digits are repeated in the nose in a different typeface than on '4407', and the camouflage pattern is rather different.

Above right: Close-up of the forward fuselage of '4406', showing the aerial array of the Ritsa radar detection system. Sister ship '4408' with the engine cowlings opened for maintenance is visible in the background.

Right: Close-up of the KSR-2 missile on the port pylon of '4407'.

Right: This shot of Tu-16KSR-2 '4404' dates back to an earlier period. The aircraft wears a two-tone camouflage introduced after the Six-Day War and the serial is in Arabic only, and worn on the nose instead of the rear fuselage.

Above: As distinct from true Egyptian *Badgers* in the post Six-Day War period, the aircraft operated by the 90th ODRAE ON (exemplified here by Tu-16R *Badger-E* '4378 Black') retained their natural metal finish. Repainting them in EAF camouflage colours for the brief secondment was not considered worthwhile – in peacetime at least.

Below: Quasi-Egyptian Tu-16R *Badger-E* '4376 Black' is shadowed by a US Navy F-4B from the aircraft carrier USS *John F. Kennedy* over the Mediterranean.

Above: '4387 Black', a 90th ODRAE ON Tu-16P Buket ECM aircraft. This one wears an 'anti-flash' colour scheme.

Below: Tu-16RM-2 '4392 Black' seen from a shadowing US Navy F-4. Note the variance in the rendering of the serials – probably caused by the fact that they were applied in different units before the departure to Egypt.

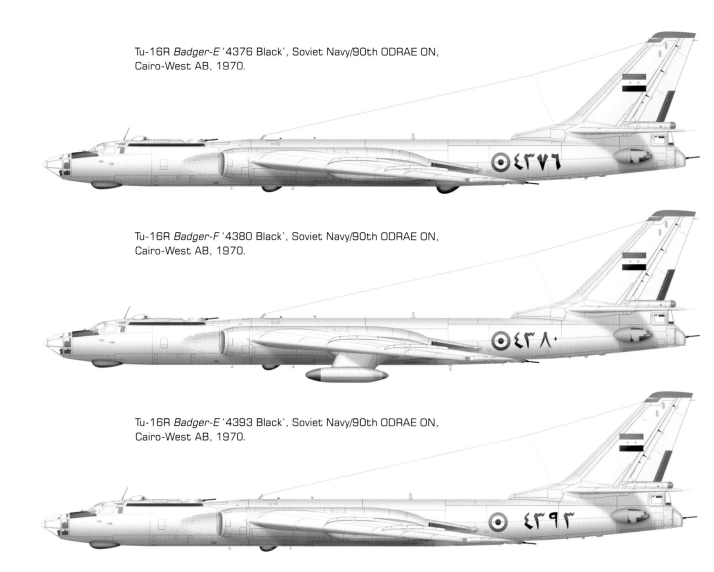

Tu-16R *Badger-E* '4376 Black', Soviet Navy/90th ODRAE ON,
Cairo-West AB, 1970.

Tu-16R *Badger-F* '4380 Black', Soviet Navy/90th ODRAE ON,
Cairo-West AB, 1970.

Tu-16R *Badger-E* '4393 Black', Soviet Navy/90th ODRAE ON,
Cairo-West AB, 1970.

sile carriers, as well as a stock of KSR-2 air-to-surface missiles. The aircraft were ferried in pairs via Hungary and Yugoslavia to Cairo-West AB, entering service with two squadrons, including the newly formed No.36 Sqn. Soviet Naval Aviation/Black Sea Fleet crews made the ferry flights, and the Egyptian personnel were trained in situ by Soviet instructors.

In addition, several Soviet Navy Tu-16R *Badger-E/-F* reconnaissance aircraft with SRS-1 and SRS-3 SIGINT sets, Tu-16RM-2 reconnaissance aircraft and Tu-16P *Badger-J* ECM aircraft were

on detachment in Egypt in keeping with an agreement signed in March 1968, gathering intelligence for both nations. The North Fleet Tu-16Rs arrived in 1968, being superseded by Black Sea Fleet aircraft in 1970, and the Baltic Fleet Tu-16Ps (at least four) followed in 1971. As mentioned in Chapter 7, despite wearing EAF markings like the rest, they were Soviet-operated, serving with the 90th Independent Special Mission Long-Range Reconnaissance Squadron (90th ODRAE ON). Originally they were based at Cairo-West AB; later some of the aircraft moved to Mersa Matruh AB.

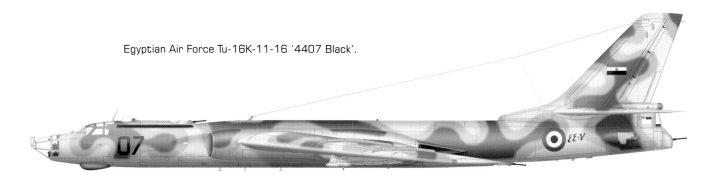

Egyptian Air Force Tu-16K-11-16 '4407 Black'.

Right: This one's Egyptian all right. Camouflaged Tu-16 '4301 Black' sits unserviceable in a revetment at Cairo-West AB partly filled with sand.

Camouflaged Egyptian Air Force Tu-16K-11-16s taxi out for a training sortie. Note the wrecked Tu-16 in natural metal finish on the left; it was probably lying there since the Six-Day War.

The *Badgers* were heavily involved in operations when Egypt unleashed the 'October War of Liberation' (6th-22nd October 1973), better known as the Holy Day War or Yom Kippur War, hoping to regain the territory annexed by Israel in 1967. During this round of hostilities the Egyptian Tu-16s launched some 25 missiles against Israeli targets on the Sinai Peninsula, destroying two radar sites and a field supply depot.

Mindful of the experience gained from the Six-Day War, the Egyptians now kept their Tu-16s at airfields south of Sinai, beyond the reach of the IDF/AF. Also, unlike the first lot of Tu-16s, which had retained their natural metal finish and were easy to detect, the *Badgers* from the second lot received two- or three-tone camouflage. According to the Egyptians, the Tu-16s suffered no losses, although the Israelis claimed one bomber destroyed.

As time passed, however, the Egyptian leaders grew at odds with the Soviet Union. In July 1972, the new Egyptian President

Above left: A different perspective of a 90th ODRAE ON Tu-16RM-2, showing the equal-sized dielectric blisters.

Left: With inevitable fighter 'escort', a quasi-Egyptian Tu-16R flies over the USS *Franklin D Roosevelt* as she cruises in the Mediterranean.

Known Egyptian Air Force/United Arab Republic Air Force Tu-16s			
Serial	**Version**	**C/n**	**Notes**
4005 Black/05	Tu-16	?	No.34 Sqn. Destroyed 5-6-1967
4009 Black	Tu-16	?	No.34 Sqn. Destroyed 5-6-1967
4012 Black	Tu-16	?	Preserved Cairo-Almaza
4027 Black	Tu-16	?	No.34 Sqn. Destroyed 5-6-1967
4030 Black	Tu-16	?	No.34 Sqn. Destroyed 5-6-1967
4035 Black/35	Tu-16	?	
4047 Black/47	Tu-16	***0402	No.34 Sqn. Destroyed 5-6-1967
4055 Black/55	Tu-16	?	No.34 Sqn. Destroyed 5-6-1967
4065 Black	Tu-16	?	No.34 Sqn. Destroyed 5-6-1967
4074 Black	Tu-16	?	No.34 Sqn. Destroyed 5-6-1967
4087 Black	Tu-16	?	No.34 Sqn. Destroyed 5-6-1967
4092 Black	Tu-16	?	No.34 Sqn. Destroyed 5-6-1967
4106 Black	Tu-16KS	?	No.35 Sqn. Destroyed 5-6-1967
4108 Black/08	Tu-16KS	?	Natural metal finish. No.35 Sqn. Destroyed 5-6-1967
4114 Black	Tu-16KS	?	No.35 Sqn. Destroyed 5-6-1967

Serial	Version	C/n	Notes
4117 Black	Tu-16KS	6203220	Natural metal finish. No.35 Sqn. Destroyed 5-6-1967
4301 Black/01	Tu-16	?	Tan/green/grey camouflage
4376 Black	Tu-16R	?	*Badger-E*, 90th ODRAE ON
4378 Black	Tu-16R	?	*Badger-E*, 90th ODRAE ON
4380 Black	Tu-16R	?	*Badger-F*, 90th ODRAE ON
4381 Black	Tu-16R	?	*Badger-E*, 90th ODRAE ON
4383 Black	Tu-16	?	
4384 Black	Tu-16R	?	*Badger-F*, 90th ODRAE ON
4386 Black	Tu-16	?	Sold to the USA for evaluation
4387 Black	Tu-16P	?	90th ODRAE ON
4392 Black	Tu-16R	?	*Badger-E*, 90th ODRAE ON
4393 Black	Tu-16R	?	*Badger-E*, 90th ODRAE ON
4402 Black	Tu-16	?	
4403 Black	Tu-16	?	
4404 Black	Tu-16KSR-2A	?	Tan/green/grey camouflage
4406 Black/06	Tu-16KSR-2-11	?	Tan/green/grey camouflage
4407 Black/07	Tu-16KSR-2-11	?	Tan/green/grey camouflage
4408 Black	Tu-16KS	?	
4409 Black	Tu-16	?	
4416 Black	Tu-16	?	

Above: Another Tu-16RM-2 from the same squadron. The camera port of the vertical camera aft of the nosewheel well appears to be open.

Above right: The nose of Tu-16R *Badger-E* '4381 Black' from the 90th ODRAE ON seen on a mission over the Med.

Right: The tail of the same aircraft, with an escorting F-4B of VF-14 in the background.

Below: An overall view of Tu-16R '4381 Black'.

Anwar Sadat banished all Soviet military staff from the country. After this, the Soviets cut off spares supplies for the military equipment they had provided. Striving to maintain their machines in operational condition, the Egyptians turned to China, which was building the Tu-16 under licence. In April 1976, an agreement was signed whereby China furnished Egypt with Xian H-6A bombers and spares for the existing *Badgers*.

Egypt used the H-6As operationally during a four-day skirmish with Libya in 1977. In early 1990 the EAF still operated sixteen Tu-16s and H-6As which equipped a bomber brigade based in the south of Egypt. They were finally retired in 2000.

Indonesia

After Indonesia had been a Dutch colony for nearly 350 years, an uprising against colonial rule began in August 1945, after the Dutch East Indies had been liberated from the Japanese, sparking a four-year liberation war; the Netherlands began what it called a 'police action' to quell the mutiny but, under international pressure, eventually recognised the country's independence on 27th December 1949. The Soviet Union established diplomatic relations with Indonesia in 1950 and, of course, the Soviet government perceived this as an opportunity to gain a foothold in the region.

The **Indonesian Air Force** (originally AURI – *Angkatan Udara Republik Indonesia*; now called TNI-AU, *Tentara Nasional Indonesia – Angkatan Udara*) was born on 17th August 1945, while the new Republic was fighting the Dutch. By the end of the liberation war most of the AURI aircraft had been destroyed. (This was when the original red/white Indonesian Air Force roundels were replaced by the current pentagonal insignia and fin flash.) Diplomatic relations with the Soviet Union were established in 1950. While Dr. Ahmed Sukarno was President in the late 1950s and early/mid-1960s, Indonesia was on fairly good terms with the Soviet Union and enjoyed Soviet military aid, including deliveries of aircraft.

In 1962 the Soviet government took the decision to dispatch a squadron of Tu-16KS missile carriers from the Long-Range Aviation's 56th *Breslavl'skaya* TBAD to Indonesia, along with a group of escort fighters, to assist in repelling a possible Dutch military intervention. The group of bombers was commanded by Col. N. I. Korobchak and senior navigator Yu. L. Deryabichev; it was composed of highly experienced crews that were hand-picked on the criteria of professionalism, good moral character and (last but not least) ideological trustworthiness. The crews were captained by Lt.-Col. A. A. Sharlapov, Lt.-Col. B. I. Sharonov,

M-1618, one of the Tu-16KS missile strike aircraft supplied to the Indonesian Air Force, with two KS-1 missiles attached. The *Badgers* were Soviet-crewed initially until the Indonesian airmen had been fully trained.

Another aspect of the same aircraft, with a sister ship visible in the background.

Maj. N. F. Akimov, Maj. N. A. Varlamov, Maj. L. V. Kotov, Capt. V. A. Lyamin, Capt. V. M. Meshkov and others.

In the summer of 1962 twelve Tu-16 *sans suffixe* bombers and twelve Tu-16KS *Badger-B* missile carriers were transferred from the Soviet Air Force to the AURI, together with a supply of KS-1 missiles. The *Badger-As* equipped the newly formed 41 SkU (*Skadron Udara* – No.41 Air Sqn) based near Jakarta, while the Tu-16KSs equipped the co-located 42 SkU; both units were part of Wing 003. Thus Indonesia became the second operator of the *Badger* after the Soviet Union and the first nation in South-East Asia to acquire strategic bombing capability. As Lt.-Col. R. J. Salatun, Secretary of Indonesia's Joint Chiefs of Staff, put it, *'With the Tu-16 our aircrew can take-off after breakfast, reach and bomb targets anywhere in our territory and return before lunch time; a long-range jet bomber is needed because there is only one airfield suitable for jet operations – Kemajoran'.*

On arrival at Jakarta the Soviet airmen made several flights over the capital to make their presence known and started preparing to wage war in West Irian where Dutch forces remained. The planned Indonesian invasion of West Irian was codenamed Operation *Trikora*. The Tu-16s redeployed to Iswahyudi AB near Ngawi, Jawa Timur Province. The airstrip on Morotai Island, which was 500 km (310 miles) from the disputed territory, was used as a forward operating location. A supply of fuel and the necessary ground support equipment for the *Badgers* was delivered to Morotai, and three Tu-16KSs with two missiles each maintained a full-time presence there, ready to launch anti-shipping sorties. As the Indonesians recalled, refuelling the Tu-16s manually at Morotai was one hell of a job, because the full fuel load was 45,000 litres (9,900 Imp gal), and the operation could take four days and four nights!

The Tu-16s were not the only bombers assigned to the operation; 18 Il-28s of the AURI were deployed at Laha AB, but soon moved to Amahai airfield on Seram Island, which had a longer runway. Apart from that, the AURI had 40 MiG-17Fs and MiG-17PFs at Morotai, Amahai and Letfuan (on the Banda Islands in the southwest of Papua) – primarily for the purpose of escorting the transports that were to airlift personnel and supplies to West Irian during the planned infiltration phase of Operation *Trikora*. Should the Netherlands go to war, the MiGs were to escort the Tu-16s and Il-28s and also neutralise the Royal Netherlands Air Force Hawker Hunter fighters based at Numfor, Biak Island (the latter base was also assigned as a target for the bombers, should negotiations with the Netherlands break down). Mil' Mi-4 *Hound* medium utility helicopters and Mi-6 *Hook* heavy transport heli-

Another fully armed Indonesian Tu-16KS (the serial digits are unfortunately obscured by the wing). Despite being anti-shipping missile carriers, the *Badger-Bs* were operated by the Air Force, not the Navy. Note how the serial prefix was carried on the rear fuselage; this was not the case with all AURI aircraft types.

Tu-16KS M-1624 retracts the landing gear on take-off.

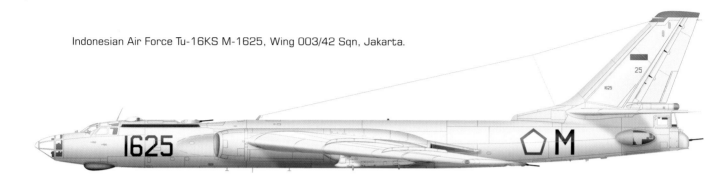

Indonesian Air Force Tu-16KS M-1625, Wing 003/42 Sqn, Jakarta.

copters were also assigned to the airlift but were not ready for action by the time the invasion was due to start.

Intelligence supplied by Taiwanese (Republic of China Air Force) Lockheed U-2 reconnaissance aircraft showed that the Dutch would probably be unable to maintain air superiority if hostilities began. Furthermore, it was estimated that six KS-1 missiles would have been enough to sink the aircraft carrier HNLMS *Karel Doorman* (R81), the flagship of the Dutch task force. *'AURI is the most dreaded Air Force in South East Asia',* wrote the Dutch aviation magazine *Vliegwereld.* This show of force was enough to make the Netherlands and the USA back down; the US Ambassador in Jakarta advised the Dutch government to avoid open warfare and transfer Irian Jaya peacefully to Indonesia. Not wishing to become involved in jungle warfare a long way from home, on 15th August 1962, the Dutch signed the New York Agreement, handing over West Irian to the United Nations Temporary Executive Authority for subsequent integration into Indonesia, and the invasion was called off.

One Tu-16 was damaged beyond repair during a night training sortie in late 1962 when it force-landed in a sugar cane field near Geneng village, Madiun, East Java Province, when one of the engines failed after take-off. Two of the crewmembers were killed; the trainee captain Suwandi narrowly escaped with his life. It turned out that the fuel had been contaminated with a certain kind of algae that clogged the fuel filters! Suwandi went on to become the Indonesian pilot with the highest number of hours on the type.

Once the New York Agreement had been signed, the Soviet crews on temporary deployment to Indonesia were given a new assignment; they were now to act as instructors, training the local

airmen to fly the Tu-16s which the Soviet government had decided to transfer to the Indonesian Air Force. This was an extremely complicated job, for the Indonesians had not flown any aircraft of a similar class before; besides, no flight charts and no interpreters proficient in aviation terminology were available initially. Still, these difficulties were overcome eventually. (Interestingly, Indonesian sources indicate that a few selected AURI pilots, including Sumarno and Suwandi, were sent to the Soviet Union, undergoing a four-month crash training course for the Tu-16 at the Long-Range Aviation's 43rd TsBP i PLS in Ryazan'. After completing the course they flew their new bombers to Jakarta as co-pilots, with multiple stops, including Irkutsk, Beijing, Kunming and Rangoon; the captains were Russian.) A practice bombing range was set up on Sumatra where the combat training took place. The aircrews of the 56th TBAD spent six months in Indonesia until the local airmen were qualified to fly the *Badger*; the ground crews stayed for another four months to keep up the operations of the bombers until local technicians had been trained. Many of the Soviet servicemen participating in the Indonesian deployment received the Order of the Red Banner of Combat for this operation.

Almost immediately, Indonesia found itself embroiled in a new conflict – an attempt to stop the formation of the Malaysian Federation; the undeclared war was called Operation *Dwikora*, and subsequently became known in Indonesia and Malaysia simply as *Konfrontasi*. The confrontation unfolded in 1962-66 along the border of Borneo (aka Kalimantan), the Malacca Strait and near the Singapore border. Borneo was the main bone of contention, with the British protectorates of Sabah and Sarawak (collectively

Left: Indonesian Air Force Tu-16s and Tu-16KSs sit in storage at Jakarta after retirement.

Right and above right: Tu-16KS M-1625 is one of the two AURI *Badgers* that have been preserved. The shed keeps out the sun and most of the bird droppings, but it also complicates photography immensely!

known as British Borneo; now East Malaysia) in the north, which were amalgamated into Malaysia along with the Federation of Malaya (now West Malaysia) and Singapore in September 1963. There were some anti-amalgamation protests in British Borneo, which Indonesia attempted to exploit.

This time the tables were turned – it was a no-win situation for Indonesia; Malaysia was backed by the UK (which dispatched a task force to the region), Australia and New Zealand. Most of the fighting took place on Borneo. There was very little offensive air action; the AURI did, however, use its An-12B transports, Mi-4 and Mi-6 helicopters to airlift troops infiltrating Sabah and Sarawak.

During Operation *Dwikora* the Indonesian Tu-16s were used for a 'show of force', making incursions into Malaysian airspace near Singapore, although they did not participate in actual combat. Two such aircraft were stationed at Medan in North Sumatra for the duration. There were two routes they would typically take when deploying from Iswahyudi AB, Madiun (East Java Province), to Medan. The north route lay over the Makassar Strait, Mindanao, West Kalimantan, North Kalimantan, the South China Sea and the Malacca Strait; the south route took the aircraft over Christmas Island (British territory), Cocos Island, Andaman Island and Nikobar.

During one such sortie in 1964 the Indonesians discovered how sturdy the *Badger* was. As a Tu-16 captained by Damanik Shah Alam flew over the Malacca Strait, heading towards Kuala Lumpur, two Gloster Javelin interceptors of the Royal Air Force's

No.60 Sqn scrambled from RAF Butterworth on the coast of Penang Island and chased the bomber, as they would occasionally. The Indonesian crew had no doubts that the Javelins were trying to force the Tu-16 to land either in Singapore or at Butterworth. The situation became very tense; Damanik ordered his gunners to return fire if the British jets attacked. In the meantime, he got a better idea. Without warning he yanked the control wheel, pulling the bomber up into a sharp climb, which surprised the Javelin pilots; the Tu-16 vanished into thick clouds and headed back towards Medan. *'The tail gunner and other crew members were screaming because they were undergoing high Gs when the jet shot up. But it was much better than being forced to land by the British'*, said Damanik. However, the RAF used the Javelins as a deterrent, warning the Tu-16s not to cross the border.

As part of Operation *Dwikora*, in mid-1963 three Tu-16 *Badger-As* flew a psychological warfare mission. One bomber captained by Lt.-Col. Sardjono went to Kinabalu and Sandakan (both in Borneo), another to Sarawak; they were tasked with distributing propaganda leaflets. Taking off at midnight, Sardjono's aircraft cruised at 11,000 m (36,090 ft) but descended to 400 m (1,310 ft) before reaching Sandakan.

The objective of the third jet captained by Air Commodore Suwondo was Australia; this aircraft carried materiel such as parachutes, communication sets and canned food, which it was to drop near Alice Springs, right in the middle of Australia – exactly to prove that AURI was able to reach the heart of the continent. The mission seemed crazy, as Alice Springs had an OTH radar

The Indonesian Air Force Tu-16s			
Serial	**Type**	**C/n**	**Notes**
M-1601	Tu-16	?	
M-1602	Tu-16	?	
M-1603?	Tu-16	?	Existence not confirmed but likely
M-1604?	Tu-16	?	Existence not confirmed but likely
M-1605?	Tu-16	?	Existence not confirmed but likely
M-1606?	Tu-16	?	Existence not confirmed but likely
M-1607	Tu-16	?	
M-1608?	Tu-16	?	Existence not confirmed but likely
M-1609?	Tu-16	?	Existence not confirmed but likely
M-1610?	Tu-16	?	Existence not confirmed but likely
M-1611	Tu-16	?	
M-1612?	Tu-16	?	Existence not confirmed but likely; serial M-1613 probably not assigned for superstitious reasons
M-1614	Tu-16KS?	*20****	Preserved Iswahyudi AB, Madiun, minus pylons, marked '630427' on fin
M-1615?	Tu-16KS	*20****	Existence not confirmed but likely
M-1616	Tu-16KS	*20****	
M-1617?	Tu-16KS	*20****	Existence not confirmed but likely
M-1618	Tu-16KS	*20****	
M-1619	Tu-16KS	*20****	
M-1620	Tu-16KS	*20****	
M-1621	Tu-16KS	*20****	
M-1622	Tu-16KS	*20****	
M-1623?	Tu-16KS	*20****	Existence not confirmed but likely
M-1624	Tu-16KS	*20****	
M-1625	Tu-16KS	*20****	Made last Tu-16 flight in Indonesia 10-1970. Preserved TNI-AU Museum, Adisutjipto AB, Yogyakarta; marked '63427' on fin, reported in error as c/n 7203427
M-16...	Tu-16KS	6203414?	One of the above aircraft. Ex-Soviet Air Force '08 Black'; marked 3414 on fin when still operational

Left: An Iraqi Air Force Tu-16 without missile pylons shows off its two-tone camouflage scheme.

Below: Iraqi Xian B-6Ds make a flypast during a military parade.

system to monitor the whole Asia-Pacific region. Nevertheless, taking off from Iswahyudi AB at 0100 hrs local time, the Tu-16 got through unscathed at low altitude, encountering no opposition from Royal Australian Air Force F-86 Sabres or Bloodhound SAMs, and returned to base at around 0800 hrs. All three bombers returned home safely.

However, after an unsuccessful communist coup attempt against President Sukarno on 30th September 1965 (the so-called 30th September Movement), a violent wave of repressions against civilian and military communist sympathisers swept the country. The death toll was at least 500,000 (many of the victims were members of the armed forces), and Soviet support was promptly withdrawn. Predictably, all Soviet-built aircraft were soon grounded by lack of spares. From then on, President Sukarno slowly lost power and the staunchly anti-Communist Maj.-Gen. Mohammed Suharto seized power in March 1966, installing a military dictatorship; Suharto favoured the USA as an arms supplier.

Realising that they were outmatched by the Commonwealth forces, the Indonesians gradually shifted the focus of their operations from offensive to defensive. When President Sukarno was replaced by Gen. Suharto, the Indonesian interest in continuing *Konfrontasi* began to decline, as it had been largely a sabre-rattling exercise meant to divert public attention from the problems on the home front. Eventually a peace treaty was signed in Bangkok in August 1966, whereby Indonesia accepted the formation of Malaysia.

After the break between Indonesia and the USSR the Tu-16s remained operational until October 1970, when the farewell flight took place; after that they remained in storage for some time, grounded by lack of spares. When Indonesia acquired new Western air technology, all but two of the *Badgers* were scrapped. The two preserved aircraft are marked '630427' and '63427'; presumably this denotes 27th April 1963, a date of some importance to the TNI-AU.

Although the Indonesian Tu-16KSs never fired in anger, a test launch of a KS-1 missile took place on Arakan Island, between Bali and Ujung Pandang, in 1964 or 1965. The missile homed in accuracy and tore a gaping hole in the middle of the steel platform used as the target.

Iraq

The **Iraqi Air Force** (IrAF, or *al Quwwat al-Jawwiya al-Iraqiya*) originated as the Royal Iraqi Air Force in 1931, changing its name after the revolution on 14th July 1958, in which King Faisal II was assassinated, along with the greater part of his family and the Minister of Defence, and the Republic of Iraq was established. After the revolution, the Soviet Union and its Warsaw Pact allies (notably Czechoslovakia) established ties with the new republic and started supplying armaments right away; these included aircraft for the IrAF. Shortly after the revolution the new Commander-in-Chief of the IrAF, Brig. Gen. J. Awqati, arranged a large order for MiG-15 and MiG-17 fighters, Il-28 bombers and other military hardware.

In 1960 the 'extremely progressive' regime of Gen. Abd al-Karim Qasim degenerated into a military dictatorship. Actually Qasim was communist-minded and pro-Soviet. In 1960 he made the fatal mistake of nationalising the Iraqi Petroleum Company – a step which the IPC's Anglo-American owners would not tolerate.

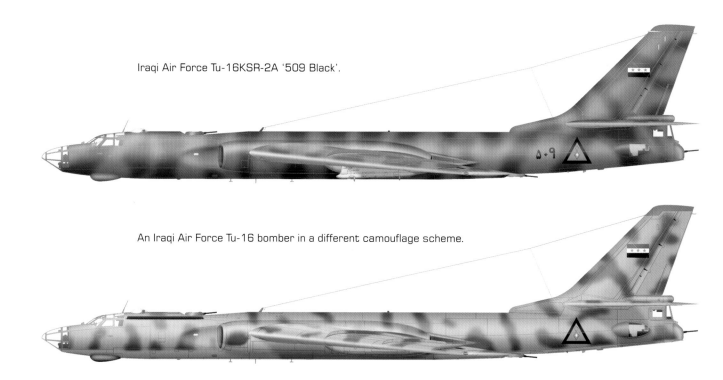

Iraqi Air Force Tu-16KSR-2A '509 Black'.

An Iraqi Air Force Tu-16 bomber in a different camouflage scheme.

On 8th-9th February 1963, Qasim was unseated and executed in a coup led by the Ba'ath Party (the Arab Socialist Renaissance Party), reportedly with backing from the British government and the CIA. The Ba'ath Party was ousted from government just seven months later. However, relations with the Soviet Union improved again when the Ba'ath Party returned to power after the 17th July 1968, coup and Saddam Hussein became head of state.

In the 1960s, the Iraqi Air Force acquired eight Tu-16KSR-2-11 *Badger-G* missile strike aircraft, which were operated by No.10 Sqn at Habbaniya. On the morning of 5th June 1967 – the opening day of the Six-Day War – several Iraqi Air Force aircraft were destroyed on the ground by an Israeli strike at the so-called H-3 base cluster west of Baghdad. In retaliation, the Tu-16 bombers – then operating from al-Walid AB (aka 'H-3 Main') 435 km (270 miles) west of Baghdad – delivered a strike against Israeli airbases on 6th June. One of these bombers captained by Sqn Ldr

Hussein Mohammad Hussein was shot down by IDF/AF Dassault Mirage IIICJ fighters over Ramat David AB.

The *Badgers* that survived the Six-Day War were used during the Iran-Iraq War of 1980-88 to bomb Iranian positions, as well as military and civilian targets in Iran. In particular, the Tu-16s bombed Teheran airport and carried out several missile launches against Iranian objectives. Subsequently, Iraq purchased four examples of the *Badger-G*'s Chinese-built equivalent – the Xian B-6D, together with a large number of C-601 and C-611 ASMs; these were operated by the same No.10 Sqn. The type was reportedly used operationally against Iranian shipping during the Iran-Iraq War (1980-88). After the disintegration of the Soviet Union, China supplied Iraq with spares for its Tu-16/B-6D fleet. By 1991 virtually all Iraqi Tu-16s had run out of service lives. Three of them were damaged or destroyed on the ground by Allied air strikes during the First Gulf War of 1990-91 (Operation *Desert Storm*).

Known Iraqi Air Force Tu-16s			
Serial	Version	C/n	Notes
509 Black	Tu-16KSR-2-11	?	Grey/green camouflage
547 Black	Tu-16	?	No.10 Sqn
548 Black	Tu-16	?	No.10 Sqn
558 Black	Tu-16	?	No.10 Sqn
559 Black	Tu-16	?	No.10 Sqn
560 Black	Tu-16	?	No.10 Sqn
561 Black	Tu-16	?	No.10 Sqn
562 Black	Tu-16	?	No.10 Sqn
563 Black	Tu-16	?	No.10 Sqn
566 Black	Tu-16	?	No.10 Sqn
638 Black	Tu-16	?	No.10 Sqn

Opposite page:

Top and centre: This series of four photos shows the wreckage of an Iraqi Tu-16 shot down by Iranian air defences during a raid against Iran on 23rd September 1980. The local residents have gathered to take a look at the fallen aggressor.

Bottom: Kurdish Peshmerga warriors examine the wreckage of a Tu-16 downed in Iraqi Kurdistan.

Appendix 1

Tu-16 production list

The Tu-16's production run amounted to 1,510 – two Moscow-built prototypes (plus a static test airframe), and 1,507 production machines (including 799 Kazan'-built aircraft, 543 Kuibyshev-built aircraft and 165 Voronezh-built aircraft). These are listed in construction number order. Unfortunately, far from all c/n to serial tie-ups are known; therefore, to save space, production batches with few or no identified aircraft are listed as 'from this to that c/n', only positively identified aircraft being included. Crashed or destroyed examples are indicated by 'RIP crosses' where known, with the date of the accident.

C/n	Serial/tactical code/ registration	Version	Manufacture date	Notes
1. MMZ No.156, Moscow				
0001?	no serial	Tu-16		First flight 27-4-1952. Damaged 30-3-1953, repaired
0002?	no serial	Tu-16		F/F 6-4-1953
2. Kazan' aircraft factory No.22				
System 1: 8.2.041.05 = year of manufacture 1958, plant No.22, Batch 041, 05th aircraft in the batch				
3200101	?	Tu-16	30-12-1953	203rd TBAP, Baranovichi; to ?th TBAP, Kiev-Borispol' AP
3200102	?	Tu-16	30-12-1953	?th TBAP; converted to, see next line
		Tu-16A		71st Test Range/35th OSBAP, Bagerovo AB
3200103	?	Tu-16	?-1-1954	?th TBAP; converted to, see next line
		Tu-16A		71st Test Range/35th OSBAP, Bagerovo AB
3200104	?	Tu-16	?-1-1954	203rd TBAP, Baranovichi
3200105	1 Black	Tu-16	?-1-1954	LII, ejection system testbed; reconverted to standard; see next line
	?			402nd TBAP, Balbasovo AB
4200201	no code; ?	Tu-16	?-2-1954	203rd TBAP, Baranovichi
4200202	?	Tu-16	?-2-1954	402nd TBAP, Balbasovo AB † 6-4-1954
4200203	?	Tu-16	?-2-1954	402nd TBAP, Balbasovo AB; to GK NII VVS
4200204	22 Red	Tu-16	24-3-1954	203rd TBAP, Baranovichi; to 402nd TBAP, Balbasovo AB
	no code			GIA RIIGA[1], Riga-Skulte
4200205	?	Tu-16	24-3-1954	203rd TBAP, Baranovichi
4200301	?	Tu-16	?-3-1954	203rd TBAP, Baranovichi
4200302	?	Tu-16	?-3-1954	203rd TBAP, Baranovichi
4200303	36 Black	Tu-16	?-4-1954	203rd TBAP, Baranovichi; to 402nd TBAP; see next line
				71st Test Range/35th OSBAP, Bagerovo AB; to Tupolev OKB/Kazan' branch
4200304	?	Tu-16	?-4-1954	203rd TBAP, Baranovichi
4200305	no code	Tu-16KS	?-4-1954	Prototype, Tupolev OKB; converted Tu-16 *sans suffixe*
4200401	41 Red	Tu-16	?-5-1954	Became, see next line
	72 Red			?th TBAP, Engels-2 AB. Became, see next line
	no code			Ground instructional airframe IVATU,[1] Irkutsk, later scrapped
4200402	–	Tu-16	–	Delivered to plant No.1 as CKD kit, see c/n 1880002
4200403	no code	Tu-16	?-5-1954	Transferred to NISO[1]
4200404	44 Red	Tu-16	?-5-1954	LII, aerodynamics testbed
4200405	?	Tu-16KS	?-5-1954	2nd prototype?
4200501	?	Tu-16	?-6-1954	Converted to, see next line
	77 Red	Tu-16T	3-8-1954	Prototype, NII AVMF, Feodosia
4200502	?	Tu-16A	?-6-1954	402nd TBAP, Balbasovo AB
4200503	71 Red (Ukraine AF)	Tu-16A	?-6-1954	Tu-16A pattern aircraft; became, see next line
		Tu-16V		To 251st GvTBAP
4200504	?	Tu-16A	?-7-1954	Tupolev OKB; to 71st Test Range/35th OSBAP, Bagerovo AB
4200505	–		–	Delivered to plant No.1 as CKD kit, see c/n 1880001

Batch 6 (Tu-16As 4200601 to 4200605)

4200601	72 Red	Tu-16A	?-6-1954	
4200602	?	Tu-16A	?-7-1954	402nd TBAP, Balbasovo AB. Became, see next line
	29 Blue (Ukraine AF)			251st GvTBAP
4200603	?	Tu-16A	?-6-1954	402nd TBAP, Balbasovo AB
4200604	?	Tu-16A	?-7-1954	?th TBAP, Kiev-Borispol' AP

Batch 7 (Tu-16As 4200701 to 4200705)

4200702	?	Tu-16A	?-7-1954	?th TBAP, Kiev-Borispol' AP
4200703	40 Red (Ukraine AF)	Tu-16K-26	?-8-1954	Preserved Belaya Tserkov' AB
4200704	?	Tu-16A	?-8-1954	402nd TBAP, Balbasovo AB
4200705	15	Tu-16KSR-2-5-11?	?-8-1954	Originally Tu-16A. Possibly Tu-16KSR-2-11, Tu-16K-11-16 or Tu-16K-26

Batch 8 (Tu-16As 4200801 to 4200805)

4200801	42 Red	Tu-16A	?-8-1954	
4200804	?	Tu-16A	?-8-1954	† 15-2-1955
4200805	83 Red (Ukraine AF)	Tu-16A	?-8-1954	260th TBAP, Stryy

Batch 9 (Tu-16As 4200901 to 4200905, mfd September 1954) – no aircraft identified

Batch 10 (4201001 to 4201005, mfd September-October 1954)

4201001	?	Tu-16KS	?-9-1954	
4201002	?	Tu-16A	?-11-1954	Pattern aircraft for 1955. Became, see next line
	02 Blue	Tu-16LL		LII. WFU Zhukovskiy
4201004	?	Tu-16K-11-16	?-9-1954	Converted Tu-16A. Converted to, see next line
	53 Blue	Tu-16K-26		Preserved Central Russian Air Force Museum, Monino

Batch 11 (Tu-16As 4201101 to 4201110, mfd October-November 1954)

4201101	?	Tu-16KS	?-10-1954	
4201102	?	Tu-16KS	?-10-1954	
4201105	23 Red	Tu-16A	?-10-1954	
4201106	?	Tu-16KS	?-10-1954	
4201109	?	Tu-16A	?-11-1954	† 15-2-1955
4201110	74 Red (Ukraine AF)	Tu-16A	?-11-1954	251st GvTBAP, operational 1989 but version unknown

Batch 12 (Tu-16As 4201201 to 4201210, mfd November-December 1954)

4201204	20	Tu-16A	?-12-1954	
4201207	58	Tu-16KSR-2-5-11?	?-12-1954	Originally Tu-16A. Possibly Tu-16KSR-2-11, Tu-16K-11-16 or Tu-16K-26; SPS-5 jammer
4201208	14 Red?	Tu-16A; M-16?	?-12-1954	

Batch 13 (Tu-16As 4201301 to 4201303 and 5201304 to 5201310, mfd December 1954/February 1955)

4201301	12 Red	Tu-16A	?-12-1954	Eventually converted to, see next line
	74	Tu-16KSR-2-11?		Ritsa system, SPS-5 jammer, 'Excellent aircraft' badge
5201305	55 Red	Tu-16K-26P	?-2-1955	Siren'-D jammer (forward hemisphere), Rogovitsa system
5201308	65 Red, 17 Red	Tu-16A	?-2-1955	
5201309	?	Tu-16M	?-2-1955	Converted by plant No.22
5201310	?	Tu-16M	?-2-1955	Converted by plant No.22

Batch 14 (5201501 to 5201410, mfd February-March 1955)

5201404	63 Red	?	?-2-1955	
5201406	70 Red	Tu-16A	?-2-1955	
5201408	81 Red	Tu-16A	?-2-1955	
5201410	07 Blue	Tu-16A	?-3-1955	

Batch 15 (5201501 to 5201510, mfd March 1955)

| 5201508 | 12 | Tu-16A? | ?-3-1955 | ChVVAUSh/605th UAP. † 14-5-1974 |
| 5201510 | 32 Blue | Tu-16A | ?-3-1955 | |

Batch 16 (5201601 to 5201610, mfd March 1955)

5201602	?		?-3-1955	† 30-5-1957
5201603	–		–	Delivered to plant No.64 as CKD kit, see c/n 5400001
5201604	25 Blue	Tu-16KSR-2_	?-3-1955	'Order 684/1' update (BD3-16K racks on wing pylons)
5201605	?		?-3-1955	184th GvTBAP, Priluki. † 17-8-1957

5201607	?	Tu-16A	?-3-1955	'Order 684/1' update
5201610	08	Tu-16K-11	?-3-1955	251st GvTBAP? C/n painted on in error as 6201610 after overhaul
Batch 17 (5201701 to 5201710, mfd April 1955)				
5201705	?	Tu-16KSR-2-5	?-4-1955	Siren'-D (forward hemisphere) and SPS-5 jammers, Rogovitsa system
Batch 18 (5201801 to 5201810, mfd April-May 1955)				
5201810	14 Red	Tu-16KSR-2?	?-5-1955	
Batch 19 (5201901 to 5201910, mfd May-June 1955)				
5201902	?		?-5-1955	† 23-12-1958?
5201904	19 Red	Tu-16A	?-5-1955	
5201907	?	Tu-16P 'Buket'	?-5-1955	
5201908	13 Red?		?-5-1955	
5201910	21 Red	Tu-16A	?-6-1955	Ground instructional airframe Yegor'yevsk Civil Aviation Air Technical School
Batch 20 (5202001 to 5202010, mfd June 1955)				
5202008	?	Tu-16K-11-16	?-6-1955	
5202009	52 Red	Tu-16K-11-16	?-6-1955	
5202010	65 Red	Tu-16KSR-2A	?-6-1955	Converted to, see next line
	?	Tu-16KSR-2-5		
Batch 21 (5202101 to 5202110, mfd June-July 1955)				
5202104	35	Tu-16A	?-6-1955	
5202110	66 Red	Tu-16KSR-2-5	?-7-1955	Check-up tests at GK NII VVS
Batch 22 (5202201 to 5202210, mfd July 1955) – no aircraft identified				
Batch 23 (5202301 to 5202310, mfd July-August 1955)				
5202301	?	Tu-16A	?-7-1955	† 10-1-1957?
5202310	?	Tu-16A	?-8-1955	† 2-2-1956
Batch 24 (5202401 to 5202410, mfd September 1955) – no aircraft identified				
Batch 25 (Tu-16As 5202501 to 5202510, mfd September 1955)				
5202501	28 Blue	Tu-16K-11-16?	?-9-1955	Possibly Tu-16KSR-2-11; SPS-100 Rezeda (in tail fairing) and SPS-5 jammers
5202506	15 Red	Tu-16A	?-9-1955	GNIKI VVS, Akhtoobinsk; special version or testbed with flattened boxy fairings under wings
Batch 26 (mostly Tu-16As, 5202601 to 5202620, mfd September-October 1955)				
5202605	11 Red	Tu-16A	?-9-1955	Preserved Engels-2 AB base museum
5202616	?	Tu-16KS	?-10-1955	
5202617	?	Tu-16KS	?-10-1955	
5202618	?	Tu-16KS	?-10-1955	
5202619	?	Tu-16KS	?-10-1955	
Batch 27 (Tu-16As 5202701 to 5202720, mfd October-November 1955)				
5202703	?	Tu-16A	?-10-1955	184th GvTBAP, Priluki. † 17-4-1956
5202715	20 Blue	Tu-16KSR-2-11	?-11-1955	Rogovitsa system, SPS-5 jammer
5202716	?	Tu-16KS	?-10-1955	Tail number 5014. Converted to, see next line
	85	Tu-16KSR-2		
Batch 28 (mostly Tu-16As, 5202801 to 5202820, mfd November-December 1955)				
5202808	?	Tu-16A	?-11-1955	185th GvTBAP, Poltava. † 26-6-1956
5202809	?	Tu-16P	?-11-1955	Converted Tu-16A. 200th TBAP, operational 1989
5202811	?	Tu-16KS	?-11-1955	
5202812	?	Tu-16KS	?-11-1955	
5202813	?	Tu-16KS	?-11-1955	
5202818	63 Red	Tu-16K-26P	?-12-1955	
5202819	no code	Tu-16K-26P	?-12-1955	Preserved city park Ternopol', the Ukraine
Batch 29 (Tu-16As 5202901 to 5202914 and 6203915 to 6202920, mfd December 1955/February 1956)				
5202901	?	Tu-16A	?-12-1955	† 3-2-1957?
5202905	?	Tu-16A	?-12-1955	† 28-9-1957
5202907	17 Red	Tu-16K-26P	?-12-1955	Siren'-D jammer (forward hemisphere), Siren'-MD jammer in UKhO fairing (rear hemisphere), Rogovitsa system, SPS-5 jammer. GNIKI VVS, used in 'Elektron' R&D programme
5202908	14 Red	Tu-16A	?-12-1955	200th TBAP, Bobruisk. † 10-2-1956 (damaged beyond repair; used as mock-up for Tu-16K-11-16, 1-1962)

5202911	?	Tu-16A	?-12-1955	† 10-4-1958
6202917	?	Tu-16A	?-2-1956	† 18-1-1956

Batch 30 (Tu-16As 6203001 to 6203020, mfd February-March 1956)

6203001	72	Tu-16K-26P	?-2-1956	Ritsa system, Rogovitsa system, SPS-5 jammer
6203004	54 Red	Tu-16KSR-2-5-11?	?-2-1956	Originally Tu-16A. Possibly Tu-16KSR-2-11, Tu-16K-11-16 or Tu-16K-26. Ritsa system, Rogovitsa system, SPS-5 jammer
6203010	?	Tu-16A	?-2-1956	260th TBAP, Stryy. † 26-7-1956
6203016	10 Red	Tu-16A	?-3-1956	Ground instructional airframe Kazan' Aviation Institute
6203017	47	Tu-16K-...	?-3-1956	ChVVAUSh/605th UAP, 1982
6203020	?	Tu-16A	?-3-1956	260th TBAP, Stryy. † 21-3-1957

Batch 31 (mostly Tu-16As, 6203101 to 6203130, mfd March-June 1956)

6203101	35 Red	Tu-16A	?-3-1956	
6203102	18 Red	Tu-16K-26P	?-3-1956	Originally Tu-16A. Rogovitsa system, Siren'-D jammer (forward hemisphere), SPS-5 jammer
6203106	?	Tu-16K-...	?-3-1956	303rd TBAP. † 24-8-1981
6203110	02 Red	Tu-16KS	?-5-1956	
		Tu-16K-11-16		
6203111	?	Tu-16KS	?-5-1956	
6203112	02	Tu-16KS	?-5-1956	
		Tu-16K-11-16		
6203114	?	Tu-16A	?-4-1956	402nd TBAP, Balbasovo AB. † 4-7-1957
6203116	?	Tu-16KS	?-6-1956	
6203117	?	Tu-16KS	?-6-1956	
6203119	02 Blue	Tu-16KSR-2-5-11?	?-5-1956	Originally Tu-16A. Possibly Tu-16KSR-2-11, Tu-16K-11-16 or Tu-16K-26. Ritsa system, SPS-5 jammer 260th TBAP?
6203120	?	Tu-16A	?-4-1956	† 6-7-1956
6203121	04 Red	Tu-16A	?-5-1956	
6203123	71 Red	Tu-16KSR-2-5-11?	?-5-1956	Originally Tu-16A. Possibly Tu-16KSR-2-11, Tu-16K-11-16 or Tu-16K-26. Ritsa system, SPS-5 jammer
6203125	25 Blue	Tu-16KS	?-5-1956	
6203126	?	Tu-16KS	?-5-1956	
6203127	16 Blue	Tu-16KS	?-8-1956	
6203128	12	Tu-16KSR-2-5-11?	?-5-1956	Originally Tu-16A. Possibly Tu-16KSR-2-11, Tu-16K-11-16 or Tu-16K-26. SPS-5 jammer
6203130	?	Tu-16KS	?-6-1956	Converted to, see next line
		Tu-16KSR-2		Converted to, see next line
		Tu-16KSR-2-5		

Batch 32 (mostly Tu-16As, 6203201 to 6203230, mfd June-November 1956)

6203201	?	Tu-16KS	?-6-1956	
6203202	?	Tu-16KS	?-6-1956	
6203203	19	Tu-16KSR-2-5?	?-6-1956	AVMF. Originally Tu-16A. Possibly Tu-16K-11-16; converted to, see next line
	CCCP-42355	Tu-16 Tsiklon-N		Converted to, see next line
		Tu-16 Tsiklon-NM		WFU Chkalovskaya AB 1997; scrapped 2005
6203204	?	Tu-16A	?-6-1956	840th TBAP, Sol'tsy AB. † 24-8-1957
6203208	?	Tu-16KSR-2-5	?-6-1956	AVMF. Originally Tu-16A. Possibly Tu-16K-11-16; converted to, see next line
	CCCP-42484	Tu-16 Tsiklon-N		SOC Belaya Tserkov' 1986, scrapped 1995
6203209	?	Tu-16KS	?-7-1956	
6203210	?	Tu-16KS	?-7-1956	Tail number 6035. Converted to, see next line
	85 Red	Tu-16KSR-2-5-11?		Possibly Tu-16KSR-2-11, Tu-16K-11-16 or Tu-16K-26
6203212	?	Tu-16A	?-6-1956	444th TBAP, Vozdvizhenka AB. † 25-2-1957
6203216	?	Tu-16KS	?-8-1956	
6203218	24 Red	?	?-7-1956	303rd TBAP, Tu-16K-... or Tu-16P, operational 1989
6203220	?	Tu-16KS	?-10-1956	Transferred to Egypt as, see next line
	Egyptian AF 4117			
6203223	?	Tu-16KS	?-11-1956	

6203224	?	?	?-8-1956	402nd TBAP, Tu-16K-... or Tu-16P, operational 1989
6203225	?	Tu-16KS	?-10-1956	
6203226	?	Tu-16KS	?-10-1956	
6203227	?	Tu-16KS	?-11-1956	
6203228	86 Red	Tu-16KSR-2-5-11?	?-8-1956	Originally Tu-16A. Possibly Tu-16K-11-16 or Tu-16K-26. Ground instructional airframe Yegor'yevsk Civil Aviation Aviation Technical School; Ritsa system but no pylons
6203230	?	Tu-16KS	?-11-1956	
Batch 33 (6203301 to 6203330, mfd September-December 1956)				
6203303	?	Tu-16KS	?-9-1956	
6203305	?	Tu-16KS	?-9-1956	
6203306	?	Tu-16A	?-8-1956	444th TBAP, Vozdvizhenka AB.† 31-8-1957
6203308	08	Tu-16KSR-2-5	?-9-1956	
6203310	85 Blue?	Tu-16K-11-16?	?-9-1956	
6203314	?	Tu-16A	?-9-1956	
6203315	?	Tu-16KS	?-10-1956	
6203316	?	Tu-16A	?-9-1956	?th TBAP, Skomorokhi AB. † 29-5-1958?
6203317	?	Tu-16KS	?-10-1956	
6203319	?	Tu-16KS	?-10-1956	
6203320	48 Red	Tu-16K-??? (ZA)	?-9-1956	Originally Tu-16A. 'Excellent aircraft' badge; Ritsa system, Rogovitsa system,
6203324	?	?	?-11-1956	† 16-3-1958
6203326	31 Red	M-16	?-11-1956	Camera pods under wings; Siren'-D jammer (forward hemisphere), L-shaped aerial under nose
6203330	27	Tu-16B	?-12-1956	LII
Batch 34 (6203401 to 6203418 and 7203419 to 7203430, mfd November 1956/February 1957)				
6203403	01 Red	Tu-16A?	?-12-1956	'Excellent aircraft' badge; Rogovitsa system, SPS-5 jammer
6203405	18 Blue	Tu-16KS	?-12-1956	
6203408	?	Tu-16K-...	?-12-1956	AVMF/Black Sea Fleet, 124th MRAP, Gvardeiskoye AB. † 31-8-1957
6203414	08 Black	Tu-16KS	?-12-1956	AVMF. Transferred to Indonesia as, see next line
	Indonesian AF M-16...			
6203415	26 Blue	Tu-16KSR-2-5	?-1-1957	
6203416	?	?	?-12-1956	219th ODRAP?
7203422	?	Tu-16KS	?-1-1957	Tail number 7102. Converted to, see next line
	21 Red	Tu-16KSR-2		SPS-5 jammer
7203423	?	?	?-2-1957	† 12-2-1958
7203426	?	?	?-2-1957	43rd TsBP i PLS
7203427	not known	Tu-16KS	?-2-1957	
7203428	?	Tu-16A	?-2-1957	
	02 Red	Tu-16N		Rogovitsa system, SPS-5 jammer
7203430	?	?	?-2-1957	132nd TBAP, Tu-16K-... or Tu-16P, operational 1989
Batch 35 (7203501 to 7203530, mfd February-April 1957)				
7203510	?	?	?-2-1957	† 13-1-1959?
7203513	?	?	?-3-1957	ECM equipment testbed
7203514	34 Red	Tu-16A	?-3-1957	SPS-100 (in tail fairing) and SPS-5 jammers, 'order 2624' mod
7203516	61	Tu-16KSR-2	?-3-1957	Preserved Zavitinsk
7203524	30 Red	Tu-16Ye	?-3-1957	
7203527	07 Red	Tu-16KSR-2	?-4-1957	Tail number 7121
Batch 36 (7203601 to 7203630, mfd April-June 1957)				
7203601	?	?	?-4-1957	Reinforced engine nacelles
7203602	?	?	?-4-1957	Reinforced engine nacelles
7203603	?	?	?-4-1957	Reinforced engine nacelles. † 10-8-1957
7203605	71 Red	Tu-16KSR-2	?-4-1957	Tail number 7122?
7203606	?	Tu-16KSR-2	?-4-1957	Tail number 7123?

7203608	no code	Tu-16KS	?-5-1957	Tail number 7124. Converted to, see next line
	no code	Tu-16KSR		Prototype. Converted to, see next line
	49 Black	Tu-16KSR-2		Prototype. Converted to, see next line
	21 Blue (Ukraine AF)?			251st GvTBAP? (also reported as Ground instructional airframe IVATU)
7203616	32 Red	M-16 'Orbita'	?-5-1957	
7203617	83 Blue	Tu-16KSR-2-5-11	?-5-1957	AVMF. Possibly Tu-16K-11-16; SPS-5 jammer
7203620	20 Red	Tu-16K-26P	?-6-1957	GNIKI VVS. Rogovitsa system, Siren'-D (forward hemisphere) and SPS-5 jammers
7203624	19 Red (Ukraine AF)	Tu-16A	?-6-1957	251st GvTBAP. Converted to, see next line
		Tu-16K-26		Siren'-MD jammer in UKhO fairing (rear hemisphere)
7203625	65 Black		?-6-1957	AVMF
7203626	?		?-6-1957	† 8-8-1960 (8-8-1961?)
7203630	30 Blue	Tu-16KS	?-6-1957	LII, testbed for exploring the heat signature of targets
Batch 37 (7203701 to 7203730, mfd June-August 1957)				
7203710	09 Red	Tu-16KSR-2(-5)	?-7-1957	Unusual typeface of tactical code (similar to AdverGothic font)
7203712	73 Red (Ukraine AF)	?	?-7-1957	251st GvTBAP
7203722	?	Tu-16A	?-8-1957	Converted to, see next line
	?	Tu-16K-11-16		Converted to, see next line
	70 Red	Tu-16K-26		
7203724	56 Red	Tu-16A	?-8-1957	Myasishchev OKB, landing gear testbed for M-50. Reconverted to standard; became, see next line
	07 Red (Ukraine AF)			WFU Kiev-Gostomel'
7203725	21 Black	Tu-16K-16	?-8-1957	
7203730	62 Red	Tu-16KS	?-8-1957	Tail number 7153
Batch 38 (7203801 to 7203830, mfd August-October 1957)				
7203804	?	Tu-16KS	?-9-1957	Converted to, see next line
	71 Red	Tu-16KSR-2-5		Converted to, see next line
	10 Red	Tu-16K-26P		Rogovitsa system, Siren'-D jammer (forward hemisphere)
7203805	no code	Tu-16K-10	?-9-1957	1st prototype
7203806	no code	Tu-16K-10	?-12-1957	2nd prototype. Possibly became, see next line
	74 Red?			
7203810	?	Tu-16A	?-9-1957	RBP-6 Lyustra and PRS-2 Argon-2 radars. Converted to, see next line
	06 Red	Tu-16K-26P		Ritsa system, Rogovitsa system, SPS-5 jammer
7203811	?	Tu-16KS	?-9-1957	Converted to, see next line
	?	Tu-16KSR-2-5-11?		Possibly Tu-16KSR-2-11, Tu-16K-11-16 or Tu-16K-26
7203812	03 Red	Tu-16A	?-9-1957	'Excellent aircraft' badge
7203817	10 Red (Ukraine AF)	?	?-9-1957	WFU Kiev-Gostomel'
7203818	24 Blue	Tu-16KS	?-9-1957	Tail number 7163
7203820	65 Red	Tu-16KS	?-9-1957	Tail number 7164. Converted to, see next line
	55 Blue	Tu-16KSR-2-5		Siren'-D (forward hemisphere) and SPS-5 jammers
7203822	47 Blue	?	?-9-1957	
7203827	08 Blue	Tu-16KS	?-10-1957	
7203829	06 Red (Ukraine AF)	Tu-16A (Tu-16Z?)	?-10-1957	251st GvTBAP
Batch 39 (7203901 to 7203930, mfd October-December 1957)				
7203903	07 Red (Ukraine AF)	?	?-10-1957	251st GvTBAP
7203907	15 Black;	Tu-16A	?-10-1957	Became, see next line
	08 Red (Ukraine AF)	?		251st GvTBAP
7203908	26 Blue (Ukraine AF)	?	?-10-1957	260th TBAP
7203914	04 Red (Ukraine AF)	?	?-12-1957	251st GvTBAP
7203920	25 Red	Tu-16KSR-2-5	?-12-1957	Tail number 7182. 'Order 476' update [2]
7203930	?	Tu-16KSR-2-5?	?-12-1957	'Order 476' update
Batch 40 (7204001 to 7204007 and 8204008 to 8204030, mfd December 1957/March 1958)				
7204002	?	?	?-12-1957	† 5-6-1958

7204003	17 Red (Ukraine AF)	?	?-12-1957	251st GvTBAP
7204005	18 Red (Ukraine AF)	Tu-16KSR-2-5?	?-12-1957	'Order 476' update, 251st GvTBAP
7204006	?	Tu-16KSR-2-5?	?-12-1957	'Order 476' update
7204007	?	Tu-16KSR-2-5?	?-12-1957	'Order 476' update
8204008	99 Red	Tu-16P 'Buket'	?-1-1958	Additional SPS-5 jammer
8204009	?	?	?-1-1958	444th TBAP, operational 1989
8204010	54 Red	Tu-16P	?-4-1958	Reported in error as '1st production Tu-16K-10'
8204014	25 Blue	Tu-16K-11-16	?-2-1958	Preserved Ukraine Air Force Museum, Poltava
8204016	96 Red	Tu-16P 'Buket'	?-1-1958	
8204018	?	?	?-3-1958	444th TBAP, operational 1989
8204021	?	Tu-16P	?-3-1958	200th TBAP, operational 1989
8204022	?	Tu-16A	?-2-1958	Tail number 8191. Converted to, see next line
	?	Tu-16K-11-16		Converted to, see next line
	54 Red	Tu-16K-26		Ground instructional airframe Kiev Air Force Institute
8204023	?		?-2-1958	Tail number 8192. † 5-11-1960
8204024	05 Red	?	?-2-1958	Tail number 8193
8204026	?	Tu-16KRM	?-3-1958	
8204029	?	Tu-16K-10 (ZA)	?-8-1958	Pre-production aircraft, converted Tu-16A
Batch 41 (8204101 to 8204130, mfd March-June 1957)				
8204102	?	Tu-16A (ZA)	?-3-1958	
8204103	?	Tu-16K-10 (ZA)	?-12-1958	Pre-production aircraft, converted Tu-16A
8204104	?	Tu-16R 'Romb'	?-4-1958	'Order 261' update
8204105	05 Blue	Tu-16LL	?-4-1958	'Order 226' mod, LII
8204108	23 Red;	Tu-16Ye	?-4-1958	Converted to, see next line
	90 Red	M-16		
8204110	?	Tu-16K-...	?-4-1958	444th TBAP, operational 1989
8204111	16 Red	Tu-16KSR-2-5	?-4-1958	Tail number 8211. Converted to, see next line
		Tu-16KRM		Prototype
8204112	27 Red	Tu-16K-11-16	?-4-1958	Tail number 8212
8204117	?	Tu-16LL	?-4-1958	'Order 226' mod, LII; crashed, date unknown
8204124	?	Tu-16P	?-5-1958	52nd GvTBAP; operational in 1989
8204130	47 Red	Tu-16P	?-6-1958	
Batch 42 (8204201 to 8204222, mfd June-December 1958)				
8204201	?	?	?-6-1958	† 5-11-1960
8204203	90 Red	?	?-6-1958	
	77 Red	M-16-2		Siren'-D jammer (forward hemisphere), Siren'-DM jammer in UKhO fairing (rear hemisphere), Rogovitsa system
8204206	40 Red	Tu-16P 'Buket'	?-6-1958	Additional Siren'-D (forward hemisphere) and SPS-5 jammers
8204208	23 Blue	Tu-16Ye 'Azaliya'	?-6-1958	Ventral Azaliya jammer antennas, Siren'-D jammer (forward hemisphere), Siren'-DM jammer in UKhO fairing (rear hemisphere), SPS-5 jammer, Rogovitsa system
8204210	39 Red (Ukraine AF)	Tu-16SPS	?-7-1958	251st GvTBAP
8204211	?	?	?-7-1958	† 10-10-1959
8204212	80 Red	?	?-7-1958	Siren'-D jammer (forward hemisphere), Rogovitsa system
		M-16-3		
8204213	19 Red	Tu-16 Yolka (ZA)	?-7-1958	SPS-100 and SPS-5
8204214	69 Blue	Tu-16Ye 'Azaliya'	?-7-1958	Siren'-D jammer (forward hemisphere), Siren'-DM jammer in UKhO fairing (rear hemisphere), SPS-5 jammer, Rogovitsa system
8204215	51 Red	Tu-16Ye	?-7-1958	132nd TBAP
8204216	09	Tu-16K-10 (ZA)	?-12-1958	Pre-production aircraft, converted Tu-16A
8204222	?	Tu-16K-10 (ZA)	?-12-1958	Pre-production aircraft, converted Tu-16A

System 2: 2.74.3.05.4 = 2 means nothing, Batch 74, year of manufacture 1963, 05th aircraft in the batch, 4 means nothing (= f/n 7405)

Batch 51 (f/ns 5101 to 5105, mfd June-July 1961)

1511012	?	Tu-16K-10 (ZA)	?-6-1961	F/n 5101. † 20-6-1961
2511023?	?	Tu-16K-10	?-6-1961	F/n 5102; c/n not confirmed but likely
3511034	?	Tu-16K-10	?-7-1961	F/n 5103. Converted to, see next line
	41 Blue	Tu-16K-10-26		

Batch 52 (f/ns 5201 to 5205, mfd July-September 1961) – no aircraft identified

Batch 53 (f/ns 5301 to 5305, mfd September 1961) – no aircraft identified

Batch 54 (f/ns 5401 to 5405, mfd October 1961) – no aircraft identified

Batch 55 (f/ns 5501 to 5505, mfd October-November 1961)

2551023	52	Tu-16K-10	?-11-1961	F/n 5502

Batch 56 (f/ns 5601 to 5605, mfd December 1961)

2561024	04 Red (Ukraine AF)	Tu-16K-10	?-12-1961	F/n 5602
3561035	92 Red	Tu-16K-10	?-12-1961	F/n 5603, North Fleet

Batch 57 (f/ns 5701 to 5705, mfd February 1962) – no aircraft identified

Batch 58 (f/ns 5801 to 5805, mfd February-March 1962) – no aircraft identified

Batch 59 (f/ns 5901 to 5905, mfd March 1962) – no aircraft identified

Batch 60 (f/ns 6001 to 6005, mfd April 1962) – no aircraft identified

Batch 61 (f/ns 6101 to 6105, mfd April-May 1962)

...61204...	?	Tu-16K-10	?-5-1962	F/n 6104. Pacific Fleet. †

Batch 62 (f/ns 6201 to 6205, mfd May-June 1962)

...62203...	11	Tu-16K-10	?-6-1962	F/n 6203

Batch 63 (f/ns 6301 to 6305, mfd June-July 1962)

2632024	12 Blue	Tu-16K-10	?-6-1962	F/n 6302. SPS-100 (in tail fairing) and SPS-5 jammers, 'order 2624' mod

Batch 64 (f/ns 6401 to 6405, mfd July-August 1962)

4642012	?	Tu-16K-10	?-7-1962	F/n 6401

Batch 65 (f/ns 6501 to 6505, mfd August-September 1962)

4652012	?	Tu-16K-10	?-8-1962	F/n 6501
4652042	57 Red	Tu-16K-10(ZA)	?-8-1962	F/n 6504. To Myasishchev OKB, converted to 17LL-2 avionics/weapons testbed

Batch 66 (f/ns 6601 to 6605, mfd September 1962) – no aircraft identified

Batch 67 (f/ns 6701 to 6705, mfd September-October 1962)

5672032?	?, 20 Red	Tu-16K-10	?-10-1962	F/n 6703; c/n not 100% clearly readable

Batch 68 (f/ns 6801 to 6805, mfd October-November 1962) – no aircraft identified

Batch 69 (f/ns 6901 to 6905, mfd November-December 1962) – no aircraft identified

Batch 70 (f/ns 7001 to 7005, mfd December 1962) – no aircraft identified

Batch 71 (f/ns 7101 to 7105, mfd January 1963)

1713014	50 Red	Tu-16K-10	?-1-1963	F/n 7101
2711041?	01	Tu-16K-10		F/n 7104; not 100% clearly readable (painted on with wrong year of manufacture?)

Batch 72 (f/ns 7201 to 7205, mfd February 1963) – no aircraft identified

Batch 73 (f/ns 7301 to 7305, mfd February-March 1963)

2733045	13, later 01 Blue	Tu-16K-10	?-3-1963	F/n 7304. Pacific Fleet. † 28-7-1963

Batch 74 (f/ns 7401 to 7405, mfd April-May 1963)

2743054	?	Tu-16K-10	?-5-1963	F/n 7405. Converted to, see next line
	?	Tu-16K-10D	Converted to, see next line	
	?	Tu-16K-10-26		

Batch 75 (f/ns 7501 to 7505, mfd May 1963) – no aircraft identified

Batch 76 (f/ns 7601 to 7605, mfd June-July 1963) – no aircraft identified

Batch 77 (f/ns 7701 to 7705, mfd July 1963) – no aircraft identified

Batch 78 (f/ns 7801 to 7805, mfd August-September 1963) – no aircraft identified

Batch 79 (f/ns 7901 to 7905, mfd October-November 1963)

1793014	15 Red	Tu-16K-10	?-10-1963	F/n 7901. Converted to, see next line
	?	Tu-16K-10D		Converted to, see next line
	?	Tu-16K-10-26		

1793041?	?	Tu-16K-10	?-10-1963	F/n 7904
Batch 80 (f/ns 8001 to 8005, mfd December 1963) – no aircraft identified				

3. Kuibyshev aircraft factory No.1

1.88.11.10 = plant No.1, 'aircraft 88' (Tu-16), Batch 11, 10th aircraft in the batch

1880001	?	Tu-16	?-10-1954	Built from Kazan' CKD kit (c/n 4200505), Tupolev OKB; converted to, see next line
	?	Tu-16Z		
1880002	?	Tu-16	?-11-1954	Ground instructional airframe IVATU, Irkutsk; later scrapped
1880101	57 Red	Tu-16	?-10-1954	Tupolev OKB
		Tu-16Z		
Batch 2 (1880201 and 1880203, mfd November-December 1954)				
1880201	?	Tu-16Z	?-11-1954	GK NII VVS
1880301	?	Tu-16Z	?-12-1954	
1880302	50 Red	Tu-16R-1	?-12-1954	Prototype, Tupolev OKB; converted to, see next line
		Tu-16R-2		Preserved Central Russian Air Force Museum, Monino
Batch 4 (1880401 to 1880405, mfd December 1954/February 1955)				
1880402	?	Tu-16	?-12-1954	?th TBAP, Kiev-Borispol' AP
1880403	ЛЗ Blue/43 Blue	Tu-16LL	?-12-1954	LII ('order 226' mod); code 'L3' on fuselage and '43' on tail
Batch 5 (1880501 to 1880505, mfd February-March 1955) – no aircraft identified				
Batch 6 (1880401 to 1880605, mfd March 1955)				
1880602	76 Black	?	?-3-1955	?th TBAP, Dyagilevo AB. † 20-2-1958
1880605	?	?	?-3-1955	Ground instructional airframe, location unknown
Batch 7 (1880701 to 1880705, mfd March-April 1955)				
1880701	?	Tu-16P 'Buket'	?-3-1955	185th GvTBAP, Poltava. † ?-6-1956
Batch 8 (1880801 to 1880805, mfd April 1955)				
1880802	76	?	?-4-1955	185th GvTBAP, Poltava. † 19-8-1955
1880803	?	Tu-16SPS	?-4-1955	
1880804	01 Blue	Tu-16	?-4-1955	
Batch 9 (1880901 to 1880905, mfd May 1955)				
1880901	14 Red	?	?-5-1955	
1880902	47 Blue	?	?-5-1955	AVMF/Pacific Fleet, 183rd MRAP/Sqn 3, Vladivostok-Knevichi AP
1880904	09 Red	?	?-5-1955	AVMF
Batch 10 (1881001 to 1881005, mfd May 1955)				
1881004	?	?	?-5-1955	402nd TBAP, Balbasovo AB † 11-11-1959 (8-12-1959?)
Batch 11 (1881101 to 1881110, mfd June 1955)				
1881102	?	?	?-6-1955	† 23-12-1958?
1881110	10 Red	Tu-16LL	?-6-1955	LII
Batch 12 (1881201 to 1881210, mfd July 1955)				
1881209	?	?	?-7-1955	† 15-7-1957
1881210	19 Red	?	?-7-1955	GNIKI VVS
Batch 13 (1881301 to 1881310, mfd July-September 1955)				
1881301	?	Tu-16	?-7-1955	Converted to, see next line
	CCCP-Л5411	Tu-16G		Ground instructional airframe KIIGA, Kiev-Zhulyany
1881303	?	Tu-16-UB	?-7-1955	
1881304	58 Red	?	?-9-1955	Bomb fuse arming system tests (1957). Ground instructional airframe KIIGA
1881305	?	Tu-16SPS	?-7-1955	Converted to, see next line
	42 Red	Tu-16P 'Buket'		Siren'-D jammer (forward hemisphere), Siren'-MD jammer in UKhO fairing (rear hemisphere), SPS-5 jammer, Rogovitsa system
Batch 14 (1881401 to 1881410, mfd September 1955)				
1881407	43 Red	?	?-9-1955	402nd TBAP, Balbasovo AB?
1881410	?	Tu-16SPS	?-9-1955	Converted to, see next line
	34 Blue (?)	Tu-16P 'Buket'		402nd TBAP? SPS-22, SPS-5 jammer, Rogovitsa system

Batch 15 (1881501 to 1881510, mfd September 1955)				
1881503	35 Red	Tu-16Ye 'Azaliya'	?-9-1955	Siren'-D jammer (forward hemisphere), SPS-5 jammer, probably Siren'-MD jammer in UKhO fairing (rear hemisphere)
1881509	02 Red	Tu-16Ye 'Azaliya'	?-9-1955	Siren'-D jammer (forward hemisphere), Siren'-MD jammer in UKhO fairing (rear hemisphere), SPS-5 jammer
Batch 16 (1881601 to 1881610, mfd September-October 1955)				
1881602	10 Blue	Tu-16P 'Buket'	?-9-1955	SPS-22, SPS-5 jammer, Rogovitsa system
1881605	23 Blue	Tu-16 Yolka	?-10-1955	
Batch 17 (1881701 to 1881710, mfd September 1955)				
1881703	32 Red	Tu-16	?-10-1955	Converted to, see next line
		Tu-16SPS	?-11-1955	New manufacture date as Tu-16SPS
1881704	?	Tu-16	?-10-1955	Converted to, see next line
		Tu-16SPS	?-11-1955	New manufacture date as Tu-16SPS
1881705	?	Tu-16	?-10-1955	Converted to, see next line
		Tu-16SPS	?-11-1955	New manufacture date as Tu-16SPS
1881706	?	Tu-16	?-10-1955	Converted to, see next line
		Tu-16SPS	?-11-1955	New manufacture date as Tu-16SPS
1881707	?	Tu-16	?-10-1955	Converted to, see next line
		Tu-16SPS	?-11-1955	New manufacture date as Tu-16SPS
1881708	?	Tu-16	?-10-1955	Converted to, see next line
		Tu-16SPS	?-11-1955	New manufacture date as Tu-16SPS
1881709	?	Tu-16	?-10-1955	Converted to, see next line
		Tu-16SPS	?-11-1955	New manufacture date as Tu-16SPS
1881710	?	Tu-16	?-10-1955	Converted to, see next line
		Tu-16SPS	?-11-1955	New manufacture date as Tu-16SPS
Batch 18 (1881801 to 1881810, mfd November-December 1955)				
1881809	12 Red	Tu-16Ye	?-12-1955	GNIKI VVS. Rogovitsa system. Preserved Vladimirovka AB, Akhtoobinsk (929th GLITs)
Batch 19 (1881901 to 1881910, mfd December 1955)				
1881901	?	?	?-12-1955	† 13-3-1959
1881907	46 Red	Tu-16	?-12-1955	Modified for *Bar'yer neizvesnosti* movie
Batch 20 (1882001 to 1882020, mfd December 1955/February 1956)				
1882013	32 Red	Tu-16Ye	?-2-1956	
1882017	?, 15 Red	Tu-16 Yolka	?-2-1956	Additional SPS-4 jammer
Batch 21 (1882101 to 1882120, mfd February-March 1956)				
1882101	30 Black	Tu-16Z	?-2-1956	
1882106	?	Tu-16 'Silikat'	?	Prototype. Converted to, see next line
		Tu-16 'Fonar''		Prototype
1882108	26 Red	Tu-16Z	?-3-1956	
1882120	44	Tu-16	?-3-1956	One ASO-16/3 chaff dispenser
Batch 22 (1882201 to 1882220, mfd April-May 1956)				
1882202	?	Tu-16N	?-4-1956	Converted 4-1970, upgraded September-December 1970
1882205	01 Red	Tu-16P 'Buket'	?-4-1956	Unit unknown
	28 Red			52nd GvTBAP. Gate guard Shaikovka AB
1882213	?	Tu-16Z	?-9-1956	184th GvTBAP, Priluki. † 17-8-1957
1882214	?	Tu-16Z	?-9-1956	
1882216	61 Red	M-16-2	?-5-1956	Siren'-D jammer (forward hemisphere), Siren'-DM jammer in UKhO fairing (rear hemisphere), Ritsa system (!)
1882218	?	Tu-16P	?-5-1956	200th TBAP, operational 1989
Batch 23 (1882301 to 1882320, mfd May-June 1956)				
1882302	41 Red/41 Blue	Tu-16NN	?-5-1956	SPS-5 jammer, Rogovitsa system, R-832M radio
1882305	?	Tu-16R 'Romb'	?-6-1956	
1882306	09 Red	Tu-16Ye	?-5-1956	SRS-1, SPS-5 jammer, Rogovitsa system
1882307	?	?	?-6-1956	Siren'-D jammer (forward hemisphere)

1882309	?	?	?-5-1956	† 6-10-1956
1882311	?	?	?-6-1956	† 3-7-1959
1882313	?	?	?-6-1956	260th TBAP, operational 1989
1882315	34 Red	Tu-16Z	?-6-1956	SPS-5 jammer
Batch 24 (1882401 to 1882420, mfd July-September 1956)				
1882401	?	Tu-16N	?-7-1956	Prototype. Delivered to 251st GvTBAP
1882402	23 Red	Tu-16R (SRS-3)	?-7-1956	
1882405	33 Blue	Tu-16 Yolka	?-7-1956	
1882406	73	Tu-16P 'Buket'	?-7-1956	SPS-5 jammer, Siren'-D jammer (forward hemisphere), Rogovitsa system
1882408	?	Tu-16SPS	?-7-1956	Converted to, see next line
	?	Tu-16P 'Buket'		
1882409	?	Tu-16SPS	?-7-1956	Converted to, see next line
	?	Tu-16P 'Ficus'		Siren'-DM jammer in UKhO fairing (rear hemisphere)
1882411	45 Red	Tu-16Ye	?-8-1956	Converted Tu-16A. SPS-1 or SPS-2 and SPS-5 jammers
1882420	?	Tu-16R (SRS-3)	?-8-1956	Ground instructional airframe IVATU, Irkutsk; later scrapped
Batch 25 (1882501 to 1882520, mfd September-November 1956)				
1882503	?	Tu-16	?-9-1956	Converted to, see next line
	45 Blue	Tu-16NN		251st GvTBAP. SPS-5 jammer
1882504	?	?	?-9-1956	† 14-10-1959
1882509	51 Red	Tu-16A	?-10-1956	
1882515	?	?	?-10-1956	444th TBAP, Vozdvizhenka AB
Batch 26 (1882601 to 1882620, mfd November 1956/January 1957)				
1882612	21 Blue	Tu-16R?	?-12-1956	185th GvTBAP; gate guard Priluki AB
1882615	78	Tu-16Ye	?-12-1956	SPS-1, SPS-4 and SPS-5 jammers
Batch 27 (1882701 to 1882720, mfd January-February 1957)				
1882708	?	?	?-1-1957	219th ODRAP, Spassk-Dal'niy † 21-2-1984
1882710	26 Red	Tu-16Ye	?-1-1957	Converted Tu-16A. SPS-5 jammer
1882713	?	?	?-2-1957	† 25-6-1957
Batch 28 (1882801 to 1882820, mfd February-April 1957)				
1882801	30 Blue	Tu-16Z	?-2-1957	SPS-5 jammer
1882808	08 Red	?	?-3-1957	LII; RD-3MR engines with thrust reversers
1882809	?	?	?-3-1957	† 12-9-1958
1882819	?	Tu-16P?	?-4-1957	52nd GvTBAP, operational 1989? Not confirmed – possibly c/n 5202819
1882820	16	?	?-4-1957	
Batch 29 (1882901 to 1882920, mfd April-May 1957)				
1882906	?	Tu-16Z	?-5-1957	
1882907	?	Tu-16Z	?-5-1957	
1882908	?	Tu-16Z	?-5-1957	
1882909	?	Tu-16Z	?-5-1957	
1882914	?	?	?-5-1957	† ?-11-1957
1882917	33 Red	Tu-16Z	?-5-1957	
1882919	93 Red	Tu-16P 'Buket'	?-6-1957	
Batch 30 (1883001 to 1883020, mfd June-July 1957)				
1883001	?	?	?-9-1957	Reinforced engine nacelles
1883002	?	?	?-6-1957	Reinforced engine nacelles
1883003	?	?	?-6-1957	Reinforced engine nacelles
1883004	42	Tu-16R	?-11-1957	Reinforced engine nacelles, late manufacture date. AVMF/Pacific Fleet, 183rd MRAP/Sqn 3, Vladivostok-Knevichi AP
1883005	?	?	?-6-1957	Reinforced engine nacelles
1883006	?	?	?-6-1957	Reinforced engine nacelles
1883007	?	?	?-6-1957	Reinforced engine nacelles
1883012	?	Tu-16Z	?-7-1957	
1883014	39 Blue	Tu-16R	?-7-1957	

1883020	45	Tu-16P	?-7-1957	AVMF/Pacific Fleet
Batch 31 (1883101 to 1883120, mfd July-October 1957)				
1883101	?	Tu-16Z	?-7-1957	
1883102	?	Tu-16P	?-7-1957	200th TBAP, operational 1989
1883103	32 Red	?	?-7-1957	Scrapped
1883106	?	Tu-16 (ZA)	?-8-1957	219th ODRAP, Spassk-Dal'niy
1883108	50 Red	Tu-16A	?-8-1957	Gate guard Dyagilevo AB, Ryazan'
1883117	?	Tu-16P (ZA) 'Ficus'	?-8-1957	52nd GvTBAP; in service 1989
1883118	83 Red	Tu-16A	?-8-1957	
1883119	16 Red	Tu-16R???	?-8-1957	SPS-5 jammer
Batch 32 (1883201 to 1883220, mfd September-October 1957)				
1883204	12 Red	?	?-9-1957	
1883205	28	Tu-16R (ZA)	?-9-1957	Converted to, see next line
		Tu-16RR (ZA)		Siren'-D jammer (forward hemisphere), SPS-5 jammer
1883207	22	Tu-16R (SRS-1)	?-9-1957	SRS-4 SIGINT set retrofitted; SPS-5 jammer. Became, see next line
	24 Blue			
1883210	08	Tu-16RP	?-9-1957	Siren'-D jammer (forward hemisphere), Siren'-MD jammer in UKhO fairing (rear hemisphere), SPS-5 jammer
1883213	06	?	?-10-1957	
1883218	?	?	?-10-1957	† 13-10-1958
Batch 33 (1883301 to 1883320, mfd October-December 1957)				
1883301	29 Red	?	?-10-1957	
1883302	30 Red	?	?-10-1957	Converted to, see next line
	86 Blue	Tu-16RM-2		
1883303	31 Blue	Tu-16R (SRS-1)	?-10-1957	SRS-4 SIGINT set retrofitted
1883304	12 Red	Tu-16R (ZA) (SRS-1)	?-10-1957	SRS-4 SIGINT set retrofitted. Became, see next line
	39 Red			
1883305	27 Blue	Tu-16R (ZA)	?-10-1957	219th ODRAP. Converted to, see next line
	28 Red	Tu-16RR (ZA)		
1883307	43 Red	?	?-11-1957	
1883308	87 Red	Tu-16SPS (ZA)	?-11-1957	
1883309	29 Blue?	Tu-16Ye?	?-11-1957	
1883310	21 Black	Tu-16R	?-11-1957	
1883312	28 Blue		?-11-1957	
1883313	35 Red	Tu-16R (ZA) (SRS-3)	?-11-1957	Became, see next line
	23			
1883314	23 Red	Tu-16R (ZA) (SRS-3)	?-11-1957	Ground instructional airframe KIIGA, Kiev-Zhulyany
1883315	09 Red	Tu-16R (ZA) (SRS-3)	?-11-1957	219th ODRAP/Sqn 1
1883316	02 Red	Tu-16R (SRS-3)	?-11-1957	219th ODRAP/Sqn 1. Converted to, see next line
		Tu-16RR		
1883317	?	Tu-16R (ZA)	?-11-1957	
1883318	25 Red	Tu-16R (SRS-3)	?-12-1957	
1883319	22 Blue	?	?-12-1957	219th ODRAP; scrapped
Batch 34 (1883401 to 1883420, mfd December 1957/February 1958)				
1883402	23 Red	Tu-16R (ZA) (SRS-3)	?-12-1957	SPS-5 jammer
1883403	25 Blue	Tu-16R (SRS-3)	?-12-1957	Scrapped
1883404	22 Red	Tu-16R (ZA)	?-12-1957	219th ODRAP/Sqn 2
1883405	05 Blue	Tu-16R (ZA) (SRS-3)	?-12-1957	219th ODRAP/Sqn 1. Siren'-D jammer (forward hemisphere), Siren'-MD jammer in UKhO fairing (rear hemisphere) added later, SPS-5 jammer
1883408	20 Red	Tu-16R (ZA)	?-12-1957	219th ODRAP
1883409	04 Red	Tu-16R (ZA) (SRS-3)	?-12-1957	'Excellent aircraft' badge
1883410	07 Red	Tu-16R (ZA) (SRS-1)	?-1-1958	SRS-4 SIGINT set retrofitted. Siren'-D jammer (forward hemisphere), Siren'-MD jammer in UKhO fairing (rear hemisphere), SPS-5 jammer

1883411	21	Tu-16RR (ZA)	?-1-1958	SRS-1/SRS-4 SIGINT sets
1883412	?	?	?-1-1958	Rogovitsa system; scrapped
1883414	?	Tu-16R (ZA)	?-1-1958	
1883415	?	Tu-16R (SRS-3)???	?-1-1958	Siren'-D jammer (forward hemisphere)
1883416	03	Tu-16Ye?	?-1-1958	Siren'-D jammer (forward hemisphere), SPS-5 jammer
1883418	26 Black	Tu-16R	?-1-1958	
Batch 35 (1883501 to 1883520, mfd February-March 1958)				
1883501	?	Tu-16R (ZA)	?-2-1958	
1883504	44?, 41 Red	Tu-16R (ZA) (SRS-3)	?-2-1958	SPS-5 jammer
1883506	26	?	?-2-1958	
1883508	14 Red	Tu-16R (ZA) (SRS-1)	?-2-1958	SRS-4 SIGINT set retrofitted; SPS-5 jammer
1883511	29 Red	Tu-16R (ZA)	?-3-1958	SRS-1/SRS-4 sets, SPS-100M jammer in tail fairing, R-832M radio. Became, see next line
	04 Red/04 Black			219th ODRAP/Sqn 1. Preserved Long-Range Aviation Museum, Dyagilevo AB, Ryazan'
1883512	?	Tu-16R	?-3-1958	
1883513	03 Red	Tu-16RM-2	?-3-1958	AVMF
Batch 36 (1883601 to 1883620, mfd March-May 1958)				
1883601	69 Red	Tu-16AFS	?-3-1958	Based Zhukovskiy; derelict by 8-1993, scrapped
1883606	?	Tu-16 Yolka	?-4-1958	Converted to, see next line
	29 Red	Tu-16P (ZA) 'Buket'		C/n not worn visibly
1883612	?	?	?-5-1958	† 14-11-1960
Batch 37 (1883701 to 1883720, mfd February-October 1959)				
1883701	18 Red (Russian AF)	Tu-16Ye	?-2-1959	GNIKI VVS. Siren'-D jammer (forward hemisphere, 'bone through the nose' version)
1883702	10 Red (Russian AF)	Tu-16Ye	?-2-1959	52nd GvTBAP. Siren'-D jammer (forward hemisphere), SPS-1 and SPS-4 jammers
1883704	08 Red (Russian AF)	Tu-16 Yolka	?-2-1959	99th GvORAP/Sqn 1. Named after Pyotr Ivanovich Gavrilov (HSU). Converted to, see next line
		Tu-16KRME		PVO/1076th SAM Systems Test Centre. Siren'-D jammer (forward hemisphere, 'bone through the nose' version)
1883705	?	Tu-16Ye	?-2-1959	
1883706	?	Tu-16Ye	?-3-1959	
1883707	?	Tu-16Ye	?-4-1959	
1883708	16 Red (Russian AF)	Tu-16Ye	?-4-1959	GNIKI VVS. Siren'-D jammer (forward hemisphere, 'bone through the nose' version)
1883709	?	Tu-16Ye	?-5-1958	
1883710	?	Tu-16Ye	?-5-1959	
1883711	10 Red (Russian AF)	Tu-16Ye	?-5-1959	GNIKI VVS. Siren'-D jammer (forward hemisphere, 'bone through the nose' version) plus ECM antennas near the engine nozzles
1883712	?	Tu-16Ye	?-5-1959	
1883713	?	Tu-16Ye	?-6-1959	
1883714	?	Tu-16K-10 (ZA)	?-9-1959	
1883715	?	Tu-16K-10 (ZA)	?-10-1959	
1883716	03 Blue	Tu-16K-10 (ZA)	?-9-1959	
1883717	?	Tu-16K-10 (ZA)	?-10-1959	
1883718	?	Tu-16K-10 (ZA)	?-9-1959	
1883719	?	Tu-16K-10 (ZA)	?-10-1959	
1883720	?	Tu-16K-10 (ZA)	?-10-1959	
Batch 38 (Tu-16K-10 (ZA)s, 1883801 to 1883820, mfd November 1959/February 1960)				
1883820	12 Red	Tu-16K-10 (ZA)	?-2-1960	
Batch 39 (Tu-16K-10 (ZA)s, 1883901 to 1883920, mfd January-April 1960)				
1883905	02 Red (Ukraine AF)	Tu-16K-10 (ZA)	?-7-1960	AVMF/33rd TsBP i PLS, Nikolayev. Converted to, see next line
		Tu-16K-10D		
1883915	05 Red (Ukraine AF)	Tu-16K-10 (ZA)	?-3-1960	AVMF/33rd TsBP i PLS?
Batch 40 (Tu-16K-10 (ZA)s, 1884001 to 1884012, mfd April-June 1960) – no aircraft identified				

4. Voronezh aircraft factory No.64

7.4.021.04 = year of manufacture 1957, plant No.64, Batch 021, 04th aircraft in the batch

Batch 0 (5400001 to 5400003, mfd April-July 1955)				
5400001	08	Tu-16	?-5-1955	Ground instructional airframe Achinsk VATU
Batch 1 (5400101 only, mfd December 1955) – aircraft not identified				
Batch 2 (5400201 to 5400205, mfd August-September 1955) – no aircraft identified				

Batch 3 (5400301 to 5400305, all except first aircraft Tu-16Ts, mfd September-October 1955) – no aircraft identified

Batch 4 (Tu-16Ts 5400401 to 5400405, mfd October-December 1955) – no aircraft identified

Batch 5 (Tu-16Ts 5400501 to 5400505, mfd November-December 1955) – no aircraft identified

Batch 6 (Tu-16Ts 5400601 to …400605, mfd December 1955/January 1956) – no aircraft identified [3]

Batch 7 (Tu-16Ts 6400701 to 6400705, mfd February 1956) – no aircraft identified

Batch 8 (Tu-16Ts 6400801 to 6400805, mfd February-March 1956) – no aircraft identified

Batch 9 (Tu-16Ts 6400901 to 6400905, mfd March-May 1956)

6400903	?	Tu-16T	?-3-1956	Converted to, see next line
	?	Tu-16P 'Buket'		Later retrofitted with 'Pilon' system (12 RPZ-59 rockets)

Batch 10 (Tu-16Ts 6401001 to 6401005, mfd May 1956)

6401002	16 Red	Tu-16T	?-5-1956	

Batch 11 (mostly Tu-16Ts, 6401101 to 6401105, mfd May-June 1956)

6401101	33 Red	Tu-16A?	?-5-1956	

Batch 12 (Tu-16Ts 6401201 to 6401210, mfd June-July 1956)

6401201	?	Tu-16	?-6-1956	† 11-12-1956
6401208	14 Red	Tu-16KSR-2-5?	?-7-1956	GNIKI VVS; converted to avionics testbed with trapezoidal aerials above/below centre fuselage (2 each) and on starboard side of nose

Batch 13 (mostly Tu-16Ts, 6401301 to 6401310, mfd July-August 1956)

6401309	09 Red	Tu-16T	?-8-1956	LII; to ?th TBAP, Skomorokhi AB. † 27-7-1958

Batch 14 (6401401 to 6401410, mfd August-October 1956)

6401401	01 Blue	Tu-16LL	?-8-1956	LII; WFU Zhukovskiy
6401404	04 Blue	Tu-16	?-9-1956	LII, testbed with spin recovery parachute
6401406	?	Tu-16	?-10-1956	WFU and transferred for repeat static tests
6401408	08 (Blue?)	Tu-16LL	?-10-1956	LII; fate unknown
6401410	41 Red	Tu-16LL	?-10-1956	LII; WFU Zhukovskiy

Batch 15 (mostly Tu-16Ts, 6401501 to 6401510, mfd October-December 1956)

6401501	01 Red	Tu-16LL	?-10-1956	LII; WFU Zhukovskiy
6401502	no code	Tu-16T?	?-10-1956	AVMF
6401503	32 Red	Tu-16T	?-10-1956	
6401504	54 Blue	Tu-16T	?-12-1956	AVMF/Pacific Fleet, 49th MRAP, Vladivostok-Knevichi AP
6401505	?	Tu-16T	?-10-1956	

Batch 16 (6401601 to 6401610, mfd November-December 1956)

6401602	?	Tu-16	?-11-1955	† 10-6-1957 or 30-5-1957
6401607	10 Red	Tu-16RT	?-12-1956	
6401610	24 Red	Tu-16	?-12-1956	

Batch 17 (Tu-16Ts 6401701 to 6401705 and 7401706 to 7401710, mfd December 1956/February 1957)

7401706	21	Tu-16T	?-12-1956	Converted to, see next line
	?	Tu-16P 'Buket'		SPS-22N jammer
7401707	?	Tu-16T	?-12-1956	

Batch 18 (7401801 to 7401810, mfd February-March 1957) – no aircraft identified

Batch 19 (7401901 to 7401910, mfd March-May 1957)

7401903		?	?-4-1957	568th MTAP, Mongokhto AB † 29-1-1958

Batch 20 (Tu-16 (ZA)s 7402001 to 7402012, mfd May-August 1957) – no aircraft identified

Batch 21 (7402101 to 7402110, mfd August-October 1957)

7402011	?	?	?-8-1957	† 3-7-1959
7402101	44	Tu-16Z	?-9-1957	
7402104	35 Blue	?	?-9-1957	

Batch 22 (7402201 to 7402210, mfd October-December 1957)

7402209	48 Blue	?	?-12-1957	AVMF/Pacific Fleet, 367th MRAP/Sqn 3, Vladivostok-Knevichi AP, 1988

Notes:

1. RIIGA = *Rizhskiy institoot inzhenerov grazhdahnskoy aviahtsiï* – Riga Civil Aviation Engineers Institute; KIIGA = *Kiyevskiy institoot inzhenerov grazhdahnskoy aviahtsiï* – Kiev Civil Aviation Engineers Institute; IVATU = *Irkootskoye voyennoye aviatsionno-tekhnicheskoye oochilishche* – Irkutsk Military Aviation Technical Staff College; NISO = *Naoochnyy institoot spetsiahl'novo oboroodovaniya* – Special Equipment Research Institute

2. Unfortunately no information is available as to the nature of the 'order 476' conversion job

3. Despite the fact that the aircraft were accepted by the military in early 1957, they could still have c/ns commencing 6

Appendix 2

Tu-16 accident attrition

Unfortunately the Tu-16 has suffered heavy accident attrition during the course of its 40-year service career. As mentioned earlier, no fewer than 122 aircraft were lost in fatal and non-fatal accidents; this amounts to just over 8% of the flyable Tu-16s built. The accident rate was particularly high in 1957-60 when about ten machines were lost each year, which was due both to the learning curve and to the *Badger*'s teething troubles. Then the accident rate fell sharply; in the 1960s and 1970s the average annual attrition was one or two. The causes varied; some Tu-16s crashed due to critical hardware failures, while other accidents were caused by the tell-tale human factor – pilot error or the faulty actions of ground personnel. Some aircraft were lost by sheer bad luck.

Some of the accidents are listed below in chronological order; far from all have been included due to space limitations. Unfortunately in many cases no details are known (except if the accident was fatal or not). Combat losses are not included here.

• The first loss of an operational Tu-16 occurred even before the type's official service entry. On 6th April 1954, a 45th TBAD/402nd TBAP Tu-16 (c/n 4200202) dived into the ground near Kazeki village not far from its home base (Bolbasovo AB) due to spontaneous deflection of the elevator trim tab, killing the crew of six captained by Col. V. Ya. Shurookhin.

• As mentioned earlier, on 28th September 1954, the first pre-production Kuibyshev-built Tu-16 (c/n 1880001) stalled and flicked into a spin while making a test flight from Kuibyshev-Bezymyanka for the purpose of determining the machine's G limits. When recovery appeared impossible, part of the crew ejected, the aircraft's captain Lt.-Col. Gheorgiy S. Molchanov and GRO V. D. Kalachov losing their lives; co-pilot Maj. Aleksandr I. Kazakov managed a recovery to straight and level flight and brought the aircraft back to base, landing safely. The bomber stood up to the abuse and, after examination, was returned to flight status.

• On 30th January 1955, the nose gear unit of Tu-16 c/n 4201302 collapsed on landing at the GK NII VVS airfield in Akhtoobinsk.

• On 15th February 1955, Tu-16A c/n 4200804 suffered an uncontained failure of the starboard AM-3 engine as the latter was being ground-run. The ensuing fire destroyed the aircraft completely; the crew escaped unhurt.

• That same day another Tu-16A (c/n 4201109), apparently from the 326th TBAD/132nd TBAP, crashed fatally at Tartu.

• On 19th August 1955, a 13th GvTBAD Tu-16 serialled '76' (c/n 1880802) crashed fatally at Poltava AB when the AP-5-2M autopilot failed.

• On 18th January 1956, a brand-new Tu-16A (c/n 6202917) took off from Kazan'-Borisoglebskoye at 0904 hrs local time on a pre-delivery test flight to the GK NII VVS test range at Vladimirovka AB which involved bombing, gunnery and checks of the radio and radar equipment. Eleven minutes later the bomber dived into the ground near Koshchakovo village, killing the crew – captain Leonid A. Cherkasov, co-pilot Mir'yaf Yu. Chavkin, navigator/bomb-aimer V. I. Aristov, Nav/Op B. A. Vasil'yev, GRO G. V. Ryzhkevich and tail gunner M. Ye. Klyukin. For four days it was impossible to approach

the crash site because of the exploding ammunition and the burning fuel. The aircraft had dug a crater 6 m (19 ft) deep measuring 42 x 14 m (137 x 46 ft); most of the wreckage was within a 250-m (820-ft) radius, and some fragments were found 3 km (1.86 miles) away. Bits and pieces of the wreckage had been looted by the local populace who believed they might come in handy, and they would not turn in the loot until KGB agents threatened them with prosecution.

The cause of the crash was not determined because the aircraft was totally destroyed and there had been no distress call. Eyewitnesses said the aircraft was not burning or disintegrating in mid-air when it fell out of the clouds with strong right bank. Engine failure or control system failure was ruled out after examination of the wreckage. The most likely cause was loss of attitude awareness in the clouds – possibly due to a partial failure of the artificial horizon. That day the cloudbase was at 250 m and horizontal visibility was no more than 4 km (2.5 miles), and the crew's lack of experience in IMC flying was a contributing factor. So was poor crew resources management – Cherkasov, who was originally to be the co-pilot, acted as a stand-in for the 'proper' captain Pyotr S. Yakovlev, who had failed to show up; in turn, the young pilot Chavkin subbed for Cherkasov, and the two had not flown together before.

• On 2nd February 1956, an almost new Tu-16A (c/n 5202310) was written off in a non-fatal accident when an air filter in the front pressure cabin caught fire due to an excessive oxygen content in the cabin air. Some of the crew members suffered burns and injuries.

• Eight days later a 200th TBAP Tu-16A coded '14 Red' (c/n 5202908) was likewise lost in a non-fatal accident.

• On 17th April 1956, a 184th GvTBAP Tu-16A (c/n 5202703) captained by Capt. N. Yu. Voytetskiy crash-landed at its home base of Priluki after a night proficiency check flight. When the pilot made an error and the machine touched down 8 m (26 ft) short of the runway, the main gear bogies striking the raised runway threshold, the forward fuselage failed at frames 18-20, the flight deck section breaking away; GRO V. P. Belkin lost his life. The cause was the insufficient structural strength that affected the early-production Tu-16s.

• In June 1956, a Tu-16P ECM aircraft from the 185th GvTBAP was lost in a fatal crash.

• One more Tu-16A (c/n 6203120) belonging to the 840th TBAP was written off in a crash landing at Sol'tsy AB on 6th July 1956 when the forward fuselage failed, the flight deck section breaking away. luckily the entire crew captained by 840th TBAP CO Col. Gheorgiy G. Agamirov was unhurt.

• On 26th June 1956, a 185th GvTBAP Tu-16A (c/n 5202808) was flying a training sortie from Poltava. At 10,000 m (32,810 ft) the bomber ran into a storm front; both engines flamed out and the aircraft crashed, killing the crew of six captained by Maj. Bondarenko.

• An uncanny repetition of Voytetskiy's accident occurred on 15th July (some sources say 13th July) 1956, when a 185th GvTBAP Tu-16A crash-landed at Poltava. Again, the aircraft undershot and hit the elevated runway threshold, the fuselage breaking at frame 20. Co-pilot Lt. Tsaryov and GRO Pvt Sinitsyn lost their lives.

• On 26th July 1956, the DA lost another Tu-16A, a 260th TBAP aircraft from Stryy (c/n 6203010).

• The first loss of a Kuibyshev-built *Badger* was on 6th October 1956, when Tu-16 c/n 1882309 crashed fatally. Apparently this aircraft was one of two Tu-16s involved in an IFR operation (either the Tu-16Z tanker or the receiver aircraft). In the midst of the operation the tanker's hose snagged the other aircraft's port aileron, causing the machine to roll uncontrollably and collide with the tanker. Both crews were killed.

• The first loss of a Voronezh-built Tu-16 (c/n 6401201) occurred on 11th December 1956 – also a fatal accident.

• On 23rd December 1956, a 341st TBAP Tu-16 captained by Maj. Lomiya and co-piloted by 15th TBAD Deputy CO Col. Yakov A. Shashlov (HSU) as instructor crashed during a night sortie in poor weather, killing the crew. The cause was apparently controlled flight into terrain (CFIT).

• On 10th January 1957, Tu-16A c/n 5202301 was lost in a fatal crash.

• Some sources report that Tu-16A c/n 5202901 crashed fatally on 3rd February 1957.

• On 25th February 1957, the 444th TBAP at Vozdvizhenka AB lost Tu-16A c/n 6203212 in a fatal crash.

• On 2nd March 1957, a 260th TBAP Tu-16A (c/n 6203020) was returning to Stryy AB after a night training sortie in IMC when it entered heavy overcast. Knowing there were mountains ahead, the captain executed an excessively sharp manoeuvre, causing the aircraft to lose control and crash with 90° right bank, killing the crew. The accident date was also reported in error as 21st March 1957.

• On 30th May 1957, Tu-16A c/n 6401602 captained by Maj. A. S. Loychikov was making a flight along a predetermined route as part of a 36-strong group of bombers flying in line astern formation with a horizontal separation of 1 km (0.62 miles). As the aircraft approached Groznyy, Chechen-Ingush ASSR, it entered storm clouds when descending from the cruise altitude of 11,300 m (37,070 ft). The starboard engine flamed out in turbulence and the bomber lost control, entering a flat spin from which the pilots could not recover due to disorientation in the clouds. Two of the crewmembers managed to eject; the other four were killed when the aircraft slammed into the ground. Some sources, though, give a different date for this accident (10th June 1957).

• On 25th June 1957, Tu-16A c/n 1882713 was lost in a fatal crash.

• On 4th July 1957, the 402nd TBAP lost another *Badger* when Tu-16A c/n 6203114 crashed immediately after take-off from runway 23 at Bolbasovo AB, having climbed to 20-25 m (65-82 ft). All six crew members were killed and the aircraft destroyed three houses in Len'kovichi village located 2 km (1.24 miles) south-west of the base as it fell. The original theory was single-engine failure compounded by crew error, but this was not substantiated later

• Tu-16 c/n 1881209 crashed fatally on 15th July 1957.

• Tu-16 c/n 7203603 crashed fatally on 10th August 1957.

• A week later the 184th GvTBAP lost two *Badgers* in a single day – Tu-16A c/n 5201605 and Tu-16Z c/n 1882213. This was not a mid-air collision during aerial refuelling – the aircraft crashed independently in identical circumstances, stalling in severe turbulence while trying to 'jump over' a storm front into which they had been mistakenly directed by an inept ATC officer. Both crews were killed.

• A 840th TBAP Tu-16A from Sol'tsy AB (c/n 6203204) crashed on 24th August 1957, after losing control in storm turbulence, killing the crew of six. The aircraft, which was one of four *Badgers* flying a sortie nears Lodeynoye Pol'e (Leningrad Region), entered the storm clouds at 11,500 m (37,730 ft); the cloud top was at 12,000 m (39,370 ft) and the cloudbase at only 135 m (440 ft)!

• Two *Badgers* were lost in isolated accidents (both of them fatal) on 31st August 1957. The first aircraft was an Air Force (444th TBAP) bomber (c/n 6203306). The other aircraft was an AVMF/Black Sea Fleet machine from the 88th MTAD DD/5th GvMTAP DD at Gvardeyskoe AB which crashed near Anapa on the Crimea Peninsula.

• Tu-16A c/n 5202905 crashed fatally on 28th September 1957.

Right and above right: This Tu-16 coded '25 Blue' overran on landing at Mirgorod, collapsing the landing gear. The crew used the dorsal hatches to exit the aircraft.

• The most unusual loss of a *Badger* in 1957 was Tu-16 c/n 1882914 which was accidentally shot down by a Soviet Air Defence Force MiG-19 interceptor in a 'friendly fire' incident. A different account says this was not a shootdown but a mid-air collision between a 477th OAP RTR Tu-16R ELINT aircraft captained by Maj. Bokhantsev and a MiG-15 fighter 50 km (31 miles) from Mirgorod. Only the navigator ejected and survived.

• On 29th January 1958, an AVMF/Pacific Fleet Tu-16 (c/n 7401903) from the 568th MTAP crashed near its home base of Mongokhto AB. The aircraft was posing as an intruder for a practice intercept by MiG-19 fighters from a PVO unit. After the practice attack one of the MiG-19s came within close range of the *Badger*, allegedly for the purpose of escorting it. Afterwards the fighter pilot reported that the Tu-16 suddenly yawed and entered a descending spiral with increasing bank until it collided with the ground; none of the six crew survived. The weather was clear, with no turbulence that might have been considered as a cause.

• Another AVMF Tu-16, a Baltic Fleet machine (c/n 7203423), crashed near Ostrov AB on 12th February 1958, killing the crew.

• On 20th February 1958, a Tu-16A coded '76 Black' (c/n 1880602) and operated by the 43rd TsBP i PLS crashed fatally shortly after taking off from Dyagilevo AB, its home base. The cause was traced to loss of control due to failure of a push-pull rod in the elevator control circuit. Only the GRO and the tail gunner, both in the rank of private, survived; the tail gunner had the curiously Finnish-sounding name of Urho O. Tuomi, being a native of the Karelian ASSR – a region that used to be part of Finland.

• Tu-16 c/n 6203324 was lost in a fatal crash on 16th March 1958.

• Tu-16A c/n 5202911 crashed on 10th April 1958, killing the crew of six. The cause was a defective fuel line which had become disconnected in flight, causing the engines to quit.

• As recounted in Chapter 7, on 26th April 1958, a 52nd GvTBAP Tu-16A coded '04 Red' and captained by Col. Anton A. Alekhnovich was damaged in a collision with an Aeroflot/Polar Aviation Il-14T transport on the runway of the drifting ice station SP-6. When repairing it on site proved impossible, the aircraft was eventually destroyed on 16th April 1959 to prevent capture.

The tail of Tu-16K-10 '01 Blue' which crashed in the Soviet Far East on 28th July 1963.

• On 29th May 1958, Tu-16A c/n 6203316 crashed fatally near Skomorokhi AB.

• Tu-16 c/n 7204002 was lost in a fatal crash on 5th June 1958.

• On 13th June 1958, an AVMF/North Fleet Tu-16R captained by Capt. V. I. Volkov was making a test flight from Chkalovskaya AB where it was undergoing check-up tests at GK NII VVS. When the weather began deteriorating the ATC officer ordered the captain to abort the mission and return to base. When the aircraft turned onto finals for runway 12, approaching the base from the nearby town of Shcholkovo, the rain intensified from a drizzle to a downpour and horizontal visibility diminished to 50 m (164 ft). This was way below Volkov's rated weather minima, which were a cloudbase of 500 m (1,640 ft) and a horizontal visibility of 5 km (3.1 miles). The crew attempted an ILS approach but the aircraft descended below glide path and struck the rooftops of Khotovo village before crashing in an open field beyond. In addition to the crew of six, eight people on the ground were killed in their homes. The commanders of GK NII VVS had to take the rap for the accident.

• On 27th July 1958, Tu-16T '09 Red' (c/n 6401309) crashed fatally near Skomorokhi AB.

• On 2nd August 1958, a Tu-16 operated by one of the Long-Range Aviation units suffered structural failure at an altitude of some 400 m (1,310 ft), the starboard flap breaking away as the bomber turned onto finals. The result was inevitably an irrecoverable departure; rolling to the right, the aircraft impacted with 45° bank in a forest and exploded, killing the crew of six.

• On 12th September 1958, a 56th TBAD Tu-16 (c/n 1882809) operated by the 45th TBAP or 173rd TBAP took off from runway 25 at Migalovo AB. Immediately after passing the inner marker beacon for the reciprocal heading (runway 07) at an altitude of 60-80 m (200-260 ft) the aircraft rolled to port and started losing altitude, crashing and burning in a forest some 1.5 km (0.9 miles) beyond the runway. All six crewmen lost their lives.

• On 13th October 1958, another Kuibyshev-built Tu-16 (c/n 1883218) was lost in a crash somewhere in the Soviet Far East. As it descended from its cruise altitude of 11,000 m (36,090 ft), the aircraft started banking of its own accord. The pilots managed to restore a wings-level attitude, but not for long; going out of control, the aircraft crashed into the ground in a 70-80° dive. Again, there were no survivors.

• According to some sources, two Tu-16s (c/ns 5201902 and 1881102) crashed fatally on 23rd December 1958, though this is unconfirmed.

• Sometime in 1958, a Soviet Air Force Tu-16 was to fly a sortie over northern China from Ookraïnka AB in the Soviet Far East, posing as an intruder for the purpose of training PLAAF fighter pilots (the Soviet Union was then on good terms with China, which made such co-operation in military matters possible). However, the port engine failed when the aircraft was on the point of rotation during the take-off run; the take-off was aborted but the bomber overran the runway, ending up in a swamp and collapsing the nose gear unit. A fuel tank ruptured and a fire ensued; luckily the crew managed to exit the aircraft before it was engulfed.

• According to an unconfirmed report, Tu-16 c/n 7203510 crashed fatally on 13th January 1959.

• Exactly two months later, on 13th March, Tu-16 c/n 1881901 was lost in a fatal crash.

• Again, two months later, on 13th May 1959, a 402nd TBAP Tu-16 crashed at Bolbasovo AB during a training sortie, killing the crew (Capt. N. N. Foorgaïlo, Lt. P. Ye. Pan'kov, Lt. V. F. Bibikov, Lt (SG) G. N. Krivosheyin, Lt. P. F. Golubev, W/O N. A. Chivilyov and SSgt N. G. Khodosevich. Golubev was not a member of the flight crew but a technician who was aboard for some reason.

• Two Tu-16s (c/ns 1882311 and 7402011) were lost on 3rd July 1959 – probably as a result of a mid-air collision; there were fatalities in both crews.

• A week later, on 10th July 1959, a 132nd TBAP Tu-16 captained by Maj. Kovalenko crashed on take-off at Tartu, its home base. The co-pilot, navigator/bomb-aimer and Nav/Op ejected and survived; the captain and the occupants of the rear cabin were killed.

• Tu-16 c/n 8204211 was lost in a fatal crash on 10th October 1959.

• Four days later a 251st GvTBAP Tu-16 (c/n 1882504) captained by Maj. I. T. Khizhnyak crashed near Belaya Tserkov' AB, killing the entire crew, when the aileron control linkage became disconnected, rendering the bomber uncontrollable.

• On 11th November 1959, a 402nd TBAP Tu-16 (c/n 1881004) crashed when an elevator bellcrank broke and the aircraft became uncontrollable; again, the entire crew perished. The accident date was also reported as 8th December 1959.

• Two Tu-16s from the 184th GvTBAP at Priluki crashed during IFR operations sometime in 1959; there were no survivors in either crew. It is not known if this was an accident involving the tanker and the receiver or two isolated accidents on different dates.

• Also at an unspecified date in 1959, a Tu-16 from the 226th TBAP was similarly lost with all hands in an in-flight refuelling accident.

• On 27th February 1960, a 1229th TBAP/Sqn 2 Tu-16 captained by V. V. Chernykh was making a check flight from Belaya AB after maintenance of the elevator trim tabs. On take-off from runway 15 the aircraft proved reluctant to rotate, the pilots experiencing higher-than-usual forces on the control yokes. The captain deflected the elevator trim tabs all the way but this only made matters worse, the elevator control force reaching 300 kgf (660 lbf), and the aircraft only barely managed to become airborne. Climbing to 70 m (230 ft), it crossed the rivers Belaya and Angara before colliding with a hill; the rear fuselage broke away, whereupon the aircraft pitched up, briefly becoming airborne again, then fell and exploded. The explosion tore off the flight deck section which was propelled forward about 100 m (330 ft). The captain, co-pilot N. Petrooshin and navigator/bomb-aimer D. F. Kanzyuda were killed; Nav/Op O. V. Selivanov, GRO V. Perepyolkin and tail gunner I. Stoopin survived with injuries.

• On 2nd March 1960, a 185th GvTBAP Tu-16 captained by Capt. A. A. Chernysh made a go-around after landing approach on a training sortie. After retracting the landing gear the captain allowed the forward speed to decay to 360 km/h (223 mph) at an altitude of 9,400 m (30,840 ft), whereupon the bomber pitched up into a stalled attitude and flicked into a spin. All spin recovery attempts proved futile; when the captain ordered an ejection only

The remains of a 185th GvTBAP Tu-16A (c/n 5202808) which crashed on 26th June 1956.

the co-pilot, the GRO and the tail gunner managed to eject, the other three crew members losing their lives when the aircraft impacted in a wings-level attitude and exploded.

• On 28th April 1960, pilot Starostenko, a cadet of the LII Test Pilots School (ShLI – *Shkola lyotchikov-ispytahteley*), messed up a landing at Zhukovskiy in an 8-m/sec (16-kt) crosswind. The Tu-16 ran off the side of the runway and collided with a pile of frozen peat; navigator/bomb-aimer Milov was killed outright and the aircraft was a total loss.

• On 8th August 1960, Tu-16 c/n 7203626 was lost in a fatal crash. (It is possible that the report has got the year wrong and the correct date is 8th August 1961!)

• On 5th November 1960, two Tu-16s were lost in isolated fatal accidents. One was Tu-16KS c/n 8204023 (tail number 8192). The other aircraft was a Tu-16R (c/n 8204201) operated by the 290th GvODRAP which crashed at its home base of Zyabrovka AB.

• On 14th November 1960, a 303rd TBAP Tu-16 (c/n 1883612) captained by Capt. G. M. Roodkov was coming in to land at Khorol' AB. When communicating with the crew the ATC officer supplied them with an erroneous QNH (barometric pressure above

The starboard wing of a Tu-16 lucky enough to land in one piece after colliding with trees at low altitude.

sea level) value, which the crew duly set on the altimeter, causing it to give incorrect readings. As a result, the aircraft flew lower than it should. After making the turn onto the base leg of the landing pattern the bomber collided with a hill rising 433 m (1,420 ft) above the airfield level; there were no survivors.

• On 23rd January 1961, a 341st TBAP Tu-16 captained by Capt. L. V. Bykov was making a night landing approach to Ozyornoye AB in IMC; the captain lacked the proper training for the existing weather minima. Bykov messed up the first approach and made a go-around; in so doing he executed turns with large bank angles, causing the aircraft to lose altitude. The Tu-16 collided with the ground 450 m (1,476 ft) beyond the outer marker beacon, killing four of the six crew.

• Two days later a Tu-16 captained by Capt. V. Ya. Chaika was to make practice circuits of the airfield at night in IMC. Immediately after take-off the aircraft unexpectedly started descending after climbing to only 100 m (330 ft); the bomber impacted 1.8 km (1.12 miles) beyond the runway and burst into flames. The GRO and tail gunner managed to exit the aircraft and rescue the captain; the other crew members perished.

• On 8th August 1961, a 52nd GvTBAP Tu-16 captained by Lt (SG) Kazantsev was lost in a fatal crash.

• On 2nd October 1961, another 303rd TBAP Tu-16 captained by Capt. B. N. Sokolov topped up its fuel tanks from a Tu-16Z over the sea. After receiving 4,000 litres (880 Imp gal) of fuel and breaking contact normally the aircraft inexplicably rolled right 70-80° and dived vertically into the sea, taking its crew with it.

• A month later a 402nd TBAP Tu-16 captained by Capt. N. V. Laskaryov was taking off from Bolbasovo AB at night. Apparently the climb angle was too small; shortly after take-off the aircraft began losing altitude and crashed 1.9 km (1.18 miles) beyond the runway. There were no survivors among the six crew.

• On 20th June 1961, Tu-16K-10 (ZA) c/n 1511012 (f/n 51-01) was to make contact with a Tu-16Z tanker over the Kirov Region of Russia during a test flight from Kazan'-Borisoglebskoye. After two failed attempts the captain, Kazan' factory test pilot Col. Anvar I. Karimov, decided to abort the mission, citing crew fatigue as the reason. Yet the tanker's captain Amir Kh. Karimov, another Kazan' factory test pilot, persuaded him to make one more attempt. On the third try Anvar Karimov placed his port wingtip on the hose too sharply and the hose formed a loop, snagging the port aileron and sending the aircraft plummeting to the ground in a steep left-hand spiral. The co-pilot, V. A. Sviridov, managed to eject but was struck by the horizontal tail immediately afterwards, losing his legs and his life; the rest of the crew (Anvar I. Karimov, V. S. Demidov, A. I. Vorob'yov, G. A. Bad'yanov and I. D. Stolyarov) could not eject because of the high G loads. Investigation of the accident showed that the tanker's hose supplied by the Kuibyshev factory was substandard, not having passed quality control, which is why it folded all too easily.

• On 29th January 1962, a 182nd GvTBAP Tu-16 captained by Maj. Sh. T. Shugayev (the commander of one of the regiment's squadrons) was returning to Nezhin after a night flight along a predetermined route. The approach to the base was obscured by low clouds, and the crew let the aircraft drop below the glideslope on final approach. The bomber ran out of altitude between the

outer and inner marker beacons; only one of the six crewmembers survived.

• On 11th April 1962, another 182nd GvTBAP Tu-16 captained by Capt. K. V. Sevast'yanov was cruising at 11,000 m (36,090 ft) as part of a bomber formation. Realising he was catching up on the aircraft ahead, the captain throttled back the engines – and apparently overdid it, causing the aircraft to lose speed and stall. As the Tu-16 entered a spin, Sevast'yanov ordered the crew to eject. The co-pilot, navigator, Nav/Op and GRO did it successfully but the tail gunner ejected too late and was killed. The captain stayed with the aircraft, trying to the last to recover from the spin, but the Tu-16 hit the ground before he could manage it.

• On 27th April 1962, a Tu-16 captained by Lt.-Col. D. K. Ustyshkin undershot on landing and struck the elevated runway threshold, overstressing the fuselage which broke at frame 26. As the flight deck section separated, the throttle control cables went taut and the engines went to full power; the 'headless' aircraft pitched up and lifted off, flying 500 m (1,640 ft) before crashing from an altitude of 25-30 m (80-100 ft). The tail gunner (W/O Pavlov) was killed when his ejection seat fired him into the ground; the other crewmembers survived, sustaining injuries.

• On 15th August 1962, a 52nd GvTBAP Tu-16 captained by Maj. Ye. G. Maksimov collided with a sister ship captained by Capt. M. G. Karimov when flying in too close formation. Both aircraft crashed, all 12 crewmembers losing their lives.

• Another mid-air collision with fatal results for the crews occurred on 25th August 1962, when two AVMF/Pacific Fleet Tu-16 missile carriers of the 183rd MRAP (one of them captained by Lt.-Col. Antipin) were making a flypast over the Amur Bay in Vladivostok as part of the Soviet Navy Day celebrations. The crews lost sight of each other when the *Badgers* entered heavy cloud over Roosskiy Island.

• On 14th January 1963, a pair of 303rd TBAP Tu-16s was flying in echelon starboard formation at night at 9,300-9,600 m (30,510-31,500 ft). Suddenly the wingman switched to echelon port formation and then dived into the ground, killing the crew headed by Maj. D. F. Popko.

• The next day (some sources say 16th January 1963) a 1229th TBAP Tu-16 captained by regiment CO Maj. D. G. Shakhov rolled to port immediately after becoming airborne at Belaya AB, clipped the ground with the port wingtip and crashed, killing the crew. The cause was traced to the aileron trim tab drive motor whose power supply had been cross-wired to the wrong contacts.

• On 13th June 1963, a 226th TBAP Tu-16 returning to Poltava AB from a practice bombing sortie at night mistakenly descended to 200 m (660 ft) instead of the 1,200 m (3,940 ft) required in the airfield circuit. The weather was good but the pilots had closed the flight deck blinds for a simulated IMC approach. The aircraft collided with the ground 17 km (10.5 miles) from the runway, killing the crew headed by Capt. M. V. Zinov'yev.

• On 28th July 1963, a Pacific Fleet Tu-16K-10 coded '01 Blue' (c/n 2733045, f/n 7304) collided with high ground on approach to Khorol' AB.

• On 17th January 1964, a 173rd TBAP Tu-16 captained by Capt. V. N. Koginov was making a maximum gross weight take-off from Migalovo AB. On rotation the captain hauled back on the yoke too hard, causing overrotation; immediately after becoming airborne the bomber rolled to the port and crashed inverted. Four of the crew perished.

• On 19th February 1964, a Tu-16R of the 219th ODRAP captained by Capt. I. L. Cherednikov crashed when the captain accidentally deployed the flaps at excessive speed after take-off, causing them to fail catastrophically. All seven occupants were killed; there are claims that one of them was an illegal female passenger who had been given a joyride!

• On 15th July 1964, an AVMF/Pacific Fleet Tu-16R captained by Maj. L. Kozharin crashed into the Sea of Japan immediately after the crew reported sighting an American carrier group 200 km (124 miles) east of the Japanese coast. There were no survivors among the crew of seven.

• On 29th January 1965, a 200th TBAP Tu-16 captained by Capt. Yu. M. Oovarov was making a maximum gross weight take-off from a dirt airstrip at an auxiliary airfield. Immediately after lift-off the aircraft pitched up sharply and rolled, crashing 450 m (1,480 ft) from the unstick point with 60-70° left bank. The two gunners in the rear cabin survived, the other four crewmen perishing.

• Three months later, on 29th April, an AVMF/Pacific Fleet Tu-16 was flying a night weather reconnaissance sortie from Mongokhto AB. A group of Tu-16s departed the base on a regular sortie later, but on the way back Mongokhto shut down because of bad weather and the *Badgers* were ordered to land at Khorol' AB which was the alternate airfield. The weather recce aircraft took a different route to Khorol', approaching later than the leader of the main group; the ATC officer mistook the latter's blip on the radarscope for the weather recce aircraft, authorising the latter to descend. Its crew did not sense anything amiss because the ADF was behaving as it should in a normal approach. As a result, the Tu-16 hit a hillside, killing captain Maj. Ye. Tikhonov, co-pilot Lt (SG) Berestenko, navigator Capt. Yusupov, Nav/Op Lt.-Col. Kravtsov, GRO seaman Shul'ga and tail gunner W/O Shchadenko.

• On 27th May 1965, a 260th TBAP Tu-16 captained by regiment CO Col. N. I. Fomin ran into a swath of dense fog during a night approach to Stryy AB. Trying to switch off the landing lights which were creating a 'reflection screen', the captain involuntarily increased the sink rate to 14-15 m/sec (2,755-2,950 ft/min); dropping below the glideslope, the bomber clipped some trees and came down in the middle of the runway's approach lights. There were no fatalities but the aircraft was totalled.

• In December 1965, the crew of a Baltic Fleet/57th MRAD Tu-16 misread the altimeter reading during a night approach to Bykhov AB and judged the altitude to be 1,000 m (3,280 ft) greater than it was. The result was CFIT; only the tail gunner survived.

• On 3rd August 1966, a 132nd TBAP Tu-16 captained by Capt. S. V. Denisyuk suffered a catastrophic structural failure on landing at Zheludok auxiliary airfield. The flight deck section broke away when the fuselage failed at frames 22-26; the rest of the airframe zoomed to an altitude of 20-25 m (65-80 ft), stalled and crashed 590 m (1,935 ft) from the touchdown point. The navigator, GRO and tail gunner were killed; the pilots and the Nav/Op survived.

• On 3rd March 1967, a 185th GvTBAP Tu-16 diverting to Priluki (because Poltava had shut down due to bad weather) was forced to make a go-around when the weather at Priluki turned foul as well. In so doing the aircraft lost altitude and struck the outer marker beacon building with its starboard main gear bogie and flaps, suffering damage to the latter; this caused it to roll to starboard and dive into the ground from an altitude of 100 m (330 ft). The crew headed by Capt. L. P. Pasynkov was killed.

• On 27th June 1967, a pair of Tu-16Ps from Mirgorod captained by Maj. V. P. Shoomkov (lead aircraft) and Lt (SG) I. A. Vinogradov (wingman) were flying a special sortie from Vladimirovka AB over the GNIKI VVS test range in Akhtoobinsk, setting up ECM for fighters. On the way back to Vladimirovka AB the pilots of the lead aircraft saw a fighter ahead on a collision course. Without warning the leader performed an evasive manoeuvre, losing speed and causing the wingman to collide with it. Only two of the 12 men aboard the two aircraft survived when they were thrown clear of the disintegrating aircraft, their parachutes opening automatically.

• On 25th May 1968, another naval Tu-16R captained by Col. Pliyev was lost near Newfoundland after overflying a US Navy CTF led by the aircraft carrier USS *Essex*. There was suspicion that the aircraft had been shot down by the US Navy air defences, but this allegation was refuted by the Americans. Wreckage of the aircraft collected during the ensuing SAR operation was transferred to the Soviet Navy/Baltic Fleet ASW destroyer SNS *Kazanets* (hull number 311).

• On 15th July 1968, a North Fleet/924th MRAP Tu-16 missile carrier crashed into mountains on the Kola Peninsula about 50 km (31 miles) from its home base, Olen'ya AB. The crew of six was killed.

• On 4th October 1968, a 185th TBAP Tu-16 captained by Capt. V. P. Yashchukov was making a positioning flight from Priluki to Poltava. After entering clouds the aircraft started climbing and descending erratically, eventually colliding with the ground. The only survivor was the tail gunner who ejected on his own at 1,200 m (3,940 ft) after sensing that something was wrong.

• On 14th April 1970, a Tu-16 operated by the 43rd TsBP i PLS took off from Dyagilevo AB, making a circuit of the field; it was flown by trainee pilot Lt (SG) A. F. Mel'gunov and QFI Maj. Novosyolov. The cloudbase was at 500 m (1,640 ft) and the cloud top at 1,400 m (4,590 ft). After climbing to 700 m (2,300 ft) and turning onto the downwind leg of the circuit the aircraft unexpectedly entered a dive with negative G and hit the ground in a 60° nose-down attitude with a speed of 720 km/h (447 mph), killing the crew. Eyewitness accounts say the aircraft was on fire when it fell out of the clouds; thus, the crash was apparently caused by hardware failure.

• Ten days later a Tu-16 being ferried from Shaikovka AB to Vladivostok-Knevichi airport went missing over Siberia. The last thing the crew reported before radio contact was lost was that they were observing a UFO... No aircraft or wreckage was ever found.

• On 1st February 1971, a Tu-16LL engine testbed operated by LII crashed on landing approach due to a malfunction of the flaps, killing the test crew captained by Sultan Amet-Khan.

• Another Tu-16LL engine testbed was lost on 15th April 1971, when the development engine caught fire. The test crew captained by Sergey N. Anokhin ejected.

• On 19th September 1971, a 444th TBAP Tu-16 captained by Maj. Ye. G. Tatarchuk crashed in the Sea of Okhotsk off Sakhalin Island when operating as part of a group. The cause of the crash was an incorrect QNH setting on the altimeter which led the pilots to descend too low in the darkness; the aircraft struck the water with the port wing while making a steep turn.

• In May 1973, a Black Sea Fleet/124th MRAP Tu-16 crashed on approach to Gvardeiskoye AB due to a faulty artificial horizon.

• On 4th November 1973, a North Fleet/967th ODRAP Tu-16R captained by Lt.-Col. A. P. Sviridov was flying a sortie over the Norwegian Sea in search of a US Navy CTF led by the carrier USS *John F. Kennedy*. When the *Badger* approached the CTF at 100 m (330 ft), a McDonnell Douglas F-4 Phantom II fighter launched from the carrier to intercept it. The fighter pilot favoured a 'wait until you can see the whites of their eyes' tactic – the F-4 manoeuvred dangerously, approaching within 4-6 m (13-20 ft) of the Tu-16R. Eventually, positioning himself under the *Badger*'s starboard wing, the pilot gunned the throttles and pitched the fighter up, apparently trying to intimidate the Soviet crew. However, he misjudged the manoeuvre and the F-4 struck the Tu-16 with its fin, damaging the wing skin. Unable to land normally on the carrier, the Phantom had to make a forced landing in Norway; the Tu-16R also managed to return to Severomorsk-3 AB, despite the danger of fire and explosion. For this sortie Sviridov was awarded the Order of the Red Banner of Combat.

• On 14th May 1974, Tu-16 '12 Red' (c/n 5201508) operated by the Chelyabinsk VVAUSh/605th UAP crashed on landing at Travyany airfield near Kamensk-Ural'skiy where the regiment was based.

• In early May 1975, a group of new MiG-23M fighters staged through Belaya AB on delivery to the Soviet Air Force's 126th IAP based at Choiren, Mongolia. When one of the MiGs, which had suffered a malfunction, was having its engine check-run after repairs, the MAP technician sitting in the cockpit accidentally engaged the afterburner. Unrestrained by chocks, the fighter careened across the flight line and collided with one of the resident Tu-16s which was fully fuelled and with bombs ready for loading alongside (the bomber unit was due to fly a sortie). Both aircraft burst into flames; burning fuel spread across the hardstand and the bombs began exploding. As a result, three Tu-16s were completely destroyed and a fourth damaged beyond repair. For this accident 8th OTBAK Commander Lt.-Gen. Leonid I. Agoorin and regiment CO Lt.-Col. L. P. Kazakov were removed from office.

• On 21st November 1975, a 444th TBAP Tu-16 was flying a night sortie; Capt. O. A. Lebedev was in the left-hand seat, with QFI Maj. Zhuravlyov checking his flying skills. After climbing to 12,500 m (41,010 ft) the pilots initiated a descent, the aircraft accelerating to Mach 0.91; then the pilots hauled back on the control yokes and throttled back to idle power. This caused the aircraft to enter a spin, the engines flaming out. At 9,800 m (32,150 ft) the captain ordered an ejection; because of the G loads he and the navigator were unable to eject (the other four crewmembers ejected safely).

• On 14th May 1976, the nose gear unit of a Tu-16 captained by Maj. Alfeyev jammed halfway through retraction on take-off. All attempts to re-extend it proved fruitless, and eventually the pilots made an emergency landing on the unpaved reserve runway in which the aircraft suffered irreparable damage to the starboard wing. On the plus side, the crew was unhurt.

• On 6th September 1976, the North Fleet's 987th MRAP was to redeploy in full strength from Severomorsk-3 AB to Beryozovka auxiliary airfield near Kirovsk (Murmansk Region) during an exercise. Beryozovka had no navaids, and when the 19 Tu-16K-10s came in to land in the darkness, trouble started. In IMC some of the *Badgers* missed the runway and had to go around, creating congestion in the airfield circuit; the contradictory orders of an inept ATC officer certainly did not help. Realising they might never get a chance to land, the crews of three *Badger-Cs* chose to return to Severomorsk; two aircraft reached the base on the last dregs of fuel but the third machine captained by Maj. Rybin ran out of fuel on final approach, crash-landing in a swamp 2.5 km (1.55 miles) out. The crew walked away but the aircraft was a total loss.

However, the crew of Capt. Aleksandr Uspenskiy fared even worse, losing their bearings in the darkness. There's no telling what prompted Uspenskiy to direct the aircraft northwards and order the crew to eject over the sea when the fuel ran low. Only the WSO survived, using an inflatable dinghy to reach the shore; the Nav/Op also used a dinghy but lost his nerve and, not believing he would be rescued, shot himself. The other crewmen were never found…

• On 27th July 1980, a Pacific Fleet Tu-16R captained by Maj. G. Karakozov crashed into the Sea of Japan 70 km (43.5 miles) from Sado Island while shadowing a US Navy CTF, killing the crew of six. Again, the cause was never determined.

• On 24th August 1981, a 55th TBAD/303rd TBAP Tu-16K-something-or-other (c/n 6203106) collided with an Aeroflot/Far Eastern Civil Aviation Directorate An-24RV twin-turboprop airliner registered CCCP-46653 (c/n 47309204) near Zavitinsk, Amur Region. The collision occurred in thick overcast and the pilots were unable to take evasive action. The crash was caused by poor interaction between civil and military air traffic controllers who, unbeknownst to each other, had cleared both aircraft to use the same flight level. The bomber's crew perished; so did all aboard the An-24 except one female passenger who incredibly survived a fall from high altitude, albeit with injuries, after being thrown clear of the aircraft as it disintegrated and landing in deep snow. Interestingly, at the time of the crash the Tu-16 was using the ATC callsign CCCP-07514; in reality this registration belonged to an An-2TP utility biplane (c/n 1G 15242) built in December 1973.

• On 21st February 1984, a 219th ODRAP Tu-16 (c/n 1882708) was lost in a fatal crash at Spassk-Dal'niy.

• The last crash of a Tu-16 occurred on 10th November 1990. The aircraft was a 132nd TBAP machine which the crew was to ferry from Tartu AB to a storage depot for disposal. Yet, it almost seems the aircraft sensed this and had different views, preferring to crash rather than be scrapped. Immediately after take-off the bomber rolled sharply and impacted with 40° bank, killing captain Lt.-Col. Khakimov, co-pilot Lt. Kolesnik, navigator Maj. Il'demenov and Nav/Op Lt. Okorokov; the GRO and tail gunner survived. It turned out that an aileron crank had failed, rendering the machine uncontrollable.